Instructor's Resource Guide
Volume 1

for

Understanding Business

Tenth Edition

William G. Nickels
University of Maryland

James M. McHugh
St. Louis Community College at Forest Park

Susan M. McHugh
Applied Learning Systems

Prepared by
Pam McElligott
St. Louis Community College at Meramec

Molly McHugh

McGraw-Hill
Irwin

McGraw-Hill
Irwin

Instructor's Resource Guide, Volume 1 for
UNDERSTANDING BUSINESS
William G. Nickels, James M. McHugh, and Susan M. McHugh

Published by McGraw-Hill/Irwin, an imprint of The McGraw-Hill Companies, Inc., 1221 Avenue of the
Americas, New York, NY 10020. Copyright © 2013, 2012, 2010, 2008, 2005, 2002 by The McGraw-Hill Companies, Inc.
All rights reserved. Printed in the United States of America.

1 2 3 4 5 6 7 8 9 0 QDB/QDB 10 9 8 7 6 5 4 3 2

ISBN: 978-0-07-747438-6
MHID: 0-07-747438-4

www.mhhe.com

Contents

Preface

PART 1

Business Trends: Cultivating a Business in Diverse, Global Environments

PART 2

Business Ownership: Starting a Small Business

PART 3

Business Management: Empowering Employees to Satisfy Customers

PART 4

Management of Human Resources: Motivating Employees to Produce Quality Goods and Services

Preface

Teaching an introduction to business class can be satisfying and challenging because this is the first business course for many of your students. You have the important task of introducing them to a broad range of topics and helping them learn the business terms necessary to understand the business literature. Throughout the course, you will be helping them explore and prepare for their careers.

The volume and speed of changes in today's world requires that continuous education be an integral part of each of our lives. We cannot tell our students as we hand them their degrees. Here, now you know all you need to know. Even if we were successful in teaching them what we thought they needed to know, much of it will be obsolete before their diplomas are framed. The best way that we can make sure that our students develop the skills needed to succeed is to teach them how to learn, how to think, how to question.

Helping students learn how to think is what *Understanding Business,* strives to do. The design of the text and this instructor's manual is based on learning principles that put the responsibility for learning where it belongs: on the students' shoulders.

Secretary's Commission on Necessary Skills (Scans)

The Secretary of Labor appointed a commission, the Secretary's Commission on Achieving Necessary Skills (SCANS), to identify the skills people need to succeed in the workplace. SCANS fundamental purpose is to encourage a high-performance economy characterized by high-skill, high-wage employment. The commission's message to educators is this: Help your students connect what they learn in class to the world outside.

To help educators prepare their students for the workplace, SCANS identified five workplace competencies that should be taught: (1) Resources ability to allocate time, money, materials, space, and staff; (2) Interpersonal skills ability to work on teams, teach others, serve customers, lead, negotiate, and work well with people from culturally diverse backgrounds; (3) Information ability to acquire and evaluate data, organize and maintain files, interpret and communicate, and use computers to process information; (4) Systems understanding of social, organizational, and technological systems; ability to monitor and correct performance and to design or improve systems; and (5) Technology ability to select equipment and tools, apply technology to specific tasks, and maintain and troubleshoot equipment. The pedagogical tools in the text and this instructor's manual are designed to facilitate these SCANS competencies.

Perhaps it is because we use these materials in our own classrooms that we were so meticulous with their preparation. Jim taught traditional-size classes of 30-50 students in an urban community college and Bill taught large classes of 250 in lecture halls in a four-year institution. As a result, everything in this instructor's manual is designed to help instructors be more effective and make this course more practical and interesting for students. To accomplish this integration, the authors designed and contributed to the instructor's manual by implementing suggestions from other users and focus group participants. We want to thank Gayle Ross and Molly McHugh for the stellar job they did in revising the lecture outlines, writing new lecture links, adding supplemental exercises and cases, and putting the numerous pieces of this complicated document together in such an attractive and functional format.

Components of the Instructor's Resource Manual

Below is a brief overview of the components for each chapter:

chapter contents

The first page of each chapter answers the question, What's in this thing anyway? The list of chapter contents gives all of the materials contained in the Instructor's Resource Manual chapter.

brief chapter outline and learning goals

This abbreviated outline provides a quick overview of the topics covered in the chapter. Chapter learning goals are included at the appropriate points.

lecture outline and lecture notes

To make the system easy to use, the detailed lecture outline contains marginal notes recommending where to use supplementary cases, lecture links, and critical thinking exercises. When the instructor's manual is opened flat, the lecture outline is on the left-side page. If all you want is a thorough outline of the chapter, you can ignore the notations and material on the facing page. The lecture outline remains uninterrupted since all of the references to supplements and article summaries, etc. are on the right-side Lecture Notes pages.

PowerPoint slide notes

There are over 1,000 PowerPoint slides available on the Instructor's Resource CD and in the Instructor Resource area of the Online Learning Center (www.mhhe.com/ub10e) to help you animate your lectures. There are two types of PPT slides: slides that focus directly on the key points and/or figures within the text, and slides that expand the text with outside examples or illustrations. The slides that contain outside material have a different background color (purple) than the rest of the slides in that chapter. All PPT slides from outside the text have teaching notes to help you better understand how they might fit in your lectures.

lecture links

The lecture links are fresh examples or extended discussions of topics in the text that you can use to enhance your lectures. A brief description of each lecture link is integrated in the lecture notes pages (of course, they include page references for where you can find the complete lecture enhancer in the folder).

critical thinking exercises

These exercises are designed to get the students actively involved in the learning process as recommended by SCANS. The exercises help students relate the concepts covered in the text to their own experiences in their own communities. The critical thinking exercises can be used as class activities or outside assignments for individual students or teams of students.

bonus cases

These cases provide opportunity for additional discussion. The cases can be reproduced for seminar-style classes or for outside assignments.

You will find that there is much more material than you could possibly use in this manual. That gives you the flexibility to pick and choose what to cover and how to cover it.

Standford Erickson says in his book, *The Essence of Teaching*, that students learn what they care about and remember what they understand. Our job as teachers, therefore, is to show students why they should care about a subject and then help them understand it. We sincerely hope this instructor's manual and the entire integrated teaching and testing system provides you with the materials you need to make your job easier and your students the most caring you've had in your career!

Bill Nickels

Jim McHugh

Susan McHugh

Other
Teaching Tools

instructor's supplements:

MONTHLY NEWSLETTER:

The business world has always been in a constant state of change, but the changes brought on by the recent economic crisis seem even more rapid and powerful. In order to help you and your students keep up with these changes, we offer you a monthly newsletter that contains abstracts of current articles, links to new videos, a file of supporting PPT slides, and plenty of discussion questions (and possible answers, of course).

INSTRUCTOR'S SUPPLEMENTS ORIENTATION VIDEO – ONLINE:

Instructors can access this online orientation guide. Great for instructors new to using the text, or for adjuncts/full-timers not sure what all is available in this supplements package! Jim McHugh and Jeffrey Jones, another St. Louis CC professor who served 4 years as an adjunct, walk through every one of the supplements available with the text and discuss how they can be effective teaching tools, what's included in each, etc. The video is available at the OLC (www.mhhe.com/ub10e)

TEST BANK:

The print test bank includes over 4000 questions, reviewed for accuracy. The questions are organized by learning objective and by the level of learning (definition, application, etc). Test Tables are included for each chapter as well that organize every question in that chapter in a table so professors can see – at a glance – which questions test on which learning objective and which level of learning. And, it is indicated which questions test on boxed material, which are essay questions, m-c questions, true-false questions, and which questions test on cases in the book, etc.

Assurance of Learning Ready

Many educational institutions today are focused on the notion of *assurance of learning*, an important element of some accreditation standards. *Understanding Business* is designed specifically to support your assurance of learning initiatives with a simple, yet powerful solution. Each test bank question for *Understanding Business* maps to a specific chapter learning outcome/objective listed in the text. You can use our test bank software, EZ Test and EZ Test Online, to easily query for learning outcomes/objectives that directly relate to the learning objectives for your course. You can then use the reporting features of EZ Test to aggregate student results in similar fashion, making the collection and presentation of assurance of learning data simple and easy.

AACSB Statement

The McGraw-Hill Companies is a proud corporate member of AACSB International. Understanding the importance and value of AACSB accreditation, *Understanding Business* recognizes the curricula guidelines detailed in the AACSB standards for business accreditation by connecting selected questions to the six general knowledge and skill guidelines in the AACSB standards. The statements contained in *Understanding Business* are provided only as a guide for the users of this textbook. The AACSB leaves content coverage and assessment within the purview of individual schools, the mission of the school, and the faculty. While *Understanding Business* and the teaching package make no claim of any specific AACSB qualification or evaluation, we have within *Understanding Business* labeled selected questions according to the six general knowledge and skills areas.

EZTEST ONLINE:

McGraw-Hill's EZ Test Online is a flexible and easy-to-use electronic testing program. The program allows instructors to create tests from book specific items, accommodates a wide range of question types, and enables instructors to add their own questions. Multiple versions of the test can be created and any test can be exported for use with course management systems such as WebCT, BlackBoard or any course management system. EZ Test Online is accessible to busy instructors virtually anywhere via the Web, and the program eliminates the need for them to install test software. Utilizing EZ Test Online also allows instructors to create and deliver multiple-choice or true/false quiz questions using iQuiz for iPod. For more information about EZ Test Online, please see the website at: www.eztestonline.com.

IRCD:

The Instructor's Resource CD includes the Instructor's Resource Manual, Computerized Test Bank, PPT slides, video notes, and digital asset library (all figures from the text).

VIDEOS:

Videos are included for each of the chapters in the text. Videos include a variety of companies and organizations – from small businesses to large corporations. **ALL videos are closed-captioned.**

MEDIA RESOURCE GUIDE:

The Media Resource Guide includes detailed teachings notes for each of the videos that accompany the book, along with instructional information on using Investments Trader (see below). The material can be found within the Instructor Resources of the Online Learning Center at www.mhhe.com/ub10e.

CONNECT INTERACTIVE APPLICATIONS

If you have chosen to use Connect with your course, interactive applications are available for your students. Each interactive is offered in three versions, allowing you to create assignment pools from which Connect will randomly select an activity for each student. Pooling reduces student collaboration, if that's one of your goals. Assignments in Connect are autograded, saving you time for more teaching.

LEARNSMART

McGraw-Hill's LearnSmart™ is an adaptive system that helps students efficiently build their knowledge to achieve course mastery. LearnSmart's personalized study environment is tailored to your students' needs; detecting concepts they have missed and providing further practice with them. This practice builds students' mastery and helps them retain new concepts. To get the most out of LearnSmart, McGraw-Hill recommends that you:

- assign LearnSmart to your students and make their performance part of their final course grade.

- share your plans to use LearnSmart with students by including your expectations for their use of LearnSmart in the syllabus and discussing LearnSmart with them during the first week of class.

- align assignment start and end dates with your syllabus and lectures so as to expose students to the foundational terminology, concepts and principles in *Understanding Business.*

- encourage students to return to previous LearnSmart assignments to practice challenging topics, refresh their knowledge, and increase their retention of course concepts.

BUSINESS PLANNING SOFTWARE:

For instructors who incorporate a business plan project into their class, the New Business Mentor and the Business Plan Pro are both available as packaging options with the text. Both software packages include sample business plans and resources to help you as you start your business, along with financial worksheets and help along the way.

MCGRAW-HILL INVESTMENTS TRADER:

The Investments Trader can be accessed from the Online Learning Center at www.mhhe.com/ub10e. Students receive $100,000 to trade with for their semester and they compete with students using Understanding Business around the country. Students can trade stocks or mutual funds. Teaching notes are included in the Media Resource Guide.

student's supplements:

STUDENT ASSESSMENT AND LEARNING GUIDE:

The print study guide is designed to help students study important material from the chapters and give them an edge in the course. Each chapter contains learning goals, key term review, assessment checks, critical thinking exercises, practice quizzes, internet research exercises, and answers to all of these questions so students can study on their own.

IPOD CONTENT:

Chapter summaries, PowerPoints, and quizzes can be downloaded from the Online Learning Center to students' iPods to help them study.

special packaging:

WALL STREET JOURNAL EDITION:

Students can go to www.wsjstudent.com to subscribe to the print and online journal for $29.95. They have the option to pay by credit card or to be billed for the subscription. Students will be required to fill in their school and professor information during the registration process, and professors will receive a free subscription to the *Journal* after 10 students register.

EBOOKS:

eBooks, or digital textbooks, are exact replicas of the print version, and can offer substantial savings to your students off the cost of their textbook. *Understanding Business* offers the following:

COURSESMART EBOOK:

With the CourseSmart eTextbook version of this title, students can save up to 50% off the cost of a print book, reduce their impact on the environment, and access powerful web tools for learning. Faculty can also review and compare the full text online without having to wait for a print desk copy. CourseSmart is an online eTextbook, which means users need to be connected to the internet in order to access. Students can also print sections of the book for maximum portability.

PRIMIS:

Primis Online allows you to build your own custom textbook if you don't use the entire text. Select the content and chapters that you are interested in from this book, arrange them in the order that's most effective for your class, personalize them with the information from your course, and request a complimentary print copy for your review and approval. Visit www.primisonline.com or talk to your McGraw-Hill/Irwin sales representative for more details.

online supplements:

ONLINE LEARNING CENTER: www.mhhe.com/ub10e

The Online Learning Center is designed to be a study resource for students and houses additional downloadable supplements and teaching information for professors. The student side of the OLC contains video clips, quizzes, news and company resources, the Investments Trader, and chapter summaries, etc. The Instructor side also contains the downloadable supplements and sample syllabi.

The material presented online is meant to explain and enhance the chapter material from the text and make it more understandable by providing students with new and engaging examples to which they can relate. The Learning Objectives and chapter summaries from each chapter are used in the chapter presentations. Self-check feedback refers students back to specific pages in the text where they can (re)read to gain a better understanding of concepts with which they are struggling. Reading assignments from each chapter also link back to specific pages within Nickels/McHugh/McHugh: *Understanding Business*. See below in the Online Supplements section for more information on the Online Learning Center.

The Online Learning Center works with any major Course Management System that is in use today. The following CMS's will all function with our Understanding Business Online content:

- Blackboard

- Blackboard (CE) Campus Edition (formerly WebCT)

- Moodle

- Angel

- Desire2Learn (D2L)

- Sakai

- eCollege

The content will upload into your Course Management System and you can add your own content or hide some of the content that has been provided.

The entire course is 508 compliant. Section 508 requires that Federal agencies' electronic and information technology is accessible to people with disabilities.

Be sure to ask your McGraw-Hill Sales Representative about the many packaging options for *Understanding Business* and the Online Learning Center.

MANAGER'S HOTSEAT ONLINE - www.mhhe.com/mhs:

The Manager's Hot Seat Online is an interactive application that allows students to watch 15 real managers apply their years of experience in confronting certain management and organizational behavior issues. Students assume the role of the manager as they watch the video and answer multiple-choice questions that pop up during the segment, forcing them to make decisions on the spot. Students learn from the manager's mistakes and successes, and then do a report critiquing the manager's approach by defending their reasoning. Manager's HotSeat is available as Premium Content on the text website.

MCGRAW-HILL CONNECT BUSINESS:

Less Managing. More Teaching. Greater Learning.

McGraw-Hill Connect Business is an online assignment and assessment solution that connects students with the tools and resources they'll need to achieve success. McGraw-Hill Connect Business helps prepare students for their future by enabling faster learning, more efficient studying, and higher retention of knowledge.

McGraw-Hill *Connect Business* features

Connect Business offers a number of powerful tools and features to make managing assignments easier, so faculty can spend more time teaching. With *Connect Business*, students can engage with their coursework anytime and anywhere, making the learning process more accessible and efficient. *Connect Business* offers you the features described below.

Simple assignment management

With *Connect Business,* creating assignments is easier than ever, so you can spend more time teaching and less time managing. The assignment management function enables you to:

- Create and deliver assignments easily with selectable end-of-chapter questions and test bank items.

- Streamline lesson planning, student progress reporting, and assignment grading to make classroom management more efficient than ever.

- Go paperless with the eBook and online submission and grading of student assignments.

Smart grading

When it comes to studying, time is precious. *Connect Business* helps students learn more efficiently by providing feedback and practice material when they need it, where they need it. When it comes to teaching, your time also is precious. The grading function enables you to:

- Have assignments scored automatically, giving students immediate feedback on their work and side-by-side comparisons with correct answers.

- Access and review each response; manually change grades or leave comments for students to review.

- Reinforce classroom concepts with practice tests and instant quizzes.

Instructor library

The *Connect Business* Instructor Library is your repository for additional resources to improve student engagement in and out of class. You can select and use any asset that enhances your lecture. The *Connect Business* Instructor Library includes:

- Instructor's Manual

- Testbank

- PowerPoint presentation

- Videos

- eBook

Student study center

The Connect Business Student Study Center is the place for students to access additional resources. The Student Study Center:

- Offers students quick access to lectures, practice materials, eBooks, and more.

- Provides instant practice material and study questions, easily accessible on the go.

- Gives students access to the Personalized Learning Plan described below.

Diagnostic and adaptive learning of concepts: LearnSmart

Students want to make the best use of their study time. The LearnSmart adaptive self-study technology within *Connect Business* provides students with a seamless combination of practice, assessment, and remediation for every concept in the textbook. LearnSmart's intelligent software adapts to every student response and automatically delivers concepts that advance the student's understanding while reducing time devoted to the concepts already mastered. The result for every student is the fastest path to mastery of the chapter concepts. LearnSmart:

- Applies an intelligent concept engine to identify the relationships between concepts and to serve new concepts to each student only when he or she is ready.

- Adapts automatically to each student, so students spend less time on the topics they understand and practice more those they have yet to master.

- Provides continual reinforcement and remediation, but gives only as much guidance as students need.

- Integrates diagnostics as part of the learning experience.

- Enables you to assess which concepts students have efficiently learned on their own, thus freeing class time for more applications and discussion.

Student progress tracking

Connect Business keeps instructors informed about how each student, section, and class is performing, allowing for more productive use of lecture and office hours. The progress-tracking function enables you to:

- View scored work immediately and track individual or group performance with assignment and grade reports.

- Access an instant view of student or class performance relative to learning objectives.

- Collect data and generate reports required by many accreditation organizations, such as AACSB.

Lecture capture

Increase the attention paid to lecture discussion by decreasing the attention paid to note taking. For an additional charge Lecture Capture offers new ways for students to focus on the in-class discussion, knowing they can revisit important topics later. Lecture Capture enables you to:

- Record and distribute your lecture with a click of button.

- Record and index PowerPoint presentations and anything shown on your computer so it is easily searchable, frame by frame.

- Offer access to lectures anytime and anywhere by computer, iPod, or mobile device.

- Increase intent listening and class participation by easing students' concerns about note-taking. Lecture Capture will make it more likely you will see students' faces, not the tops of their heads.

McGraw-Hill Connect Plus Business

McGraw-Hill reinvents the textbook learning experience for the modern student with Connect Plus Business. A seamless integration of an eBook and Connect Business, Connect Plus Business provides all of the Connect Business features plus the following:

- An integrated eBook, allowing for anytime, anywhere access to the textbook.

- Dynamic links between the problems or questions you assign to your students and the location in the eBook where that problem or question is covered.

- A powerful search function to pinpoint and connect key concepts in a snap.

In short, *Connect Business* offers you and your students powerful tools and features that optimize your time and energies, enabling you to focus on course content, teaching, and student learning. *Connect Business* also offers a wealth of content resources for both instructors and students. This state-of-the-art, thoroughly-tested system supports you in preparing students for the world that awaits.

For more information about Connect, go to **www.mcgrawhillconnect.com,** or contact your local McGraw-Hill sales representative.

TEGRITY CAMPUS: LECTURES 24/7

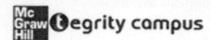

Tegrity Campus is a service that makes class time available 24/7 by automatically capturing every lecture in a searchable format for students to review when they study and complete assignments. With a simple one-click start-and-stop process, you capture all computer screens and corresponding audio. Students can replay any part of any class with easy-to-use browser-based viewing on a PC or Mac.

Educators know that the more students can see, hear, and experience class resources, the better they learn. In fact, studies prove it. With Tegrity Campus, students quickly recall key moments by using Tegrity Campus's unique search feature. This search helps students efficiently find what they need, when they need it, across an entire semester of class recordings. Help turn all your students' study time into learning moments immediately supported by your lecture.

To learn more about Tegrity watch a 2-minute Flash demo at **http://tegritycampus.mhhe.com**.

McGraw-Hill Customer Care Contact Information

At McGraw-Hill, we understand that getting the most from new technology can be challenging. That's why our services don't stop after you purchase our products. You can e-mail our Product Specialists 24 hours a day to get product-training online. Or you can search our knowledge bank of Frequently Asked Questions on our support website. For Customer Support, call **800-331-5094**, e-mail **hmsupport@mcgraw-hill.com**, or visit **www.mhhe.com/support**. One of our Technical Support Analysts will be able to assist you in a timely fashion.

Pretest

Before beginning the text, you might take a few minutes to have your students take the short test on the following page. This test will give them some indication of their current business I.Q. and will introduce the types of material they will be studying.

The answers are:

1. d
2. c
3. a
4. b
5. b
6. a
7. a
8. c
9. b
10. a
11. c
12. b
13. d
14. d
15. c
16. b
17. b
18. a
19. b
20. a
21. c
22. b
23. c
24. d
25. d

Pretest Your Business I.Q.

1. _____ is the unfavorable balance of trade that occurs when a country's imports exceed its exports.
   - a. Trade surplus
   - b. Trade protectionism
   - c. The nation's debt
   - d. Trade deficit

2. In the United States, what signal tells farmers and other producers what to produce?
   - a. supply
   - b. demand
   - c. price
   - d. news reports

3. Which of the following refers to taxes and spending by the government?
   - a. fiscal policy
   - b. monetary policy
   - c. national policy
   - d. deficit policy

4. What are people who take the risk of starting and managing a business called?
   - a. bureaucrats
   - b. entrepreneurs
   - c. speculators
   - d. designers

5. What is the term used to describe working four 10-hour days instead of five 8-hour days ever week?
   - a. job sharing
   - b. compressed workweek
   - c. flextime
   - d. weekending

6. Which of the following utilities provided by marketers brings strawberries to the market in winter?
   - a. time
   - b. place
   - c. possession
   - d. information

7. Which of the following marketing terms describes a product that's better for the environment than competing products?
   - a. green products
   - b. pure products
   - c. eco-friendly products
   - d. crystal-clear products

8. Which kind of goods are consumers more likely to go out of town to find?
   - a. convenience goods
   - b. shopping goods
   - c. specialty goods
   - d. dry goods

9. Which kind of marketing intermediary is most likely to sell to consumers like you and me?
   - a. wholesalers
   - b. retailers
   - c. sales agents
   - d. manufacturing agents

10. What are TV programs devoted exclusively to selling goods and services called?
    - a. infomercials
    - b. advertorials
    - c. promotional videos
    - d. sales pitches

11. Which of the following leadership styles involves making decisions without consulting others?
    - a. democratic
    - b. laissez-faire
    - c. autocratic
    - d. participative

12. Making goods using less input is called:
    a. skimping
    b. lean manufacturing
    c. downsizing
    d. short-changing

13. Companies use _____ to compare their practices and products against the best in the industry.
    a. outsourcing
    b. operations management
    c. distribution
    d. benchmarking

14. Which form of business provides limited liability to the owners?
    a. sole proprietorship
    b. partnership
    c. cooperative
    d. corporation

15. Who controls the money supply of the United States?
    a. Congress
    b. The President
    c. The Federal Reserve
    d. Local banks

16. The organizational structure that is described on the organization chart is the:
    a. matrix structure
    b. line organization
    c. informal organization
    d. critical structure

17. What do accountants call items such as trucks and machinery?
    a. liabilities
    b. assets
    c. revenues
    d. goods

18. Which function in business is responsible for obtaining money and deciding how it should be spent?
    a. finance
    b. accounting
    c. credit
    d. logistics

19. It is illegal and unethical for insiders use private company information to further their own fortunes or those of their family and friends, a practice called:
    a. liability reporting
    b. insider trading
    c. facilitating
    d. trading short

20. A company's profit is calculated by subtracting expenses from the total:
    a. revenue
    b. liabilities
    c. assets
    d. income

21. The most powerful tactic a union can use to achieve its objectives is the _____ in which workers refused to go to work.
    a. boycott
    b. lockout
    c. strike
    d. decertification

22. People who report illegal or unethical behavior are called:
    a. security officers
    b. whistleblowers
    c. stakeholders
    d. auditors

23. _____ is a motivational strategy that emphasizes motivating the worker through the job itself.
    a. Equity theory
    b. Flexible staffing
    c. Job enrichment
    d. Telecommuting

24. To motivate employees, the organization should set goals that are: d
   a. easy to meet
   b. subjective and vague
   c. too high to reach
   d. ambitious but attainable

25. The owners of a corporation are the:
   a. government
   b. creditors
   c. corporate officers
   d. stockholders

Suggested Class Schedules

16-WEEK TERM

WEEK	TOPICS	CHAPTER ASSIGNMENT
1	Introduction to Course and Text Taking Risks and Making Profits within the Dynamic Business Environment Understanding How Economics Affects Business	1, 2
2	Understanding How Economics Affects Business (continued) Doing Business in Global Markets Demanding Ethical and Socially Responsible Behavior	2, 3, 4
3	Demanding Ethical and Socially Responsible Behavior (continued) Exam I How to Form a Business	4, 5
4	How to Form a Business (continued) Entrepreneurship and Starting a Small Business Section Review and Recap Exam II	5, 6
5	Management and Leadership Structuring Organizations for Today's Challenges	7, 8
6	Structuring Organizations for Today's Challenges (continued) Production and Operations Management Section Review and Recap Exam III	8, 9
7	Motivating Employees and Building Self-Managed Teams Human Resource Management: Finding and Keeping the Best Employees	10, 11
8	Human Resource Management: Finding and Keeping the Best Employees (continued) Dealing with Union and Employee–Management Issues	11, 12

WEEK	TOPICS	CHAPTER ASSIGNMENT
9	Section Review and Recap Exam IV Marketing: Helping Buyers Buy	13
10	Developing and Pricing Goods and Services Distributing Products	14, 15
11	Using Effective Promotions Section Review and Recap	16
12	Exam V Understanding Accounting and Financial Information	17
13	Financial Management Using Securities Markets for Financing and Investing Opportunities	18 19
14	Money, Financial Institutions, and the Federal Reserve Section Review and Recap Exam VI	20
15	Working within the Legal Environment Using Technology to Manage Information Managing Risk	A, B, C
16	Managing Your Personal Finances Section Review and Recap Exam VII or Final Exam	D

14-WEEK TERM

WEEK	TOPICS	CHAPTER ASSIGNMENT
1	Introduction to Course and Text Taking Risks and Making Profits within the Dynamic Business Environment Understanding How Economics Affects Business	1, 2
2	Doing Business in Global Markets Demanding Ethical Behavior and Social Responsibility Section Review and Recap	3, 4
3	Exam I How to Form a Business Entrepreneurship and Starting a Small Business	5, 6
4	Section Review and Recap Exam II Management and Leadership	7
5	Structuring Organizations for Today's Challenges Production and Operations Management Section Review and Recap	8, 9
6	Exam III Motivating Employees and Building Self-Managed Teams Human Resource Management: Finding and Keeping the Best Employees	10, 11
7	Human Resource Management: Finding and Keeping the Best Employees (continued) Dealing with Union and Employee–Management Issues Section Review and Recap	11, 12
8	Exam IV Marketing: Helping Buyers Buy Developing and Pricing Goods and Services	13, 14

WEEK	TOPICS	CHAPTER ASSIGNMENT
9	Developing and Pricing Goods and Services (continued) Distributing Products Using Effective Promotions	14, 15, 16
10	Using Effective Promotions (continued) Section Review and Recap Exam V Understanding Accounting and Financial Information	16, 17
11	Understanding Accounting and Financial Information (continued) Financial Management Using Securities Markets for Financing and Investing Opportunities	17, 18, 19
12	Using Securities Markets for Financing and Investing Opportunities (continued) Money, Financial Institutions, and the Federal Reserve Section Review and Recap	19, 20
13	Exam VI Working within the Legal Environment Using Technology to Manage Information	A, B
14	Managing Risk Managing Your Personal Finances Section Review and Recap Exam VII or Final Exam	C, D

10-WEEK TERM

WEEK	TOPICS	CHAPTER ASSIGNMENT
1	Introduction to Course and Text Taking Risks and Making Profits within the Dynamic Business Environment Understanding How Economics Affects Business Doing Business in Global Markets	1, 2, 4
2	Demanding Ethical Behavior and Social Responsibility Section Review and Recap Exam I How to Form a Business	4, 5
3	How to Form a Business (continued) Entrepreneurship and Starting a Small Business Section Review and Recap Exam II Management and Leadership	5, 6, 7
4	Management and Leadership (continued) Structuring Organizations for Today's Challenges Production and Operations Management Section Review and Recap	7, 8, 9
5	Exam III Motivating Employees and Building Self-Managed Teams Human Resource Management: Finding and Keeping the Best Employees	10, 11
6	Dealing with Union and Employee–Management Issues Section Review and Recap Exam IV Marketing: Helping Buyers Buy	12, 13
7	Developing and Pricing Goods and Services Distributing Products Using Effective Promotions Section Review and Recap	14, 15, 16
8	Exam V Understanding Accounting and Financial Information Financial Management Using Securities Markets for Financing and Investing Opportunities	17, 18, 19

WEEK	TOPICS	CHAPTER ASSIGNMENT
9	Using Securities Markets for Financing and Investing Opportunities (continued) Money, Financial Institutions, and the Federal Reserve Section Review and Recap Exam VI Working within the Legal Environment	19, 20, A
10	Using Technology to Manage Information Managing Risk Managing Your Personal Finances Section Review and Recap Exam VII or Final Exam	B, C, D

8-WEEK TERM

WEEK	TOPICS	CHAPTER ASSIGNMENT
1	Introduction to Course and Text Taking Risks and Making Profits within the Dynamic Business Environment Understanding How Economics Affects Business Doing Business in Global Markets Demanding Ethical Behavior and Social Responsibility	1, 2, 3, 4
2	Demanding Ethical Behavior and Social Responsibility (continued) Section Review and Recap Exam I How to Form a Business Entrepreneurship and Starting a Small Business Section Review and Recap	4, 5, 6
3	Exam II Management and Leadership Structuring Organizations for Today's Challenges Production and Operations Management	7, 8, 9
4	Section Review and Recap Exam III Motivating Employees and Building Self-Managed Teams Human Resource Management: Finding and Keeping the Best Employees	10, 11
5	Dealing with Union and Employee–Management Issues Section Review and Recap Exam IV Marketing: Helping Buyers Buy Developing and Pricing Goods and Services Distributing Products	12, 13, 14, 15
6	Using Effective Promotions (continued) Section Review and Recap Exam V Understanding Accounting and Financial Information Financial Management	16, 17, 18

WEEK	TOPICS	CHAPTER ASSIGNMENT
7	Using Securities Markets for Financing and Investing Opportunities Money, Financial Institutions, and the Federal Reserve Section Review and Recap Exam VI	19, 20
8	Working within the Legal Environment Using Technology to Manage Information Managing Risk Managing Your Personal Finances Section Review and Recap Exam VII or Final Exam	A, B, C, D

6-WEEK TERM

WEEK	TOPICS	CHAPTER ASSIGNMENT
1	Introduction to Course and Text Taking Risks and Making Profits within the Dynamic Business Environment Understanding How Economics Affects Business Doing Business in Global Markets Demanding Ethical Behavior and Social Responsibility Section Review and Recap Exam I	1, 2, 3, 4
2	How to Form a Business Entrepreneurship and Starting a Small Business Section Review and Recap Exam II Management and Leadership Structuring Organizations for Today's Challenges	5, 6, 7, 8
3	Production and Operations Management Section Review and Recap Exam III Motivating Employees and Building Self-Managed Teams Human Resource Management: Finding and Keeping the Best Employees Dealing with Union and Employee–Management Issues	9, 10, 11, 12
4	Dealing with Union and Employee–Management Issues (continued) Section Review and Recap Exam IV Marketing: Helping Buyers Buy Developing and Pricing Goods and Services Distributing Products Using Effective Promotions	12, 13, 14, 15, 16
5	Using Effective Promotions (continued) Section Review and Recap Exam V Understanding Accounting and Financial Information Financial Management Using Securities Markets for Financing and Investing Opportunities	16, 17, 18, 19

WEEK	TOPICS	CHAPTER ASSIGNMENT
	Money, Financial Institutions, and the Federal Reserve	
	Section Review and Recap	
	Exam VI	
	Working within the Legal Environment	
6	Using Technology to Manage Information	20, A, B, C, D
	Managing Risk	
	Managing Your Personal Finances	
	Section Review and Recap	
	Exam VII or Final Exam	

Taking Risks and Making Profits within the Dynamic Business Environment

chapter 1

what's new in this edition

additions to the 10th edition:

- Getting to Know Monif Clarke of Monifc.com
- Name That Company: Grameen Bank and Muhammad Yunus
- Spotlight on Small Business: Networking of Minority Businesses
- Social Media in Business: JCPenney Keeps in Touch
- Video Case

revisions to the 10th edition:

- Text was revised to eliminate redundancy and tighten discussions.
- Statistical data and examples throughout the chapter were updated to reflect current in-formation.

deletions from the 9th edition:

- Name That Company: Hyundai
- Spotlight on Small Business
- Figure 1.4 How Competition Changes Business

brief chapter outline and learning goals

Taking Risks and Making Profits within the Dynamic Business Environment

Getting To Know MONIF CLARKE of MONIFC.COM

learning goal 1
Describe the relationship between profit and risk, and show how businesses and nonprofit organizations can raise the standard of living for all..

I. ENTREPRENEURSHIP AND WEALTH BUILDING
   A. Revenues, Profits, and Losses
   B. Matching Risk with Profit
   C. Standard of Living and Quality of Life
   D. Responding to the Various Business Stakeholders
   E. Using Business Principles in Nonprofit Organizations

learning goal 2
Compare and contrast being an entrepreneur and working for others.

II. ENTREPRENEURSHIP VERSUS WORKING FOR OTHERS
   A. Opportunities for Entrepreneurs
   B. The Importance of Entrepreneurs to the Creation of Wealth.

III. THE BUSINESS ENVIRONMENT

learning goal 3
Analyze the effects of the economic environment and taxes on businesses.

   A. The Economic and Legal Environment

learning goal 4
Describe the effects of technology on businesses.

   B. The Technological Environment
      1. How Technology Benefits Workers and You
      2. The Growth of E-Commerce
      3. Using Technology to Be Responsive to Customers

learning goal 5

Demonstrate how businesses can meet and beat competition.

C.   The Competitive Environment

1.   Competing by Exceeding Customer Expectations

2.   Competing by Restructuring and Empowerment

learning goal 6

Analyze the social changes affecting businesses.

D.   The Social Environment

1.   Managing Diversity

2.   The Increase in the Number of Older Citizens

3.   The Increase in the Number of Single-Parent Families

learning goal 7

Identify what businesses must do to meet global challenges, including war and terrorism.

E.   The Global Environment

1.   War and Terrorism

2.   How Global Changes Affect You

3.   The Ecological Environment

learning goal 8

Review how past trends are being repeated in the present and what they mean for tomorrow's college graduates.

IV. THE EVOLUTION OF U.S. BUSINESS

A.   Progress in the Agricultural and Manufacturing Industries

B.   Progress in the Service Industries

C.   Your Future in Business

V. SUMMARY

Getting to Know MONIF CLARKE of MONIFC.COM

Monif Clarke couldn't find flattering clothing in the size she needed. She decided to fill the need by creating her own line. With a $30,000 loan from her parents, she started Monif C. Con-temporary Plus Sizes. She received lots of publicity when her fashions appeared on TLC's What Not to Wear, but she struggled with getting her clothes into leading department stores. Instead she turned to the Internet where she's developed a strong online presence. .

NAME THAT company

This microlending organization provides small loans to entrepreneurs too poor to qualify for traditional loans. The person who started the organization has started 30 of what he calls social businesses that do not have profit as their goal. Name that organization and its founder.

(Students should read the chapter before guessing the company's name: Grameen Bank and Muhammad Yunus*)*

learning goal 1

Describe the relationship between profit and risk, and show how businesses and nonprofit organizations can raise the standard of living for all.

I. ENTREPRENEURSHIP AND WEALTH BUILDING

A. BASIC CONCEPTS:

1. Success in business involves finding a need and filling it.

2. A business provides needed goods, jobs, and services to people in the area.

    a. **_GOODS_** are tangible products such as computers, food, clothing, cars, and appliances.

    b. **_SERVICES_** are intangible products that can't be held in your hand, such as education, health care, insurance, recreation, and travel and tourism.

3. Successfully filling a need may make you rich.

PPT 1-1
Chapter Title

PPT 1-2
Monif Clarke

(See complete PowerPoint slide notes on page 1.36.)

PPT 1-3
Learning Goals

(See complete PowerPoint slide notes on page 1.36.)

PPT 1-4
Learning Goals (Cont'd)

(See complete PowerPoint slide notes on page 1.37.)

PPT 1-5
Name That Company

(See complete PowerPoint slide notes on page 1.37.)

PPT 1-6
Goods and Services

(See complete PowerPoint slide notes on page 1.37.)

4. A ***BUSINESS*** is any activity that seeks to provide goods and services to others while operating at a profit.

5. An ***ENTREPRENEUR*** is a person who risks time and money to start and manage a business.

B. **REVENUES, PROFITS, AND LOSSES**

1. ***REVENUE*** is the total amount of money a business takes in during a given period by selling goods and services.

2. ***PROFIT*** is the amount a business earns above and beyond what it spends for salaries and other expenses.

3. **REVENUE – EXPENSES = PROFIT.**

4. A ***LOSS*** occurs when a business's expenses are more than its revenues.

5. Approximately 80,000 businesses in the U.S. fail each year (although this number may be overstated).

C. **MATCHING RISK WITH PROFIT**

1. ***RISK*** is the chance an entrepreneur takes of losing time and money on a business that may not prove profitable.

2. *The text uses the example of selling hot dogs during the summer—paying for supplies, rent, salaries, and only then making a profit.*

3. Not all enterprises make the same amount of profit.

4. The more **RISKS** you take, the **HIGHER THE REWARDS** may be.

PPT 1-7
Business and Entrepreneurship

(See complete PowerPoint slide notes on page 1.38.)

PPT 1-8
Revenue, Profit, and Loss

(See complete PowerPoint slide notes on page 1.38.)

lecture link 1-1
THE WORLD'S RICHEST PEOPLE

These are the world's 20 richest people—their wealth, age, residence, and country of citizenship. (See the complete lecture link on page 1.55 in this manual.)

critical thinking exercise 1-1
HOW MUCH PROFIT?

The text defines profit as the amount a business earns above and beyond what it spends for salaries and other expenses. Students often have a very inaccurate idea of how much profit businesses actually make. This exercise leads students to find this actual profit percentage. (See complete exercise on page 1.65 of this manual.)

PPT 1-9
Risk

(See complete PowerPoint slide notes on page 1.38.)

D. **STANDARD OF LIVING AND QUALITY OF LIFE**

1. Entrepreneurs **PROVIDE EMPLOYMENT** for other people.

2. They also **PAY TAXES** that are used for schools, hospitals, and other facilities.

3. Businesses are part of an economic system that helps **CREATE A HIGHER STANDARD OF LIVING** and quality of life for everyone.

4. _**STANDARD OF LIVING**_ is the amount of goods and services people can buy with the money they have.

5. Potential businesspeople must find a location with the right level of taxes and regulations.

6. _**QUALITY OF LIFE**_ is the general well-being of a society in terms of political freedom, natural environment, education, health care, safety, amount of leisure, and rewards that add to the satisfaction and joy that other goods and services provide.

7. The combined efforts of businesses, nonprofit organizations, and government agencies are required to maintain a high quality of life.

E. **RESPONDING TO THE VARIOUS BUSINESS STAKEHOLDERS**

1. _**STAKEHOLDERS**_ are all the people who stand to gain or lose by the policies and activities of a business and whose concerns the business needs to address.

PPT 1-10
How Is Tax Money Used?

(See complete PowerPoint slide notes on page 1.39.)

PPT 1-11
Standard of Living

(See complete PowerPoint slide notes on page 1.39.)

PPT 1-12
Quality of Life

(See complete PowerPoint slide notes on page 1.39.)

lecture link 1-2
**COMMUNITY COLLEGES
THRIVE IN HARD TIMES**

During the recent recession, more students are turning toward community colleges to prepare for four-year schools and improve their quality of life. (See the complete lecture link on page 1.55 in this manual.)

PPT 1-13
Stakeholders

(See complete PowerPoint slide notes on page 1.40.)

2. Stakeholders include customers, employees, stockholders, suppliers, bankers, people in the local community, environmentalists, and elected leaders.

3. The challenge for companies in the 21st century will be to recognize and respond to the needs of their stakeholders.

4. To stay competitive, businesses may **OUT-SOURCE** jobs to other countries.

   a. ***OUTSOURCING*** means contracting with other companies (often in other countries) to do some or all of the functions of the firm, like its production or accounting tasks.

   b. Many companies have set up design and production facilities here in the United States, a practice known as **INSOURCING**.

   c. The decision whether to outsource or to insource is based on what is best for all the stakeholders.

F. **USING BUSINESS PRINCIPLES IN NONPROFIT ORGANIZATIONS**

   1. **NONPROFIT ORGANIZATIONS**—such as government agencies, public schools, charities, and social causes—make a major contribution to the welfare of society.

   2. A ***NONPROFIT ORGANIZATION*** is an organization whose goals do not include making a personal profit for its owners or organizers.

TEXT FIGURE 1.1
A Business and its Stakeholders
(Text page 6)

This text figure shows all the people who stand to gain or lose by the policies and activities of a business.

PPT 1-14
Outsourcing and Insourcing

(See complete PowerPoint slide notes on page 1.40.)

PPT 1-15
Nonprofit Organizations

(See complete PowerPoint slide notes on page 1.41.)

PPT 1-16
**Well-Known Nonprofits in the
United States**

(See complete PowerPoint slide notes on page 1.41.)

PPT 1-17
**Keeping Strong Employees at
Nonprofits**

(See complete PowerPoint slide notes on page 1.41.)

lecture link 1-3
**UNEMPLOYED CLERGY ON THE
RISE**

As donations drop, nonprofits, especially churches, are feeling the pinch and many clergy are out searching for jobs (See the complete lecture link on page 1.56 in this manual.)

3. **SOCIAL ENTREPRENEURS** are people who use business principles to start and manage organizations that are not for profit and who help countries with their social issues.

4. You need the **SAME SKILLS** to work in nonprofit organizations that you need in business, including information management, leadership, marketing, and financial management.

5. Businesses, nonprofit organizations, and volunteer groups often strive to accomplish the same objectives.

<u>**learning goal** 2</u>

Compare and contrast being an entrepreneur and working for others.

II. ENTREPRENEURSHIP VERSUS WORKING FOR OTHERS

A. **THERE ARE TWO WAYS TO SUCCEED IN BUSINESS:**

1. One way is to **RISE UP THROUGH THE RANKS** of a large company.

2. The riskier path is to **START YOUR OWN BUSINESS.**

B. **OPPORTUNITIES FOR ENTREPRENEURS**

1. Millions of people have taken the entrepreneurial risk and succeeded.

2. The number of Hispanic-owned businesses in the United States has grown dramatically.

3. Increases have also been made by Asians, Pacific Islanders, American Indians, and Alaska Natives.

bonus case 1-1
THE WORLD'S LARGEST CHARITY

Three of the wealthiest people in the world are busy giving away their wealth through the Bill and Melinda Gates Foundation. (See the complete case, discussion questions, and suggested answers beginning on page 1.70 of this manual.)

PPT 1-18
Social Entrepreneurs

(See complete PowerPoint slide notes on page 1.42.)

lecture link 1-4
SOCIAL ENTREPRENEURSHIP: MERCY CORPS

Programs such as Yunus's GrameenBank are known as microfinance institutions (MFIs). Mercy Corps provides these institutions with organization and resources. (See the complete lecture link on page 1.56 of this manual.)

lecture link 1-5
SOCIAL ENTREPRENEURSHIP: IMPROVING WORLD HEALTH WITHOUT PROFITS

Victoria Hale has created a nonprofit organization, OneWorldHealth, to finance necessary prescription drugs that have no profit potential. (See complete lecture link on page 1.57 of this manual.)

progress assessment
(Text page 8)

PPT 1-19
Progress Assessment

(See complete PowerPoint slide notes on page 1.42.)

PPT 1-20
The Ups and Downs of Entrepreneurship

(See complete PowerPoint slide notes on page 1.43.)

PPT 1-21
Who Takes the Entrepreneurial Challenge?

(See complete PowerPoint slide notes on page 1.43.)

4. Women now own over one-third of all businesses.

5. Businesses owned by minority women are growing twice as fast as minority men and over four times faster than nonminority entrepreneurs.

C. **THE IMPORTANCE OF ENTREPRENEURS TO THE CREATION OF WEALTH**

1. The ***FACTORS OF PRODUCTION*** are the resources used to create wealth:

   a. **LAND** *(or natural resources)*

   b. **LABOR** *(workers)*

   c. **CAPITAL**

      i. This includes machines, tools, buildings, or whatever is used in the production of goods, but not money.

      ii. Money is used to buy factors of production.

   d. **ENTREPRENEURSHIP**

   e. **KNOWLEDGE**

2. Some experts, including the late Peter Drucker, believe that the most important factor of production is **KNOWLEDGE.**

3. Some countries are rich in land or labor, but these aren't critical to wealth creation.

4. What makes rich countries rich is not land, labor, or capital; it is a combination of **ENTREPRENEURSHIP** and the effective use of **KNOWLEDGE**.

5. Entrepreneurship also helps make some states and cities rich while others remain relatively poor.

critical thinking exercise 1-2
JOB AND CAREER VERSUS OWNING A BUSINESS

This exercise guides the student through the decision-making process of evaluating various career options. (See complete exercise on page 1.67 of this manual.)

SPOTLIGHT ON small business
(Text page 10)

PPT 1-22
Networking of Minority Businesses

(See complete PowerPoint slide notes on page 1.43.)

PPT 1-23
Five Factors of Production

(See complete PowerPoint slide notes on page 1.44.)

TEXT FIGURE 1.2
The Five Factors of Production
(Text page 10)

This text figure shows the five resources used to create wealth: land, labor, capital, entrepreneurship, and knowledge.

progress assessment
(Text page 11)

PPT 1-24
Progress Assessment

(See complete PowerPoint slide notes on page 1.44.)

III. THE BUSINESS ENVIRONMENT

A. The **_BUSINESS ENVIRONMENT_** consists of the surrounding factors that either help or hinder the development of business; they are:

1. The economic and legal environment
2. The technological environment
3. The competitive environment
4. The social environment
5. The global business environment

Businesses that create jobs and wealth grow and prosper in a healthy environment.

learning goal 3

Analyze the effects of the economic environment and taxes on businesses.

B. **THE ECONOMIC AND LEGAL ENVIRONMENT**

1. People are willing to risk starting businesses if they feel that the risk is acceptable.

2. **GOVERNMENTS CAN LESSEN THE RISK** of starting a business and increasing entrepreneurship and wealth by:

   a. Minimizing spending and keeping **TAXES AND REGULATIONS** to a minimum.

   b. Allowing **PRIVATE OWNERSHIP** of business.

   c. Passing **LAWS** that enable businesspeople to write enforceable contracts.

   d. Establishing a **CURRENCY** that is tradable in world markets.

   e. **MINIMIZING CORRUPTION** in business and government.

TEXT FIGURE 1.3
Today's Dynamic Business
Environment
(Text page 12)

This text figure illustrates the four environments of business (economic and legal, technical, competitive, and social), bounded by the global business environment.

PPT 1-25
What Is the Business Environment?

(See complete PowerPoint slide notes on page 1.44.)

lecture link 1-6
AMERICA'S LOST DECADE

The business environment of the "Oughts" has been seen as an enormous step backward for the United States. (See the complete lecture link on page 1.57 in this manual.)

PPT 1-26
Government's Role in Business

(See complete PowerPoint slide notes on page 1.45.)

3. **CORRUPT AND ILLEGAL ACTIVITIES** negatively affect the business community and the economy.

4. The capitalist system relies heavily on honesty, integrity, and high ethical standards.

   a. The recent faltering economy was partially caused by mortgage bankers pushing borrowers into subprime mortgages.

   b. The ripple effects reduced the value of housing and led to a freeze in credit markets.

learning goal 4

Describe the effects of technology on businesses.

C. **THE TECHNOLOGICAL ENVIRONMENT**

1. Few technical changes have had a more lasting impact on businesses than **INFORMATION TECHNOLOGY.**

2. Innovations such as the iPhone, BlackBerry, Facebook, and Twitter have changed how people communicate.

3. **HOW TECHNOLOGY BENEFITS WORKERS AND YOU**

   a. ___TECHNOLOGY___ means everything from phones and copiers to computers, medical imaging devices, personal digital assistants, and various software programs that make business processes more efficient and productive.

      i. **EFFECTIVENESS** means producing the desired result.

      ii. **EFFICIENCY** means producing goods and services using the least amount of resources.

PPT 1-27
Corruption Worldwide

(See complete PowerPoint slide notes on page 1.45.)

MAKING
ethical decisions
(Text page 14)

PPT 1-28
Ethics Begins with You

(See complete PowerPoint slide notes on page 1.45.)

critical thinking exercise 1-3
MAKING ETHICAL DECISIONS

This exercise raises the question: What does the student do when he or she comes to a Making Ethical Decisions box in the text? (See complete exercise on page 1.68 of this manual.)

PPT 1-29
Benefits of Technology

(See complete PowerPoint slide notes on page 1.46.)

b. **_PRODUCTIVITY_** is the amount of output you generate given the amount of input (such as hours worked).

c. The average worker in the U.S. contributes over $63,000 to GDP.

d. Tools and technology increase productivity.

e. Farmers use high technology to increase production and profit.

4. **THE GROWTH OF E-COMMERCE**

a. **_E-COMMERCE_** is buying and selling of goods over the Internet.

b. There are two types of e-commerce transactions:

   i. **BUSINESS-TO-CONSUMER (B2C)**

   ii. **BUSINESS-TO-BUSINESS (B2B)**

c. **B2B E-COMMERCE** consists of selling goods and services from one business to another.

d. Traditional businesses need to learn how to deal with competition from B2B and B2C firms.

5. **USING TECHNOLOGY TO BE RESPONSIVE TO CUSTOMERS**

a. The businesses that are most responsive to customer wants and needs will succeed.

b. Businesses can use technology *(such as UPC bar codes on products)* to become more responsive.

c. A **_DATABASE_** is an electronic storage file for information; one use of databases is to store vast amounts of information about consumers.

bonus case 1-2
**NETWORKING OUTSIDE THE
NET**

Though a lot of business networking is now done through social media, it's no replacement for real human interaction. (See the complete case, discussion questions, and suggested answers beginning on page 1.72 of this manual.)

**social
media in
business**
(Text page 15)

PPT 1-30
JCPenney
Keeps in Touch

(See complete PowerPoint slide notes on page 1.46.)

lecture link 1-7
**EDUCATION'S NEW
WHITEBOARD**

Technology is also revolutionizing the educational sector. (See the complete lecture link on page 1.58 in this manual.)

PPT 1-31
E-Commerce

(See complete PowerPoint slide notes on page 1.46.)

    d.   Databases also allow stores to carry fewer items and less inventory.

    e.   However, gathering personal information about people has led to ***IDENTIFY THEFT***, obtaining individuals' personal information, such as Social Security and credit card numbers, for illegal purposes.

    f.   The Federal Trade Commission says that millions of Americans are victims of identify theft each year.

learning goal 5

Demonstrate how businesses can meet and beat competition.

D. **THE COMPETITIVE ENVIRONMENT**

    1.   Making quality products is not enough to stay competitive in world markets—now you have to offer quality products and outstanding service at competitive prices.

    2.   **COMPETING BY EXCEEDING CUSTOMER EXPECTATIONS**

        a.   Customers today want good quality at low prices plus great service.

        b.   Business is becoming **CUSTOMER-DRIVEN**—customers' wants and needs come first.

        c.   Successful companies must **LISTEN TO CUSTOMERS** to determine their wants and needs and then adjust their products, policies, and practices to meet these demands.

PPT 1-32
Databases and Identify Theft

(See complete PowerPoint slide notes on page 1.47.)

PPT 1-33
Protect Yourself from Identity Theft

(See complete PowerPoint slide notes on page 1.47.)

lecture link 1-8
PREVENTING IDENTITY THEFT

How to reduce identity theft and what to do when it happens (See the complete lecture link on page 1.59 in this manual.)

lecture link 1-9
MAGAZINES PLEAD PRINT'S CASE

Few industries are feeling the sting of competition like print media and they're scrambling to find ways to adapt to a digital world. (See the complete lecture link on page 1.61 in this manual.)

3. **COMPETING BY RESTRUCTURING AND EMPOWERMENT**

   a. To meet the needs of customers, firms must enable their frontline workers to **RESPOND QUICKLY TO CUSTOMER REQUESTS.**

   b. **_EMPOWERMENT_** is giving frontline workers the responsibility, authority, freedom, training, and equipment they need to respond quickly to customer requests.

   c. It sometimes takes years to restructure an organization to empower numbers.

learning goal 6

Analyze the social changes affecting businesses.

E. **THE SOCIAL ENVIRONMENT**

   1. **_DEMOGRAPHY_** is the statistical study of the human population in regard to its size, density, and other characteristics, such as age, race, gender, and income.

   2. **MANAGING DIVERSITY**

      a. Today diversity includes many more population groups, including seniors, people with disabilities, singles, the devout, and so on.

      b. The number of legal and illegal **IMMIGRANTS** has had a dramatic impact on cities and businesses.

   3. **THE INCREASE IN THE NUMBER OF OLDER CITIZENS**

      a. U.S. citizens aged 65–74 are the richest demographic group in U.S. society.

PPT 1-34
Using Empowerment to Compete in
Today's Market

(See complete PowerPoint slide notes on page 1.47.)

PPT 1-35
Demography

(See complete PowerPoint slide notes on page 1.48.)

lecture link 1-10
THE LANGUAGE OF BUSINESS

More businesses are looking for bilingual employees. (See the complete lecture link on page 1.61 of this manual.)

PPT 1-36
Demography of the U.S. by Age

(See complete PowerPoint slide notes on page 1.48.)

     b. By 2020, 22.8% of the population will be over 60 years old.

     c. Think of the career opportunities of providing goods and services for older adults.

     d. Paying Social Security to seniors will drain huge amounts of money from the economy.

     e. Soon there will be **LESS MONEY COMING INTO** the Social Security system than will **BE GOING OUT.**

4. **THE INCREASE IN THE NUMBER OF SINGLE-PARENT FAMILIES**

     a. **SINGLE PARENTS** have encouraged businesses to implement family-friendly programs such as **FAMILY LEAVE** and **FLEXTIME.**

learning goal 7

Identify what businesses must do to meet global challenges, including war and terrorism.

F. **THE GLOBAL ENVIRONMENT**

1. Two important environmental changes in recent years have been the **GROWTH OF GLOBAL COMPETITION** and the **INCREASE OF FREE TRADE** among nations.

     a. Improvements in transportation and communication have led to more trade.

     b. World trade (**GLOBALIZATION**) has significantly improved living standards around the world.

     c. World trade has both benefits and costs, as will be discussed in Chapter 3.

PPT 1-37
Projected Demography of the U.S. by Race in 2050

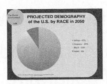

(See complete PowerPoint slide notes on page 1.48.)

PPT 1-38
The Rise of the U.S. Hispanic Population

(See complete PowerPoint slide notes on page 1.49.)

PPT 1-39
U.S. Population Changes

(See complete PowerPoint slide notes on page 1.49.)

PPT 1-40
Who Will Support Social Security?

(See complete PowerPoint slide notes on page 1.49.)

PPT 1-41
Worried about Social Security?

(See complete PowerPoint slide notes on page 1.50.)

PPT 1-42
Important Changes to the Global Environment

(See complete PowerPoint slide notes on page 1.50.)

PPT 1-43
World's Largest Cities Back in the Day and Today

(See complete PowerPoint slide notes on page 1.50.)

2. **WAR AND TERRORISM**

   a. The wars in Iraq and Afghanistan have drawn billions of dollars from the American economy.

   b. The threat of terrorism makes people more fearful and cautious and adds to a business's organizational costs.

   c. Businesspeople benefit from a peaceful and prosperous world.

G. **THE ECOLOGICAL ENVIRONMENT**

   1. **_CLIMATE CHANGE_** is the movement of the temperature of the planet up or down over time.

   2. **_GREENING_** is saving energy and producing products that cause less harm to the environment.

   3. These concepts will be highlighted throughout this text.

H. **HOW GLOBAL CHANGES AFFECT YOU**

   1. Expanding global commerce will create many career opportunities for American college graduates.

   2. Students must prepare themselves to compete in changing global environments.

learning goal 8

Review how past trends are being repeated in the present and what they mean for tomorrow's college graduates.

IV. THE EVOLUTION OF U.S. BUSINESS

A. American businesses have become so productive that fewer workers are needed in the industrial sector to produce goods.

PPT 1-44
Increasing Costs of the Global Environment

(See complete PowerPoint slide notes on page 1.51.)

PPT 1-45
Global Greening

(See complete PowerPoint slide notes on page 1.51.)

thinking green
(Text page 20)

PPT 1-46
Getting Involved Personally

(See complete PowerPoint slide notes on page 1.51.)

lecture link 1-11
THE HIGH DEMAND FOR GREEN DEGREES

As the job crunch was experienced by recent grads, students still in school started enrolling in sustainability programs. (See the complete lecture link on page 1.62 of this manual.)

progress assessment
(Text page 19)

PPT 1-47
Progress Assessment

(See complete PowerPoint slide notes on page 1.52.)

B. **PROGRESS IN THE AGRICULTURAL AND MANUFACTURING INDUSTRIES**

1. The use of **TECHNOLOGY** made the agricultural industry so **PRODUCTIVE** that the number of farmers dropped from about a third of the population to about 1%.

2. **AGRICULTURE** is still a major industry in the U.S., but fewer and larger farms have replaced millions of small farms.

3. Many farmers lost their jobs and went to work in factories.

4. Now **TECHNOLOGY** is making manufacturing more productive and workers again losing their jobs.

C. **PROGRESS IN THE SERVICE INDUSTRIES**

1. The fastest growing firms provide services in areas like law, health, telecommunications, entertainment, and finance.

2. **SERVICES** make up over 70% of the value of the U.S. economy and have generated almost all the increases in employment.

3. Service-sector growth has slowed, but is still the largest area of growth.

4. There are more high-paying jobs in the service sector than in the goods-producing sector.

D. **YOUR FUTURE IN BUSINESS**

1. The service sector now seems to be losing out to a new era.

2. This information-based global revolution will alter the way business is done in the future.

lecture link 1-12
MILESTONES IN BUSINESS

Some important dates in the history of business. (See the complete lecture link on page 1.63 of this manual.)

PPT 1-48
The Evolution of Business

(See complete PowerPoint slide notes on page 1.52.)

PPT 1-49
The Agricultural Era

(See complete PowerPoint slide notes on page 1.53)

PPT 1-50
The Manufacturing Era

(See complete PowerPoint slide notes on page 1.53)

PPT 1-51
The Service Era

(See complete PowerPoint slide notes on page 1.53)

lecture link 1-13
EARNING AN HONEST McPAYCHECK

While many food service businesses struggled during the recent recession, McDonald's flourished. (See the complete lecture link on page 1.63 of this manual.)

3. Most of the **CONCEPTS AND PRINCIPLES** that make business more effective and efficient are also applicable in government agencies and non-profit organizations.

V.   SUMMARY

PPT 1-52
The Information Technology Era

(See complete PowerPoint slide notes on page 1.54.)

TEXT FIGURE 1.4
What Is the Service Sector?
(Text page 22)

This text figure gives a representative list of services as classified by the government.

**progress
assessment**
(Text page 22)

PPT 1-53
Progress Assessment

(See complete PowerPoint slide notes on page 1.54.)

PowerPoint slide notes

PPT 1-1
Chapter Title

PPT 1-2
Monif Clarkes

PPT 1-3
Learning Goals

LEARNING GOALS

Chapter One

1. Describe the relationship between profit and risk, and show how businesses and nonprofits can raise the standard of living for all.

2. Compare and contrast being an entrepreneur and working for others.

3. Analyze the effects of the economic environment and taxes on businesses.

4. Describe the effects of technology on businesses.

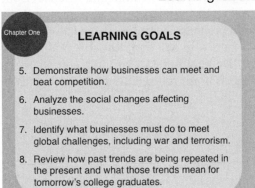

Answer: Grameen Bank and Muhammad Yunus

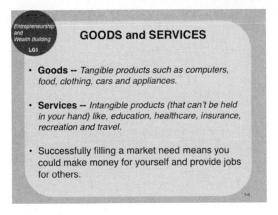

It is important to make sure that students understand the difference between goods and services. Emphasize that goods are tangible (can be held or touched) like Nike athletic shoes, while services are intangible (cannot be held in your hand) like a haircut.

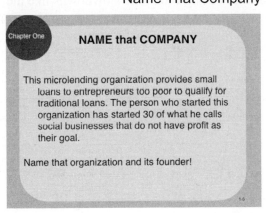

PPT 1-7
Business and Entrepreneurship

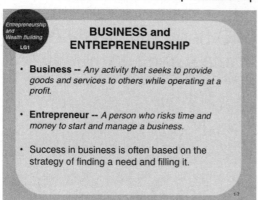

In the United States the entrepreneur is held in high regard. Most students have heard of Sam Walton and Michael Dell, but it often adds to the classroom experience if they understand how these entrepreneurs started their businesses. Sam Walton started Walmart with just one store in Arkansas in the 1960s. Michael Dell got his start building computers in his University of Texas dorm room, ultimately leading to the creation of Dell, Inc.

PPT 1-8
Revenue, Profit, and Loss

About 80,000 businesses in the United States close each year. Even more close during economic slowdowns like the one that started in 2008.

PPT 1-9
Risk

Irish entrepreneur Denis O'Brien makes billions by selling cell phones in the poorest and most violent countries in the world. Big risk, big profit.

PPT 1-10
How Is Tax Money Used?

Entrepreneurs provide jobs for others and the taxes they pay benefit the community.

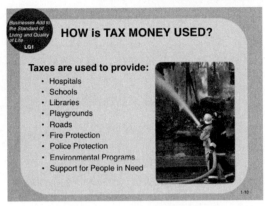

PPT 1-11
Standard of Living

Workers in Japan may make more than Americans, but a bottle of beer may cost $7 in Japan.

PPT 1-12
Quality of Life

The more money businesses create, the more is available to improve the quality of life for all citizens.

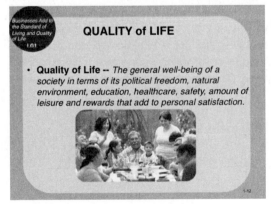

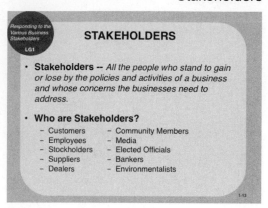

1. Outsourcing is the contracting with other companies to do some of the firm's functions. As the slide states, these companies are often in other countries. For example, Dell Computers and many other companies outsource support services to call centers in India and other Asian nations. This can be an emotional issue and one that students often do not understand. When discussing this topic with students, it is important for students to understand that outsourcing has occurred for years and does not always involve a company from the United States locating jobs in another country.

2. Once students understand outsourcing, the concept of insourcing can be discussed. For example, Hyundai operates plants in the United States. Its design and engineering headquarters are in Detroit, and it produces cars in Montgomery, Alabama, all of which employ American workers. Insourcing benefits the American worker such as when Toyota and Honda decided to build automobile manufacturing plants in Kentucky and Ohio rather than in Japan.

Nonprofit Organizations

Nonprofits use the same principles and skills you will learn in this class.

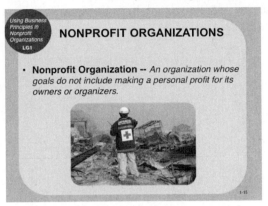

Well-Known Nonprofits in the United States

1. This slide provides a listing of well-known nonprofit organizations in the United States.

2. Some of the better known nonprofit organizations include Salvation Army, United Way, and the American Red Cross.

3. Ask students to identify smaller, local nonprofit organizations and discuss how they contribute to the community's quality of life.

Keeping Strong Employees at Nonprofits

1. Since few nonprofits can compete for qualified employees by offering higher salaries, they must find other ways to recruit, hire, and retain workers.

2. Many nonprofit workers choose to accept lower wages in exchange for the feeling that they are helping a good cause.

3. Since nonprofit work is often exhausting, managers need to find ways to help employees relax and celebrate their good works.

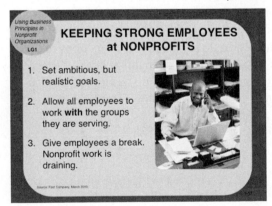

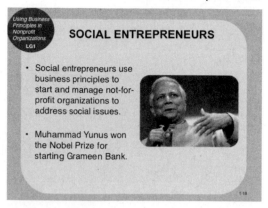

Muhammad Yunus and Grameen Bank are the answer to the Name That Company section at the top of this chapter and presentation. He has started 30 social businesses that do not have profit as their goal.

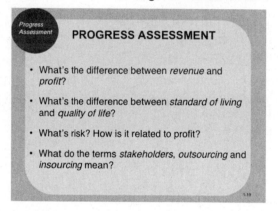

1. Revenue is the total amount of money a business takes in during a given period of time. Profit is the amount of money a business earns above and beyond what it spends for salaries and other expenses during a given period.

2. Standard of living is the amount of goods and services a person can buy with the money he or she has. Quality of life refers to the general well-being of society in terms of its political freedom, natural environment, education, health care, safety, amount of leisure, and rewards that add to the satisfaction and joy that other goods and services provide.

3. Risk is the chance an entrepreneur takes in losing time and money on a business that may not prove profitable. Usually, entrepreneurs willing to take the most risk make the highest profit.

4. Stakeholders are all the people who stand to gain or lose by the policies and activities of a business and whose concerns the business needs to address. Outsourcing is contracting with other companies (often in other countries) to do some or all the functions of a firm, like its production or accounting tasks. Insourcing is when foreign companies set up design and production facilities in the United States.

PPT 1-20
The Ups and Downs of Entrepreneurship

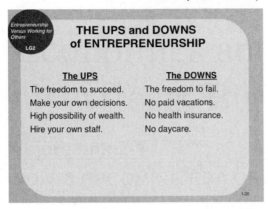

THE UPS and DOWNS of ENTREPRENEURSHIP

Entrepreneurship Versus Working for Others
LG2

The UPS	The DOWNS
The freedom to succeed.	The freedom to fail.
Make your own decisions.	No paid vacations.
High possibility of wealth.	No health insurance.
Hire your own staff.	No daycare.

PPT 1-21
Who Takes the Entrepreneurial Challenge?

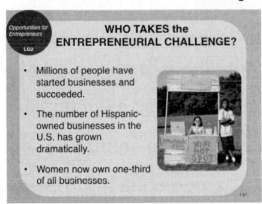

WHO TAKES the ENTREPRENEURIAL CHALLENGE?

Opportunities for Entrepreneurs
LG2

- Millions of people have started businesses and succeeded.
- The number of Hispanic-owned businesses in the U.S. has grown dramatically.
- Women now own one-third of all businesses.

PPT 1-22
Networking of Minority Businesses

NETWORKING of MINORITY BUSINESSES
(Spotlight on Small Business)

- Carol's Daughter, a company that creates and sells hair care and beauty products, was started by Lisa Price.
- Price experimented with fragrances in her Brooklyn kitchen.
- Through networking, Price found investors like Will Smith and Jay-Z.

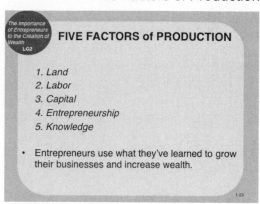

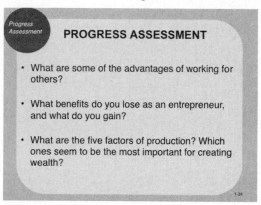

1. When working for others, someone else assumes the entrepreneurial risk and provides you with benefits (life health insurance, vacation time, etc.).

2. As an entrepreneur you have the freedom to make your own decisions and the potential for creating wealth, while sacrificing the benefits that working for others often provides.

3. The factors of production are land, labor, capital, entrepreneurship, and knowledge. Of these, entrepreneurship and knowledge seem to be the most important for creating wealth.

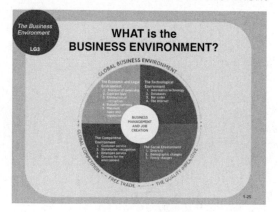

PPT 1-26
Government's Role in Business

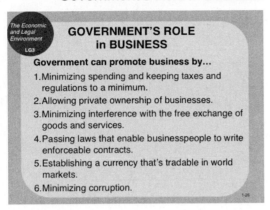

GOVERNMENT'S ROLE in BUSINESS

The Economic and Legal Environment — LG3

Government can promote business by...

1. Minimizing spending and keeping taxes and regulations to a minimum.
2. Allowing private ownership of businesses.
3. Minimizing interference with the free exchange of goods and services.
4. Passing laws that enable businesspeople to write enforceable contracts.
5. Establishing a currency that's tradable in world markets.
6. Minimizing corruption.

PPT 1-27
Corruption Worldwide

Canada is the 6th least corrupt, the United States is 22nd, and Mexico is 98th out of 178 countries.

CORRUPTION WORLDWIDE

The Economic and Legal Environment — LG3

Least Corrupt	Most Corrupt
1. Denmark	1. Somalia
2. New Zealand	2. Myanmar
3. Singapore	3. Afghanistan
4. Finland	4. Iraq
5. Sweden	5. Uzbekistan

Source: Transparency International, June 2011.

PPT 1-28
Ethics Begins with You

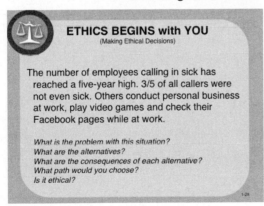

ETHICS BEGINS with YOU
(Making Ethical Decisions)

The number of employees calling in sick has reached a five-year high. 3/5 of all callers were not even sick. Others conduct personal business at work, play video games and check their Facebook pages while at work.

What is the problem with this situation?
What are the alternatives?
What are the consequences of each alternative?
What path would you choose?
Is it ethical?

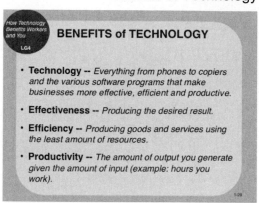

BENEFITS of TECHNOLOGY

How Technology Benefits Workers and You
LG4

- **Technology --** *Everything from phones to copiers and the various software programs that make businesses more effective, efficient and productive.*

- **Effectiveness --** *Producing the desired result.*

- **Efficiency --** *Producing goods and services using the least amount of resources.*

- **Productivity --** *The amount of output you generate given the amount of input (example: hours you work).*

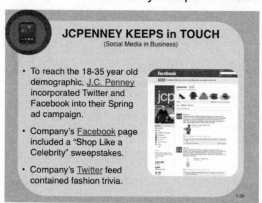

JCPENNEY KEEPS in TOUCH
(Social Media in Business)

- To reach the 18-35 year old demographic, J.C. Penney incorporated Twitter and Facebook into their Spring ad campaign.

- Company's Facebook page included a "Shop Like a Celebrity" sweepstakes.

- Company's Twitter feed contained fashion trivia.

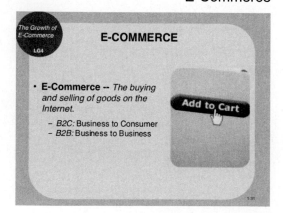

E-COMMERCE

The Growth of E-Commerce
LG4

- **E-Commerce --** *The buying and selling of goods on the Internet.*
  - *B2C:* Business to Consumer
  - *B2B:* Business to Business

Add to Cart

PPT 1-32

Databases and Identity Theft

1. The number of ID theft cases is rising every year. The Federal Trade Commission estimates that 9 million people per year have their identities stolen.

2. About 39% of the victims were between the ages of 18 and 39 (the same age group of many students).

PPT 1-33

Protect Yourself from Identity Theft

3. Approximately 16% of the victims had a personal relationship with the thief.

4. Top five states for identity theft (per capita) are Arizona, California, Nevada, Texas, and Florida.

5. Ask the students, How often do you throw away mail or other documents with your personal information on it without shredding it? *(It is becoming imperative that we shred all documents with personal info and keep the sharing of private info such as credit card and bank account information and Social Security numbers to a limited number of people.)*

PPT 1-34

Using Empowerment to Compete in Today's Market

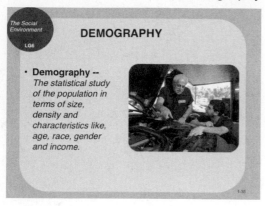

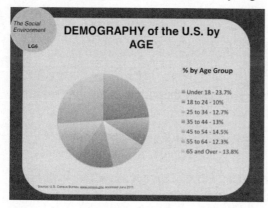

1. This slide highlights the age of the population in the United States.

2. Demography is the statistical study of the human population in terms of its size, density, and other characteristics such as age, race, gender, income, and so on.

3. The slide gives insight into the aging of the population with 66% of the population older than 24 years old.

4. Ask the students, How will the aging of the population impact businesses? *(Businesses will need to re-examine their approach to marketing and human resources in order to meet the challenges facing them. While some businesses will fail, other new businesses will emerge creating new opportunities.)*

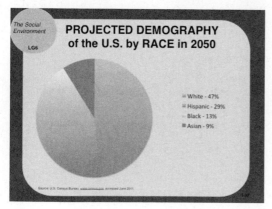

1. This slide gives insight into the changing ethnic landscape of the United States.

2. Legal and illegal immigrants have had a dramatic effect on many states.

3. Many local services, such as health care and education, are making efforts to adapt. Some changes include changing signs, brochures, and websites to reflect this change in demographics.

4. Ask the students, What changes have you noticed in your particular city? *(Answers may vary, but might include bilingual signs in government offices and the use of emergency room translators in local hospitals.)*

PPT 1-38
The Rise of the U.S. Hispanic Population

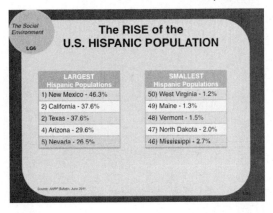

1. This slide expands on the previous slides, giving insight into the changing ethnic landscape of the United States.

2. Ask the students, Why to you think the southwestern states have the highest Hispanic populations, while the East Coast states are among the lowest? (Most students will probably note the obvious proximity of the southwestern states to Mexico.)

PPT 1-39
U.S. Population Changes

When discussing how demographic changes experienced in this country over the past 30 years have affected businesses, it often helps to use the grocery store as an example. The grocery store has evolved from a market selling primarily raw materials used to produce a meal into stores that now serve premade products that simply involve "heating and eating." Why? Some would argue this change has more to do with the two-income and single-parent household than any other environmental factor. Engaging students in this discussion is often useful to their understanding of how businesses must adapt to changing demographic circumstances.

PPT 1-40
Who Will Support Social Security

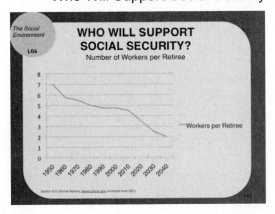

1. The number of workers per retiree has dropped dramatically since 1950.

2. Ask the students, What impact will the decline of the number of workers per retiree have in the future? (In the future, government might have to raise taxes and reduce benefits for individuals or use a means test in an effort to prevent Social Security payments from bankrupting the government.)

Worried About Social Security?

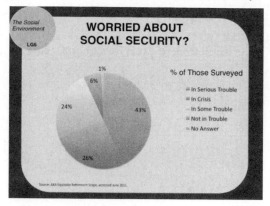

1. This slides shows that almost everybody in the United States thinks that Social Security is in trouble (only 6% think the system is not in trouble).

2. Ask the students, What do you think should be done to make sure that Social Security is around when you need it?

PPT 1-42

Important Changes to the Global Environment

PPT 1-43

World's Largest Cities Back in the Day and Today

Today Tokyo is three times larger than New York was in 1950 (when New York was the largest city in the world). New York doesn't even rank in the top five largest cities today. How will this changing population affect global trade?

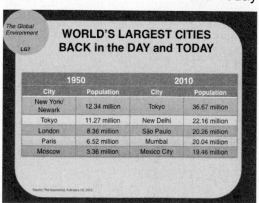

PPT 1-44

Increasing Costs of the Global Environment

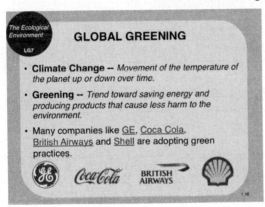

Ask the students, Can terrorism and an economic crisis like the one that began in 2008 decrease economic cooperation and free trade among nations? *(This question is at the same time alarming and thought provoking. Given recent events, asking students this question will get them thinking about how the world and events in faraway places can impact their lives.)*

PPT 1-45

Global Greening

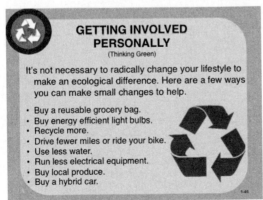

Links go to each company website's "green" section.

PPT 1-46

Getting Involved Personally

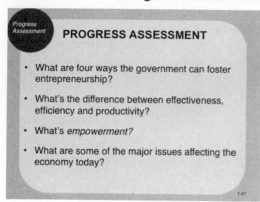

1. The government can foster entrepreneurship by:
   - Allowing private ownership of business
   - Passing laws that enable businesses to write enforceable contracts
   - Establishing a currency that is tradable in world markets
   - Minimizing corruption in business and in its own ranks

2. Effectiveness means producing the desired results. Efficiency means producing goods and services using the least amount of resources. Productivity is the amount of output you generate given the amount of input, such as the number of hours you work.

3. Empowerment is allowing workers to make decisions essential to producing high-quality goods and services.

4. Technology changes, identity theft, changing demographics, diversity, climate change, war, and terrorism are several issues of concern.

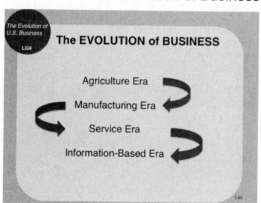

This slide, along with the next four, gives students a sense of perspective into the evolution of the U.S. economy.

PPT 1-49
The Agricultural Era

Agriculture was the leading industry in the United States in the 1800s. Technology has made farming so efficient, the number of farmers has dropped from about 33% of the population to about 1%. However, it is still a major industry in the United States.

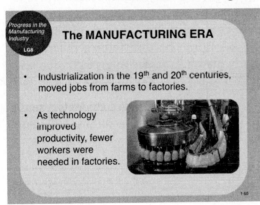

PPT 1-50
The Manufacturing Era

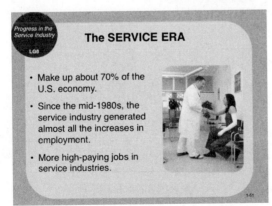

PPT 1-51
The Service Era

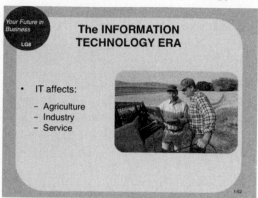

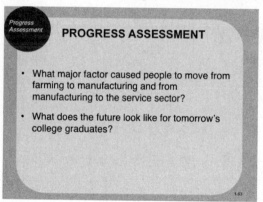

1. Efficiencies in agriculture led to the reduction in farms and growth in industry that caused workers to leave the farm and come to the cities. The growth of efficiencies in production had the same effect as in agriculture. As factories became more efficient and technologically driven, workers migrated to the service sector.

2. The information-based global revolution will alter all sections of the economy. It will be an interesting opportunity for college graduates.

lecture links

lecture link 1-1

THE WORLD'S RICHEST PEOPLE

In 2011, there were over 1,200 billionaires in the world. According to *Forbes* magazine, their combined worth was $4.5 trillion.[1]

RANK	NAME	COUNTRY OF CITIZENSHIP	AGE	WORTH ($ BILLIONS)
1	Carlos Slim Helu and family	Mexico	71	$74.0
2	William Gates III	United States	55	56.0
3	Warren Buffett	United States	80	50.0
4	Bernard Arnault	France	62	41.5
5	Lawrence Ellison	United States	67	39.5
6	Lakshmi Mittal	India	61	31.1
7	Amancio Ortega	Spain	71	31.0
8	Eike Batista	Brazil	54	30.0
9	Mukesh Ambani	India	54	27.0
10	Christy Walton and family	United States	56	26.5

lecture link 1-2

COMMUNITY COLLEGES THRIVE IN HARD TIMES

Community colleges have long been an integral part of the American higher educational system. The affordability and accessibility of community colleges drew many students to these institutions in the past, but never more so than in these tough economic times. The tightening of wallets across the country is sending an unprecedented number of bright young students, many originally bound for four-year schools, into the community college system. And while younger students may fret about their local college's lack of brand-name prestige, many are finding out that community colleges have even more to offer students than their four-year counterparts.

Forty-six percent of students on community college campuses are now younger than 21, up from 42.5% in 2003. Overall enrollment rose 17% on average. For most, the biggest advantage to enrolling at a community college is the cost. Average annual tuition at a community college clocks in at $2,554, compared to $7,000 annually at public four-year institutions and much more at private schools. But just because the price tag is lower doesn't mean students are getting a lower quality education. For one, community college professors tend to be free from the pressures of publishing scholastic research and therefore can spend more time in and outside the classroom with students. And while instructor workloads are sometimes larger at two-year institutions, community colleges still teach the same critical thinking and studying skills as four-year schools.

Community colleges can also act as a good starting point for students planning to earn a bachelor's degree. Students can complete two years at a community college, then transfer to a four-year college to finish their education. Many community colleges also offer affordable study-abroad programs, such as Montgomery College just outside of Washington, D.C. Students in the Montgomery Scholars program receive full scholarships to the school as well as a free summer trip to study at Cambridge University in England, one of the oldest and most well-regarded learning institutions in the world. With community colleges, one needn't travel too far from home to receive a world-class education.[ii]

lecture link 1-3

UNEMPLOYED CLERGY ON THE RISE

The hardship of the recent recession isn't exclusive to the secular world. Churches across the country are feeling the financial pinch as donations and attendance in many Christian denominations drop. As a result, an increasing number of churches have been forced to trim costs wherever they can. Unfortunately for some, that means laying off clergy. In 2009, the government estimated that about 5,000 clergy were looking for jobs, up from 2,000 in 2005. Additionally, a survey of the National Association of Church Business Administration found that one in every five members of the 3,000-member organization laid off staff due to the recession.

As the recession takes its toll on congregations across the nation, the coffers of many churches get barer by the day. Thirty percent of surveyed church attendees said they reduced their giving since the beginning of the financial crisis. Consequently, nearly half of the members of the National Association of Church Business Administration said they reduced or froze salaries and benefits for many employees. For recently sacked clergy, the job search can be daunting. The Presbyterian Church in America estimates that each of its 54 job openings has at least five pastors vying for the position.

Despite the recession-driven rise in jobless clergy, the 1.2% unemployment rate among clergy pales in comparison to the double-digit national average. But the path of a jobless clergyperson can often be more difficult than it would for the average layperson. For one, churches are exempt from unemployment taxes, so laid-off workers can't collect unemployment benefits. Some churches can afford to let clergy stay on the payroll until they find a new job, but many are too cash-strapped to even provide severance assistance. Most churches are so reluctant to lay off clergy in the first place that by the time the axe drops they don't have the cash to adequately provide for pink-slipped preachers.[iii]

lecture link 1-4

SOCIAL ENTREPRENEURSHIP: MERCY CORPS

In Indonesia, where 100 million people live on less than $2 a day, microfinance has become a crowded, chaotic field. More than 50,000 microfinance institutions (MFIs) operate, reaching 50 million poor people. An Oregon-based antipoverty group Mercy Corps saw an answer to the fractured approach in 2008, buying a struggling Balinese bank and reopening it as a wholesale bank exclusively serving MFIs. The mission of this "bank of banks" was to cut MFIs' costs and inefficiencies, and provide them with the capital, financial tools, and tech platforms they need to improve and expand their services. Says CEO Neal Keny-Guyer, "We wanted real impact." Keny-Guyer argues that microfinance needs such improvements to become a sustainable industry. The bank's first loans were distributed in the fall of 2008, and the program is being expanded to China, Nepal, and the Philippines.

lecture link 1-5

SOCIAL ENTREPRENEURSHIP: IMPROVING WORLD HEALTH WITHOUT PROFITS

Knowing that Victoria Hale was a pharmaceutical scientist, a friend called her, desperate. Their 13-year-old daughter had been diagnosed with a deadly form of cancer called Ewing's sarcoma. The daughter's doctors were offering little hope, and the cancer was spreading fast. Could Hale help? With the aid of a former FDA colleague, she began searching for experimental compounds that might offer any ray of hope. They found two substances that had shown initial promise in fighting the cancer, but both were sitting idle on laboratory shelves. No one was working to develop the compounds into drugs. The cancer was too rare to create an attractive market for new treatments.

The young girl lost her battle with cancer, and Hale was determined to change things. She created OneWorldHealth, the first U.S. nonprofit pharmaceutical company.

Hale identified five disease categories that she believed could benefit from an aggressive drug development effort, but would not be profitable. Her plan was this: Find research on these diseases that had already been conducted, but nothing had been done because the drug would not be profitable. She would then persuade the pharmaceutical company to donate the information to her in return for tax write-offs. Finally, she would seek funding from foundations and others to make those drugs available.

Hale got $4.7 million from the Bill and Melinda Gates Foundation for researching diseases in the developing world. She also negotiated deals with the World Health Organization and the National Institutes of Health to do some clinical trials. Hale hopes that she can sell some drugs at a profit in order to continue her work.

As scientists and companies heard about the organization's efforts, many began calling to say "We've got something you might be interested in." Many scientists are also volunteering their time and expertise. Hale doesn't find this surprising. "Most pharmaceutical researchers got into the business because they wanted to ease suffering and save lives. Systems may be flawed, but most people want to do the right thing," says Hale.

All organizations need money to operate. One of the major sources of money is investors who give money to firms in order to make a profit. Those firms have to be profitable. Nonprofit organizations usually rely on the donations from others to keep operating. Often that money comes from profit-making companies, like Celera, who are concerned about disease prevention, but can't stay in business unless they make a profit. Hale has found a way to link these organizations. [iv]

lecture link 1-6

AMERICA'S LOST DECADE

It's no secret that the past few years have been rough on the U.S. economy. Sadly, though, the American financial sector's recent rockiness tells only a portion of the decade's dire story. When looked at as a whole, the time known by some as the "Oughts" (2000–2009) was an enormous step backward for the economy. While every decade since the 1940s has seen job growth of at least 20%, from December 1999 on there has been zero net job creation in the United States. Adjusted for inflation, middle-income households made less money in 2008 than in 1999, marking the first decade to see falling median incomes since the data were first gathered in the 1960s. Finally, the net worth of American assets, such as the value of their houses and retirement funds, has also declined, another unprecedented occurrence in recent American economic history.

Some of these sobering figures could be attributed to poor timing, seeing as the prosperous 1990s gave way to the burst of the dot-com bubble in the early 2000s. But while bad luck may have a little to do with America's disastrous decade, most of the Oughts' stagnation stemmed from the trillions of dollars funneled into housing investment and consumer spending. The money that made its way into these markets found no sustainability, eventually creating a distorted depiction of economic growth that failed to reflect America's toxic addiction to debt. In total, household debt increased 117% from 1999 to its peak in 2008. At the same time, corporate debt spiraled out of control as financial firms engaged in fruitless buyouts and dumped billions into commercial real estate. The 2008 burst of the housing bubble eventually brought the financial world back to reality, where it has been struggling to pick up the pieces ever since.

For all its destructive elements, the economic debacle of the 2000s has succeeded in providing government officials, financial experts, and the public with some much-needed perspective. Due to the magnitude of the Oughts' financial failures, economists will be unraveling all its lessons for some time. However, one obvious source of reform for regulators is the banking industry. Instead of monitoring individual banks closely, regulators must now observe the banking industry as a whole to measure its overall effect on the economy. Reforms to Federal Reserve policy are also expected, but Fed officials are still uncertain how to implement them.[v]

lecture link 1-7
EDUCATION'S NEW WHITEBOARD

Technology advances have revolutionized the telecommunication industry, the computer industry, agriculture, manufacturing, and so on. Rarely mentioned, but just as surely transformed, is the non-profit sector, specifically education.

What's causing the latest buzz is an interactive whiteboard, the most coveted piece of educational equipment on the market today. The electronic chalkboards are essentially giant computer touch screens that let teachers display and change data with the touch of a finger. (Think of the interactive maps that the networks use on election eve.)

At schools fortunate enough to have them, interactive whiteboards are a blessing for educators struggling to engage a generation of students raised with the Internet. In the United Kingdom 70% of all primary and secondary classrooms have interactive whiteboards, compared with just 16% in the United States. Students in those classrooms made the equivalent of five months' additional progress in math. Multiple studies suggest that the devices boost attendance rates and classroom participation. At Dorchester School District 2 in Summerville, South Carolina, 1,200 interactive boards have been installed in the classrooms. "Students were bored" before the touch screens arrived, says Superintendent Joe Pye. "Trips to the principal's office are almost nonexistent now."

But holding back universal deployment is the cost of the devices, currently about $3,000. For cash-strapped school districts, the cost is prohibitive. Teachers have taken to old-fashioned fund-raising to buy the new whiteboards. At Cartier Elementary School in London, Ontario, three elementary school teachers agreed to be duct-taped to the gym wall while students hit them with pies.

Another roadblock—the steep learning curve with the device. A generation gap has opened with teachers who are still more comfortable creating lesson plans with pencil and paper. Many older educators are afraid of the boards. Training is essential. Otherwise, it's just another underused, expensive gizmo.[vi]

PREVENTING IDENTITY THEFT

Each year, millions of Americans fall prey to identity theft. Your identity is not just your unique DNA and fingerprints. It is also your Social Security number, credit card numbers, driver's license number, telephone calling records, date of birth, home address, phone numbers, and passwords. An identity thief can use those bits of information to take over your credit rating, bank account, and credit card accounts.

For example, personal information on about 650,000 customers of JCPenney and up to 100 other retailers could have been compromised when a computer disk went missing. GE Money, which handled credit card operations for JCPenney and many other retailers, reported that the missing information included Social Security numbers for about 150,000 people.

The Identity Theft Resource Center says there has been a sixfold increase in the number of credit breaches in the United States.

HOW IDENTITY IS STOLEN

Thieves often rely on hacking vulnerable computer systems to harvest information. In 2005, the credit card processing agency CardSystems revealed that it improperly kept information on credit card customers for research. When hackers breached the system, over 40 million customers were exposed.

In January 2009, Heartland Payment announced that the company's card processing system had been hacked. En route to Heartland's processing centers, data-sniffing software captured credit card information from the card's magnetic strip. This included everything needed to duplicate a card: card number, expiration date, and internal bank codes. Since the company handles more than 1.2 billion credit card transactions ranging from restaurants to retailers to payroll systems, chances are someone in every state was affected by this data loss.

Con artists can also pose as legitimate debt collectors or insurance agencies, scamming businesses into sending them sensitive information. In 2004, ChoicePoint sent thousands of reports stocked with names, Social Security numbers, and financial information to con artists.

Thieves can also harvest your individual information in a number of creative ways. "Dumpster diving" involves sorting through trash bins for loan applications, credit card documents, or anything printed with Social Security numbers. Crooks can lurk at ATMs or phone booths and "shoulder surf," picking off PINs, credit card numbers, and passwords. Some talented con artists have even attached data storage devices to ATMs to steal credit and debit card numbers. "Phishing," posing by e-mail or phone as a legitimate company and claiming that there is a problem with a customer's account, regularly takes in gullible consumers. Then there is the low-tech technique of stealing credit cards, tax info, and financial correspondence by rifling through unprotected mailboxes. Finally there is the good old-fashioned method of stealing wallets and purses.

HOW YOU CAN PROTECT YOURSELF

1. Place the contents of your wallet on a photocopy machine. Do both sides of each license, credit card, and so on. That way you will know what you had in your wallet and all of the account numbers and phone numbers to call and cancel. Keep the photocopy in a safe place.

2. Don't use the last four digits of your Social Security number, your mom's maiden name, birthdate, or pet's name as your password or PIN.

3. Shred financial documents and paperwork with personal information before your discard them; in fact, shred every piece of trash containing your credit card number, bank account number, Social Security number, or tax information.

4. Review your bills each month for misuse; store canceled checks safely; shred preapproved credit offers before throwing them away.

5. The next time you order checks, have your checks printed with only your initials (instead of first name) and last name. If someone takes your checkbook, he or she will not know if you sign your checks with just your initials or your first name, but your bank will know how you sign your checks.

6. Do not sign the back of your credit cards. Instead, put "PHOTO ID REQUIRED."

7. When you are writing checks to pay on your credit card accounts, do not put the complete account number on the "For" or "Memo" line. Instead, just put the last four numbers. The credit card company knows the rest of the number. That way no one who might be handling your check as it passes through the entire check-processing channel will have access to it.

8. Put your work phone number on your checks instead of your home phone. If you have a Post Office box, use that instead of your home address. If you do not have a P.O. Box, use your work address. Never have your Social Security number printed on your checks. You can add it at the checkout if it is absolutely necessary (and it usually is NOT). But if you have it printed, anyone can get it.

9. Never click on links sent in unsolicited e-mails; instead, type in a Web address you know. Use firewalls, antispyware, and antivirus software to protect your home computer.

10. Most states are now moving away from using Social Security numbers on driver's licenses. When you renew your license, ask about using a substitute number.

SIGNS THAT YOUR IDENTITY MIGHT HAVE BEEN STOLEN

Be alert to signs that require immediate attention such as:

1. Bills that do not arrive as expected

2. Unexpected credit cards or account statements

3. Denials of credit for no apparent reason

4. Calls or letters about purchases you did not make

WHAT TO DO IF YOUR IDENTIFY IS STOLEN[vii]

1. Immediately cancel your credit cards. The key is having the toll-free numbers and your card numbers on hand so you know whom to call. Keep those where you can find them. Follow up in writing with copies of supporting documents. Choose new passwords for new accounts.

2. File a police report immediately in the jurisdiction where your credit cards were stolen. This proves to credit providers that you were diligent, and this is the first step toward an investigation.

3. Call the three national credit reporting organizations immediately to place a fraud alert on your name and Social Security number. The alert means any company that checks your credit knows your information was stolen, and it has to contact you by phone to authorize new credit.

4. File a complaint with the Federal Trade Commission, and report the fraud to the Social Security Administration.

Below are the important telephone numbers you will need to begin rebuilding your credit:

Equifax: 1-800-766-0008 (www.equifax.com)

Experian: 1-888-EXPERIAN (www.experian.com)

Trans Union: 1-800-680-7289 (www.transunion.com)

Federal Trade Commission 1-877-ID-THEFT (www.ftc.gove/idtheft)

Social Security Administration (fraud line): 1-800-269-0271 (www.ssa.gov)

lecture link 1-9

MAGAZINES PLEAD PRINT'S CASE

For years, print media publications have been scrambling to find suitable ways to adapt to the digital age. In anticipation of Apple's iPad, for example, a group of magazine publishers combined their efforts to devise a way to migrate magazines from the paper issue to the electronic tablet. But another group of publishers, headed by *Rolling Stone* founder Jann Wenner, is defending the legitimacy of their current medium with an unprecedented joint ad campaign. Along with publishers like Conde Nast, Meredith, and Time Inc., Wenner and company aim to remind readers about the "power of print."

The publishers pooled $90 million to purchase over 1,400 pages in ads that will appear in magazines like *Vogue* and *People* throughout the year. The ads push the immersive experience of reading a physical copy of a magazine as opposed to the fleeting experience of casually browsing the Web. For instance, one ad featuring swimmer Michael Phelps includes the tagline, "We surf the Internet. We swim in magazines." This new stance on print may seem counterproductive after publishers have been touting the bright digital future of magazines for years. But instead of viewing the new campaign as a step back, publishers see it as a public reinforcement of print journalism as their greatest asset.

The companies will still need to search for new ways to harness technology to endure into the future, though. The Internet's share of global ad spending is expected to rise to 16% by 2012, up from 12% in 2009. By the middle of the decade, experts predict the Internet will finally usurp newspapers as the world's second largest advertising medium next to television. Nevertheless, the "power of print" publishers are right to say that print isn't dead yet. Magazine readership rose 4.3% last year. Also, after a dry two years, magazine ad sales are on the rise once again.[viii]

lecture link 1-10

THE LANGUAGE OF BUSINESS

The population of the United States is becoming increasingly diverse. Today Hispanics are the fastest-growing minority population. These consumers have significantly increased the demand for bilingual salespersons and professionals throughout the economy.

One such business is Arise Virtual Solutions, a call center that provides customer service for about 40 companies. About a third of the independent contractors who work for the company are bilingual, many of them immigrants or first-generation Americans who grew up speaking the language of their parents' homelands.

According to Mary Bartlett, talent manager for Arise, by far the biggest demand is for Spanish. Companies want someone who can "really connect with the customer." Among her employees is Susan Mattingly, who grew up speaking and writing in both English and Spanish because her Cuban-born mother wanted to keep the family's Latino heritage alive. Mattingly is among an estimated 11% of Americans who speak English and a second language fluently, according to the Census Bureau.

Most workers in the United States don't need to speak or write a second language. But recruiters say some telemarketing, banking, engineering, and financial service companies are looking for workers and managers with bilingual skills because of the growing immigrant population of the United States or because they are doing more business in foreign countries. According to Manpower Professional, the *Fortune* 500 companies are asking more frequently for managers who speak Spanish, Portuguese, and Mandarin Chinese.

Kevin Hendzel, spokesperson for the American Translators Association, says demand is up for skilled people who can read and write in a foreign language. He attributes that to increased international trade and an executive order that requires federally funded institutions and agencies to provide bilingual services to clients with limited English skills. Professional translators and interpreters usually not only take college-level language classes but also attend professional language schools that require their students to live in the countries whose languages they want to become proficient in. "It takes a long time and a lot of effort to master a language," says Hendzel.

States with the highest percentage of persons speaking a language other than English at home are:

California, 42.5%

New Mexico, 36.5%

Texas, 33.6%

New York, 28.8%

Arizona, 28%

States with the lowest percentage include:

West Virginia, 2.3%

Mississippi, 3.1%

Kentucky, 4.1%

Alabama, 4.2%

Montana, 4.7%[ix]

lecture link 1-11

THE HIGH DEMAND FOR GREEN DEGREES

We all know the job market has been tough on new college grads the past few years. Despite drive and degrees, many graduates left school only to find few opportunities for the young and inexperienced. In order to avoid the job crunch, currently enrolled students are beginning to seek majors that are more likely to promise success in the job market after graduation. One such area is environmental sustainability, which the Obama administration estimates will have 52% job growth through 2016. As a result, more schools are adding green majors to their curriculums, and students are filling the classes in droves.

In 2005 only three schools had energy and environmental sustainability degree programs. In 2008 though, colleges big and small created more than 100 major, minor or certificate programs in green studies. Even cash-strapped schools that have cut other majors are adding sustainability degrees to their curriculum. The idea is too good for many colleges to pass up: Students want to take the classes, and employers actually want to hire the trained students. For example, Arizona State University established an undergrad program in sustainability studies. Now the school has about 600 sustainability majors on campus, an unprecedented number for a new degree program.

Similar programs have been established in top-flight schools like MIT and the University of California–Berkeley. Some colleges, such as Illinois State University, have received grant money from the Department of Energy to start up sustainability course plans. For several of these schools, renewable energy and environmental majors can be among the most selective degree programs. But as long as green jobs stay in demand, which by all accounts they should, green degrees are expected to turn up at even more schools.[x]

lecture link 1-12

MILESTONES IN BUSINESS

190	Development of the abacus
1776	American Revolution
1790	First patent laws are passed
1830s	Labor begins to organize
1834	McCormick patents wheat harvester
1841	First American advertising agency
1867	Invention of the typewriter
1876	Invention of the phone
1903	Wright brothers invent airplanes
1911	Invention of air conditioning
1930	First supermarket/Beginning of Depression
1946	A general-purpose computer is available
1950s	The service economy takes off
1955	Disneyland opens
1963	Equal pay for equal work
1972	E-mail is invented
1976	Apple Computers are introduced
1981	IBM PCs enter the fray
1996–2000	Fastest-growing industries are in services: computer and data processing, health, public relations, residential care, etc.
2003	Genetic engineering growing in importance
2007–2008	Housing market collapses; stock market falls over 50%; government nationalizes major financial institutions
2009	Stem cell research is approved

lecture link 1-13

EARNING AN HONEST McPAYCHECK

McJobs, a term that refers to low-paying, advancement-free work, came into prominence in the United States as the recession ravaged the job market. Understandably, McDonald's didn't appreciate the association very much. After all, as the company's vice president for the Boston area Robert Garcia said, "with a McJob comes a McPaycheck." And while unemployment continues to soar, McDonald's did its part to spur on growth on April 19, 2011, by hiring 50,000 people in a single day.

While many food-service businesses struggled during the downturn, McDonald's flourished as a low-cost option for penny-pinchers who still wanted to eat out occasionally. The company began receiving record numbers of employment applications from college grads, professionals and others needing to supplement their incomes. One hiring spree on the West Coast in 2010 brought in more than 60,000 applications for 13,000 positions.

Analysts note that it's wise for the company to make such a big hiring push now. Although unemployment still remains high nationally, in some regions the restaurant industry is beginning to hire again. By making such a big splash now, McDonald's is putting its name ahead of other companies that graduates might consider. Contrary to the popular view, McDonald's actually offers many opportunities for job advancement. More than three-quarters of its managers and half its franchise owners started behind a grill and worked their way up. And with managers pulling in $50,000 or more annually, many are beginning to see McDonald's in a new light.[xi]

critical
thinking exercises

Name: _____

Date: _____

critical thinking exercise 1-1
HOW MUCH PROFIT?

The text defines profit as "the amount a business earns above and beyond what it spends for salaries and other expenses." Choose a large corporation representing each of the following types of companies. Using the above profit definition, how much profit as a percentage of sales do you think each corporation earns? In other words, out of every dollar a company earns, how much does it keep?

1. **BANKING**

   Corporation _____   Percent Estimated Profit _____

2. **FOOD MANUFACTURER**

   Corporation _____   Percent Estimated Profit _____

3. **AIRLINE**

   Corporation _____   Percent Estimated Profit _____

4. **COMPUTER COMPANY**

   Corporation _____   Percent Estimated Profit _____

5. **OIL AND PETROLEUM**

   Corporation _____   Percent Estimated Profit _____

notes on critical thinking exercise 1-1

Students often have a much-exaggerated idea of the amount of profit big corporations make. This exercise should help set the record straight.

Each spring, *Fortune* magazine publishes a comprehensive listing of the largest U.S. corporations along with annual income, profit, employees, and so on. There are several financial references on the Web, such as www.moneycentral.msn.com/investor, www.biz.yahoo.com, or www.marketwatch.com. You can also find the information on each corporation's website. You can use these resources to find the most recent profit figures for comparison.

critical thinking exercise 1-2
JOB AND CAREER VERSUS OWNING A BUSINESS

To help make a decision about the advantages of pursuing a career and the advantages of owning your own business, use the list below to answer some basic questions. At the end, look at your two choices and see where you might have a reason to pursue your anticipated career or where you might find an interest and potential desire to be a small-business owner.

1. **CAREER SALARY OPPORTUNITIES** (circle one)

    Beginning Salary (average/good/excellent)

    Upper Job Salary (average/good/excellent)

2. **CAREER JOB OPPORTUNITIES** (circle one)

    Growing Field (yes/no)

    Requires Trade School/Associate Degree/Bachelor's Degree (yes/no)

    Best-Sized Company for Career Job (small/middle-sized/large)

3. **SMALL-BUSINESS OWNERSHIP OPPORTUNITIES** (circle one)

    Requires Up-Front Investment (small investment/medium-sized investment/large investment)

    Potential Franchise Has a Good Business Model (yes/no)

    Competition from Other Franchise Owners Will Be (nonexistent/some competition/will be very competitive)

4. **POTENTIAL RETURN ON THE SMALL-BUSINESS PURCHASE** (circle one)

    Provides Purchase of Additional Locations (yes/no)

    Has Name Recognition (yes/no)

    Has a Good Support System (yes/no)

5. If you could, would pursuing your ideal career be worth the investment? (yes/no)

6. Are you willing to make the investment (more schooling) and work for moderate pay to get the knowledge and experience to make this investment pay off? (yes/no)

7. If you could investment in your own business, would you and could you obtain the necessary finances to make this happen? (yes/no)

8. Is the risk of the unknown in the business environment worth the pursuit of your time, money, and family adjustment to own your own business? (yes/no)

9. Given the two choices, what direction would you rather pursue?

critical thinking exercise 1-3
MAKING ETHICAL DECISIONS

Throughout the textbook, you will see a box in each chapter called Making Ethical Decisions. You will be given a short description of a situation and then asked what you would do in that situation. These boxes may or may not be assigned by your professor, but you will benefit greatly by reading them and answering the questions. If they are assigned, you probably won't be required to hand in a written report. Your professor will probably have no real way of knowing if you read the boxes and answered the questions. You are likely to be "on your honor."

This is your first ethical situation in this course: You come to a Making Ethical Decisions box in your text. What do you decide to do—read and answer the questions, or skip it and go on?

Use the questions below to help you make your decision.

1.   What is the problem?

2.   What are your alternatives?

3.   What are the effects of each alternative? (What will happen if you choose that alternative?)

4.   Which alternative will you choose? Why?

5.   Is your choice ethical? (Would you want your family and professor to know of your decision? Would you want it printed in the school paper? Is it fair to all parties involved?)

notes on critical thinking exercise 1-3

It is easy to skip ethical boxes in a text because they don't seem to have any direct relationship to your main goal in this class—to learn about business so you can get a good job and make good money. The problem is that businesspeople tend to have the same attitude. They don't want to waste their time making ethical decisions—they want to make decisions that result in more profit for the firm. There comes a time, however, when society must recognize the need for making moral and ethical decisions and puts so much pressure on people that they conform. This can take the form of laws, but it is much easier to permit more freedom for people to choose to act morally and ethically on their own. You should encourage your students to choose what is right always, and what is right in this case is to consider the moral and ethical ramifications of their business decisions so that it becomes automatic. "Is it right?" should be heard in corporate offices as often as "Is it profitable?"

bonus cases

bonus case 1-1
THE WORLD'S LARGEST CHARITY

Bill Gates is one of the wealthiest people in the world. According to Forbes magazine, his net worth is $56 billion. But at age 50, Bill Gates earned respect in a new way. Along with his wife Melinda, the chair of Microsoft became the greatest philanthropist in history. Melinda, a former Microsoft colleague, has a bachelor's degree in computer science and economics and a master's in business from Duke University. (Bill dropped out of Harvard at the end of his sophomore year to run Microsoft.)

In its short existence, the Bill and Melinda Gates Foundation has already helped save at least 700,000 lives in poor countries through its investments in vaccinations. In the United States, its library project has brought computers and Internet access to 11,000 libraries. The fund sponsored the biggest privately funded scholarship program in history, sending over 9,000 high-achieving minority students to college. It is the largest foundation in the world, with an endowment of about $35 billion. Each year the Gates Foundation spends almost the same amount as the World Health Organization (WHO).

In 1993, advisers gave Bill Gates a copy of the 1993 World Bank Development report. The document explained how many millions of people in poor countries die from diseases that already have cures. Then it listed the most cost-effective methods of preventing those deaths, from immunization to AIDS prevention to nutrition. The document reads like a blueprint for the Gates foundation.

In June 2006, Bill Gates announced that he was stepping down from full-time duties at Microsoft, giving up his role as chief software architect, to devote more attention to the Gates Foundation.

The Gateses run the Seattle-based foundation like a business. They are fluent in the science of public health, and both use the language of business to describe their philanthropic work. "There is no better return on investment than saving the life of a newborn," said Melinda.

The foundation has been able to instill a rare level of accountability from its grantees. In India, the foundation runs an HIV AIDS-prevention program, headed by Ashok Alexander. Alexander calls the program's clinics "franchises." In 2005, Alexander cut off funding to three nongovernmental organizations because they did not meet agreed-upon milestones. "People are not used to being terminated for nonperformance," says Alexander.

Gates did not keep his title of top philanthropist for long. In the same month that Gates left Microsoft, Warren Buffett announced that he planned to give away his stake in Berkshire-Hathaway, the company he founded, worth more than $44 billion. Buffett will divide the gift over five foundations, but the largest amount will go to the Gates Foundation. Buffett's donation exceeds the amounts given by the great philanthropists of the past. Andrew Carnegie's giving totaled about $380 million—$7.6 billion in today's dollars. Based on the Berkshire stock price on the day the gift was announced, Buffett's gifts would be worth $37 billion. Because the donation is in the form of Berkshire stock shares given over time, the total donation could grow in value as the company grows.

According to Buffett, he always intended to have his wife oversee his charitable giving when he died. But after she died in 2004, he saw an opportunity to invest in "an existing well-respected foundation run by two ungodly bright people." He changed plans and started giving away his fortune in 2006.

Buffett credits his late wife Susan for his change in priority. "We agreed with Andrew Carnegie, who said that huge fortunes that flow in large part from society should in large part be returned to society," said Buffett.

The gift more than doubled the size of the Gates Foundation. "We are awed by our friend Warren Buffett's decision to use his fortune to address the world's most challenging inequities," Bill and Melinda Gates said in a statement. "As we move forward with the work, we do so with a profound sense of responsibility. Working with Warren and with our partners around the world, we have a tremendous opportunity to make a positive difference in people's lives." [xii]

discussion questions for bonus case 1-1

1. How do Bill and Melinda Gates use basic business principles to run the Gates Foundation?

2. Since the foundation does not earn a profit, how should its success be judged?

3. Most philanthropists are wealthy individuals who begin their charitable work late in life after years of building an enterprise. Why do you think Gates started so early in his life?

4. Why do you think Buffett chose the Gates Foundation for his record-breaking donation?

notes on discussion questions for bonus case 1-1

1. *How do Bill and Melinda Gates use basic business principles to run the Gates Foundation?*

   They use business principles such as return on investment, responsibility, and accountability. Running a philanthropic enterprise is much the same as running a business. You have the same kind of goals, the same need for good workers, the same need to measure performance, and the same need to fire incompetent workers.

2. *Since the foundation does not earn a profit, how should its success be judged?*

   Performance measures will differ based on the goals established. One goal may be to provide medicine for a certain number of people. Another might be to develop a vaccine for malaria within six months. Each goal calls for a different measure of success. One measure may be simply to raise the public's interest in an issue—such as poor schools, or poverty in the United States.

3. *Most philanthropists are wealthy individuals who begin their charitable work late in life after years of building an enterprise. Why do you think Gates started so early in his life?*

   Gates was encouraged to do so by other entrepreneurs. Bill and Melinda have a passion for certain causes, and are willing and able to back their wants with the finances necessary. Gates did not leave his business until it was running smoothly and people were in place to keep it going. In fact, new people may add new innovations and help the company to grow, creating more wealth for the Gates family, and more donations to worthy causes.

4. *Why do you think Buffett chose the Gates Foundation for his record-breaking donation?*

   The Gates Foundation is run like a business, with clear mission, strategies, and controls. This appeals to a businessperson like Buffett. Also, the donation is so huge, most charities do not have the infrastructure to absorb it. The Gates Foundation already has a large global network in place.

bonus case 1-2
NETWORKING OUTSIDE THE NET

On the surface, people appear to network with one another now more than ever. Social media dominate many people's lives while smartphones ensure that everybody can get in touch with everyone else anywhere at anytime. Nevertheless, digital interaction is no replacement for genuine human contact. As social media become more prevalent and accessible, the information they disseminate runs the risk of losing its value. To put it another way, Which carries more weight: a handshake or a Facebook poke?

For recent grads and experienced rat race veterans alike, nothing beats the old networking maxim "See and be seen." Industry events and conferences provide invaluable face time and can be found listed in trade magazines and, ironically, on social networks. Though living one's professional life solely online can be detrimental, Facebook and Twitter are useful for finding solid networking spots, especially informal gatherings. Green Drinks, for instance, regularly hosts casual get-togethers for green industry professionals to meet and exchange information.

Networking face-to-face also means maintaining a professional image. Not only does that entail dressing well and speaking clearly, it also includes promptly returning correspondence and clearing your Facebook page of any regrettable photos. Again, it's important to remember that social media and "real life" are not separate things. Social networking practices like "tweetups" help bridge the gap by putting people in physical contact with those who have active online personas. Finally, keep in mind that networking goes both ways. If people come off too aggressive about their own ambitions, they may appear too wrapped up in their own endeavors to care much about their contacts. Young professionals are advised to be ready to give assistance first rather than asking for it on the first meeting. That way they can build a rapport of equality that could pay off in the long term.

discussion questions for bonus case 1-2

1.   What can we conclude about digital interaction and human contact?

2.   Why is it important to keep your Facebook account professional?

notes on discussion questions for bonus case 1-2

1.   *What can we conclude about digital interaction and human contact?*

It's obvious that, used correctly, the two can go together like peanut butter and jelly. As the abstract notes, industry events and conferences provide valuable face time with peers and contacts. Social media can keep you informed about such opportunities and also facilitate valuable follow-up after key events.

2   *Why is it important to keep your Facebook account professional?*

Your Facebook page provides a image of you in the same way your personal appearance does. Regrettable photos or postings can come back to hurt a person's image and perhaps his or her career.

endnotes

[i] *Source:* "The World's Billionaires," *Forbes*, March 2011.

[ii] *Source:* Michelle R. Davis, "The Alternative: Younger Students Give Community College a Second Look," *The Washington Post Magazine*, April 11, 2010.

[iii] *Source:* Joe Light, "Joblessness Hits the Pulpit," *The Wall Street Journal*, May 17, 2010.

[iv] *Sources:* Allison Overholt, "Health and the Profit Motive," *Fast Company,* February 2003, p. 38; Victoria Hale, "Creating More Paths to Hope," *Newsweek*, December 6, 2004.

[v] *Source:* Neil Irwin, "A Lost Decade for U.S. Economy, Workers," *The Washington Post,* January 1, 2010.

[vi] *Source:* Matthew Philips, "It Makes Teachers Touchy," *Newsweek*, September 22, 2008.

[vii] *Sources:* "Your Privacy for Sale," *Consumer Reports*, July; "Deter, Detect, Defend: Avoid ID Theft," The Federal Trade Commission, www.ftc.gov; Sid Kirchheimer, "Phishing Phrenzy," *AARP Bulletin,* February 2007; David Koenig, "Data Lost on 650,000 Credit Card Holders," Associated Press, January 18, 2008; "Major Data Breach Puts Millions at Risk," CBS News, January 23, 2009; Brennon Slattery, "Heartland Has No Heart for Violated Customers," *PC World*, www.PCWorld.com, January 21, 2009; Elinor Mills, "Three Data Breaches Hit Florida, One Hits the Feds," *CNET News,* www.CNET.com, February 20, 2009; Erik Larkin, "Keep Tabs on Your Financial Data to Fight Identity Theft," *PC World*, www.PCWorld.com, August 15, 2008; Elinor Mills, "'SMiShing' Fishes for Personal Data Over Cell Phone," *CNET News,* www.CNET.com.

[viii] *Source*: Russell Adams and Shire Ovide, "Magazines Team Up to Tout 'Power of Print,'"*The Wall Street Journal,* March 1, 2010.

[ix] *Sources:* "Firms Seek More Bilingual Workers," Gannett News Service, *Clarion-Ledger,* May 13, 2007; DatabankUSA, *AARP Bulletin,* April 2008; U.S. Census Bureau, www.census.gov.

[x] *Source:* Julie Schmidt, "As Colleges Add Green Majors and Minors, Classes Fill Up," *USA Today,* December 28, 2009.

[xi] *Source:* Katie Johnston Chase, "Fast-Food King Has Openings," *The Boston Globe,* April 19, 2011.

[xii] *Sources*: Amanda Ripley, "*Time* Persons of the Year: From Riches to Rags," *Time*, December 26, 2005–January 2, 2006, pp. 72–88; Liv Grossman, "Bill Gates: Giving It Away in Style," *Time*, April 18, 2005; Steven Levy, "Bill Gates Goes Part Time at Microsoft," *Newsweek,* June 17, 2006; Yuki Noguchi, "Gates Foundation to Get Bulk of Buffett's Fortune," *The Washington Post*, June 26, 2006; Carol J. Loomis, "Warren Buffett Gives Away His Fortune," *Fortune*, June 25, 2006; "The World's Billionaires," *Forbes*, March 2011; information from www.gatesfoundation.org, accessed August 2011.

Understanding Economics and How It Affects Business

chapter 2

critical thinking exercises

bonus case

what's new in
this edition

additions to the 10th edition:

- Getting to Know John Maynard Keynes, Economist

- Discussion of state capitalism in section Understanding Free-Market Capitalism

- Reaching Beyond Our Borders: China's Changing Economy

revisions to the 10th edition:

- Text was revised to eliminate redundancy and tighten discussions.

- Statistical data and examples throughout the chapter were updated to reflect current information.

- Spotlight on Small Business: A Small Loan Can Make a Big Difference

- Thinking Green: Bringing in the Green with Green Products

- Making Ethical Decisions: Corruption's Effect on the Economy

deletions from the 9th edition:

- Getting to Know Muhammad Yunus, Founder of the Grameen Bank

- Discussion of chained consumer price index from section Key Economic Indicators

- Reaching Beyond Our Borders

brief chapter outline and learning goals

Understanding Economics and How It Affects Business

Getting To Know JOHN MAYNARD KEYNES, ECONOMIST

learning goal 1
Explain basic economics.

I. HOW ECONOMIC CONDITIONS AFFECT BUSINESSES
   A. What Is Economics?
   B. The Secret to Creating a Wealthy Economy
   C. Adam Smith and the Creation of Wealth
   D. How Businesses Benefit the Community

learning goal 2
Explain what capitalism is and how free markets work.

II. UNDERSTANDING FREE-MARKET CAPITALISM
   A. The Foundations of Capitalism
   B. How Free Markets Work
   C. How Prices Are Determined
   D. The Economic Concept of Supply
   E. The Economic Concept of Demand
   F. The Equilibrium Point, or Market Price
   G. Competition within Free Markets
   H. Benefits and Limitations of Free Markets

learning goal 3
Compare socialism and communism.

III. UNDERSTANDING SOCIALISM
   A. The Benefits of Socialism
   B. The Negative Consequences of Socialism

IV. UNDERSTANDING COMMUNISM

learning goal 4

Analyze the trend toward mixed economies.

V. THE TREND TOWARD MIXED ECONOMIES

learning goal 5

Discuss the economic system of the United States, including the significance of key economic indicators (especially GDP), productivity, and the business cycle.

VI. UNDERSTANDING THE U.S. ECONOMIC SYSTEM

    A. Key Economic Indicators

        1. Gross Domestic Product

        2. The Unemployment Rate

        3. Inflation and Price Indexes

    B. Productivity in the United States

    C. Productivity in the Service Sector

    D. The Business Cycle

learning goal 6

Contrast fiscal policy and monetary policy, and explain how each affects the economy.

    E. Stabilizing the Economy through Fiscal Policy

    F. Fiscal Policy in Action During the Recent Economic Crisis

    G. Using Monetary Policy to Keep the Economy Growing

VII. SUMMARY

lecture outline

Getting to Know JOHN MAYNARD KEYNES, ECONOMIST

Keynes was one of the economists who had a great influence on U.S. economic policy. He believed if the economy was in a recession, the government should increase spending and cut taxes to stimulate the economy. Keynesian theory has been in and out of favor since the 1930s and what Presidents Bush and Obama had in mind when they attempted to stimulate the economy.

NAME THAT company

This organization lends small amounts of money to people in poor countries. For example, it loaned a woman in Uganda enough to buy a refrigerator. She was able to sell fresh food from the refrigerator and make enough money for her family to succeed. Name this organization.

Students should read the chapter before guessing the company's name: Foundation for International Community Assistance (FINCA)

learning goal 1
Explain basic economics.

I. HOW ECONOMIC CONDITIONS AFFECT BUSINESSES

A. An economic system either promotes or hinders business activity.

B. Much of America's business success is due to an economic and social climate that allows businesses to operate freely.

  1. Any change in the U.S. economic system has a major influence on the business system.

  2. Also, **GLOBAL ECONOMICS** and **WORLD POLITICS** have a major influence on U.S. business.

C. **WHAT IS ECONOMICS?**

  1. **ECONOMICS** is the study of how society chooses to employ resources to produce goods and

PPT 2-1
Chapter Title

PPT 2-2
Learning Goals

(See complete PowerPoint slide notes on page 2.44.)

PPT 2-3
Learning Goals

(See complete PowerPoint slide notes on page 2.44.)

PPT 2-4
John Maynard Keynes

(See complete PowerPoint slide notes on page 2.45.)

PPT 2-5
Name That Company

(See complete PowerPoint slide notes on page 2.45.)

services and distribute them for consumption among various competing groups and individuals.

2. **_MACROECONOMICS_** is the part of economic study that looks at the operation of a nation's economy as a whole.

3. **_MICROECONOMICS_** is the part of economic study that looks at the behavior of people and organizations in particular markets.

4. "Economics" is sometimes defined as the allocation of scarce resources.

5. **_RESOURCE DEVELOPMENT_** is the study of how to increase resources and to create the conditions that will make better use of those resources.

6. Businesses help economic systems by inventing products and services that expand available resources *(example: mariculture, raising fish in ocean pens.)*

D. **THE SECRET TO CREATING A WEALTHY ECONOMY**

1. The English economist Thomas Malthus believed that population growth would outstrip resources.

    a. In response, Thomas Carlyle called economics **"THE DISMAL SCIENCE."**

    b. Many still believe, like Malthus, that the solution to poverty is birth control.

    c. **WORLD POPULATION** is currently growing more slowly than expected.

    d. But population in the **DEVELOPING WORLD** will continue to climb quickly.

PPT 2-6
The Major Branches of Economics

(See complete PowerPoint slide notes on page 2.45.)

PPT 2-7
Resource Development

(See complete PowerPoint slide notes on page 2.46.)

PPT 2-8
Examples of Ways to Increase Resources

(See complete PowerPoint slide notes on page 2.46.)

PPT 2-9
Thomas Malthus and the Dismal Science

(See complete PowerPoint slide notes on page 2.46.)

critical thinking exercise 2-1
KNOW YOUR HISTORY OF ECONOMICS

This Internet exercise is designed to help students gather information about economics from a historic perspective. (See complete exercise on page 2.71 of this manual.)

lecture link 2-1
INDIA'S UPCOMING ERA OF GROWTH

India is a burgeoning economic powerhouse with one of the fastest growing working-age populations. However, they must overcome some bumps in the road. (See the complete lecture link on page 2.65 in this manual.)

2. Others believe that a large population can be a valuable resource, especially if people are educated.

3. The **SECRET TO ECONOMIC DEVELOPMENT** can be summed up in the saying, *"give a man a fish and you feed him for a day, but teach a man to fish and you feed him for a lifetime."*

4. Business owners provide **JOBS AND ECONOMIC GROWTH** for their employees as well as for themselves.

5. Economists and governments examine what makes some countries relatively rich and other countries relatively poor, then develop policies that lead to **INCREASED PROSPERITY** for everyone.

E. **ADAM SMITH AND THE CREATION OF WEALTH**

1. **ADAM SMITH** believed wealth could be created through entrepreneurship.

   a. Rather than dividing *fixed* resources, Smith envisioned creating *more* resources so that everyone could be wealthier.

   b. In 1776, Smith wrote ***THE WEALTH OF NATIONS,*** in which he outlined steps for creating prosperity.

2. Smith believed that **FREEDOM** was vital to the survival of any economy.

3. Also, he believed that people will work hard if they have **INCENTIVES** for doing so.

PPT 2-10
Population as a Resource

(See complete PowerPoint slide notes on page 2.47.)

**thinking
green**
(Text page 32

PPT 2-11
Bringing in the
Green with Green
Products

(See complete PowerPoint slide notes on page 2.47.)

lecture link 2-2
**THE GRADUAL RETURN OF
AMERICAN OPTIMISM**

The U.S. is banking on the "give a man a fish" philosophy by extending the tax cuts from the 2009 stimulus package. (See the complete lecture link on page 2.65 in this manual.)

PPT 2-12
Adam Smith the Father of
Economics

(See complete PowerPoint slide notes on page 2.47.)

**critical thinking
exercise 2-2**
**APPLYING ECONOMIC
PRINCIPLES TO EDUCATION**

Principles such as competition and productivity apply to nonprofit organizations, such as schools, as well as businesses. (See complete exercise on page 2.72 of this manual.)

4. Smith is considered to be the **FATHER OF MODERN ECONOMICS.**

F. **HOW BUSINESSES BENEFIT THE COMMUNITY**

1. The ***INVISIBLE HAND*** is a phrase coined by Adam Smith to describe the process that turns self-directed gain into social and economic benefits for all.

2. Basically, this meant that a person working hard to make money for his or her own **PERSONAL INTEREST** would *(like an invisible hand)* also **BENEFIT OTHERS.**

    a. *For example, a farmer trying to make money would grow as many crops as possible.*

    b. This would provide jobs and needed food for others.

    c. If everyone worked hard in his or her own self interest, Smith said, society as a whole would prosper.

3. Smith assumed that as people become wealthier, they would reach out to help the less fortunate, but that hasn't always happened.

    a. Many U.S. businesspeople are becoming concerned about social issues and their obligation to return to society some of what they've earned.

    b. It is important for businesses to be ethical as well as generous.

PPT 2-13
The Invisible Hand Theory

(See complete PowerPoint slide notes on page 2.48.)

PPT 2-14
Understanding the Invisible Hand Theory

(See complete PowerPoint slide notes on page 2.48.)

lecture link 2-3

A NEW CROP OF CONSUMERS IN AFRICA

Africa has a growing middle class that rivals both China and India. Despite the persisting wealth disparities, more Africans have disposable incomes in which they can buy goods from others. (See the complete lecture link on page 2.66 in this manual.)

MAKING

ethical
decisions
(Text page 34)

PPT 2-15
Corruption's Effect on the Economy

(See complete PowerPoint slide notes on page 2.48.)

progress
assessment
(Text page 34)

PPT 2-16
Progress Assessment

(See complete PowerPoint slide notes on page 2.49.)

Explain what capitalism is and how free markets work.

II. UNDERSTANDING FREE-MARKET CAPITALISM

A. Following the ideas of Adam Smith, businesspeople created more wealth than every before.

1. But **GREAT DISPARITIES** in wealth remained or even increased.

2. Although it is not easy, opportunities to start one's own business have always been there, especially in a free market.

3. ***CAPITALISM*** is an economic system in which all or most of the factors of production and distribution are privately owned and operated for profit.

    a. In capitalist countries, businesspeople decide how to use their resources and how much to charge.

    b. No country is purely capitalist, but the foundation of the U.S. is capitalism.

    c. Capitalism is also the foundation for the economics of England, Canada, Australia, and most developed nations.

    d. Some countries are practicing **STATE CAPITALISM** where the state runs some businesses instead of private owners (i.e. China).

B. **THE FOUNDATIONS OF CAPITALISM**

1. People under free-market capitalism have **FOUR BASIC RIGHTS:**

    a. The right to **PRIVATE PROPERTY**

bonus case 2-1
FOUNDATIONS OF THE CAPITALIST SYSTEM

What are the moral, ethical, and spiritual foundations of capitalism? (See the complete case, discussion questions, and suggested answers beginning on page 2.79 of this manual.)

PPT 2-17
Capitalism

(See complete PowerPoint slide notes on page 2.49.)

PPT 2-18
State Capitalism

(See complete PowerPoint slide notes on page 2.49.)

SPOTLIGHT ON
small
business
(Text page 38

PPT 2-19
A Small Loan
Can Make a Big
Difference

(See complete PowerPoint slide notes on page 2.50)

    b. The right to **OWN A BUSINESS** and to keep all of that business's profits after taxes

    c. The right to **FREEDOM OF COMPETITION**

    d. The right to **FREEDOM OF CHOICE**

2. One benefit of such rights is that people are willing to take more **RISKS** than they would otherwise.

3. President Franklin Roosevelt believed **FOUR ADDITIONAL FREEDOMS** were essential:

    a. Freedom of **SPEECH AND EXPRESSION**

    b. Freedom to **WORSHIP IN YOUR OWN WAY**

    c. Freedom from **WANT**

    d. Freedom from **FEAR**

C. **HOW FREE MARKETS WORK**

1. In a free-market system, decisions about what to produce and in what quantities are made by **THE MARKET.**

2. **CONSUMERS** send signals to **PRODUCERS** about what to make, how many, and so on through the mechanism of **PRICE.** *(Text example: t-shirts supporting favorite baseball teams.)*

3. In a free market. the **PRICE** tells producers how much to produce, reducing the chances of a long-term shortage of goods.

D. **HOW PRICES ARE DETERMINED**

1. Prices in a free market are not determined by sellers; rather buyers and sellers negotiating in the marketplace determine them.

PPT 2-20
Capitalism's Four Basic Rights

(See complete PowerPoint slide notes on page 2.50.)

PPT 2-21
Roosevelt's Four Additional Rights

(See complete PowerPoint slide notes on page 2.50.)

PPT 2-22
Free Markets

(See complete PowerPoint slide notes on page 2.51.)

lecture link 2-4
THE CIRCULAR FLOW MODEL

The Circular Flow Model is used to explain how businesses and individuals interact in a free market economy. (See the complete lecture link on page 2.66 of this manual.)

PPT 2-23
Circular Flow Model

(See complete PowerPoint slide notes on page 2.51.)

PPT 2-24
Pricing

(See complete PowerPoint slide notes on page 2.52.)

    2. Price is determined through the economic concepts of supply and demand.

E. **THE ECONOMIC CONCEPT OF SUPPLY**

    1. ***SUPPLY*** refers to the quantity of products that manufacturers or owners are willing to sell at different prices at a specific time.

    2. The amount supplied will **INCREASE** as the price **INCREASES** (**DIRECT** relationship.)

    3. The quantity producers are willing to **SUPPLY** at certain prices is illustrated on a **SUPPLY CURVE.**

F. **THE ECONOMIC CONCEPT OF DEMAND**

    1. ***DEMAND*** refers to the quantity of products that people are willing to buy at different prices at a specific time.

    2. The quantity demanded will **DECREASE** as the price **INCREASES** (**INVERSE** relationship.)

    3. The quantities consumers are willing to buy at certain prices are illustrated on a **DEMAND CURVE.**

G. **THE EQUILIBRIUM PRICE, OR MARKET PRICE**

    1. The key factor in determining the quantity supplied and the quantity demanded is **PRICE.**

        a. At the **EQUILIBRIUM POINT**, the supply and demand curves cross, and the quantity demanded equals the quantity supplied.

        b. ***MARKET PRICE*** is the price determined by supply and demand.

    2. In free-market economies it is the **INTERACTION** between **SUPPLY** and **DEMAND** that determines

TEXT FIGURE 2.1
The Supply Curve at Various Prices
(Text page 38)

This text figure shows a simple supply curve for T-shirts. The curve rises from left to right. The higher the price, the more will be supplied.

PPT 2-25
Supply Curves

(See complete PowerPoint slide notes on page 2.52.)

TEXT FIGURE 2.2
Demand Curves
(Text page 38)

This is a simple demand curve showing the quantity of T-shirts demanded at different prices. The demand curve falls from left to right.

PPT 2-26
Demand Curves

(See complete PowerPoint slide notes on page 2.52.)

TEXT FIGURE 2.3
The Equilibrium Point
(Text page 38)

This text figure shows the equilibrium point, the point at which the supply and demand curves intersect—where quantity demanded equals quantity supplied.

PPT 2-27
Equilibrium

(See complete PowerPoint slide notes on page 2.53.)

**critical thinking
exercise 2-3**
FINDING THE EQUILIBRIUM POINT

How does the equilibrium price of a product change when forces in the economy change? (See complete exercise on page 2.73 of this manual.)

the market price in the long-run.

   a. If **SURPLUSES** (too many products) develop, a signal is sent to sellers to **LOWER** the price.

   b. If **SHORTAGES** (not enough products) develop, a signal is sent to sellers to **INCREASE** the price.

   c. Eventually, supply will again equal demand.

3. *The text uses the example of gas prices after the recent Gulf oil spill.*

4. In countries without a free-market system, there is no such mechanism, so there are often **SHORTAGES OR SURPLUSES.**

5. When government interferes in free markets, surpluses and shortages may develop.

H. **COMPETITION WITHIN FREE MARKETS**

1. Competition exists in different degrees, ranging from perfect to nonexistent.

2. **_PERFECT COMPETITION_** is the degree of competition in which there are many sellers in a market and none is large enough to dictate the price of a product.

   a. Sellers produce products that appear to be **IDENTICAL**.

   b. *There are no true examples of perfect competition, but agricultural products are often used as an example.*

3. **_MONOPOLISTIC COMPETITION_** is the degree of competition in which a large number of sellers

<u>lecture link 2-5</u>

**THE ECONOMIC IMPACT OF THE
2010 OIL SPILL**

The 2010 oil leak from BP's Deepwater Horizon didn't just affect gas prices, property values and the fishing industry were also hit hard. (See complete lecture link on page 2.67 of this manual.)

PPT 2-28
Four Degrees of Competition

(See complete PowerPoint slide notes on page 2.53.)

produce very similar products that buyers nevertheless perceive as different.

    a. **PRODUCT DIFFERENTIATION**, making buyers think similar products are different, is a key to success.

    b. *The fast food industry is an example.*

4. An **_OLIGOPOLY_** is a degree of competition in which just a few sellers dominate a market.

    a. The **INITIAL INVESTMENT** required to enter the market is usually high.

    b. Prices among competing firms tend to be close to the same.

    c. *Examples include breakfast cereal and soft drinks.*

5. A **_MONOPOLY_** is a degree of competition in which only one seller controls the total supply of a product or service, and sets the price.

    a. U.S. laws prohibit the creation of monopolies, but do permit **APPROVED MONOPOLIES** in markets for public utilities.

    b. New laws have ended the monopoly status of utilities in some areas, creating intense competition among utility companies.

    c. **DEREGULATION** is meant to increase competition and lower prices for consumers.

I. **BENEFITS AND LIMITATIONS OF FREE MARKETS**

1. The free market allows open competition among companies.

2. Free-market capitalism provides opportunities for

<u>critical thinking
exercise 2-4</u>
**STANDARD OF LIVING
COMPARISON**

This exercise asks students to research key economic indicators for a capitalist country, a socialist country, and a communist country. (See complete exercise on page 2.75 of this manual.)

PPT 2-29
Free Market Benefits and
Limitations

(See complete PowerPoint slide notes on page 2.53.)

poor people to work their way out of poverty.

3. Capitalism also creates **INEQUITIES** between those who have gained wealth and those who are not able to.

4. Not all businesspeople agree on how to deal with this **INEQUITY**.

5. Greed has led some businesspeople to engage in **UNETHICAL PRACTICES** and deceive the public.

6. Some government **REGULATIONS ARE NECES-SARY** to protect stockholders and vulnerable citizens.

<u>**learning goal** 3</u>

Compare socialism and communism.

III. UNDERSTANDING SOCIALISM

A. *SOCIALISM* is an economic system based on the premise that some, if not most, basic businesses should be owned by the government so that profits can be distributed among the people.

1. Entrepreneurs can own small businesses, but their profits are **STEEPLY TAXED** to pay for social programs.

2. Advocates of socialism acknowledge the major benefits of capitalism, but believe that **WEALTH SHOULD BE MORE EVENLY DISTRIBUTED.**

B. The **MAJOR BENEFIT** of socialism is **SOCIAL EQUALITY**.

1. Income is taken from the wealthier people and redistributed to the poorer members of the population.

PPT 2-30
The Government Needs

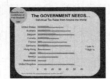

(See complete PowerPoint slide notes on page 2.54.)

PPT 2-31
Atypical Taxes

(See complete PowerPoint slide notes on page 2.54.)

progress
assessment
(Text page 41)

PPT 2-32
Progress Assessment

(See complete PowerPoint slide notes on page 2.55.)

PPT 2-33
Socialism

(See complete PowerPoint slide notes on page 2.55.)

2. Workers in socialist countries are given free education, free health care, free child care, and more employee benefits.

C. **THE NEGATIVE CONSEQUENCES OF SOCIALISM**

1. Socialism may create **EQUALITY**, but it **TAKES AWAY SOME WORK INCENTIVES**.

2. Tax rates in some nations once reached 83%.

3. Because wealthy professionals have very high tax rates, many of them leave socialist countries for countries with lower taxes.

4. The loss of the best and brightest people to other countries is called **_BRAIN DRAIN_**.

5. Socialist systems can result in **FEWER INVENTIONS AND LESS INNOVATION**.

IV. UNDERSTANDING COMMUNISM

A. **_COMMUNISM_** is an economic and political system in which the government makes almost all economic decisions and owns almost all the major factors of production.

B. **PROBLEMS WITH COMMUNISM**

1. The government has no way of knowing what to produce because prices don't reflect **SUPPLY** and **DEMAND**.

2. **SHORTAGES** of many items may develop.

3. Communism doesn't inspire businesspeople to work hard, and is slowly disappearing as an alternative economic form.

PPT 2-34
Benefits of Socialism

(See complete PowerPoint slide notes on page 2.56.)

PPT 2-35
Negatives of Socialism

(See complete PowerPoint slide notes on page 2.56.)

PPT 2-36
Communism

(See complete PowerPoint slide notes on page 2.56.)

C. Most communist countries today are **SUFFERING SEVERE ECONOMIC DEPRESSION**, including North Korea and Cuba.

1. Some countries, such as Venezuela, are moving toward communism.

2. The former Soviet Union is moving toward free markets.

3. Russia now has a flat tax of 13%, a much lower tax rate than the U.S. has.

4. The trend toward free markets is growing.

<u>**learning goal** 4</u>

Analyze the trend toward mixed economies.

V. THE TREND TOWARD MIXED ECONOMIES

A. There are two dominant economic systems:

1. **FREE MARKET ECONOMIES**

   a. ***FREE MARKET ECONOMIES*** are economic systems in which the market largely determines what goods and services get produced, who gets them, and how the economy grows.

   b. This system is commonly known as **CAPITALISM.**

2. **COMMAND ECONOMIES**

   a. ***COMMAND ECONOMIES*** are economic systems in which the government largely decides what goods and services will be produced, who will get them, and how the economy will grow.

PPT 2-37
Two Major Economic Systems

(See complete PowerPoint slide notes on page 2.57.)

        b.   These economies are known as **SOCIALISM** and **COMMUNISM**.

B. No one economic system is perfect by itself.

    1. Free-market mechanisms haven't been responsive enough to a nation's social and economic needs and haven't adequately protected the environment.

    2. Socialism and communism haven't always created enough jobs or wealth to keep economies growing fast enough.

    3. Socialist and communist countries have moved toward **CAPITALISM**.

    4. So-called capitalist countries tend to move toward **SOCIALISM**.

    5. No country is purely capitalist or purely capitalist, rather some **MIX OF THE TWO SYSTEMS**.

    6. The result has been a **BLEND** of capitalism and communism.

C. **_MIXED ECONOMIES_** are economic systems in which some allocation of resources is made by the market and some by government.

D. **THE U.S. HAS A MIXED ECONOMY.**

    1. The role of government in many parts of the economy is a matter of some debate.

    2. For instance, the government has become the largest employer in the U.S.

PPT 2-38
Mixed Economies

(See complete PowerPoint slide notes on page 2.57.)

PPT 2-39
Trending Toward Mixed Economies

(See complete PowerPoint slide notes on page 2.57.)

REACHING BEYOND
our borders
(Text page 44

PPT 2-40
China's Changing
Economy

(See complete PowerPoint slide notes on page 2.58.)

TEXT FIGURE 2.4
Comparisons of Key Economic
Systems
(Text page 45)

This text figure compares capitalism, socialism, communism, and mixed economies on five key elements.

progress
assessment
(Text page 46)

PPT 2-41
Progress Assessment

(See complete PowerPoint slide notes on page 2.58.)

lecture outline

Discuss the economic system of the United States, including the significance of key economic indicators (especially GDP), productivity, and the business cycle.

VI. UNDERSTANDING THE U.S. ECONOMIC SYSTEM

A. KEY ECONOMIC INDICATORS

1. **GROSS DOMESTIC PRODUCT (GDP)**

   a. **_GROSS DOMESTIC PRODUCT (GDP)_** is the total value of final goods and services produced in a country in a given year.

   b. Both domestic and foreign-owned companies can produce goods and services included in GDP.

   c. A major influence on the growth of GDP is how productive the work force is.

   d. The total U.S. GDP is $14 trillion.

2. **THE UNEMPLOYMENT RATE**

   a. The **_UNEMPLOYMENT RATE_** is the number of civilians at least 16 years old who are unemployed and tried to find a job within the prior four weeks.

   b. There are four types of unemployment: frictional, structural, cyclical, and seasonal (as seen in **Text Figure 2.6.)**

   c. The U.S. tries to protect those who are unemployed because of recessions, industry shifts, and other cyclical factors.

3. **INFLATION AND PRICE INDEXES**

   a. **THE PRICE INDEXES** help measure the health of the economy.

PPT 2-42
Gross Domestic Product

(See complete PowerPoint slide notes on page 2.58.)

PPT 2-43
The United States GDP

(See complete PowerPoint slide notes on page 2.59.)

PPT 2-44
Playing Catch Up

(See complete PowerPoint slide notes on page 2.59.)

PPT 2-45
Unemployment

(See complete PowerPoint slide notes on page 2.59.)

TEXT FIGURE 2.5
U.S. Unemployment Rate
1989-2011
(Text page 47)

This text figure shows the unemployment rate for the years from 1989 to 2011.

PPT 2-46
Unemployment Rate of the U.S.

(See complete PowerPoint slide notes on page 2.60.)

TEXT FIGURE 2.6
Four Types of Unemployment
(Text page 49)

This figure describes the four types of unemployment: frictional, structural, cyclical, and seasonal.

PPT 2-47
Best and Worst Cities for a Job
Search

(See complete PowerPoint slide notes on page 2.60.)

b. _**INFLATION**_ is a general rise in the prices of goods and services over time.

c. _**DISINFLATION**_ is a situation in which price increases are slowing *(the inflation rate is declining.)*

d. _**DEFLATION**_ is a situation in which prices are declining, occurring when countries produce so many goods that people cannot afford to buy them all.

e. _**STAGFLATION**_ is a situation when the economy is slowing, but prices keep going up anyhow.

f. **CONSUMER PRICE INDEX (CPI)**

   i. The _**CONSUMER PRICE INDEX (CPI)**_ are monthly statistics that measure the pace of inflation or deflation.

   ii. Some wages, rents, government benefits, and interest rates are based on the CPI.

   iii. **CORE INFLATION** is the CPI minus food and energy costs.

e. The _**PRODUCER PRICE INDEX (PPI)**_ is an index that measures prices at the wholesale level.

B. **PRODUCTIVITY IN THE UNITED STATES**

   1. U.S. productivity has gone up in recent years because computers have made production faster.

   2. The **HIGHER PRODUCTIVITY** is, the **LOWER COSTS** are in producing goods and services, and the lower prices can be.

PPT 2-48
Inflation

(See complete PowerPoint slide notes on page 2.60.)

lecture link 2-6
OTHER ECONOMIC INDICATORS

In addition to the GDP, CPI, and unemployment indicators, there are other economic indicators that can forecast changes in the economy. (See the complete lecture link on page 2.67 of this manual.)

lecture link 2-7
NEW ECONOMIC MEASURES

Michael Gelobter thinks that the GDP, unemployment levels, and price indices should be replaced with the "genuine progress indicator (GPI)." (See the complete lecture link on page 2.68 in this manual.)

PPT 2-49
Consumer Price Index

(See complete PowerPoint slide notes on page 2.61)

TEXT FIGURE 2.7
How the Consumer Price Index is Put Together
(Text page 48)

This text figure how the Consumer Price Index is figured out and released.

PPT 2-50
Producer Price Index

(See complete PowerPoint slide notes on page 2.61)

PPT 2-51
Productivity

(See complete PowerPoint slide notes on page 2.61)

3. The U.S. economy is a **SERVICE ECONOMY**—very labor intensive—creating productivity issues.

C. **PRODUCTIVITY IN THE SERVICE SECTOR**

   1. Technologies may add to the quality of the services but not to the **OUTPUT PER WORKER** which is the definition of productivity.

   2. New measures of productivity for the service economy are needed to measure **QUALITY** as well as **QUANTITY** of output.

D. **THE BUSINESS CYCLE**

   1. ___BUSINESS CYCLES___ are the periodic rises and falls that occur in economies over time.

   2. Joseph Schumpter identified **FOUR PHASES OF BUSINESS CYCLES:**

      a. In an **ECONOMIC BOOM,** there is strong business activity.

      b. A ___RECESSION___ is two or more consecutive quarters of decline in the GDP.

      c. A ___DEPRESSION___ is a severe recession, usually accompanied by deflation.

      d. A **RECOVERY** occurs when the economy stabilizes.

   3. The goal of economists is to predict these fluctuations, which can be very difficult.

   4. Fluctuations in the economy are **INEVITABLE.**

   5. The government uses **FISCAL** and **MONETARY** policy to minimize these disruptions.

PPT 2-52
Productivity in the Service Sector

(See complete PowerPoint slide notes on page 2.62.)

PPT 2-53
Business Cycles

(See complete PowerPoint slide notes on page 2.62.)

lecture link 2-8
CHINA'S POTENTIAL REAL ESTATE BUST

After years of growth, financial experts are afraid the Chinese real estate boom could turn into a bust. (See the complete lecture link on page 2.69 in this manual.)

lecture link 2-9
WHAT IS A DEPRESSION?

There is a well-established definition for a recession. A depression is, well, not so easy to define. (See the complete lecture link on page 2.69 in this manual.)

lecture outline

Contrast *fiscal policy* and *monetary policy*, and explain how each affects the economy.

E. **STABILIZING THE ECONOMY THROUGH FISCAL POLICY**

1. ***FISCAL POLICY*** is the federal government's efforts to keep the economy stable by increasing or decreasing taxes or government spending.

2. The first half of fiscal policy involves **TAXATION.**

   a. **HIGH TAX RATES** may discourage small business ownership.

   b. **LOW TAX RATES** would tend to give the economy a boost.

   c. The **PERCENTAGE OF GDP** taken by all levels of government through taxes is about **28%.**

3. The second half of fiscal policy involves **GOVERNMENT SPENDING.**

   a. The **NATIONAL DEFICIT** is the amount of money that the federal government spends over and above the amount it gathers in taxes.

   b. The ***NATIONAL DEBT*** is the sum of government deficits over time.

   c. The national debt of the U.S. is over **$14 TRILLION**.

4. One way to lessen the annual deficits is to **CUT GOVERNMENT SPENDING**, but there is a continuing need for social programs and for military spending.

F. **FISCAL POLICY IN ACTION DURING THE ECONOMIC CRISIS OF 2008-2011**

PPT 2-54
Fiscal Policy

(See complete PowerPoint slide notes on page 2.62.)

**critical thinking
exercise 2-5**
**BALANCING THE FEDERAL
BUDGET**

Can your students balance the federal budget? This exercise presents figures and asks them to make adjustments in spending and income to do just that. (See complete exercise on page 2.76 of this manual.)

TEXT FIGURE 2.8
The National Debt
(Text page 51)

This text figure shows the national debt—the sum of government deficits over time—for years 1980 to 2011.

PPT 2-55
National Deficits, Debt, and Surplus

(See complete PowerPoint slide notes on page 2.63.)

PPT 2-56
What's Our National Debt?

(See complete PowerPoint slide notes on page 2.63.)

1. President George Bush basically followed the basic economic principles of free markets.

    a. However, the economy plummeted and President Bush approved spending almost $1 trillion to revive the failing economy.

    b. President Barack Obama promised to spend additional funds.

2. ***KEYNESIAN ECONOMIC THEORY*** is the theory that a government policy of increasing spending and cutting taxes could stimulate the economy in a recession.

G. **USING MONETARY POLICY TO KEEP THE ECONOMY GROWING**

    1. The **FEDERAL RESERVE SYSTEM (THE FED)** is a semiprivate organization that decides how much money to put into circulation.

    2. ***MONETARY POLICY*** is the management of the monetary supply and interest rates; it is controlled by the Fed.

        a. When the economy is booming, the Fed tends to **RAISE INTEREST RATES.**

        b. **LOWERING INTEREST RATES** encourages more business borrowing.

        c. Raising and lowering interest rates helps control the rapid ups and downs of the economy.

        d. In 2010-2011, the Fed kept interest rates near zero, but the economy remained sluggish.

PPT 2-57

What Can a _____ Dollars Buy

(See complete PowerPoint slide notes on page 2.63.)

PPT 2-58

Monetary Policy

(See complete PowerPoint slide notes on page 2.64.)

lecture link 2-10

CONTROLLING YOUR PERSONAL MONEY SUPPLY

Controlling your personal money supply is harder than you may think. (See the complete lecture link on page 2.70 of this manual.)

3. The Federal Reserve also controls the **MONEY SUPPLY**.

   a. The **MORE MONEY** the Fed makes available to businesspeople, the **FASTER THE ECONOMY GROWS.**

   b. To **SLOW THE ECONOMY**, the Feds **LOWERS** the money supply.

4. The economic goal is to keep the economy growing.

VII. SUMMARY

progress
assessment
(Text page 52)

PPT 2-59
Progress Assessment   (See complete PowerPoint slide notes on page 2.64.)

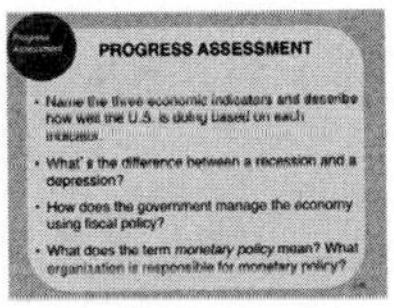

PowerPoint slide notes

PPT 2-1
Chapter Title

PPT 2-2
Learning Goals

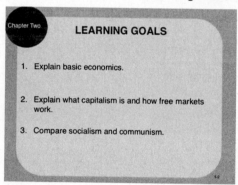

PPT 2-3
Learning Goals

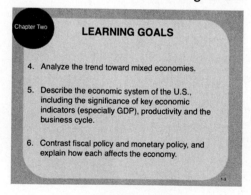

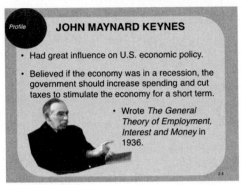

Organization: Foundation for International Community Assistance (FINCA)

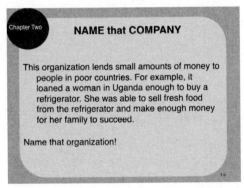

This slide gives students insight into the definition of economics. When going over this definition it often helps to further define the term resources. The term resources ties back into Chapter 1 and the factors of production: land, labor, capital, knowledge and entrepreneurship.

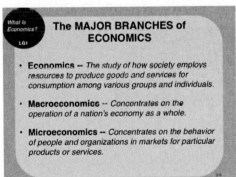

Businesses can contribute to an economic system by inventing new products that increase the availability of resources.

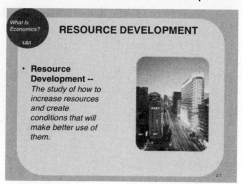

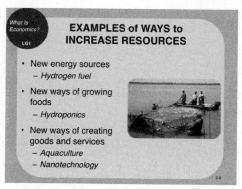

Thomas Malthus believed that if people were left to their own devices there would be chaos; therefore the government needed to be heavily involved in controlling the economy. Malthus' ideas are still with us. Neo-Malthusian ideas of overpopulation are prevalent in books such as Paul Ehrlich's *The Population Bomb* which contains ideas similar to those presented by Thomas Malthus 200 years ago.

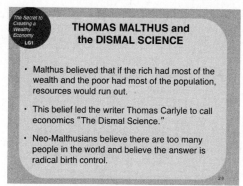

PPT 2-10
Population as a Resource

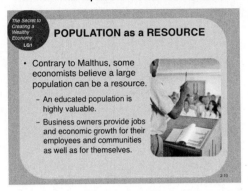

Malthus viewed a large population as a negative. However, many economists today see a highly educated population as a valuable, scarce resource. Countries like Japan and Germany are examples of nations that have become economically successful due to large well-educated populations producing sophisticated high-value products.

PPT 2-11
Bringing in the Green with Green Products

PPT 2-12
Adam Smith the Father of Economics

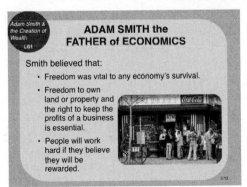

Adam Smith's ideas were laid out in his seminal book, An Inquiry into the Nature and Causes of the Wealth of Nations. Smith believed strongly in more "natural liberty" and less government intervention into the economy {an idea that was an anathema to Malthus}. Smith argued that allowing people the freedom to own land and the right to keep profit would not create chaos as Malthus had argued, but rather would create greater resources for all.

PPT 2-13
The Invisible Hand Theory

The invisible hand was at the heart of Adam Smith's theory describing the process of turning self-directed gain into social and economic benefits for all.

The INVISIBLE HAND THEORY

How Businesses Benefit the Community — LG1

- As people improve their own situation in life, they help the economy prosper through the production of goods, services and ideas.

- **Invisible Hand --** *When self-directed gain leads to social and economic benefits for the whole community.*

2-13

PPT 2-14
Understanding the Invisible Hand Theory

UNDERSTANDING the INVISIBLE HAND THEORY

How Businesses Benefit the Community — LG1

- A farmer earns money by selling his crops.
- To earn more, the farmer hires farmhands to produce more crops.
- When the farmer produces more, there is plenty of food for the community.
- The farmer helped his employees and his community while helping himself.

2-14

PPT 2-15
Corruption's Effect on the Economy

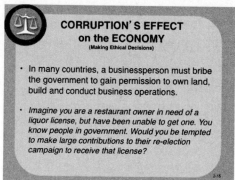

CORRUPTION'S EFFECT on the ECONOMY
(Making Ethical Decisions)

- In many countries, a businessperson must bribe the government to gain permission to own land, build and conduct business operations.

- *Imagine you are a restaurant owner in need of a liquor license, but have been unable to get one. You know people in government. Would you be tempted to make large contributions to their re-election campaign to receive that license?*

2-15

PPT 2-16
Progress Assessment

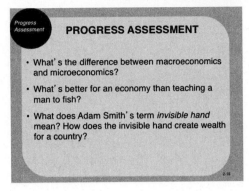

1. Macroeconomics looks at the operations of a nation's economy as a whole. Microeconomics looks at the behavior of people and organizations in markets for particular products or services.

2. To create wealth in an economy, it is better to teach a man to start a fish farm, whereby he will be able to feed a village for a lifetime.

3. The invisible hand is the term used by Adam Smith to describe the processes that turns self-directed gains into social and economic benefits for all. To become wealthy, people working in their own self-interest producing goods and services expand by hiring others that provides employment and increases the well-being of others. They also tend to reach out to help the less fortunate over time.

PPT 2-17
Capitalism

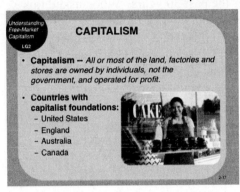

PPT 2-18
State Capitalism

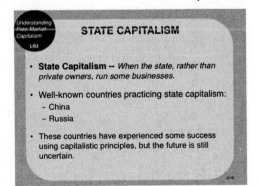

PPT 2-19
A Small Loan Can Make a Big Difference

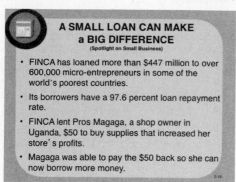

A SMALL LOAN CAN MAKE a BIG DIFFERENCE
(Spotlight on Small Business)

- FINCA has loaned more than $447 million to over 600,000 micro-entrepreneurs in some of the world's poorest countries.
- Its borrowers have a 97.6 percent loan repayment rate.
- FINCA lent Pros Magaga, a shop owner in Uganda, $50 to buy supplies that increased her store's profits.
- Magaga was able to pay the $50 back so she can now borrow more money.

PPT 2-20
Capitalism's Four Basic Rights

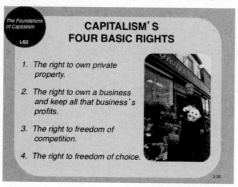

CAPITALISM'S FOUR BASIC RIGHTS

1. The right to own private property.
2. The right to own a business and keep all that business's profits.
3. The right to freedom of competition.
4. The right to freedom of choice.

The four basic rights under a capitalist system are straightforward, but which of the four basic rights has been weakened in the United States over the past 30 years? When asked this question, rarely do students touch on the concept of eminent domain and the weakening of the right to own private property due to the Kelo vs. New London Supreme Court case from 2005. If time permits students can explore this case and the potential impact the case may have on America capitalism.

PPT 2-21
Roosevelt's Four Additional Rights

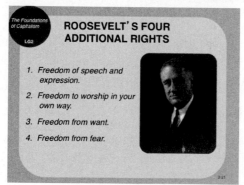

ROOSEVELT'S FOUR ADDITIONAL RIGHTS

1. Freedom of speech and expression.
2. Freedom to worship in your own way.
3. Freedom from want.
4. Freedom from fear.

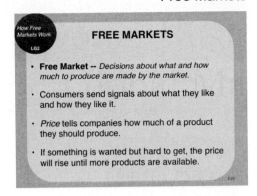

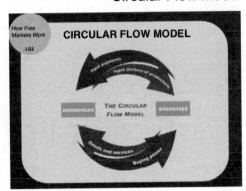

In a free market economy, business activity involves two major players: individuals (**households**) who own the resources that are the inputs into the productive process, and **businesses** who use these inputs (factors of production) to create goods and services.

1. In the **Resource Market** (top part of the model)

   a. Businesses demand resources.

   b. Households own the resources (factors of production).

   c. Income from providing these resources flows back to the households.

   d. The price of these resources set by laws of supply and demand.

2. In the **Product Market** (lower part of the model)

   a. Businesses use these resources to create goods and services.

   b. Households (individuals) demand these goods and services.

   c. Individuals use their income to purchase goods and services.

PPT 2-24
Pricing

Prices are determined by consumers negotiating with the sellers.

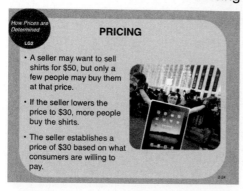

PPT 2-25
Supply Curves

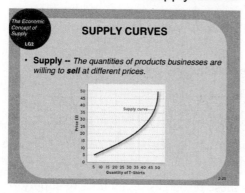

PPT 2-26
Demand Curves

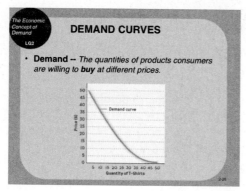

PPT 2-27
Equilibrium

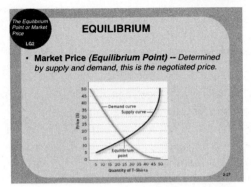

EQUILIBRIUM

The Equilibrium Point or Market Price
LG2

- **Market Price *(Equilibrium Point)* --** *Determined by supply and demand, this is the negotiated price.*

PPT 2-28
Four Degrees of Competition

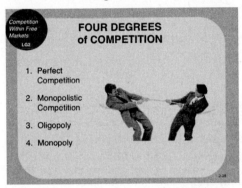

Competition Within Free Markets
LG2

FOUR DEGREES of COMPETITION

1. Perfect Competition

2. Monopolistic Competition

3. Oligopoly

4. Monopoly

PPT 2-29
Free Market Benefits and Limitations

Benefits and Limitations of Free Markets

FREE MARKET BENEFITS and LIMITATIONS

Benefits:
- It allows for open competition among companies.
- Provides opportunities for poor people to work their way out of poverty.

Limitations:
- People may start to let greed drive them.

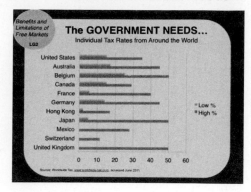

PPT 2-30
The Government Needs...

1. This slide compares some world's lowest and highest individual tax rates.

2. Students may be surprised at the difference between the rates in the U.S. and many other countries. For example the U.S. rate seems low compared to Belgium's rate which is 50%.

3. To help explain the difference between the U.S. rate and Belgium's higher rate, you can discuss some of the differences between capitalism and socialism. (*Socialism believes that the government should provide increased services for people by redistributing income from the richer people to the poor. Explain to the students that in socialist countries citizens are given free education, free health care, and more employee benefits (like longer vacations and family leave). Therefore they must pay higher taxes to support these benefits.*

4. Point out the major disadvantages of socialism:

   - Reduced incentives to work harder resulting in less innovation.

   - Marginal tax rates are higher and can sometimes approach 85% after a person reaches a certain amount of income (in other words, eight-five cents of each dollar earned is paid in taxes.

   - The term "brain drain" refers to the loss of professionally trained individuals due to higher taxes.

PPT 2-31
Atypical Taxes

A little bit about the lighter side of taxes.

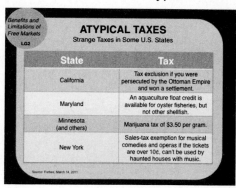

PPT 2-32
Progress Assessment

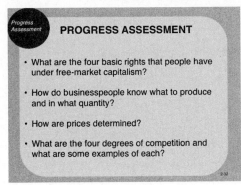

1. The four rights are: the right to own private property, the right to own a business and keep all that business's profits, the right to freedom of choice, and the right to freedom of competition.

2. Decisions about what to produce and in what quantity are decided by the market, consumers sending signals about what to make, how many in what color, and so on.

3. Prices are determined by the economic concepts of supply and demand.

4. The four degrees of competition are:

   • Perfect competition – such as a farmer's market where good are indistinguishable. Today, however, there are no good examples of perfect competition.

   • Monopolistic competition – such as fast-food restaurants where products are similar but consumers perceive the products to be different. Product differentiation is a key here.

   • Oligopoly – a situation where just a few major producers dominate a market such as tobacco, gasoline, automobiles, etc. A few sellers dominate because the initial investment to enter such a market is significant.

   • Monopoly – a situation where only one producer exists in a market. U.S. law prohibits the creation of monopolies.

PPT 2-33
Socialism

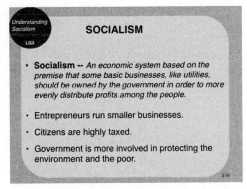

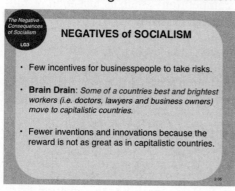

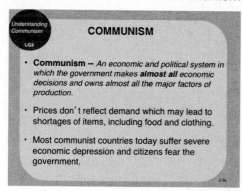

PPT 2-37
Two Major Economic Systems

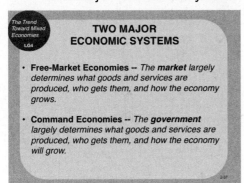

TWO MAJOR ECONOMIC SYSTEMS

- **Free-Market Economies --** *The **market** largely determines what goods and services are produced, who gets them, and how the economy grows.*

- **Command Economies --** *The **government** largely determines what goods and services are produced, who gets them, and how the economy will grow.*

PPT 2-38
Mixed Economies

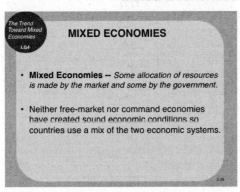

MIXED ECONOMIES

- **Mixed Economies --** *Some allocation of resources is made by the market and some by the government.*

- Neither free-market nor command economies have created sound economic conditions so countries use a mix of the two economic systems.

PPT 2-39
Trending Toward Mixed Economies

TRENDING TOWARD MIXED ECONOMIES

- Communist governments are disappearing.

- Socialist governments are cutting back on social programs, lowering taxes and moving toward capitalism.

- Capitalist countries are increasing social programs and moving more toward socialism.

PPT 2-40
China's Changing Economy

PPT 2-41
Progress Assessment

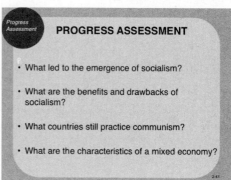

1. Socialists believe that the distribution of wealth should be more evenly distributed than in free-market capitalism. Government should be empowered to carry out the distribution of wealth.

2. Free education through college, free health care, and free child-care are some of the benefits of socialism. The key drawback of socialism is high taxes often causing a "brain drain" in the economy. Socialism also tends to inspire less innovation.

3. Most nations have drifted away from communism but North Korea, Cuba still espouse communism. Russia, Vietnam, and China still have some communist ideals in place.

4. Mixed economies have systems where the allocation of resources is made by the market and some by the government. Like most nations of the world, the United States is a mixed economy.

PPT 2-42
Gross Domestic Product

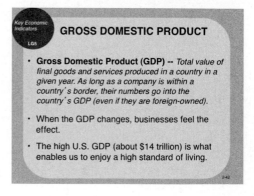

1. In 2010, the U.S. gross domestic product was $14.1 trillion.

2. This compares to the GDP of $ 5.8 trillion in 1990 and $ 2.8 trillion in 1980. As can be seen on the slide, the U.S. GDP has grown over 400% since 1980.

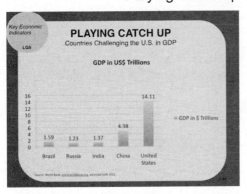

1. America is often referred to as *"the engine that runs the world's economy." It is easy to see the truth in this statement* with gross domestic product far exceeding the four countries listed on the slide.

2. While China has grown dramatically since 1975, their economy is still dwarfed by that of the United States.

3. Much is made of the economic growth of China, India, Russia and Brazil, but students must understand the sum of these four countries gross domestic products is approximately half that of the United States.

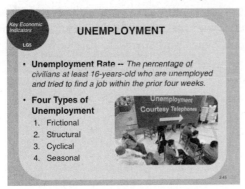

While the term unemployment seems simple enough, the Bureau of Labor Statistics (BLS) has a very specific definition. According to the BLS unemployment is the percentage of civilians at least 16-years-old who are unemployed and tried to find a job within the prior four weeks. The BLS figure does not include workers who had to take part-time jobs because they couldn't find full-time work, those who are underemployed (working at jobs far below their qualifications), or those workers who gave up looking for jobs altogether. If that was not confusing enough there are four types of unemployment which students are often surprised to discover.

The U.S. unemployment rate reached its lowest point in 30 years at 3.9% in 2000. By 2010, however, it had risen to over 10%. In 2011, it still hovered over 9%.

PPT 2-46
U.S. Unemployment Rate

The unemployment rate in the United States over the past 50 plus years has been as low as 3.9 percent, but more recently has climbed past 10 percent. Although the unemployment rate is climbing in the United States, it still has a long way to go to reach the unemployment rate in Zimbabwe (80 percent).

PPT 2-47
Best and Worst Cities for a Job Search

PPT 2-48
Inflation

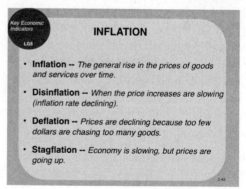

When discussing inflation, disinflation, deflation and stagflation, introducing the term hyperinflation is particularly interesting to students. Historical examples of countries suffering from hyperinflation post-World War I and currently Zimbabwe bring this topic to life.

PPT 2-49
Consumer Price Index

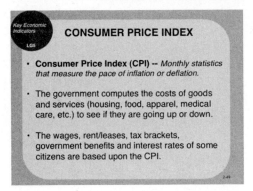

After discussing hyperinflation in the previous slide, students can appreciate the importance of monitoring a nation's inflation rate to prevent it from spiraling out of control. As inflation is increasing, it acts as a hidden tax increase eroding the purchasing power of the population.

PPT 2-50
Price Index

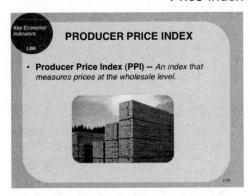

PPT 2-51
Productivity

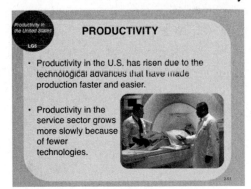

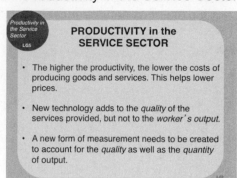

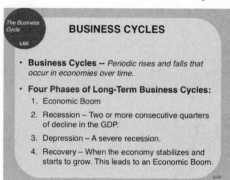

Yes, it is true that a recession is two or more consecutive quarters of contracting gross domestic product, but students will be interested in knowing that for a recession to be officially labeled a recession it must be declared by the National Bureau of Economic Research. Their website, www.nber.org, provides numerous resources to further explain this part of the business cycle.

In the U.S., the percentage of the GDP the government takes through taxes at all levels is about 28%. However, when you count all fees, taxes on the highest-earning citizens could exceed 50%.

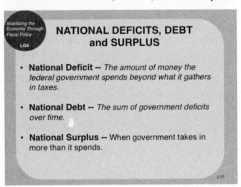

1. Discuss with the class the size of the national debt and what impact this has on the economy. (*Increased borrowing by the government takes money out of the consumer and business markets, impacting the cost of borrowing.*)

2. The national debt has continued to increase roughly $4 billion per day since September 28, 2007.

3. On a per person basis, each citizen's share of this debt is roughly $46,000.

4. A family of four shares the debt burden of about $184,000.

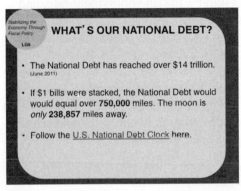

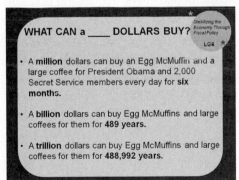

1. Before showing the slide, ask students, "If you were a rich, generous person who wanted to treat President Obama and his 2,000 Secret Services members to an Egg McMuffin every morning, how many days could you treat them if you decided to spend a million dollars? A billion dollars? A trillion dollars?"

2. Students are usually surprised to see how much a million, billion, or trillion dollars can buy.

MONETARY POLICY

- **Monetary Policy** -- *The management of the money supply and interest rates by the Federal Reserve Bank (the Fed).*

- **The Fed's most visible role is increasing and lowering interest rates.**
    - When the economy is booming, the Fed tends to increase interest rates.
    - When the economy is in a recession, the Fed tends to decrease the interest rates.

PROGRESS ASSESSMENT

- Name the three economic indicators and describe how well the U.S. is doing based on each indicator.

- What's the difference between a recession and a depression?

- How does the government manage the economy using fiscal policy?

- What does the term *monetary policy* mean? What organization is responsible for monetary policy?

1. The three key economic indicators are the Gross Domestic Product (GDP), the unemployment rate, and the price indexes. The U.S. GDP is approximately $14 trillion. Our high GDP allows citizens to enjoy a high standard of living. In 2000, the U.S. reached it lowest unemployment rate in over 30 years. However, the recent recession could lead unemployment to at least 10 percent. The consumer price index (CPI) has not risen to high levels keeping inflation in check. However the recession has caused fears of deflation.

2. A recession is two or more consecutive quarters of decline in the GDP. A depression is a severe recession, usually accompanied by deflation.

3. Fiscal policy refers to the government's efforts to keep the economy stable by increasing or decreasing taxes or government spending.

4. Monetary policy is the management of the nation's money supply and interest rates. The Federal Reserve controls the money supply in the United States.

lecture
links

"It's a recession when your neighbor loses his job; it's a depression when you lose your own."
Harry S. Truman

"Three groups spend other people's money: children, thieves, politicians. All three need parental supervision."
Dick Army, politician

lecture link 2-1

INDIA'S UPCOMING ERA OF GROWTH

By all accounts, India is destined for massive growth over the next decade. Yet India is always measured in the shadow of its neighbor and fellow burgeoning economic superpower, China. After all, by 2030 the two nations are estimated to account for 34% of the globe's total economic output. Experts assert that China will be on top, however, and is on target to overtake the U.S. with 24% of world GDP by the same year.

But China's massive growth could ultimately be hindered by its one-child policy. With population escalation stunted, the pool of Chinese citizens eligible for work will shrink just as the nation surges towards GDP dominance. India, on the other hand, will experience one of the fastest growths of working-age populations in the world between 2010 and 2050. India's upcoming spike of work-eligible citizens could provide it with a much-needed advantage over not only China, but also the fully developed economies of the U.S. and Europe. Small countries with low birth rates like Sweden, Austria and Denmark could eventually drop off the list of the 30 biggest economies in the world. Instead, high population and expanding nations like India could take up the economic mantle in the next decade and beyond.

That is if India can suitably develop its crumbling infrastructure. Cracked roads and bridges present the biggest impediment towards India's growth. While India nearly matched China in total economic expansion last year at 9.7%, its dire infrastructure is ranked 91st out of 139 nations, behind Ethiopia and Indonesia. Even worse, despite its vast population India lacks the skilled labor to repair and rebuild. Though laborers abound, many Indians look down on the profession since those jobs were previously performed by lower classes. Therefore parents want their kids to upgrade to life as an engineer rather than a mason or a carpenter. In an effort to combat their skilled worker shortage, Indian companies are forming their own training schools that will hopefully convert standard laborers into capable contractors and foremen.[i]

lecture link 2-2

THE GRADUAL RETURN OF AMERICAN OPTIMISM

The debate over the Bush-era tax cuts raged in Congress for months, ending at last in December 2010 with a compromise between the Obama administration and Republicans. According to the new legislation, the tax laws instated by President Bush will continue for two more years along with a number of provisions from the 2009 stimulus package. Critics fear the extension of the cuts will deprive the government of the cash it so desperately needs to shrink the deficit. But for big business leaders, the tax breaks and stimulus expansion are cause for newfound optimism.

The new financial law comes hot on the heels of a string of surprisingly good news for the American economy. Stocks on the S&P 500 index were up an average of 12.8% at the end of 2010. Plus, after President Obama signed the new financial legislation into law, Goldman Sachs' notoriously bearish chief economist raised his 2011 forecast of American stocks' growth from 2% to 3.4%.

Most importantly, though, the U.S. is reemerging as a stable, dominant force on the global market. As Europe continues to struggle to untangle a knot of sovereign debt, the worst aspects of the American financial crisis seem to be over. And while the dollar has managed to find some steady footing, inflation woes loom large over developing countries like China and India. Still, the recent economic stimulus certainly won't stay exclusively within our nation's borders. American businesses will inevitably invest a good chunk of the bill's $858 billion into growing operations overseas. Additionally, the unencumbered growth of Chinese and Indian companies fueled by foreign cash will have global repercussions on the commodities and energy markets. As these nations' economies expand, their increased demand for resources will drive up prices around the world. So while America's economic outlook for 2011 looks relatively stable, there are several outside factors preventing it from becoming totally secure.[ii]

lecture link 2-3

A NEW CROP OF CONSUMERS IN AFRICA

While a great deal of focus has been given to burgeoning economic superpowers like India and China, Africa has a growing middle class that rivals both those countries. Thanks to open markets and greater political stability, economists estimate Africa's middle class (those who spend $2-20 a day) makes up 34% of the continent's population. A new study shows that this 313-million strong middle class, which has grown 60% over the last decade, is upwardly mobile and in the market for foreign goods.

However, this isn't to say that Africa is prosperous. Sixty-one percent of Africa's 1 billion people continue to live on less than $2 a day. Vast wealth disparities persist as well. The net worth of 100,000 of the continent's richest citizens accounts for 60% of its gross domestic product. A further 180 million people can only afford to spend $2 to $4 a day, making them vulnerable to economic shifts that could knock them out of the middle class. Even those firmly entrenched in the new consumer class are far from rich with daily spending budgets between $4 and $20.

To many, the fact that a significant portion of Africa's population has disposable income at all is cause for celebration. In fact, some analysts credit this new breed of consumer for buffering Africa against much of the global financial crisis. Also with jobs on the rise, rural Africans are flocking to cities. The U.S. ambassador to South Africa even claims that Africa is now nearly as urbanized as China. Again, all this newfound growth must be viewed alongside current stories of tragedies against citizens in Uganda and Nigeria as well as the violent repressions in Libya. Still, one can only hope that much of the violence and chaos that has defined Africa for decades is now in the past, leaving the future open for more political freedom and economic growth.[iii]

lecture link 2-4

THE CIRCULAR FLOW MODEL

(**PPT 2-23** presents this simplified Circular Flow Model.)

Economists often used "models" to explain economic principles. A model is like a map of a concept. A *road map* shows you the major highways and waterways, not every tree. An *economic model* presents an economic concept as a bare-bones "map," containing only the major elements. Thus a model does not contain all the detail and complexity of the concept, just the simplified major elements.

One such economic model is the "Circular Flow Model," a simplified presentation of the basic transactions in a free-market economy. The two major elements are **consumers** (presented in the model as "households,") and the **businesses** that create goods and services.

Each of the factors of production mentioned in the text has a price. To use *land*, a business must make rent or mortgage payments (simplified as "*rent*.") *Labor* must be paid salary or *wages*. The buildings, equipment, production lines, etc. (*capital*) are financed by paying *interest*. Finally, the entrepreneur expects to earn a *profit* from using his or her *entrepreneurship*. However, this resource payment is not guaranteed. If costs exceed income, the business may suffer a *loss*. (Some newer versions of this model include "knowledge" as a factor of production; older versions usually don't.)

Businesses demand resources in order to produce products and services. In a capitalist economy, the households own the factors of production and must be compensated. This income flows back into the households. The prices of resources are set by the interaction of supply and demand.

The goods and services which households demand are created by business. The consumers in these households use the income from their factors of production to purchase goods and services.

Thus, business activity flows in a circle, which is illustrated by the Circular Flow Model. The market for resources (top arrows) is known as the *resource market*. The bottom flow is referred to as the *product market*.

This is a simplified model of pure capitalism, and it ignores a major player—government. Purchases of goods and services by all levels of government amount to about 20% of the nation's gross domestic product. More sophisticated models include the government's role in diverting resource payments as taxes and spending on government programs, which creates a more realistic representation of a mixed economy.

lecture link 2-5

THE ECONOMIC IMPACT OF THE 2010 OIL SPILL

The crude oil that spilled from BP's Deepwater Horizon rig is one of the most tragic environmental disasters in human history. The full effect of the spill on the region's wildlife and coastlines is still speculative. The only givens at this point are that the repercussions to the region will be overwhelmingly negative and vast.

That sad fact may not be true for the nation's economy as a whole, though. According to a study by Moody's Economy, the spill isn't expected to have a significant effect on the nation's gross domestic product. The coastline of Louisiana, Florida, Alabama, and Mississippi accounts for just 1% of the GDP. The study also points out that jobs lost in the fishing industry could be made up for in oil recovery jobs. But despite what the oil spill's effect on the national economy ultimately amounts to, the local impact of the spill on the Gulf region is nothing short of catastrophic. Approximately 33% of federal waters in the Gulf were closed off to commercial fishing, crippling the region's $2.4 billion commercial fishing industry.

On the shore, meanwhile, commercial property values are expected to tank 10% in the next three years. Property losses could total north of $4.3 billion on the coastline from Louisiana to Florida. Even before the spill, lot values on the 600-mile stretch were ailing as the recession leveled prices by almost 34% from the peak of U.S. residential sales. As for BP, experts estimate the spill may cost the company $37 billion in cleanup and restitution to local businesses. We can only hope that the nation's outrage and BP's insistence on maintaining a positive public image can take a backseat until a solution to the problem is devised by a mutual collaboration between corporate America, the federal government, and the public.[iv]

lecture link 2-6

OTHER ECONOMIC INDICATORS

In addition to the key economic indicators mentioned in the text—CPI, GDP, unemployment rate—there are other indicators measure different segments of the economy. Below are some of the more important ones.

KEY ECONOMIC INDICATORS

Producer Price Index	Monthly index that measures changes in wholesale prices
Prime Interest Rate	Lowest interest rate that banks charge preferred borrowers on short-term loans
Housing Starts	Tracks how many new single-family homes or buildings were constructed during the month and can detect trends in the economy looking forward
Durable-Goods Orders	New orders for goods that last more than three years
Balance of Trade	Total value of a country's exports minus the total value of its imports, over a specific period of time
Inflation Rate	Percentage increase in prices of goods or services over a period of time
Consumer Confidence Index	Measures the degree of consumer confidence in the economy, and can indicate an upcoming increase or decrease in economic activity

THE "BEIGE BOOK"

Many economists use the Federal Reserve Board "Beige Book" to detect trends in the economy. The correct name for the report is "Summary of Commentary on Current Economic Conditions by Federal Reserve District." Each Federal Reserve Bank gathers information on current economic conditions in its district. The Beige Book summarizes this information by district and sector and is a gauge on the strength of the economy.

TIMING OF THE INDICATORS

Economic indicators can further be classified by the timing of the indicator.

Some indicators are **lagging**, meaning that they don't change direction until a few quarters *after* the economy does. An example is the unemployment rate. Unemployment tends to increase for two or three quarters after the economy starts to improve.

Coincident indicators move *at the same time* as the economy does. The Gross Domestic Product measures the economy's output as it occurs.

Leading economic indicators are indicators which change *before* the economy changes. Stock market returns are a leading indicator, as the stock market usually begins to fall before the economy declines and they improve before the economy begins to pull out of a recession. Housing starts and the consumer confidence index are other leading economic indicators.[v]

lecture link 2-7

NEW ECONOMIC MEASURES

Michael Gelobter, the Executive Director of Redefining Progress, doesn't believe we are using the right measures of progress in the United States. He thinks that GDP, unemployment levels, and price indexes don't capture real economic progress or decline. He prefers what he calls the genuine progress indicator (GPI). To other economic measures, he would add the three E's: environment, economy, and equity. Gelobter would look at GDP, but he would also measure prison time, heart attacks, and clear-cut forests. Any increases would subtract from real progress, he believes. Furthermore, he would add to economic growth if there were more volunteerism and more time spent with families.

From GDP, he would like to subtract social costs such as crime, automobile accidents, commuting, family breakdown, lost leisure time, and underemployment. He would also subtract the depletion of nonrenewable resources, the cost of long-term environmental damage, and the cost of ozone depletion, lost farmlands, and lost wetlands. Housework and parenting would be added to the GDP, as would volunteer work.

You can see that there would be much controversy over such measures. Do you agree that such measures would help track social progress along with economic progress? Which measures do you agree with? Disagree with? Which measures do you think would be most difficult to gather?[vi]

lecture link 2-8

CHINA'S POTENTIAL REAL ESTATE BUST

Last year, Chinese banks lent a staggering $1.4 trillion, much of it going to the development of skyscrapers and other commercial property. At the time, government leaders championed the economic expansion. Now Chinese officials are trying to rein in commercial lending by raising the reserve requirements for the nation's banks. Why the sudden change of heart? After years of unprecedented growth, financial experts are afraid that the Chinese real estate boom could quickly turn into a bust. The office vacancy rate in Beijing clocks in at 22.4%, with over 60 office buildings sitting completely empty. Even worse, the current numbers don't include building projects that are already underway, such as the 74-story China World Tower 3 that will soon become Beijing's tallest building.

With a further 13 million square feet of office space entering the market in Beijing later this year, the Chinese economy could sustain considerable damage if the market bottoms out. Experts predict that a 10% drop in property values would triple the number of delinquent mortgages in Shanghai alone. So far, though, Chinese officials have only dissuaded banks from issuing further real estate loans rather than ordering them to halt any current or future construction projects. In fact, some Chinese officials balk that claims of market saturation are overblown. In some cases, local governments are even spurring the growth themselves. For instance, eastern Beijing government officials are hoping to add an additional 10 million square feet of office space this year, despite a 35% vacancy rate in the area.

If China does nothing to stave off runaway development, the country could suffer a fate similar to that of Dubai. From 2002 to mid-2008, Dubai residential real estate prices quadrupled thanks to a glut of foreign buyers. Developers carelessly flipped properties as banks kept them solvent with over $16 billion in residential mortgages. Once the recession hit, though, property values plunged 52%, emptying skyscrapers and sending much of the sheikdom's burgeoning expatriate workforce back home. 12% of Dubai's 27,000 residential mortgages are expected to default within the next year. In January, Barclays won Dubai's first foreclosure case, opening the floodgates for further foreclosures that could send the sheikdoms already shaky real estate market spiraling even further down.[vii]

lecture link 2-9

WHAT IS A DEPRESSION?

In 2009 with the stock marketing falling, banks failing, and unemployment soaring, many people wondered if the U.S. economy was suffering not from a recession, but from a much worse condition, a depression. Economists say that a depression is, well, nobody really has a formal description for a depression. A depression is when things are really, really bad.

While recessions are easy to define, there are no firm rules for what makes a depression. Everyone at least seems to agree there hasn't been one since the epic hardship of the 1930s. According to economist Peter Morici, a business professor at the University of Maryland, you'll know you've been in a recession when you see it behind you. "It's not going to be acknowledged until years go by. "

No one disputes the definition of a recession, and the economic downturn of 2008-2010 surely qualified. Recessions have two handy definitions—two straight quarters of economic contraction, or when the National Bureau of Economic Research makes the call.

Declaring a depression is much trickier.

- By one definition, it is a downturn of three years or more with a 10% drop in economic output and unemployment above 10%.

- Another definition says a depression is a sustained recession during which the populace has to dispose of tangible assets to pay for everyday living.

- Morici says a depression is a recession that "does not self-correct" because of fundamental structural problems in the economy, such as broken banks or a huge trade deficit.

- Or maybe a depression is whatever corporate America says it is.

The Great Depression still maintains top ranking. Unemployment peaked at more than 25%. From 1929 to 1933, the economy shrank 27%. The stock market lost 90% of its value from boom to bust. The 2008-2010 recession came no where near those figures. And government policy makers argue that safeguards in place today weren't there in the 1930s: deposit insurance, unemployment insurance, and an ability by government to hurl trillions of dollars at the problem.

Before the 1930s, any serious economic downturn was called a depression or a "panic." The term "recession" didn't come into common use until "depression" became burdened by memories of the 1930s. When the economy collapsed again in 1937, people didn't want to call that a new depression, and that's when the term "recession" was first used. According to Millsaps College professor Robert McElvaine, "People also use 'downward blip.' Alan Greenspan once called it a 'sideways waffle'."[viii]

Government officials are extremely cautious in using the D-word. Alfred Kahn, a top economic advisor to President Carter, learned that lesson in 1978 when he warned that rampaging inflation might lead to a recession or even "deep depression." When presidential aides asked him to use another term, Kahn promised he'd come up with something completely different.

"We're in danger," he said, "of having the worst banana in 45 years."

lecture link 2-10

CONTROLLING YOUR PERSONAL MONEY SUPPLY

Controlling your personal money supply is harder than you may think. In a recent study, nearly half of those asked said they lose track of how they spend their pocket cash, on average more than $2,000 a year. The study was commissioned by the Visa credit card group, part of their campaign to get Americans to use debit cards to manage money.

A dollar here, a dollar there, everyone loses track of some cash. What surprised the survey's authors was how much cash goes unaccounted for at the end of a week. The survey asked over 2,000 respondents to estimate their "mystery spending," or money they couldn't keep track of. Of those, 48% said they couldn't account for an average of $2,340 a year. At the extreme end of the spectrum were 7% who said they lost track of more than $100 per week, or $5,000 per year.

People 34 and under are the biggest offenders. Men lost track of an average of $50 a week, or $3,078 a year. Over half of them said they blew the cash during a night out. Young women spent $42 in mystery cash a week, or $2,709 a year. Two-thirds of the women blamed shopping trips.[ix]

critical
thinking exercises

Name: _____

Date: _____

critical thinking exercise 2-1
KNOW YOUR HISTORY OF ECONOMICS

Go to the Internet and look up the following economists: Adam Smith, Jeremy Bentham, David Ricardo and T.R. Malthus. Choose one of these economists and answer the following questions that describe their contributions to the field of economics.

1. Describe the personality of your chosen economist.

2. What major contributions did this chosen economist contribute to the field of economics regarding:

    a. Micro economics

    b. Macro economics

3. How does the works of your chosen economist have any relevance to our economy today?

4. How did your chosen economist further the field of economic study?

critical thinking exercise 2-2
APPLYING ECONOMIC PRINCIPLES TO EDUCATION

Recently, the U.S. Supreme Court ruled that cities could have voucher programs that give money directly to parents, and the parents can then choose between competing schools: public and private. The idea for promoting such a ruling was to create competition among schools. As with businesses, schools were expected to improve their products (how effectively they teach) to win students from competitors. Supposedly, that would mean an improvement in all schools, private and public, and would benefit many students.

1. Do you believe that such economic principles apply in both private and public organizations? Be prepared to defend your answer.

2. Are there other public functions that might benefit from more competition, including competition from private firms?

critical thinking exercise 2-3
FINDING THE EQUILIBRIUM POINT

In 2011, Knight Electronics sold 350,000 digital video recorders (DVRs.) Based on the company's analysis of the DVR market, the company believed that $160 was the equilibrium price based on the following supply and demand schedules.

2011 PRICE	AMOUNT SUPPLIED	AMOUNT DEMANDED
$120	290,000	390,000
$140	320,000	370,000
$160	350,000	350,000
$180	380,000	330,000
$200	410,000	310,000
$220	440,000	290,000

As the price of gasoline rose and the economy hit the skids, consumers began driving less and going out less frequently for entertainment. With more people staying at home, DVR usages increased. In 2012 Knight revised its estimate of the amount of product demanded. At each of the above price points, they estimate that consumers will purchase (demand) 50,000 more DVRs. For instance, at $140, now 420,000 DVRs will be sold. The price/amount supplied relationship remains the same.

1. Describe what has happened to the supply and demand curves for Knight DVRs in 2011.

2. What is the new equilibrium price?

3. How many DVRs will be produced at the new equilibrium price?

4. Knight revised its estimate of the amount of product demanded for 2012 as described above. In 2013 a new technology become available enabling DVRs to communicate over cell phones and the Internet. Knight's competitors are selling this new DVR, called SuperDVR, for $150. What will happen to the supply and demand curves for Knight DVRs now?

notes on critical thinking exercise 2-3

1. *Describe what has happened to the supply and demand curves for Knight DVRs in 2011.*

    Supply remained unchanged. Demand shifted right, showing the increased quantity demanded at every price.

2. *What is the new equilibrium price?*

    The quantity demanded and quantity supplied are now identical at $180, a higher price. At that price the quantity supplied remains stable at 380,000. However, the quantity demanded at that price is increased by 50,000 to 380,000. The equilibrium price will now be $180.

2012 PRICE	AMOUNT SUPPLIED	AMOUNT DEMANDED
$120	290,000	440,000
$140	320,000	420,000
$160	350,000	400,000
$180	*380,000*	*380,000*
$200	410,000	360,000
$220	440,000	350,000

3. *How many DVRs will be produced at the new equilibrium price?*

    At $180, 380,000 DVRs will be produced.

4. *Knight revised its estimate of the amount of product demanded for 2012 as described above. In 2013 a new technology become available enabling DVRs to communicate over cell phones and the Internet. Knight's competition are selling this new DVR, called SuperDVR, for $150. What will happen to the supply and demand curves for Knight DVRs now?*

    With a more advanced DVR available from competitors, demand for Knight DVRs will decrease at the same price. The demand curve shifts to the left, and the equilibrium price falls.

critical thinking exercise 2-4
STANDARD OF LIVING COMPARISON

Is the standard of living different in capitalist, socialist, and communist economies? Which economic system provides the highest standard of living? One way of answering these questions is by comparing economic data you might find in the library or on the Internet. (Hint: try the CIA Web site.) Choose one capitalist country, one socialist country, and one communist country. Use the following chart to record your findings.

	CAPITALIST COUNTRY	SOCIALIST COUNTRY	COMMUNIST COUNTRY
Country Chosen			
Gross Domestic Product			
Consumer Prices			
Unemployment Rate			
Average Income			
Average Education			

critical thinking exercise 2-5

BALANCING THE FEDERAL BUDGET

The Federal government's historical budget deficit is discussed and debated endlessly. Everyone has an opinion on how to balance the budget. Figures are presented on the next page. Rearrange the figures to eliminate the $2,079,500,000,000 ($2.079 trillion) deficit and balance the budget. You can either cut money going out or increase money coming in, but *interest payments on the national debt cannot be adjusted*. Good luck.

critical thinking exercise 2-5 (continued)

FEDERAL GOVERNMENT REVENUE AND SPENDING, 2010

MONEY COMING IN (RECEIPTS) (all figures in $millions)	2010	Proposed Value
Individual income taxes	1,732,600	
Corporation income taxes	179,600	
Unemployment taxes	45,200	
Excise taxes	71,600	
Estate and other taxes	187,500	
TOTAL, FEDERAL RECEIPTS	**2,216,500**	

MONEY GOING OUT (OUTLAYS) (all figures in $millions)		
Defense	830,400	
Health and Human Service	857,600	
Social Security	753,900	
Treasury	372,900	
Veterans Affairs	336,900	
Labor	179,000	
Agriculture	130,600	
Education	89,500	
Transportation	79,800	
Homeland Security	55,700	
Foreign Aid and Development	10,500	
Justice and State	53,800	
Science and Energy	44,200	
Housing, Interior, and Commerce	87,900	
All other outlays	198,500	
Interest on National Debt (CANNOT BE CHANGED)	**214,800**	**214,800**
TOTAL, FEDERAL OUTLAYS	**4,296,000**	

SURPLUS (DEFICIT)	**(2,079,500)**	**0.0**

notes on critical thinking exercise 2-5

There is no "right" or "wrong" answer to this exercise. Each student will modify the budget figures based on their individual beliefs and attitudes. It is interesting to assign this exercise as a group project and have the groups negotiate an equitable balance.

You can also update the figures with the current year's data by visiting Websites such as www.fmb.treas.gov, www.whitehouse.gov/omb/budget/, or www.gpoaccess.gov/usbudget. [x] You may have a hard time finding reliable totals, as different sources use different categorization methods.

bonus case

bonus case 2-1

FOUNDATIONS OF THE CAPITALIST SYSTEM

Throughout history of capitalism, there has been one persistent criticism. The whole system seems to be based on selfishness—the more one works, the more one prospers. If one is unable to work, the system seems to have no answer to his or her problems. Furthermore, there does not seem to be any moral or spiritual foundation to the system. Where do businesses get their values? What about concepts such as sharing, helping neighbors, and protecting the environment?

It is important to make a distinction between plain capitalism and democratic capitalism. Democratic capitalism is a system based on three components: (1) free enterprise; that is, freedom to own your own businesses and farms and freedom to keep the profits, (2) a freely elected government that has internal checks and balances, and (3) moral, ethical, and spiritual values that are part of the very fabric of the country and the business system. Plain capitalism is a system where there is free enterprise, but no freely elected government and no foundation of moral, ethical, and spiritual values. There are several "capitalist" countries headed by right-wing dictators that do not have democratic capitalism and do not have the relative prosperity and social justice that we have in the United States.

Let's explore democratic capitalism in more detail so that you can understand how the system works. One of the most important elements of democratic capitalism is its moral and spiritual base. When the U.S. was being settled, there was so much religious debate and rivalry among religions that people were tortured and killed for their beliefs. When it came time to establish a free and separate U. S., however, the founding fathers were adamant about freedom of religion. They were very religious people themselves.

Thomas Jefferson was proud of his religious heritage and his fight for religious freedom in the U.S. He asked that his epitaph should read: "Author of the Declaration of Independence, of the Statute of Virginia for Religious Freedom, and Father of the University of Virginia." Jefferson felt that freedom of religion was one of his most important contributions. He felt it was as important as being President of the United States.

Democratic capitalism cannot work effectively and fairly without all three components. With all three, the democratic capitalist system can become the most fair and equitable economic system in the world. Not everyone agrees on the role of government in the democratic system and on how much of the total gross national product the government should control. (Recent history indicates that somewhere between 20% and 25% of GDP gives the government the funds it needs to create more social justice and more equitable distribution of wealth.) A freely elected government is important to democratic capitalism because if the people feel that the system is not fair, they can elect new politicians to change the rules.

discussion questions for bonus case 2-1

1. Do you see any evidence that the moral, ethical, and spiritual foundation of the American democratic capitalist system is eroding? How does that affect the ability of capitalist proponents to promote capitalism in other countries such as China and India?

2. Why is it so necessary to have a freely elected government for democratic capitalism to create a prosperous and fair economy?

3. Go through the three components of democratic capitalism and picture an economy without each one. What happens to freedom, fairness, and moral and ethical behavior? Which part of the system seems weakest today? What can be done about it?

notes on discussion questions for bonus case 2-1

1. *Do you see any evidence that the moral, ethical, and spiritual foundation of the American democratic capitalist system is eroding? How does that affect the ability of capitalist proponents to promote capitalism in other countries such as China and India?*

   When one of the authors was in elementary school, the codes of what was moral forbid him to see "The Moon Is Blue" because the movie used the word "virgin" in it. Now movies include more adult language and more violence and sexual content. In fact, many such movies are now available in prime time on TV. There does seem to be an erosion of moral and ethical behavior in business, witness the Merck, Enron, WorldCom, Tyco, and Martha Stewart scandals. It could be a function of more media reporting of such behavior, but the impression is clear—moral decay is spreading.

   When other countries see moral decay in capitalist countries, they are hesitant to adopt capitalism. They do not want the immorality, the crime, and the music that they see as corrupting of the spiritual values of their countries.

2. *Why is it so necessary to have a freely elected government for democratic capitalism to create a prosperous and fair economy?*

   Because any kind of dictatorship hinders the operation of free markets, or at least tends to do so. Free choice in the market is based on a value system that includes free choice in it, including free choice of leaders.

3. *Go through the three components of democratic capitalism and picture an economy without each one. What happens to freedom, fairness, and moral and ethical behavior? Which part of the system seems weakest today? What can be done about it?*

   Without free enterprise, shortages develop and the whole economy tends to slow. Poverty, hunger and starvation often result. Without a freely-elected government, the arbitrary allocation of resources can lead to the same problems as an absence of free markets. But what is needed in any economy is a moral and ethical base. Without that base, the market mechanism falters.

endnotes

[i] *Sources:* Peter Coy, "If Demography is Destiny, Then India has the Edge," *Bloomberg BusinessWeek*, January 13, 2011; Madelene Pearson and Malavika Sharma, "Where Are India's Skilled Laborers?" *Bloomberg BusinessWeek*, January 6, 2011.

[ii] *Source*: Rich Miller and Simon Kennedy, "For the U.S., the Future Suddenly Seems Brighter," *Bloomberg BusinessWeek*, December 29, 2010.

[iii] *Source:* Peter Wonacott, "A New Class of Consumers Grows in Africa," *The Wall Street Journal*, May 2, 2011.

[iv] *Sources:* John Gittleshon, "Oil Spill May Cost $4.3 Billion in Property Values," *Bloomberg Businessweek*, June 11, 2010; Alice Gomstyn and Daniel Arnall, "Oil Spill Won't Hurt National Economy," *ABC News*, May 20, 2010; "Oil Spill Closes More Gulf Waters to Fishing," The Associated Press, June 5, 2010; Elizabeth Campbell and Yi Tian, "Shrimp Prices to Rise After BP Oil Spill Forces Fishing Curbs," *Bloomberg Businessweek*, May 3, 2010.

[v] *Sources*: Mike Moffatt, "A Beginner's Guide to Economic Indicators," *About.com*, May 16, 2006; "Economic Indicators," *Investopedia.com*; "Leading Indicators Index Shows Economy Braking," *The Clarion-Ledger*, May 19, 2006, p. 3C; and "Economic Indicators," *GPOAccess,* Council of Economic Advisors, www.gpoaccess.gov.

[vi] *Source:* Scott Burns, "New Measurement of Economy Urged," *The Washington Times*, October 23, 2002, p. C9.

[vii] *Sources:* Michael Forsythe and Kevin Hamlin, "The Building Bubble in China," *Bloomberg BusinessWeek*, March 1, 2010; Zainab Fattah, "Dubai: The First Foreclosure," *Bloomberg BusinessWeek*, January 25, 2010.

[viii] *Sources:* Tom Raym "The D-Word: Will Recession Become Something Worse?" *ABC News*, March 2, 2009; and "Fed's Yellen: Economy Similar to Great Depression," *CNNMoney.com*, February 7, 2009.

[ix] *Source*: "Half of Americans 'Lose' $2,000 in Cash a Year," *CNNMoney.com*, September 13, 2007.

[x] The Internet is a dynamic, changing information source. Web links noted in this manual were checked at the time of publication, but content may change over time. Please review the website before recommending it to your students.

Doing Business in Global Markets

chapter 3

critical thinking exercises

3.83

bonus cases

3.89

what's new in this edition

additions to the 10th edition:

- Getting to Know Yang Lan, Cofounder and Chair of Sun Media Group
- Name That Company: Yum! Brands
- Discussion of BRIC as an economic term added to section The Future of Global Trade
- Spotlight on Small Business: A Small Business with a Big Vision
- Reaching Beyond Our Borders: Golden Arches Glowing across the Globe
- Video Case

revisions to the 10th edition:

- Text was revised to eliminate redundancy and tighten discussions.
- Statistical data and examples throughout the chapter were updated to reflect current information.
- Making Ethical Decisions: See the Sights, Meet the Doctors

deletions from the 9th edition:

- Getting to Know Sheikha Lubna al-Qasimi, Foreign Trade Minister of the United Arab Emirates
- Name That Company: Starbucks and Howard Schultz
- Spotlight on Small Business
- Reaching Beyond Our Borders
- Legal Briefcase

brief chapter outline
and learning goals

Doing Business in Global Markets

Getting To Know YANG LAN, COFOUNDER AND CHAIR OF SUN MEDIA GROUP

learning goal 1

Discuss the importance of the global market and the roles of comparative advantage and absolute advantage in global trade.

I. THE DYNAMIC GLOBAL MARKET

II. WHY TRADE WITH OTHER NATIONS?

A. The Theories of Comparative and Absolute Advantage

learning goal 2

Explain the importance of importing and exporting, and understand key terms used in global business.

III. GETTING INVOLVED IN GLOBAL TRADE

A. Importing Goods and Services

B. Exporting Goods and Services

C. Measuring Global Trade

learning goal 3

Illustrate the strategies used in reaching global markets and explain the role of multinational corporations.

IV. STRATEGIES FOR REACHING GLOBAL MARKETS

A. Licensing

B. Exporting

C. Franchising

D. Contract Manufacturing

E. International Joint Ventures and Strategic Alliances

F. Foreign Direct Investment

Getting to Know YANG LAN of SUN MEDIA GROUP

Known as the Chinese Oprah, Lan's show attracts 200 million viewers. Her media success has led Lan to purchase various publications and websites. In 2000, she launched her own television network. The network, Sun TV, failed and Lan sold it in 2003. She bounced back and used her entrepreneurial talents to succeed in other areas. Sun Media Group produces television shows and contains a jewelry and credit card line. Lan believes the growth of Chinese media will eventually lead to a more open press.

 NAME THAT company

We franchise 37,000 of our KFC, Taco Bell, and Pizza Hut restaurants in 109 countries around the world. It didn't take us long to learn that customers around the globe have very different tastes when it comes to their food. We found in Japan that a favorite pizza enjoyed by our patrons was topped with squid and sweet mayonnaise. In China it's a must to serve a "dragon twister" with our world-famous chicken. Name our company.

(Students should read the chapter before guessing the company's name: Yum! Brands.*)*

learning goal 1

Discuss the importance of the global market and the roles of comparative advantage and absolute advantage in global trade.

I. THE DYNAMIC GLOBAL MARKET

A. THE IMPORTANCE OF INTERNATIONAL MARKETS

1. Whereas there are over 310 million people in the U.S., there are 6.9 billion potential customers in the world.

2. U.S. customers buy billions of dollars in goods from China.

3. Companies such as UPS and sports teams in the NBA, MLB, and NFL operate extensively overseas.

B. The U.S. is the **THIRD LARGEST EXPORTING NATION** in the world; it is the world's largest importer as well.

PPT 3-1
Chapter Title

PPT 3-2
Learning Goals

(See complete PowerPoint slide notes on page 3.52.)

PPT 3-3
Learning Goals

(See complete PowerPoint slide notes on page 3.52.)

PPT 3-4
Yang Lan

(See complete PowerPoint slide notcs on page 3.53.)

PPT 3-5
Name That Company

(See complete PowerPoint slide notes on page 3.53.)

PPT 3-6
Business in the Global Market

(See complete PowerPoint slide notes on page 3.53.)

PPT 3-7
World Population by Continent

TEXT FIGURE 3.1
World Population by Continent
(Text page 61)

(See complete PowerPoint slide notes on page 3.54.)

lecture link 3-1

CHINA BESTS THE UNITED STATES IN AUTO SALES

China has overtaken Germany as the world's largest exporter. With its growing economic clout, China has dethroned the United States as the world's largest car market. (See the complete lecture link on page 3.76 in this manual.)

1. ***IMPORTING*** is buying products from another country.

2. ***EXPORTING*** is selling products to another country.

3. **COMPETITION IS INTENSE**: The U.S. must compete against aggressive global competitors.

C. The purpose of this chapter is to discuss the potential and challenges of international business.

II. WHY TRADE WITH OTHER NATIONS?

A. Reasons **FOR** trading with other nations include:

1. No nation can produce all the products that its people need.

2. Nations seek trade with countries to meet the needs of their people.

3. **MUTUALLY BENEFICIAL EXCHANGE**

    a. Some nations have abundant natural resources and lack technological know-how.

    b. Others have sophisticated technology but few natural resources.

    c. Global trade relations enable countries to produce what they can and buy the rest in a mutually beneficial exchange.

4. ***FREE TRADE*** is the movement of goods and services among nations without political or economic obstruction.

B. **THE THEORIES OF COMPARATIVE AND ABSOLUTE ADVANTAGE**

1. Nations exchange goods and services, art, sports, and much more.

PPT 3-8
Importing and Exporting

(See complete PowerPoint slide notes on page 3.54.)

PPT 3-9
Pleasure Doing Business

(See complete PowerPoint slide notes on page 3.54.)

PPT 3-10
Can You Spare a Dime?

(See complete PowerPoint slide notes on page 3.55.)

PPT 3-11
Trading with Other Nations

(See complete PowerPoint slide notes on page 3.55.)

TEXT FIGURE 3.2
The Pros and Cons of Tree Trade
(Text page 62)

This text figure shows some arguments for and against free trade.

PPT 3-12
How Exports Affect the GDP (U.S.)

(See complete PowerPoint slide notes on page 3.55.)

PPT 3-13
How Exports Affect the GDP
(China)

(See complete PowerPoint slide notes on page 3.56.)

PPT 3-14
How Exports Affect the GDP
(Germany)

(See complete PowerPoint slide notes on page 3.56.)

2. **_COMPARATIVE ADVANTAGE THEORY_** states that a country should sell to other countries those products that it produces most effectively and efficiently and should buy from other countries those products that it cannot produce as effectively or efficiently.

   a. The U.S. has a **COMPARATIVE ADVANTAGE** in producing goods and services.

   b. It lacks a comparative advantage in growing coffee or making shoes.

3. **_ABSOLUTE ADVANTAGE_** is the advantage that exists when a country has a monopoly on producing a specific product or is able to produce it more efficiently than all other countries.

   a. South Africa once had an **ABSOLUTE ADVANTAGE** in diamond production.

   b. Today there are very few instances of absolute advantage.

learning goal 2

Explain the importance of importing and exporting, and understand key terms used in global business.

III. GETTING INVOLVED IN GLOBAL TRADE

A. The real potential in global markets may be with **SMALL BUSINESSES.**

   1. Small businesses generate about 30% of exports, yet only 1% of the 29 million small businesses take part.

   2. President Obama wants to double exports by 2015.

PPT 3-15
How Free Trade Benefits the World

(See complete PowerPoint slide notes on page 3.56.)

PPT 3-16
Comparative and Absolute
Advantage

(See complete PowerPoint slide notes on page 3.57.)

PPT 3-17
Going Global with a Small Business

(See complete PowerPoint slide notes on page 3.57.)

PPT 3-18
Whom Does the U.S. Owe?

(See complete PowerPoint slide notes on page 3.57.)

3. Getting started in global trade can be through observation, determination, and risk.

B. **IMPORTING GOODS AND SERVICES**

1. Foreign students attending U.S. schools often notice some products widely available in their countries are not available here.

2. Importing these goods into the U.S. can be quite profitable.

3. Howard Schultz brought the idea of neighborhood coffee bars to the U.S. as Starbucks.

C. **EXPORTING GOODS AND SERVICES**

1. **WHAT CAN YOU SELL TO OTHER COUNTRIES?**

   a. Just about anything that is used in the United States can be sold in other countries.

   b. Competition abroad is often not as intense for U.S. producers as it is at home.

   c. *The text offers the example of snowplows to Saudi Arabia for sand removal on driveways.*

2. Exporting creates **GREAT OPPORTUNITIES** and is a terrific boost to the U.S. economy.

3. Selling in global markets, however, involves many **HURDLES.**

4. The text supplies several sources of information about exporting, including a government pamphlet, trade magazine, and several websites.

SPOTLIGHT ON
small
business
(Text page 64)

PPT 3-19
A Small
Business with a
Big Vision

(See complete PowerPoint slide notes on page 3.58.)

PPT 3-20
Getting Involved in Importing

(See complete PowerPoint slide notes on page 3.58.)

PPT 3-21
Getting Involved in Exporting

(See complete PowerPoint slide notes on page 3.58.)

bonus case 3-1
MAKING A MINT ON MAKE-BELIEVE

The popularity of KidZania, a brand of "edutainment" theme parks headquartered in Mexico, has taken off with parents and kids all around the world. (See the complete case, discussion questions, and suggested answers beginning on page 3.89 of this manual.)

lecture link 3-2
URBAN OUTFITTERS'S EUROPEAN EXPANSION

Urban Outfitters jumped the cultural hurdles of selling in Europe by designing clothes with a European appeal and not just offering the same products as in American stores. (See the complete lecture link on page 3.76 in this manual.)

critical thinking exercise 3-1
WHICH COUNTRY?

This exercise asks students to use Internet research to evaluate a possible expansion into one of two countries (See complete exercise on page 3.83 of this manual.)

D. **MEASURING GLOBAL TRADE**

1. **_BALANCE OF TRADE_** is the total value of a nation's exports compared to its imports measured over a particular period.

   a. A favorable balance of trade, or **_TRADE SURPLUS_**, exists when the value of a nation's exports exceeds its imports measured over a particular period.

   b. **_TRADE DEFICIT_** is an unfavorable balance of trade; **it** occurs when the value of a country's imports exceeds that of its exports.

2. **_BALANCE OF PAYMENTS_** is the difference between money coming into a country (from exports) and money leaving the country (for imports) plus money flows from other factors such as tourism, foreign aid, military expenditures, and foreign investment.

   a. **A FAVORABLE BALANCE OF PAYMENTS** means more money is flowing into than flowing out of the country.

   b. Likewise, an **UNFAVORABLE BALANCE OF PAYMENTS** means more money is leaving than coming into the country.

3. Since 1975 the U.S. has run a trade **DEFICIT.**

4. The U.S. exports a much **LOWER PERCENTAGE** of its products than other countries do.

5. Like other nations, the U.S. tries to make sure global trade is conducted fairly.

   a. The U.S. has laws to prohibit unfair practices such as **_DUMPING,_** the practice of selling products in a foreign country at lower prices than those charged in the producing country.

PPT 3-22
How to Measure Global Trade

(See complete PowerPoint slide notes on page 3.59.)

TEXT FIGURE 3.3
The Largest Trading Nations in the
World and Largest U.S. Trade
Partners
(Text page 65)

This text figure lists the major trading countries in the world.

PPT 3-23
Balance of Payments

(See complete PowerPoint slide notes on page 3.59.)

PPT 3-24
Unfair Trade Practices

(See complete PowerPoint slide notes on page 3.59.)

b. There is also evidence that some governments subsidize certain industries to sell goods in global markets for less.

<u>**learning goal** 3</u>

Illustrate the strategies used in reaching global markets and explain the role of multinational corporations.

IV. STRATEGIES FOR REACHING GLOBAL MARKETS

A. The following are some ways an organization can participate in global trade.

B. **LICENSING**

1. *__LICENSING__* is a global strategy in which a firm (the licensor) allows a foreign company (the licensee) to produce its products in exchange for a fee (a royalty).

2. The **ADVANTAGES** of licensing:

a. A company can gain additional revenues from a product it would not have normally produced domestically.

b. The firm can sell start-up supplies, component materials, and consulting services *(examples: Coca-Cola and Fredrick's of Hollywood).*

c. The licensor spends little or no money to produce and market the product; licensees bear the costs.

3. The **PROBLEMS** of licensing:

a. Often a firm must grant licensing rights to its product for an extended period.

progress
assessment
(Text page 66)

PPT 3-25
Progress Assessment

(See complete PowerPoint slide notes on page 3.60.)

PPT 3-26
Key Strategies for Reaching Global
Markets

TEXT FIGURE 3.4
Strategies for Reaching Global
Markets
(Text page 67)

(See complete PowerPoint slide notes on page 3.60.)

PPT 3-27
Licensing

(See complete PowerPoint slide notes on page 3.61.)

      b. If a product experiences remarkable growth in the foreign market, the bulk of the revenues goes to the licensee.

      c. If the foreign licensee learns the technology, it may break the agreement and begin to produce a similar product on its own.

C. EXPORTING

1. The Department of Commerce created **EXPORT ASSISTANCE CENTERS (EACs)** to provide hands-on exporting assistance and trade-finance support for small and medium-sized businesses.

2. An EAC network exists in more than 109 U.S. cities and 80 countries.

3. To overcome small firms' reluctance, **EXPORT-TRADING COMPANIES** can match buyers and sellers from different countries.

4. An export-trading company is a good place to get career training in global trade.

D. FRANCHISING

1. **FRANCHISING** is a contractual arrangement whereby someone with a good idea for a business sells the rights to use the business name.

2. Franchising is popular both domestically and in global markets.

3. *Examples: Subway, Holiday Inn, and Dunkin' Donuts.*

4. Franchisers must adapt in the countries they serve.

5. *Domino's Pizza found that Japanese people enjoyed squid and sweet mayonnaise pizza.*

lecture link 3-3
DISNEY'S SECOND TRY IN CHINA

When Disneyland Hong Kong was opened, cultural disconnects were discovered. As Disney licenses another park in Asia, it aims to correct its mistakes. (See the complete lecture link on page 3.77 in this manual.)

PPT 3-28
Export Assistance Centers and Export Trading Centers

(See complete PowerPoint slide notes on page 3.61.)

PPT 3-29
Franchising

(See complete PowerPoint slide notes on page 3.61.)

PPT 3-30
Time to Make the Donuts …

(See complete PowerPoint slide notes on page 3.62.)

REACHING BEYOND
our borders
(Text page 69

PPT 3-31
Golden Arches Glowing across the Globe

(See complete PowerPoint slide notes on page 3.62.)

PPT 3-32
That's at McDonalds?

(See complete PowerPoint slide notes on page 3.62.)

E. **CONTRACT MANUFACTURING**

1. ***CONTRACT MANUFACTURING*** involves a foreign country's production of private-label goods to which a domestic company then attaches its brand name or trademark; also called outsourcing *(text examples: Dell, Xerox, and IBM).*

2. By using contract manufacturing a company can often experiment in a new market **WITHOUT HEAVY START-UP COSTS.**

3. A firm can also use contract manufacturing temporarily to **MEET AN UNEXPECTED INCREASE IN ORDERS.**

4. Also, labor costs are low.

F. **INTERNATIONAL JOINT VENTURES AND STRATEGIC ALLIANCES**

1. A ***JOINT VENTURE*** is a partnership in which two or more companies (often from different countries) join to undertake a major project.

2. *The text offers the example of the joint venture between Disney and Shanghai Shendi Group.*

3. A unique joint venture is that between University of Pittsburgh and the government of Italy to build a medical transplant center in Sicily.

4. The **BENEFITS** of joint venture:

   a. Shared technology and risk

   b. Shared marketing and management expertise

   c. Entry into markets where foreign companies are not allowed unless their goods are produced locally

PPT 3-33
Contract Manufacturing

(See complete PowerPoint slide notes on page 3.63.)

PPT 3-34
Joint Ventures

(See complete PowerPoint slide notes on page 3.63.)

5. The **DRAWBACKS**:

    a. One partner can learn the technology and practices of the other and **LEAVE TO BECOME A COMPETITOR.**

    b. A shared technology may become **OBSOLETE.**

    c. The partnership may be **TOO LARGE TO BE AS FLEXIBLE** as needed.

6. A ***STRATEGIC ALLIANCE*** is a long-term partner-ship between two or more companies established to help each company build competitive market advantages.

    a. Alliances can provide access to markets, capi-tal, and technical expertise.

    b. Strategic alliances are **FLEXIBLE** and can be effective between firms of different sizes.

    c. *The text uses the example of Hewlett-Packard's strategic alliances with Hitachi and Samsung.*

G. **FOREIGN DIRECT INVESTMENT**

1. ***FOREIGN DIRECT INVESTMENT*** is buying per-manent property and business in foreign nations.

2. A ***FOREIGN SUBSIDIARY*** is a company owned in a foreign country by another company (**PARENT COMPANY**).

    a. **THE LEGAL REQUIREMENTS** of both the **PARENT (HOME)** and the **FOREIGN (HOST) COUNTRIES** must be observed.

PPT 3-35
Strategic Alliances

(See complete PowerPoint slide notes on page 3.64.)

PPT 3-36
Foreign Direct Investment

(See complete PowerPoint slide notes on page 3.64.)

b. The **ADVANTAGE** of foreign subsidiaries is that the **COMPANY MAINTAINS COMPLETE CONTROL** over any technology or expertise it may possess.

c. The major **SHORTCOMING** is that the firm's assets could be **EXPROPRIATED**, taken over by the foreign government, if relations with the host country fail.

d. *As an example of a company with many foreign subsidiaries, the text uses the example of consumer giant Nestlé.*

3. **MULTINATIONAL CORPORATIONS**

a. A **_MULTINATIONAL CORPORATION_** is an organization that manufactures and markets products in many different countries and has multinational stock ownership and multinational management.

b. Only firms that have manufacturing capacity or other physical presence in different nations can truly be called multinational.

4. **SOVEREIGN-WEALTH FUNDS (SWFs)**

a. One of the fastest-growing forms of foreign direct investment is the use of sovereign wealth funds (SWFs).

b. SWFs are investment funds controlled by governments holding large stakes in foreign companies.

c. SWFs from Kuwait, Singapore, and China have purchased significant portions of U.S. companies, such as Citigroup.

critical thinking exercise 3-2
EVALUATING GLOBAL EXPANSION

One company is faced with the decision of whether or not to enter a joint venture with a Latin American country. (See complete exercise on page 3.84 of this manual.)

PPT 3-37
Multinational Corporations

(See complete PowerPoint slide notes on page 3.64.)

TEXT FIGURE 3.5
The Largest Multinational Corporations in the World
(Text page 71)

This text figure lists the 10 largest multinational corporations in the world.

bonus case 3-2
GAP'S EVOLVING VIEW OF ETHICS

Facing a flood of stories focusing on wage and safety violations in its overseas factories, Gap responded by procducing a "social-responsibility" report, honestly detailing the problems facing the company (See the complete case, discussion questions, and suggested answers beginning on page 3.91 of this manual.)

PPT 3-38
Sovereign Wealth Funds

(See complete PowerPoint slide notes on page 3.64.)

> d. There is concern that the size and government ownership of these funds could be used for achieving geopolitical objectives.

5. Different strategies reflect different levels of ownership, financial commitment, and risk.

<u>**learning goal** 4</u>

Evaluate the forces that affect trading in world markets.

V. FORCES AFFECTING TRADING IN GLOBAL MARKETS

A. Succeeding in any business takes work and effort with many challenges.

B. **SOCIOCULTURAL FORCES**

1. The term **CULTURE** refers to the set of values, beliefs, rules, and institutions held by a specific group of people.

2. Culture can include social structures, religion, manners and customs, values and attitudes, language, and personal communication.

3. American businesspeople are notoriously bad at adapting to cultural differences among nations.

   a. Some have been accused of **ETHNOCENTRICITY**, an attitude that our culture is superior to all others.

   b. In contrast, foreign businesspeople are very good at adapting to U.S. culture.

   c. *Example: German, Japanese, and Korean carmakers have adapted to the U.S. market, but U.S. carmakers have not been as successful adapting their products to other cultures.*

**progress
assessment**
(Text page 72)

PPT 3-39
Progress Assessment (See complete PowerPoint slide notes on page 3.65.)

PPT 3-40
Forces Affecting Global Trade

(See complete PowerPoint slide notes on page 3.66.)

lecture link 3-4
FOREIGN ETIQUETTE TIPS

The author of *Business Etiquette for Dummies* gives tips for avoiding embarrassing cultural gaffes (See the complete lecture link on page 3.78 of this manual.)

PPT 3-41
Cultural Differences

(See complete PowerPoint slide notes on page 3.66.)

PPT 3-42
Lost in Translation

(See complete PowerPoint slide notes on page 3.66.)

4. **RELIGION** is an important part of any society's culture and can have a significant impact on business operations *(example: misunderstandings about Muslim culture)*.

5. **SOCIOCULTURAL DIFFERENCES** can also impact business decisions involving human resource management.

6. Learning about sociocultural perspectives regarding time, change, competition, natural resources, achievement, and even work itself can help.

7. A sound global philosophy is *never assume what works in one country will work in another*.

C. **ECONOMIC AND FINANCIAL FORCES**

1. Due to economic conditions, global opportunities may not be viable opportunities at all.

   a. Global financial markets do not have a worldwide currency.

   b. The **U.S. DOLLAR** is a dominant and stable currency.

2. The ***EXCHANGE RATE*** is the value of one nation's currency relative to the currencies of other countries.

   a. A **HIGH VALUE OF THE DOLLAR** means the products of foreign producers would be cheaper, but U.S.-produced goods would be more expensive.

   b. A **LOW VALUE OF THE DOLLAR** means foreign goods become more expensive because it takes more dollars to buy them.

lecture link 3-5
BLOOD TYPE MATTERS IN JAPAN

In Japan, a person's blood type is a popular way of categorizing personalities. Some companies even base business assignments on a person's blood type. (See complete lecture link on page 3.79 of this manual.)

PPT 3-43
Ready to Travel Abroad?

(See complete PowerPoint slide notes on page 3.67.)

TEXT FIGURE 3.6
Oops, Did We Say That?
(Text page 73)

This text figure shows some classic blunders in translating advertising campaigns for global markets.

PPT 3-44
Do as the Germans...

(See complete PowerPoint slide notes on page 3.67.)

PPT 3-45
Exchange Rates

(See complete PowerPoint slide notes on page 3.68.)

3. Global financial markets operate under a system of **FLOATING EXCHANGE RATES** in which currencies "float" according to supply and demand in the global market for currency.

    a. Changes in currency values impact global commerce in numerous ways.

    b. Currency fluctuations can be especially tough for developing economies.

    c. These changes cause other problems; labor costs can vary as currency values shift.

4. ***DEVALUATION*** is lowering the value of a nation's currency relative to other currencies.

    a. In many developing nations the only trade possible is **BARTERING**, trading merchandise for merchandise with no money involved.

    b. ***COUNTERTRADING*** is a complex form of bartering in which several nations may be involved, each trading goods for goods or services for services.

    c. Approximately 20% of the global exchanges involve countertrading.

    d. *The text uses the example of the Ford Motor Company trading vehicles to Jamaica for bauxite.*

D. **LEGAL AND REGULATORY FORCES**

1. In global markets, several groups of laws and regulations may apply.

    a. Global markets are governed by a myriad of **LAWS AND REGULATIONS** that are often **INCONSISTENT**.

critical thinking
exercise 3-3
CURRENCY SHIFTS

This exercise asks students to track the exchange rates for six currencies for 30 days. (See complete exercise on page 3.86 of this manual.)

PPT 3-46
Devaluation and Countertrading

(See complete PowerPoint slide notes on page 3.68.)

PPT 3-47
Legal Concerns Overseas

(See complete PowerPoint slide notes on page 3.68.)

    b. Important legal questions are interpreted differently country to country.

  2. American businesspeople are bound to follow **U.S. LAWS AND REGULATIONS** in conducting business globally.

    a. The **FOREIGN CORRUPT PRACTICES ACT OF 1978** prohibits "questionable" or "dubious" payments to foreign officials to secure business contracts.

    b. This law runs contrary to beliefs and practices in many countries.

    c. The **ORGANIZATION FOR ECONOMIC COOPERATION AND DEVELOPMENT (OECD)** and **TRANSPARENCY INTERNATIONAL** have led the effort to fight corruption and bribery in foreign markets.

  3. To be successful in global markets it is often important to **CONTACT LOCAL BUSINESSPEOPLE** and gain their cooperation.

E. **PHYSICAL AND ENVIRONMENTAL FORCES**

  1. Technological constraints may make it difficult to build a large global market.

  2. Some developing nations have **PRIMITIVE TRANSPORTATION AND STORAGE SYSTEMS** that make distribution ineffective.

  3. Certain **TECHNOLOGICAL DIFFERENCES** affect exportable products (*such as the difference between 110 and 220 voltage electricity*).

TEXT FIGURE 3.7
Countries Rated Highest on
Corrupt Business
(Text page 75)

This text figure lists the 10 countries rated highest on corrupt business practices.

lecture link 3-6
BRIBERY PITFALLS

The Sarbanes-Oxley Act has focused corporate executives' attention on uncovering and preventing bribery. (See the complete lecture link on page 3.79 of this manual.)

bonus case 3-3
COOLING OFF THE SWEAT SHOPS

Apparel leaders such as Nike, Reebok, and Liz Claiborne are responding to critics by joining the Fair Labor Association, a sweatshop-monitoring organization. (See the complete case, discussion questions, and suggested answers beginning on page 3.93 of this manual.)

PPT 3-48
Environmental Forces

(See complete PowerPoint slide notes on page 3.69)

progress assessment
(Text page 75)

PPT 3-49
Progress Assessment

(See complete PowerPoint slide notes on page 3.69)

VI. TRADE PROTECTIONISM

A. **_TRADE PROTECTIONISM_** is the use of government regulations to limit the import of goods and services.

1. **ADVOCATES** believe that trade protectionism allows domestic producers to survive and grow, producing more jobs.

   a. Countries often use trade protectionism measures to **PROTECT THEIR INDUSTRIES** against dumping and foreign competition.

   b. Some are wary of foreign competition in general.

2. Business, economics, and politics have always been closely linked.

   a. For centuries businesspeople advocated an economic principle called **MERCANTILISM,** selling more goods to other nations than you bought from them; that is, to have a favorable balance of trade.

   b. The expected result was a flow of money to the country that sold the most globally.

   c. Governments charged a **_TARIFF_**, a tax on imports, making imported goods more expensive.

3. There are two kinds of **TARIFFS**:

   a. **PROTECTIVE TARIFFS** are import taxes designed to raise the price of imported products so that domestic products can be more competitively priced.

PPT 3-50
Trade Protectionism

(See complete PowerPoint slide notes on page 3.70)

lecture link 3-7
DOES TRADE PROTECTION PROTECT OR RISK YOUR FUTURE?

This reading focuses on the consequences of the 1930 Smoot-Hawley Act. (See the complete lecture link on page 3.80 in this manual.)

PPT 3-51
Tariffs

(See complete PowerPoint slide notes on page 3.70)

b. Tariffs are intended to save jobs and protect the country's infant industries.

c. **REVENUE TARIFFS** are designed to raise money for the government.

4. **QUOTAS** are more restrictive.

a. An ***IMPORT QUOTA*** is a limit on the number of products in certain categories that a nation can import.

b. Nations also **PROHIBIT** the export of specific products.

c. **ANTITERRORISM LAWS** and the **U.S. EXPORT ADMINISTRATION ACT OF 1979** prohibit exporting goods like high-tech weapons.

d. An ***EMBARGO*** is a complete ban on the import or export of a certain product or stopping all trade with a particular country *(example: the U.S. embargo against trade with Cuba since 1962)*.

5. **NONTARIFF BARRIERS**

a. **NONTARIFF BARRIERS** are not as specific or formal as tariffs but can still be detrimental to free trade.

b. *India imposes a number of restrictive standards to inhibit the sale of imported products.*

c. *China omits many American-made products from government catalogs.*

d. An impending free trade agreement with South Korea will open the market to U.S. producers.

PPT 3-52
Import Quotas and Embargos

(See complete PowerPoint slide notes on page 3.70)

6. Overcoming trade constraints creates business opportunities.

B. **THE WORLD TRADE ORGANIZATION (WTO)**

1. Leaders from 23 countries formed the General Agreement on Tariffs and Trade (GATT).

2. The ***GENERAL AGREEMENT ON TARIFFS AND TRADE (GATT)*** is a 1948 agreement that established a forum for negotiating mutual reductions in trade restrictions.

3. The 1986 **URUGUAY ROUND OF GATT TALKS** were convened to deal with the renegotiation of trade agreements.

   a. After eight years, 124 nations agreed to a new GATT agreement.

   b. The agreement **LOWERS TARIFFS** on average by 38% worldwide.

4. Created by the Uruguay Round on January 1, 1995, the ***WORLD TRADE ORGANIZATION (WTO)*** is the international organization that replaced the General Agreement of Tariffs and Trade and was assigned the duty of mediating trade disputes.

5. WTO acts as an independent player that oversees key cross-border issues and global business practices.

6. The formation of the WTO did not totally eliminate national laws that **IMPEDE TRADE EXPANSION.**

   a. The 2001 WTO Round addressed many unresolved issues.

PPT 3-53
World Trade Organization

(See complete PowerPoint slide notes on page 3.71)

    b.   The Doha Round ended in 2008 with no significant agreements.

C. **COMMON MARKETS**

    1.   A **_COMMON MARKET_** is a regional group of countries that have a common external tariff, no internal tariffs, and the coordination of laws to facilitate exchange among member countries (also called a **TRADING BLOC**).

    2.   The **EUROPEAN UNION (EU)** is a group of 27 nations in Western Europe.

        a.   When combined, the European Union nations have a population of over 500 million and GDP of $16.4 trillion.

        b.   The objective was to make Europe an even stronger competitor in global commerce.

    3.   The **PATH TO UNIFICATION** has been slow and difficult, yet significant progress has been made.

        a.   In 1999, the EU officially launched its **JOINT CURRENCY,** the **EURO**.

        b.   The adoption of the euro eliminated currency conversion problems and saved billions of dollars.

        c.   In 2010–2011, the EU faced **DEBT, DEFICIT, AND GROWTH PROBLEMS** due to financial difficulties in Greece, Ireland, Portugal, and Spain.

    4.   Another common market is **MERCOSUR**, a group that includes Brazil, Argentina, Paraguay, Uruguay, Chile, Bolivia, Columbia, Ecuador, and Peru.

        a.   Ambitious economic goals included single currency.

PPT 3-54
Common Markets

(See complete PowerPoint slide notes on page 3.71)

PPT 3-55
EU Members

TEXT FIGURE 3.8
Members of the European Union
(Text page 78)

(See complete PowerPoint slide notes on page 3.71)

5. The **ASSOCIATION OF SOUTHEAST ASIAN NATIONS (ASEAN)** was established in 1967.

    a. ASEAN creates economic cooperation among its five original members (Indonesia, Malaysia, Philippines, Singapore, and Thailand).

    b. ASEAN has expanded to include Brunei, Cambodia, Lao PDR, Myanmar, and Vietnam.

6. **COMESA** is a 19-member African trading bloc with a GDP of $740 billion and population of 533 million.

D. **THE NORTH AMERICAN AND CENTRAL AMERICAN FREE TRADE AGREEMENTS**

1. The **_NORTH AMERICAN FREE TRADE AGREEMENT (NAFTA)_** is the agreement that created a free-trade area among the United States, Canada, and Mexico, signed in 1994.

2. **NAFTA OPPONENTS** believe the agreement caused loss of U.S. jobs and capital.

3. The **OBJECTIVES OF NAFTA** were to:

    a. Eliminate trade barriers

    b. Promote conditions of fair competition

    c. Increase investment opportunities

    d. Provide effective protection of intellectual property rights

    e. Establish a framework for further regional trade cooperation

    f. Improve working conditions in North America

PPT 3-56
NAFTA

(See complete PowerPoint slide notes on page 3.72)

4. The combination of the United States, Canada, and Mexico created a **MARKET OF OVER 450 MILLION PEOPLE** with a gross domestic product of over $17 trillion.

5. NAFTA has experienced both **SUCCESS** and **DIFFICULTIES.**

   a. U.S. exports to NAFTA partners have increased from $289 billion to $1 trillion since the agreement was signed.

   b. However, the U.S. has lost almost 750,000 jobs since signing NAFTA.

   c. **INEQUITIES** still exist between Mexico and the U.S. in income and working conditions.

6. The **CENTRAL AMERICAN FREE TRADE AGREEMENT** seeks to create a free-trade zone with the Central American nations of Costa Rica, the Dominican Republic, El Salvador, Guatemala, Honduras, and Nicaragua.

   a. **CRITICS** again warned of lost jobs.

   b. **SUPPORTERS** hope that it will open markets and reduce trade regulations.

   c. This agreement remains stalled due to U.S. political considerations.

7. Some economists praise such unions, while others feel that the world is **DIVIDING ITSELF INTO MAJOR TRADING BLOCKS**.

PPT 3-57
CAFTA

(See complete PowerPoint slide notes on page 3.70)

PPT 3-58
New Free Trade Agreements

(See complete PowerPoint slide notes on page 3.70)

progress
assessment
(Text page 79)

PPT 3-59
Progress Assessment (See complete PowerPoint slide notes on page 3.70.)

lecture outline

Discuss the changing landscape of the global market and the issue of offshore out-sourcing.

VII. THE FUTURE OF GLOBAL TRADE

A. New markets present new opportunities for trade and development.

1. **ADVANCED COMMUNICATIONS** have made distant markets instantly accessible, particularly China.

   a. China's 1.3 billion population represents a tremendous business opportunity.

   b. The risk of foreign direct investment in China has been significantly reduced.

   c. **400** of the Fortune 500 companies have invested in over 2,000 projects in China.

   d. China has dethroned Germany as the world's largest exporter.

   e. **CONCERNS** still remain about China's one-party political system, trade imbalances, and human rights policies.

   f. China has significant problems with product piracy and counterfeiting.

   g. China is becoming a key driver of the world economy.

2. **OTHER POTENTIAL MARKETS and BRIC**

   a. **INDIA'S** 1.1 billion population and **RUSSIA'S** 150 million potential customers are prized by global traders.

PPT 3-60
Future of Global Trade

(See complete PowerPoint slide notes on page 3.70)

lecture link 3-8

EGYPT AND THE RELIABILITY OF SOCIAL MEDIA

The Egyptian revolution in 2010 showed how powerful advance communications can be for information circulation of both the good and the bad. (See the complete lecture link on page 3.80 in this manual.)

lecture link 3-9

GOOGLE VS. CHINA

Ever since Google started a Chinese version of its service, the company has been beset with ethical dilemmas. (See the complete lecture link on page 3.81 in this manual.)

    b. **RUSSIA** is receiving much attention from multinationals like Chevron, ExxonMobil, and BP because of Russia's rich oil reserves.

    c. The term **BRIC** refers to **Brazil, Russia, India,** and **China**—four major up-and-coming economies.

    d. Brazil and Russia are expected to dominate as suppliers of raw materials. China and India will be leading suppliers of manufactured goods.

    e. **OTHER POTENTIAL MARKETS** include Indonesia, Thailand, Singapore, the Philippines, Korea, Malaysia, and Vietnam.

B. **THE CHALLENGE OF OFFSHORE OUTSOURCING**

  1. **OUTSOURCING** is the purchase of goods and services from sources outside a firm rather than providing them within the company.

    a. U.S. companies have outsourced functions such as payroll and manufacturing.

    b. **OFFSHORE OUTSOURCING,** shifting functions to markets outside the U.S., is more controversial.

  2. The first phase was outsourcing simplified manufacturing overseas.

  3. The "second wave" of offshore outsourcing involves more skilled, well-educated workers in service-sector jobs.

  4. The two major outsource markets are China and India.

bonus case 3-4
AFRICA: THE NEW INDIA

While many big corporations are focusing on the Indian market, some are giving their attention to a region much like India 20 years ago. (See the complete case, discussion questions, and suggested answers beginning on page 3.95 of this manual.)

PPT 3-61
Outsourcing

(See complete PowerPoint slide notes on page 3.7470)

TEXT FIGURE 3.9
The Pros and Cons of Offshore Outsourcing
(Text page 82)

There are advantages and disadvantages to the trend toward offshore outsourcing.

MAKING
ethical
decisions
(Text page 83)
PPT 3-62
See the Sights, Meet the Doctors

(See complete PowerPoint slide notes on page 3.74.)

lecture link 3-10
INDIAN CALL CENTERS EXPAND TO THE UNITED STATES

Indian companies are opening call centers in the United States and hiring American workers to staff them. (See the complete lecture link on page 3.55 of this manual.)

5. Outsourcing will impact the future of many U.S. businesses.

C. **GLOBALIZATION AND YOUR FUTURE**

1. Students are encouraged to study foreign languages, foreign cultures, and international businesses.

2. Small and medium-sized businesses are often better prepared to enter global markets.

VIII. SUMMARY

PPT 3-63
Plan for Your Global Career

(See complete PowerPoint slide notes on page 3.74.)

progress
assessment
(Text page 83)

PPT 3-64
Progress Assessment

(See complete PowerPoint slide notes on page 3.75.)

PowerPoint slide notes

PPT 3-1
Chapter Title

PPT 3-2
Learning Goals

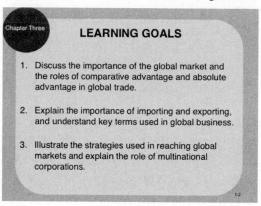

PPT 3-3
Learning Goals

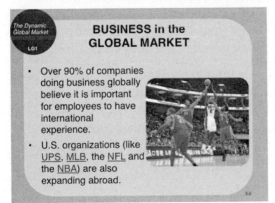

1. The U.S. is a market of over 310 million potential customers, but the world market is over 6.9 billion.

2. It is easy for students in the United States to lose sight of the importance of the global market. This slide helps them see that the international marketplace offers businesses opportunities due to the size of the market. Companies like Procter & Gamble and Wal-Mart have found the international market offers opportunities for additional revenue growth.

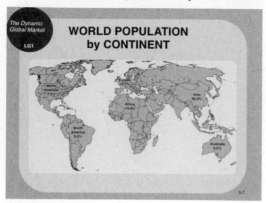

The United States follows China and Germany in exports.

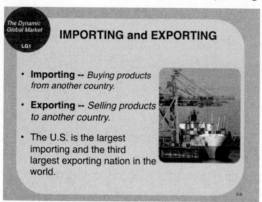

Forbes's ranking was determined by the business climate, red tape, corruption, property rights, and innovation of 128 nations. This slide shows the top 10 of their study. Notice that the United States slipped from number 2 to number 9, citing high tax rates and poor trade showings.

It might also be helpful to point out to students that none of the 10 top countries experienced any GDP growth in 2009. Number 1, Denmark, registered –4.7%, number 6, Ireland, –7.6%, and number 9, the United States, –2.6%.

PPT 3-10
Can You Spare a Dime?

1. The United States has the most billionaires in the world.

2. Ask the students, Why does the United States have more billionaires than any other country in the world? *(There are many reasons why this is true. We have a larger population than some of the other countries on the slide, so it would stand to reason that we would have more billionaires than those countries. However, some of the countries listed have a larger population than the United States, namely India and China. In the United States there is less regulation on businesses and wages/salaries are much higher.)*

PPT 3-11
Trading with Other Nations

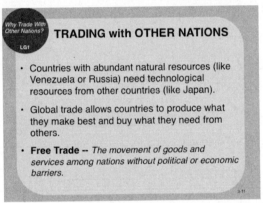

No nation can produce all the products its people want and need.

PPT 3-12
How Exports Affect the GDP (U.S.)

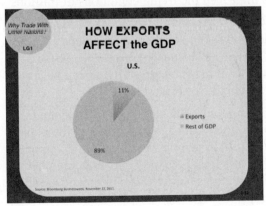

1. Often it is difficult for students to see how trade affects nations. This slide illustrates how much world trade accounts for a country's GDP.

2. The United States is a largely domestic economy (exporting 11.1% of GDP) whereas Singapore (not illustrated) exports 156.4%—it imports some resources and then exports them right back out.

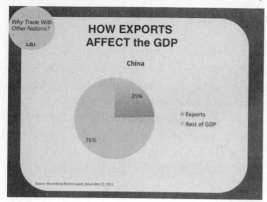

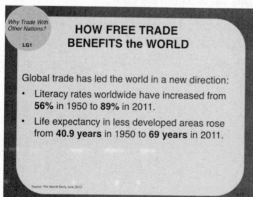

1. Often it is difficult for students to see how world trade has improved the living conditions of millions of the world's poorest individuals.

2. This slide shows some of the improvement in literacy rates and life expectancy since 1950. These improvements in the standard of living can be somewhat attributed to free trade.

3. From *The Economist,* January 26, 2008, print edition: Twenty-five years ago two-thirds of the population or 600 million people were living in extreme poverty (on less than $1 a day). Now, the number living on $1 a day is below 180 million and yet the world's population has increased.

4. To start a discussion ask the students: Why has China been able to improve the living conditions of so many of its citizens in the last twenty-five years? *(More liberal economic policies have led to greater economic growth and an increase in the standard of living for individuals.)*

Comparative and Absolute Advantage

David Ricardo expanded on Adam Smith's theory of absolute advantage with the theory of comparative advantage. This theory can be difficult for students to grasp. A country should produce only what it can produce efficiently, buying what it cannot produce as efficiently. This theory of international trade, along with Adam Smith's Theory of Absolute Advantage, has been a guiding tenet of international trade since the late 1700s.

Going Global with a Small Business

Whom Does the U.S. Owe?

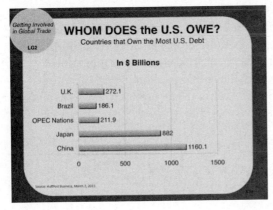

1. As the world's largest debtor nation the United States relies on other countries' purchasing debt as an investment.

2. OPEC nations include Algeria, Angola, Ecuador, Indonesia, Iran, Iraq, Kuwait, Libya, Nigeria, Qatar, Saudi Arabia, UAE, and Venezuela.

3. Ask the students, *What are the ramifications of U.S. indebtedness on its population? (Answers to this question will vary but may include lost sovereignty, weakening of the U.S. dollar and a loss of purchasing power as import prices rise, inflation, and an increase in taxes.)*

A Small Business with a Big Vision

VisionSpring is still growing, but it operates at a loss. Donations are still essential to maintain operations.

A SMALL BUSINESS with a BIG VISION
(Spotlight on Small Business)

- Jordan Kassalow visited Mexico and saw how the lack of eyeglasses affected the local workers.

- He founded VisionSpring, part charity and part franchisor, with a partner.

- VisionSpring employs mostly women needing additional income. They buy glasses from VisionSpring and then sell them to locals.

- This gives eyesight to those who need it and stimulates the local economy.

Getting Involved in Importing

Starbucks CEO, Howard Shultz, found his importing opportunity in Italy. He transformed a coffee shop in Seattle to mimic the European cafes.

GETTING INVOLVED in IMPORTING

- Students attending schools abroad tend to notice products that they're used to are unavailable in their new country.

- By working with producers in their native country, some become importers while still in school.

Getting Involved in Exporting

One website that can bring a lecture on exporting alive is http://tse.export.gov. The TradeStats Express website is presented by the U.S. Commerce Department and gives students a look at any number of statistics on exporting. One example that may surprise students is that snow-plows/snow-blowers have been sold in Middle Eastern countries like Saudi Arabia. They are used to clear sand from driveways.

GETTING INVOLVED in EXPORTING

- Exporting provides a great boost to the U.S. economy.

- It's estimated every $1 billion in U.S. exports generate over 7,000 U.S. jobs.

PPT 3-22
How to Measure Global Trade

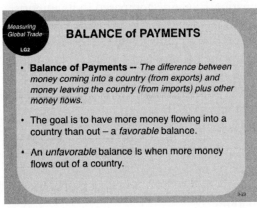

PPT 3-23
Balance of Payments

Since 1975, the U.S. has bought more goods from other nations than it has sold and thus has a trade deficit.

PPT 3-24
Unfair Trade Practices

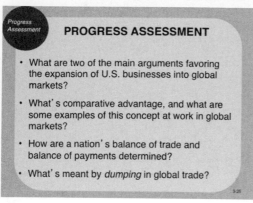

PPT 3-25
Progress Assessment

1. One major argument favoring the expansion of U.S. business is that the sheer size of the global market (6.9 billion people) is too large to ignore. Plus it's difficult for an economy, even one as large as the U.S. economy, to produce all the goods and services its citizens desire.

2. Comparative advantage theory was proposed by David Ricardo and simply states that a country should sell to other countries those products it produces most effectively and efficiently, and buy from other countries those products it cannot produce as effectively and efficiently. Examples include the U.S. producing goods and services such as software and engineering services and buying goods, such as coffee and shoes, from other nations.

3. The balance of trade is the difference in the total value of a nation's exports compared to its imports. The balance of payments is the difference between money coming into a country (from exports) and money leaving the country (for imports) plus money flows coming into or leaving a country from other factors such as tourism, foreign aid, military expenditures, and foreign investment.

4. Dumping is the selling of products in foreign countries at lower prices than those charged in the producing country. This tactic is sometimes used to reduce surplus products in foreign markets or gain a foothold in a new market.

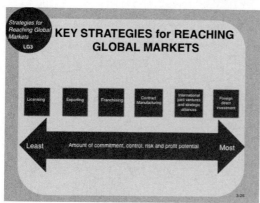

PPT 3-26
Key Strategies for Reaching Global Markets

When senior management elects to expand internationally, it has a wide range of options available. Such options range from licensing with the least risk all the way to foreign direct investment with the most risk. A few examples to be shared during this portion of the lecture include Coca-Cola's use of licensing, McDonald's use of franchising, Nike's use of contract manufacturing, Volkswagen's joint venture in China, and Toyota's foreign direct investment in the United States.

Coca-Cola has entered into licensing agreements with over 300 licensees that have extended into long-term service contracts that sell over $1 billion of the company's products each year.

Links on the slide take you to KFC–Japan, Taco Bell–India, and Pizza Hut–Hong Kong.

Time to Make the Donuts …

1. Students should enjoy this slide. It shows the cultural influence with donuts preferences.

2. Ask the students: What type of donuts do you enjoy? Would your prefer sweet potato, or green apple, or mango in your donuts?

3. Ask the students: What modifications do companies need to make when you go to different countries like the ones shown in this slide? *(Students should point out the need to understand and research the market and cultural/customer preferences and then offer what the customers want.)*

Golden Arches Glowing Across the Globe

Students may find it interesting that McDonald's Hamburger University is more selective than Harvard (62 out of 1,000 applicants make it in).

That's at McDonalds?

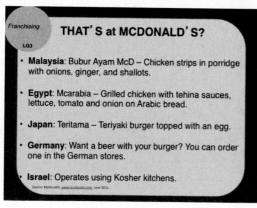

1. McDonald's is a leader in franchising and the company operates in 117 different countries.

2. This slide gives students an insight into some of the changes McDonald's has made to its menu when operating in the world market.

3. Ask the students, Why does the leading provider of American-style fast-food adopt different menu items? *(Like all successful companies, McDonald's adapts its menu to meet the different needs of its customers worldwide.)*

PPT 3-33
Joint Ventures

Joint ventures can also have drawbacks: (1) One partner can learn the other's practices and then use the knowledge to its own advantage; (2) a shared technology may become obsolete; and (3) the joint venture may become too large to be as flexible as needed.

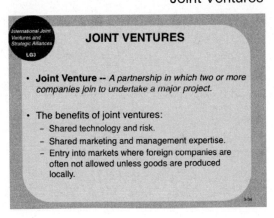

PPT 3-34
Joint Ventures

Joint ventures can also have drawbacks: (1) One partner can learn the other's practices and then use the knowledge to its own advantage; (2) a shared technology may become obsolete; and (3) the joint venture may become too large to be as flexible as needed.

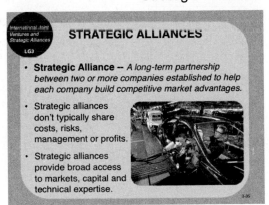

PPT 3-35
Strategic Alliances

PPT 3-36
Foreign Direct Investment

FOREIGN DIRECT INVESTMENT

- **Foreign Direct Investment (FDI) --** *The buying of permanent property and businesses in foreign nations.*
- **Foreign Subsidiary --** *A company owned in a foreign country by another company called the parent company.* The most common form of FDI.
  - Primary Advantage: Parent company maintains complete control over its technology or expertise.
  - Primary Disadvantage: Must commit funds and technology within foreign boundaries.

PPT 3-37
Multinational Corporations

MULTINATIONAL CORPORATIONS

- **Multinational Corporation --** *A company that manufactures and markets products in many different countries and has multinational stock ownership and management.*
- Not all large global businesses are multinational.
- Only firms that have *manufacturing capacity* or some other physical presence in different nations can truly be multinational.

PPT 3-38
Sovereign Wealth Funds

 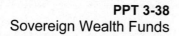

SOVEREIGN WEALTH FUNDS

- **Sovereign Wealth Funds (SWFs) --** *Investment funds controlled by governments holding large stakes in foreign companies.*
- The size of the funds and the fact that they are government-owned make some fear they might be used for:
  - Geopolitical objectives.
  - Gaining control of strategic natural resources.
  - Obtaining sensitive technologies.
  - Undermining the management of the companies in which they invest.

PROGRESS ASSESSMENT

- What are the advantages of using licensing as a method of entry in global markets? What are the disadvantages?
- What services are usually provided by an export-trading company?
- What's the key difference between a joint venture and a strategic alliance?
- What makes a company a multinational corporation?

1. The key advantages of using licensing as a method of entry into global markets are (a) a firm can often gain revenues in a market it would not have generated in its home market; (b) licensees must purchase start-up supplies and consulting services from the licensing firm; and (c) licensors spend little or no money to produce and market their products. Disadvantages to licensing include (a) if a product is extremely successful in another market, the licensor does not receive the bulk of the revenues; and (b) if the foreign licensee learns the company's technology and product secrets, it may break the agreement and begin producing similar products on its own.

2. Export trading companies provide such services as assistance in associating and establishing the desired trading relationships, matching buyers and sellers from different countries, and help dealing with foreign customs offices, documentation, and weights and measures.

3. A joint venture is a partnership between two or more companies whereby they undertake a major project. Joint ventures generally involve (a) sharing technology and risk, (b) sharing marketing and management expertise, and (c) entering into markets where foreign companies are often not allowed unless goods are produced locally. In a strategic alliance partners do not share costs, risks, management, or even profits. The purpose is to gain advantages in building competitive market advantages.

4. A multinational corporation manufactures and markets products in many different countries and has multinational stock ownership and management. Only firms that have manufacturing capacity or other physical presence in other countries can be called multinational.

What makes operating in the international environment more complex than operating only in the domestic market is the addition of new uncontrollable forces. Examples of these forces include sociocultural, economic, financial, legal, regulatory, physical, and environmental.

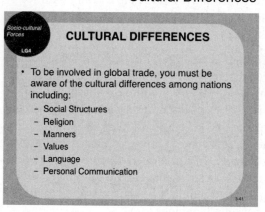

A lack of cultural understanding can create problems with working in the international market; even the color or type of flower can have a different meaning. One book that provides numerous examples to share with students is titled *Kiss, Bow or Shake Hands: How to Do Business in Sixty Countries*. Never assume what works in one country will work in another.

1. Culture refers to the set of values, beliefs, rules, and institutions held by a specific group of people.

2. One of the basic elements of culture is language and language delineates cultures.

3. To operate successfully in the international marketplace, a company must never assume what works in one country will work in another.

4. To avoid the funny and sometimes disastrous advertisements listed above, shrewd marketers must use back translations. Back translation is a process in which the first translation is made by a bilingual native, after which the work will then be translated back by a bilingual foreigner to see how it compares with the original.

Ready to Travel Abroad?

1. Some fascinating cultural and social differences exist in other nations.

2. Discuss the following interesting points:

    - A smile in Japan can mean that a person is uncomfortable or sad.

    - When traveling to Sweden, make appointments two weeks in advance.

    - Lack of punctuality is a fact of life in Brazil. Become accustomed to waiting.

3. Review the following helpful hints when dealing globally:

    - Be culturally savvy. Learn about the culture, language, and dress code.

    - Recognize the importance of dealing with cultural differences and consequences of taking no action.

    - Manage and learn to appreciate various cultures.

4. Build a database of information about each country where you have business relationships.

Do as the Germans…

PPT 3-45
Exchange Rates

EXCHANGE RATES

Economic and Financial Forces
LG4

- **Exchange Rate --** *The value of one nation's currency relative to the currencies of other countries.*

- *High value of the dollar –* Dollar is trading for more foreign currency; foreign goods are *less* expensive.

- *Low value of the dollar –* Dollar is trading for less foreign currency; foreign goods are *more* expensive.

- Currencies float in value depending on the supply and demand for them in the global market.

3-45

The floating exchange rate system creates transaction risk. If the U.S. dollar is trading for more foreign currency, it is said to be getting stronger. When the U.S. dollar is trading for less foreign currency, it is said to be getting weaker. Since the breakdown of the Bretton Woods agreement in 1971, the value of the U.S. currency has generally trended downward versus major world currencies.

PPT 3-46
Devaluation and Countertrading

DEVALUATION and COUNTERTRADING

Economic and Financial Forces
LG4

- **Devaluation --** *Lowers the value of a nation's currency relative to others.*

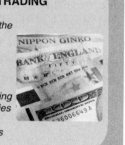

- **Countertrading --** *Complex form of bartering in which several countries each trade goods or services for other goods or services.*

3-46

It's estimated that countertrading accounts for over 20% of all global exchanges, especially in developing countries. One famous example of countertrading involved Pepsi and Russian vodka. Pepsi received the right to market Russian vodka in the United States as payment for Pepsi being sold in Russia. More information on countertrading can be found at www.londoncountertrade.org.

PPT 3-47
Legal Concerns Overseas

LEGAL CONCERNS OVERSEAS

Legal and Regulatory Forces
LG4

- There's no global system of laws.

- Laws may be inconsistent.

- U.S. businesses must follow U.S. laws while conducting global business.

- The Organization for Economic Cooperation and Development (OECD) and Transparency International fight to end corruption and bribery in foreign markets and have had limited success.

3-47

PPT 3-48
Environmental Forces

ENVIRONMENTAL FORCES

Physical and Environmental Forces
LG4

- Developing countries have transportation and storage systems that make international distribution difficult or impossible.

- Often, technological capabilities are far from those in the U.S. which make for a tough business environment.

3-48

PPT 3-49
Progress Assessment

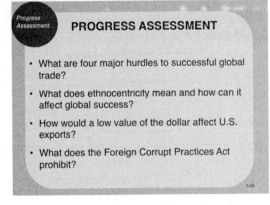

PROGRESS ASSESSMENT

Progress Assessment

- What are four major hurdles to successful global trade?

- What does ethnocentricity mean and how can it affect global success?

- How would a low value of the dollar affect U.S. exports?

- What does the Foreign Corrupt Practices Act prohibit?

3-49

1. Four major hurdles to successful global trade are sociocultural forces, economic and financial forces, legal and regulatory forces, and physical and environmental forces.

2. Ethnocentricity is an attitude that your nation's culture is superior to other cultures. It can affect global trade because all nations are proud of their cultures and do not aspire to be like other countries. Thus it's easy to offend potential customers by being ethnocentric.

3. A low value of the dollar would make U.S. exports cheaper in foreign markets and may lead to higher demand for U.S. products.

4. The Foreign Corrupt Practices Act prohibits "questionable" or "dubious" payments to foreign officials to secure business contracts. Other nations do not have to follow this law, causing some disadvantages for U.S. businesses.

The Great Depression was exacerbated by the passage of the Glass-Steagall Act. The Glass-Steagall Act of 1933 raised the tariff rates on thousand of products imported into the United States. This led to other nations enacting similar protectionist measures, effectively shutting down world trade. Many fear that the economic contraction the world is currently experiencing will lead to similar laws.

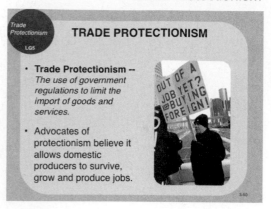

While a tariff may end up raising revenue for the government, it ultimately costs consumers more money in the long run. Due to tariff rates on the importation of sugar, consumers in the United States end up paying close to 50% more for sugar than the rest of the world.

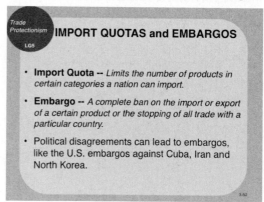

WORLD TRADE ORGANIZATION

The World Trade Organization LG5

- **General Agreement on Tariffs and Trade (GATT) --**
  A global forum for reducing trade restrictions on goods, services, ideas and cultural problems.

- **World Trade Organization (WTO) --**
  Headquartered in Geneva, the WTO is an independent entity of 153 member nations whose purpose is to oversee cross-border trade issues and global business practices.

COMMON MARKETS

Common Markets LG5

- **Common Market --** *A regional group of countries with a common external tariff, no internal tariffs and coordinated laws to facilitate exchange among members.*

- The European Union (EU), Mercosur, the ASEAN and the COMESA are common markets.

EU MEMBERS

Common Markets LG5

Free traders hope CAFTA will lead to the creation of a Free Trade Area of the Americas (FTAA).

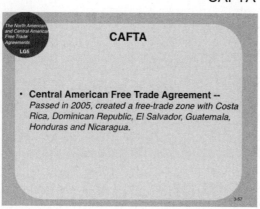

PPT 3-59
Progress Assessment

PROGRESS ASSESSMENT

- What are the advantages and disadvantages of trade protectionism and of tariffs?

- What's the primary purpose of the WTO?

- What's the key objective of a common market like the EU?

- Which three nations comprise NAFTA?

1. Trade protectionism is the use of government regulations to limit the import of goods and services. It can be a barrier to global trade. Trade protectionism often involves the use of tariffs or taxes on imported goods that makes them more expensive to buy. Protective tariffs can be an advantage to workers in certain industries since it makes the products they produce more cost competitive with imported products. American labor unions have sought certain protective tariffs. Revenue tariffs are designed as a source of revenue for the government. Most economists do not favor the use of tariffs; instead they are in favor of free trade.

2. The World Trade Organization (WTO) was established to mediate trade disputes among nations.

3. The purpose of a common market like the EU is to have common external tariffs, no internal tariff, and coordinated laws to facilitate exchange between member nations. This enables smaller nations to compete as a group against large economies like the United States, China, and Japan.

4. NAFTA is comprised of the United States, Canada and Mexico.

PPT 3-60
Future of Global Trade

FUTURE of GLOBAL TRADE

LG6

- With over 1.3 billion people, China has transformed the world economic map. Many multinationals invest heavily in China.

- India has seen huge growth in information technology, pharmaceuticals and biotechnology.

- Russia is a large oil producing country with many multinationals interested in developing there.

- Brazil is expected to be one of the wealthier economies by 2030.

BRIC has been an acronym for these countries. However, BRIC nations are not the only areas of opportunity. Other countries to look at include Indonesia, Thailand, Singapore, the Philippines, South Korea, Malaysia, and Vietnam.

PPT 3-61
Outsourcing

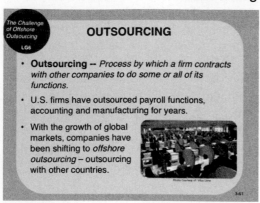

OUTSOURCING

The Challenge of Offshore Outsourcing

LG6

- **Outsourcing --** *Process by which a firm contracts with other companies to do some or all of its functions.*

- U.S. firms have outsourced payroll functions, accounting and manufacturing for years.

- With the growth of global markets, companies have been shifting to *offshore outsourcing* – outsourcing with other countries.

PPT 3-62
See the Sights, Meet the Doctors

**SEE the SIGHTS,
MEET the DOCTORS**
(Making Ethical Decisions)

- Some insurance companies encourage patients to seek medical care in foreign countries.

- Procedures are cheaper and involve top-flight doctors at state-of-the-art facilities.

- Would it be ethical to force patients to travel to other countries to save money?

PPT 3-63
Plan for Your Global Career

Globalization and Your Future **PLAN for YOUR GLOBAL CAREER**

LG6

- Study foreign languages.

- Learn about foreign cultures.

- Take global business courses.

PROGRESS ASSESSMENT

- What are the major threats to doing business in global markets?

- What key challenges must India and Russia face before becoming global economic leaders?

- What does the acronym *BRIC* stand for?

- What are the two primary concerns about offshore outsourcing?

3-64

1. The major threats to doing business in global markets are terrorism, nuclear proliferation, rogue states, and other issues.

2. India must relax its difficult trade laws and inflexible bureaucracy. Russia is plagued by political, currency, corruption, and social problems.

3. *BRIC* stands for Brazil, Russia, India, and China.

4. The key concern surrounding offshore outsourcing is the loss of jobs. Today such loss includes professional services as well as production jobs. Questions also linger about outsourcing sensitive products like airline maintenance and medical devices. Consumers' fears about quality and product safety keep the issue center stage.

lecture links

lecture link 3-1

CHINA BESTS THE UNITED STATES IN AUTO SALES

Over the last 20 years, China has become an undisputed financial powerhouse. In 2009 it overtook Germany as the world's largest exporter, and in 2011 it is predicted to surpass Japan as the world's second largest economy. As China's economic clout has increased, so has its growing population of middle-class urbanites' demand for Western goods. Recently experts even went so far as to predict that this demand could result in China topping the United States in auto sales by 2020. As it turns out, the experts were right, only they underestimated the date by about a decade. In 2009 total vehicle sales in China topped out at an estimated 13.6 million, compared to 10.4 million for the United States. This event marks the first time in history that another nation has surpassed the United States in auto sales and effectively crowns China as the world's largest auto market.

Several factors spurred China's 45% jump in auto sales. For one, China's $586 billion government stimulus package helped the economy grow by more than 8% even as the rest of the world floundered in recession. Next, government officials slashed taxes for smaller, fuel-efficient cars while also granting $730 million in subsidies for purchasers of SUVs, trucks, and vans. By all accounts the Chinese government is planning to keep the auto market stimulated by keeping taxes low and granting further subsidies.

Despite America's 21% plunge in 2009 auto sales, Chinese demand for vehicles has nevertheless become a major boon for American auto companies. As domestic demand for cars has waned, U.S. companies have found new growth opportunities with the Chinese urban elite. In 2009 GM saw sales in China grow by 67% while Ford sales increased by 44%. American automakers aren't the only ones benefiting from this surge in Chinese car buying; German car company Volkswagen claimed that China is currently its biggest market as well. Foreign-made cars remain superior in quality and safety than Chinese cars, ensuring that China will continue to be a major market for car manufacturers worldwide. Chinese auto companies are growing, however, with some hoping to break into Western auto markets once they are able to satisfy safety and emissions standards.[i]

lecture link 3-2

URBAN OUTFITTERS'S EUROPEAN EXPANSION

For many American retail chains, Europe presents an alluringly deceptive market. On the surface, "the Continent" appears to be flush with young, fashionable consumers who share similar tastes with their American counterparts. In reality, Europe is a complex and incredibly varied market that doesn't always jibe with current U.S. styles or brands. For example, Gap has 180 locations on the Continent that stock the same clothes as the chain's American locations. European sales for Gap have fallen steadily since 2005. Wal-Mart adopted a similar strategy when it expanded into Germany, only to give up on the venture entirely in 2006.

Urban Outfitters, on the other hand, used a vastly different method when it came to Europe. Before the company cut the ribbon on its first European location in 1998, Urban Outfitters created a separate design department in London so its clothes could cater more to local European tastes. While designing and operating the new line hurt the company's initial European expansion, the strategy paid off as Urban Outfitters started to stand out from the pack of other American retailers. Also, instead of glutting the market with hundreds of locations like Gap, Urban Outfitters has opted to build its base slowly. To date the company only has 16 Urban Outfitters locations in Europe. Over the next 10 years, the company hopes to open 100 European locations for both Urban Outfitters and Anthropologie.

Breaking into the European market further will be an essential element to Urban Outfitters's future growth. The company has weathered the recession fairly well, expanding sales by 6% in 2009. But while sales at its Anthropologie stores rose by 10% last year, Urban Outfitters saw a 1% slip in sales at its namesake chain. The company's European expansion will help only its bottom line, with European sales already accounting for 10% of total revenue. Furthermore, Urban Outfitters scouts recently started surveying tastes in China, Japan, and Korea, paving the way for a possible Asian location by 2013.[ii]

lecture link 3-3

DISNEY'S SECOND TRY IN CHINA

When Disney opened up Disneyland Hong Kong in 2005 executives thought the project was a guaranteed slam-dunk. After all, more than 260 million Chinese viewers tune in to TV shows featuring the company's iconic characters each week. But poor planning led to a disastrous debut. Disney underestimated just how many people would visit the park, leading to a lack of enough sitting space and food at restaurants. Although the park is expanding with attendance climbing 13% last year, it lost $92.3 million in 2010.

Disney has no plans to make the same mistakes again with its latest Chinese venture, the Shanghai Disney Resort. The Chinese market is simply too big to fail for the company. Experts estimate that by 2015 China's growing middle class will spend $200 billion annually on leisure travel. And with a population of 300 million people living within a 3-hour drive of Shanghai, the new location will need all the space it can get. The $4.4 billion park will encompass nearly 85 acres, about 50% larger than Disneyland Hong Kong.

Besides space issues, Disney also suffered from a cultural disconnect in Hong Kong. Seemingly ignoring the mistakes of Disneyland Resort Paris in the 1990s, the company simply copied and pasted some of the most famous aspects of its American parks in Asia. Soon enough, though, Disney realized it was time to cut down on its supply of hot dogs and begin serving more dim sum and noodle dishes. To narrow the cultural divide, a team of Chinese "imagineers" has joined the design team for the Shanghai park. Along with new attractions derived from Chinese culture, Shanghai Disney will not include such American staples as Main Street USA. If all goes according to plan, Disney hopes to rake in $200 million of management fees from the park within a decade.[iii]

lecture link 3-4

FOREIGN ETIQUETTE TIPS

As more businesses engage in global trade, cultural pitfalls increase. Every day business deals are jeopardized or lost when foreign associates are offended by Americans unaware of other countries' customs, culture, or manners. Sue Fox, the author of *Business Etiquette for Dummies*, provides the following tips for avoiding embarrassing gaffes.

Argentina: It is rude to ask people what they do for a living. Wait until they offer the information.

Bahrain: Never show signs of impatience, because it is considered an insult. If tea is offered, always accept.

Cambodia: Never touch or pass something over the head of a Cambodian, because the head is considered sacred.

China: As in most Asian culture, avoid waving or pointing chopsticks, putting them vertically in a rice bowl, or tapping them on the bowl. These actions are considered extremely rude.

Dominican Republic: When speaking to someone, failure to maintain good eye contact may be interpreted as losing interest in the conversation.

France: Always remain calm, polite, and courteous during business meetings. Never appear overly friendly, because this could be construed as suspicious. Never ask personal questions.

Greece: If you need to signal a taxi, holding up five fingers is considered an offensive gesture if the palm faces outward. Face your palm inward with closed fingers.

India: Avoid giving gifts made from leather, because many Hindus are vegetarian and consider cows sacred. Also, keep this in mind when taking Indian clients to restaurants. Don't wink, because it is seen as a sexual gesture.

Japan: Never write on a business card or shove the card into your back pocket when you are with the giver. This is considered disrespectful. Hold the card with both hands and read it carefully. It's considered polite to make frequent apologies in general conversation.

Malaysia: If you receive an invitation from a business associate from Malaysia, always respond in writing. Avoid using your left hand because it is considered unclean.

Mexico: If visiting a business associate's home, do not bring up business unless the associate does.

Singapore: If you plan to give a gift, always give it to the company. A gift to one person is considered a bribe.

Spain: Always request your check when dining out in Spain. It is considered rude for wait staff to bring your bill beforehand.

Vietnam: Shake hands only with someone of the same sex who initiates it. Physical contact between men and women in public is frowned upon.[iv]

lecture link 3-5

BLOOD TYPE MATTERS IN JAPAN

Among the more unusual cultural behaviors is the Japanese obsession with blood type. In Japan, "What's your type?" can be an important question in everything from matchmaking to getting a job. Although the belief has been scientifically debunked, there is still a widely held notion that blood tells all.

In 2008, four of Japan's top 10 best sellers were about how blood type determines personality. The books' publisher, Bungeisha, says the series—one each for types B, O, A, and AB—has combined sales of well over 5 million copies.

As defined by the books, type As are sensitive perfectionists but overanxious. Type Bs are cheerful but eccentric and selfish. Os are curious, generous, but stubborn. ABs are arty but mysterious and unpredictable.

Blood type turns up in surprising places in Japanese culture, including on "lucky bags" of women's accessories tailored to blood type. A TV network developed a comedy about women seeking husbands according to blood type.

Matchmaking agencies provide blood-type compatibility tests. Children at some kindergartens are divided up by blood type, and some companies make decisions about assignments based on employees' blood types.[v]

lecture link 3-6

BRIBERY PITFALLS

The passage of the Sarbanes-Oxley Act in 2002 raised the stakes for corporate responsibility. CEOs and CFOs now have to personally sign off on company financials, making those executives much warier of letting a bribe slide through. Conducting business globally exposes U.S. companies to all sorts of potential minefields that don't exist at home.

The Corruption Perception Index—based on bribery data and surveys conducted by the Transparency International, a nongovernment organization dedicated to fighting bribery—finds signs of "rampant corruption" in no fewer than 60 countries. Bangladesh and Haiti are the worst of that group. Russia and several other former Soviet republics are included.

Non-U.S. companies face far fewer constraints when dealing with this shadowy business world. While the 35 signatories of the Organization for Economic Cooperation and Development 1997 convention made it a crime to bribe foreign officials, there has been little enforcement of new laws by national governments, other than by the United States.

That bribery gap has been costly for American companies. During a 12-month period in 2004, according to the U.S. Commerce Department, competition for 47 contracts worth $18 billion may have been affected by bribes that foreign firms paid to foreign officials.

Since 1977, the Foreign Corrupt Practices Act has barred all issuers of U.S.-traded equities from bribing foreign government officials to acquire or retain business. But while it is illegal for U.S.-listed companies and employees to take part in bribes, some authorities suggest that until a few years ago companies didn't routinely report corruption in their overseas operations. The concept was that companies didn't have to turn themselves in on a potential crime.

SEC policy and the Sarbanes-Oxley rules, however, now call for disclosure of both the incidents and the steps a company takes to address them.[vi]

lecture link 3-7

DOES TRADE PROTECTION PROTECT OR RISK YOUR FUTURE?

No topic in this chapter generates more differing opinions than that of trade protectionism. Whenever the topic is reintroduced, stories in newspapers and commentators on television begin referring again to "Smoot-Hawley." When trade protection comes up, this question is inevitably asked: "What is Smoot-Hawley and why does this term appear every so often?" Some history may help clarify the issue.

The date: June 13, 1930 (Friday the 13th). The time: 2:13 p.m. The place: the U.S. Senate. The Great Depression had started, and the air was full of talk about trade protection. Over 1,000 economists warned the government that protectionism was dangerous and petitioned it not to pass the Smoot-Hawley Act. (Hawley was a professor of economics at Willamette University. Smoot was a banker and wool manufacturer.) But, by a vote of 44 to 42, the bill passed. It was an act conceived by Republican congressmen, passed by a Republican Congress, and signed into law by conservative, Republican President Herbert Hoover.

The bill imposed duties of up to 60% on almost everything imported into the United States. The concept was to protect the western beet sugar farmer by raising the duty for sugar; protect the northwestern wheat farmer by raising the duty on wheat; and protect the Imperial Valley cotton farmer by raising the duty on cotton from Egypt. The list went on: cattle and dairy products, hides, shoes, velvet, silk, china, pocket knives, watch parts, and so on.

The result was world trade fell by one-third, and a global trade war started. Exports dropped from $4.8 billion to $1.7 billion from 1929 to 1932. Imports dropped from $5.4 billion to $2.4 billion. Other countries were plunged into depression as world trade fell. In 1934, Congress passed the Reciprocal Trade Agreement Act to reduce tariffs, but it was too little too late.

The issue of world trade regulation continued. From 1987 until 1993, the General Agreement on Tariffs and Trade (GATT) discussions often reached impasse points or stalemates. A collapse of the negotiations would have actually pleased protectionists. Instead, the GATT agreement was passed by 124 nations in 1994. Still the growth of several key trading blocs such as NAFTA and the EU raised the fear that a new wave of protectionism might surface. These trading blocs allow for free trade among nations in the same trading bloc, but may lead to greater protectionist legislation and less free trade between nations in competing trading blocs. Many wondered if Smoot-Hawley is lifting its head again.[vii]

lecture link 3-8

EGYPT AND THE RELIABILITY OF SOCIAL MEDIA

The extent to which social media sites like Facebook and Twitter contributed to the actual organization of the recent Egyptian revolution remains to be seen. Ultimately, the uprising was a product of years of simmering dissent among the people of Egypt who came together at a key moment in history to topple oppression. Though social media provided a common rallying point, it is the Egyptians, not the feats of Western technology, who deserve the lion's share of credit for this immense undertaking.

From an American perspective, though, it's easy to see why media consumers and creators alike heralded the information bonanza provided by Facebook and Twitter. The social networks facilitated a riveting stream of on-site appraisals of the uprising from dangerous locales otherwise inaccessible to traditional media outlets. Nevertheless, one essential element missing from the nonstop barrage of tweets coming from Egypt was authenticity. After all, anyone can make a social media account and post whatever they want from whichever perspective they choose, genuine or not. That's not to say the social media flood from Egypt was untrustworthy on the whole. However, when these false accounts show up among the thousands of other tweets about the revolution, it's difficult to parse the reality from the fiction among the inundation of information.

The hallmark of social media is their unparalleled ability to compile and circulate information. Not all news is equal, though, which is why arbiters like journalists are instrumental in presenting all the facts in order and context. Social media, unfortunately, have no single judge of content. Instead, they foist that position on the user. This leads to confusion and, at worst, mass dissemination of false information. So for social media–obsessed businesses, governments, and citizens alike, the data deluge of Facebook and Twitter can provide a wealth of information, but it still requires a keen, scrutinizing eye before it can pass into the realm of fact.[viii]

lecture link 3-9

GOOGLE VS. CHINA

Ever since Google began a Chinese version of its website in 2006, the company has been beset with ethical dilemmas. Chinese law required that Google self-censor its search results against subjects considered to be pornographic or subversive, such as the 1989 Tiananmen Square Massacre. Critics felt Google's collusion with Chinese censors betrayed the company's famous "Don't Be Evil" slogan, but for Google, the world's largest market of Internet users was too big to pass up. Then on January 12, 2010, Google discovered that it and 20 other U.S. companies had been attacked by computer hacks originating in China. Google even found that the hackers attempted to break into the Gmail accounts of prominent human rights activists working in China, leading some to speculate that the Chinese government played a role in the attacks.

News of the espionage outraged Google, which vowed to take action against the Chinese government. Retaliation arrived the following March when the company shut down Google.cn, redirecting users to its uncensored Hong Kong site. Chinese officials immediately denounced the attack, accusing Google of sparking an "Internet war" and working with the U.S. government to hamstring Chinese innovation. Google's chief legal officer, on the other hand, justified the company's actions as being in accordance with Chinese law and Google policy rather than an act of defiance. Also, in some parts of the country the elimination of Google.cn may just be a symbolic blow to Chinese censorship. Images deemed inappropriate by Chinese authorities are still blocked by government firewalls in parts of Mainland China.

The move damaged Google's non-search-related endeavors in China as well. The day after Google.cn went down, China Mobile, the country's largest telecommunications company, dropped Google as the default search engine on its new line of smartphones. The nation's second-largest mobile company, China Unicom, also halted production on a phone based on Google's Android. Still, Google's engineering and sales offices in China will remain open as the company tries to keep a toehold in the country by selling Chinese language ads. Nevertheless, there's no guarantee that even those operations won't be hurt in some way by government intervention. Besides making a seismic ethical statement, the other silver lining for Google is that China accounted for only $300 million to $600 million of Google's annual sales of $24 billion. But only time will tell how the Chinese market will grow and how Google's decision will affect its future in the country.[ix]

lecture link 3-10

INDIAN CALL CENTERS EXPAND TO THE UNITED STATES

More than a few of America's established business practices were topsy-turvy when the U.S. economy turned from boom to bust in the 2000s. Among the most common practices that were impacted was outsourcing. For years, American companies exported jobs to countries with cheaper workforces and lower overhead. But as jobs became scarce on the home front and domestic companies lacked the ability to grow, businesses in developing nations took advantage of the U.S. lull and began to plan their own expansions. Foreign manufacturers began to set up shop in the United States to make use of the newly cheap labor. Now, in perhaps the ultimate outsourcing irony, Indian companies are opening call centers in the United States and hiring American workers to staff them.

As India's $60 billion software-exporting industry continues to grow, Indian companies have been regularly expanding operations overseas, including in the United States. The vast majority don't hire locally, however, choosing instead to import their staff from back home using H-1B and L-1 visas. But at Aegis Communications, executives have begun to tout the company's new practice of "cross-shoring" and "near-sourcing." The idea was actually born years ago as call centers in the United States were liquidating in droves. In the early 1990s an Aegis exec convinced the Ruia brothers, owners of the company's parent the Essar Group, to buy a delinquent Texas call center. After two decades of similar acquisitions, Aegis now employs 5,000 people at nine call centers in the United States with plans to triple its staff in the coming years.

Recent studies have found that a number of Indian companies may have abused provisions of the Immigration Act of 1990. In 2008, for instance, a government inquiry found that 20.7% of H-1B applications contained fraud or technical violations. Furthermore, H-1B visas were originally intended to entice high-level foreign talent to work challenging technical jobs. Now that companies use the visas to bring in low-skill call center workers, however, lawmakers are attempting to curb H-1B applications. One such roadblock set in place by the Obama administration adds a $2,000 fee for every H-1B applied for by large companies.[x]

critical
thinking exercises

Name: _____

Date: _____

critical thinking exercise 3-1
WHICH COUNTRY?

The Internet gives students access to endless information sources. One of the most surprising sources is the online database maintained by the CIA. The agency's *World Factbook* gives extensive data about each country's geography, government, economy, communications, and so on. Go to the CIA Factbook website (www.cia.gov/cia/publications/factbook/index.html).[xi] (Sometimes the Web address for a location changes. You might need to search to find the exact location mentioned.)

For this exercise assume you are the owner of a small electronics firm based in the American Midwest. Your research department has developed a cellular phone that translates conversations into any of 24 languages. From conversations with business associates and friends, you have identified two especially attractive overseas markets—Brazil and Australia.

Use the CIA *World Factbook* to research these two countries.

1. What is the total population for each country? Which country's population is growing the fastest? What is the median age?

2. Compare the government types for each country. What type of legal system does each have?

3. Which country has the largest number of cellular phones in use? What percentage of the population uses cellular phones?

4. Based on your research, which country, Brazil or Australia, would you choose to introduce your product? Why?

critical thinking exercise 3-2
EVALUATING GLOBAL EXPANSION

Greenwich Industries entered the Latin American market in the 1950s by forming a joint venture with Industro Viejes in Santo Ignezeto to manufacture bicycle parts. The joint venture flourished in the 1960s, and Greenwich eventually bought out 100% ownership. The company earned steady profits from the Latin American subsidiary until a military junta overthrew the government in the late 1970s. The ruling generals expropriated all foreign-owned companies, including the Santo Ignezeto bicycle parts plant.

Today Santo Ignezeto is ruled by a democratic government that has been in power for 10 years. Industro Viejes has approached Greenwich about another joint venture. The government is offering an attractive incentive package to attract foreign investment.

You have been assigned to travel to Santo Ignezeto and begin planning and staffing.

1.   What are the potential problems that face the new venture?

2.   What are the potential advantages of this venture for the company?

3.   Would you recommend entering the joint venture? Why or why not?

4.   If Greenwich Industries partners with Industro Viejes, would you recommend hiring local managers or American managers for the top and middle management positions? Why?

notes on critical thinking exercise 3-2

1. *What are the potential problems that face the new venture?*

    All of the risks of international commerce are here—currency shifts, cultural differences, infra-structure, and so on. In the previous joint venture, Greenwich Industries had its plant expropri-ated, so this will be an ongoing concern, despite the current government stability.

2. *What are the potential advantages of this venture for the company?*

    Locating a plant in a Latin American country will probably mean lower-cost labor, thus reducing the cost of producing bicycle parts and lowering the prices to consumers. There is also the poten-tial for expanding Greenwich's consumer base. In most Latin American countries, low per-capita income means fewer people can afford a car. Bicycle transportation is more common and presents an opportunity to enter a new market with both production and revenue potential.

3. *Would you recommend entering the joint venture? Why or why not?*

    Using the answers to questions 1 and 2, balance the risks and potential advantages, and make the decision.

4. *If Greenwich Industries partners with Industro Viejes, would you recommend hiring local man-agers or American managers for the top and middle management positions? Why?*

    Local managers would be more in touch with the area job market and local customs. In a new enterprise, however, more control and oversight is needed in the early years. A compromise might involve American top management at the beginning, shifting to local managers as the business matures.

critical thinking exercise 3-3
CURRENCY SHIFTS

As the text discusses, one of the hurdles of international trade is the constant shift in exchange rates. Just how much do exchange rates change over a 30-day period? Let's find out by choosing five countries of interest to you and recording the exchange rate for their currency (Great Britain's pound, Japan's yen, Mexico's peso, or the European euro) for 30 days. The rates are available daily in *The Wall Street Journal* (in the "Currency Markets" chart in the "Money and Investing" section). They are also available on many websites, such as Yahoo Finance (www.finance.yahoo.com) or CNNMoney (http://money.cnn.com/markets/currencies/). The published chart shows the amount of foreign currency per dollar. What effect would such currency shifts have on your business trade with each of these countries? (Sometimes the Web address for a location changes. You might need to search to find the exact location mentioned.)

Country (Currency)	Country (Currency)	Country (Currency)	Country (Currency)	Country (Currency)
_____	_____	_____	_____	_____
(____)	(____)	(____)	(____)	(____)

1. _____ _____ _____ _____ _____

2. _____ _____ _____ _____ _____

3. _____ _____ _____ _____ _____

4. _____ _____ _____ _____ _____

5. _____ _____ _____ _____ _____

6. _____ _____ _____ _____ _____

7. _____ _____ _____ _____ _____

8. _____ _____ _____ _____ _____

9. _____ _____ _____ _____ _____

10. _____ _____ _____ _____ _____

11. _____ _____ _____ _____ _____

12. _____ _____ _____ _____ _____

13. _____ _____ _____ _____ _____

	Country (Currency)	Country (Currency)	Country (Currency)	Country (Currency)	Country (Currency)
	_____	_____	_____	_____	_____
	(_____)	(_____)	(_____)	(_____)	(_____)
14.	_____	_____	_____	_____	_____
15.	_____	_____	_____	_____	_____
16.	_____	_____	_____	_____	_____
17.	_____	_____	_____	_____	_____
18.	_____	_____	_____	_____	_____
19.	_____	_____	_____	_____	_____
20.	_____	_____	_____	_____	_____
21.	_____	_____	_____	_____	_____
22.	_____	_____	_____	_____	_____
23.	_____	_____	_____	_____	_____
24.	_____	_____	_____	_____	_____
25.	_____	_____	_____	_____	_____
26.	_____	_____	_____	_____	_____
27.	_____	_____	_____	_____	_____
28.	_____	_____	_____	_____	_____
29.	_____	_____	_____	_____	_____

notes for critical thinking exercise 3-3

What effect would such currency shifts have on your business trade with each of these countries?

The principle is this: If the currency of another country goes up, that means it can buy more U.S. goods more cheaply, and that is good for exporters. If the value of its currency goes down, that means goods and services from the United States are more expensive, and that would hurt your business.

bonus
cases

bonus case 3-1
MAKING A MINT ON MAKE-BELIEVE

Chances are that when most Americans think of theme parks, they envision places like Disney World where all the fun aspects of *childhood* are celebrated. However, at KidZania, a new brand of "edutainment" theme parks headquartered in Mexico, role-playing activities based on all the trappings of *adulthood* attract millions of patrons a year. The parks are kid-sized replicas of real cities where children role-play a variety of careers such as firefighters, dentists, painters, and more than 100 other occupations.

Xavier Lopez Ancona got the idea for KidZania after a friend approached him about investing in a line of day care centers focused on role-play. Ancona, a former private equity trader, soon realized that no one, not even Disney, owned the market on children's role-playing activities. In 1999 he opened the first KidZania in Mexico City with tremendous success. The park exceeded all projections by a significant margin thanks to KidZania's immersive atmosphere. At the box office parents purchase a "plane ticket" for their child's passage into the nation of KidZania. After receiving a check for 50 kidZos (the local currency), the visitors take a trip to the career center. After a quiz determines their best-fitting pretend career paths, the children set off to earn kidZos that can be used to buy goods and services. KidZanians can increase their earning potential by obtaining degrees up to the doctoral level.

Seven years after its Mexico City location took off, KidZania opened up a new outpost in Tokyo, followed shortly by locations in Dubai, Seoul, and several other cities. The company has 10 more parks currently under construction as well as plans for an undisclosed American location. In order to house a KidZania, a region must have a significant number of young families as well as a few generous corporations. The company relies heavily on corporate sponsorship to provide funds for the high production values of their parks' role-playing pavilions. Although the company makes a third of its money from marketing deals, Ancona insists that the sponsorship is not a form of advertising. Coca-Cola, for instance, sponsors a pretend bottling plant in five KidZanias and insists it is not targeting children with marketing messages. On the other hand, at the Mexico City location, Procter & Gamble sponsors a section where kids are encouraged to keep their hands clean by using the company's Safeguard soap. A representative from Procter & Gamble said she hopes the exposure turns children into lifelong customers of the brand.[xii]

discussion questions for bonus case 3-1

1. Would "edutainment" parks like KidZania find success in the United States?

2. Is corporate sponsorship at KidZania intended only to build future customers?

notes on discussion questions for bonus case 3-1

1. *Would "edutainment" parks like KidZania find success in the United States?*

   Worldwide, kids are kids. If we think of the popularity of Disney characters globally, there's no reason to think that the KidZania concept would not be successful in the United States.

2. *Is corporate sponsorship at KidZania intended only to build future customers?*

   As P&G's representative states, it hopes to turn children into lifelong customers. There's no doubt that much of the corporate sponsorship relates to marketing efforts at KidZania. However, the same corporate sponsors are present at parks like Disney World. Learning to live like adults would not be the same without well-known brands.

bonus case 3-2

GAP'S EVOLVING VIEW OF ETHICS

In the 1990s, shoe and clothing retailers faced a flood of stories focusing on wage and safety violations in their overseas factories. Did Nike use child labor? Were Kathy Lee's sweaters produced in "sweatshops"? Companies were forced to confront critics and repair the damage to their reputations.

The first reaction of Gap, the corporate parent of Old Navy and Banana Republic, was to clam up and go into fix-it mode. It built an elaborate monitoring system, which performs more than 8,500 factory inspections. But the company gradually realized that this internal monitoring system was not changing public and industry perceptions. Although Gap monitored 100% of its overseas factories for abuses, no one outside the company knew it.

Recently the company was targeted again when Domini Social Investments and other investors filed a shareholder resolution requesting greater transparency from the company. Gap was forced to publish a "social-responsibility" report. However, instead of producing a sanitized report glossing over the problems, Gap decided to produce a warts-and-all profile of the problems facing the company.

The report found persistent wage, health, and safety violations in most regions where it does business, including China, Africa, India, and Central and South America. The infractions ranged from failure to provide proper protective equipment to physical abuse. Although discoveries of the worst violations were rare, Gap reported that it had pulled its business from 136 factories and turned down bids from more than 100 others when they failed to meet its labor standards.

The clothing retailer also committed to making changes that are more sweeping. Most significantly, Gap has agreed to rethink accepted garment-industry business practices, which include unrealistic production cycles that drive such abuses as unpaid overtime.

Even the company's harshest critics welcome the company's candor. "Instead of dealing with a black box, we now have a window into data that can really help us make a judgment on how the company is progressing in handling of these issues," says Conrad MacKerron, a director at As You Sow, a non-profit shareholder advocacy group. "This will put pressure on other retailers to do the same."

In 2006, Gap Inc. was named as one of the "100 Best Corporate Citizens" among major U.S. companies by *Business Ethics* magazine.[xiii]

discussion questions for bonus case 3-2

1. Are you impressed with the effort that Gap has made to respond to the need to have more worker-friendly suppliers? Would such information lead you to buy more goods from Gap, or are things like price and quality and value more important?

2. Gap explored wage, health, and safety issues in its plants. What other issues might the company explore if it wants to ensure the best working conditions possible?

3. If you were a stockholder in Gap Inc., would you be as impressed with its efforts to satisfy the needs of its workers? Would you be more interested in revenues and profits than good wages and working conditions? What concerns might a Gap employee working in one of its stores have because of its social stance?

1.   *Are you impressed with the effort that Gap has made to respond to the need to have more worker-friendly suppliers? Would such information lead you to buy more goods from Gap, or are things like price and quality and value more important?*

It is one thing to talk about the importance of taking care of workers (talking the talk). It is quite another to actually do your part to help (walk the walk). Students often go to stores that offer the latest in fashion or the best prices and could care less about working conditions for the people who made the goods. It may be difficult, but worthwhile, to explore how your students feel.

2.   *Gap explored wage, health, and safety issues in its plants. What other issues might the company explore if it wants to ensure the best working conditions possible?*

In addition to wage, health, and safety issues, there are the issues of child labor, equal pay for equal work, assistance with getting to work, educational advancement, training, and more. What other issues would you add?

3.   *If you were a stockholder in Gap Inc., would you be as impressed with its efforts to satisfy the needs of its workers? Would you be more interested in revenues and profits than good wages and working conditions? What concerns might a Gap employee working in one of its stores have because of its social stance?*

Stockholders are almost exclusively focused on issues such as revenues and profits and price–earnings ratios. They might resent the company spending more money on workers since the costs of production may go up. Employees may also be concerned about competitive pricing, quality, and value. Not everyone is focused on the needs of the world's workers. Is that a good thing or not?

bonus case 3-3

COOLING OFF THE SWEATSHOPS

In the late 1800s and early 1900s, labor conditions in the United States were certainly less than ideal. The average workweek was 60 hours, but it was not unusual for workers to spend 80 hours on the job every week. Children toiled in unsafe conditions sometimes 10 hours a day, six days a week; wages were low and fears of unemployment high; and job benefits such as sick leave and medical care were nonexistent. Labor unions, religious groups, and social reformers were active, attempting to ignite efforts to reform the workplace and end the existence of "sweatshops," where workers often spent their entire lives in atrocious working conditions. Efforts by reformers, plus the publication of the novel *The Jungle* by Upton Sinclair, heightened public awareness of the abuses existing in the workplace. Sinclair portrayed the dark side of Chicago's meat-packing industry, whose inhuman conditions often destroyed the lives and spirit of workers.

A real-life tragedy at the Triangle Shirtwaist Company on March 25, 1911, also intensified the efforts aimed at eliminating sweatshops in the United States. Triangle employed young women in the garment industry. A fire at the company's factory led to the death of 126 young women, who could not exit the building due to locked doors and the lack of a fire escape. News reports faulted the company and brought to light the harsh conditions in which these women worked. The fallout from Sinclair's book and the Triangle Shirtwaist Company fire generated an impassioned public outcry and eventually led to strong federal legislation that improved working conditions throughout the United States.

The issue of sweatshops again is a hot topic in the media. However, today's issue does not deal directly with U.S. workers. The issue also is championed not just by unions and other such organizations but also by college students. At college campuses across the country, students are demanding assurances that clothing bearing their universities' names and logos are produced under humane conditions in global markets. United Students Against Sweatshops (USAS) represents students at some 100 colleges across the nation. The organization demands that universities employ a vigorous monitoring campaign that forces companies to publicly disclose the location of foreign factories so human rights groups can independently monitor their actions. They also demand that employers pay a so-called living wage that meets the basic needs of workers in various global markets.

Apparel industry leaders Nike, Reebok, and Liz Claiborne responded by agreeing to join the Fair Labor Association (FLA), a sweatshop-monitoring group established by a presidential task force of apparel makers and human rights groups. Students, however, argue that this group is nothing more than a publicity stunt, with a weak code of conduct and very little accountability. The USAS and UNITE (the largest garment-workers union in the United States) founded the Workers Rights Consortium (WRC) in 1999 as an alternative to the Fair Labor Association.

Apparel companies contend that their businesses involve thousands of factories operating in very diverse economies. They claim the idea of establishing a formal living-wage structure is impossible and could in fact place significant burdens on the industry and workers in the global economies they seek to help. Edward Graham, a senior fellow at the Institute for International Economics, agrees. He says that multinational companies offer the best-paying jobs around in developing countries. If they did not, workers would refuse to take them. Political leaders in many developing nations fear that if wage standards are imposed on companies like Nike, Levi Strauss, and others, it could price them out of global markets. Since these countries depend on foreign investment money, the loss of such investment could shatter their nation's economies. Economists fear that the concept of a living wage will cost many workers their jobs. They also agree that it is difficult to define a living wage down to the penny and say that the term *living wage* is an emotional term rather than a definable economic term. Still, Juan O. Somavia, director-general of the International Labor Organization, predicts that in five years labor rules around the globe will establish standards. This emotional debate will certainly rage on.[xiv]

discussion questions for bonus case 3-3

1. An argument can be offered that developed (industrialized) countries in the world experienced poor working conditions as their economies matured. Therefore, over time, workers in developing countries will gain the same benefits as their counterparts in countries such as the United States, Germany, and Japan. What's your opinion?

2. What role, if any, should the U.S. government take in this issue of setting fair wages in developing countries? What is your definition of a "fair" (living) wage? Would it vary by country?

3. Would you buy an apparel item with your college name or logo on it if you knew it was produced in a country where workers toiled in sweatshops? Why or why not?

notes on discussion questions for bonus case 3-3

1. *An argument can be offered that all developed (industrialized) countries in the world experienced poor working conditions as their economies matured. Therefore, over time, workers in developing countries will gain the same benefits as their counterparts in countries such as the United States, Germany, and Japan. What's your opinion?*

    This should open quite a discussion in class because the topic is current and emotion laden. It is important to look at this issue from all sides, so several student opinions should be aired. There is no doubt that more can be done to help workers in other countries achieve better working conditions, but is it possible to set wages without knowing in detail the local market?

2. *What role, if any, should the U.S. government taking in this issue of setting fair wages in developing countries? What is your definition of a "fair" (living) wage? Would it vary by country?*

    The U.S. government can urge other countries to establish fair wages, but it has no authority to demand such wages. The U.S. government, on the other hand, can and should investigate and solve and problems with below-standard wages and conditions in the United States. Teaching by example is the key.

    Each student will have his or her own definition of "fair' wages. Students who have already been out in the real job market may have a different interpretation than those who have never worked. There may also be differences in student responses depending on the age of the student, geographic location, and other variables.

3. *Would you buy an apparel item with your college name or logo if you knew it was produced in a country where workers toiled in sweatshops? Why or why not?*

    This is an opinion question, but, again, one that should generate lively debate. The apparel should be less expensive if produced in such a country, but what are the moral issues? And what, exactly, is a "sweatshop"? Does the definition change from country to country? What is a "fair" wage? These are issues that can be explored, but not necessarily answered.

UNDERSTANDING BUSINESS: Instructor's Resource Manual

bonus case 3-4
AFRICA: THE NEW INDIA?

Recognizing that they had hundreds of millions of underserved consumers in their own backyard, Indian companies initiated decades of economic expansion. While many of the nation's big corporations are still focusing on the Indian market, some are turning their attention to a place with an economic situation almost identical to India's 20 years ago—Africa. The typical Indian business model of low cost and high efficiency seems tailor-made for the African continent where consumers are clamoring for goods. Economists predict that consumer spending in Africa could double to as much as $1.8 trillion by 2020, or the equivalent of adding a market the size of Brazil.

Facing tough competition at home, Indian companies see Africa as the perfect opportunity to continue expansion. The $15 billion conglomerate Essar Group has made a substantial foothold already, snatching up coal mines in Mozambique, an oil refinery in Kenya, and soon a power plant in Nigeria. The company now boasts 2,000 African employees. Meanwhile India's largest cell phone provider bought the African cellular operations of Kuwait's Zain Company for $9 billion. In total, Indian companies have invested $16 billion on the continent since 2005.

While some see Africa as an opportunity for growth, others see it as a sort of insurance plan. The idea is that if the Indian economy takes a U-turn sometime soon, operations in Africa will provide a reliable source of income bolstered by its capacity for expansion. Indian government bureaucracy also has companies heading west after squabbles with landowners left them mired in red tape. For instance, Karuturi Global, the world's largest rose producer, couldn't secure enough land in India to compete with its rivals in other countries. After it purchased a small piece of property in Ethiopia, Karuturi's sales increased elevenfold. The company now leases a tract of land larger than the state of Rhode Island.[xv]

discussion questions for bonus case 3-4

1.   Is Indian expansion in Africa a sign India is becoming a dominant global competitor?

2.   What is the major problem India faces as it expands economically?

notes on discussion questions for bonus case 3-4

1. *Is Indian expansion in Africa a sign India is becoming a dominant global competitor?*

   The expansion into Africa is certainly a sign that India is looking to a future in the global market. The population of Africa is soaring and by 2020 the continent could be an almost $2 trillion economy. The Indian model seems like a perfect fit for Africa.

2. *What is the major problem India faces as it expands economically?*

   India's biggest challenge may be transforming itself into a business-friendly nation. Government bureaucracy has been a major obstacle in business expansion in India and many companies are heading out of India to do business.

endnotes

i *Source:* "China Surpasses U.S. in 2009 Auto Sales," Associated Press, January 8, 2010.

ii *Sources:* Michael Arndt, "Urban Outfitters' Grow-Slow Strategy," *Bloomberg Businessweek*, March 1, 2010; Urban Outfitters, www.urbanoutfitters.com, accessed November 7, 2011.

iii *Source:* Ronald Grover, Stephanie Wong, and Wendy Leung, "Disney Gets a Second Chance in China," *Bloomberg Businessweek*, April 14, 2011.

iv *Source:* Gary Stoller, "Doing Business Abroad? Simple Faux Pas Can Sink You," *USA Today*, August 24, 2007.

v *Source:* Mari Yamaguchi, "In Japan, You Are Your Blood Type," *The (Baton Rouge) Advocate*/Associated Press, February 8, 2009.

vi *Source:* David M. Katz, "The Bribery Gap," *CFO*, January 2005.

vii *Sources:* Louis S. Richman, "What's Next After GATT's Victory?" *Fortune*, January 10, 1994, pp. 66–71; Tim Lang, "The New Protectionism: Global Trade Rules Protect Corporations," *The Nation*, July 15, 1996, p. 29; John McGinnis, "Restraining Leviathan: If Free Trade Is Federalism's Heir, Protectionism Is the Best Way to Ensure a Future for Big Government," *National Review*, March 11, 1996, p. 40; Robert W. Staiger, "Economic Theory and the Interpretation of GATT/WTO," *The American Economist*, September 22, 2002; Mohamed Ariff, "Pitfalls Aplenty on the Fast Track to Trade," *New Strait Times*, April 11, 2006.

viii *Source:* Bob Sullivan, "Told in Tweets, Egypt Conflict Riveting, Confusing," *MSNBC Red Tape Chronicles*, February 4, 2011.

ix *Sources:* Michael Liedtke and Jessica Mintz, "Google Ends Four Years of Censorship in China," Associated Press, March 22, 2010; Miguel Helft and Michael Wines, "Google Faces Fallout as China Reacts to Shift," *The New York Times*, March 23, 2010.

x *Source:* Paul Glader, "As Indian Companies Grow in the U.S., Outsourcing Comes Home," *The Washington Post*, May 20, 2011.

xi The Internet is a dynamic, changing information source. Web links noted of this manual were checked at the time of publication, but content may change over time. Please review the website before recommending it to your students.

xii *Source:* Dana Rubinstein, "Playing Grown-Up at KidZania," *Bloomberg Businessweek*, May 19, 2011.

xiii *Sources*: Cheryl Dahle, "Gap's New Look: The See-Through," *Fast Company*, September 2004, pp. 69–71; Kimberly Terry, "Gap Inc. Makes 2006 '100 Best Corporate Citizens' List," *CNNMoney.com*, April 27, 2006.

xiv *Sources:* Diana Fu, "Sweatshops Provoke More Than a Moral Outcry," *University Wire*, January 29, 2003; Nicholas Stein, "Now Way Out of Competition to Make Products for Western Companies Has Revised an Old Form of Abuse: Debt Bondage," *Fortune*, January 20, 2003, pp. 102–110; Douglas Lavin, "Globalization Goes Upscale," *The Wall Street Journal*, February 1, 2002, p. A18; Beth Coombs, "USC Questions Possible WRC Membership," *University Wire*, June 5, 2002.

xv *Source:* Mehul Srivastava and Subramaniam Sharma, "Corporate India Finds Greener Pastures—In Africa," *Bloomberg Businessweek*, November 4, 2010.

Demanding Ethical and Socially Responsible Behavior

chapter 4

what's new in this edition

additions to the 10th edition:

- Getting to Know Blake Mycoskie, Founder of TOMS Shoes

- Name That Company: Xerox

- Discussion of Dodd-Frank Wall Street Reform and Consumer Protection Act added to section Setting Corporate Ethical Standards

- Discussion of changes of forms of corporate philanthropy added to section Corporate Social Responsibility

- Discussion of use of social media to communicate corporate social responsibility efforts added to section Responsibility to Customers

- Discussion of socially conscious research organizations

- Making Ethical Decisions: Facebook or Fakebook?

revisions to the 10th edition:

- Text was revised to eliminate redundancy and tighten discussions.

- Statistical data and examples throughout the chapter were updated to reflect current information.

- Expanded discussion of Nike's efforts to improve overseas factory conditions in section International Ethics and Social Responsibility

- Legal Briefcase: Cost of Corruption

- Thinking Green: Sustainable or Suspect: Greenwashing

deletions from the 9th edition:

- Getting to Know Steve Ells, Founder and CEO of Chipolte Mexican Grill

- Name That Company: Enron

- Discussion of Citizen Corps deleted from section Corporate Social Responsibility

- Making Ethical Decisions

brief chapter outline and learning goals

Demanding Ethical and Socially Responsible Behavior

Getting To Know BLAKE MYCOSKIE, Founder of TOMS SHOES

learning goal 1

Explain why obeying the law is only the first step in behaving ethically.

I. ETHICS IS MORE THAN LEGALITY.

A. Ethical Standards Are Fundamental.

learning goal 2

Ask the three questions to answer when faced with a potentially unethical action.

B. Ethics Begins with Each of Us.

learning goal 3

Describe management's role in setting ethical standards.

II. MANAGING BUSINESSES ETHICALLY AND RESPONSIBLY

learning goal 4

Distinguish between compliance-based and integrity-based ethics codes, and list the six steps in setting up a corporate ethics code.

A. Setting Corporate Ethical Standards

learning goal 5

Define *corporate social responsibility* and compare corporations' responsibility to various stakeholders.

III. CORPORATE SOCIAL RESPONSIBILITY

A. Responsibility to Customers
B. Responsibility to Investors
C. Responsibility to Employees
D. Responsibility to Society and the Environment
E. Social Auditing

learning goal 6

Analyze the role of U.S. businesses in influencing ethical behavior and social responsibility in global markets.

IV. INTERNATIONAL ETHICS AND SOCIAL RESPONSIBILITY

V. SUMMARY

lecture outline

Getting to Know BLAKE MYCOSKIE, Founder of TOMS SHOES

TOMS's mission is simple: For every pair of shoes sold, give a free pair to a child in need. So far, the company has been wildly successful and Mycoskie has helped in giving away over 1 million shoes. Mycoskie was entrepreneurial before TOMS, opening an ad agency and an online driver's education system. But it was while participating in CBS's Amazing Race where he saw how much children around the world needed his help. Mycoskie and his entrepreneurial spirit started TOMS in 2006.

NAME THAT company

This company has a program it calls Social Service Leave that allows employees to take up to a year off to work for a nonprofit organization while earning their full salary and benefits, including job security. Name that company.

(Students should read the chapter before guessing the company's name: Xerox.*)*

learning goal 1

Explain why obeying the law is only the first step in behaving ethically.

I. ETHICS IS MORE THAN LEGALITY.

A. HISTORY OF SCANDALS

1. In the early 2000s scandals at WorldCom, Tyco, and ImClone focused attention on the subject of **ETHICS.**

2. In recent years, greedy borrowers and lenders helped precipitate a worldwide financial crisis.

3. What can be done to restore trust in the free-market system?

   a. Those who have broken the law need to be **PUNISHED ACCORDINGLY.**

   b. Also helpful are new laws making accounting records more transparent and more laws making businesspeople more accountable.

PPT 4-1
Chapter Title

PPT 4-2
Learning Goals

(See complete PowerPoint slide notes on page 4.38.)

PPT 4-3
Learning Goals

(See complete PowerPoint slide notes on page 4.38.)

PPT 4-4
Blake Mycoskie

(See complete PowerPoint slide notes on page 4.39.)

PPT 4-5
Name That Company

(See complete PowerPoint slide notes on page 4.39.)

PPT 4-6
Life After Scandal

(See complete PowerPoint slide notes on page 4.39.)

    c. Laws alone don't make people honest, reliable, or truthful.

  4. Ethical behavior is not the same as following the law.

    a. Ethical behavior goes **BEYOND** the law.

    b. **ETHICS** deals with the proper relations with and responsibilities toward other people.

    c. **LEGALITY** deals with much narrower issues.

    d. It refers only to laws we have written to protect ourselves—many **UNETHICAL ACTS FALL WITHIN OUR LAWS.**

B. **ETHICAL STANDARDS ARE FUNDAMENTAL.**

  1. _**ETHICS**_ are the standards of moral behavior; that is, behavior that is accepted by society as right versus wrong.

  2. Many Americans have few moral absolutes and make **DECISIONS SITUATIONALLY.**

  3. Even in today's diverse culture, there are still **COMMON STANDARDS OF ETHICAL BEHAVIOR.**

    a. Integrity, respect for human life, self-control, honesty, courage, and self-sacrifice are **RIGHT**.

    b. Cheating, cowardice, and cruelty are **WRONG**.

  4. All major religions support a version of the **GOLDEN RULE**: "Do unto others as you would have them do unto you."

legal
briefcase
(Text page 91)

PPT 4-7
Cost of
Corruption

(See complete PowerPoint slide notes on page 4.40.)

PPT 4-8
What Is a Ponzi Scheme?

(See complete PowerPoint slide notes on page 4.40.)

PPT 4-9
What Are Ethics?

(See complete PowerPoint slide notes on page 4.40.)

PPT 4-10
Basic Moral Values

(See complete PowerPoint slide notes on page 4.41.)

lecture link 4-1
GIVING ONLINE WITH CAUSES

Giving and volunteerism are prominent in American culture. In an effort to reach more Americans, Causes links 119 users to charities around the world. (See the complete lecture link on page 4.54 in this manual.)

critical thinking
exercise 4-1
EXPLORING COMMUNITY
SERVICE

This exercise encourages students to use the Internet to explore opportunities for community service. (See complete exercise on page 4.61 of this manual.)

<u>**learning goal**</u> 2

Ask the three questions one should answer when faced with a potentially unethical action.

C. **ETHICS BEGINS WITH EACH OF US.**

1. Americans in general are not always honest and honorable.

   a. A recent study identified low managerial ethics as a major factor in America's competitive problems.

   b. Another survey revealed that 3/4 of the population **NEVER GAVE TIME** to their communities.

   c. The most common form of cheating is plagiarizing material from the Internet.

   d. In a recent study, 38% of teens felt that lying, cheating, plagiarizing, or behaving violently are sometimes necessary.

   e. Many schools now require a certain number of hours of community service to graduate.

2. It is important to **KEEP ETHICS IN MIND** when making a business decision.

   a. There is not always an easy choice.

   b. Sometimes the obvious solution from an ethical point of view has drawbacks from a personal or professional point of view.

   c. Sometimes there is no desirable alternative, a situation referred to as an **ETHICAL DILEMMA**.

3. Three **"ETHICS CHECK QUESTIONS"** can help

PPT 4-11
Ethics and You

(See complete PowerPoint slide notes on page 4.41.)

lecture link 4-2

**CHINA CONFRONTS ITS
ETHICAL DEMONS**

As China grows in economic clout, it must improve its dismal record on corruption and environmental issues. (See the complete lecture link on page 4.55 in this manual.)

MAKING
ethical
decisions
(Text page 93)

PPT 4-12
Facebook or
Fakebook

(See complete PowerPoint slide notes on page 4.41.)

critical thinking
exercise 4-2

ETHICAL DILEMMAS

This exercise presents 10 examples of ethical dilemmas for students to evaluate. (See complete exercise on page 4.62 of this manual.)

TEXT FIGURE 4.1
Ethical Orientation Questionnaire
(Text page 95)

This figure presents a nine-question quiz to identify one's style of recognizing and resolving ethical dilemmas.

individuals and organizations be sure their decisions are ethical:

    a. Is my proposed action **LEGAL**?

    b. Is it **BALANCED**?

    c. How will it make me **FEEL ABOUT MYSELF**?

4. Individuals and companies that develop a strong ethics code tend to behave more ethically than others.

<u>**learning goal 3**</u>
Describe management's role in setting ethical standards.

II. MANAGING BUSINESSES ETHICALLY AND RESPONSIBLY

A. ORGANIZATIONAL ETHICS BEGINS AT THE TOP.

1. People learn their standards and values from observing what others do, not what they say.

2. Corporate values are instilled by the leadership and example of strong top managers.

3. Any trust and cooperation between workers and managers must be based on **FAIRNESS, HONESTY, OPENNESS, AND MORAL INTEGRITY.**

4. Some managers think ethics is a personal matter—that they are not responsible for an individual's misdeeds.

    a. Individuals do not usually act alone—they need the implied, if not the direct, cooperation of others to behave unethically in a corporation.

PPT 4-13
Facing Ethical Dilemmas

(See complete PowerPoint slide notes on page 4.42.)

PPT 4-14
Bribery Bad Boys

(See complete PowerPoint slide notes on page 4.42.)

progress
assessment
(Text page 94)

PPT 4-15
Progress Assessment

(See complete PowerPoint slide notes on page 4.42.)

PPT 4-16
Ethics Start at the Top

(See complete PowerPoint slide notes on page 4.43.)

PPT 4-17
Factors Influencing Managerial
Ethics

(See complete PowerPoint slide notes on page 4.43.)

b. *The text uses the example of cell phone sales reps who unethically pressure customers.*

5. In some corporations, corporate standards may encourage dishonesty.

learning goal 4

Distinguish between compliance based and integrity based ethics codes, and list the six steps in setting up a corporate ethics code.

B. SETTING CORPORATE ETHICAL STANDARDS

1. Most corporations have **WRITTEN CODES OF ETHICS.**

2. Although ethics codes vary greatly, they can be classified into **TWO MAJOR CATEGORIES**: compliance-based and integrity-based.

   a. ***COMPLIANCE-BASED ETHICS CODES*** are ethical standards that emphasize preventing unlawful behavior by increasing control and by penalizing wrongdoers.

   b. ***INTEGRITY-BASED ETHICS CODES*** are ethical standards that define the organization's guiding values, create an environment that supports ethically sound behavior, and stress a shared accountability among employees.

3. A **6-STEP PROCESS** can help improve America's business ethics.

   a. Step 1: **TOP MANAGEMENT** must adopt and unconditionally support an explicit code of conduct.

   b. Step 2: **EMPLOYEES** must understand that expectations for ethical behavior begin at the top and all employees are expected to act ethically.

TEXT FIGURE 4.2
Overview of Johnson &
Johnson's Code of Ethics
(Text page 97)

This text figure is an overview of Johnson & Johnson's code of ethics, what it calls its Credo.

TEXT FIGURE 4.3
Strategies for Ethics
Management
(Text page 97)

This text figure presents a comparison of compliance-based and integrity-based ethics codes.

lecture link 4-3
SELECTED CODES OF ETHICS

Codes of ethics are as unique as the companies that write them. This Lecture Link presents samples of ethics codes for several major U.S. companies. (See the complete lecture link on page 4.55 in this manual.)

PPT 4-18
Ethics Codes

(See complete PowerPoint slide notes on page 4.43.)

critical thinking
exercise 4-3
RESEARCHING CODES OF
ETHICS

Most companies now publish codes of ethics to provide ethical guidelines for employees. This Internet exercise directs students to research these codes of ethics on the Internet. (See complete exercise on page 4.66 of this manual.)

c. Step 3: **MANAGERS** and others must be trained to consider the ethical implications of all business decisions.

d. Step 4: **AN ETHICS OFFICE** must be set up.

　　i. **_WHISTLEBLOWERS_** (insiders who report illegal or unethical behavior) must feel protected from retaliation.

　　ii. The **CORPORATE AND CRIMINAL FRAUD ACCOUNTABILITY ACT** (Sarbanes-Oxley, 2002) contains protections for corporate whistleblowers and the Dodd-Frank Act includes a "bounty" for whistleblowers if the information given results in a successful enforcement action.

e. Step 5: **OUTSIDERS** such as suppliers, subcontractors, distributors, and customers must be told about the ethics program.

f. Step 6: **THE ETHICS CODE MUST BE ENFORCED.**

　　i. If rules are broken, **CONSEQUENCES** should follow quickly.

　　ii. **ENFORCEMENT** shows that the code is serious and cannot be broken.

4. A company's ethics code is worthless **IF NOT ENFORCED**.

a. *Enron's management sent the message to employees that unethical behavior would be tolerated.*

PPT 4-19
How to Improve America's
Business Ethics

(See complete PowerPoint slide notes on page 4.44.)

PPT 4-20
How to Improve America's
Business Ethics

(See complete PowerPoint slide notes on page 4.44.)

    b. *Johnson & Johnson's response to the cyanide poisoning crisis in the 1980s enhanced its bottom line.*

  5. An important factor to encourage ethical behavior is the selection of **AN ETHICS OFFICER** who:

    a. Sets a positive tone, communicates effectively, relates well with employees

    b. Serves as a counselor or as an investigator

  6. **EFFECTIVE ETHICS OFFICERS** are people who:

    a. Can be trusted to maintain confidentiality, conduct objective investigations, and ensure the process is fair

    b. Can demonstrate to stakeholders that ethics are important

learning goal 5

Define corporate social responsibility and compare corporations' responsibilities to various stakeholders.

III. CORPORATE SOCIAL RESPONSIBILITY

A. BASICS OF SOCIAL RESPONSIBILITY

  1. *CORPORATE SOCIAL RESPONSIBILITY (CSR)* is a business's concern for the welfare of society.

    a. It is based on a company's concern for the welfare of all its stakeholders, not just the owners.

    b. Some **CRITICS** of CSR believe that a manager's sole role is to compete and win.

    c. Milton Friedman stated that the only social

PPT 4-21
How to Prevent Unethical
Behaviors

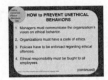

(See complete PowerPoint slide notes on page 4.44.)

PPT 4-22
How to Prevent Unethical
Behavior

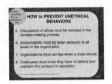

(See complete PowerPoint slide notes on page 4.45.)

progress
assessment
(Text page 98)

PPT 4-23
Progress Assessment

(See complete PowerPoint slide notes on page 4.45.)

PPT 4-24
Corporate Social Responsibility

(See complete PowerPoint slide notes on page 4.46.)

responsibility of business is to make money for stockholders.

  d. **DEFENDERS** argue that CSR makes more money for investors in the long run.

  e. One study showed a positive correlation between corporate social performance and corporate financial performance.

2. **SOCIAL PERFORMANCE** of a company has several dimensions:

  a. ***CORPORATE PHILANTHROPY*** is the dimension of social responsibility that includes charitable donations.

  b. ***CORPORATE SOCIAL INITIATIVES*** are enhanced forms of corporate philanthropy directly related to the company's competencies.

  c. ***CORPORATE RESPONSIBILITY*** is the dimension of social responsibility that includes everything from hiring minority workers to making safe products.

  d. ***CORPORATE POLICY*** is the dimension of social responsibility that refers to the position a firm takes on social and political issues.

3. **IMPACT OF CORPORATIONS ON SOCIETY**

  a. Many people get a one-sided view of the impact that companies have on society.

  b. Few people see the **POSITIVE IMPACTS**, such as the commitments of many companies to volunteerism, *such as Xerox's Social Service Leave program.*

lecture link 4-4
APPROACHES TO SOCIAL RESPONSIBILITY

Corporations can take several approaches toward social responsibility: reaction, defense, accommodation, and proaction (See the complete lecture link on page 4.57 of this manual.)

PPT 4-25
Corporate Philanthropy and Social Initiatives

(See complete PowerPoint slide notes on page 4.46.)

PPT 4-26
Corporate Responsibility and Policy

(See complete PowerPoint slide notes on page 4.46.)

critical thinking exercise 4-4
ETHICS MINICASES

This exercise presents five short cases about real-world ethical dilemmas. It also makes a good group exercise. (See complete exercise on page 4.67 of this manual.)

PPT 4-27
Positive Impacts of Companies

(See complete PowerPoint slide notes on page 4.47.)

    c. The recent recession has changed corporate philanthropy: Companies have cut donations since 2008 and are encouraging employees to volunteer more.

    d. Two-thirds of MBA students surveyed said that they would take a lower salary to work for a socially responsible company.

    e. Social responsibility is seen differently through the eyes of various **STAKEHOLDERS** to whom businesses are responsible.

B. RESPONSIBILITY TO CUSTOMERS

  1. President John F. Kennedy proposed four basic rights of consumers:

    a. The right to **SAFETY**

    b. The right to **BE INFORMED**

    c. The right to **CHOOSE**

    d. The right to be **HEARD**

  2. Business is responsible to **SATISFY CUSTOMERS** with goods and services of real value, not an easy task.

  3. Many new businesses fail—perhaps because their owners failed to please their customers.

  4. Social media are a growing way companies communicate their social efforts: over **70%** use social media.

  5. *The text uses the example of how Celestial Seasoning ignored its image of social responsibility when it poisoned prairie dogs.*

PPT 4-28
Helping Hands

(See complete PowerPoint slide notes on page 4.47.)

PPT 4-29
Generous Guys

(See complete PowerPoint slide notes on page 4.47.)

lecture link 4-5
**CORPORATE RESPONSIBILITY
IN THE CLASSROOM**

Social responsibility is becoming a hallmark of many companies. Many top graduate-level business schools are adding CSR to their curricula. (See complete lecture link on page 4.57 of this manual.)

PPT 4-30
Life After Tragedy

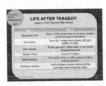

(See complete PowerPoint slide notes on page 4.48.)

PPT 4-31
President Kennedy's Basic Rights
of Consumers

(See complete PowerPoint slide notes on page 4.48.)

bonus case 4-1
**WAL-MART'S VIRGINIA
BATTLEGROUND**

Customers exercised their right to be heard in Virginia as Wal-Mart announced plans to construct a new Supercenter near a Civil War battle site. (See the complete case, discussion questions, and suggested answers beginning on page 4.76 of this manual.)

6. Customers prefer to do business with companies they trust.

C. **RESPONSIBILITY TO INVESTORS**

1. **ETHICAL BEHAVIOR** is good for shareholder wealth.

2. **UNETHICAL BEHAVIOR** does financial damage.

3. Some believe that **BEFORE** you can do good you must **DO WELL**.

4. Others believe that **BY DOING GOOD**, you can also **DO WELL** *(example: Bagel Works)*.

5. Many people believe that it makes **FINANCIAL** as well as **MORAL** sense to invest in socially responsible companies.

6. Another ethical concern is **INSIDER TRADING**.

   a. **_INSIDER TRADING_** is an unethical activity in which insiders use private company information to further their own fortunes or those of their family and friends.

   b. The text uses these examples:

      i. *Raj Rajaratnam was accused of masterminding an insider trading ring that made his hedge fund $45 million richer.*

      ii. *An IBM secretary benefited from advance knowledge of the Lotus merger.*

   c. In response to insider trading scandals, the SEC adopted **REGULATION FD** for "fair disclosure."

   d. If companies tell something to **ANYONE**, they must tell **EVERYONE**—at the same time.

lecture link 4-6
PHARMACEUTICAL OR FOOD?

Companies are infusing foods with beneficial substances and selling them as "healthy" even if they don't live up to the advertising promises. (See the complete lecture link on page 4.58 of this manual.)

PPT 4-32
How Do Customers Know?

(See complete PowerPoint slide notes on page 4.48.)

PPT 4-33
Social Customer Contact

(See complete PowerPoint slide notes on page 4.49.)

PPT 4-34
Insider Trading

(See complete PowerPoint slide notes on page 4.49.)

lecture link 4-7
MERCK AND ETHICS (PART I)

When Merck researchers discovered a drug that treated river blindness, there was no profitable market for it. Instead, Merck donated the drug to treat millions of people in Africa. (See the complete lecture link on page 4.58 of this manual, and see **Bonus Case 4-2** on page 4.78 for the second part of the Merck story.)

bonus case 4-2
MERCK AND ETHICS (PART II)

What happened to Merck? The well-respected company's reputation for socially responsible behavior (see Lecture Link 4-7) was tarnished by its handling of the Vioxx controversy. (See the complete case, discussion questions, and suggested answers beginning on page 4.78 of this manual.)

    e. Companies can **MISUSE INFORMATION FOR THEIR OWN BENEFIT** at investors' expense, as in the case of WorldCom's fraudulent accounting practices.

D. **RESPONSIBILITY TO EMPLOYEES**

  1. **RESPONSIBILITIES OF BUSINESSES:**

    a. Businesses have a responsibility to **CREATE JOBS.**

    b. Businesses have an obligation to see that **HARD WORK AND TALENT ARE FAIRLY REWARDED.**

  2. A company's effectiveness and financial performance depends on human resource management.

  3. If a company **TREATS EMPLOYEES WITH RESPECT**, they will respect the company.

    a. In their book *Contented Cows Give Better Milk*, Bill Catlette and Richard Hadden compared "contented cow" companies with "common cow" companies.

    b. The **"CONTENTED COW"** companies grew faster and earned more than **"COMMON COW"** companies.

  4. Replacing employees costs between 150% and 250% of their annual salary, so retaining workers is good for business.

  5. By giving employees salaries and benefits that help them **REACH THEIR PERSONAL GOALS**, the employer shows commitment and caring.

critical thinking
exercise 4-5
**SOCIAL RESPONSIBILITY
SUCCESSES AND FAILURE**

This Internet exercise encourages students to use the Internet to research companies that have succeeded or have failed to be socially responsible. (See complete exercise on page 4.72 of this manual.)

PPT 4-35
Responsibility to Employees

(See complete PowerPoint slide notes on page 4.50.)

lecture link 4-8
**APP-GATE AT UNIVERSITY OF
MISSOURI**

Should the rules of intellectual property be the same for students as it is for professors? The University of Missouri struggled with this question and how talent should be rewarded to both student and university. (See the complete lecture link on page 4.59 in this manual.)

PPT 4-36
America's Most Admired
Companies

(See complete PowerPoint slide notes on page 4.50.)

6. When employees feel they've been **TREATED UNFAIRLY**, they strike back.

    a. **DISSATISFIED WORKERS** relieve their frustrations in subtle ways.

    b. **EMPLOYEE FRAUD** causes 30% of business failures.

E. **RESPONSIBILITY TO SOCIETY AND THE ENVIRONMENT**

1. A major responsibility of business to society is to **CREATE NEW WEALTH.**

    a. Most nonprofits own shares of publicly held companies.

    b. As those share prices increase, funds are available to benefit society.

2. There is also a growing **GREEN MOVEMENT**.

    a. A product's **CARBON FOOTPRINT** (the amount of carbon released during production, distribution, consumption, and disposal) defines how green it is.

    b. No specific guidelines define the carbon footprint of products and businesses, but many companies are making **GREEN PRODUCTS** available.

3. Business is responsible for contributing to making its **OWN ENVIRONMENT** a better place.

4. *The text uses the example of Ciba Specialty Chemicals developing a low-salt textile dye that could be sold at a premium price.*

bonus case 4-3

A GLANCE INTO THE FUTURE: YOUR COMPUTER KNOWS

Microsoft has applied for a patent on a new application—software capable of remotely monitoring a worker's productivity, physical well-being, and competence. (See the complete case, discussion questions, and suggested answers beginning on page 4.80 of this manual.)

PPT 4-37

When Employees Are Upset …

(See complete PowerPoint slide notes on page 4.50.)

PPT 4-38

Society and the Environment

(See complete PowerPoint slide notes on page 4.50.)

PPT 4-39

Responsibility to the Environment

(See complete PowerPoint slide notes on page 4.51.)

5. Not all environmental efforts are financially successful, *such as StarKist's failed "tuna-safe" initiative.*

6. The green movement has had a positive impact on the U.S. labor force.

7. To publicize their commitment to society, many corporations **PUBLISH REPORTS** that document their net social contribution.

F. **SOCIAL AUDITING**

1. How can you measure how well organizations are incorporating social responsiveness into top management's decision making?

2. A ***SOCIAL AUDIT*** is a systematic evaluation of an organization's progress toward implementing socially responsible and responsive programs.

3. Many **SOCIAL AUDITS** consider such things as:
   a. Workplace issues
   b. The environment
   c. Product safety
   d. Communications
   e. Military weapons contracting
   f. International operations
   g. Human rights

4. Some suggest that positive actions be added up and negative effects subtracted to get a **NET SOCIAL CONTRIBUTION.**

5. **FIVE GROUPS** serve as "**WATCHDOGS**" monitoring how well companies enforce their ethical

thinking green
(Text page 104)

PPT 4-40
Sustainable or Suspect Greenwashing

(See complete PowerPoint slide notes on page 4.51.)

PPT 4-41
Worthy Causes

(See complete PowerPoint slide notes on page 4.51.)

PPT 4-42
Social Auditing

(See complete PowerPoint slide notes on page 4.52.)

critical thinking exercise 4-6
SURVEYING PUBLIC INTEREST ORGANIZATIONS

This exercise asks students to research two organizations involved in public interest activities. (See complete exercise on page 4.73 of this manual.)

and social responsibility policies:

   a. **SOCIALLY CONSCIOUS INVESTORS,** who insist that companies extend the company's own high standards to all their suppliers.

   b. **SOCIALLY CONSCIOUS RESEARCH ORGANIZATIONS,** that analyze and report on CSR efforts.

   c. **ENVIRONMENTALISTS,** who apply pressure by naming names of companies that don't abide by the environmentalists' standards.

   c. **UNION OFFICIALS,** who hunt down violations and force companies to comply to avoid negative publicity.

   d. **CUSTOMERS,** who take their business elsewhere if a company demonstrates socially irresponsible practices.

6. Bob McDonald of P&G believes sustainability isn't optional anymore. It's essential.

7. It isn't enough for a company to be right when it comes to ethics and social responsibility—it also has to convince customers that it's right.

learning goal 6

Analyze the role of U.S. businesses in influencing ethical behavior and social responsibility in global markets.

IV. INTERNATIONAL ETHICS AND SOCIAL RESPONSIBILITY

   A. **ETHICAL PROBLEMS ARE NOT UNIQUE TO THE UNITED STATES.**

   1. *The text gives the examples of recent "influence peddling" in Japan, South Korea, Zaire, China, and others.*

progress
assessment
(Text page 105)

PPT 4-43
Progress Assessment   (See complete PowerPoint slide notes on page 4.52.)

2. What is new is that leaders are being held to new, higher standards.

B. Many American businesses, *such as Sears* and *Dow Chemical*, are demanding socially responsible behavior from international suppliers.

1. They make sure their suppliers **DO NOT VIOLATE U.S. HUMAN RIGHTS AND ENVI-RONMENTAL STANDARDS.**

2. In contrast, companies like *Nike* have been criticized for the low pay, long hours, and unsafe working conditions for factory workers in Asia.

3. *Nike has been monitoring efforts to improve labor conditions since the 1990s and in 2005 released names and locations of factories to encourage transparency.*

4. Should international suppliers be required to adhere to U.S. ethical standards? What about countries where child labor is accepted? What about multinational corporations?

   a. None of these questions are easy to answer.

   b. They show how complex social responsibility issues are in international markets.

5. Many U.S. executives complain that the Foreign Corrupt Practices Act put their businesses at a competitive disadvantage.

6. **STANDARDS ON SOCIAL RESPONSIBILITY:**

   a. International organizations, such as the Organization of American States, have adopted the **INTER-AMERICAN CONVENTION AGAINST CORRUPTION.**

PPT 4-44
International Ethics

(See complete PowerPoint slide notes on page 4.52.)

REACHING BEYOND
our borders
(Text page 108

PPT 4-45
Ethical Culture
Clash

(See complete PowerPoint slide notes on page 4.53.)

b. The **INTERNATIONAL ORGANIZATION FOR STANDARDIZATION (ISO)** has developed a set of standards for social responsibility, but these are voluntary.

V.   SUMMARY

progress
assessment
(Text page 109)

PPT 4-46
Progress Assessment   (See complete PowerPoint slide notes on page 4.53.)

PowerPoint slide notes

LEARNING GOALS

Chapter Four

1. Explain why obeying the law is only the first step in behaving ethically.

2. Ask the three questions you need to answer when faced with a potentially unethical action.

3. Describe management's role in setting ethical standards.

LEARNING GOALS

Chapter Four

4. Distinguish between compliance-based and integrity-based ethics codes, and list the six steps in setting up a corporate ethics code.

5. Define *corporate social responsibility* and compare corporations' responsibilities to various stakeholders.

6. Analyze the role of U.S. businesses in influencing ethical behavior and social responsibility in global markets.

Company: Xerox

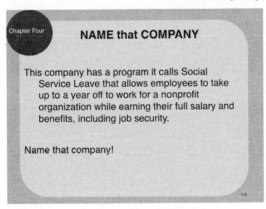

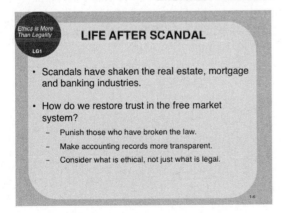

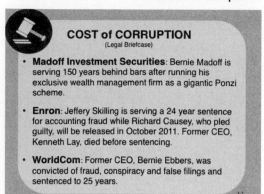

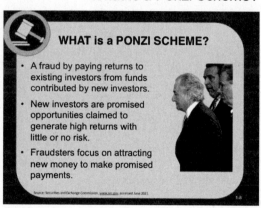

The reputations of American businesses have been under assault due to numerous scandals over the past 20 years. Following the law is only the first step in being ethical. Ethics are standards of moral behavior and are accepted by society as right versus wrong.

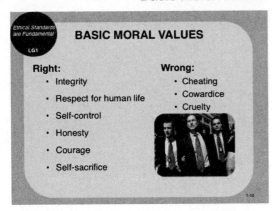

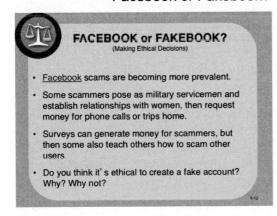

Asking and answering these three questions will prevent many people from making unethical decisions.

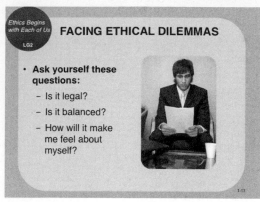

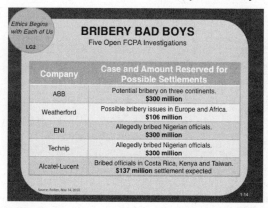

1. The Justice Department has 150 open Foreign Corrupt Practices Act (FCPA) cases.

2. This slide highlights five of the current cases and the amount that these companies have reserved to cover any settlements.

3. To promote discussion, you can discuss how these companies are first extorted by the officials in foreign nations and then punished for their actions back at home. It is illegal for U.S. companies to participate in bribery, yet it is common practice in some countries. How are Americans supposed to deal with these issues? What is the ethical dilemma here?

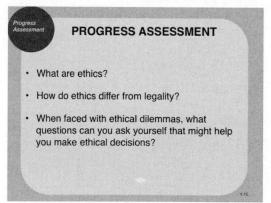

1. Ethics are society's accepted standards of behavior, in other words behaviors accepted by society as right rather than wrong.

2. Ethics reflect people's proper relationships with one another. Legality is narrower in that it refers to laws we have written to protect ourselves from fraud, theft, and violence.

3. It helps to ask the following questions when faced with an ethical dilemma: Is the proposed action legal? Is it balanced? Would I want to be treated this way? How will it make me feel about myself?

Ethics Start at the Top

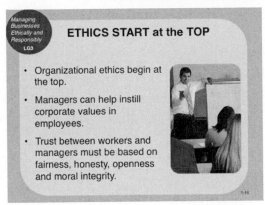

Leadership helps instill corporate values in employees. So, like many aspects of business, ethical behavior practiced and modeled by managers and executives will often trickle down to the employees at large.

Factors Influencing Managerial Ethics

1. Before you put this slide up, you may want to ask the students: What factors influence managerial ethics?

2. Ethics begins with the individual, but are influenced by the organization and the environment in which the business operates.

3. To bring the discussion to the present, you may ask: How can the firm's reward system impact ethical behavior? How did these reward systems at large banks and other financial institutions exacerbate the financial crisis in this country? *(Students should be able to discuss this point. Excessive risk taking imperiled all of the stakeholders of various financial institutions as well as the world economy.)*

Ethics Codes

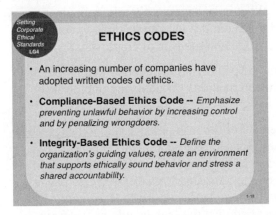

How to Improve America's Business
Ethics

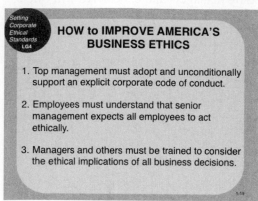

How to Improve America's Business
Ethics

How to Prevent Unethical Behaviors

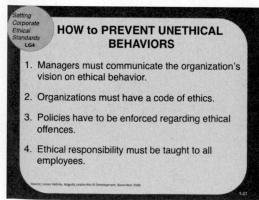

1. Before you put this slide up, you may want to ask the students: What is management's role in preventing unethical behaviors? What can be done to deter un-ethical behaviors on the part of employees?

2. Increasing the penalty and educating employees are among the top methods for deterring unethical behaviors.

3. Thirty percent of the respondents in a poll suggested adding new laws to deter unethical behaviors. Ask the students: If ethics is more than legality, would new laws help? *(Students should be able to argue this point. Although ethics is more than legality, if something is against the law, people may refrain from such behavior. However, it should be pointed out that ethics should be the way of life, i.e., it needs to be ingrained in the employees through culture and role modeling by managers and executives.)*

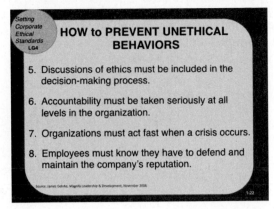

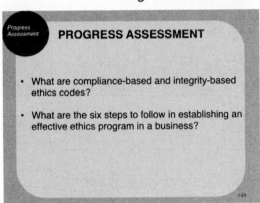

1. Compliance-based ethics codes emphasize preventing unlawful behavior by increasing control and penalizing wrongdoers. Integrity-based ethics codes define the organization's guiding values, create an environment that supports ethically sound behavior, and stress shared accountability.

2. The six steps many believe will improve U.S. business ethics are: (1) Top management must adopt and unconditionally support an explicit corporate code of conduct; (2) Employees must understand that expectations for ethical behavior begin at the top and that senior management expects all employees to act accordingly; (3) Managers and others must be trained to consider the ethical implications of all business decisions; (4) An ethics office must be set up with which employees can communicate anonymously; (5) Outsiders such as suppliers, subcontractors, distributors, and customers must be told about the ethics program; (6) The ethics code must be enforced with timely action if any rules are broken.

PPT 4-24
Corporate Social Responsibility

Many for-profit companies have philanthropic endeavors as a part of their mission. Communities often depend on companies to help with social programs that make the lives of people in the community better. It stands to reason that businesses that strengthen their communities, as proponents of CSR argue, will grow stronger as their communities improve.

PPT 4-25
Corporate Philanthropy and Social Initiatives

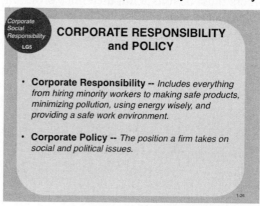

PPT 4-26
Corporate Responsibility and Policy

CORPORATE RESPONSIBILITY and POLICY

- **Corporate Responsibility --** *Includes everything from hiring minority workers to making safe products, minimizing pollution, using energy wisely, and providing a safe work environment.*

- **Corporate Policy --** *The position a firm takes on social and political issues.*

PPT 4-27
Positive Impacts of Companies

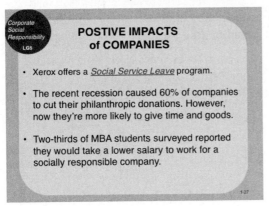

An ultimate example of a company helping the community is Xerox's program, Social Service Leave, which allows employees to leave for up to a year and work for a non-profit while still earning full salary, including benefits and job security.

PPT 4-28
Helping Hands

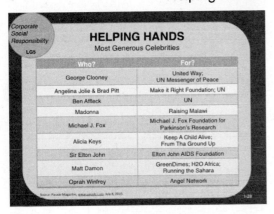

1. Students will find it interesting to see on this slide what some of their favorite celebrities have donated.

2. Oprah Winfrey earns well over $200 million per year and donates nearly $50 million.

3. The talk-show host and entertainment mogul is the founder of the Angel Network, a charity that raises money for poverty-stricken children, and she has raised money to open schools for girls in South Africa.

PPT 4-29
Generous Guys

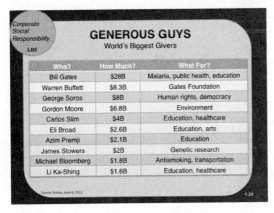

1. Students may be surprised how much billionaires donate and the causes they support. You could prompt discussion by asking students why they believe billionaires give so much to education while celebrities choose more social causes.

2. Bill Gates's net worth is over $56 billion and he's donated $28 billion!

Life after Tragedy

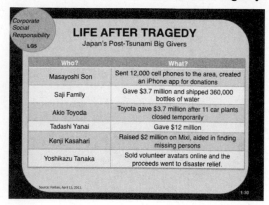

1. Japan was left devastated after an earthquake and tsunami destroyed cities and ports.

2. Japanese tycoons and their companies quickly did their part in aiding those affected by the disaster.

3. Some of their companies were even shut down. Tadashi Yanai's stock dip cut his worth from $6.3 billion to $1.3 billion.

PPT 4-31
President Kennedy's Basic Rights of Consumers

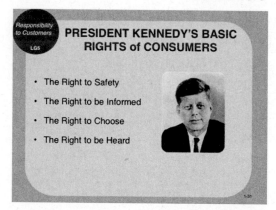

PPT 4-32
How Do Customers Know?

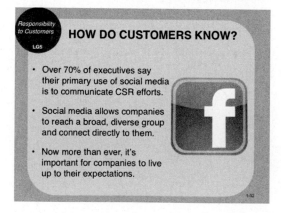

PPT 4-33
Social Customer Contact

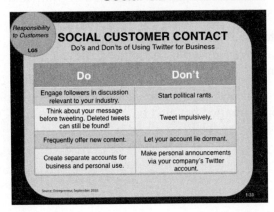

SOCIAL CUSTOMER CONTACT
Do's and Don'ts of Using Twitter for Business

Responsibility to Customers — LG5

Do	Don't
Engage followers in discussion relevant to your industry.	Start political rants.
Think about your message before tweeting. Deleted tweets can still be found!	Tweet impulsively.
Frequently offer new content.	Let your account lie dormant.
Create separate accounts for business and personal use.	Make personal announcements via your company's Twitter account.

Source: Entrepreneur, September 2010

PPT 4-34
Insider Trading

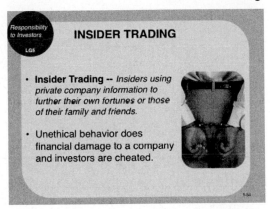

INSIDER TRADING

Responsibility to Investors — LG5

- **Insider Trading** -- *Insiders using private company information to further their own fortunes or those of their family and friends.*

- Unethical behavior does financial damage to a company and investors are cheated.

PPT 4-35
Responsibility to Employees

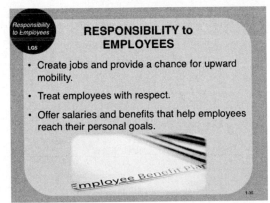

RESPONSIBILITY to EMPLOYEES

Responsibility to Employees — LG5

- Create jobs and provide a chance for upward mobility.

- Treat employees with respect.

- Offer salaries and benefits that help employees reach their personal goals.

Employee Benefit Plan

America's Most Admired Companies

1. Before you put up this slide you may want to ask the students, Are the ideals of maximization of profit and social responsibility in conflict?

2. Corporate social responsibility is the concern businesses have for the welfare of society, not just for their owners.

3. The vast majority of the companies listed in this slide are not only admired but also financially successful.

When Employees Are Upset ...

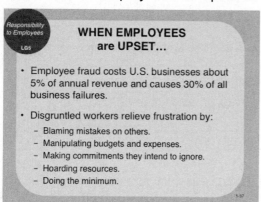

Society and the Environment

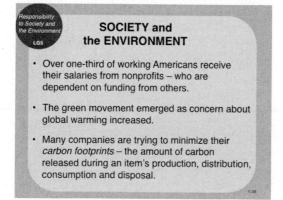

PPT 4-39
Responsibility to the Environment

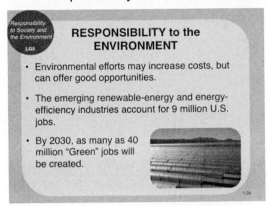

PPT 4-40
Sustainable or Suspect: Greenwashing

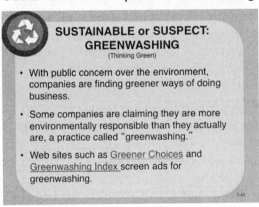

PPT 4-41
Worthy Causes

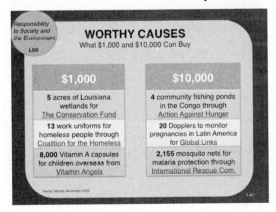

1. Sometimes it's difficult to imagine just how far our donation money can go. This slide can give students insight into what some American families are able to give.

2. It's not uncommon to think that donations under $1,000 will not go far. But when students see how much good $1,000 can do, they see smaller donations are still worth it.

3. To promote discussion, navigate through the websites linked to the slide and check out what smaller and bigger donations provide for these groups.

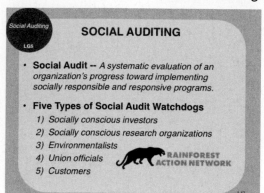

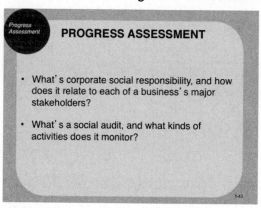

1. Corporate social responsibility (CSR) is the concern businesses have for the welfare of society, not just for their owners. CSR defenders believe that businesses owe their existence to the societies they serve and cannot succeed in societies that fail. CSR must be responsible to all stakeholders, not just investors in the company.

2. A social audit is a systematic evaluation of an organization's progress toward implementing socially responsible and responsive programs. Many feel a social audit should measure workplace issues, the environment, product safety, community relations, military weapons contracting, international operations and human rights, and respect for the rights of local people.

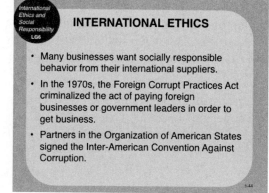

ETHICAL CULTURE CLASH
(Reaching Beyond Our Borders)

- Almost half of Motorola's employees live outside the U.S.

- A Motorola employee returns to his home country to work and the company reimburses living expenses so he can live in a safe area. The employee is trying to do the honorable thing for his family and the company is trying to keep the employee safe.

- If the employee uses the money to help his family instead, is it right for the company to stop payment?

1-45

PROGRESS ASSESSMENT

- How are U.S. businesses demanding socially responsible behavior from their international suppliers?

- Why is it unlikely that there will be a single set of international rules governing multinational companies soon?

1-46

1. Many U.S. businesses now demand that international suppliers do not violate U.S. human rights and environmental standards.

2. It's unlikely there will be a single set of international rules governing multinational companies because of the widespread disparity among global nations as to what constitutes ethical behavior. For example, a gift in one culture can be a bribe in another. In some nations child labor is expected and an important part of a family's standard of living. The fairness of adhering to U.S. standards of ethical behavior is not as easy as you may think.

lecture links

"A business that makes nothing but money is a poor kind of business."

Henry Ford

"Commitment in and of itself, irrespective or whether you win or not, is something that truly makes your life worthwhile."

Pete Seeger

"We make a living by what we get, but we make a life by what we give."

Winston Churchill

"Life is all one piece. Men err when they think they can be inhuman exploiters in their business life, and loving husbands and fathers at home. For achievement without love is a cold and tight-lipped murderer of human happiness everywhere."

Smiley Blanton

lecture link 4-1

GIVING ONLINE WITH CAUSES

As most of the business world has embraced technology over the last decade, it's difficult to believe there are entire industries that haven't adapted accordingly. But of the $263 billion Americans donated to charity in 2009, only 5.7% of that cash came from online coffers. In spite of vast, accessible technological progress, the giving industry solicits potential donors primarily through old-fashioned means like direct mail and telemarketing. The target audience of many charities explains some of the story: The majority of donations to nonprofits like Save the Children come from middle-aged and older people.

Still, older Americans are flocking to once strong online bastions of youth like Facebook and getting involved in the digital world more deeply. And as the massive viral donation movement in the wake of the Haiti earthquake proved, not only can the Internet be a powerful philanthropic tool, but young people can make significant contributions as well. In an effort to unite these two groups, the social media application Causes links its 119 million users to a bevy of charities across the world, streamlining and centralizing giving like never before.

Founded in 2007, Causes facilitates approximately $1 million in donations a month in addition to corporate-sponsored fundraising campaigns that attract donations from $50,000 to $300,000 apiece. Unlike most socially conscious institutions, Causes operates as a for-profit company in order to avoid the financing bottlenecks associated with nonprofits. Doing so has netted Causes nearly $9 million in venture capital that will allow the company's staff to expand beyond its initial 16-person workforce. Aside from its corporate sponsors, Causes makes money by asking donors for a voluntary "tip" of 10% or more when they give to a charity through the service. And along with its online presence, Causes recently entered the retail market through gift cards that allow the receiver to donate to one of its thousands of affiliated charities. In fact, Causes's birthday app, which encourages users to ask for donations rather than gifts, has generated more than $7.6 million.[i]

lecture link 4-2

CHINA CONFRONTS ITS ETHICAL DEMONS

China recently surpassed Japan to become the world's second largest economy, behind only the United States. As China grows in economic clout, the famously insular nation is expanding its role in global business in ways beyond manufacturing and exporting. But with new international ventures comes the need to adhere to new customs, business practices, and ethical standards.

In order for the still developing nation to modernize itself within the 21st-century business environment, China must improve its dismal record on corruption and environmental issues. For example, China recently came under fire regarding the recent floods caused by landslides. Though described as natural disasters by the state, geologists found that the catastrophic landslides are a direct result of forest destruction, farmland expansion, and overdevelopment of hydroelectric power. The general public isn't fooled, either, with 82.4% of respondents in a recent poll believing that the floods and landslides were human-made. As a result of the outcry, China shut down 2,087 factories with low energy efficiency, taking its first steps toward finding sustainable ways to do business.

According to cases filed under the Foreign Corruption Practices Act (FCPA), China ranks only behind Iran and Nigeria for most criminal corruption prosecutions. Over the years the Chinese business practice of gift giving often devolved into outright bribery. But as the United States and other countries gain footholds within China (and vice versa), the FCPA is used to target major bribery offenders. Under the FCPA, any company, foreign or otherwise, that lists securities on U.S. exchanges is susceptible to prosecution. This allows the FCPA to target major violators like Siemens, which was ordered to pay $450 million in fines for bribery in China and other nations. Chinese bribery laws have also been strengthened in recent years, sometimes resulting in prosecution under both the FCPA and Chinese law. So although Chinese efforts to curb corruption and environmental hazards still linger in their beginning stages, the country is now taking a more active role in targeting some of its most outright offenders.

lecture link 4-3

SELECTED CODES OF ETHICS

Codes of ethics are as unique as the companies that write them. There is no firmly established format for these codes. Below are samples of ethics codes for several major U.S. companies.

ETHICS CODE FOR DELL COMPUTERS

Just as The Soul of Dell articulates our values and beliefs, the following Code of Conduct provides guidance to ensure we meet our higher standard and conduct business the Dell Way—the right way; which is "Winning with Integrity." Simply put, we want all members of our team, our shareholders, customers, suppliers and other stakeholders to understand that they can believe what we say and trust what we do. Our higher standard includes several key components and characteristics that both underpin The Soul of Dell and provide the foundation for our Code of Conduct.

- **Trust**. Our word is good. We keep our commitments to each other and to our stakeholders.

- **Integrity.** We do the right thing without compromise. We avoid even the appearance of impropriety.

- **Honesty.** What we say is true and forthcoming—not just technically correct. We are open and transparent in our communications with each other and about business performance.

- **Judgment.** We think before we act and consider the consequences of our actions.

- **Respect.** We treat people with dignity and value their contributions. We maintain fairness in all relationships.

- **Courage.** We speak up for what is right. We report wrongdoing when we see it.

- **Responsibility.** We accept the consequences of our actions. We admit our mistakes and quickly correct them. We do not retaliate against those who report violations of law or policy.

All of us—regardless of grade level, position, or geographic location—should base our daily actions and conduct on these standards, which support The Soul of Dell and our ultimate success.

CODE OF ETHICS FOR MERCK & COMPANY

1. **Our business is preserving and improving human life.** All of our actions must be measured by our success in achieving this goal. We value, above all, our ability to serve everyone who can benefit from the appropriate use of our products and services, thereby providing lasting consumer satisfaction.

2. **We are committed to the highest standards of ethics and integrity.** We are responsible to our customers, to Merck employees and their families, to the environments we inhabit, and to the societies we serve worldwide. In discharging our responsibilities, we do not take professional or ethical shortcuts. Our interactions with all segments of society must reflect the high standards we profess.

3. **We are dedicated to the highest level of scientific excellence and commit our research to improving human and animal health and the quality of life.** We strive to identify the most critical needs of consumers and customers, and we devote our resources to meeting those needs.

4. **We expect profits, but only from work that satisfies customer needs and benefits humanity.** Our ability to meet our responsibilities depends on maintaining a financial position that invites investment in leading-edge research and that makes possible effective delivery of research result.

5. **We recognize that the ability to excel—to most competitively meet society's and customers' needs—depends on the integrity, knowledge, imagination, skill, diversity and teamwork of our employees, and we value these qualities most highly.** To this end, we strive to create an environment of mutual respect, encouragement and teamwork—an environment that rewards commitment and performance and is responsive to the needs of our employees and their families.

(See **Lecture Link 4-7** on page 4.58 and **Bonus Case 4-2** on page 4.78 of this manual for more on Merck, www.merck.com.)

CODE OF ETHICS FOR JCPENNEY

J. C. Penney founded the retailing company in 1903. In 1913, with 34 stores and 325 employees, he presented his first written code of ethics—"The Penney Idea."

The Penney Idea

- To serve the public, as nearly as we can, to its complete satisfaction

- To expect for the service we render a fair remuneration and not all the profit the traffic will bear

- To do all in our power to pack the customer's dollar full of value, quality and satisfaction

- To continue to train ourselves and our associates so that the service we give will be more and more intelligently performed

- To improve constantly the human factor in our business

- To reward men and women in our organization through participation in what the business produces

- To test our every policy, method and act in this wise: "Does it square with what is right and just?"

CODE OF ETHICS FOR *BUSINESSWEEK* MAGAZINE

1. Our integrity is of the highest caliber.

2. We base our unique brand of journalism on accurate information, gathered honestly and presented fairly.

3. Our professional conduct is unassailable.

4. Our personal conduct, as it reflects on *BusinessWeek*, is beyond reproach.[ii]

lecture link 4-4

APPROACHES TO SOCIAL RESPONSIBILITY

Corporations can take several approaches toward social responsibility:

1. **Reaction**. In this approach, an organization basically has no strategy for social responsibility. It merely reacts to outside influences that might occur.

2. **Defense**. A corporation responds to challenges to its effect on the community only to defend whatever it has been doing.

3. **Accommodation**. Here corporations adapt their policies and behaviors to comply with public policy and regulations. They are attempting to be responsive to what their customers and the public expect.

4. **Proaction**. Organizations with this approach take a leadership role in anticipating what they might do to improve the welfare of their community. They take the initiative in forming their own policy of social responsibility.

lecture link 4-5

CORPORATE RESPONSIBILITY IN THE CLASSROOM

Businesspeople have long debated the role companies should play in the betterment of society. After all, renowned economist Milton Friedman once asserted that a business's only responsibility was to make money for its stockholders. But in these days of mounting environmental concerns and unscrupulous corporate behavior, social responsibility is quickly becoming a hallmark of many companies. In response, some of the nation's top graduate-level business schools added programs on corporate social responsibility to their overall curriculum.

For many companies, getting involved in social concerns can be more than just a reputation booster. Fair business practices like environmental sustainability can increase a company's bottom line as well. And that's exactly what high-level MBA programs across the country are teaching the future executives of America. Schools teach students about corporate social responsibility through case studies with actual companies that have seen overall growth or brand awareness stem from their social initiatives. Campbell Soup Company, for example, is conducting a study on sustainable agriculture and packaging with students at the University of Pennsylvania's Wharton School. Additionally, the nonprofit Net Impact, a global network of business leaders, expanded onto 157 MBA campuses in an effort to get students to work with companies on social issues.

For students, working with these companies can act as brief internships as they move past classroom theory into the reality of today's business environment. Still, most recruiters admit that skills in corporate social responsibility aren't required for new hires. Even aspiring MBAs participating in these programs won't likely seek out jobs in the green sector or other socially responsible industries. Instead, schools hope that students will impart these skills to whatever company they end up working for. Some companies, such as Campbell, are going so far as to train new hires in social concerns with the goal that such knowledge will someday be required in recruiting.[iii]

lecture link 4-6

PHARMACEUTICAL OR FOOD?

As organic and local food movements gain steam, some food companies are responding by providing the consumer public with "healthier" options, even in snack foods. Traditional prepackaged snacks have never been a favorite with nutritionists. Most are high in sugar and fat and provide little nutritional value to the average human. But instead of just cutting down on the fatty stuff that make snack foods so unhealthy, some companies are injecting snacks with supposedly beneficial substances. The result is a line of snacks marketed more as medicine than food. For example, a yogurt-like beverage called ProBugs touts itself as a healthy snack packed with stomach-healing probiotics that help fight antibiotic-associated diarrhea in children.

Besides its less than appetizing marketing campaign, ProBugs simply does not work as advertised. A study commissioned by Lifeway, owners of ProBugs, and published by Georgetown University found that the yogurt does little to curb stomach problems or missed days in school. Other foods like Flax Plus cereal and Sara Lee's Soft & Smooth Plus white bread claim to be rich in heart-protecting omega-3 fatty acids, only they're not the same beneficial fats found primarily in fish. Another product, Dream Water, advertises three additives that can lead to more satisfying sleep. In reality, the data on those additives are mixed at best, with one ingredient not even entering into the brain.

Food companies can make such broad claims thanks to a 1994 law allowing companies to promote the ways their products affect the normal "structure and function" of the body. However, the law prohibits companies from making outright claims that a product can treat disease. Regardless, medicines masquerading as snacks have become big business for food companies, pulling in more than $160 billion worldwide annually. For now the FDA can't do anything to stop these dubious claims due to another law that exempts foods from pharmaceutical-style regulation. In the meantime, consumers are once again warned not to believe everything they read on a product's packaging. Many businesses fail because they fail to please customers. If these products don't live up to promises, do you think they will thrive or disappear?[iv]

lecture link 4-7

MERCK AND ETHICS (PART I)

River blindness is a parasitic disease transmitted to humans through the bite of the common blackfly found along riverbanks. Unlike many other water-born diseases, river blindness occurs only around fast-flowing rivers and not in pools of stagnant water.

Once the parasite is in the bloodstream, it multiples and spreads throughout the body. The adult parasite, which can survive for up to 15 years, produces offspring called microfilaria. The microfilarias cause skin rashes, itching, and blindness. River blindness is most prevalent in sub-Saharan Africa, where 28 countries are affected. The World Health Organization estimates that river blindness afflicts 18 million people worldwide. It is the leading cause of blindness in the developing world.

In the early 1970s researchers at the pharmaceutical company Merck were looking for drugs to treat a host of resistant worm parasites in livestock. The researchers imported bacteria from around the world, more than 100,000 species. Fermented in broths, the organisms produced new compounds. These were tried, one by one, in worm-infested mice. In 1975, they hit the jackpot with a soil bacterium from Japan. The new drug, ivermectin, not only killed all the worms inside the animal, but it also killed biting insects on the skin of the animals after a single dose.

Ivermectin became a financial success with sales greater than those of any other animal health product in the world. It is used against animal parasites in most domestic animals—including cattle, horses, pigs, and dogs.

In 1978, researchers discovered that the drug worked against a parasitic worm in horses, similar to the one that causes river blindness in humans. Researchers at Merck suggested ivermectin be tried on humans. Doctors conducted a human study in Dakar, Senegal, that produced excellent results. Within a year doctors had given the new drug to a few patients with excellent results. Ivermectin does not kill the adult parasitic worms in the patient's body, so it is not a total cure. What it does do is kill off the microworms to keep the adults from producing more offspring. It also showed that a once-a-year dose might be enough to prevent the disease.

Because of these studies, Merck knew that ivermectin could potentially prevent river blindness. But this disease is prevalent among the poorest people in the world. In some of these poverty-stricken countries, only $1 per year per person can be budgeted for public health. These people could not afford the drug even at a price of pennies per year. Merck then asked governments in Africa, Europe, and the United States to purchase ivermectin from Merck (at a low price), but no government agreed to this.

Faced with the fact that it had a drug that could potentially eradicate the disease, Merck announced in 1987 that it would provide ivermectin without charge to as many people as needed it for as long as river blindness remained a threat. "Merck is demonstrating the kind of social responsibility that I hope will spread in the pharmaceutical community," said Merck researcher Dr. William Foege.

The Merck donation program is the largest ongoing medical donation program in history. Treatment programs now exist in 34 countries, and more than 40 million people receive ivermectin to treat river blindness each year. Merck has formed a partnership with the Bill and Melinda Gates Foundation to distribute the drugs. The foundation will put up $50 million, matched by $50 million from Merck. In 2002, Celestina Hiza, a Tanzanian grandmother, received the 250 millionth free dose of the drug.[v]

(See **Bonus Case 4-2** on page 4.78 of this manual for the second part of the Merck story.)

lecture link 4-8

APP-GATE AT UNIVERSITY OF MISSOURI

By their nature, colleges are meant to foster thought and instill in students applicable knowledge that will serve them well outside the university halls. Also hard at work within academic institutions are scholars and researchers who, similar to their pupils, push past the current limits of human understanding in order to better serve the world at large. Some would say that the only distinction between scholar and student is that one is paid to gather information while the other pays for the privilege.

What happens, though, when the two intersect and the student begins making money off the fruits of his or her knowledge and skills? A proud professor may mark the achievement as the sign of a job well done, but the university's bursar office may view it a bit differently. After all, many colleges claim a percentage of the profits from all ventures undertaken by faculty members who use school resources. Why shouldn't the same principles apply to students?

Administrators at the University of Missouri asked this same question when they demanded a 25% ownership stake and two-thirds of any profits from a student-made iPhone app. Undergraduate Tony Brown devised the idea for a smartphone search engine of apartment listings in class and created the app on his own time with three fellow students. Since its launch in March 2009, the app has had hundreds of thousands of downloads and has led to a wealth of job offers for its creators. But the demands of the university had Brown and company shaking as they squared off with an institution far older and better funded than the lot of them. Luckily for the young entrepreneurs, resulting public outcry caused college officials eventually to relent. Mizzou subsequently implemented a policy that keeps the college's hands off any student project spawned from a school contest, extracurricular activity, or individual initiative. This issue is far from resolved nationwide, however, as hundreds of other schools lack similarly explicit policies on their books.[vi]

critical
thinking exercises

Name: _____

Date: _____

critical thinking exercise 4-1
EXPLORING COMMUNITY SERVICE

One of the most common reasons people give for not contributing more of their time to their community is that they don't know where to go to volunteer. You can find out about volunteer options in your zip code by visiting these Internet sites—www.volunteermatch.org, www.1-800-volunteer.org, or www.networkforgood.org.[vii] (Sometimes the Web address for a location changes. You might need to search to find the exact location mentioned.)

1. Go to one of these volunteer websites. Use the site's search tools to see what types of volunteer options are available in your area. If your area is not yet included in the site's database, choose a nearby zip code so that you have an idea of what types of agencies you can contact to offer your services. Write down several volunteer opportunities and the skills required.

2. A new trend in community service is virtual volunteering. Click on the virtual link and search for volunteer opportunities you can do from your computer. Are virtual volunteer opportunities more or less attractive to you than actual hands-on activities? Why?

3. The best way to learn about volunteering is by volunteering, so put your community service plan into action by offering your services to one of the agencies in your area.

critical thinking exercise 4-2
ETHICAL DILEMMAS

Below are several situations that present ethical questions in a business. Discuss each situation (a) from the strictly legal viewpoint, (b) from a moral and ethical viewpoint, and (c) from the point of view of what is best in the long run for the company. Be sure to consider both short- and long-range consequences. Also look at each situation from the perspective of all groups concerned: customers, stockholders, employees, government, and community.

1. A disgruntled employee of your major competitor mails top-secret information or new product samples to you. Do you begin to do a dance on your desktop or do you immediately mail the information back to your competitor? What would you do?

    a. Throw the plans or secrets away.

    b. Send them to your research department for analysis.

    c. Notify your competitor about what is going on.

    d. Call the FBI.

2. You are the general manager of a regional chemical company. In the course of producing your bulk chemicals, large amounts of particles and smoke are emitted through your plant's smoke-stack. The level of pollutants is below current EPA regulations, and you are violating no laws, but neighborhood groups are complaining about minor health problems caused by the smoke. After investigating numerous alternatives, you find the most effective solution would be to install a "scrubber" system, which will remove 90% of the pollutants and ash. Cost: $1 million. Do you install the system?

3. You are a general manager in a cosmetics firm. The results of a study show that your major brand could cause skin cancer. What do you do?

4. You have the opportunity to offer a job to a friend who really needs it. Although you believe that the friend could perform adequately, there are more qualified applicants. What would you do?

5. You are the vice president of a beer company in a state that sets the legal drinking age at 21. Your boss asks you to organize a lobbying effort to have the drinking age reduced to 18. What would you do?

6. Because of a loophole in federal laws you find that you could legally pay your workers less than the minimum wage. The cost savings you recommend may mean your getting a choice promotion. What would you do?

7. You are an accountant in a large firm. Your boss tells you to use a controversial accounting practice, which will make the company's profits seem higher. She tells you it is only to impress stockholders and will not be used in statements submitted to the IRS. What would you do?

8.   You are required to fire a worker for persistent absenteeism, but you know that her absence is because she is caring for her father who is in the advanced stage of Alzheimer's disease. You feel that the organization is being inhumane in its attitude, but your boss remains insistent. What would you do?

9.   A worker is repeatedly late for work. You know she has family problems and is going through a difficult period with an alcoholic husband. Her work is inconsistent—sometimes average, often excellent. She has been with the company for nine years. On Monday she was two hours late for work. What would you do?

10. You believe that your (male) boss is overly friendly with a (female) member of your staff and that she is taking advantage of the situation. What would you do?

notes on critical thinking exercise 4-2

Each of these situations may have several possible solutions. The best solution from the company's point of view may be quite different from one's own philosophical point of view. Below are some discussion points.

1. This actual situation is at the heart of a dispute between rivals 3M Corporation and Johnson & Johnson. It seems a 3M employee named Philip Stegora mailed samples he stole of a new casting tape to J&J and three other competitors. He offered to meet and explain the technology for a fee of $20,000.

   Here's what happened in the 3M and J&J case: None of the contacted companies reported his scheme to 3M. Instead, an outside source contacted 3M, who then turned the case over to the FBI. The case could have ended there, but in patent-infringement proceedings, 3M found that J&J had done chemical tests on the sample Stegora had sent. 3M sued and was awarded $116.3 million from J&J for infringing on its patent and misappropriating trade secrets. Sounds like someone should have sent the tape back to J&J in the first place.

2. In considering whether to install the scrubber, both the short- and long-term consequences should be addressed. While the level of pollution is legal today, is it likely to be regulated tomorrow? What would be the public relations impact for the company if it installed the system? If it did not? Should the company publicize the scrubber installation or avoid discussing pollution at all?

3. The key word in this question is *could*. The evidence is inconclusive. How would the company be affected if the product were pulled prematurely? How would it be affected if the product causes dozens of cancers and results in huge lawsuits?

4. This is a gray area. Hiring a friend may smack of favoritism. However, with a friend you already know about his or her background, reputation, experience, and work ethic. The friend may be the best one for the job if you value his or her abilities. The downside is that you may have to fire your friend, losing an employee and a friendship.

5. Eighteen- to 21-year-olds represent a huge market for liquor. But, again, the public reaction should be considered.

6. Many smaller companies are exempt from minimum wage laws but still pay the prevailing wage. The supply and demand for workers is a more important price factor. A company that pays less than minimum wage will not be able to attract as many qualified workers as one that does.

7. This is the only black and white dilemma. To use dual accounting practices to deceive investors is illegal.

8. This is a direct order from your superior. You might take a meeting with the supervisor to explain the extenuating circumstances, but if there's no change in his or her position, you will have to fire the employee or be ready to leave your job.

9. This worker is going through a difficult time. Her work is, however, "often excellent." The costs of training a replacement worker must be weighed against her possibly temporary reduction in productivity.

10.   Your boss is guilty of sexual harassment. The female member of your staff may be taking advantage of it, but that does not change the reality. The boss's actions may open up your company to a sexual harassment law suit. Fighting it will be costly and generate bad publicity. The boss needs to be warned, although you might not be the one to do it. If you have a mentor in the firm or a sympathetic friend in upper management, you might approach him or her, confidentially, about the situation. If you decide to talk to the boss yourself, how would you handle the encounter? What could your first sentence possibly be?

critical thinking exercise 4-3
RESEARCHING CODES OF ETHICS

Most companies now publish codes of ethics to provide ethical guidelines for employees. Many of the larger companies publish these codes on their websites, but they may be hard to find.

The Center for the Study of Ethics in the Professions (CSEP) has collected over 850 codes of ethics and put them on its website (http://ethics.iit.edu/codes/). (Sometimes the Web address for a location changes. You might need to search to find the exact location mentioned.) The collection includes codes of ethics for professional societies, corporations, government, and academic institutions. Earlier versions of codes of ethics of some organizations are available so you can study the development of codes.

(Some of the more interesting codes of ethics that CSEP has collected are the codes of ethics for the CIA and for Enron.)

1. Locate the codes of ethics for an educational institution, a media organization, and a business organization. What do the three codes have in common? In what ways do they differ?

2. Find a company for which a previous code is available (such as IBM). Review the key sections. How has the code changed?

critical thinking exercise 4-4
ETHICS MINICASES

Below are six short cases about real-world ethical dilemmas. For each minicase, consider what decision you would make or action you would take.

MINICASE 1. Recycling and Unintended Consequences

In 2009, the United States switched from analog to digital TV transmission. The digital signals provide a much clearer picture and allow broadcasters to squeeze more channels into existing transmission bands. In order to receive the new signal, however, the viewer must have a TV that accepts digital signals or purchase a converter box to convert analog signals from older TVs into digital form.

Televisions that are carelessly disposed of can be toxic to the environment. A huge backlog of unused older TVs were sitting around in people's homes in 2008, as many as 99 million, according to the Environmental Protection Agency (EPA). With the switch to analog, the number of unwanted TVs skyrocketed as consumers upgraded to sets capable of receiving high-definition broadcasts.

Though a TV set is benign in the living room, it can be dangerous when broken up to reach the reusable materials inside. There's a lot of lead, a bit of barium, cadmium, chromium, traces of gold, and even mercury. The best way to deal with them is not to throw them away at all but to keep using them, says the EPA.

Under EPA rules, cathode-ray tube TVs aren't supposed to be put into landfills, but households are exempt. It's also illegal to export them for recycling unless the destination country agrees and the EPA has been notified. But the Government Accountability Office (GAO) found that recycling companies routinely circumvent the rule. The problem, according to a GAO report last year, is that the EPA's enforcement is notably lacking.

The GAO report found that although some electronics are handled responsibly, "a substantial quantity ends up in countries where disposal practices are unsafe to workers and dangerous to the environment."[viii]

1.   If you were a member of the state legislature, what would you do, if anything?

2.   If you were a public official (county or parish), what would you do, if anything?

3.   If you were the CEO of a company manufacturing TVs, what would you do, if anything?

MINICASE 2. Wireless Wardriving

A car equipped with a laptop computer, a portable GPS receiver, and a wireless network card drives through your neighborhood. Unknown to onlookers, the people in this car are actually "wardriving," scanning for any wireless access points. Anyone with a wireless router is vulnerable.

Since the wireless router is designed to extend the radio signal providing an Internet connection, its range can reach up to 150 feet—into the street, the yard, even the neighbors' houses. The mobile computer is looking for an SSID, the wireless network name people assign to their home networks. The SSID is constantly broadcast by the network's access point, letting computers know of its presence. The wardriver uses software to scan the airwaves for SSIDs. Using the GPS receiver, he or she records the coordinates of the strong signal. Once the SSID and GPS are collected, wardrivers usually post open wireless access point locations online, documenting their successes. The wardriver can use the victim's Internet access and can explore computers on the network. If files are shared within someone's private network, all that information is available to the wardriver, including the user's passwords and credit card numbers used on the Internet. Wireless network vulnerability has become a major problem—10 million American homes use a wireless router.

Most wardrivers think of themselves as freewheeling rebels. They drive along, using their technical savvy to embarrass careless network administrators. If they find an unprotected company network, some wardrivers then notify companies when they find vulnerable networks. This form of wardriving in itself is legal. In 2004, CNET, the computing and technology news service, hired a research assistant to search out open wireless networks. In a suburban five-block drive, the research assistant found 40 access points. Only 8 of them had any kind of encryption turned on. The remaining access points were wide open, including 8 in a local school and 1 in a firehouse.

Gathering information is no crime, but it's illegal to access found networks. In 2003 Paul Timmins and Adam Botbyl, members of the Michigan 2600 group of hackers, found this out. They were wardriving in Southfield, Michigan, when they came upon a Lowe's hardware store with an open wireless network. What Timmins did next was technically illegal: He used the Lowe's network to check his e-mail. When he realized it was Lowe's private network, however, he disconnected. Lowe's became aware of the breach and contacted the FBI, who charged Timmins with one count of unauthorized computer access.

Some insiders believe that Lowe's was partially responsible for the breach for not ensuring its private wireless network was not leaking information. Others ask why consumers should not be able to sue companies that are negligent with their personal data. California has passed a law that makes companies more responsible for protecting personal information, with stiff penalties for failure to report any compromises.[ix]

1.   Who is more responsible for breach in wireless security—the drivers who search for unsecured networks or the owners/managers who leave their networks unprotected?

2.   Are the wardrivers' actions ethical? Explain.

3.   Do you believe wardriving is harmless or a crime?

MINICASE 3. Funding Cancer Research

In October 2006, Dr. Claudia Henschke released a study that showed that 80% of the lung cancer deaths could be prevented through widespread use of CT scans. Lung cancer, by far the biggest cause of cancer deaths in the United States, kills 160,000 people a year. The death rate is particularly depressing because so few lung cancers can be cured—most are discovered too late for treatment to be effective.

Dr. Henschke, of the Weill Cornell Medical College, published the study in the *New England Journal of Medicine*. Henschke's study involved screening 31,567 people from seven countries with a specialized CT scanning procedure, called "spiral CT screening." The screening uncovered 484 lung cancers, 412 of them at a very early stage. Three years later, most of those patients were still alive.

Dr. Henschke's work, while controversial among cancer researchers, has been embraced by many lung cancer advocacy organizations, which have pushed for legislation in California, New York, and Massachusetts to pay for lung cancer screening. However, critics question her survival projections and her assumption that all would have died without screening. CT scans also have radiation risks and sometimes detect cancers that would not have progressed, leading to risky medical procedures that may not be needed.

The small print at the end of the study noted that it had been financed in part by a little-known charity called the Foundation for Lung Cancer: Early Detection, Prevention & Treatment. Dr. Henschke and her longtime collaborator, Dr. David Yankelevitz, were both officers of the foundation, which was formed so quickly that its 2000 tax return stated "not yet organized."

A review of tax records by the *New York Times* revealed that the foundation was underwritten almost entirely by $3.6 million in grants from the parent company of the Liggett Group, maker of Liggett Select, Eve, Grand Prix, Quest, and Pyramid cigarette brands.

An increasing number of universities do not accept grants from cigarette makers. A growing awareness of the influence that companies can have over research outcomes has led nearly all medical journals and associations to demand that researchers accurately disclose financing sources. Following the *New York Times* article publication, the *Journal of the American Medical Association* published corrections about unreported financial disclosures of. Dr. Henschke and Dr. Yankelevitz. The editor's note stated that the journal was not aware of Dr. Henschke's association with Liggett.[x]

1. Should the funding for the study have been disclosed? Why or why not?

2. Do you believe that the funding source affected the results?

3. What was the responsibility of the medical journals to determine the study's validity and funding?

MINICASE 4. Off-Label Drug Prescriptions

Before it can be prescribed in the United States, a pharmaceutical manufacturer must convince the Food and Drug Administration (FDA) that a drug is both safe and effective against at least one disease. Any potential new drug must undergo a demanding sequence of tests to win FDA approval. If the preliminary first stage test-tube trials go well, the proposed medicine then moves into clinical trials using human subjects. Many drugs fail in preliminary or clinical trial levels. This kind of drug trial is considered the "gold standard" of proof for a drug's value. According to industry estimates, it costs around $800 million to bring a drug to market. Once the drug is approved for one use, the race is on to profit from the investment before the patent expires.

When the new drug enters the U.S. market, doctors are legally free to prescribe it "off-label" for any other condition. Prescribing drugs for off-label uses is nothing new. Doctors have been doing it for decades to treat rare diseases, pediatric disorders (for which medicines are often not specifically approved), and various cancers. Many doctors feel the practice can save lives. Statins, for example, were initially approved to lower cholesterol but are now heavily prescribed to prevent heart attacks and strokes (and blessed by regulators). Since 1998, the number of off-label prescriptions has nearly doubled. By some estimates, off-label use of prescription medications occurs in about one in every five prescriptions filled in the United States.

The potential for abuse can be seen in the case of Warner-Lambert's drug Neurontin. The drug was initially approved only for treating epilepsy, a relatively small market. However, in the 1990s, Warner-Lambert salespeople paid doctors to prescribe Neurontin for ailments ranging from manic depression to restless leg syndrome, although the company had evidence that the drug was ineffective for those ailments. The firm also hired ghost writers to draft articles promoting off-label uses. They then located doctors to willingly lend their names as authors for a $1,000 "honorarium." Neurontin sales came in at $2.7 billion in 2003, with off-label prescriptions accounting for an estimated 90%.[xi]

1.   Should the practice of prescribing drugs off-label be restricted or regulated? Why or why not?

2.   Did Warner-Lambert sales personnel act ethically in encouraging off-label use for Neurontin? Unethically? Explain.

3.   What are the prescribing physicians' ethical responsibilities in writing off-label prescriptions?

4.   Should physicians be required to disclose to patients when they have been compensated by a drug company?

notes on critical thinking exercise 4-4

MINICASE 1.

The students' reactions to this case will depend upon their view on regulation. Interesting discussion topic in today's political environment.

MINICASE 2.

Several states have passed laws to deter wardrivers. In California, there are laws forbidding the publication of networks without the network owner's permission, thus eliminating the widespread practice of posting open network addresses on the Internet. Nevada is also considering such a law.

If a wardriver enters the network without permission, laws already exist to protect businesses and individuals from invasion of privacy or theft of information. From the legal point of view, companies have a "presumed expectation of privacy." If a company installs the basic safeguards—such as antivirus software and a firewall—they have fulfilled their responsibility to protect their proprietary information. If someone gets onto their network, it is considered "intrusion," the electronic version of breaking and entering. Laws that are more specific are needed to define the concept of intrusion and to set realistic penalties if the law is broken.

MINICASE 3.

Regardless of the validity of this study, the results will be questioned because of the tobacco funding. Sad result—wasted resources and no progress in medical care.

MINICASE 4.

In 2004, Warner-Lambert pled guilty to two counts of violating the Food, Drug, and Cosmetic Act by misbranding Neurontin, failing to provide adequate directions for use, and participating in interstate commerce of an unapproved drug. Immediately after the verdict, Judge Richard Stearns sentenced the company to pay a $240 million fine, the second largest criminal fine ever imposed in a health care fraud prosecution.

critical thinking exercise 4-5

SOCIAL RESPONSIBILITY SUCCESSES AND FAILURES

Name at least one example of a company that succeeded or failed to be socially responsible in each of the categories below. Describe the success or failure. Record the exact URL (Web address) of the site you visit.

CATEGORY	SUCCESS	FAILURE
Corporate Philanthropy	Company: URL: Description:	Company: URL: Description:
Employee Health and Safety	Company: URL: Description:	Company: URL: Description:
Environmental Stewardship	Company: URL: Description:	Company: URL: Description:
Minority and Women's Employment and Advancement	Company: URL: Description:	Company: URL: Description:

<u>critical thinking exercise 4-6</u>
SURVEYING PUBLIC INTEREST ORGANIZATIONS

Newspapers and the Internet are full of stories about individuals and organizations that are not socially responsible. What about those individuals and organizations that do take social responsibility seriously? We don't read about them as often. Do a little investigative reporting of your own. List two of the public interest power groups in your community and identify their officers, their objectives, their sources, and the amount of financial support they receive, the size and characteristics of their membership, and examples of their recent actions and/or accomplishments.

1.   **ORGANIZATION**   Sources of Funds   Annual Budget

_____   _____   _____

Officers

_____

_____

Size and Characteristics of Membership _____

_____

Objectives

_____

_____

_____

Recent Actions and/or Accomplishments _____

_____

_____

2.   **ORGANIZATION**   Sources of Funds   Annual Budget

_____   _____   _____

Officers
_____

_____

Size and Characteristics of Membership _____

_____

Objectives
_____

_____

_____

Recent Actions and/or Accomplishments _____

_____

_____

notes on critical thinking exercise 4-6

Students can research these organizations on the Internet or call the local Chamber of Commerce or Better Business Bureau for help. Also, they can call local government agencies or visit government websites and see what private firms are operating in your area that have the public interest in mind. For example, there are likely to be environmental groups, animal protection groups, and political action committees.

bonus cases

bonus case 4-1

WAL-MART'S VIRGINIA BATTLEGROUND

Although many criticisms have been lodged against Wal-Mart, perhaps the most common complaint is the negative effects the retail giant's stores have on the small communities they inhabit. After all, Wal-Mart has long been the enemy of local businesses that can't compete with the company's low prices. But recently in Fredericksburg, Virginia, anti-Wal-Mart troops gathered to combat another form of encroachment on the community—the construction of a new Supercenter near a Civil War battle site.

Nearly 150 years ago 185,000 Union and Confederate troops fought at the Battle of the Wilderness, a clash that took some 30,000 lives and marked the beginning of the end of the Civil War. Though the proposed store would lie one mile from the battle site's national park entrance, historical preservationists and residents protested the plans even after Orange County officials approved construction. A lawsuit filed against the county's decision soon garnered support from hundreds of historians as well as celebrities like actor Robert Duvall and filmmaker Ken Burns. According to the plaintiffs, county supervisors ignored the input of preservationists, who claim the proposed store site served as the Union's "nerve center" during the battle.

Wal-Mart and government officials countered their opponents by claiming the land was zoned for commercial use and located in an area that already had a retail presence. With both sides armed and anxious, a looming January 27 court date set the stage for a lengthy legal struggle to overturn the county's controversial 2009 decision. But a day before the trial was to begin, Wal-Mart abruptly announced it was abandoning plans to build on the site. The company's sudden withdrawal came with a low-key response from a spokesperson saying, "We just felt it was the right thing to do." Rather than face a protracted courtroom melee and an unsure outcome, Wal-Mart simply waved the white flag over the whole affair.[xii]

discussion questions for bonus case 4-1

1. Why did Wal-Mart give up the fight to build near the historic site? Discuss.

2. What type of research does Wal-Mart do before picking a site for a new store?

3. Do you think that Wal-Mart had a right to build on a site that was near an official historic site and that already had other retail stores? Explain.

notes on discussion questions for bonus case 4-1

1. *Why did Wal-Mart give up the fight to build near the historic site? Discuss.*

    Only Wal-Mart knows the exact answer to that question, but our guess is that they believed the publicity that the construction near the historic site would generate was not worth the effort.

2. *What type of research does Wal-Mart do before picking a site for a new store?*

    Wal-Mart conducts extensive research and collects information about traffic patterns, population demographics, local government attitude, and many more factors before deciding to build a new store.

3. *Do you think that Wal-Mart had a right to build on a site that was near an official historic site and that already had other retail stores? Explain.*

    Answers will vary.

MERCK AND ETHICS (PART II)

Discovered in a Merck lab in 1994, the drug was one of a new class of painkillers called COX-2 inhibitors, which reduce pain and inflammation without the side effects—ulcers and gastrointestinal bleeding—that painkillers such as ibuprofen can cause. Vioxx worked beautifully in clinical trials with arthritis patients and was approved by the FDA in 1999. Edward Scolnick, president of Merck Research Labs, even let it be known that he was taking Vioxx himself for back pain.

But in September 2004, Merck removed Vioxx from the market after a study found a higher rate of heart attacks and strokes in patients taking the drug. Vioxx, on the market for five years, had been marketed in 80 countries with worldwide sales totaling $2.5 billion in 2003. When it was pulled from the market, 2 million Americans were taking Vioxx.

The pharmaceutical industry was astonished that the well-respected company had marketed a drug known to cause higher rates of cardiac events. Almost 20 years earlier Merck established a reputation for social responsibility by donating a treatment for river blindness to patients in developing countries.

Still more shocking was the admission that as far back as 1998 Merck knew the drug had problems. Even before FDA approval, researchers outside Merck had found evidence that it might increase the risk of a heart attack. In 1998 a group at the University of Pennsylvania discovered that COX-2 inhibitors interfere with enzymes thought to ward off cardiovascular disease. A 2001 study testing the drug against nonprescription naproxen showed that Vioxx was safer than naproxen, but it also found that Vioxx doubled the risk of cardiovascular problems. Merck put a positive spin on the data, highlighting the lower risk of side effects, not the cardiac complications.

By April 2002, the FDA mandated that Merck note a possible link to heart attacks and strokes on Vioxx's label. At the time, Merck was spending more than $100 million a year on direct-to-consumer advertising building the "blockbuster" status of the drug.

Merck continued to minimize the problems up until a month before withdrawing the drug. The deathblow to the drug was the results of APPROVe, a database analysis of 1.4 million patients. Ironically, this study was designed to test whether Vioxx reduced the risk of colon polyps. Instead, it showed that patients who took the drug for at least 18 months had double the risk of heart attacks and strokes as those who took the placebo. For a few weeks, Merck focused on the fact that it took 18 months for Vioxx to cause problems. However, Merck researchers continued crunching the data and concluded that the safety window might be as little as three months.

The researchers who told Merck CEO Ray Gilmartin about the APPROVe results pointed out that the company was under no obligation to recall the drug. Merck could take the data to the FDA and have the labeling changed. In fact, the majority of outside clinicians whom Merck consulted in the first few days suggested it do just that, since there were millions of people who were benefiting from Vioxx and not getting heart attacks. But Gilmartin decided that withdrawing the drug was the responsible thing to do.

Since the drug was withdrawn, investigators have linked Vioxx to more than 27,000 heart attacks or sudden cardiac deaths nationwide from the time it came on the market in 1999 through 2003. Over 11,000 lawsuits have been filed against Merck.[xiii]

discussion questions for bonus case 4-2

1.   If Merck can donate $50 million in free doses of ivermectin, what does that say about the amount of revenue the company generates in the drug research and distribution industry?

2.   In the case of Vioxx, known serious side effects were being reported and yet the company was slow to suspend or remove the drug from the market. What does this say about the approval process of drugs to the market and why companies would be reluctant to give up the revenue stream for a commonly used drug like Vioxx?

3.   Merck finally pulls Vioxx from the market and has 11,000 lawsuits to handle. How would you feel if you were the company president and you were a known name and face of a company that was responsible for the stroke or heart attack of a past user of the drug?

notes on discussion questions for bonus case 4-2

1.   *If Merck can donate $50 million in free doses of ivermectin, what does that say about the amount of revenue the company generates in the drug research and distribution industry?*

Drug companies are some of the highest revenue producers and very profitable if they get their drugs into the mainstream use without any major problems. In the case of Merck, it appears to be one of these types of drug companies. However, the process of research and FDA approval can be tedious and costly with no guarantees that their products are going to be successes on the market.

2.   *In the case of Vioxx, known serious side effects were being reported and yet the company was slow to suspend or remove the drug from the market. What does this say about the approval process of drugs to the market and why companies would be reluctant to give up the revenue stream for a commonly used drug like Vioxx?*

Market success, as already mentioned, is a conclusion to a commitment of research and numerous expenses for the low percentage that they will have a successful drug reach the marketplace. As a result, getting to this level is a huge potential payoff for the company and therefore a difficult reality to remove this product from the most sought after objective of the company—market approval and market success.

3.   *Merck finally pulls Vioxx from the market and has 11,000 lawsuits to handle. How would you feel if you were the company president and you were a known name and face of a company that was responsible for the stroke or heart attack of a past user of the drug?*

The president of Merck works at such a high level and has such responsibilities, especially to the stockholders of the company, that his business training and business acumen allow him or her to handle these types of situations. The average person would be too emotional and would not be equipped to deal with these types of situations, as compared to the seasoned company president or CEO.

bonus case 4-3

A GLANCE INTO THE FUTURE: YOUR COMPUTER KNOWS

Microsoft has been on a patent roll. In recent years, it has been one of the U.S. Patent and Trademark Office's biggest customers.

But it's one particular filing that has been grabbing headlines recently. That is a patent application filed by the company for a computer system that links workers to their computers via wireless sensors that measure their metabolism. The system would allow managers to monitor employees' performance by measuring their heart rate, body temperature, movement, facial expression, and blood pressure.

Technology allowing constant monitoring of workers was previously limited to pilots, firefighters, and NASA astronauts. This is believed to be the first time a company has proposed developing such software for mainstream workplaces.

Microsoft submitted a patent application for a "unique monitoring system" that could link workers to their computers. Wireless sensors could read "heart rate, galvanic skin response, EMG, brain signals, respiration rate, body temperature, movement facial movements, facial expressions, and blood pressure," the application states.

The system could also "automatically detect frustration or stress in the user" and "offer and provide assistance accordingly." Physical changes to an employee would be matched to an individual psychological profile based on a worker's weight, age, and health. If the system picked up an increase in heart rate or facial expressions suggestive of stress or frustration, it would tell management that he or she needed help.

Microsoft, which typically does not comment on individual applications, did offer a bit of comment on this patent. According to Horacio Gutierrez, Microsoft's vice president of intellectual property and licensing, this application could monitor a user heart rate, among other physical states, detect when users need assistance with their activities, and offer assistance by putting them in touch with other users who may be able to help. "It is important to keep in mind that with most organizations in the business of innovation, some of our patent applications reflect inventions that are currently present in our products, and other applications represent innovations being developed for potential future use."

Trolling through filings can offer a glimpse of where a company is headed, but seeing something in a patent application is far from a guarantee of what will eventually ship. The U.S. Patent Office will decide whether to grant the patent in about a year.[xiv]

discussion questions for bonus case 4-3

1. Do you think Microsoft's patent application should be approved by the U.S. Patent and Trademark Office? Why or why not?

2. Do you think monitoring of employees in this way is ethical or unethical? Legal or illegal? Explain.

3. Would you work for a company if you knew a computer system was monitoring your performance and measuring your vital signs? Why or why not?

notes on discussion questions for bonus case 4-3

1. *Do you think Microsoft's patent application should be approved by the U.S. Patent and Trademark Office? Why or why not?*

   Generally, to qualify for a patent the product must be "new, inventive, and useful or industrially applicable." The Patent Office does not decide whether the product or idea is ethical or unethical—simply whether it is new and innovative.

2. *Do you think monitoring of employees in this way is ethical or unethical? Legal or illegal? Explain.*

   Interesting discussion. On one hand, the monitoring system will improve productivity by reducing employee time spent in nonwork activities. On the other hand, such a system will be intrusive and smacks of "big brother."

3. *Would you work for a company if you knew a computer system was monitoring your performance and measuring your vital signs? Why or why not?*

   Each student will have an individual opinion, based on his or her interpretation of individual privacy versus employer rights.

endnotes

[i] *Source:* Douglas MacMillan, "Philanthropy: Causes, the Socially Conscious Network," *Bloomberg Businessweek*, October 21, 2010.

[ii] *Sources*: Corporate websites.

[iii] *Source:* Alina Dizik, "Social Concerns Gain New Urgency," *The Wall Street Journal*, March 4, 2010.

[iv] *Source:* Matthew Harper and Rebecca Ruiz, "Snake Oil in Your Snacks," *Forbes*, June 7, 2010.

[v] *Sources:* Erick Eckholm, "River Blindness: Conquering an Ancient Scourge," *The New York Times*, January 8, 1989; P. Roy Vagelos, "Social Benefits of a Successful Biomedical Research Company: Merck," *Proceedings of the American Philosophical Society,* Vol. 145, December 2001; "Commitment to Society: Merck Expands Its Commitment to Eliminate River Blindness," Merck corporate website, www.merck.com; David Shook, "How Merck Is Treating the Third World," *BusinessWeek,* October 10, 2002; Daniel Dickinson, "River Blindness Drug Revives Village Life," *BBC News*, September 15, 2002.

[vi] *Source:* Associated Press, "Colleges Going to School on Apps," *Investors Business Daily*, January 24, 2011.

[vii] The Internet is a dynamic, changing information source. Web links noted of this manual were checked at the time of publication, but content may change over time. Please review the website before recommending it to your students.

[viii] *Sources:* Elizabeth Weise, "Old TVs Cause New Problems," *USA Today*, January 26, 2009; "Buyback Programs Turn Electronic Trash to Cash," *ZDNet News,* March 23, 2008.

[ix] *Sources*: Matt Lake, "When Does Wardriving Cross the Double Yellow Line?" *CNET Reviews*, June 29, 2004; Robert Vamosi, "Real-World Wardriving Arrests," *ZDNet AnchorDesk,* September 17, 2004; Zackary Anderson, "What Is Wardriving and How Can You Prevent It?" *webpronews.com*, August 18, 2004; Corilyn Shropshire, "Hot Spots for Hackers: Wireless Networks," *Pittsburgh Post-Gazette*, March 27, 2005; D. Brian Burghrt, "Wardriving Is Not a Crime," RN&R *Newsreview.com*.

[x] *Source:* Gardiner Harris, "Cigarette Company Paid for Lung Cancer Study," *The New York Times*, March 26, 2008.

[xi] *Sources*: Daren Fonda and Barbara Kiviat, "Curbing the Drug Marketers," *Time*, July 5, 2004; "'Off-Label Prescription Drug Use Common," *Forbes*, May 8, 2006; Bernadette Tansy, "Why Doctors Prescribe Off Label," *San Francisco Chronicle*, May 1, 2005; "Warner-Lambert Pleads Guilty and Is Sentenced for Criminal Health Care Fraud Relating to Off-Label Promotion of Drug Neurontin, Reports U.S. Attorney," *PR Newswire*, June 7, 2004; Rita Rubin, "Study: Off-Label Drugs Should Be Researched for Safety," *USA Today,* November 24, 2008.

[xii] *Sources*: Kenneth H. Hammonds, "Harry Kraemer's Moment of Truth," *Fast Company*, November 2002, p. 93; Michael Arndt, "How Does Baxter's Harry Kraemer Do It?" *BusinessWeek Online*, July 22, 2002; "Baxter Announces Harry Kraemer to Resign as Chairman and CEO," *PR Newswire*; Keith Hammonds, "Moment of Truth?" *Fast Company*, April 2004; Bruce Japsen, "Baxter International Works to Resolve Drug-Delivery Pump Issues," *Chicago Tribune*, October 21, 2005.

[xiii] *Sources*: Rita Rubin, "How Did Vioxx Debacle Happen?" *USA Today*, October 12, 2004; John Simons and David Stipp, "Will Merck Survive Vioxx?" *Fortune*, October 18, 2004; Matthew Herper, "The Vioxx Maelstrom," *Forbes,* May 22, 2006; "Vioxx Risk Seen With Short-Term Use—Report," *Reuters*, May 17, 2006.

[xiv] *Sources*: Alexi Mostrous and David Brown, "Microsoft Seeks Patent for Office 'Spy' Software," *The Times of London*, January 16, 2008; Ina Fried, "Microsoft Revs Its Patent Machine," http://news.cnet.com, January 16, 2008; www.uspto.gov.

How to Form a Business

chapter 5

what's new in this edition

additions to the 10th edition:

- Getting to Know Mary Ellen Sheets, Founder of Two Men and a Truck
- Name That Company: H&R Block
- Discussion of online franchising added to section E-Commerce in Franchising
- Social Media in Business: Franchise Expansion on Facebook
- Video Case

revisions to the 10th edition:

- Text was revised to eliminate redundancy and tighten discussions.
- Statistical data and examples throughout the chapter were updated to reflect current information.
- Legal Briefcase: Virtual Companies
- Thinking Green: Play Ball but Play Green
- Spotlight on Small Business: The Ties That Bind

deletions from the 9th edition:

- Getting to Know Brian Scudmore, Founder of 1-800-GOT-JUNK
- Name That Company: Mary Ellen Sheets and Two Men and a Truck

brief chapter outline
and learning goals

How to Form a Business

Getting To Know MARY ELLEN SHEETS of the TWO MEN AND A TRUCK

I. BASIC FORMS OF BUSINESS OWNERSHIP

learning goal 1

Compare the advantages and disadvantages of sole proprietorships.

II. SOLE PROPRIETORSHIPS

A. Advantages of Sole Proprietorships

B. Disadvantages of Sole Proprietorships

learning goal 2

Describe the differences between general and limited partners, and compare the advantages and disadvantages of partnerships.

III. PARTNERSHIPS

A. Advantages of Partnerships

B. Disadvantages of Partnerships

learning goal 3

Compare the advantages and disadvantages of corporations, and summarize the differences between C corporations, S corporations, and limited liability companies.

IV. CORPORATIONS

A. Advantages of Corporations

B. Disadvantages of Corporations

C. Individuals Can Incorporate

D. S Corporations

E. Limited Liability Companies

learning goal 4

Define and give examples of three types of corporate mergers, and explain the role of leveraged buyouts and taking a firm private.

V. CORPORATE EXPANSION: MERGERS AND ACQUISITIONS

learning goal 5

Outline the advantages and disadvantages of franchises, and discuss the opportunities for diversity in franchising and the challenges of global franchising.

VI. FRANCHISES

- A. Advantages of Franchises
- B. Disadvantages of Franchises
- C. Diversity in Franchising
- D. Home-Based Franchises
- E. E-Commerce in Franchising
- F. Using Technology in Franchising
- G. Franchising in Global Markets

learning goal 6

Explain the role of cooperatives.

VII. COOPERATIVES

VIII. WHICH FORM OF OWNERSHIP IS FOR YOU?

IX. SUMMARY

lecture outline

Getting to Know MARY ELLEN SHEETS of TWO MEN AND A TRUCK

Mary Ellen Sheets started her company when her sons were in college. They were looking for ways to make some money so she bought a truck for $350 and placed an advertisement under "Movers" in the classified section of the newspaper. When the boys went back to school, she found more men to fill the trucks. Now it's a large company bringing in $193.3 million annually with 215 franchise locations.

Around April 15 every year, we are a very sought out company. With thousands of locations in the United States we make tax filing much easier. Most people are unaware that we are actually a Canadian franchise even though we have our headquarters in the United States.

(Students should read the chapter before guessing the company's name: H&R Block)

I. BASIC FORMS OF BUSINESS OWNERSHIP

A. About 600,000 new businesses are started in the U.S. each year.

B. The form of business ownership can make a difference in the success of the business.

C. The **THREE MAJOR FORMS OF BUSINESS OWNERSHIP** are:

   1. A **_SOLE PROPRIETORSHIP_** is a business that is owned, and usually managed, by one person; it is the most common form.

   2. A **_PARTNERSHIP_** is a legal form of business with two or more owners.

   3. A **_CORPORATION_** is a legal entity with authority to act and have liability separate from its owners.

D. Each form of business ownership has its advantages and its disadvantages.

PPT 5-1
Chapter Title

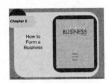

PPT 5-2
Learning Goals

(See complete PowerPoint slide notes on page 5.44.)

PPT 5-3
Learning Goals

(See complete PowerPoint slide notes on page 5.44.)

PPT 5-4
Mary Ellen Sheets

(See complete PowerPoint slide notes on page 5.45.)

PPT 5-5
Name That Company

(See complete PowerPoint slide notes on page 5.45.)

PPT 5-6
Major Forms of Ownership

(See complete PowerPoint slide notes on page 5.45.)

PPT 5-7
Forms of Business Ownership

TEXT FIGURE 5.1
Forms of Business Ownership
(Text page 116)

(See complete PowerPoint slide notes on page 5.46.)

lecture link 5-1
THE *FORTUNE* LIST OF MOST ADMIRED CORPORATIONS

Each year *Fortune* magazine asks industry experts which corporations it admires. This lecture link gives the *Fortune* listing for 2006 to 2011. (See the complete lecture link on page 5.62 in this manual.)

<u>**learning goal** 1</u>

Compare the advantages and disadvantages of sole proprietorships.

II. SOLE PROPRIETORSHIPS

A. ADVANTAGES OF SOLE PROPRIETORSHIPS

1. Ease of **STARTING AND ENDING** the business.

   a. After you rent or buy the equipment, all you need is a permit from the local government.

   b. To get out of business, you just quit.

2. **BEING YOUR OWN BOSS.** Working for yourself is exciting.

3. **PRIDE OF OWNERSHIP**. Sole proprietors take the risk and deserve the credit.

4. **LEAVING A LEGACY** behind for future generations.

5. **RETENTION OF COMPANY PROFITS**. You don't have to share profits with anyone.

6. **NO SPECIAL TAXES.** Profits of the business are taxed as the personal income of the owner.

B. DISADVANTAGES OF SOLE PROPRIETORSHIPS

1. Unlimited liability—the risk of personal losses

   a. You and the business are one.

   b. <u>***UNLIMITED LIABILITY***</u> is the responsibility of business owners for all of the debts of the business.

2. **LIMITED FINANCIAL RESOURCES**: Financing is limited to the funds that the sole owner can gather.

3. **MANAGEMENT DIFFICULTIES**: Many owners are not skilled at management and with details such as accounting.

PPT 5-8
Ethnic Business Centers

(See complete PowerPoint slide notes on page 5.46.)

PPT 5-9
Major Benefits of Sole
Proprietorship

(See complete PowerPoint slide notes on page 5.46.)

PPT 5-10
Disadvantages of Sole
Proprietorship

(See complete PowerPoint slide notes on page 5.47.)

4. **OVERWHELMING TIME COMMITMENT**

    a. The owner has no one with whom to share the burden.

    b. A business owner may work 12 hours a day.

5. **FEW FRINGE BENEFITS:**

    a. You have no paid vacation or health insurance.

    b. Fringe benefits can add up to 30% of a worker's compensation.

6. **LIMITED GROWTH:** Expansion is slow.

7. **LIMITED LIFE SPAN.** If the sole proprietor dies or leaves, the business ends.

learning goal 2

Describe the differences between general and limited partners, and compare the advantages and disadvantages of partnerships.

III. PARTNERSHIPS

A. A **PARTNERSHIP** is a legal form of business with two or more owners.

B. **TYPES OF PARTNERSHIPS**

1. A ***GENERAL PARTNERSHIP*** is a partnership in which all owners share in operating the business and in assuming liability for the business's debts.

2. A ***LIMITED PARTNERSHIP*** is a partnership with one or more general partners and one or more limited partners.

    a. A ***GENERAL PARTNER*** is an owner (partner) who has unlimited liability and is active in managing the firm.

Progress
assessment
(Text page 119)

PPT 5-11
Progress Assessment   (See complete PowerPoint slide notes on page 5.47.)

PPT 5-12
Major Types of Partnerships

(See complete PowerPoint slide notes on page 5.47.)

    b.   A **_LIMITED PARTNER_** is an owner who invests money in the business but does not have any management responsibility or liability for losses beyond the investment.

    c.   **_LIMITED LIABILITY_** is the responsibility of a business's owners for losses only up to the amount they invest; limited partners and shareholders have limited liability.

3. **_MASTER LIMITED PARTNERSHIP (MLP)_** is a partnership that looks much like a corporation (in that it acts like a corporation and is traded on a stock exchange) but is taxed like a partnership and thus avoids the corporate income tax.

4. A **_LIMITED LIABILITY PARTNERSHIP (LLP)_** is a partnership that limits partners' risk of losing their personal assets to only their own acts and omissions and the acts and omissions of the people under their supervision.

    a.   Your partner's malpractice will not cost you your personal assets.

    b.   In some states, personal protection does not extend to contract liabilities such as bank loans.

5. **UNIFORM PARTNERSHIP ACT (UPA)**

    a.   All states except Louisiana have adopted the Uniform Partnership Act to replace laws relating to partnerships.

PPT 5-13
Types of Partners

(See complete PowerPoint slide notes on page 5.48.)

PPT 5-14
Other Forms of Partnerships

(See complete PowerPoint slide notes on page 5.48.)

     b. The UPA defines the **THREE KEY ELE-MENTS** of any general partnership:

        i.   Common ownership

        ii. Shared profits and losses

        iii. The right to participate in managing the operations of the business

C. **ADVANTAGES OF PARTNERSHIPS**

   1. **MORE FINANCIAL RESOURCES:** Two or more people can pool their money and credit.

   2. **SHARED MANAGEMENT AND POOLED/ COMPLEMENTARY KNOWLEDGE**: Partners give each other time off and provide different skills and perspectives.

   3. **LONGER SURVIVAL**: Partners are four times as likely to succeed as sole proprietorships.

   4. **NO SPECIAL TAXES:** All profits of partners are taxed as personal income of the owners.

D. **DISADVANTAGES OF PARTNERSHIPS**

   1. **UNLIMITED LIABILITY**

     a. Each **GENERAL PARTNER** is liable for the debts of the firm, no matter who was responsible for causing those debts.

     b. You are liable for your partners' mistakes as well as your own.

   2. **DIVISION OF PROFITS**: Sharing profits can cause conflicts.

PPT 5-15
Advantages of Partnerships

(See complete PowerPoint slide notes on page 5.48.)

critical thinking
exercise 5-1
PICKING PARTNERS

This exercise explores the personal skills and capital that can be obtained for a business by adding a partner. (See the complete exercise on page 5.70 of this manual.)

PPT 5-16
Disadvantages of Partnerships

(See complete PowerPoint slide notes on page 5.49.)

TEXT FIGURE 5.2
How to Form a Partnership
(Text page 120)

This text figure gives some suggestions on what should be included in partnership agreements.

3. **DISAGREEMENTS AMONG PARTNERS**

   a. Disagreements can arise over division of authority, purchasing decisions, and so on.

   b. Because of potential conflicts, all terms of partnership should be spelled out **IN WRITING** to protect all parties.

4. **DIFFICULTY OF TERMINATION**

   a. It is not easy to get out of a partnership.

   b. *For example: Who gets what and what happens next?*

   c. It is best to make these decisions at the beginning.

E. Many ventures avoid the disadvantages of these forms of ownership by forming corporations.

learning goal 3

Compare the advantages and disadvantages of corporations, and summarize the differences between C corporations, S corporations, and limited liability companies.

IV. CORPORATIONS

A. A **_CONVENTIONAL (C) CORPORATION_** is a state-chartered legal entity with authority to act and have liability separate from its owners.

   1. Businesses do not have to be big to incorporate.

   2. The corporation's owners (**STOCKHOLDERS**) are not liable for the debts of the corporation beyond the money they invest.

   3. Many people can share in the ownership of a business without working there.

   4. Corporations can choose to offer ownership to outsiders or remain private.

SPOTLIGHT ON
small business
(Text page 121)

PPT 5-17
The Ties That Bind

(See complete PowerPoint slide notes on page 5.49.)

lecture link 5-2
THE DEVELOPMENT OF SEARS, ROEBUCK, AND COMPANY

Sears started out as a sole proprietorship, became a partnership, then formed a corporation. (See the complete lecture link on page 5.63 in this manual.)

progress assessment
(Text page 122)

PPT 5-18
Progress Assessment

(See complete PowerPoint slide notes on page 5.49.)

TEXT FIGURE 5.3
Corporate Types
(Text page 124)

This text figure identifies several different types of corporations.

PPT 5-19
Conventional Corporations

(See complete PowerPoint slide notes on page 5.50.)

B. **ADVANTAGES OF CORPORATIONS**

1. **LIMITED LIABILITY**

   a. Limited liability is probably the **MOST SIGNIFICANT ADVANTAGE** of corporations.

   b. The owners of a business are responsible for losses only up to the amount they invest.

2. **ABILITY TO RAISE MORE MONEY FOR INVESTMENT**

   a. To raise money, a corporation sells **OWNERSHIP (STOCK)** to anyone interested.

   b. It is also easier for corporations to obtain loans.

   c. Corporations can also borrow money from investors by issuing **BONDS**.

3. **SIZE**

   a. Because corporations can raise large amounts of money, they can build modern facilities.

   b. They can also hire experts in all areas of operation.

   c. They can buy other corporations in other fields to diversify their risk.

   d. Corporations have the size and resources to take advantage of opportunities anywhere in the world.

   e. Corporations do not have to be large to have these benefits.

4. **PERPETUAL LIFE**: The death of one or more owners does not terminate the corporation.

PPT 5-20
Advantages of Corporations

(See complete PowerPoint slide notes on page 5.50.)

lecture link 5-3
**FORTUNE 500 LARGEST
CORPORATIONS**

Fortune magazine also publishes a listing of the largest U.S. companies ranked by annual revenue. For 2011, Wal-Mart Stores topped the list. (See the complete lecture link on page 5.64 in this manual.)

TEXT FIGURE 5.4
How Owners Affect Management
(Text page 125)

PPT 5-21
How Owners Affect Management

(See complete PowerPoint slide notes on page 5.50.)

PPT 5-22
The Big Boys of Business

(See complete PowerPoint slide notes on page 5.51.)

5. **EASE OF OWNERSHIP CHANGE:** Selling stock to someone else changes ownership.

6. **EASE OF DRAWING TALENTED EMPLOYEES:** Corporations can offer benefits such as **STOCK OPTIONS**—the right to purchase shares of the corporation for a fixed price.

7. **SEPARATION OF OWNERSHIP FROM MANAGEMENT**: Corporations can raise money from investors without having them involved in management.

C. **DISADVANTAGES OF CORPORATIONS**

1. **INITIAL COST**

    a. Incorporation may cost thousands of dollars and involve lawyers and accountants.

    b. There are less expensive ways of incorporating in certain states.

2. **EXTENSIVE PAPERWORK**

    a. A corporation must keep detailed records.

    b. Many firms incorporate in Delaware and Nevada because favorable laws make the process easier.

3. **DOUBLE TAXATION:** Corporate income is taxed twice.

    a. The **CORPORATION PAYS TAX** on income before it can distribute any dividends to stockholders.

    b. The **STOCKHOLDERS PAY TAX** on the income they receive from the corporation.

bonus case 5-1
BUILDING COMPUDYNE

A small manufacturer of precision screws grew into one of the biggest and most successful security companies in the United States. (See the complete case, discussion questions, and suggested answers beginning on page 5.75 of this manual.)

PPT 5-23
Privacy Please

(See complete PowerPoint slide notes on page 5.51.)

PPT 5-24
Disadvantages of Corporations

(See complete PowerPoint slide notes on page 5.51.)

PPT 5-25
Even the Big Guys Make Mistakes

(See complete PowerPoint slide notes on page 5.52.)

      c.   States often tax corporations more harshly than other enterprises.

  4. **TWO TAX RETURNS:** A corporate owner must file both a corporate tax return and an individual tax return.

  5. **SIZE**: Large corporations sometimes become inflexible and too tied down in red tape.

  6. **DIFFICULTY OF TERMINATION**: A corporation is relatively difficult to end.

  7. **POSSIBLE CONFLICT WITH STOCKHOLDERS AND BOARD OF DIRECTORS.**

      a.   The board chooses the company's officers.

      b.   An entrepreneur can be forced out of the very company he or she founded.

  8. Many people feel the hassles of incorporation outweigh the advantages.

D. **INDIVIDUALS CAN INCORPORATE**

  1. By incorporating, individuals such as doctors and lawyers can save on taxes and receive other benefits of incorporation.

  2. Small corporations usually do not issue stock to outsiders, so they don't have all the same advantages and disadvantages of large corporations.

  3. It is wise to consult a lawyer when incorporating.

  4. It takes, on average, about 30 days to incorporate.

E. **S CORPORATIONS**

  1. An **_S CORPORATION_** is a unique government creation that looks like a corporation but is taxed like sole proprietorships and partnerships.

<u>critical thinking
exercise 5-2</u>
**INDEPENDENT RESEARCH:
SMALL BUSINESS OWNERSHIP**

This exercise asks students to select a local businessperson and interview that individual about his or her business structure. (See complete exercise on page 5.71 of this manual.)

<u>lecture link 5-4</u>
OUSTED FOUNDERS

Rod Canion (Compaq) and the late Steve Jobs (Apple) both were removed as heads of the companies they founded. (See the complete lecture link on page 5.65 of this manual.)

PPT 5-26
Who Can Incorporate?

(See complete PowerPoint slide notes on page 5.52.)

TEXT FIGURE 5.5
How to Incorporate
(Text page 127)

This text figure lists some common items included in the articles of incorporation.

      a. S corporations have shareholders, directors, and employees.

      b. However, the profits are taxed as the personal income of the shareholders.

      c. They also have the benefit of limited liability.

  2. **S CORPORATIONS MUST:**

      a. Have no more than 100 shareholders

      b. Have shareholders who are individuals or estates and are citizens or permanent residents of the U.S.

      c. Have only one class of stock

      d. Not have more than 25% of income derived from passive sources (rents, royalties, interest, etc.)

  3. The **TAX STRUCTURE** of an S corporation isn't attractive to all businesses.

  4. The benefits of S corporations change every time the tax rules change.

F. **LIMITED LIABILITY COMPANIES**

  1. A ***LIMITED LIABILITY COMPANY (LLC)*** is a company similar to an S corporation but without the special eligibility requirements.

      a. LLCs were introduced in Wyoming in 1977.

      b. By 1996, all 50 states recognized LLCs.

      c. More than half of new business registrations in some states today are LLCs.

  2. **ADVANTAGES OF LLCs:**

      a. **LIMITED LIABILITY**: Personal assets are protected.

PPT 5-27
Oldies But Goodies

(See complete PowerPoint slide notes on page 5.52.)

PPT 5-28
S Corporations

(See complete PowerPoint slide notes on page 5.53.)

PPT 5-29
Who Can Form S Corporations?

(See complete PowerPoint slide notes on page 5.53.)

PPT 5-30
Limited Liability Companies

(See complete PowerPoint slide notes on page 5.53.)

    b. **CHOICE OF TAXATION:** LLCs can choose to be taxed as partnerships or as corporations.

    c. **FLEXIBLE OWNERSHIP RULES:** LLCs do not have to comply with ownership restrictions as S corporations do.

    d. **FLEXIBLE DISTRIBUTION OF PROFITS AND LOSSES:** Profit and losses don't have to be distributed in proportion to the money each person invests.

    e. **OPERATING FLEXIBILITY:** Reporting requirements are less than for a corporation.

3. **DISADVANTAGES OF LLCs:**

    a. **NO STOCK**

       i. LLC ownership is nontransferable.

      ii. LLC members need the approval of the other members in order to sell their interest.

    b. **LIMITED LIFE SPAN:** LLCs have to identify dissolution dates in the articles of organization.

    c. **FEWER INCENTIVES:** LLCs can't deduct the cost of fringe benefits or use stock options.

    d. **TAXES:** LLC members must pay self-employment taxes on profits.

    e. **PAPERWORK:** More paperwork is required than for sole proprietors.

4. The start-up cost for an LLC varies.

PPT 5-31
Disadvantages of LLCs

(See complete PowerPoint slide notes on page 5.54.)

legal
briefcase
(Text page 129)

PPT 5-32
Virtual
Companies

(See complete PowerPoint slide notes on page 5.54.)

TEXT FIGURE 5.6
Comparison of Forms of Business
Ownership
(Text page 130)

This text figure presents the advantages and disadvantages of the major forms of business ownership.

progress
assessment
(Text page 129)

PPT 5-33
Progress Assessment

(See complete PowerPoint slide notes on page 5.54.)

lecture outline

Define and give examples of three types of corporate mergers, and explain the role of leveraged buyouts and taking a firm private.

V. CORPORATION EXPANSION: MERGERS AND ACQUISITIONS

A. The 1990s merger mania reached its peak in 2000.

1. Most of the deals involved companies trying to expand within their own fields or enter a new market.

2. Two-thirds of the mergers of the late 1990s failed to meet their goals.

3. A **MERGER** is the result of two firms forming one company.

4. An **ACQUISITION** is one company's purchase of the property and obligations of another company.

B. **THREE MAJOR TYPES OF CORPORATE MERGERS**

1. **VERTICAL MERGER** is the joining of two companies involved in different stages of related businesses (*example: merger of a soft drink company and a company producing artificial sweetener*).

2. **HORIZONTAL MERGER** joins two firms in the same industry.

    a. It allows the firms to diversify or expand their products.

    b. *Example: merger of a soft drink and a mineral water company.*

3. **CONGLOMERATE MERGER** is the joining of firms in completely unrelated industries thereby diversifying business operations (*example: merger of a soft drink company and a snack food producer*).

PPT 5-34
Mergers and Acquisitions

(See complete PowerPoint slide notes on page 5.55.)

<u>lecture link 5-5</u>
MICROSOFT GAMBLES WITH SKYPE PURCHASE

Looking to expand into online ventures, Microsoft acquired Skype in 2011 and spent more than four times the company's value to get it. (See the complete lecture link on page 5.66 of this manual.)

PPT 5-35
Keep Growing . . .

(See complete PowerPoint slide notes on page 5.55.)

PPT 5-36
Types of Mergers

(See complete PowerPoint slide notes on page 5.55.)

TEXT FIGURE 5.7
Types of Mergers
(Text page 132)

This text figure illustrates the differences among the three types of mergers.

C. Rather than merge, some corporations decide to **MAINTAIN CONTROL** of the firm internally, **TAKING IT PRIVATE**.

    1. A ***LEVERAGED BUYOUT*** is an attempt by employees, management, or a group of investors to purchase an organization primarily through borrowing.

        a. Borrowed funds are used to buy out the stockholders in the company.

        b. Employees, managers, or a group of investors then become the owners of the firm.

    2. Merger mania has also involved foreign companies purchasing U.S. companies.

    3. Some international mergers are controversial *(such as the failed 2005 merger of a U.S. oil company and a Chinese oil company).*

<u>**learning goal** 5</u>

Outline the advantages and disadvantages of franchises, and discuss the opportunities for diversity in franchising and the challenges of global franchising.

VI. FRANCHISES

A. A ***FRANCHISE AGREEMENT*** is an arrangement whereby someone with a good idea for a business sells the rights to use the business name and sell a product or service to others in a given territory.

    1. **DEFINITIONS**:

        a. The ***FRANCHISOR*** is a company that develops a product concept and sells others the rights to make and sell the product.

lecture link 5-6
JAM AND COFFEE

In a natural brand coupling, Smucker's is adding Folgers coffee to its product line using an unusual financial vehicle called a "reverse Morris Trust." (See the complete lecture link on page 5.66 of this manual.)

PPT 5-37
Leveraged Buyouts

(See complete PowerPoint slide notes on page 5.56.)

lecture link 5-7
EMPLOYEE STOCK OWNERSHIP PLANS (ESOPS)

ESOPs are essentially employee-owned businesses. In theory, worker-owners will be more productive and earn more money than other employees. (See the complete lecture link on page 5.67 in this manual.)

PPT 5-38
Franchising

(See complete PowerPoint slide notes on page 5.56.)

    b. The ***FRANCHISE*** is the right to use a specific business's name and sell its products or services in a given territory.

    c. The ***FRANCHISEE*** is the person who buys a franchise.

2. Franchising may be an alternative for people who like to own their own businesses but want more assurance of success.

3. More than 825,000 franchised businesses operate in the U.S. That's 1 in every 10 businesses.

4. The most popular businesses for franchising are restaurants, gas stations, retail stores, hotels and motels, and automotive parts and service centers.

5. Senior care is a fast-growing sector.

B. **ADVANTAGES OF FRANCHISES**

  1. **MANAGEMENT AND MARKETING ASSISTANCE**, providing a greater chance of success through:

    a. An established product

    b. Help in choosing a location

    c. Assistance in all phases of operation

    d. Intensive training

    e. Local marketing efforts

  2. **PERSONAL OWNERSHIP:** You are still your own boss, although you must follow the rules, regulations, and procedures of the franchise.

<u>lecture link 5-8</u>
SUSTAINABLE FRANCHISING

Companies have been making efforts to be "greener" and the International Franchise Association has seen a huge jump in green-based franchises. (See the complete lecture link on page 5.68 in this manual.)

<u>bonus case 5-2</u>
FRANCHISE OR INDEPENDENT? WHAT FITS YOUR MOLD?

A husband and wife team opens a restaurant and discovers how big a job it is. (See the complete case, discussion questions, and suggested answers beginning on page 5.77 of this manual.)

PPT 5-39
Make Way for the Newbies

(See complete PowerPoint slide notes on page 5.56.)

3. **NATIONALLY RECOGNIZED NAME**: You get instant recognition and support.

4. **FINANCIAL ADVICE AND ASSISTANCE**

    a. Franchisees get assistance arranging financing and learning to keep records.

    b. Some franchisors will even provide financing to potential franchisees.

5. **LOWER FAILURE RATE**

    a. Historically, the failure rate for franchises has been lower than that of other business ventures.

    b. However, because many weak franchises have entered the field, care is needed.

C. **DISADVANTAGES OF FRANCHISES**

1. **LARGE START-UP COSTS**

    a. Most franchises charge a fee for the rights to the franchise.

    b. Start-up costs can be as high as $2 million *(for a Dunkin' Donuts franchise).*

2. **SHARED PROFIT**: The franchisor often demands a large share of the profits, or **ROYALTY**, based on sales, not profit.

3. **MANAGEMENT REGULATION**

    a. Some franchisees find the company's rules and regulations burdensome.

    b. In recent years, franchisees have banded together to resolve their grievances with franchisors.

thinking
green
(Text page 133)
PPT 5-40
Play Ball but Play
Green

(See complete PowerPoint slide notes on page 5.57.)

PPT 5-41
Advantages of Franchising

(See complete PowerPoint slide notes on page 5.57.)

c. In 2010, the KFC National Council & Advertising Cooperative sued KFC to gain control of advertising strategies.

4. **COATTAIL EFFECTS**

a. The actions of other franchisees have an impact on the franchise's future growth and level of profitability, a phenomenon known as a **COATTAIL EFFECT**.

b. Franchisees must also watch for competition from fellow franchisees.

5. **RESTRICTIONS ON SELLING**

a. Many franchisees face restrictions when re-selling their franchises.

b. Franchisors often insist on approving the new owner, who must meet their standards.

6. **FRAUDULENT FRANCHISORS**

a. Most franchisors are not large systems; many are small, obscure companies.

b. There has been an increase in complaints to the FTC about franchisors that delivered little or nothing that they promised.

D. **DIVERSITY IN FRANCHISING**

1. **WOMEN IN FRANCHISING**

a. Women are underrepresented in larger franchises due to lack of money—the **"GREEN CEILING."**

b. However, firms owned by women have grown at twice the rate of all companies.

PPT 5-42
Disadvantages of Franchising

(See complete PowerPoint slide notes on page 5.57.)

TEXT FIGURE 5.8
Buying a Franchise
(Text page 136)

This text figure provides some tips on evaluating a franchise.

PPT 5-43
Women in Franchising

(See complete PowerPoint slide notes on page 5.58.)

      c. Women are becoming **FRANCHISORS** as well.

      d. *The text uses the example of the franchise Two Men and a Truck, founded by entrepreneur Mary Ellen Sheets.*

  2. **MINORITY FRANCHISE OWNERSHIP** is growing at more than six times the national average.

  3. Nearly 20% of the franchises in the U.S. are owned by African Americans, Latinos, Asians, and Native Americans.

  4. Franchisors are increasingly focusing on recruiting minority franchisees.

E. **HOME-BASED FRANCHISES**

  1. Home-based businesses offer advantages but may leave owners with a feeling of isolation.

  2. Home-based **FRANCHISES** feel less isolated.

F. **E-COMMERCE IN FRANCHISING**

  1. Today, Internet users worldwide can obtain franchises to open online retail stores.

  2. Many franchisees with existing brick-and-mortar stores are expanding online.

  3. Some franchisors prohibit franchisee-sponsored websites, however, which can lead to conflicts between franchisors and franchisees.

  4. Traditional brick-and-mortar franchises require finding real estate. Online franchises require little training and franchise fees.

PPT 5-44
Minority-Owned Franchises

(See complete PowerPoint slide notes on page 5.58.)

PPT 5-45
Home-Based Franchises

(See complete PowerPoint slide notes on page 5.58.)

PPT 5-46
Home Sweet Home

(See complete PowerPoint slide notes on page 5.59.)

PPT 5-47
E-Commerce in Franchising

(See complete PowerPoint slide notes on page 5.59.)

G. **USING TECHNOLOGY IN FRANCHISING**

1. Franchisors are using technology, including social media, to meet the needs of customers and franchisees.

2. Franchise websites streamline communication with employees, customers, and vendors.

3. Using a website, every franchisee has immediate access to every subject that involves the franchise operation.

H. **FRANCHISING IN GLOBAL MARKETS**

1. Canada is by far the most popular market because of proximity and language.

2. The costs of franchising are high in these markets, but these are counterbalanced by less competition and rapidly expanding consumer base.

3. Newer, smaller franchises are also going international, *such as Auntie Anne's and Build-A-Bear Workshop.*

4. Convenience and a predictable level of service and quality are what make international franchising successful.

5. Franchisors must be careful to adapt to the region.

6. Foreign franchises are also expanding to the U.S.

learning goal 6

Explain the role of cooperatives.

VII.   COOPERATIVES

A. A **_COOPERATIVE_** is a business owned and controlled by the people who use it—producers, consumers, or workers with similar needs who pool their resources for mutual gain.

social
media in
business
(Text page 139

PPT 5-48
Franchise
Expansion on
Facebook

(See complete PowerPoint slide notes on page 5.59.)

PPT 5-49
Global Franchising

(See complete PowerPoint slide notes on page 5.60.)

lecture link 5-9
FRANCHISING AROUND THE
WORLD

It's worth the time and risk to franchise internationally and now small companies, like Wing Zone, are breaking into international markets. (See the complete lecture link on page 5.68 in this manual.)

PPT 5-50
What to Choose?

(See complete PowerPoint slide notes on page 5.60.)

PPT 5-51
High Flyers

(See complete PowerPoint slide notes on page 5.60.)

1. There are about 750,000 cooperatives worldwide.

2. Members democratically control these businesses by electing a board of directors that hires professional management.

B. Some cooperatives are formed to give members **MORE ECONOMIC POWER** than they would have as individuals *(e.g., farm cooperatives).*

   1. The **FARM COOPERATIVE** began with farmers joining together to get better prices for their food products.

   2. Farm cooperatives now buy and sell other products needed on the farm.

   3. Cooperatives are still a major force in agriculture today.

VIII.   WHICH FORM OF OWNERSHIP IS FOR YOU?

A. There are **RISKS TO EVERY FORM** of business ownership.

B. The freedom and incentives of capitalism make risks acceptable to many people.

IX.   SUMMARY

PPT 5-52
Cooperatives

(See complete PowerPoint slide notes on page 5.61.)

<u>critical thinking</u>
<u>exercise 5-3</u>
CHOOSING A FORM OF
BUSINESS OWNERSHIP

This exercise presents eight types of businesses and asks the student to consider which form of business ownership would be right for each one. (See the complete exercise on page 5.72 of this manual.)

progress
assessment
(Text page 141)

PPT 5-53
Progress Assessment

(See complete PowerPoint slide notes on page 5.61.)

PowerPoint slide notes

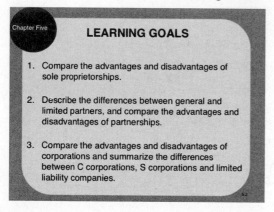

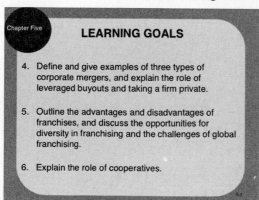

Company: H&R Block

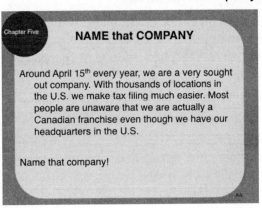

More than 600,000 businesses are started each year.

Forms of Business Ownership

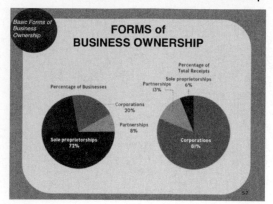

Although corporations make up only 20% of the total number of businesses, they make up 81% of the total receipts. Sole proprietorships are the most common form (72%), but they earn only 6% of the receipts.

PPT 5-8
Ethnic Business Centers

1. This slide presents Forbes's 2011 top five U.S. cities for minority-run businesses.

2. Most of these cities are situated in the South. However, we tend to hear a lot about the high population numbers of Asians in San Francisco or Hispanics in Los Angeles.

3. Milwaukee, Wisconsin, was listed last at number 40 in ethnic population growth.

4. To promote discussion ask the students, Why do you think these cities attract minority-run companies? Don't just focus on the businesses, also look at the total population and customer base.

PPT 5-9
Major Benefits of Sole Proprietorship

This slide helps students understand why sole proprietorships account for the largest number of businesses in the United States.

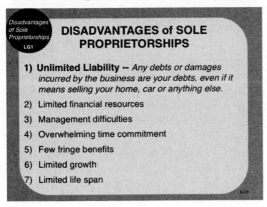

Since the main advantage of sole proprietorships is the ease by which they can be started, this slide gives students the reason why this form of ownership accounts for such a small percentage of overall total revenue. Special emphasis should be given to the disadvantage of unlimited liability (personal assets at risk), and to the time commitment (24 hours, 7 days per week, and 365 days per year).

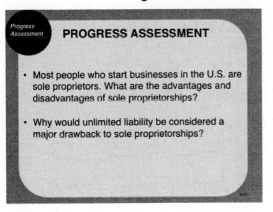

1. The primary advantages of sole proprietors are ease of starting and ending the business, being your own boss, pride of ownership, leaving a legacy, retention of company profits, no special taxes. Disadvantages include unlimited liability, limited financial resources, management difficulties, overwhelming time commitment, few fringe benefits, limited growth, limited life span.

2. With unlimited liability, the sole proprietor is liable for all debts and obligations of the business and must pay them even if it means selling your home, car, or whatever else you own.

Each type of partnership has advantages and disadvantages. In a general partnership resources are pooled and liability is spread among all partners. However, in this type of partnership there is the possibility for disagreement and/or personality conflicts. A limited partnership is made up of a mixture of general partners and limited partners. Limited partners cannot actively take part in business dealings.

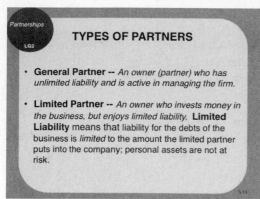

The limited partner is not able to exercise any management control over the partnership, but maintains limited liability. A limited partner's liability is limited to the amount invested in the partnership.

There are two less common forms of partnerships outlined in this slide: master limited partnership and the limited liability partnership. The master limited partnership is unique because it combines the tax benefits of a more traditional partnership and the liquidity of a publicly traded security. One example of a master limited partnership is Kinder Morgan Energy Partners, which is engaged in energy storage and operates 26,000 miles of pipelines.

Partnerships have some distinct advantages. The key advantage is that partnerships have access to more resources such as financial resources, management skills, and knowledge

Disadvantages of Partnerships

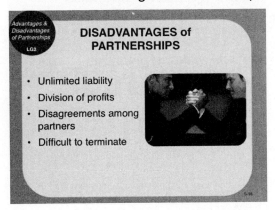

Like the sole proprietorship, a partnership has some serious disadvantages such as unlimited liability and division of profits. One disadvantage that students might not consider is disagreement among partners.

The Ties That Bind

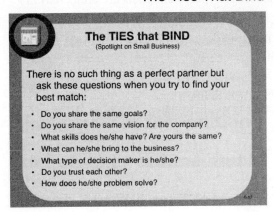

Successful partnerships start with a shared vision. In order to develop a successful partnership all partners must be honest with each other and bring a variety of different skills to the partnership. Suggestions to discuss with students regarding partnerships include:

- Partnership agreements must be in writing!

- Each individual's responsibilities to the company must be in writing and included as part of the contract.

Make certain that provisions are in place if one or more partners want to terminate the agreement. (Information outlining the terms and conditions of terminating any agreement should be outlined in the original contract.)

Progress Assessment

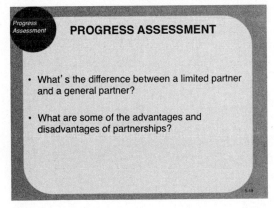

1. A general partner is an owner who has unlimited liability and can be active in managing the firm. A limited partner is an owner who invests money in the business, but does not have any management responsibility or liability for losses beyond his or her investment.

2. Some of the advantages of partnerships are more financial resources, shared management and pooled/complementary skills and knowledge, longer survival, no special taxes. Disadvantages of partnerships include unlimited liability (for general partners), division of profits, disagreements among partners, difficulty of termination.

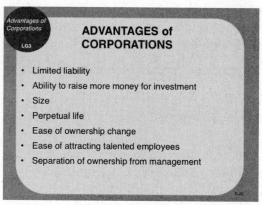

1. The major advantage of corporate ownership is limited liability protection (personal assets are protected).

2. Interesting facts regarding incorporating a business: the cost for a business to incorporate ranges from about $50 to over $300, plus states' fees. Over half of Fortune 500 companies choose to incorporate in Delaware because the state's laws make the process easier than it is in other states.

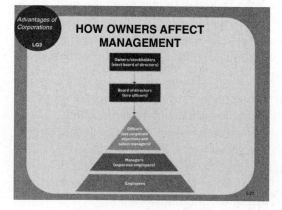

The Big Boys of Business

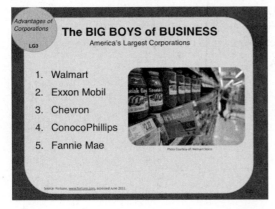

1. This slide presents *Fortune*'s 2011 top five U.S. corporations.

2. Ask the students, Several of the companies in the top five deal with similar products and services; how are the products and services these companies sell similar? *(ExxonMobil, Chevron, and ConocoPhillips are all oil companies.)*

Privacy Please

1. This slide presents America's top ten private companies in 2011.

2. Ask the students to debate why a company may want to remain private. (Some of the reasons may be control, privacy, no external pressure, and preference.)

Disadvantages of Corporations

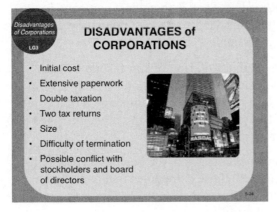

Double taxation is a major disadvantage of corporations. A corporation is taxed on income earned, and then shareholders are taxed on any dividends the company may pay.

Even the Big Boys Make Mistakes

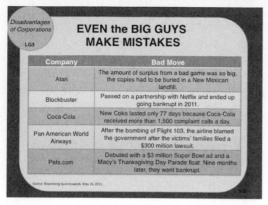

1. This slide presents examples of mistakes made by big corporations.

2. Sometimes mistakes can be rectified (as in the case of Coca-Cola withdrawing New Coke), but sometimes they contribute to the company going out of business.

Who Can Incorporate?

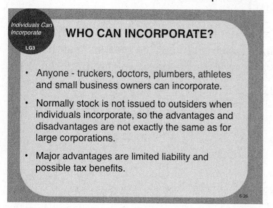

Oldies But Goodies

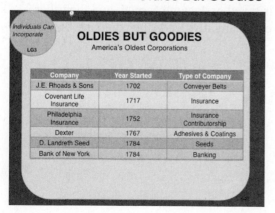

1. A few facts you may wish to address with the students are:

    - JE Rhoads & Sons is the oldest company in the United States and started off tanning leather for Buggy Whips.

    - Philadelphia Contributorship Insurance was formed based on a suggestion by Benjamin Franklin regarding the establishment of a volunteer fire brigade, which eventually developed into an insurance company.

2. Environmental changes in the business world will always happen; those companies that *embrace change* and provide quality goods and services will continue to profit.

3. Discuss with the students the significant amount of commitment a company must be prepared to make to stay in business. *(Some areas that must continually be addressed are changes in societal culture, competition, economy, laws/politics, and technology changes.)*

S CORPORATIONS

S Corporations
LG3

- **S Corporation --** *A unique government creation that looks like a corporation, but is taxed like sole proprietorships and partnerships.*

- S corporations have shareholders, directors and employees, plus the benefit of limited liability.

- Profits are taxed only as the personal income of the shareholder.

An S corporation looks like a corporation, but is taxed like a sole proprietorship or partnership. The primary advantage of an S corporation is that it avoids the double taxation of a C corporation. Approximately 3 million U.S. companies operate as S corporations.

WHO CAN FORM S CORPORATIONS?

S Corporations
LG3

- **Qualifications for S Corporations:**
  - Have no more than 100 shareholders.
  - Have shareholders that are individuals or estates and are citizens or permanent residents of the U.S.
  - Have only one class of stock.
  - Derive no more than 25% of income from passive sources.

- If an S corporation loses its S status, it may not operate under it again for at least 5 years.

Originally to qualify as an S Corporation, the number of shareholders was limited to 75. This has now been amended to no more than 100.

LIMITED LIABILITY COMPANIES

Limited Liability Companies
LG3

- **Limited Liability Company (LLC) --** *Similar to a S corporation, but without the eligibility requirements.*

- **Advantages of LLCs:**
  - Limited liability
  - Choice of taxation
  - Flexible ownership rules
  - Flexible distribution of profits and losses
  - Operating flexibility

Advantages and disadvantages of LLCs are listed in this slide. The biggest advantages of LLCs are limited liability and flexibility.

Primary disadvantages from entrepreneurs' perspectives would be limited life span and paperwork.

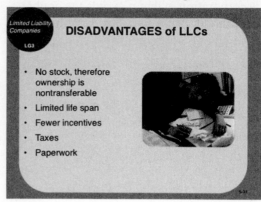

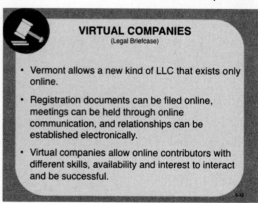

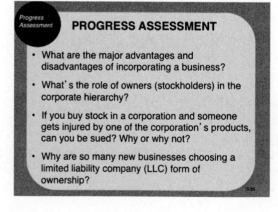

1. Advantages of incorporating a business include limited liability, ability to raise more money for investment, size, perpetual life, ease of ownership change, ease of attracting talented employees, separation of ownership from management. Disadvantages of incorporating are initial cost, extensive paperwork, double taxation, two tax returns, size, difficulty to terminate, possible conflict with stockholders and board of directors.

2. Stockholders do not have to be employees of the corporation. They are investors who have limited liability. Stockholders elect the board of directors of a company who select the management to control the company.

3. Stockholders in a corporation have limited liability, meaning as owners they are responsible for its losses only up to the amount they invested. The corporation could be sued and forced out of business but the stockholder would lose only what he or she invested.

4. Limited liability companies have become a popular way to form a business since all 50 states now recognize LLCs. Some of the advantages of LLCs are limited liability, choice of taxation (can be taxed as a partnership or corporation), flexible ownership rules, flexible distribution of profit and losses, operating flexibility.

Merger mania of the late 1990s reached its peak in 2000. By 2009, the U.S. economy caused the volume of mergers and acquisitions to plummet 86%! In 2010, mergers increased 14%.

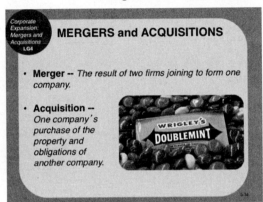

1. This slide covers the amount spent on acquisitions by big businesses and the number of completed or pending deals since 2005.

2. Much of corporate growth relies on acquisitions.

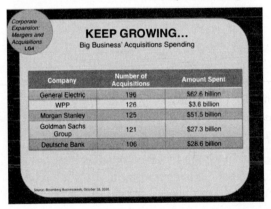

There are three types of mergers. Horizontal mergers take place in the same industry (i.e., one competitor merging with another). An example of this would be Daimler Mercedes-Benz merging with Chrysler to create DaimlerChrysler in the 1990s. Vertical merger takes place between companies in a value chain—for example, a supplier and a distributor merging. Conglomerate merger has no relationship between companies; both Tyco and General Electric operate as conglomerates.

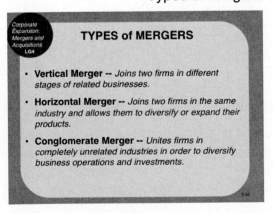

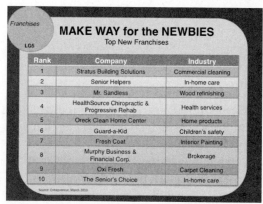

1. New franchise opportunities pop up all the time and this slide shows the top ten new companies from *Entrepreneur*'s Franchise 500.

2. Take notice that all the listed companies here are in the service sector. This can promote discussion on the evolution of American business.

3. Ask the students, Why do you think there is growth in these service franchises, such as senior in-home care and health?

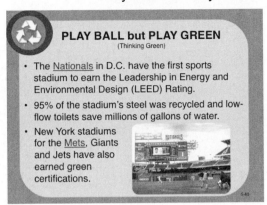

Franchising has a lower failure rate because the franchisee has support from the franchisor. This support can range from marketing to financial.

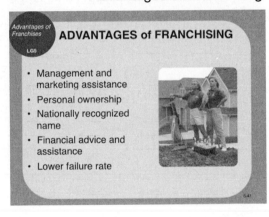

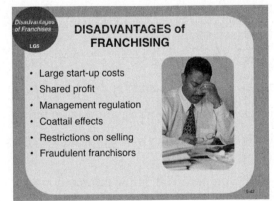

PPT 5-43
Women in Franchising

PPT 5-44
Minority-Owned Franchises

Franchising has a lower failure rate because the franchisee has support from the franchisor. This support can range from marketing to financial.

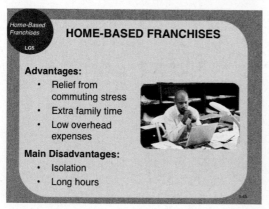

PPT 5-45
Home-Based Franchises

Home-based businesses are growing at an enormous rate. This slide helps clarify some of the reasons why. Share with the class some tips on getting started:

- Decide on a business idea.
- Set goals for the business.
- Determine how many hours you want to work.
- Decide how many employees you want to hire.
- Decide how much money you will need to get started.

Visit www.e-myth.com for more online information regarding start-ups.

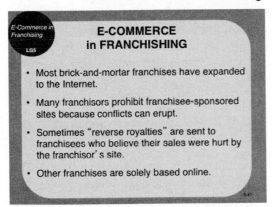

1. Many franchisees are looking toward home-based businesses.

2. These 10 franchises have held their own despite the recent economic crisis.

3. Some of these companies, like Jazzercise, require franchisees to rent space for client-based activities. However, the businesses can be run from the home

GLOBAL FRANCHISING

Franchising in International Markets
LG5

- Canada is the most popular target for U.S.-based franchises. China, South Africa, the Philippines and the Middle East are becoming popular despite high cost.

- Franchising is successful when the product is convenient, high quality, great service is included and the franchisee adapts to the region.

- International franchising goes both ways – some foreign franchises have come to the U.S.

PPT 5-50
What to Choose?

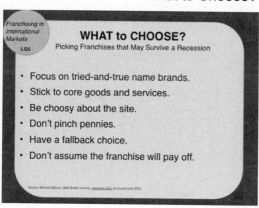

WHAT to CHOOSE?
Picking Franchises that May Survive a Recession

Franchising in International Markets
LG5

- Focus on tried-and-true name brands.
- Stick to core goods and services.
- Be choosy about the site.
- Don't pinch pennies.
- Have a fallback choice.
- Don't assume the franchise will pay off.

Source: Richard Gibson, Wall Street Journal, www.wsj.com, accessed June 2011.

1. This is valuable information that must be examined by anyone wishing to purchase a franchise.

2. The number one reason why franchises fail is due to miscalculation of start-up costs and operating costs. Examine all costs carefully. It is important to understand that all franchise opportunities are not created equal.

3. Suggest to the class that anyone interested in a franchise should also follow these additional guidelines:

   - Have an attorney experienced in franchise contracts review the agreement.

   - Hire a CPA to review all financial statements. This is commonly referred to as performing a "Due Diligence."

   - Interview other franchise owners.

   - Have experience in the industry.

PPT 5-51
High Flyers

HIGH FLYERS
Ten High-Performing Franchises

Franchising in International Markets
LG5

1. Hampton Hotels
2. AMPM
3. McDonald's
4. 7-Eleven
5. Supercuts
6. Days Inn
7. Vanguard Cleaning Systems
8. Servpro
9. Subway
10. Denny's

Photo Courtesy of: Hampton Hotels

Source: Entrepreneur, January 2011.

1. This slide lists 10 high-performing franchises.

2. As mentioned earlier, not all franchises are created equal and require careful investigation before considering an investment.

3. Websites like www.franchise.com provide information such as the cost of thousands of franchise systems.

4. Ask the students, What makes an effective franchisor? *(Answers will vary, but should include name recognition, financial stability, innovative product, and effective business management.)*

COOPERATIVES

- **Cooperatives --** *Businesses owned and controlled by the people who use it – producers, consumers, or workers with similar needs who pool their resources for mutual gain.*

- Worldwide, 750,000 co-ops serve 730 million members – 120 million in the U.S.

- Members democratically control the business by electing a board of directors that hires professional management.

PROGRESS ASSESSMENT

- What are some of the factors to consider before buying a franchise?

- What opportunities are available for starting a global franchise?

- What's a cooperative?

1. Before buying a franchise be sure to check a company's (franchisor's) resources and reputation. There are many franchising scams. The checklist on page 136 of the text gives advice about things to consider before buying a franchise.

2. Successful franchising in global markets offers the same opportunities as in domestic markets. However, franchisors must be careful to adapt to the region where they wish to expand. McDonald's, for example, has more than 32,000 restaurants in 117 countries.

3. A cooperative is a form of business that is owned and controlled by the people who use it—producers, consumers, or workers with similar needs who pool their resources for mutual gain. Cooperatives are a major force in agriculture and other industries today.

lecture links

lecture link 5-1

THE *FORTUNE* LIST OF MOST ADMIRED CORPORATIONS

Each year *Fortune* magazine asks top executives, outside directors, and securities analysts to evaluate the companies in their industries on each of eight criteria. These criteria are added together to obtain an overall "admired" score. Below are the top 10 companies for 2011.[i]

For the 50 most admired companies overall, *Fortune*'s survey asked businesspeople to vote for the companies that they admired most, from any industry.

2011 MOST ADMIRED COMPANIES

1	Apple	6	Coca-Cola
2	Google	7	Amazon
3	Berkshire Hathaway	8	FedEx
4	Southwest Airlines	9	Microsoft
5	Procter & Gamble	10	McDonald's

The Most Admired Companies in previous years:

2010

1	Apple	6	Proctor & Gamble
2	Google	7	Toyota Motor
3	Berkshire Hathaway	8	Goldman Sachs
4	Johnson & Johnson	9	Wal-Mart
5	Amazon	10	Coca-Cola

2009

1	Apple	6	Proctor & Gamble
2	Berkshire Hathaway	7*	Southwest Airlines
3	Toyota Motor	7*	FedEx
4	Google	9	General Electric
5	Johnson & Johnson	10	Microsoft

2008

1	Apple	6	Starbucks
2	Berkshire Hathaway	7	FedEx
3	General Electric	8	Proctor & Gamble
4	Google	9	Johnson & Johnson
5	Toyota Motor	10	Goldman Sachs

2007

1	General Electric	6	FedEx
2	Starbucks	7	Apple
3	Toyota Motor	8	Google
4	Berkshire Hathaway	9	Johnson & Johnson
5	Southwest Airlines	10	Procter & Gamble

2006

1	General Electric	6	Johnson & Johnson
2	FedEx	7	Berkshire Hathaway
3	Southwest Airlines	8	Dell
4	Procter & Gamble	9	Toyota Motor
5	Starbucks	10	Microsoft

lecture link 5-2

THE DEVELOPMENT OF SEARS, ROEBUCK, AND COMPANY

WATCHMAKER WANTED

with references

who can furnish tools.

State age, experience, and salary required.

T39, Daily News

The above ad appeared in the Help Wanted section of the *Chicago Daily News* of April 11, 1887. It was placed by Richard W. Sears of Chicago and was answered by Alvah Roebuck, a watch assembler and repairman from Indiana.

Sears was a railroad stationmaster and telegraph operator in Redwood, Minnesota, where a shipment of watches remained unclaimed by the owner. Sears sold the watches to nearby farmers. This effort was so successful and rewarding that he started ordering and "peddling" watches. He soon quit his railroad job and moved to Minneapolis, where he founded the R. W. Sears Watch Company.

In 1887, Sears moved to Chicago, placed the above ad, and he and Roebuck formed a partnership. Sears was the hyperactive, brilliant advertiser, promoter, and salesman while Roebuck was the quiet, reserved organizer. As their business boomed, they expanded into diamonds and general jewelry, general household and farm goods, musical instruments, and anything else the customers ordered. The main business was done by catalog and mail orders, which required extensive advertising, low prices, and a "money-back guarantee."

Sears would take the orders and then rush around to find the goods to fill them. This pressure caused Roebuck to sell out to Sears in 1895 for $25,000. Sears then required an organizer and manager. He hired Julius Rosenwald, who played a key role in the firm's development. Rosenwald, who was noted for his business skills, became president in 1908 when Sears resigned after a disagreement with him. Rosenwald brought in General Robert E. Wood, the quartermaster who had masterminded the Panama Canal construction, to lead the firm into a new era.

After Roebuck went broke in the 1929 crash, his old company, now a thriving mail-order firm, put him on the publicity department payroll to make goodwill tours.

Largely as a result of the automobile and the mobility created by World War I, there was a migration from the farms to the cities in the 1920s. Sensing that this shift would vitally affect them, Rosenwald shifted the firm's emphasis from mail-order business to urban merchandising. Later, the firm opened up stores outside the cities where there was plenty of parking space.

Realizing the effects of World War II's "G.I. Bill" on U.S. business, General Wood started a modernization and expansion program in the late 1940s that put Sears out in front of Montgomery Ward and other competitors for over two decades. Wood also got Sears into auto service, operations in Latin America, home and auto insurance, auto rental, pest control, gardening, and house decorating.

By the mid-1980s, Sears had become prominent in real estate and securities investing through acquiring Dean Witter Reynolds, the nation's seventh-largest securities brokerage firm, and Coldwell Banker and Co., the largest independent real estate services company. It already was a force in the insurance field through its Allstate Insurance subsidiary.

The 1990s saw another crisis for Sears. In 1990 it slipped to the nation's number three retailer from number two the years before. Shareholder groups pressured Sears's board to spin-off some businesses and undertake a makeover of the retail operations. The restructuring eventually resulted in the closure of Sears's huge catalog operations and closing 113 stores.

lecture link 5-3

FORTUNE 500 LARGEST CORPORATIONS

Each year *Fortune* also lists the 500 largest corporations in the United States, based on annual revenue. For 2011, the largest corporation was Wal-Mart Stores. The retail giant topped the revenue listing with $421.8 billion. It also earned a $16 billion profit. That's $16,000,000,000—nine zeroes.

Here are the top ten largest corporations in 2011:[ii]

RANK	COMPANY	REVENUES ($ MILLIONS)	PROFITS ($ MILLIONS)
1	**Wal-Mart Stores**	**$421,849.0**	**$ 16,389.0**
2	ExxonMobile	354,674.0	30,460.0
3	Chevron	196,337.0	19,024.0

4	ConocoPhillips	184,966.0	11,358.0
5	Fannie Mae	153,825.0	−14,014.0
6	General Electric	151,628.0	11,644.0
7	Berkshire Hathaway	136,185.0	12,967.0
8	General Motors	135,592.0	6,172.0
9	Bank of America Corp.	134,194.0	−2,238.0
10	Ford Motor	128,954.0	6,561.0

lecture link 5-4
OUSTED FOUNDERS

Rod Canion and two friends founded Compaq Computers in 1981. However, in October of 1991 Rod Canion was replaced as president and CEO of the company. The move followed an announcement that Compaq had lost $70 million in the third quarter and planned lay-offs of more than 1,400 employees. The board of directors stated it "decided it was time for a change." Canion eventually was paid $3.6 million in severance pay. (Compaq merged with Hewlett-Packard in 2001.)

Canion went on to found Insource Technology Group, a consulting services company, in 1992 and served as chair and CEO. In 1999, he led the initial funding drive for Questia Media, Inc., the first comprehensive research service for college students doing research papers in the humanities and social sciences.

The late **Steve Jobs** was a cofounder of Apple Computers, but was ousted from the company in 1985. Jobs was stripped of his chairmanship by CEO John Sculley after slow sales of the Macintosh computer led to pressure from the board for Sculley to act. Jobs sold 850,000 shares of his stock for about $14 million.

In 1985, Jobs began NeXT Computers and bought Pixar, a computer animation company, from LucasFilm. While the NeXT computer was not a commercial success, the company's focus was changed to software, and in 1997 it was bought by Apple. Pixar grew into Pixar Animation Studios and, in partnership with Walt Disney Co., made blockbuster movies like the *Toy Story* series, *Cars, Wall-E,* and *Finding Nemo.*

In an ironic twist of fate, Jobs returned to Apple in 1997. Apple also bought NeXT Computers and its NeXT operating system. Jobs returned to his forte—developing cutting-edge products. The revolutionary iMac was introduced in 1998, followed by the iPod. The company has become the single dominant force in selling music online through its iTunes Music Store.

Even the nonprofit Habitat for Humanity ousted its founder **Millard Fuller** in 2005. Fuller, who founded Habitat for Humanity in 1976, was fired after more than a year of tension sparked by allegations that he sexually harassed a female colleague. The charge was never substantiated, and Fuller denies it.

The dismissals of Fuller and his wife, Linda, created a rift in the charity's large fundraising base. Habitat chapters around the world have a combined annual budget of about $748 million, but some long-time donors say they're upset about Fuller's dismissal and will stop giving money to the global nonprofit. Habitat has built nearly 200,000 houses for 1 million people.[iii]

lecture link 5-5

MICROSOFT GAMBLES WITH SKYPE PURCHASE

In today's hyper-valued tech world, it can be difficult to determine what a particular business is actually worth. Although many tech companies don't actually earn a profit, that doesn't stop financial experts from placing a figure on the "potential" worth of an up and coming enterprise. Nowhere was this problem more apparent than during the popping of the dot-com bubble in the early 2000s. Companies that had been given valuations in the billions one day became worthless the next. Now as today's giants like Facebook and Groupon sport multi-billion-dollar valuations of their own, the debate over the value of future profits versus genuine assets rages on.

Most recently, Microsoft became embroiled in this issue with its $8.5 billion purchase of Skype. eBay first acquired the Internet telephony company in 2005 for $2.6 billion. After failing to integrate the software into its core online retailing business, eBay sold 70% of Skype to venture capitalists for a little less than $2 billion in 2009. The fact that Microsoft spent more than four times the company's value (not to mention ten times Skype's 2010 revenues) has many shareholders shaking their heads. None of Microsoft's online ventures have taken off substantially, including its heavily touted search engine Bing, leaving its Web division continually operating in the red. Also, new Internet services from other companies, namely Google, threaten to usurp the dominance of Microsoft's established Windows and Office brands.

Nevertheless, the Skype acquisition is not without its positives. For one, Microsoft has cash reserves to the tune of $42 billion sitting in banks overseas. Reluctant to bring the money into the United States and face the 35% corporate tax rate, the company instead lets it languish in vaults, not creating jobs or acquiring start-ups. The purchase of Skype puts some of that offshore cash to use in the United States. Perhaps most importantly, though, is that Microsoft finally has a big name Internet brand. There are precious few big time names in online branding—think Netflix, Twitter, or Craigslist—and hardly any of them are for sale. With Skype, Microsoft finally has the potential to get its online enterprise off the ground.[iv]

lecture link 5-6

JAM AND COFFEE

In a natural brand coupling, Smucker's is adding Folgers coffee to its product line. J. M. Smucker, the jelly and jam outfit, is buying the Folgers coffee business from Procter & Gamble, creating a breakfast food combo. Sounds simple, but the $3.3 billion transaction is complex and sophisticated.

The purchase was structured as a "reverse Morris Trust," an arcane financial vehicle used for a sophisticated bit of financial planning.

Until about 2000, regular Morris Trust deals—in which a company would divide itself into two pieces, one of which would be swapped for stock in an unrelated company—were a mergers-and-acquisitions mainstay. But in 1997, after a series of Morris Trust deals threatened to turn a once-reasonable loophole into a major tax drain, Congress cracked down. Merger dealers spent a few years evolving hybrid Morris Trusts, more difficult, complicated, and rare.

Technically, Smucker's isn't buying Folgers from P&G. Such a sale would have required P&G to pay capital gains taxes of $1 billion or so. Instead, Smucker's will acquire a new, independent company that P&G will create to own Folgers. This company creation, owned by some or all of P&G's existing shareholders, would be a tax-free transaction.

Then, a nanosecond after the Folgers company is created, Smucker's will buy it for about 63 million newly issued Smucker's shares. That stock-for-stock deal will be tax-free, also. When the dust settles, Smucker's will own Folgers, and Folgers shareholders will own about 53% of Smucker's.

UNDERSTANDING BUSINESS: Instructor's Resource Manual

Why would a family-controlled public company like Smucker's think of turning over more than half its stock to outsiders? Won't this hopelessly dilute the family's control? Not really, thanks to unusual provisions in Smucker's corporate charter that give long-term holders (like the Smucker family) ten votes a share on key issues, while short-term holders have only one vote.

Smucker's revels in its midwestern aura. Its corporate symbol is a big red strawberry, and its headquarters are at 1 Strawberry Lane in Orrville, Ohio. But little Smucker's "purchase" of Folgers proves that it can play with the big boys.v

lecture link 5-7
EMPLOYEE STOCK OWNERSHIP PLANS (ESOPs)

No matter how hard workers fight for better pay, they will never become as wealthy as the people who actually own the company. At least that is the theory behind employee stock ownership plans (ESOPs). An ESOP enables employees to buy part or total ownership of the firm. Louis O. Kelso, a San Francisco lawyer and economist, conceived the idea of ESOPs about 50 years ago. His plan was to turn workers into owners by selling them stock. Using this concept, he helped the employees of a newspaper buy their company. Since then, the idea of employees taking over all or some of the ownership of their companies has gained favor—there are approximately 11,500 ESOPs today.

Employee participation in ownership has emerged as an important issue in many different industries and every type of company. Many people consider ESOPs examples of capitalism at its best. Some benefits of ESOPs include:

- Increased employee motivation
- Shared profitability through ownership of the firm
- Improved management–employee relations
- Higher employee pride in the organization
- Better customer relations

The fact is, however, that not all ESOPs work as planned. When used correctly, ESOPs can be a powerful strategy for improving company profitability and increasing employee satisfaction, participation, and income. But potential problems with ESOPs include:

- Lack of employee stock voting rights within the firm
- Lack of communication between management and employees
- Little or no employee representation on the company board of directors
- Lack of job security assurances

The saga of Weirton Steel illustrates what can happen when an ESOP goes wrong. In 1983, the employees of Weirton Steel voted to take a 20% pay cut to save their jobs. Through an Employee Stock Ownership Plan, they purchased the ailing company. Full of hope and confidence, the workers believed their sacrifices would eventually secure their future. Weirton became the largest ESOP in the United States.

Things looked good initially. Weirton earned about $500 million profit between 1984 and 1990, of which workers shared $170 million. The mill also provided 8,000 jobs. Several observers described the mill's participative practices in glowing terms.

However, profits then steadily turned to into large losses, $230 million in 1993, $320 million in 2001, and almost $700 million in 2003. Management cut the workforce by two-thirds, and Weirton's employee-owners lost their investments. In May 2003, the company filed bankruptcy.

Today Weirton's stock is practically worthless, thousands of jobs have been eliminated, and the company's officers and directors have been subject to multiple lawsuits. Members of top management were criticized for bad accounting and personal enrichment, while the employee-owners watched their net worth erode year after year. Long before Arthur Andersen's poor auditing became legendary, the firm's auditors helped Weirton Steel's management waste millions of the employee-owners' value.[vi]

lecture link 5-8

SUSTAINABLE FRANCHISING

Over the last few years, companies big and small have made a concerted effort toward conducting business in a more environmentally friendly manner. "Going green" is becoming more and more acceptable in the business world, so much so that the International Franchise Association has seen a significant rise in inquiries regarding green-based franchises. More so than just a blanket term for any business that separates out its recycling, green franchises base their entire enterprise around environmental sustainability.

But it's that same commitment to keeping green that makes opening a green franchise so tricky. While shaping a company around an environmental ideal may be noble, a business must first and foremost possess a viable concept that can serve a particular market. Though some green franchises, such as restaurants and stores, have clear-cut benchmarks on which to judge their success, other new green businesses like energy auditors or waterless car washes have limited frames of reference with which to predict their potential for success. Regardless of the uncertainty of their business, however, several of these experimental green franchises are blossoming into thriving operations.

Another pitfall for potential green franchisees are "greenwashed" companies, or businesses that claim to adhere to strictly sustainable guidelines but are actually doing little to make their operations entirely green. Franchisees run the risk of being exposed as frauds if their environmentally conscious company turns out to be greenwashed. In order to avoid such bad press, franchisees must look closely at how their potential franchise limits its impact on the environment, such as the company's method of waste reduction or its use of solar panels. But despite its dangers, the time for opening a green franchise has never been better, especially since the 2009 economic stimulus package offers several incentives for green businesses.[vii]

lecture link 5-9

FRANCHISING AROUND THE WORLD

For a small restaurant chain like the Atlanta-based Wing Zone, the thought of international expansion would have been laughable ten years ago. However, in November 2010 the company opened up its first franchise outside the United States in Panama City, Panama. Although establishing a global business presence is easier now than it once was, Wing Zone will likely have to wait 2 to 3 years before its international business turns a profit.

Still, it is well worth the time and risk for the company to hedge its bets on foreign soil. For years the world's rising middle class has been turned on to Western tastes by large chains like McDonald's and KFC. These big brands paved the way for smaller companies to break through as well, but several other factors have also contributed to the global franchising push. Economic stagnation at home has made the United States less appealing for businesses wanting to expand their brand. Also, in America Wing Zone has to compete head to head with a number of domestic competitors such as Wing Stop, Buffalo Wild Wings, Hooters, and many others. By going global, companies can gain access to a largely untapped marketplace.

Setting up shop in just any international market won't do, however. For Wing Zone, it needed a country with a strong middle class that enjoyed spicy tastes and poultry. The company also gave itself a wide 18-month window to correct any problems that might come up before the grand opening. Wing Zone's careful planning paid off. The Panama City restaurant's first week of operation was the busiest week for any location in the history of the company. Wing Zone's initial success spurred an expansion spree with stores opening soon in England, Saudi Arabia, and El Salvador. The company even has plans to open up as many as 50 restaurants in and around Tokyo.[viii]

critical
thinking exercises

Name: _____

Date: _____

critical thinking exercise 5-1
PICKING PARTNERS

Did you ever think you might like to go into business for yourself? What kind of business would you like to start? What resources (both personal skills and capital) would you need to make your business a success? Sometimes it helps to have a partner to share the burdens of starting a business. What skills would you need to look for in your partner?

Use the space below to list the personal skills and capital needed for your proposed business. Put your initials next to the skills and capital you would bring to the business. Think of a friend who might be interested in joining you as a partner. Put your friend's initials next to the skills and capital he or she can offer. What capital or skills are missing?

Type of business:_____

Proposed partner:_____

Personal skills needed: **Capital needed:**

_____   _____

_____   _____

_____   _____

_____   _____

_____

What skills and/or capital are missing? _____

_____

What can you do to get what is needed? _____

_____

_____

_____

UNDERSTANDING BUSINESS: Instructor's Resource Manual

critical thinking exercise 5-2
INDEPENDENT RESEARCH: SMALL-BUSINESS OWNERSHIP

Choose a business in either your hometown or a town or city near your school. Approach the owner and request an interview about his or her business. Here are a couple of tips:

- Offer to submit questions in advance.
- A businessperson is very busy—use allotted time wisely.
- Ask permission to talk with employees or visit parts of the business.
- Recognize the need for secrecy.
- Don't assume that you, as a business student, are the expert.

1. What type of business ownership does the business use?

2. Why was this form of ownership chosen?

3. If sales were to double, would the business then choose another form?

   a. If so, which form?

   b. Why?

4. How many hours per week does the owner spent at his or her business?

5. Does the owner plan to have the business continue in the family? If yes, describe the plan.

6. If the owner could change one thing in building his or her business, what would that be?

7. What advice does he or she have for a new entrepreneur?

8. Prepare a short recommendation about business ownership in this specific business for presentation to the class.

critical thinking exercise 5-3

CHOOSING A FORM OF BUSINESS OWNERSHIP

The needs of the businessperson starting a new business are a major consideration when deciding the best form of business ownership. The kind of business being started is also important to consider when deciding to make your new business a sole proprietorship, partnership, or corporation. Look at the list of new businesses below. Indicate the form of ownership you think would be best for each business. Give the reason for your selection.

BUSINESS	FORM	REASON
Swimming pool repair		
Flower shop		
Internet-based specialty store		
Termite control service		
Textbook publishing company		
Law firm		
Underwear manufacturer		
Child care center		

notes on critical thinking exercise 5-3

SWIMMING POOL REPAIR

A swimming pool repair company would probably operate best as a sole proprietorship or partnership initially. There is no great need for capital at first, so a partner may not be needed. A good way to start would be to hire a few good people and begin work. If many jobs came in, you could hire more workers. If the managerial task became too much, you could hire an accountant or office manager. A partner would be good if you wanted an expert in marketing or some other function. Also, it is often fun to have a partner to share ideas and successes with.

FLOWER SHOP

A flower shop would likely do best as a partnership. The reason is that retail stores demand that someone be there all the time. Since stores are open as much as seven days a week, 12 hours a day, it helps to have a partner to share the managerial responsibilities. A partner is also helpful in raising the initial capital. A sole proprietor could succeed if he or she found an excellent manager or two to help.

INTERNET-BASED SPECIALTY STORE

The answer to this would depend on the size envisioned for the specialty store. A small seller of a few specialty products could operate as a sole proprietorship, if the owner had the necessary skills. Orders could be taken without human assistance. Initial investment, excluding inventory, would be low.

If the store were larger and carried more extensive product lines, the owner would need assistance, perhaps from a partner. Maybe the best choice would be the limited liability partnership. Without limited liability, the owner(s) would be liable for all the business's debts, and personal assets would be at risk.

TERMITE CONTROL SERVICE

A termite control service is much like the swimming pool company, a consumer service. One can start out small with little capital and build as the business grows. A sole proprietor can do fine with some good employees. A partner can be of assistance in marketing and sharing the burden if the business grows rapidly. A partner is good for sharing thoughts and worries and joys, but is not necessary.

TEXTBOOK PUBLISHING COMPANY

A textbook publishing company calls for a corporate type of structure because the costs of publishing a text are so high. The cost of publishing this text plus all the supplements—instructor's manual, study guide, test bank, videos, computer projects, and so on—comes to $1 million dollars or so. It is very difficult for a sole proprietor or a partnership to raise such funds. The production facilities and other physical spaces are subject to accidents that could lead to lawsuits. A corporation protects its owners from losses beyond what they invest. All in all, a corporate form is probably best in this situation.

LAW FIRM

Law firms can be sole proprietorships, but the growth would be severely limited. Besides, there would be no one to cover when the owner gets sick or goes on vacations. In this case, it is best to have a partner or several partners. In fact, that is what most law firms do. Whether or not the partners decide to incorporate has much to do with taxes and liability. The need for capital is not that great.

UNDERWEAR MANUFACTURER

An underwear manufacturer would likely need buildings and equipment that could not be obtained without much capital. That calls for incorporating and raising those funds through the sale of stock. This is much like the publishing case.

CHILD CARE

A child care center could very well be a sole proprietorship if it was small enough. Employees could be hired to do all that was necessary. On the other hand, a partner may be needed to help finance the building, if the building is not rented. A partner could help in many other ways as well, being there when you can't be, sharing ideas, and so on. Incorporation would be necessary only to protect against liability, which can be important, or for tax purposes if the center expands to make lots of money. An S corporation may be a good idea in that case. Of course, a child care center could also be a cooperative if the parents are willing.

S corporations could be used for the swimming pool company, the flower shop, and the Internet specialty store as well. The basic goal is to minimize taxes. Such a decision is best left to a small-business expert who is also a lawyer or accountant or both.

bonus cases

bonus case 5-1
BUILDING COMPUDYNE

The global security firm Compudyne is one of the biggest and most successful security companies in the world, which produces prison equipment and surveillance gear and helps protect government buildings against terrorism. After the 1998 bombings of two U.S. embassies in Africa, Compudyne's business supplying blast-resistant windows and doors to most of the embassies around the world doubled. After the terrorist attack on the U.S.S. *Cole* in 2000, the company was hired to provide shoreline protection for the U.S. Navy and Air Force. And following the attacks on the World Trade Center and the Pentagon on September 11, 2001, Compudyne started fielding calls from federal and state government agencies around the country asking for help in protecting "at-risk assets" like nuclear power plants.

Considered the industry leader in the market for physical and electronic security, Compudyne took in $141 million in revenues in 2005, compared to $127 million in revenues in 2001. That performance becomes even more impressive when you consider that the company was near bankruptcy in 1995. Compudyne was founded as a defense contractor back in the early 1950s. For decades, it stuck mostly to security projects, but in the 1980s, when big conglomerates like Gulf & Western were popular, the company's management made an ill-fated attempt to branch off into new businesses. Some of the choices weren't entirely inane, like a home-improvement division, but others were, billboards and plastic extrusion. The diversification strategy turned out to be a disaster. By 1995, the loss of focus had combined with some management missteps had driven revenues down to just $12 million, and book value was literally zero.

In large part, the credit for Compudyne's resurgence goes to Marty Roenigk. A former investment executive at Travelers, he took over the company in 1995, streamlined its operations, made a series of strategic acquisitions, and encouraged the discovery of new technologies that could fight new threats. Some of the company's recent success is undoubtedly due to being in the right business at the right time, but the better part goes to Roenigk's ability to figure out a simple strategy and execute it extremely well.

Roenigk owned a private manufacturer called MicroAssembly Systems, which made tiny screws originally used to assemble cameras. Roenigk had built the company to about $1.6 million in revenues and had deals with AT&T and Hewlett-Packard when a stockbroker told him about Compudyne. Roenigk saw an opportunity to fold his small company into something much bigger. MicroAssembly had a core strategy and a good balance sheet, while Compudyne was an ugly collection of assets that didn't belong together. In a reverse merger—a deal in which a bigger company buys a smaller one but the smaller company retains control—Roenigk took over. He immediately got rid of the management team and sold off everything not related to security (including his old company.)

After he sold off all the unrelated pieces, Roenigk started shopping for new ones that would fit better. Compudyne's first purchase was a firm that sold electronic security systems for prisons. Roenigk also wanted to buy Norment Industries, a company that made bullet- and blast-resistant products as well as prison locks and doors. He spent about two years lobbying for the deal, finally closing it in late 1998. After each deal, Roenigk was smart enough to leave the new divisions mostly intact.

With lingering terrorism fears, Compudyne enjoyed a surging demand for its security products. In January 2004 the firm secured Army and Navy orders for security bollards and pop-up barriers that sent its stock up 14%. But the company's financial position has recently deteriorated. Compudyne reported a "sharp curtailment" of prison and jail construction contracts. For 2005 the company reported a loss of $8.2 million.

Although most of its business is still in the nuts and bolts of security, such as blast-proof doors and pop-up barriers, the company has continued to bolster its work in security software. It recently acquired 90 Degrees and its emergency medical information software for public safety agencies.[ix]

discussion questions for bonus case 5-1

1. What does this case teach you about finding opportunities for forming your own business?

2. Is being in the right place at the right time an accident, or are some people more clever than others at being in the right place at the right time?

3. What does this case teach you about making the most of a bad thing?

notes on discussion questions for bonus case 5-1

1. *What does this case teach you about finding opportunities for forming your own business?*

    The world is constantly creating new challenges and opportunities. Some people are just overwhelmed by it all and tend to stick to what they are doing no matter what. Others seek new challenges and profit from them. You may be running a successful company when you see a new opportunity. Will you seize that opportunity when it comes or stay where you are safe and secure? The biggest successes are often based on taking risks and getting out of the safe and secure path. That is what this case illustrates. You can even buy a bigger business than you are. Who would have thought it?

2. *Is being in the right place at the right time an accident, or are some people more clever than others at being in the right place at the right time?*

    Being at the right place at the right time is sometimes an accident. But, more often than not, people create opportunities so it just looks like they were in the right place at the right time. There were probably a couple of dozen other people in the same place at the same time who did not seize the opportunity. So being there is not enough. You have to act! It's often uncomfortable reaching out to grab an opportunity, but it's very rewarding when it works. However, it doesn't always work. You may be in the right place at the wrong time.

3. *What does this case teach you about making the most of a bad thing?*

    Most people pulled back from their activities when they heard about terrorist attacks around the world and in the United States. Terrorist attacks were a bad thing, but they did call for new ways of stopping such attacks. And this case shows that one man can really make a difference. You not only solve the problems as best you can, but you search for other synergistic ways of solving problems to enable growth.

bonus case 5-2

FRANCHISE OR INDEPENDENT? WHAT FITS YOUR MOLD?

In 2003, Rusty and Beth Adcock opened up the fourth franchised unit of Country Fisherman, a small, Mississippi-based, family-owned restaurant group. Rusty and Beth were switching gears from the corporate worlds of electrical wholesale distribution and retail marketing. Obviously there would be a learning curve.

They had looked at several business opportunities and decided on the restaurant business because it was a cash-basis business. There was not going to be a lot of money tied up in inventory and there would be minimal to no accounts receivables. This would bode well for cash flow.

The Country Fisherman Restaurant originated in 1987 in Prentiss, a small town in south central Mississippi. Peggy Tuma started it and built it with hard work and a deep background in food preparation. By the time her new husband Harold came along in the early 1990s, Peggy had worked out enough kinks that Harold encouraged and assisted her in expanding. Gradually they expanded into two other markets—Mendenhall and Jackson, Mississippi. It was at this time they realized the need to formulate franchise agreements.

When the Adcocks and Tumas worked out their deal with the Brookhaven franchise, it was the first franchise agreement sold subsequent to the restaurant being established. At the time, the Tumas had initially owned all of the first three restaurants. Later they sold the Mendenhall unit to a relative. So, basically, the deal being done with the Adcocks was the first independently run unit the Tumas would be selling.

While the Tumas had created a franchise model for their enterprise, the Adcocks were in charge of their own destiny. The Tumas provided simple menu plans, inventory guidelines, and volume pricing contracts with their franchise agreement. During the first week or two after opening the Brookhaven unit, the Tumas did help with hands-on assistance to make sure the unit got under way as the others they had opened. However, once the "wheels were in motion," the Adcocks were virtually on their own. The Tumas would provide answers to questions and solutions to problems when called upon.

As time went by, Rusty and Beth picked up on the ins and outs of the restaurant business. Moreover, through nobody's efforts but their own, Rusty and Beth became fairly well known in the community. And in 2007, it became evident that the franchise business model the Adcocks were a part of might not be the best answer for them now. There were some inconsistencies in the decision making for all Country Fisherman units. Therefore, Rusty and Beth felt poor decisions independently made by the other franchisees could adversely affect their unit. If the consistency was not going to be upheld by the Tumas, maybe it was time to disassociate their Brookhaven unit from the others.

In March of 2008, Rusty and Beth took the plunge. After coming to an agreement with the Tumas on terms for separation, the Country Fisherman restaurant became Rusty's Family Restaurant. Though there were some patrons of the restaurant who were confused of the change at first, it quickly became apparent that the restaurant's loyal supporters were truly more worried about who was in charge than what the name was. Once they realized Rusty and Beth were still operating the business, any concerns slipped away. It seemed that the people who operate businesses can create a very strong bond with the customers who support that business. In Rusty and Beth's case, that turned out to be a good thing.

Being independent has its drawbacks. There's no support system to lean on such as large franchise systems. Of course, as small as Country Fisherman was, the support system was not that large. Because of the relationships Rusty had built with the food suppliers, the volume discounts given up with the franchise system were basically negated with other promotions he could take advantage of that he couldn't before.

Staying involved in the community your business is a part of is important. Over time it will be apparent to those people in that community that you are a part of them. In turn, they will support you. It is sometimes as simple as "do unto others as you would have them do unto you." Of course, this means hours of hard work, too.[x]

discussion questions for bonus case 5-2

1. What are the advantages of buying a franchise operation? What are the disadvantages?

2. What do you think is key to any business, whether franchise or independent?

3. What are the advantages of owning your own independent business? What are the disadvantages?

4. If you decided to start your own or buy a business, which route would you take? Franchise or uniquely you? Cash-based, service-based, or inventory retail/wholesale? Why?

notes on discussion questions for bonus case 5-2

1. *What are the advantages of buying a franchise operation? What are the disadvantages?*

    When buying a franchise, the buyer is paying for a system that is in place and proven to work. The initial setup work has been tried and tested. Once the buyer learns the system, he or she should be able to clone it and mimic it to produce similar results. Disadvantages would be that the franchisors have not done enough homework and testing in different markets to have recognized that their system might not work for all markets. What worked in the original market setting and even several other similar markets might not do well in a different market. Sustaining power is hard to judge in different market climates. Also, if the franchisors are not true to the consistency of their offering through all of their franchisees, it can be a detriment to the whole organization.

2. *What do you think is key to any business, whether franchise or independent?*

    The key to any business is how that business treats their customers. Customer service in any market will be remembered more by the patrons of that business than any other characteristic of that business. The way a customer is treated is paramount. Furthermore, if you can create unique ways to make that customer feel important and appreciated, the retention of that customer is virtually automatic.

3. *What are the advantages of owning your own independent business? What are the disadvantages?*

    No question—if you are the owner, it's simple, the buck stops with you. The inventory you buy, the expenses you authorize, the decorating you choose, the services you provide, it's all you and no one can tell you differently. (Well, except for the IRS; it dictates your taxes whether you're independent or not.) The world (at least this little part of it) is your oyster.

    The disadvantage of being independent is that "the buck stops with you." There is added pressure on you because the blame game has nowhere to go. You are "the man." You shoulder all the responsibility and must suffer the consequences of any bad decisions.

4. *If you decided to start your own or buy a business, which route would you take? Franchise or uniquely you? Cash-based, service-based, or inventory retail/wholesale? Why?*

    Each student will have to answer this for himself or herself.

UNDERSTANDING BUSINESS: Instructor's Resource Manual

endnotes

[i] *Source:* "Most Admired Companies," *Fortune,* March 21, 2011.

[ii] *Source:* "Fortune 500 Companies," *Fortune,* May 23, 2011.

[iii] *Sources:* Jim Mallory, "Compaq Board Ousts Rod Canion," *Newsbytes News Network,* October 25, 1981; Alan Goldstein, "Houston Firm Plans to Create Virtual Library," *The Dallas Morning News,* April 6, 2000, p. D10; Nancy Perry, "Steven Jobs: Seeding a New Apple?" *Fortune,* September 2, 1985, p. 11; Philip Elmer-DeWitt, "Computers: The Love of Two Desk Lamps," *Time,* September 1, 1986, p. 66; February 7, 2005; Peter Burrows, "Apple: What's Steve Jobs Up To?" *BusinessWeek,* March 17, 1997; John Cook, "Many Young Start-Up Founders Making Way for Seasoned CEOs," *Seattle Post-Intelligence,* August 25, 2000; Ron Grover, "Is Steve Jobs About to Move His Cheese?" *BusinessWeek Online,* February 10, 2003; Jim Jewell, "Questions Follow Fuller's Firing from Habitat for Humanity," *Christianity Today*; Matthew Yi, "Jobs Return Rejuvenates Firm," *San Francisco Chronicle*, March 26, 2006.

[iv] *Source:* Eric Savitz, "Skype Me," *Forbes,* May 18, 2011.

[v] *Source:* Allan Sloan, "Smucker Adds Coffee to Its Breakfast Lineup—And Does It Tax Free," *WashingtonPost.com,* June 10, 2008.

[vi] *Sources:* Amey Stone, "The Joys of an ESOP," *BusinessWeek,* November 1, 2004; Lois Alete Fundis, "A Short History of the Weirton Area," Mary H. Weir Public Library, Weirton, West Virginia; ESOP Association, www.esopassociation.org.

[vii] *Source:* Gwen Moran, "Franchising's Green Scene," *Entrepreneur*, August 2009.

[viii] *Source:* Jason Daley, "Despite the Slowdown at Home, U.S. Franchises Expand Abroad," *Entrepreneur*, May 2011.

[ix] *Sources:* Carlye Adler, "Safe and Sound," *Fortune Small Business,* July/August 2002, pp. 46–49; "Compudyne Corporation," *Washington Post Company,* www.washingtonpost.com, 2005; "DefenseWeb's Strong Q2 Results Driven by New Contract Wins, Partnership Agreements with Industry Leaders," Freshnews.com/San Diego/Orange County, July 17, 2006.

[x] *Sources:* Rhonda Abrams, "Focus on Success, Not Failure," *USA Today,* May 6, 2004; "New Study Finds Restaurants' Failure Rate Lower than Expected," *Entrepreneur,* September 22, 2003; "Adcocks come home to Mississippi, Get 'Hooked' on Restaurant," *Brookhaven Daily Leader,* April 30, 2004, page 13P; interviews with the owners.

Entrepreneurship and Starting a Small Business

chapter **6**

critical thinking exercises

bonus cases

what's new in this edition

additions to the 10th edition:

- Getting to Know Jay-Z, Rapper and Founder of Roc Nation

- Name That Company: McDonald's

- Discussion of Self-Employment Assistance (SEA) and Startup America programs added in section Encouraging Entrepreneurship: What Government Can Do

- Discussion of community development financial institutions (CDFIs) added to section Getting Money to Fund a Small Business

- Spotlight on Small Business: Success Knows No Age

- Social Media in Business: Social Lending

- Reaching Beyond Our Borders: Emerging Markets, Emerging Entrepreneurship

- Video Case

revisions to the 10th edition:

- Text was revised to eliminate redundancy and tighten discussions.

- Statistical data and examples throughout the chapter were updated to reflect current information.

deletions from the 9th edition:

- Getting to Know Sheila C. Johnson, Cofounder of Black Entertainment Television (BET)

- Name That Company: Art Fry and 3M

- Spotlight on Small Business

- Thinking Green

- Reaching Beyond Our Borders

brief chapter outline
and learning goals

Entrepreneurship and Starting a Small Business

Getting To Know JAY-Z, Rapper and Cofounder of ROC NATION

I. THE AGE OF THE ENTREPRENEUR

II. THE JOB-CREATING POWER OF ENTREPRENEURS IN THE UNITED STATES

learning goal 1

Explain why people take the risks of entrepreneurship; list the attributes of successful entrepreneurs; and describe entrepreneurial teams, intrapreneurs, and home- and Web-based businesses.

III. WHY PEOPLE TAKE THE ENTREPRENEURIAL CHALLENGE

A.   What Does It Take to Be an Entrepreneur?

B.   Turning Your Passion and Problems into Opportunities

C.   Entrepreneurial Teams

D.   Micropreneurs and Home-Based Businesses

E.   Web-Based Businesses

F.   Entrepreneurship within Firms

G.   Encouraging Entrepreneurship: What Government Can Do

learning goal 2

Discuss the importance of small business to the American economy and summarize the major causes of small-business failure.

IV. GETTING STARTED IN SMALL BUSINESS

A.   Small versus Big Business

B.   Importance of Small Businesses

C.   Small-Business Success and Failure

Summarize the ways to learn about how small businesses operate.

V. LEARNING ABOUT SMALL-BUSINESS OPERATIONS

A.   **Learn from Others**

B.   **Get Some Experience**

C.   **Take Over a Successful Firm**

Analyze what it takes to start and run a small business.

VI. MANAGING A SMALL BUSINESS

A.   **Begin with Planning**

B.   **Writing a Business Plan**

C.   **Getting Money to Fund a Small Business**

D.   **The Small Business Administration (SBA)**

E.   **Knowing Your Customers**

F.   **Managing Employees**

G.   **Keeping Records**

H.   **Looking for Help**

Outline the advantages and disadvantages small businesses have in entering global markets.

VII. GOING GLOBAL: SMALL-BUSINESS PROSPECTS

VIII. SUMMARY

lecture outline

Getting to Know JAY-Z, Rapper and Founder of ROC NATION

Shawn Carter, aka Jay-Z, has sold over 45 million albums worldwide and is one of the world's richest musicians. He founded Roc-A-Fella Records in 1996 and retained control over his image. When choosing endorsements, he carefully considered the products and again kept creative control. His branding expertise has helped him in all of his ventures. Being successful in business, not just music, has opened many doors and relationships (with Bill Gates, Warren Buffett, and former President Bill Clinton)!

When this company's founder had financial problems in the business's early days, he asked his suppliers to help him out. They did and they were well rewarded for their risk. Today these suppliers still service this mammoth company that has franchises all over the world. Name that company.

(Students should read the chapter before guessing the company's name: McDonald's.)

I. THE AGE OF THE ENTREPRENEUR

A. Today, young people will probably not have the traditional 30-year career in one job.

B. **_ENTREPRENEURSHIP_** is accepting the risk of starting and running a business.

II. THE JOB-CREATING POWER OF ENTREPRENEURS IN THE UNITED STATES

A. The need to **CREATE MORE JOBS** is a major issue in the U.S. today.

B. The success of great American entrepreneurs shows the **JOB-CREATING POWER** of entrepreneurship.

C. The text lists examples including PAST **ENTREPRENEURS** *George Eastman (Kodak), Henry Ford (Ford Motor Company), and Jeff Bezos (Amazon.com.)*

PPT 6-1
Chapter Title

PPT 6-2
Learning Goals

(See complete PowerPoint slide notes on page 6.46.)

PPT 6-3
Learning Goals

(See complete PowerPoint slide notes on page 6.46.)

PPT 6-4
Jay-Z

(See complete PowerPoint slide notes on page 6.47.)

PPT 6-5
Name That Company

(See complete PowerPoint slide notes on page 6.47.)

PPT 6-6
What Is Entrepreneurship?

(See complete PowerPoint slide notes on page 6.47.)

PPT 6-7
Notable Entrepreneurs

(See complete PowerPoint slide notes on page 6.48)

D. **CONTEMPORARY ENTREPRENEURIAL TALENT** *include the late Steve Jobs (Apple Computer,) Mark Zuckerberg (Facebook), and Jack Dorsey (Twitter).*

<u>**learning goal 1**</u>

Explain why people take the risks of entrepreneurship; list the attributes of successful entrepreneurs; and describe entrepreneurial teams, intrapreneurs, and home- and Web-based businesses.

III. WHY PEOPLE TAKE THE ENTREPRENEURIAL CHALLENGE

A. Reasons why people are **WILLING TO TAKE THE RISKS** of business ownership include:

1. **OPPORTUNITY** to share in the American dream through initiative and hard work

2. **PROFIT**: Entrepreneurship made Bill Gates the richest person in the world

3. **INDEPENDENCE**

   a. Many entrepreneurs don't enjoy working for someone else.

   b. Some have found more self-satisfaction in starting their own businesses.

4. **CHALLENGE**

   a. Some believe that entrepreneurs are excitement junkies who enjoy taking risks.

   b. In reality, entrepreneurs take **MODERATE, CALCULATED RISKS.**

   c. In general, entrepreneurs seek **ACHIEVEMENT** more than **POWER.**

B. **WHAT DOES IT TAKE TO BE AN ENTREPRENEUR?**

lecture link 6-1
HISTORY'S GREATEST ENTREPRENEURS

Who are the greatest entrepreneurs of all time? One news website lists its top 10. (See the complete lecture link on page 6.66 in this manual.)

SPOTLIGHT ON
small
business
(Text page 149)

PPT 6-8
Success Knows No Age

(See complete PowerPoint slide notes on page 6.48.)

PPT 6-9
You're Never Too Young to Be an Entrepreneur

(See complete PowerPoint slide notes on page 6.48.)

PPT 6-10
You're Never Too *Old* to Be an Entrepreneur Either!

(See complete PowerPoint slide notes on page 6.49.)

PPT 6-11
Why Take the Risk?

(See complete PowerPoint slide notes on page 6.49.)

lecture link 6-2
LUCKY OFFICE SPACE

According to its owners, the building at 165 University Avenue in Palo Alto, California, is blessed with "good karma." (See the complete lecture link on page 6.67 in this manual.)

1. **ENTREPRENEURIAL ATTRIBUTES** Entrepreneurs tend to be:

    a. **SELF-DIRECTED:** Be self-disciplined and comfortable being the boss.

    b. **SELF-NURTURING:** Believe in your own ideas.

    c. **ACTION-ORIENTED:** Have a desire to build the dream into reality.

    d. **HIGHLY ENERGETIC:** Be emotionally, mentally, and physically able to work long hours in order to succeed.

    e. **TOLERANT OF UNCERTAINTY:** Have the ability to take calculated risks and give up some security.

C. **TURNING YOUR PASSION AND PROBLEMS INTO OPPORTUNITIES**

    1. Many entrepreneurs see business opportunities in problems or challenges.

    2. The ideas for entrepreneurs' products and services don't usually come from some **FLASH** of inspiration—often the source of innovation is more like a **FLASHLIGHT**.

    3. Not all ideas are opportunities—an idea must meet someone else's needs.

    4. A business idea is a **GOOD OPPORTUNITY** if:

        a. It fills customers' needs

        b. You have the skills and resources to start a business

<u>critical thinking exercise 6-1</u>
WHAT DOES IT TAKE TO BE AN ENTREPRENEUR?

This exercise explores the motivations and expectations of small-business owners. (See complete exercise on page 6.73 of this manual.)

PPT 6-12
What Does It Take to Be an Entrepreneur?

(See complete PowerPoint slide notes on page 6.49.)

PPT 6-13
Five Steps to Starting Your Business in School

(See complete PowerPoint slide notes on page 6.50.)

<u>lecture link 6-3</u>
CHARLES BABBAGE: 19th-CENTURY ENTREPRENEUR

Nineteenth-century England was not ready for Charles Babbage, inventor and entrepreneur. (See the complete lecture link on page 6.67 in this manual.)

c. You can sell the product or service at a price customers are willing and able to pay and still make a profit

d. You can get your product or service to customers before your window of opportunity closes

e. You can keep the business going

5. An **ENTREPRENEURIAL READINESS QUESTIONNAIRE** is presented in the text box on text pages 153–154.

D. **ENTREPRENEURIAL TEAMS**

1. An **ENTREPRENEURIAL TEAM** is a group of experienced people from different areas of business who join together to form a managerial team with the skills needed to develop, make, and market a new product.

2. This **COMBINATION OF SKILLS** is needed to get the new company off to a great start.

3. *The text uses the example of the "smart team" of entrepreneurs who founded Apple Computers.*

E. **MICROPRENEURS AND HOME-BASED BUSINESSES**

1. **MICROPRENEURS** are entrepreneurs willing to accept the risk of starting and managing the type of business that remains small, lets them do the kind of work they want to do, and offers them a balanced lifestyle.

2. Micropreneurs are content with limited growth.

3. Many micropreneurs are **HOME-BASED BUSINESS OWNERS.**

PPT 6-14
An Idea Is a Good Opportunity If…

(See complete PowerPoint slide notes on page 6.50.)

box in text
ENTREPRENEUR READINESS QUESTIONNAIRE
(Text pages 153–154)

This questionnaire helps students determine whether they have entrepreneurial ability and in which category they fit.

PPT 6-15
Entrepreneurial Teams

(See complete PowerPoint slide notes on page 6.50.)

PPT 6-16
Micropreneurs

See complete PowerPoint slide notes on page 6.51.)

4. Many are owned by people who are trying to combine career and family.

5. Reasons for the **GROWTH OF HOME-BASED BUSINESSES**:

   a. **COMPUTER TECHNOLOGY** allows home-based businesses to look and act as big as corporations.

   b. **CORPORATE DOWNSIZING** has eroded job security, leading many to start new ventures.

   c. **SOCIAL ATTITUDES** have changed to encourage home-based businesses.

   d. New **TAX LAWS** have loosened the restrictions regarding deductions for home offices.

6. **MAJOR CHALLENGES** facing home-based businesses include:

   a. Getting new customers

   b. Managing time

   c. Keeping work and family tasks separate

   d. Abiding by city ordinances

   e. Managing risk

7. **HOME OFFICE ENTREPRENEURS SHOULD FOCUS ON:**

   a. Finding opportunity instead of accepting security

   b. Getting results instead of following routines

   c. Earning a profit instead of earning a paycheck

   d. Trying new ideas instead of avoiding mistakes

PPT 6-17
Home-Based Business Growth

(See complete PowerPoint slide notes on page 6.51.)

PPT 6-18
Home-Based Business Isn't Easy

(See complete PowerPoint slide notes on page 6.51.)

PPT 6-19
Benefits of Home-Based Businesses

(See complete PowerPoint slide notes on page 6.52.)

PPT 6-20
Downsides of Home-Based Businesses

(See complete PowerPoint slide notes on page 6.52.)

PPT 6-21
Think You're Ready to Work from Home?

(See complete PowerPoint slide notes on page 6.52.)

TEXT FIGURE 6.1
Potential Home-Based Businesses
(Text page 155)

This text figure gives some suggestions for would-be entrepreneurs.

e. Creating a long-term vision instead of seeking a short-term payoff

F. **WEB-BASED BUSINESSES**

1. The Internet has spawned many small Web-based businesses.

2. Online sales in 2010 were over $172 billion.

3. *The text uses the example of Marc Resnik's website ThrowThings.com.*

4. To succeed, Web-based businesses must offer unique products or services.

5. <u>*AFFILIATE MARKETING*</u> is an Internet-based marketing strategy in which a business rewards individuals or other businesses (**AFFILIATES**) for each visitor or customer the affiliate sends to its website.

    a. *The text uses the example of directing potential buyers to a product.*

        i. You register as an affiliate on the seller's website.

        ii. Then download a **WIDGET**, a tiny application that links your page to the seller's.

        iii. Whenever anyone clicks on the widget and buys the product, the seller pays you a commission.

    b. Setting up an online store is easier using a **SOCIAL COMMERCE SERVICE**.

        i. *An example is Lemonade Inc.'s Lemonade Stand.*

TEXT FIGURE 6.2
Watch Out for Scams
(Text page 155)

This text figure highlights clues to avoiding home-based business scams.

PPT 6-22
Online Business

(See complete PowerPoint slide notes on page 6.53.)

bonus case 6-1
DRIVING AWAY BUSINESSES WITH THE AMAZON TAX

For years, Amazon has made billions without collecting a cent of sales tax. Illinois is putting an end to that and hoping increased revenue will help the state debt. (See the complete case, discussion questions, and suggested answers beginning on page 6.78 of this manual.)

PPT 6-23
Affiliate Marketing

(See complete PowerPoint slide notes on page 6.53.)

PPT 6-24
Boosting Your Business's Online Presence

(See complete PowerPoint slide notes on page 6.53.)

       ii.   Users select which products they would like to appear in their **WIDGET PRODUCT GALLERIES**.

      iii.   Using a **WIDGET OPERATOR** saves users time and effort.

  6.   Web-based businesses are not failure-proof.

G. **ENTREPRENEURSHIP WITHIN FIRMS**

  1.   <u>*INTRAPRENEURS*</u> are creative people who work as entrepreneurs within corporations.

  2.   They launch new products and generate new profits by using company's existing resources— human, financial, and physical.

  3.   *The text focuses on the development of Post-it Notes at 3M through the entrepreneurial efforts of Art Fry.*

H. **ENCOURAGING ENTREPRENEURSHIP: WHAT GOVERNMENT CAN DO**

  1.   The government passed the **IMMIGRATION ACT OF 1990** to encourage more entrepreneurs to come to the United States.

     a.   It created a category of **"INVESTOR VISAS"** that allows 10,000 people to come to the U.S. each year if they invest $1 million in an enterprise that creates or preserves 10 jobs.

     b.   Some believe that more jobs will be created if more entrepreneurs can be lured to the U.S.

  2.   One way to encourage entrepreneurship is through **ENTERPRISE ZONES** that feature low taxes and government support.

PPT 6-25
Intrapreneurs

(See complete PowerPoint slide notes on page 6.54.)

bonus case 6-2

**3M COMPANY,
INTRAPRENEURIAL LEADER**

Each year the 3M Company produces about 60,000 products and generates $16 billion in sales by fostering employee innovation. (See the complete case, discussion questions, and suggested answers beginning on page 6.80 of this manual.)

lecture link 6-4

INVENTING FROM THE OUTSIDE

For years companies haven't given time to products created outside of their own R&D departments. As companies are downsizing, product development is shifting from intrapreneurs toward outside inventors (See the complete lecture link on page 6.68 of this manual.)

PPT 6-26
Government and Entrepreneurship

(See complete PowerPoint slide notes on page 6.54.)

      a. ***ENTERPRISE ZONES*** are specific geographic areas to which governments try to attract private business investment by offering lower taxes and other government support.

      b. The government could encourage entrepreneurship by offering investment **TAX BREAKS** to businesses that invest in creating jobs.

   3. States also provide support for entrepreneurs.

      a. State commerce departments serve as clearinghouses for information and programs.

      b. States also create incubators and technology centers to reduce start-up capital needs.

      c. ***INCUBATORS*** are centers that offer low-cost offices with basic business services (such as accounting, legal advice, and secretarial help).

      d. Incubators help companies survive because they provide assistance in the **CRUCIAL EARLY DEVELOPMENT STAGE.**

   4. A few states offer assistance under the **SELF-EMPLOYMENT ASSISTANCE (SEA)** program.

      a. SEA allows participants to collect unemployment while building their business.

      b. The checks are enough to help launch the company.

learning goal 2

Discuss the importance of small business to the American economy and summarize the major causes of small-business failure.

IV. GETTING STARTED IN SMALL BUSINESS

  A. In general, the **SAME PRINCIPLES** apply to small and large companies, government, and nonprofits.

lecture link 6-5

EX-CONTREPRENEURS

Prisoner Entrepreneurship Program (PEP) has helped inmates in state prisons by teaching them how to open their own legitimate businesses after serving their sentences. (See complete lecture link on page 6.68 of this manual.)

**progress
assessment**
(Text page 158)

PPT 6-27
Progress Assessment

PROGRESS ASSESSMENT

- Why are people willing to take the risks of entrepreneurship?
- What are the advantages of entrepreneurial teams?
- How do micropreneurs differ from other entrepreneurs?
- What are some opportunities and risks of web-based businesses?

(See complete PowerPoint slide notes on page 6.55.)

1. All organizations need:
   a. Capital
   b. Good ideas
   c. Planning
   d. Information management
   e. Budgets
   f. Accounting
   g. Marketing
   h. Employee relations
   i. Good overall managerial know-how

B. **SMALL VERSUS BIG BUSINESS**
   1. As defined by the SBA, ***SMALL BUSINESS***:
      a. Is independently owned and operated
      b. Is not dominant in its field of operation
      c. Meets certain standards of size (set by the Small Business Administration) in terms of employees or annual receipts (*for example, less than $2 million a year for service companies*)
   2. **SMALL-BUSINESS STATISTICS**
      a. There are 27.8 million small businesses in the U.S.
      b. Almost 97% of all nonfarm businesses are considered small by SBA standards.
      c. Small businesses account for over **50% OF THE GROSS DOMESTIC PRODUCT**.
      d. The first jobs of about 80% of all Americans are in small business.

lecture link 6-6
START-UPS FOR GROWN-UPS

Nearly half of the country's self-employed workers are baby boomers, and that figure is expected to climb as this generation retires. (See the complete lecture link on page 6.69 of this manual.)

PPT 6-28
Small Businesses

(See complete PowerPoint slide notes on page 6.55.)

PPT 6-29
Small-Business Statistics

(See complete PowerPoint slide notes on page 6.56.)

critical thinking
exercise 6-2
WHAT IS SMALL?

The Small Business Administration defines *small* in different ways for different industries. This exercise asks students to visit the SBA website and find definitions for several industries. (See complete exercise on page 6.74 of this manual.)

e. Small businesses generate 60 to 80% of the new jobs each year.

C. **IMPORTANCE OF SMALL BUSINESSES**

1. Small businesses have advantages over big companies—they give more personal customer service and are able to respond quickly to opportunities.

2. There is plenty of room for small businesses in **MARKET NICHES** not served by big businesses.

D. **SMALL-BUSINESS SUCCESS AND FAILURE**

1. **FAILURE RATE**

   a. There is some debate about how many new small businesses fail each year.

   b. 50% of new businesses don't last five years.

   c. However, another study by economist Bruce Kirchhoff found that data misinterpretation overestimated the failure rate.

   d. Kirchhoff's data showed that the failure rate is only 18% over the first eight years.

   e. Business failures may be much lower than traditionally reported.

2. Many small businesses fail because of managerial incompetence and inadequate financial planning.

3. Choosing the **RIGHT TYPE OF BUSINESS** is critical to success.

   a. The businesses with the lowest failure rates often require advanced training to start.

   b. High-growth businesses are not easy to start and even more difficult to keep going.

PPT 6-30
Advantages of Small over Big
Business

(See complete PowerPoint slide notes on page 6.56.)

lecture link 6-7
**A NEW KING OF BEERS IN
ST. LOUIS**

When Schlafly Beer was first started, no one thought it would last because of the hometown favorite, Budweiser. Then InBev took over A-B and doors were opened for the small brewer. (See the complete lecture link on page 6.69 in this manual.)

PPT 6-31
Business Failures Are Lower Than
the Reports Because . . .

(See complete PowerPoint slide notes on page 6.56.)

lecture link 6-8
**FAILURE IS THE BEST
MEDICINE**

One commentator believes that failure is a blessing, recycling talent for new ventures. (See the complete lecture link on page 6.70 in this manual.)

PPT 6-32
They Did What?

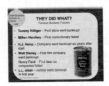

(See complete PowerPoint slide notes on page 6.57.)

TEXT FIGURE 6.3
Causes of Small-Business Failure
(Text page 160)

This text figure lists reasons for small-business failures, including managerial incompetence and inadequate financial planning.

TEXT FIGURE 6.4
Situations for Small-Business
Success
(Text page 161)

This text figure shows some factors that increase the chances of small-business success.

    c. In general, the easiest businesses to start are the ones that have the least growth and the greatest failure rate.

    d. The ones that can make you rich are both hard to start and hard to keep going.

learning goal 3

Summarize the ways to learn about how small businesses operate.

V. LEARNING ABOUT SMALL-BUSINESS OPERATIONS

A. LEARN FROM OTHERS

1. Many **LOCAL COMMUNITY COLLEGES** offer entrepreneur programs and classes.
2. Talk to **ENTREPRENEURS** who have already done it.
3. Entrepreneurs will tell you that:
   - a. Location is critical.
   - b. You should be keeping good records.
   - c. You should not be undercapitalized.

B. GET SOME EXPERIENCE

1. Go to work for others and learn all you can.
2. The general rule is: **THREE YEARS OF EXPERIENCE** in a comparable business.
3. *Cornelius Vanderbilt sold his own sailing vessels and went to work for a steamboat company so he could learn the new technology of steam.*
4. Running a small business part-time is another way of gaining experience.

C. TAKE OVER A SUCCESSFUL FIRM

1. After many years in business, some small-business owners feel stuck in their businesses.

PPT 6-33

Learning about Small Business

(See complete PowerPoint slide notes on page 6.57.)

2. The text describes a method of becoming successful small-business managers.

   a. The first step is to find a businessperson running a successful small business.

   b. Ask to serve an **APPRENTICESHIP**, a one-year training program.

   c. For another year or so, working hard to learn all about the business.

   d. At the end of two years, offer to become **ASSISTANT MANAGER.**

   e. At the end of two years, offer to manage the business when the owner retires.

   f. You can establish a profit-sharing plan for yourself plus a salary.

3. The **OWNER BENEFITS** by keeping ownership and earning profits without working.

4. If profit sharing doesn't appeal to the owner, you may want to **BUY THE BUSINESS OUTRIGHT**, basing the price of the business on:

   a. What the business owns

   b. What it earns

   c. What makes it unique

learning goal 4

Analyze what it takes to start and run a small business.

VI. MANAGING A SMALL BUSINESS

A. According to the SBA, one of the major causes of small-business failure is **"POOR MANAGEMENT."**

MAKING
ethical
decisions
(Text page 162)

PPT 6-34
Going Down with
the Ship

(See complete PowerPoint slide notes on page 6.57.)

1. This may involve poor planning, poor record keeping, poor inventory control, poor promotion, or poor employee relations.
2. The most likely cause is poor capitalization.
3. This section explores the **MAJOR FUNCTIONS OF BUSINESS** as they pertain to small business:
   a. **PLANNING** your business
   b. **FINANCING** your business
   c. **KNOWING** your customers (**MARKETING**)
   d. **MANAGING** your employees (**HUMAN RE-SOURCE DEVELOPMENT**)
   e. **KEEPING RECORDS (ACCOUNTING)**

B. **BEGIN WITH PLANNING**
   1. Small businesses start with an idea that can be developed.
   2. A **_BUSINESS PLAN_** is a detailed written statement that describes the nature of the business, the target market, the advantages the business will have in relation to competition, and the resources and qualifications of the owner(s).
   3. A business plan forces potential small-business owners to be **SPECIFIC** about the products and services they intend to offer.
   4. When talking with bankers or other investors, a business plan is mandatory.

C. **WRITING A BUSINESS PLAN**
   1. A good business plan takes a long time to write.
   2. One of the most important parts of the business plan is the **EXECUTIVE SUMMARY**, which must catch the reader's interest.

PPT 6-35
Major Business Functions

(See complete PowerPoint slide notes on page 6.58.)

PPT 6-36
Business Plans

(See complete PowerPoint slide notes on page 6.58.)

box in text

**OUTLINE OF A COMPREHEN-
SIVE BUSINESS PLAN**
(Text pages 165–166)

This text box outlines a comprehensive business plan and gives suggestions on what to include.

PPT 6-37
Writing a Business Plan

(See complete PowerPoint slide notes on page 6.58.)

critical thinking
exercise 6-3
WRITING A BUSINESS PLAN

This exercise analyzes the business plan for a small auto repair shop. (See complete exercise on page 6.75 of this manual.)

3. Computer software programs can help you get organized.

4. Getting the completed business plan in the right hands is almost as important as getting the right information in it.

5. The time and effort invested before starting a business will pay off later.

D. **GETTING MONEY TO FUND A SMALL BUSINESS**

1. New entrepreneurs have several **SOURCES OF CAPITAL,** but most start-ups receive money from friends and family.

2. **SUPPLIERS** may also be a funding source.

3. The recent credit crunch drove many potential entrepreneurs to smaller community banks, which were more likely to grant loans than larger banks were.

4. **COMMUNITY DEVELOPMENT FINANCIAL INSTITUTIONS (CDFIs)** may be a source of funding.

5. Aside from than personal savings, **INDIVIDUAL INVESTORS** are the primary source of capital for most entrepreneurs.

6. **ANGEL INVESTORS** are private individuals who invest their own money in new businesses with potential.

7. **_VENTURE CAPITALISTS_** are individuals or companies that invest in new businesses in exchange for partial ownership of those businesses.

PPT 6-38
A Family Affair

(See complete PowerPoint slide notes on page 6.59.)

PPT 6-39
Sources of Capital

(See complete PowerPoint slide notes on page 6.59.)

PPT 6-40
Funding Your Dream

(See complete PowerPoint slide notes on page 6.59.)

PPT 6-41
Community Development Financial
Institutions

(See complete PowerPoint slide notes on page 6.60.)

social media in business
(Text page 167)

PPT 6-42
Social Lending

(See complete PowerPoint slide notes on page 6.60.)

    a. Venture capitalists may demand a large share (as much as 60%) in your company in exchange for the start-up cash.

    b. Since the widespread failure of early Web start-ups, venture capitalists are willing to invest less and expect more.

  8. Smaller companies have a better chance of finding funding through an angel investor.

E. **THE SMALL BUSINESS ADMINISTRATION (SBA)**

  1. The ***SMALL BUSINESS ADMINISTRATION (SBA)*** is a U.S. government agency that advises and assists small businesses by providing management training and financial advice and loans.

  2. The SBA's **MICROLOAN PROGRAM** awards loans based on the borrowers' integrity and the soundness of their business idea.

  3. Another source of funds is a **SMALL BUSINESS INVESTMENT COMPANY (SBIC).**

    a. The ***SMALL BUSINESS INVESTMENT COMPANY PROGRAM (SBIC)*** is a program through which private investment companies licensed by the Small Business Administration lend money to small businesses.

    b. An SBIC loans to or invests in small businesses that meet its criteria.

  4. **SMALL BUSINESS DEVELOPMENT CENTERS (SBDCs),** funded jointly by the federal government and individual states, can help evaluate the feasibility of your idea, develop your business plan, and complete your funding application.

PPT 6-43
The Small Business Administration

(See complete PowerPoint slide notes on page 6.60.)

TEXT FIGURE 6.5
Types of SBA Financial Assistance
(Text page 168)

This text figure shows the types of assistance the SBA can offer to small businesses.

PPT 6-44
The Small Business Investment
Company

(See complete PowerPoint slide notes on page 6.61.)

PPT 6-45
Small Business Development
Centers

(See complete PowerPoint slide notes on page 6.61.)

5. The text gives several ways to contact the SBA, including the SBA website (www.sba.gov).

6. In February 2011, the SBA introduced the **COMMUNITY ADVANTAGE AND SMALL LOAN ADVANTAGE PROGRAM** which provides a simpler and easier way for lenders to make small loans in underserved areas.

7. One month later, funding was cut and no money was able to be used by the program.

8. For most small businesses, obtaining money from banks, venture capitalists, and government sources is very difficult.

9. Success depends on many factors, including:

   a. Knowing your customer

   b. Managing your employees

   c. Keeping records

F. **KNOWING YOUR CUSTOMERS**

1. A **_MARKET_** consists of people with unsatisfied wants and needs who have both the resources and the willingness to buy.

2. The first step in filling these needs is to identify the **WANTS AND NEEDS** of potential customers.

3. The goal of a businessperson is to **FIND A NEED AND FILL IT.**

4. Offer top quality at a fair price with great service.

5. After you have customers, you must to keep them through excellent service.

PPT 6-46
Community Advantage and Small
Loan Advantage Program

(See complete PowerPoint slide notes on page 6.61.)

PPT 6-47
Help Please!

(See complete PowerPoint slide notes on page 6.62.)

PPT 6-48
The Market

(See complete PowerPoint slide notes on page 6.62.)

lecture link 6-9
**COMPETING AGAINST
WAL-MART**

How one small hardware store found ways to compete against the world's largest retailer. (See the complete lecture link on page 6.70 in this manual.)

critical thinking
exercise 6-4
**COMPETING AGAINST
WAL-MART**

An extension of **Lecture Link 6-9** above, this exercise asks students to consider how to help a small business compete successfully against Wal-Mart. (See complete exercise on page 6.77 of this manual.)

G. **MANAGING EMPLOYEES**

1. It is not easy to **FIND, HIRE, TRAIN, AND KEEP GOOD EMPLOYEES.**

    a. Small businesses offer less money, fewer benefits, and less room for advancement than larger firms do.

    b. However, employees of small companies are often more satisfied with their jobs than their counterparts in large companies.

    c. They find their jobs are more challenging, their ideas are more accepted, and their bosses treat them with more respect.

2. As the business grows, the entrepreneur must **DELEGATE AUTHORITY**.

    a. In businesses with long-term employees, this is especially difficult.

    b. These long-term employees may not have the necessary managerial skills.

3. Family firms may be held back by attitudes such as "you can't fire family" or you must promote someone because "they're family."

4. Entrepreneurs best serve the business if they re-cruit and groom employees for management posi-tions.

5. Chapters 7 through 12 focus on managing em-ployees.

H. **KEEPING RECORDS**

1. A businessperson who sets up an **ACCOUNTING SYSTEM** early will save much grief later.

PPT 6-49
Managing Employees

(See complete PowerPoint slide notes on page 6.62.)

2. **COMPUTERS** simplify record keeping and let the business owner follow the progress of the business.

3. A good **ACCOUNTANT** can help:

   a. Decide whether to buy or lease

   b. Provide tax planning and financial forecasting

   c. Choose sources of financing

4. Chapter 17 focuses on accounting.

I. **LOOKING FOR HELP**

1. Small-business owners need help setting up their businesses early in the process.

2. A competent, experienced lawyer who knows and understands small businesses is valuable.

   a. A prepaid legal plan may be cost-effective.

   b. Online legal services are also available.

3. A **MARKETING RESEARCH STUDY** can help with key marketing decisions.

4. A **COMMERCIAL LOAN OFFICER** and an **IN-SURANCE AGENT** are also valuable experts.

5. The ***SERVICE CORPS OF RETIRED EXECU-TIVES (SCORE)*** is an SBA office with volunteers from industry, trade associations, and education who counsel small businesses at no cost (except for expenses).

6. Local college business professors may also advise small-business owners for a fee.

7. Other sources:

   a. Other small-business owners

   b. Local chambers of commerce

PPT 6-50
Accounting Assistance

(See complete PowerPoint slide notes on page 6.63.)

PPT 6-51
Legal Help

(See complete PowerPoint slide notes on page 6.63.)

PPT 6-52
Marketing Research

(See complete PowerPoint slide notes on page 6.63.)

PPT 6-53
Other Forms of Help

(See complete PowerPoint slide notes on page 6.64.)

lecture link 6-10

MAKING ENTREPRENEURSHIP A COLLEGE MAJOR

There are only 12 successful university entrepreneurial programs in the United States today. (See the complete lecture link on page 6.49 of this manual.)

    c. The Better Business Bureau

    d. National and local trade associations

learning goal 5

Outline the advantages and disadvantages small businesses have in entering global markets.

VII. GOING GLOBAL: SMALL-BUSINESS PRO-SPECTS

A. The **WORLD MARKET** is more lucrative for small businesses than the U.S. market alone.

    1. However, most small businesses still do not think internationally.

    2. Only 1% of small businesses export.

B. Technology advances, such as PayPal, have helped increase small-business exporting.

C. Many potential international businesspeople **DO NOT** enter the global market because:

    1. Financing is often difficult to find.

    2. They don't know how to get started and don't understand the cultural differences of potential markets.

    3. The bureaucratic paperwork can be overwhelming.

D. There are many good reasons for small-business owners to **CONSIDER GOING INTERNATIONAL:**

    1. Most of the world's market lies outside the U.S.

    2. Exporting can absorb excess inventory.

    3. It can soften downturns in the U.S. market.

    4. It can extend the life of products.

progress
assessment
(Text page 172)

PPT 6-54
Progress Assessment   (See complete PowerPoint slide notes on page 6.64.)

E. Small businesses have several **ADVANTAGES OVER LARGE BUSINESSES:**

1. Overseas buyers enjoy dealing with individuals rather than with large corporate bureaucracies.

2. Small companies can usually begin shipping much faster.

3. Small companies provide a wide variety of suppliers.

4. Small companies can give more personal service and more attention.

F. **SOURCES OF INFORMATION** about international business.

1. Department of Commerce's Bureau of Industry and Security (<u>www.bis.doc.gov</u>)

2. SBA's international business resources (<u>www.sba.gov</u>)

VIII. SUMMARY

PPT 6-55

Small-Business Prospects Abroad

(See complete PowerPoint slide notes on page 6.64.)

PowerPoint slide notes

PPT 6-1
Chapter Title

PPT 6-2
Learning Goals

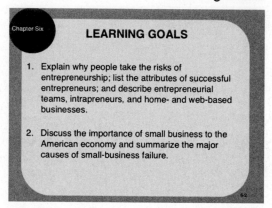

PPT 6-3
Learning Goals

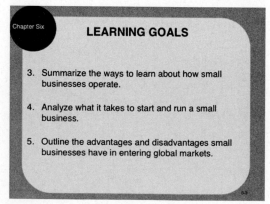

PPT 6-4
Jay-Z

JAY-Z
Roc Nation

- Founded Roc-A-Fella Records before entering into a joint venture with Def Jam.
- Maintains control over the Jay-Z brand - including his clothing line and nightclub chain.
- Regarded as a business leader, he has met with Bill Gates, Warren Buffett and former President Bill Clinton.

PPT 6-5
Name That Company   Company: McDonald's

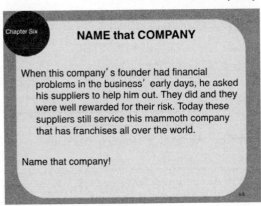

NAME that COMPANY

When this company's founder had financial problems in the business' early days, he asked his suppliers to help him out. They did and they were well rewarded for their risk. Today these suppliers still service this mammoth company that has franchises all over the world.

Name that company!

PPT 6-6
What Is Entrepreneurship?

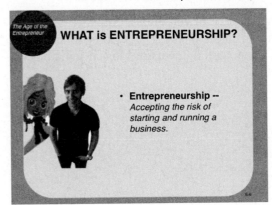

WHAT is ENTREPRENEURSHIP?

- **Entrepreneurship --** *Accepting the risk of starting and running a business.*

Notable Entrepreneurs

This slide will help start the chapter discussion. Students enjoy stories about how companies began.

Ask the students, Do you know of any interesting stories about how some other businesses got started? *(This can also be assigned as a team project to generate a good discussion.)*

PPT 6-8
Success Knows No Age

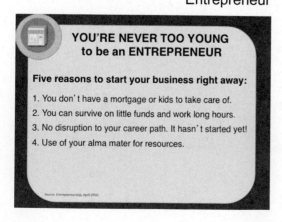

PPT 6-9
You're Never Too Young to Be an Entrepreneur

1. This slide shows the students that it's never too early to get started on your business ideas.

2. Ask the students, Can you think of other reasons you might want to start a business right after school? What are the potential downsides to starting a business right away?

PPT 6-10
You're Never Too *Old* to Be an Entrepreneur Either!

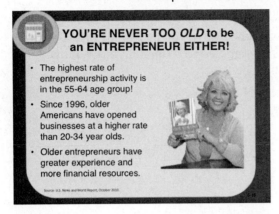

1. This slide shows that in spite of popular belief that all older Americans retire at a certain age, many start their own businesses after leaving their careers.

2. Ask the students, Can you think of reasons (other than experience and funding) that older entrepreneurs are successful? Why do you think older Americans want to start businesses at this age? What are the downsides of starting a business late?

PPT 6-11
Why Take the Risk?

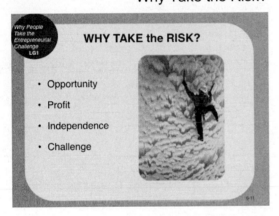

PPT 6-12
What Does It Take to Be an Entrepreneur?

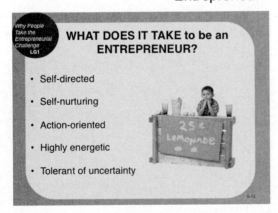

Five Steps to Starting Your Business in School

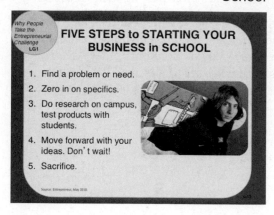

1. Just because you're still in school doesn't mean that starting a business is beyond your grasp. Many students have turned their time in college into an opportunity to create a business.

2. Ask the students, Have you had an idea for a business? What triggered it? Why did you or did you not pursue it further?

PPT 6-14

An Idea Is a Good Opportunity If . . .

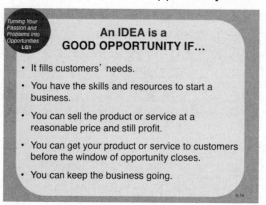

PPT 6-15

Entrepreneurial Teams

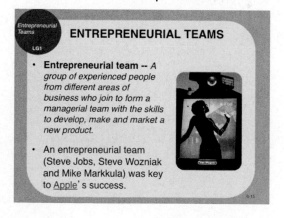

PPT 6-16

Micropreneurs

MICROPRENEURS

- **Micropreneurs** -- *Entrepreneurs willing to accept the risk of starting and managing a business that remains small, lets them do the work they want to do, and offers a balanced lifestyle.*

- About half of U.S. micropreneurs are home-based business owners – writers, consultants, video producers, architects, bookkeepers, etc.

- Nearly 60% of home-based micropreneurs are men.

6-16

PPT 6-17

Home-Based Business Growth

HOME-BASED BUSINESS GROWTH

- Computer technology has leveled the playing field.

- Corporate downsizing has led many to venture on their own.

- Social attitudes have changed.

- New tax laws have loosened restrictions on deducting expenses for home offices.

6-17

PPT 6-18

Home-Based Business Isn't Easy

HOME-BASED BUSINESS ISN'T EASY

- Getting new customers is difficult.

- Managing your time requires self-discipline.

- Work and family tasks are sometimes not separated.

- Government ordinances may restrict your business.

- Homeowner's insurance may not cover business-related claims.

6-18

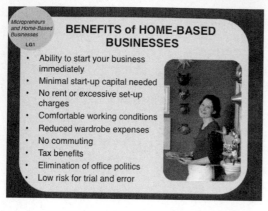

1. This slide lists some of the benefits of a home-based business.

2. Before showing this slide, have students work alone, then with a partner, then with a group (doing all three will help promote discussion of students' ideas) to see if they can come up with a list of benefits of home-based businesses. Then reveal the slide and have students compare their lists to the slide.

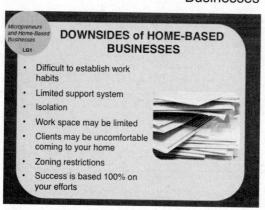

1. This slide walks students through some of the drawbacks of a home-based business.

2. Before showing this slide, have students work alone, then with a partner, then with a group (doing all three will help promote discussion of students' ideas) to see if they can come up with a list of disadvantages of home-based businesses. Then reveal the slide and have students compare their lists to the slide.

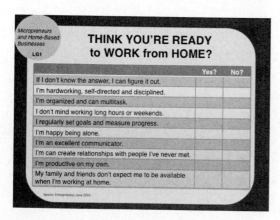

1. Running a business from home is hard work. After discussing both the ups and downs of home-based work, discuss this table with students.

2. Ask the students, What statements can you say yes and no to? What do each of these statements have to do with home business success? After looking at this table, do you think you'd be ready or want to work from home?

PPT 6-22
Online Business

It's expected that online sales will reach $250 billion by 2014.

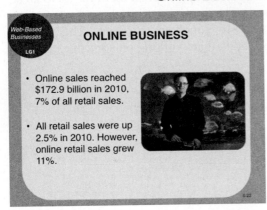

PPT 6-23
Affiliate Marketing

PPT 6-24
Boosting Your Business's Online Presence

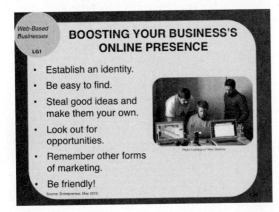

1. Activity online, both in retail and marketing, continues to grow each year. It's important that businesses (even the small ones!) have an online, user-friendly presence.

2. This slide provides some guidelines to successfully navigate the process of creating an online business identity.

3. Ask the students, Do you have any other ideas of important steps to take in creating an online personality for a business? Through Facebook? Twitter? Ads on Pandora or Hulu?

In order to develop new ideas, engineers at Google are allowed to work on projects that interest them for up to 20% of the time at work. The idea is to support creative people and ideas in an effort to launch new products. This work can be more motivating than working on someone else's ideas.

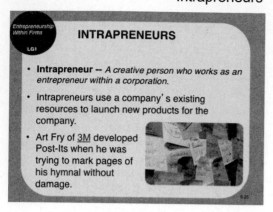

Small business is the economic engine of the U.S. economy. Due to the economic power of small businesses the government has used "investor visas," enterprise zones, and business incubators to encourage entrepreneurship. A good website to further explore incubators is www.nbia.org/.

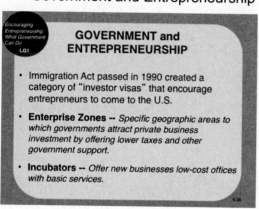

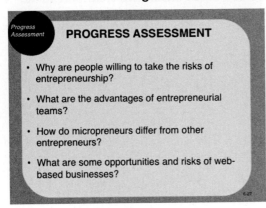

PPT 6-27
Progress Assessment

PROGRESS ASSESSMENT

- Why are people willing to take the risks of entrepreneurship?
- What are the advantages of entrepreneurial teams?
- How do micropreneurs differ from other entrepreneurs?
- What are some opportunities and risks of web-based businesses?

1. The primary reasons that people are willing to take the risk of entrepreneurship are:

   - Opportunity to share in the American dream

   - Profit, the potential to become wealthy and successful

   - Independence, becoming your own boss

   - Challenge, the desire to take a chance

2. Whereas an entrepreneur has to wear many hats and take huge responsibility, a team allows members to combine creative skills with production and marketing skills right from the start. Having a team can also ensure more cooperation and coordination later among functions in the business.

3. Most entrepreneurs are committed to the quest for growth in their business. Micropreneurs know they can be content even if their companies never appear on a list of top-ranked businesses. Many micropreneurs are home-based businesses.

4. The Internet has opened the world of entrepreneurship wider than ever. Online sales have grown six times faster than retail sales and in 2010 topped $172 billion. Today anything that can be offered in a retail environment can be offered online. However, a Web-based business is not an automatic ticket to success. It can often be a shortcut to failure. Web-based businesses must remember that they need to offer unique products or services that customers cannot easily purchase at retail locations.

PPT 6-28
Small Businesses

SMALL BUSINESSES

- **Small Business --**
  Independently owned and operated, not dominant in its field of operation and meets certain standards of size.
- Businesses are "small" in relation to other businesses in their industries.

PPT 6-29
Small-Business Statistics

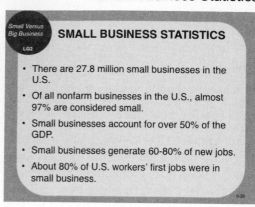

The power of small business is immense. Students are often shocked to see how small businesses contribute to the U.S. economy.

PPT 6-30
Advantages of Small over Big Business

PPT 6-31
Business Failures Are Lower Than the Reports Because . . .

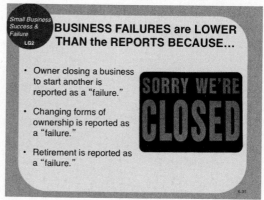

UNDERSTANDING BUSINESS: Instructor's Resource Manual

PPT 6-32
They Did What?

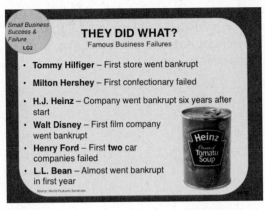

1. Starting a successful new business is never easy and many famous entrepreneurs failed at their first and subsequent attempts.

2. Ask the students, How can a business failure actually be a positive experience? *(While failure is never a goal, it often gives the entrepreneur an invaluable experience. There is an old adage, Learn from your mistakes.)*

3. Ask the students, If your first business failed, would you try again? Why or why not?

4. How can businesses survive such poor performances? *(Determination and passion of the owners and founders plays a big role.)*

PPT 6-33
Learning about Small Business

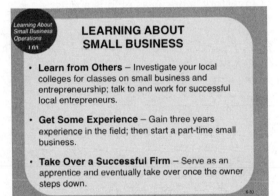

PPT 6-34
Going Down with the Ship

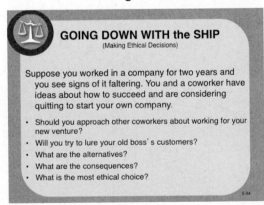

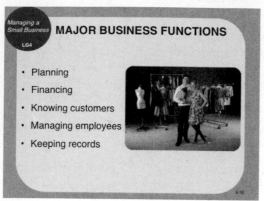

Starting a business is when the real work begins. It is important that entrepreneurs understand the major business functions such as planning, financing, understanding your customer, managing employees, and keeping good records. Many entrepreneurs create business plans that may in part outline the major business functions.

The business plan is the entrepreneur's road map to success. While a well-designed business plan will not guarantee success, the lack of one may lead to failure. To borrow money or to seek investors, a business plan is a must.

PPT 6-38
A Family Affair

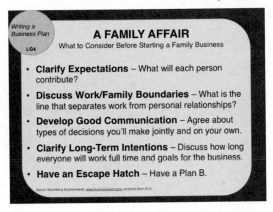

1. This slide illustrates what needs to be considered before starting a business with family members.

2. Communication and the establishment of clear expectations are the keys to making a family business work.

3. Ask the students, Why do family businesses need extra care?

PPT 6-39
Sources of Capital

One reason that businesses fail is a lack of capital. Capital can come from internal sources (personal saving, employees, etc.) or from external sources (relatives, banks, and angel investors). One source of external funding is venture capital. Venture capitalists are individuals or companies that invest in new businesses in exchange for a stake in ownership. Many well-known businesses, such as Google, Zappos, and Apple, received a first round of funding from venture capitalists.

PPT 6-40
Funding Your Dream

1. Financing is hard to come by in this economy.

2. This slide outlines Seth Godin's advice on how to self-fund start-ups.

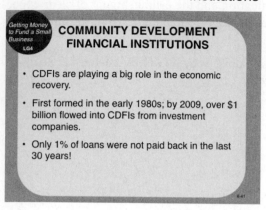

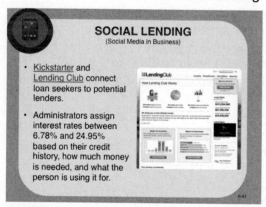

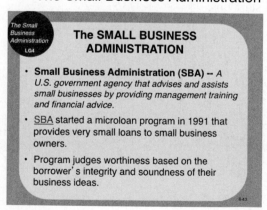

The importance of small business to the U.S. economy cannot be overstated. The SBA is the government agency that advises and assists small businesses with financial advice and management training. For more information on the SBA visit its website at www.sba.gov.

The Small Business Investment Company

The SMALL BUSINESS INVESTMENT COMPANY

- **Small Business Investment Company (SBIC) --** *A program through which private investment companies licensed by the SBA lend money to small businesses.*

  - A SBIC must have a minimum of $5 million in capital and can borrow up to $2 from the SBA for each $1 of capital it has.

  - SBICs are able to identify a business's trouble spots early, giving entrepreneurs advice, and in some cases rescheduling loan payments.

6-44

Small Business Development Centers

SMALL BUSINESS DEVELOPMENT CENTERS

- Small Business Development Centers (SBDC) are funded jointly by the federal government and individual states.

- SBDCs are able to evaluate the feasibility of your idea, develop your business plan and complete your funding application – for no charge.

6-45

Community Advantage and Small Loan Advantage Program

COMMUNITY ADVANTAGE and SMALL LOAN ADVANTAGE PROGRAM

- Announced by the SBA in February 2011, this program's aim was to provide a simpler and easier way for lenders to make smaller loans in underserved areas.

- In March 2011, the House Small Business Committee recommended the SBA budget be cut and the program couldn't be funded.

6-46

1. These are other sources for helpful information about starting and running a small business.

2. Encourage students to go to these websites to learn what services each offers.

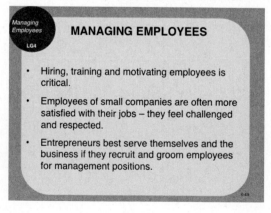

The most important assistance to small-business owners is in accounting.

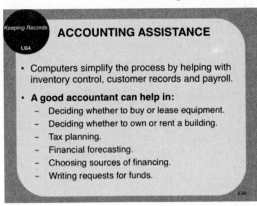

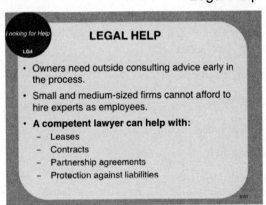

If marketing is about finding and filling customer needs, how can an entrepreneur better understand what customers need? Market research helps determine where to locate customers, whom to target as customers, and an effective strategy for reaching the market.

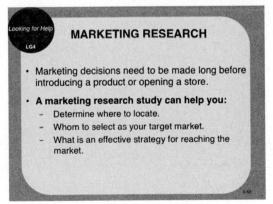

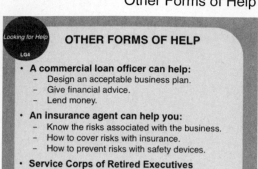

Asking good questions is the key to success in any business. Fortunately for entrepreneurs, some of the best advice comes free. Commercial loan officers can help with the creation of a business plan as well as financial advice. Insurance agents can help new entrepreneurs understand and insure against risk. One interesting and free source of information is SCORE, Service Corps of Retired Executives. To start a discussion in class, have students research SCORE (www.score.org) and the programs offered at local SCORE offices.

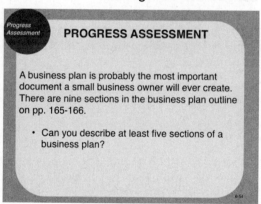

1. A business plan needs to start with a strong cover letter. The nine key sections are:

    - Executive summary

    - Company background

    - Management team

    - Financial plan

    - Capital required

    - Marketing plan

    - Location analysis

    - Manufacturing plan

    - Appendix

PPT 6-56

Emerging Markets, Emerging
Entrepreneurship

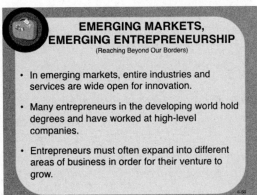

**EMERGING MARKETS,
EMERGING ENTREPRENEURSHIP**
(Reaching Beyond Our Borders)

- In emerging markets, entire industries and services are wide open for innovation.

- Many entrepreneurs in the developing world hold degrees and have worked at high-level companies.

- Entrepreneurs must often expand into different areas of business in order for their venture to grow.

PPT 6-57

Progress Assessment

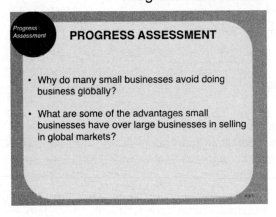

*Progress
Assessment*   **PROGRESS ASSESSMENT**

- Why do many small businesses avoid doing business globally?

- What are some of the advantages small businesses have over large businesses in selling in global markets?

1. Key reasons why many small businesses avoid doing business overseas include: (a) financing is often difficult to find, (b) would-be exporters don't know how to get started and do not understand the cultural differences between markets, and (c) the bureaucratic paperwork can threaten to bury a small business.

2. Small businesses have several advantages over large businesses in global markets. These include: (a) global buyers often enjoy dealing with individuals rather than with large corporate bureaucracies, (b) small companies can usually begin shipping much faster, (c) small companies can provide a wide variety of suppliers, and (d) mall companies can give global customers personal service and undivided attention because each overseas account is a major source of business for them.

"Our company has, indeed, stumbled onto some of its new products. But never forget that you can only stumble if you are moving."
Richard P. Carlton, Former CEO, 3M Corporation

"Imagination is more important than knowledge."
Albert Einstein

"The greater the difficulty, the more glory in surmounting it. Skillful pilots gain their reputation from storms and tempests."
Epictetus

"Keep away from small people who try to belittle your ambitions. Small people always do that, but the really great make you feel that you, too, can become great."
Mark Twain

lecture link 6-1

HISTORY'S GREATEST ENTREPRENEURS

Mention successful entrepreneurs today, and the names that come to mind include Bill Gates, Sam Walton, and Ted Turner, to name a few. But who are the greatest entrepreneurs of all time? MSNBC recently posted a listing of its picks. The finalists are men (sorry, no women) who excelled at taking capital and using it to create more capital.

10. **STEVEN JOBS** and **STEVE WOZNIAK**. Jobs and Wozniak weren't the first Silicon Valley entrepreneurs, but they were the first to successfully market a truly revolutionary device—the personal computer.

9. **H. ROSS PEROT. In** the 1990s, Perot become known for his political aspirations. However, his entrepreneurial fame involves his creation of EDS (Electronic Data Systems). Perot saw that big corporations needed data-processing help and developed an enterprise providing it.

8. **RAY KROC.** At the age of 52 Kroc bought out a small restaurant chain and launched a giant retail enterprise. Kroc's winning strategy—a limited menu, fast service, and low prices—launched McDonald's and created the fast-food industry.

7. **BENJAMIN SIEGEL. BETTER** known as "Bugsy," Siegel singlehandedly invented Las Vegas and attracted big investors to build the resorts. Unfortunately, some of these investors belonged to the Mob.

6. **HENRY FORD.** Ford revolutionized human lifestyles by making transportation affordable to the average American. He also designed the moving assembly line, a breakthrough concept in industry.

5. **THOMAS EDISON.** Edison was probably the world's greatest inventor—the electric light, the phonograph, talking motion pictures, and more than 1,300 other inventions. Unlike other inventors, he also succeeded in exploiting the profit potential of his creations, something other inventors have failed to do.

4. **P. T. BARNUM.** Americans have always loved a spectacle. Barnum catered to this fascination with the Barnum and Bailey Circus. Along the way, he invented modern advertising and became rich.

3. **BENJAMIN FRANKLIN.** Franklin is best known as one of the founders in America's early history. In addition to being a diplomat, Franklin was also a popular author, a printer, an inventor, and a savvy businessman.

2. **POPE SIXTUS IV.** Pope Sixtus was the first to realize that there was money to be made in sin and death. He saw a lucrative market selling "indulgences" for the dead. Relatives of the dead lined up and filled the Vatican's coffers. He then expanded the death market by authorizing the Spanish Inquisition. Sixtus was also the first pope to license brothels.

1. **KING CROESUS.** Croesus ruled the Asia Minor kingdom of Lydia in the sixth century B.C. He is famous for minting the world's first coinage. His extravagant lifestyle has also given generations of entrepreneurs something to shoot for—to be as "rich as Croesus."[i]

lecture link 6-2

LUCKY OFFICE SPACE

The building at 165 University Avenue in Palo Alto, California, is "blessed with good karma," according to owner Saeed Amidi. Some of the most successful Silicon Valley entrepreneurs agree. Over the years the two-story building has been home to such fledgling enterprises as PayPal, Logitech, and Google.

The Amidi family, who own a rug company on the ground floor of the building, were perceptive enough to ask for an ownership stake in the companies they housed. Their first investment was PayPal, the online payment company. When eBay bought the company for $1.5 billion, the Amidis walked away with a multimillion-dollar payout and a taste for technology investment.

Then came Logitech and Danger, which created the T-Mobile Sidekick smartphone. Amidi and his partner, Pejman Nozad, eventually created an investment fund, Amidzad, which helped bankroll over 40 companies.

Google was attracted to the building by a "for lease" sign that mentioned some of the previous tenants. When it moved into the building early in 1999, Google had six employees. By the time it left six months later, about 10 times that many were crammed into the small office space. More importantly, Sergey Brin and Larry Page had secured financing from two of Silicon Valley's best-known venture capitalists and had signed its first big partnership with the Internet browser company Netscape.

"We believe in good karma, good energy, good feeling, and believe some buildings have good energy," says Amidi. He still owns the building.[ii]

lecture link 6-3

CHARLES BABBAGE: 19TH-CENTURY ENTREPRENEUR

Nineteenth-century England was not ready for Charles Babbage. The mathematician had already proven his ingenuity by inventing the speedometer, the cowcatcher, and the first reliable life-expectancy tables when his enthusiasm turned to the problem of calculations. His first machine, which was designed to calculate logarithms, was an intricate system of gears and cogs, which he called the Differential Engine.

No sooner had the Differential Engine been completed than Babbage proposed an expanded machine: one with a central "mill" for performing logical operations, a "store" or memory to hold information, and means to put information in and retrieve it. In short, all the elements of a modern computer.

The Analytical Engine became his obsession. Along with his patron, Ada the Countess of Lovelace, he worked for nearly 40 years to perfect it. Ada, Lord Byron's mathematically gifted daughter, wrote the initial set of instructions for the Engine, the world's first computer program.

When Babbage died in 1871, all he had to show of his machine were thousands of sketches—the machine was never built. In order to perform the intricate calculations he developed, the Engine's parts had to be machined to precise tolerances. No craftsperson of the age could do so. If it had been built, the Analytical Engine would probably have been as big as a football field and would have required half a dozen locomotive engines to power it.

lecture link 6-4

INVENTING FROM THE OUTSIDE

Traditionally, independent inventors who pitch their product ideas to established companies are met with little consideration. More often than not, an inventor's idea ends up in the garbage can instead of in development. This is exactly what happened to retired ad executive Fred Sulpizio, the inventor of a trash bag ironically enough. The bag is equipped with a built-in device that prevents it from collapsing as it fills with garbage. Sulpizio shopped his prototype around to dozens of companies with a mountain of rejection letters to show for his determination.

Stories like Sulpizio's are all too common for many other would-be inventors. For years companies have trusted their own research and development divisions to devise new products and granted little regard for any idea that wasn't developed in-house. Those companies that do rarely accept proposals from outsiders do so with stringent restrictions. For example, Starbucks requires inventors to sign an agreement saying that their ideas belong entirely to the company once submitted—with no compensation to the inventors. This policy not only reduces the amount of unwanted proposals but also prevents any copyright infringement suits in the rare event that someone actually submits an idea to the company for free.

But as businesses across the country scale back on their own R&D departments, many companies are changing their tune on outside product development. For example, Greg Swartz, another trash-focused amateur inventor, devised an odor-eliminating product called the "Hang 'n' Fresh," which hooks on the inside of garbage cans. After sending an e-mail description of the product to Proctor & Gamble, Swartz received a response within 24 hours and is in negotiations to have the Hang 'n' Fresh green lighted for production. P&G is taking user-submitted ideas so seriously that it has dubbed the whole process as its Open Innovation program, with 3,704 submissions in 2009 alone and about 1,000 of those landing contracts, some worth millions. But before you send off the schematics for your robotic miracle trash can, potential applicants are advised to first get a patent for their product then submit their proposal with a business plan. A keen understanding of the company's product line is also essential.[iii]

lecture link 6-5

EX-CONTREPRENEURS

For many ex-convicts, finding an honest job after prison life can be difficult. Despite laws that prevent employers from discriminating based on a prison record, a lot of companies will bury an individual's resume if he or she has done time. This lack of steady work drives many ex-cons back to crime and, inevitably, another stint in prison.

Catherine Rohr, founder and CEO of the Prisoner Entrepreneurship Program (PEP), hopes to reduce this work-related recidivism by teaching prisoners about starting their own businesses. In 2004 Rohr visited a prison and was astounded by some prisoners' grasp of important business fundamentals they learned while dealing drugs. She soon quit her job in private equity and started PEP, which uses classroom teaching, mentoring, and a business-plan contest to help prisoners understand the workings of a legitimate business.

Of the 440 men who have completed the program, 47 have gone on to start their own businesses. For example, PEP graduate Hans Brecker, who spent a quarter of his life behind bars, started a successful landscaping business. Another 5 graduates now have jobs that pay over $100,000 a year. The program has not been a complete success, though, as 105 graduates are back in jail. Still, the lessons of entrepreneurship taught by PEP at least give ex-cons a better chance of success in a discriminating world. As difficult as starting a business is, Rohr claims the criminal who chooses to be an entrepreneur faces fewer obstacles than if he were to send out 100 resumes.[iv]

lecture link 6-6
START-UPS FOR GROWN-UPS

Move over, Google boys! Older Americans are the new entrepreneurs. Nearly half the country's self-employed workers are boomers, reports the U.S. Department of Labor. And that figure is expected to climb as people retire from one career to start another, lose their jobs, or simply want the independence and flexibility of working for themselves.

But is it wise to launch a start-up or buy a business at midlife? Experts say it's risky at any age, but for older adults, particularly those who finance their venture with savings and retirement funds, the stakes can be painfully high: If a venture goes belly-up, there's less time to work and restore retirement savings. The statistics are sobering. According to the Small Business Administration, 66% of new companies survive at least two years but only 44% last for four years.

Despite the odds, recruiter John McDorman, a managing partner at Transition Consulting in Dallas, says he often advises older clients to consider buying or starting a business if they can't find a job that pays what they think they're worth. Finding a job if you're 55 or older involves a long job search. In the nine months to a year it takes to find a job, older workers can burn through a significant amount of their savings. Says McDorman, who has counseled many older workers, "So which is more risky—the job or the venture you controlled?"

To minimize the risk, McDorman suggests buying a "fairly low-end" business with a record of success rather than financing a start-up. Examine the company's financials thoroughly and make sure it has a positive cash flow and potential for growth. McDorman says new owners often run a business better than their predecessors because they're more adept at controlling costs, expanding market share, and diversifying the product line and channels of distribution. They're motivated and fresh, he says, compared with previous owners who may be burned out.

Tom and Sue Ann McGoldrick followed McDorman's advice when they bought Paws in Heaven, a pet crematory in Texas. The McGoldricks financed the purchase with half of Tom's 401(k) retirement funds, their personal savings, and a business loan. They increased advertising and distributed brochures to veterinary clinics in neighboring counties while keeping operating costs in line—earning handsome revenues in the first year. "What I'm doing," says Tom, "it's a real labor of love."[v]

lecture link 6-7
A NEW KING OF BEERS IN ST. LOUIS

When the Belgian beer conglomerate InBev bought Anheuser-Busch in 2008, many residents in A-B's hometown of St. Louis saw the takeover as a betrayal. The brewer had been headquartered in the River City since 1852 and reigned for decades as the area's undisputed "King of Beers" with near total market dominance. But much of the city's goodwill faded fast once the company's new foreign owners dropped the axe hard on St. Louis. Of the 1,400 jobs InBev slashed just weeks after acquiring the company, 75% of those layoffs occurred at A-B's erstwhile home base.

As Budweiser's dominance of St. Louis wanes, local craft brands like Schlafly Beer are taking up the mantle as the new beer barons of the Midwest. When Schlafly first began brewing in 1991, the company's founders were seen as upstarts at best and heretics at worst. President Tom Schlafly likened the notion of opening a microbrewery in St. Louis at the time to selling a foreign car in Detroit. The brewery flourished nevertheless and soon became a staple of discerning bars across the area.

But it wasn't until A-B's merger with InBev that Schlafly managed a major push into the mainstream of America's beer capital. Once upon a time the company couldn't convince the area's fiercely loyal A-B bars to stock even one keg of Schlafly Pale Ale. Now the brewery boasts more than 2,000 taps in the St. Louis area, 30% of which were added between 2009 and 2011. Overall sales jumped the same amount in 2009 along with a 17% boost in revenue. Schlafly hasn't unseated A-B from its throne, however, with the multinational still controlling 68% of the St. Louis beer market versus Schlafly's 1.5%. The bulk of A-B's dominance comes from its immense size: In a single year its St. Louis facility brews more product than the entire craft brewing industry nationwide. Regardless of its relatively small operation, though, Schlafly is making some major headway into areas once forbidden to other brewers, such as its eight taps in St. Louis's once Bud-exclusive Busch Stadium.[vi]

lecture link 6-8

FAILURE IS THE BEST MEDICINE

Americans tend to think that failure is something to be ashamed of, a personal defeat. Paul Saffo, director of Institute for the Future, believes that failure, particularly in the high-tech companies of Silicon Valley, is a blessing.

Saffo compares failure to the cleansing fires that clean out old growth in forests and create space for new life. In the heady years of the dot-com boom, Silicon Valley was awash with too many people, too many expensive houses, too little office space, and too much money chasing too few start-ups. "Failure is the safety valve, the destructive renewing force that frees up people, ideas, and capital and recombines them, creating new revolutions," says Saffo.

Saffo points to the history of the Internet. In 1989, the World Wide Web was invented by Tim Berners-Lee, a British engineer, for use in interactive television. Half a world away, the Internet revolution gained momentum, fueled by a lucky failure. Just as Berners-Lee launched the Web, the interactive television industry was collapsing. Hundreds of millions of dollars were lost and dozens of start-ups failed. One important byproduct this collapse was a large pool of laid-off C++ programmers who were expert in multimedia design and out on the street looking for a new venture.

These revolutionaries fueled the dot-com revolution. They were Web pioneers, translating their media design talents into Internet start-ups. Many of these failed, but they spun off experienced entrepreneurs. Silicon Graphics founder Jim Clark was unemployed in 1994 after failing in another interactive-TV concept. He approached Marc Andreessen, the codeveloper of the Mosaic Internet browser, to help design a new interactive system. Instead, Andreessen refocused Clark's attention to the potential of the Web. The two collaborated to create Netscape, the first browser to commercialize the Web.

lecture link 6-9

COMPETING AGAINST WAL-MART

All across the country small retailers tell the same tale: A retail giant like Home Depot or Wal-Mart moves into the area and small businesses lose out. However, some local businesses are finding ways to compete against the giants.

Bill Fichtler, manager of the Independent Budget Food Market in Oklahoma, is surrounded by 10 Wal-Mart Supercenters, 6 Wal-Mart discount stores, and 4 Sam's Clubs. His store has served the primarily Hispanic neighborhood for more than 20 years. "We're going to do our thing and Wal-Mart can do theirs," says Fichtler.

Budget Food's customers seem to prefer his market's fresh cactus, daily baked tortillas, and other Mexican specialties to Wal-Mart's more generic selection of ethnic packaged products. The store also adds services such as check cashing and Western Union money orders.

Canadian grocery chain Loblaws differentiates itself by turning some stores into mini-lifestyle malls catering to mothers with young children. The store stocks prepared foods, a line of children's clothing, a café, on-site babysitting, and a health club.

In Fort Wayne, Dave Umber's three hardware stores also faced the big store threat. He lost $110,000 in two years. Giant superstores and home centers were chipping away at his sales. Umber held a family conference and came up with a plan to save the business.

Step one was to trim expenses. He consulted with Ace Hardware and found that successful hardware retailers spend no more than 20% of earnings on payroll. He was spending 25%. Umber recalls how hard it was to tell people who had been with him for nine years that he couldn't afford to keep them on. He scaled back health benefits and eliminated bonuses. He cut back on advertising and eliminated small luxuries such as his supper club membership. By installing energy-efficient fluorescent bulbs, he cut his lighting bill by $500.

Step two was to stock products and offer services that the big stores didn't, such as chain by the foot and paint thinner in smaller sizes. He conducts annual exit surveys to find out what his customers want. One study found that his customers were interested in bird feeders. Two weeks later, he had 24 feet of shelving devoted to them. He also keeps up with community events. At science-fair time, he stocks extra bell wire, batteries, mousetraps, springs, and magnets.

Step three was to set a pricing strategy. Umber's rule of thumb is to keep his prices within 10% of the big chains. "For 80% of the products I sell, nobody has any idea what they should cost anyway," says Umber. "If it's the difference between $1.09 and $1.29, customers don't care, particularly if it saves them from having to run across town to Home Depot."

Step four: Study the competition. He regularly visits his big competitors with a pencil and notepad, checking out products and pricing. Umber says he's never been kicked out for sleuthing, but one of his managers has.

Umber knows that his customers sometimes shop at Home Depot or Wal-Mart. One Monday when he was checking out the local Home Depot, he ran into a longtime customer Tim Stinson. After Umber explained what he was doing, Stinson told him that he needed Rustoleum chalkboard paint, a variety Umber didn't stock. Umber shook his hand and said, "Nice to see you, Tim."

"See?" said Stinson. "Nobody at Home Depot knows my name."[vii]

(*Note:* **Critical Thinking Exercise 6-4** on page 6.77 of this manual asks students to consider how they would compete against Wal-Mart.)

lecture link 6-10

MAKING ENTREPRENEURSHIP A COLLEGE MAJOR

Universities have long been dependable incubators of technological innovation. After all, Google, now one of the world's most powerful businesses, began as a Master's project at Stanford. But while all universities strive to expand human understanding, only a select few have succeeded in transferring their scholarly triumphs into entrepreneurial ones as well.

Elite schools such as Stanford, MIT, and Berkeley lead the pack in turning university-led innovation into professional ventures. While the prestige and large pool of talent at these schools help turn intellectual experimentation into viable products, these three institutions also benefit from top-flight, on-site entrepreneurship centers. Places like the Stanford Technology Ventures Program and The Deshpande Center at MIT educate academics, primarily engineers, in the art of entrepreneurship.

Unfortunately, the Kauffman Foundation, a philanthropic organization with a focus on education and entrepreneurship, estimates that there are only 12 successful university entrepreneurship programs operating in the United States today. Though intellectual talent is certainly not limited to the nation's elite schools, other academic institutions lack an in-house program centered on commercializing technology developed on campus. So as the recession wanes in the coming years and demand for quality R&D arises, many colleges won't need to worry about coming up with innovative ideas, but they may have trouble marketing them.[viii]

critical
thinking exercises

Name: _____

Date: _____

critical thinking exercise 6-1
WHAT DOES IT TAKE TO BE AN ENTREPRENEUR?

Entrepreneurship is risky business. Thousands of new businesses are started and thousands of others fail each year. Why would someone give up the security of working for others to assume the risk of business ownership? Find out by interviewing two or three small-business owners in your area. Ask them the questions listed below.

1. Did you ever work for someone else? If so, why did you stop?

2. Why did you want to go into business for yourself?

3. What expectations did you have when you started the business?

4. Which of these expectations were fulfilled?

5. Which of your expectations were not fulfilled?

6. What advice do you have for an entrepreneur thinking of starting a new business today?

critical thinking exercise 6-2
WHAT IS SMALL?

Small business is defined as an enterprise that "is independently owned and operated; is not dominant in its field of operation; and meets certain standards in terms of employees or annual receipts." Those "certain standards" are set by the Small Business Administration Office of Size Standards. In some industries, a "small" business must have fewer than 500 employees. In others, the limit is a dollar revenue figure, such as $6.5 million.

Go to the SBA website (www.sba.gov)ix and navigate to the "Size Standards" page. The size standards are listed by the NAICS U.S. industry title and code (for example, under subsection "113, Forestry and Logging," you will see a listing for "113210 Forest Nurseries"). You can find the specific code for an industry at the U.S. Bureau of the Census website (www.census.gov). Use the "NAICS Search" box in the upper left-hand corner. (Sometimes the Web address for a location changes. You might need to search to find the exact location mentioned.) Alternately, you can scroll through the table to locate the right industry.

Use the table on the SBA website to find the size limitations for the following industries:

1.   **Scheduled passenger air transport**   _____

2.   **Internet service providers**   _____

3.   **Credit unions**   _____

4.   **Breakfast cereal manufacturing**   _____

5.   **Cheese manufacturing**   _____

6.   **Florists**   _____

7.   **Aircraft manufacturing**   _____

8.   **Motorcycle and bicycle manufacturing**   _____

9.   **Cellular and wireless telecommunications**   _____

10. **Radio stations**   _____

critical thinking exercise 6-3
WRITING A BUSINESS PLAN

One of Mike McNeely's favorite pastimes as a teenager was taking his old car apart and putting it back together again. After graduation, Mike started working as a mechanic for his Uncle Larry's auto repair shop. Many of the customers have specifically asked for Mike to work on their cars because they know that he knows what he's doing and that he's honest.

It's been 10 years since Mike started his job. Now he is considering opening his own auto repair shop. He saved up some money and he thinks his rich Uncle Buck will lend him the rest. He has started writing a business plan and so far has (1) a description and appraisal of the market area, (2) an analysis of the competition, (3) a list of potential suppliers, (4) a list of purchasing and pricing procedures, and (5) a list of personnel needed and their job descriptions.

1.   What important items are missing from Mike's plans?

2.   What steps can Mike take to ensure success if he starts his own business?

notes on critical thinking exercise 6-3

1. *What important items are missing from Mike's plans?*

   The business plan should start with a brief overview stating the goals and objectives of the firm. How big does Mike want to get? How many employees? In what locations? Using what kind of financing?

   It is nice to think that a "rich uncle" will provide financing, but even rich uncles need to know how much money will be needed, how it will be spent, and what risks are involved. He may also have some interest in how the money is going to be paid back. You need a cash-flow analysis just to get some short-term money from a bank. You simply cannot be casual about funding and succeeding in a small business.

   If Mike intends to have others on his managerial team, he should describe them and their backgrounds and identify who will be responsible for what. In addition, he should mention any outside experts, such as accountants and lawyers, he may use.

   A more complete marketing program will show potential investors, including Uncle Buck, how Mike intends to promote the business. Many mistakes are made at this stage, such as not doing promotions early enough and then sitting around waiting for customers. A sales forecast is needed to show whether the goals of the firm are being met right from the start.

   In short, a business plan cannot be some casual thrown-together proposal. It takes time and effort. But the time is well spent because the business can then get off on the right foot.

2. *What steps can Mike take to ensure success if he starts his own business?*

   No one can be sure of success with a small business. That is why so many of them fail within five years. The best way to protect against failure is to have a very complete business plan at the start, to hire the best advice possible, and to set up methods along the monitor whether the business is getting off track. One of the most critical concerns is financing. But marketing and personnel are important as well, especially in this era when there are serious shortages in the labor market.

critical thinking exercise 6-4
COMPETING AGAINST WAL-MART

Lecture Link 6-9 discusses methods small businesses have used to compete against retail giants like Home Depot or Wal-Mart

Now consider this situation. You own a profitable optical outlet in a town with a population of about 12,000. Your store is in an excellent location near the downtown business district. You've just learned that a Wal-Mart Supercenter will open just outside of town in a few weeks. One of the departments in the Supercenter will be a Wal-Mart Optical Center, providing many of the same services your store does.

You know that your customers have been loyal to you throughout the 10 years you've been in operation, but you also realize that Wal-Mart will be able to undercut your prices significantly. The location of the outlet within a Wal-Mart store will give potential customers the added convenience of one-stop shopping.

1. Analyze the strengths and weaknesses of your business right now. What do you do well? Are there any gaps in services provided? Does your small business have any strategic advantages in the marketplace? Who are your customers and what do they want?

2. Prepare a six-month plan for meeting the Wal-Mart competition. How can you differentiate your business? Describe any changes you plan to make. What are the core characteristics of your enterprise that could be used to meet the competition?

3. At the end of the six-month period, what impact do you think Wal-Mart's Optical Center will have on your business? Will you still be profitable?

bonus cases

bonus case 6-1
DRIVING AWAY BUSINESSES WITH THE AMAZON TAX

Amazon's online retail empire has been a contentious issue for state governments almost since the company's founding. Amazon makes billions of dollars selling everything from books to auto parts, often without ever collecting one cent of sales tax. This is all perfectly legal thanks to a 1992 Supreme Court ruling that exempts companies without a "substantial nexus" in a state from collecting the tax. But the rules are changing in states like Illinois where money is tight and government debt soars. The Land of Lincoln's so-called Amazon tax requires the site and other online retailers to collect the state's sales tax.

Illinois government officials hope the increased tax revenue will help close the state's crippling debt gap. However, the Amazon tax may end up having the opposite effect. For instance, the website FatWallet.com directs shoppers to various deals at online retailers across the Web. The company earns an affiliate commission for each sale it directs to these sites. Until the passage of the Amazon tax, FatWallet was located in Rockton, Illinois. When the site began to sever connections with many of its Illinois affiliates, FatWallet founder Tim Storm responded by moving his company and its 54 employees five miles up the road to Beloit, Wisconsin.

This same backlash has occurred in other states as well, sometimes to even more devastating effect. When Texas claimed Amazon's Dallas warehouse counted as a "nexus" and demanded $269 million in back sales taxes, the company simply shut down the warehouse. Although the Amazon tax has many opponents, supporters include brick-and-mortar retailers like Wal-Mart and Target who have lobbied extensively for a federal law imposing a sales tax on online businesses. But their efforts may ultimately be in vain. In the end online retailers would still retain their advantage of convenience while physical stores would keep their local loyalties and the appeal of handling a product in person. With no clear-cut solution in sight, expect this to be an issue for years to come.[x]

discussion questions for bonus case 6-1

1.   Is it fair that online retailers like Amazon do not collect sales taxes?

2.   Should the U.S. Congress act to force online retailers to collect sales taxes?

notes on discussion questions for bonus case 6-1

1. *Is it fair that online retailers like Amazon do not collect sales taxes?*

   Companies like Wal-Mart and Target argue it's not fair that Amazon does not collect sales taxes. Amazon says it is following the law. While the idea of closing budget gaps through new taxes may be appealing to economic suffering states like Illinois, there is also a clear downside. Companies look carefully at the tax policies in the states where they choose to do business. Illinois better hope that the new tax doesn't cause other companies to move, taking even more tax revenues with them.

2. *Should the U.S. Congress act to force online retailers to collect sales taxes?*

   Thus far, the Congress has not moved in that direction and shows little inclination to do so at least in the near term. The decision will be up to individual states.

bonus case 6-2

3M COMPANY, INTRAPRENEURIAL LEADER

Each year the 3M Company produces about 60,000 different products from more than 40 separate divisions employing more than 5,000 engineers and scientists making $21.2 billion in sales. A multibillion-dollar company hardly sounds like an entrepreneurial hideout, but it is.

Employees are encouraged to some 15% of their work time researching new ideas without having to account for that time in any short-term way. A fifth of the R&D budget goes to basic research that has no immediate practicality. In the long term, of course, the company expects results, and results are what it gets. That's where the 60,000 products come from. Not all the discoveries are planned, however.

Patsy Sherman, for example, accidentally spilled a test chemical on her tennis shoe (people dress informally at 3M). She discovered that chemicals and dirt could not remove or stain the spot. This discovery led to the profitable Scotchgard fabric protector.

Remember those yellow Post-it notes that Art Fry developed for marking his Sunday hymnal? Art started as an intern at 3M and worked his way up to chemical engineer. A colleague, Dr. Spencer Silver, had developed a low-tack adhesive in the 1960, but the company had difficulty finding a commercial use for it. In 1977, Fry applied a coating of the adhesive to scraps of paper, and Post-it Notes were born. They are now one of the five top-selling office products in the United States.

The company's tradition of encouraging innovation goes back to one of the company's first employees, Richard Drew. 3M's first product was waterproof sandpaper. In 1923, Drew delivered samples of the sandpaper to local auto body shops for testing. Two-tone paint finishes on cars had recently been introduced and were an instant sensation. However, auto manufacturers discovered that they had no effective way to keep one color masked from the other during spray-painting. Body shops used gummed Kraft paper to shield painted areas, but removing the tape often stripped off the paint. At one body shop, a disgusted painter threw the masking tape at Drew along with some colorful language. When Drew presented the idea to 3M management, they gave Drew the time and financial backing to experiment on a more effective masking tape. He settled on an adhesive formula of cabinetmaker's glue combined with glycerin, which he applied to treated crepe paper. In 1925 3M's chief chemist brought samples of his new tape to the automakers in Detroit. They immediately placed orders for three carloads.

To give you some idea of how wide the product line is at 3M, look at some products it is working on. New product lines include fuel cells, thin-film mirrors, and a light fiber replacement for neon. 3M manufactures electrical and telecommunication products, medical devices, and office supplies. The company started out as Minnesota Mining and Manufacturing (3M) Company, but has come a long way from the mining days. Most of its success is due to intrapreneuring. In 2006, *BusinessWeek* magazine ranked 3M third in its ranking of the world's most innovative companies.[xi]

discussion questions for bonus case 6-2

1. Why is it important for laboratory people to follow their new product ideas through production and marketing?

2. How can a multibillion-dollar corporation keep its entrepreneurial spirit alive?

3. Is it healthy for a corporation to be involved in widely diverse industries such as Scotch tape and bioelectronic ears? Doesn't that prevent the corporation from having expertise in all those areas?

4. Could 3M survive without intrapreneuring?

notes on discussion questions for bonus case 6-2

1. *Why is it important for laboratory people to follow their new product ideas through production and marketing?*

    No one else in the company is as committed to that product and willing to fight to get the attention it deserves. The person who invents a product is able to generate excitement among others because his or her excitement is so high. Furthermore, following one's creation to completion gives one incentive to do it again.

2. *How can a multibillion-dollar corporation keep its entrepreneurial spirit alive?*

    One way is to give in-house entrepreneurial types free reign to create new ideas and to support the development of those ideas. Another way is to break down the larger firm into smaller divisions with relative freedom to create new product ideas and to compete as a separate unit. A combination of the two allows even the largest firms to remain entrepreneurial.

3. *Is it healthy for a corporation to be involved in widely diverse industries such as Scotch tape and bioelectronic ears? Doesn't that prevent the corporation from having expertise in all those areas?*

    It is healthy to have a diversity of products so that the failure of some will not hurt the whole firm. Expertise can be maintained in several different areas by creating specialized divisions like those at 3M.

4. *Could 3M survive without intrapreneuring?*

    3M could survive, but it wouldn't grow as rapidly as it has nor come up with so many new and helpful products. Intrapreneuring keeps the product line fresh and the company personnel on their toes. It creates excitement inside and outside the firm.

endnotes

[i] *Source:* Philipp Harper, "History's 10 Greatest Entrepreneurs," *MSNBC.com*, November 9, 2004.

[ii] *Source:* Miguel Helft, "Rental Building's Good Karma Nurtures Success," *New York Times,* September 14, 2007.

[iii] *Source:* Dyan Machan, "Inventors Wanted," *SmartMoney*, March 5, 2009.

[iv] *Source:* Mike Hofman, "Some Good Earners," *Inc.*, January/February 2009.

[v] *Sources*: Carole Fleck, "Start-Ups for Grown-Ups," *AARP Bulletin*, February 2007; the Small Business Administration, www.sba.gov.

[vi] *Source:* Angie Lau and Duane Stanford, "Challenging Bud on Its Home Turf," *Bloomberg Businessweek*, January 13, 2011.

[vii] *Sources:* Alice Z. Cuneo, "Rival Retailers, Devise Ways to Compete Against Giant," *Advertising Age,* October 6, 2003; Joshua Hyatt, "Beat the Beast," *Fortune Small Business*, September 1, 2004; Thomas Lee, "Prospect of Competing Against Wal-Mart Gives Old Rivals Some Common Ground," *Star Tribune*, April 9, 2006.

[viii] *Source*: Sramana Mitra, "Key to Innovation: Universities," *Forbes*, April 3, 2009.

[ix] The Internet is a dynamic, changing information source. Web links noted of this manual were checked at the time of publication, but content may change over time. Please review the website before recommending it to your students.

[x] *Source:* George F. Will, "Working Up a Tax Storm in Illinois," *The Washington Post*, April 29, 2011.

[xi] *Sources:* "Art Fry and the Invention of Post-It Notes," www.3M.com; Mary Bellis, "Post-It Notes: Art Fry and Spencer Silver," www.About.com; Mary Bellis, "Scotch Tape and Richard Drew," www.About.com; Beth Shery Sisk, "Engineers Find Solutions that Stick," *Engineers Week*, February 18, 2006; "3M's Seven Pillars of Innovation," *BusinessWeek,* May 10, 2006.

Management and Leadership

chapter 7

what's new in this edition

additions to the 10th edition:

- Getting to Know John Mackey of Whole Foods Market
- Name That Company: Best Buy
- Reaching Beyond Our Borders: The Japanese Crisis, Terrorism, and American Business
- Social Media in Business: Using Social Media to Build Customer Support
- Video Case

revisions to the 10th edition:

- Text was revised to eliminate redundancy and tighten discussions.
- Statistical data and examples throughout the chapter were updated to reflect current information.

deletions from the 9th edition:

- Getting to Know Indra Krishnamurthy Nooyi, CEO of PepsiCo
- Name That Company: Taco Bell
- Figure 7.2 Starbuck's Mission Statement
- Reaching Beyond Our Borders
- Spotlight on Small Business

brief chapter outline
and learning goals

Management and Leadership

Getting To Know JOHN MACKEY of WHOLE FOODS MARKET

<u>learning goal 1</u>

Describe the changes occurring today in the management function.

I.   MANAGERS' ROLES ARE EVOLVING.

<u>learning goal 2</u>

Describe the four functions of management.

II.   THE FOUR FUNCTIONS OF MANAGEMENT

<u>learning goal 3</u>

Relate the planning process and decision making to the accomplishment of company goals.

III.   PLANNING AND DECISION MAKING
   A.   Decision Making: Finding the Best Alternative.

<u>learning goal 4</u>

Describe the organizing function of management.

IV.   ORGANIZING: CREATING A UNIFIED SYSTEM
   A.   Tasks and Skills at Different Levels of Management
   B.   Staffing: Getting and Keeping the Right People

<u>learning goal 5</u>

Explain the differences between leaders and managers, and describe the various leadership styles.

V.   LEADING: PROVIDING CONTINUOUS VISION AND VALUES
   A.   Leadership Styles
   B.   Empowering Workers
   C.   Managing Knowledge

learning goal 6
Summarize the five steps of the control function of management.

VI. CONTROLLING: MAKING SURE IT WORKS

A. A Key Criterion for Measurement: Customer Satisfaction

VII. SUMMARY

lecture outline

Getting to Know JOHN MACKEY of WHOLE FOODS MARKET

John Mackey started his market with one thing in mind—to meet women. That quickly changed and he opened SaferWay Foods with his girlfriend. In 1980, SaferWay merged with another company and Whole Foods Market was born. Whole Foods now is a world leader in natural and organic foods and consistently figures in Fortune's "Best Companies to Work For" lists. Whole Foods hires good people and trains them well. In turn, its employees treat customers well.

NAME THAT company

Like many companies today, this company uses social media to communicate with customers. In one case, a customer complained on Twitter when the company sent a BlackBerry to replace an iPhone that had failed. The company responded quickly with a replacement iPhone. The customer then tweeted about the company's great customer service. Name that company

(Students should read the chapter before guessing the company's name: Best Buy)

learning goal 1

Describe the changes occurring today in the management function.

I. MANAGERS' ROLES ARE EVOLVING.

A. Managers get things done by using organizational resources—workers, financial resources, information, and equipment.

1. At one time, managers were called **BOSSES** and their job was to tell people what to do.

2. Today, managers must **GUIDE, TRAIN, SUPPORT, MOTIVATE**, and **COACH EMPLOYEES** rather than **TELLING** them what to do.

B. Most modern managers emphasize teamwork and cooperation rather than discipline and order giving.

1. Traditional long-term contracts between management and employees no longer exist.

2. Most future managers will **WORK IN TEAMS.**

PPT 7-1
Chapter Title

PPT 7-2
Learning Goals

(See complete PowerPoint slide notes on page 7.38.)

PPT 7-3
Learning Goals

(See complete PowerPoint slide notes on page 7.38.)

PPT 7-4
John Mackey

(See complete PowerPoint slide notes on page 7.39.)

PPT 7-5
Name That Company

(See complete PowerPoint slide notes on page 7.39.)

lecture link 7-1

BEWARE OF BAD BOSSES

Bad bosses have always been with us. This lecture link explains how to handle them. (See the complete lecture link on page 7.56 of this manual.)

lecture link 7-2

BEST BUSINESS LEADERS OF THE 20TH CENTURY

These are the top executives of the 20th century, as chosen through a survey of executives. (See the complete lecture link on page 7.58 of this manual.)

C. The recent economic crisis was particularly difficult for workers, who were laid off in record numbers, and managers, who had to make these difficult decisions.

D. Today's leaders are **YOUNGER**, and they tend to move from one company to another.

E. The new manager needs to be a skilled communicator and team player as well as a planner, coordinator, organizer, and supervisor.

<u>**learning goal** 2</u>
Describe the four functions of management.

II. THE FOUR FUNCTIONS OF MANAGEMENT

A. **_MANAGEMENT_** is the process used to accomplish organizational goals through planning, organizing, leading, and controlling people and other organizational resources.

B. **_PLANNING_** is a management function that includes anticipating trends and determining the best strategies and tactics to achieve organizational goals and objectives.

1. The trend today is to have **PLANNING TEAMS** monitor the environment.

2. Planning is called the **KEY MANAGEMENT FUNCTION** because the other functions depend on having a good plan.

C. **ORGANIZING** is a management function that includes designing the structure of the organization and creating conditions and systems in which everyone and everything work together to achieve the organization's goals and objectives.

lecture link 7-3
WOMEN BRINGING HOME THE BACON

As more women are taking management roles in their companies, more are becoming the primary breadwinners in their homes. (See the complete lecture link on page 7.59 of this manual.)

lecture link 7-4
THREE TYPES OF GREAT LEADERS

According to one business writer, there are three basic types of brilliant bosses. (See the complete lecture link on page 7.59 of this manual.)

PPT 7-6
What Is Management?

(See complete PowerPoint slide notes on page 7.39.)

PPT 7-7
Today's Managers

(See complete PowerPoint slide notes on page 7.40.)

PPT 7-8
Respect and How to Get It

(See complete PowerPoint slide notes on page 7.40.)

PPT 7-9
Education Matters

(See complete PowerPoint slide notes on page 7.40.)

PPT 7-10
Four Functions of Management

(See complete PowerPoint slide notes on page 7.41.)

1. Successful organizations today are designed around pleasing the customer at a profit.

2. Organizations must remain flexible and adaptable to respond to customers' changing needs.

D. _**LEADING**_ means creating a vision for the organization and guiding, training, coaching, and motivating others to work effectively to achieve the organization's goals and objectives in a timely manner.

1. Today, most managers **EMPOWER** employees, giving them as much freedom as possible.

2. This function was once known as **DIRECTING**; that is, telling employees exactly what to do.

3. Leadership is still needed to keep employees focused on the right tasks at the right time.

E. _**CONTROLLING**_ is a management function that involves establishing clear standards to determine whether or not an organization is progressing toward its goals and objectives, rewarding people for doing a good job, and taking corrective action if they are not.

F. The four functions are the heart of management.

learning goal 3

Relate the planning process and decision making to the accomplishment of company goals.

III. PLANNING AND DECISION MAKING

A. **PLANNING** involves setting the organizational vision, goals, and objectives.

1. A _**VISION**_ is an encompassing explanation of why the organization exists and where it is headed; it is more than a goal.

<u>critical thinking
exercise 7-1</u>
MANAGEMENT FUNCTIONS

This exercise asks students to organize managerial activities they have performed into the four management functions. (See the complete exercise on page 7.65 of this manual.)

TEXT FIGURE 7.1
What Managers Do
(Text page 182)

This text figure shows some tasks that managers perform while performing the four management functions.

**progress
assessment**
(Text page 183)

PPT 7-11
Progress Assessment

PROGRESS ASSESSMENT

- What are some of the changes happening in management today?
- What's the definition of management used in this chapter?
- What are the four functions of management?

(See complete PowerPoint slide notes on page 7.41.)

2. A **_MISSION STATEMENT_** is an outline of the fundamental purposes of the organization.

   a. A well-designed mission statement should address:

      i. The organization's self-concept

      ii. Company philosophy

      iii. Long-term survival

      iv. Customer needs

      v. Social responsibility

      vi. The nature of the product or service

3. **_GOALS_** are the broad, long-term accomplishments an organization wishes to attain.

4. **_OBJECTIVES_** are specific, short-term statements detailing how to achieve the organizational goals.

5. Planning is a process; it tends to follow a continuous pattern.

6. Planning answers several **FUNDAMENTAL QUESTIONS:**

   a. What is the situation now and where do we want to go?

   b. How can we get there from here?

7. **_SWOT ANALYSIS_** is a planning tool used to analyze an organization's **S**trengths, **W**eaknesses, **O**pportunities, and **T**hreats.

   a. **STRENGTHS** and **WEAKNESSES** are **INTERNAL** to the firm.

PPT 7-12
Sharing the Vision

(See complete PowerPoint slide notes on page 7.41.)

PPT 7-13
Defining the Mission

(See complete PowerPoint slide notes on page 7.42.)

lecture link 7-5
REVISITING MISSION AT VICTORIA'S SECRET

Victoria's Secret is refocusing on its original mission, ultra-feminine rather than sexy lingerie. (See the complete lecture link on page 7.60 of this manual.)

PPT 7-14
Setting Goals and Objectives

(See complete PowerPoint slide notes on page 7.42.)

PPT 7-15
Planning Answers Fundamental Questions

(See complete PowerPoint slide notes on page 7.42.)

TEXT FIGURE 7.2
SWOT Matrix
(Text page 184)

PPT 7-16
SWOT Matrix

(See complete PowerPoint slide notes on page 7.43.)

    b. **OPPORTUNITIES** and **THREATS** are often **EXTERNAL** to the firm and cannot always be anticipated.

B. **TYPES OF PLANNING**

    1. ***STRATEGIC PLANNING*** is the process of determining the major goals of the organization and the policies and strategies needed for obtaining and using resources to achieve those goals.

        a. This type of planning is usually done by top management.

        b. **POLICIES** are broad guidelines for action.

        c. **STRATEGIES** determine the best way to use resources.

        d. At this stage, top management decides:

            i.   Which customers to serve

            ii. When to serve them

            iii. What products to sell

            iv. The geographic areas in which to compete

        e. *The text uses the example of Taco Bell's successful "fourth meal" strategy and Blockbuster's lack of planning that resulted in difficulties for the company.*

        f. Because changes are occurring so fast, long-range planning has become more difficult.

        g. Shorter-term plans allow companies to respond quickly to customer needs.

    2. ***TACTICAL PLANNING*** is the process of developing detailed, short-term statements about what

critical thinking
exercise 7-2
CAREER SWOT ANALYSIS

SWOT analysis, the key tool in the strategic planning process, can also be applied to career planning. (See the complete exercise on page 7.58 of this manual.)

PPT 7-17
Planning Functions

TEXT FIGURE 7.3
Planning Functions
(Text page 185)

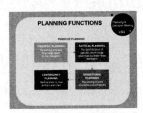

(See complete PowerPoint slide notes on page 7.43.)

PPT 7-18
Strategic and Tactical Planning

(See complete PowerPoint slide notes on page 7.43.)

bonus case 7-1
DEFENSEWEB EVALUATES A STRATEGIC EXPANSION

DefenseWeb considers a strategic move into the private sector. (See the complete case, discussion questions, and suggested answers beginning on page 7.74 of this manual.)

is to be done, who is to do it, and how it is to be done.

    a. Tactical planning is normally done by managers at **LOWER LEVELS** of the organization.

    b. *An example of tactical planning is setting annual budgets.*

3. **_OPERATIONAL PLANNING_** is the process of setting of work standards and schedules necessary to implement the company's tactical objectives.

    a. Operational planning focuses on specific supervisors and individual employees.

    b. The **OPERATIONAL PLAN** is the department manager's tool for daily operations.

4. **_CONTINGENCY PLANNING_** is the process of preparing alternative courses of action that may be used if the primary plans don't achieve the organization's objectives.

    a. An organization needs to have alternative plans ready for environmental changes.

    b. **CRISIS PLANNING**, a part of contingency planning, involves reacting to sudden changes in the environment.

5. Market-based companies stay flexible, listen to customers, and seize opportunities when they come.

    a. Instead of creating detailed strategic plans, leaders of these companies often simply set direction.

6. The opportunities, however, must fit into the company's overall goals and objectives.

PPT 7-19
Operational and Contingency Planning

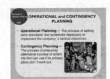

(See complete PowerPoint slide notes on page 7.44.)

REACHING BEYOND
our borders
(Text page 185)

PPT 7-20
The Japanese Crisis, Terrorism, and American Business

(See complete PowerPoint slide notes on page 7.44.)

critical thinking exercise 7-3
CRISIS MANAGEMENT

This exercise explores management reaction to rapid, unexpected change. (See the complete exercise on page 7.67 of this manual.)

C. **DECISION MAKING: FINDING THE BEST ALTER-
NATIVE**

1. All management functions involve ***DECISION
MAKING***, choosing among two or more
alternatives.

2. The **RATIONAL DECISION-MAKING MODEL** is
a series of steps managers often follow to make
logical, intelligent, and well-founded decisions.

3. **STEPS IN DECISION MAKING:**

   a. Define the situation.

   b. Describe and collect needed information.

   c. Develop alternatives.

   d. Develop agreement among those involved.

   e. Decide which alternative is best.

   f. Do what is indicated (begin implementation).

   g. Determine whether the decision was a good
   one and follow up.

4. Sometimes decisions have to be made **ON THE
SPOT** with little information available.

5. ***PROBLEM SOLVING*** is the process of solving
the everyday problems that occur; it is less formal
than the decision-making process and calls for
quicker action.

   a. Companies can use ***BRAINSTORMING***, coming up with as many solutions to a problem as
   possible in a short period of time with no cen-
   soring of ideas.

   b. Another technique is ***PMI***, listing all the **P**luses
   for a solution in one column, all the **M**inuses in
   another, and the **I**mplications in a third column.

PPT 7-21
Decision Making

(See complete PowerPoint slide notes on page 7.44.)

PPT 7-22
What Makes a Great CEO

(See complete PowerPoint slide notes on page 7.45.)

bonus case 7-2
WHEN EMPLOYEES MAKE THE DECISIONS

This case discusses how one employee-owned firm uses participative management. (See the complete case, discussion questions, and suggested answers beginning on page 7.76 of this manual.)

PPT 7-23
Rational Decision-Making Model

(See complete PowerPoint slide notes on page 7.45.)

lecture link 7-6
DECISION-MAKING TIPS

This lecture link gives some tips for enhancing decision making. (See the complete lecture link on page 7.60 of this manual.)

critical thinking exercise 7-4
EVALUATING ALTERNATIVE COURSES

Because of shrinking market share and declining profits, Monmouth Thermics, a subsidiary of a large conglomerate, needs a recovery plan. (See the complete exercise on page 7.68 of this manual.)

PPT 7-24
Problem Solving

(See complete PowerPoint slide notes on page 7.45.)

bonus case 7-3
DECISION MAKING: KLM 4805

The worst air disaster in history occurred as a result of miscommunication and bad decision making. (See the complete case, discussion questions, and suggested answers beginning on page 7.78 of this manual.)

Describe the organizing function of management.

IV. ORGANIZING: CREATING A UNIFIED SYSTEM

A. After planning a course of action, managers must **ORGANIZE** the firm—allocate resources—to accomplish their goals.

1. The **_ORGANIZATION CHART_** is a visual device that shows the relationship among people and divides the organization's work; it shows who is accountable for the completion of specific work and who reports to whom.

2. **LEVELS OF MANAGEMENT**

   a. **_TOP MANAGEMENT_** is the highest level of management, consisting of the president and other key company executives who develop **STRATEGIC PLANS.**

      i. Titles include Chief Executive Officer (CEO), Chief Operating Officer (COO), Chief Financial Officer (CFO), and Chief Information Officer (CIO).

      ii. The **CEO** is responsible for all top-level decisions in the firm.

      iii. **CEOs** are responsible for introducing change into an organization.

      iv. The **COO** is responsible for putting those changes into effect.

      v. The **CFO** is responsible for obtaining funds, planning budgets, collecting funds, and so on.

progress
assessment
(Text page 188)

PPT 7-25
Progress Assessment

(See complete PowerPoint slide notes on page 7.46.)

PPT 7-26
Organizational Charts

(See complete PowerPoint slide notes on page 7.47.)

PPT 7-27
Levels of Management

TEXT FIGURE 7.4
Levels of Management
(Text page 188)

(See complete PowerPoint slide notes on page 7.47.)

lecture link 7-7
THE 21ST-CENTURY CEO

The real economic change in our recovery will be the new crop of CEOs in American business. (See the complete lecture link on page 7.61 of this manual.)

PPT 7-28
Management Levels

(See complete PowerPoint slide notes on page 7.47.)

      vi. The **CIO** or **CKO** is responsible for getting the right information to managers so they can make good decisions. CIOs are more important than ever.

    b. ***MIDDLE MANAGEMENT*** is the level of management that includes general managers, division managers, and branch and plant managers who are responsible for tactical planning and controlling.

    c. ***SUPERVISORY MANAGEMENT*** includes managers who are directly responsible for supervising workers and evaluating their daily performance; they are also known as first-line managers.

B. **TASKS AND SKILLS AT DIFFERENT LEVELS OF MANAGEMENT**

    1. Managers are usually are not trained to be managers—they are workers with specific skills who are promoted.

    2. The higher a person moves up in the managerial ladder, the more he or she needs to be a visionary, planner, communicator, and motivator.

    3. Managers must have **THREE CATEGORIES OF SKILLS:**

       a. ***TECHNICAL SKILLS*** involve the ability to perform tasks in a specific discipline *(such as selling a product)* or department *(such as marketing).*

       b. ***HUMAN RELATIONS SKILLS*** involve communication and motivation; they enable managers to work through and with people.

PPT 7-29
Top Management

(See complete PowerPoint slide notes on page 7.48.)

PPT 7-30
America's Most Powerful Female
Managers

(See complete PowerPoint slide notes on page 7.48.)

<u>critical thinking</u>
<u>exercise 7-5</u>
**THE MOST POWERFUL WOMEN
IN BUSINESS**

Each year *Fortune* magazine lists the most powerful women in business. This exercise directs students to research the listing for the current year. (See the complete exercise on page 7.69 of this manual.)

PPT 7-31
Managerial Skills

(See complete PowerPoint slide notes on page 7.48.)

PPT 7-32
Thank You

(See complete PowerPoint slide notes on page 7.49.)

    c. ___CONCEPTUAL SKILLS___ involve the ability to picture the organization as a whole and the relationships among its various parts.

  4. **SKILLS BY LEVEL:**

    a. **FIRST-LINE MANAGERS** need fewer conceptual skills and more technical and human relations skills.

    b. **TOP MANAGERS** need fewer technical skills and more human relations and conceptual skills.

  5. Although managers need to have all three skills, the need for each skill varies at different levels.

C. **STAFFING: GETTING AND KEEPING THE RIGHT PEOPLE**

  1. To get the right kind of people, the firm has to offer the right kind of incentives.

  2. ___STAFFING___ is a management function that includes hiring, motivating, and retaining the best people available to accomplish the company's objectives.

    a. In today's high-tech world, **RECRUITING GOOD EMPLOYEES** is a critical important part of organizational success *(text examples: Google, Microsoft, Sony).*

    b. Firms with the most innovative and creative workers can develop quickly and successfully.

  3. Once they are hired, good people must be **RETAINED.**

    a. Unless they are treated well and get fair pay, employees will leave for other companies.

lecture link 7-8
LEARNING MANAGEMENT SKILLS

Another way of classifying specific management skills is presented here. (See the complete lecture link on page 7.62 of this manual.)

critical thinking exercise 7-6
RATE YOUR MANAGEMENT SKILLS

This exercise expands the classification of management skills (based on **Lecture Link 7-8** above) and asks students to rate themselves. (See the complete exercise on page 7.70 of this manual.)

PPT 7-33
Skills Needed at Various Levels of Management

TEXT FIGURE 7.5
Skills Needed at Various Levels of Management
(Text page 189)

(See complete PowerPoint slide notes on page 7.49.)

lecture link 7-9
AMERICA'S UPCOMING MANAGEMENT GAP

As upper managers are retiring, companies are worried about where the next generation of managers will come from. (See the complete lecture link on page 7.63 of this manual.)

PPT 7-34
Staffing

(See complete PowerPoint slide notes on page 7.49.)

      b. Staffing is becoming a bigger part of the managers' job.

    4. Chapter 11 is devoted to human resources issues.

learning goal 5

Explain the differences between leaders and managers, and describe the various leadership styles.

V. LEADING: PROVIDING CONTINUOUS VISION AND VALUES

  A. A person can be a good manager and not a good leader.

    1. **LEADERSHIP** involves:

      a. Creating vision for others to follow

      b. Establishing corporate values and ethics

      c. Transforming the way the organization does business in order to improve its effectiveness and efficiency

    2. **MANAGEMENT** involves carrying out the leadership's vision.

    3. Leaders must **LEAD BY DOING**, not just by saying; they must:

      a. Communicate a vision and rally others around that vision

      b. Establish corporate values

      c. Promote corporate ethics

      d. Embrace change

      e. Stress accountability and responsibility

        i. Leaders need to be held accountable for their actions.

PPT 7-38
Accountability through
Transparency

(See complete PowerPoint slide notes on page 7.51.)

PPT 7-39
Leadership Styles

(See complete PowerPoint slide notes on page 7.51.)

PPT 7-40
Various Leadership Styles

TEXT FIGURE 7.6
Various Leadership Styles
(Text page 192)

(See complete PowerPoint slide notes on page 7.51.)

PPT 7-41
Natural Born Leaders?

(See complete PowerPoint slide notes on page 7.52.)

critical thinking
exercise 7-7
**ARE LEADERS BORN OR CAN
THEY BE TAUGHT?**

This exercise explores the research and rationale behind this question. (See the complete exercise on page 7.72 of this manual.)

critical thinking
exercise 7-8
TRAITS OF LEADERS

What traits are common to great leaders? (See the complete exercise on page 7.73 of this manual.)

    c. **FREE-REIN LEADERSHIP**

        i. **_FREE-REIN LEADERSHIP_** is a leadership style that involves managers setting objectives and employees being relatively free to do whatever it takes to accomplish those objectives.

        ii. It is often successful when dealing with engineers or other professionals.

    d. Leaders rarely fit neatly into just one category.

3. Leadership is actually a **CONTINUUM** with varying amounts of employee participation.

4. **WHICH LEADERSHIP STYLE IS BEST?**

    a. The best leadership style to use **DEPENDS** on the goals and values of the firm, who is being led, and in what situations.

    b. Any one manager can use a **VARIETY OF LEADERSHIP STYLES**.

    c. Successful leaders use the leadership style that is appropriate to the situation and the employees involved.

C. **EMPOWERING WORKERS**

1. For traditional organizations, **DIRECTING** involves giving assignments, explaining routines, clarifying policies, and providing feedback on performance.

2. **PROGRESSIVE LEADERS** are less likely to give specific instructions to employees.

    a. They **EMPOWER** employees to make decisions on their own.

**social
media in
business**
(Text page 193)

PPT 7-42
Using Social
Media to Build
Customer Support

(See complete PowerPoint slide notes on page 7.52.)

PPT 7-43
Empowerment

(See complete PowerPoint slide notes on page 7.53.)

PPT 7-44
Work Smarter

(See complete PowerPoint slide notes on page 7.53.)

    b. **EMPOWERMENT** is giving employees the authority and responsibility to respond quickly to customer requests.

    c. Managers often resist empowerment because they are reluctant to give up power.

    d. ***ENABLING*** is giving workers the education and tools they need to make decisions.

D. **MANAGING KNOWLEDGE**

    1. ***KNOWLEDGE MANAGEMENT*** is finding the right information, keeping the information in a readily accessible place, and making the information known to everyone in the firm.

    2. The first step is to decide what knowledge is most important.

    3. Knowledge management tries to prevent duplicating information gathering every time a decision is made.

    4. The key to success is learning how to process information and turn it into knowledge that everyone can use.

learning goal 6

Summarize the five steps of the control function of management.

VI. **CONTROLLING: MAKING SURE IT WORKS**

A. The **CONTROL FUNCTION** is critical to the management system because it provides the feedback that lets managers adjust to any deviations from plans.

    1. The steps in controlling are:

        a. Establishing clear **PERFORMANCE STANDARDS**

PPT 7-45
Managing Knowledge

(See complete PowerPoint slide notes on page 7.53.)

PPT 7-46
Five Steps of Controlling

TEXT FIGURE 7.7
The Control Process
(Text page 195)

(See complete PowerPoint slide notes on page 7.54.)

    b. **MONITORING** and recording actual performance

    c. **COMPARING RESULTS** against plans and standards

    d. **COMMUNICATING RESULTS** and deviations to the employees involved

    e. **TAKING CORRECTIVE ACTION** when needed and **PROVIDING POSITIVE FEEDBACK** for work well done

2. The system's weak link is **SETTING STANDARDS.**

    a. In order to measure results against standards, the standards must be **SPECIFIC, ATTAINABLE**, and **MEASURABLE**.

    b. Clear, specific standards should be set during planning.

    c. Clear procedures for monitoring performance should also be established.

B. **A KEY CRITERION FOR MEASUREMENT: CUSTOMER SATISFACTION**

1. In a customer-oriented firm **CUSTOMER SATISFACTION** of both internal and external customers is the criterion for measuring success.

    a. ***EXTERNAL CUSTOMERS*** include dealers, who buy products to sell to others, and ultimate customers (or end users), who buy products for their own personal use.

PPT 7-47
Are You a Micromanager?

(See complete PowerPoint slide notes on page 7.54.)

PPT 7-48
Measuring Success

(See complete PowerPoint slide notes on page 7.54.)

      b. **<u>*INTERNAL CUSTOMERS*</u>** are individuals and units within the firm that receive services from other individuals and units.

   2. Firms now try to go beyond simply satisfying customers by "delighting" them with unexpectedly good products and services.

VII. SUMMARY

progress
assessment
(Text page 197)

PPT 7-49
Progress Assessment

(See complete PowerPoint slide notes on page 7.55.)

PowerPoint slide notes

PPT 7-1
Chapter Title

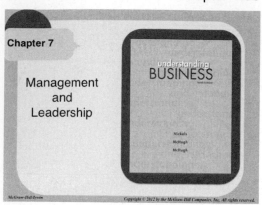

PPT 7-2
Learning Goals

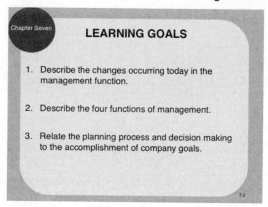

PPT 7-3
Learning Goals

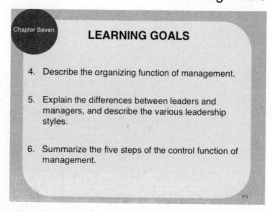

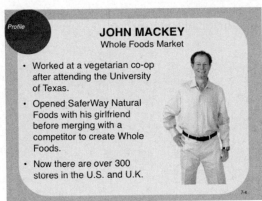

Company: Best Buy

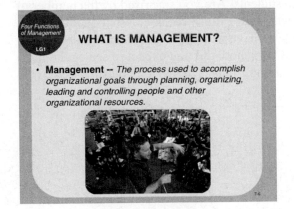

As the demographic makeup of this country changes, the typical manager is changing. Today more managers are women and less are from elite universities. Managers today act more like facilitators than supervisors.

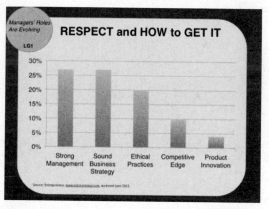

1. This slide presents the results from a study conducted by www.entrepreneur.com.

2. Ask the students. Why do you respect or not respect a manager? *(This question is certainly going to develop a discussion among students in class.)*

3. Ask the students, In your opinion why did sound business strategy and ethical practices rank so high in the study?

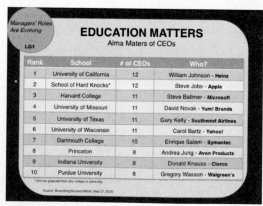

1. This slide shows the schools that have educated the most CEOs among S&P 500 companies.

2. Ask the students, Are you surprised by the number of CEOs who didn't finish college? What qualities must those CEOs have without formal education behind them? What school did you expect to see on the list that's missing? What schools are you surprised to see?

PPT 7-10
Four Functions of Management

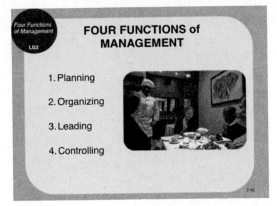

Planning: Anticipating trends and determining the best strategies and tactics to achieve organizational goals and objectives.

Organizing: Designing the structure of the organization and creating conditions and systems in which everyone and everything works together to achieve goals.

Leading: Creating a vision for the organization and communicating, guiding, training, coaching, and motivating others to achieve goals and objectives in a timely manner.

Controlling: Establishing clear standards to determine whether an organization is progressing toward its goals and objectives, rewarding people for good work, and taking corrective action if they are not performing.

PPT 7-11
Progress Assessment

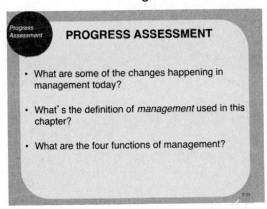

1. Some of the changes in management today include the following: managers are more facilitators than bosses; managers tend to emphasize team-building; managers tend to be younger; fewer managers attended elite schools; more managers are women; and they conduct more business globally.

2. Management is the process to accomplish organizational goals through planning, organizing, leading, and controlling people and other organizational resources.

3. The four functions of management are planning, organizing, leading, and controlling.

PPT 7-12
Sharing the Vision

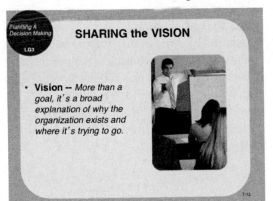

Creating vision for the company is not merely setting a goal, but rather creating a sense of purpose for the organization.

PPT 7-13
Defining the Mission

The mission statement is the foundation for setting specific goals and objectives within the organization.

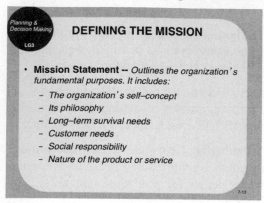

DEFINING THE MISSION

- **Mission Statement** -- *Outlines the organization's fundamental purposes. It includes:*
  - *The organization's self-concept*
  - *Its philosophy*
  - *Long-term survival needs*
  - *Customer needs*
  - *Social responsibility*
  - *Nature of the product or service*

PPT 7-14
Setting Goals and Objectives

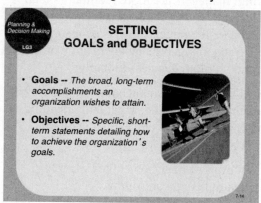

SETTING GOALS and OBJECTIVES

- **Goals** -- *The broad, long-term accomplishments an organization wishes to attain.*
- **Objectives** -- *Specific, short-term statements detailing how to achieve the organization's goals.*

PPT 7-15
Planning Answers Fundamental Questions

SWOT is an acronym for Strengths, Weaknesses, Opportunities, and Threats. As part of the internal analysis, the organization identifies the potential strengths that it can capitalize on and potential weaknesses that it should improve on. An organization, as part of an external environmental analysis, identifies the opportunities (factors that an organization can take advantage of) and threats (factors that an organization should avoid or minimize the impact of). Have the students perform a SWOT analysis on themselves. (At least the strengths and weaknesses part should be an eye-opening experience for them.)

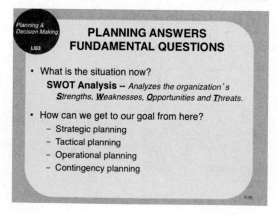

PLANNING ANSWERS FUNDAMENTAL QUESTIONS

- What is the situation now?
  SWOT Analysis -- *Analyzes the organization's Strengths, Weaknesses, Opportunities and Threats.*
- How can we get to our goal from here?
  - Strategic planning
  - Tactical planning
  - Operational planning
  - Contingency planning

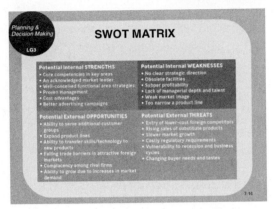

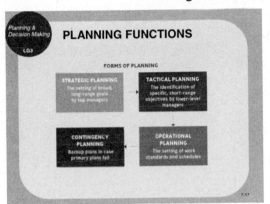

This slide covers the key areas of planning by business managers. Students should be reminded that planning requires preparation to be successful. More effort put into planning will result in greater achievement. All planning should be in writing with an estimation of time and cost. Gantt charts are often used to compare planned results with actual accomplishments. Even the best prepared plans sometimes miss the unexpected problems. Managers should always be prepared to act in the event a plan fails. Poor contingency planning may result in significant problems for a company.

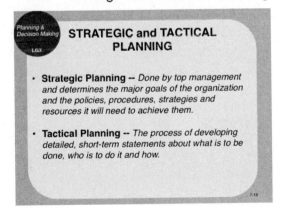

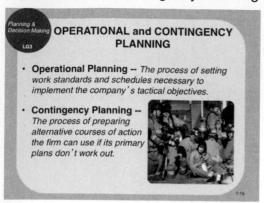

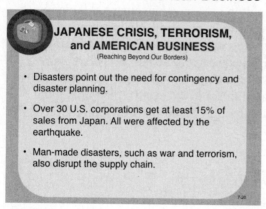

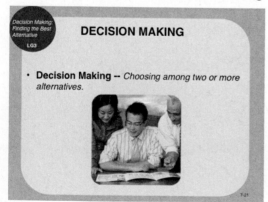

PPT 7-22
What Makes a Great CEO

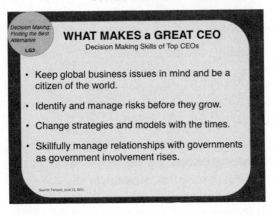

1. Since the world seems to be changing at a faster pace, it's important for CEOs to change their processes.

2. No longer can managers think small; they must think globally and plan for anything and everything.

PPT 7-23
Rational Decision-Making Model

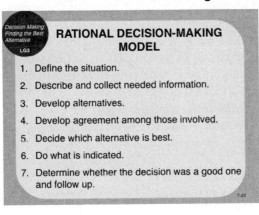

Managers don't always go through this seven-step process. However, they must always make sound decisions. But that is easier said than done. As an interesting exercise ask the students, working in groups, to go through a simple process of identifying an automobile to purchase using these steps. Everyone's input should be obtained in the group. They either can select a group manager or all can have an equal say/vote. Both scenarios should produce different, but interesting experiences for students.

PPT 7-24
Problem Solving

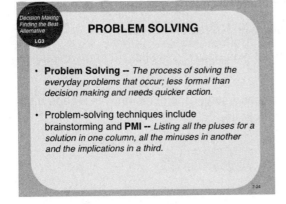

PPT 7-25
Progress Assessment

PROGRESS ASSESSMENT

- What's the difference between goals and objectives?

- What does a company analyze when it does a SWOT analysis?

- What are the differences between strategic, tactical and operational planning?

- What are the seven Ds in decision making?

7-25

1. Goals are broad, long-term accomplishments an organization wishes to attain. Objectives are specific, short-term statements detailing how the organization will achieve its goals.

2. In today's rapidly changing business environment, managers must think of planning as a continuous process. The SWOT analysis is an important part of the planning process as it evaluates an organization's strengths, weaknesses, opportunities, and threats.

3. Strategic planning is the process top management uses to determine the major goals of the organization, and the policies, procedures, strategies, and resources the organization will need to achieve them. Tactical planning is the process of developing detailed, short-term statements about what is to be done, who is to do it, and how. This type of planning is typically completed by managers at lower levels of the organization whereas strategic planning is done by the top managers. The final type of planning is operational. Operational planning is the process of setting work schedules and standards necessary to complete the organization's tactical objectives. This type of planning is the department manager's tool for daily and weekly operations.

4. What are the seven Ds in decision making? The seven Ds in decision making are as follows:

   - Define the situation.

   - Describe and collect needed information.

   - Develop alternatives.

   - Develop agreement among these involved.

   - Decide which alternative is best.

   - Do what is indicated and start the implementation.

   - Determine whether the decision was a good one and follow up.

PPT 7-26
Organizational Charts

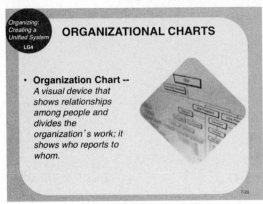

PPT 7-27
Levels of Management

This slide shows a good visual of management levels within a corporation. Note the pyramid shape and the type of job positions that are in each level. It's important for the student to know the necessary skill levels that each position in the pyramid requires. A top-level manager needs good conceptual skills, and to be able to effectively communicate goals to the entire corporation. Middle-level managers typically develop the strategies for goal attainment and develop the tactics necessary to achieve stated goals. Middle managers require good analytical skills and the ability to communicate. First-line managers are responsible for execution of business goals. Technical skills and good communications skills are necessary.

PPT 7-28
Management Levels

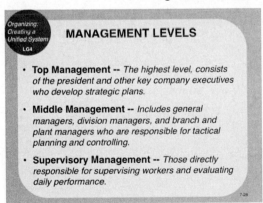

PPT 7-29
Top Management

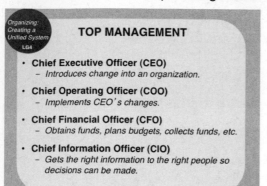

PPT 7-30
America's Most Powerful Female Managers

1. This slide illustrates the rising number of women who are in positions of power in *Fortune* 500 companies.

2. What characteristics do some women have that help them manage people?

PPT 7-31
Managerial Skills

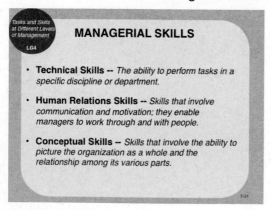

PPT 7-32
Thank You

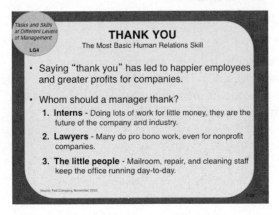

1. Customers, staff, and outside support are hard to keep happy. Who would have thought that a simple act our moms taught us would be so useful?

2. A 10-year study by Adrian Gostick and Chester Elton found that among a survey of 200,000 managers and employees, "thank yous" correlate with higher profits yet 30% still don't say it.

3. Ask the students, Why is a simple "thank you" such a powerful managerial tool?

PPT 7-33
Skills Needed at Various Levels of Management

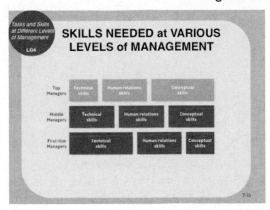

The further up the managerial ladder a person moves, the less important technical job skills become and the more important conceptual skills are.

PPT 7-34
Staffing

PPT 7-35
Staffing Is Tricky Business

PPT 7-36
Leadership

PPT 7-37
To Share or Not to Share

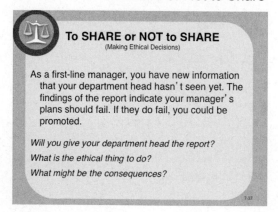

1. As we've discussed, getting and keeping the right staff is not an easy task.

2. This slide shows what managers should *not* do while staffing.

3. Ask the students, Why do you think a manager should *not* promote a longtime employee only because it's time or the manager owes him or her a favor? What's so important about feedback?

   Research tells us that determining which leadership style is best depends on what the goals and values of the firm are, who's being led, and in what situations. A successful leader in one organization may not be successful in another.

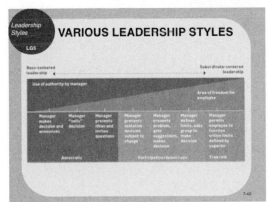

PPT 7-41
Natural Born Leaders?

1. Ask the students, Does your personality reveal how you think and work? Can it be improved? *(Tests such as Myers-Briggs profile individuals' personalities.)*

2. Williams and Deal, authors of *When Opposites Dance: Balancing the Manager and Leader Within,* identify four types of managers:

   - Rationalists, who value sound thinking and work through organizational structure to accomplish tasks.

   - Politicists, who view group dynamics from a power perspective and are adept at politics.

   - Humanists, who are attuned to organizational moods and regard people as a company's top asset.

   - Culturists, who consider culture the preeminent force in an organization and communicate through stories, ceremonies, and rituals.

3. Williams and Deal conclude that while people are predisposed to think and act in certain ways, the best executives combine different personality attributes. *(Source: CIO, November 1, 2003.)*

PPT 7-42
Using Social Media to Build Customer Support

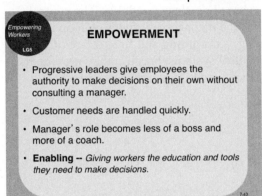

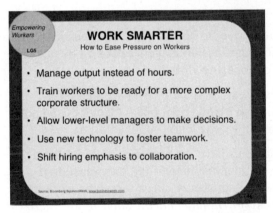

1. Managing in today's complex environment is about leading, not supervising.

2. This slide gives students insight into the process of empowering employees to work smarter.

3. Ask the students, What are the benefits of empowering employees to work smarter? *(Employees who are empowered should be more motivated and able to handle more complex tasks.)*

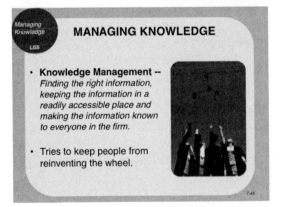

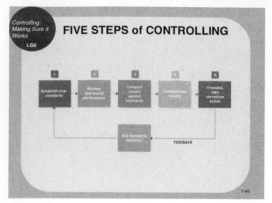

This slide presents the five steps of the control function. It should be pointed out to the students that the whole control process is based on clear standards. The control function completes the management function loop that starts with planning. Accounting and finance are often the foundations for control systems, because they provide the numbers management needs to evaluate progress.

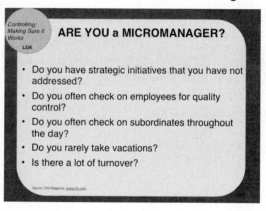

1. This slide presents a list of questions a manager can ask himself or herself to determine if he or she is a micromanager.

2. If you answer yes to any of these five questions, you are a micromanager. Managers can ask a trusted employee for honest feedback.

3. Ask the students, Have they ever worked for a micromanager? How did it make them feel and how did other employees feel?

4. Do the students have the tendency to think that if they want something done right, they must do it themselves or constantly check on others work in a team situation? *(It may indicate some of the micromanaging tendencies.)*

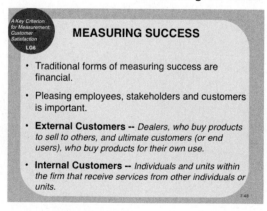

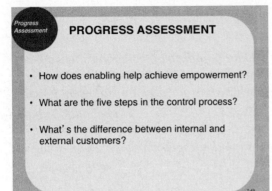

1. Enabling is the key to successfully empowering employees. Enabling means giving workers the education and the tools they need to make decisions.

2. The five steps in the control process are (1) setting clear standards, (2) monitoring and recording performance, (3) comparing performance with plans and standards, (4) communicating results and deviations to employees, and (5) providing positive feedback for a job well done and taking the corrective action necessary.

3. Not all customers come from outside the organization. Internal customers are defined as individuals and business units within the firm that receive services from other individuals or units. For example, the field salespeople are the internal customers of the marketing research units that prepare market reports for them. External customers are more traditional and include dealers, who buy products and sell to others, and ultimately customers, who buy products for their own personal use.

lecture
links

lecture link 7-1

BEWARE OF BAD BOSSES

Bad bosses—whether jerks, bullies, or micromanagers—have always been with us. Today, however, there seem to be more bad bosses than ever before. As a result of downsizing, overextended managers are both short-tempered and too busy to provide staff with the support they need. No one has as much power as a bad boss to unnerve you and wreak havoc on your sense of self-esteem. This is why it is commonly said that people don't quit jobs, they quit bosses. What makes for a bad boss? Some are just plain nasty, but often a bad boss is all in the eye of the beholder. One person's boss from hell may be another person's pin-up.

The key to getting on with a boss is to manage him or her by understanding the boss's underlying motivations, which may be different than you think. Here are some common types of bad bosses, their motivations, and strategies for dealing with them.

THE WEAK MANAGER

She won't stand up for you. She aggressively avoids taking risks. She's vague, and her commitments have the sticking power of water. But the underlying causes of her behavior can vary. Often, she simply wants to be liked by everyone and can't stand conflict. It's also possible she's too busy to understand when there is a problem or too burned out to care. Frequently, such managers are reluctant to be managers at all, and would much rather be doing their own work. They may also be ill-trained and lacking management skills.

If you are dealing with a weak manager, identify the problem. For example, if your manager needs to be liked by everyone, avoid communications that suggest contentious or highly charged emotional issues. Where you can, solve conflicts yourself. If her problem is that she is spineless and refuses to take on any leadership role, consider talking to your boss's boss.

If your boss is too burned out to care or is a reluctant manager, work around her. Take the initiative to set out the parameters of the work. Make her life easy by talking to her only about critical issues. If your boss is lacking management skills, tell her what you need from her to do your job. Then cover yourself by sending an e-mail.

THE POLITICAL MANAGER

He has an unerring ability to know what will make him look good. He will go to bat for you only on issues that serve his political agenda. He's sneaky and plays favorites. He won't think twice about using you as a sacrificial lamb to support his own career goals.

Support his high need for recognition by making him look good on strategic projects. Focus your own efforts on "high-value" work. Be prepared to share the limelight, even if it kills you. Don't trust him to have your own interests at heart. Pitch him on work you want to do by emphasizing its profile and importance to senior management.

THE OBSESSIVE MICROMANAGER

She trusts you the way you'd trust a five-year-old behind the wheel of the car. No matter how much detail you give her, or how many times you redo a piece of work, it's still not right. You're completely demotivated and have lost your sense of competence. Why is she so untrusting? Is she anxious about failing to please her boss, or is she simply a control freak? If the problem is her own insecurity, anticipate issues that will make her anxious by reassuring her that you have covered all the bases. Say, for example, "in completing this I spoke to Jane Doe and took the following issues into account. . . ." Write it down as well, as she may be too anxious to fully process what you are saying.

THE INVISIBLE MANAGER

You have no one to go to for direction. She doesn't have a clue about the volume or pace of your work. You're killing yourself, but no one notices or gives you feedback. This manager shares many of the underlying motivations of the weak manager. She may be invisible because she's too busy, or is a reluctant or unskilled manager. If she is pressed for time, do your homework before you meet with her to make the meeting as efficient as possible. Give yourself direction and feedback by setting milestones and regularly evaluating your effectiveness against them. Establish a mechanism for getting direction, whether it be weekly or monthly meetings at an agreed time. Hold her to her commitment.

THE TASK MASTER

He doesn't have a life and doesn't expect you to either. You're drowning in work, but he keeps heaping on more. His timelines are ridiculous. Sometimes an extremely task-focused manager is simply shy or preoccupied or so focused on getting the work done that he's not aware of the impact of his behavior on the people around him. Is he aware of your workload? If you've talked to him and he still doesn't get it, create your own standards for evaluating what is realistic and doable. Don't be apologetic about wanting time for a personal life. Work life balance is your right, not a privilege. If your organization wants to "be an employer of choice," remind your boss of the incongruity between policy and behavior.

THE NASTY MANAGER

She's ruthless. She seems to take pleasure in watching you squirm. She has pets, and you are not one of them. Sometimes an apparently nasty boss is simply so task-focused that she is oblivious to how her behavior makes you feel. Underneath a gruff exterior, as the saying goes, may be the heart of a pussycat. When you confront her, does she apologize or get mad?

Regardless of what type of boss you have, your first line of defense is to speak to him, as he may not be aware of his behavior. Don't make sweeping generalizations about his personality. Rather talk to the specific behavior in question and tell him how it makes you feel. You can soften your comments and avoid defensiveness by allowing your boss to save face. Introduce your statements with "You may not be aware . . ." or "You may not realize . . ." or "You may not intend. . . ."

If none of these strategies work, you have two choices. If you have good personal reasons for staying in your job—you love your work, you're learning a lot, you like the people you're working with—you can hold your nose and ignore your boss as best you can. Or, you can quit: Use the experience to learn and then move on.[i]

lecture link 7-2

BEST BUSINESS LEADERS OF THE 20TH CENTURY

Harvard Business School professors Anthony J. Mayo and Nitin Nohria set out to identify history's greatest business leaders. In their book *In Their Time: The Greatest Business Leaders of the 20th Century,* they identified 1,000 great chief executives and company founders of the 20th century. They then asked business leaders to evaluate and rank their candidates. Finally, they produced a ranking of the top 100 business leaders of the 20th century. Classic entrepreneurs who built companies from scratch dominate the list of the best. Only 1 woman—Estee Lauder—made the top 25.[ii]

1. Samuel M. Walton (Walmart)
2. Walter E. Disney (Walt Disney)
3. William H. Gates III (Microsoft)
4. Henry Ford (Ford Motor)
5. John P. Morgan (J. P. Morgan Chase)
6. Alfred P. Sloan Jr. (General Motors)
7. John F. Welch Jr. (General Electric)
8. Raymond A. Kroc (McDonald's)
9. William R. Hewlett (Hewlett-Packard)
10. David Packard (Hewlett-Packard)
11. Andrew S. Grove (Intel)
12. Milton S. Hershey (The Hershey Co.)
13. John D. Rockefeller Sr. (Standard Oil)
14. Thomas J. Watson Jr. (IBM)
15. Henry R. Luce (Time-Life Publications)
16. Will K. Kellogg (Kellogg)
17. Warren E. Buffett (Berkshire Hathaway)
18. Harland Sanders (Kentucky Fried Chicken)
19. William C. Procter (Procter & Gamble)
20. Thomas J. Watson Sr. (IBM)
21. Asa G. Candler (Coca-Cola)
22. Estee Lauder (Estee Lauder)
23. Henry J. Heinz (H. J. Heinz)
24. Daniel F. Gerber Jr. (Gerber Products)
25. James L. Kraft (Kraft Foods)

lecture link 7-3

WOMEN BRINGING HOME THE BACON

For decades women have held the purse strings of many American households. As much as 85% of all purchasing decisions are ultimately made by a female. This fact alone makes women a more than formidable market, but recent strides in social equality have facilitated a seismic shift in household dynamics that will shake the entire economy. For the first time in history, not only are women the primary purchasers, they are also the breadwinners.

The U.S. workforce became nearly half female in October 2009, with women accounting for 49.9% of all nonfarm labor jobs and 51.5% of management and professorial positions. The Bureau of Labor Statistics found that women make up the majority of the workforce in 9 of the 10 occupations slated to add the most jobs in the next eight years. And though women as a whole still earn less than men, that pay gap is finally closing in some key areas. A survey of childless city-dwelling single people in their mid-20s found that women are outearning men in metropolises like Atlanta and New York City. Many of these gains are the product of increased education. For every two men who graduate from college or attain a higher-level degree, three women do the same.

Marketing to this new crop of highly educated, independent women is a tricky task. Dell, for example, took a big misstep when it introduced Della, a dreamy, pink-laced website that highlighted the brand's "cute" laptops and offered tips on tracking calories. Within 10 days Dell took the website down after a deluge of criticism burst forth from the Twitterverse. The auto repair chain Midas, on the other hand, may have discovered a surefire way to attract and retain female customers. The discerning, cash-flush woman of today wants to know exactly what she is buying, unlike men who traditionally target a product need and fulfill it swiftly. So Midas developed a system dubbed G.E.T. (Greet, Explain, Thank) that would include women in the process of getting their car fixed. Even a standard oil change would come with a complete rundown of exactly what the mechanics were checking and adjusting. Though the G.E.T. system has been tested extensively only in Philadelphia, sales in that market are up 13% from December 2009, the month Midas implemented the system.[iii]

lecture link 7-4

THREE TYPES OF GREAT LEADERS

In their book *In Their Time: The Greatest Business Leaders of the 20th Century,* Harvard Business School professors Anthony J. Mayo and Nitin Nohria identified 1,000 great chief executives and company founders of the 20th century. (See **Lecture Link 7-2,** Best Business Leaders of the 20th Century.)

Nohria and Mayo also identified three leadership types—the entrepreneurial leader, the leader as manager, and the charismatic leader. They found that all three types exhibited what they called "contextual intelligence," the acute sensitivity to the social, political, technological, and demographic contexts that defined their eras.

The *entrepreneurial leader's* genius lies in bringing things together in a combination that no one has ever seen before. As an example of the entrepreneurial leader, they selected C. W. Post, who created Post Cereals. Post began as an itinerant salesman until he developed a caffeine-free health drink, Postum. Post differentiated his product by offering free samples to customers of general stores. He then developed a breakfast cereal and pioneered one of the first major cereal companies. But Post's real genius lay in his ability to sense that a new, national consumer was emerging in America. He saw that in the developing industrialized economy, time itself was becoming increasingly valuable. People were willing to pay for convenience. He was also one of the first leaders to recognize the power of a national brand.

Whereas entrepreneurs were company creators and agents of change, *managerial leaders* are value maximizers. They make the most out of something that already exists. Nohria and Mayo use Louis B. Neumiller as an example. Neumiller rose through the ranks of Caterpillar and became its chief executive in 1941, two months before Japan attacked Pearl Harbor. He seized on the massive global event that was World War II to build Caterpillar into a global organization. When the U.S. military approached Neumiller about converting Caterpillar's operation to artillery production, he convinced the Army that it was better served by letting Caterpillar continue to manufacture bulldozers and tractors. It turned out that the bulldozer was critical to clearing roads and building landing strips throughout the Pacific Islands. Neumiller really didn't build anything new. What he did was capitalize on the war effort to transform Caterpillar into a global giant.

America's fascination with the *charismatic leader* dates back to Lee Iacocca. When the 1970s OPEC oil embargo and the energy crisis sent shock waves through the automotive industry, Japanese automobile producers seized the opportunity to introduce smaller, fuel-efficient cars into the American market, eroding Detroit's dominance. The biggest loser was Chrysler, which posted a then record loss of $1.7 billion. Iacocca then stepped in as a larger-than-life figure who successfully turned the auto company around through the force of his personality. Iacocca persuaded the government to authorize a $1.5 billion loan guarantee using taxpayers' dollars. Then he reinvented the automobile company by changing its technology, responding to changing demographics, and reinventing the union–labor relationship. Ultimately Iacocca succeeded in turning Chrysler around and established the mold for the charismatic leader.[iv]

lecture link 7-5

REVISITING MISSION AT VICTORIA'S SECRET

Victoria's Secret, the lingerie company that introduced the Very Sexy Bra, the Fantasy Bra, and the Internet service–crashing fashion show, may have become "too sexy" for its own good, according to its chief executive officer. "We've so much gotten off our heritage," Sharen Turney, Victoria's Secret's CEO now believes, "Too sexy." . . . "We use the word sexy a lot and really have forgotten the ultra feminine."

Victoria's Secret was started in San Francisco in 1977 by Roy Raymond, who said he was embarrassed trying to buy lingerie for his wife and hoped to provide a comfortable place for men to shop. The chain was launched with the idea that "Victoria" was an aristocratic London native. Her purchases were thought to be for herself, ultra-feminine.

Turney believes that the company should get back to its heritage and think in terms of ultra-feminine and not just the word *sexy*. She believes Victoria's Secret should become more relevant to its customers. Victoria's Secret has gotten younger with a strong focus on its successful Pink line of lingerie and loungewear created for college-age women, and has tried to chase those customers.

Turney now says Victoria's Secret wants to increase its level of sophistication. "We will also reinvent the sleepwear business and focus on product quality," she says. "Our assortment will return to an ultra feminine lingerie brand to meet" customer needs.[v]

lecture link 7-6

DECISION-MAKING TIPS

Just as people are different, so are their styles of decision making. Each person is a result of all the decisions made in their life to date. Recognizing this, here are some tips to enhance your decision-making batting average.

- When making a decision you are simply choosing from among alternatives. You are not making a choice between right and wrong.

UNDERSTANDING BUSINESS: Instructor's Resource Manual

- Avoid snap decisions. Move fast on the reversible ones and slowly on the nonreversible.

- Do your decision making on paper. Make notes and keep your ideas visible so you can consider all the relevant information in making this decision.

- Be sure to choose based on what is right, not who is right.

- Write down the pros and cons of a line of action. It clarifies your thinking and makes for a better decision.

- Make decisions as you go along. Do not let them accumulate. A backlog of many little decisions could be harder to deal with than one big and complex decision.

- Consider those affected by your decision. Whenever feasible, get them involved to increase their commitment.

- Recognize that you cannot know with 100% certainty that your decision is correct because the actions to implement it will take place in the future. So make it and don't worry about it.

- Remember that not making a decision is a decision not to take action.

- Don't waste your time making decisions that do not have to be made.

- As soon as you are aware that a decision will have to be made on a specific situation, review the facts at hand then set it aside. Let this incubate in your subconscious mind until it is time to finally make the decision.

- Once you have made the decision and have started what you are going to do, put the "what if's" aside and do it with commitment.[vi]

lecture link 7-7
THE 21ST-CENTURY CEO

Economic recovery began for big businesses in 2010 as weary returns slowly transformed into relatively robust earnings. But for the most recognizable names in American business, accounting books flush with black ink aren't the only tools they'll need to forge ahead into the future. For most, real change starts at the top with a new crop of CEOs to replace the old guard.

During the recession, CEO turnover dropped from 12.7% in 2007 to just 9.4% in 2010. Boards feared that investors would construe departing high-level executives as alarm bells sounding the imminent end of the company. Now, though, big businesses are looking ahead instead of fretting about the achy economy. More often than not, companies see their future overseas in emerging global markets that require knowledge not only of other cultures, but sometimes different industries altogether. Many sitting CEOs have little experience abroad, let alone in fields other than that of their home company given the habit of big businesses to promote from within.

The 21st-century CEO is well traveled and carries a wealth of experience in fields such as marketing and sales rather than finance and manufacturing like the outgoing generation. Campbell Soup's new CEO, for instance, jumped into different positions at Procter & Gamble, Nestlé, and Kraft before finally landing at Campbell eight years ago. Connections with high-level business leaders across the globe are key as international sales start to account for more than half of some companies' total revenue. Also, studies show that executives who have lived abroad are more creative and entrepreneurial than their "monocultural" peers. Ultimately, the business hierarchy of today is built differently than when alpha-execs like General Electric CEO Jack Welch ruled the roost. Executives today are subjected to far more corporate governance than in the past, requiring today's CEOs to work closely with their boards.[vii]

LEARNING MANAGEMENT SKILLS

Now that you know some of the broad categories of skills needed by various levels of management, we can look at the more specific skills an aspiring manager needs to learn. Remember that customer satisfaction is the key to success in almost all businesses.

In general, it's a good idea to take as many courses as are available in oral communication, writing, computers, and human relations. In all managerial jobs, these are the skills in greatest demand. Naturally, it's also important to develop technical skills in some selected area. There are at least six skills students need to develop their managerial potential: verbal skills, writing skills, computer skills, human relations skills, time management skills, and other technical skills.

VERBAL SKILLS

The bulk of the duties as a manager involve communicating with others. Managers have to give talks, conduct meetings, make presentations, and generally communicate their ideas to others. To prepare for such tasks, students should take oral communication courses and become active in various student groups. It helps to become an officer and assume responsibility for conducting meetings and giving speeches. It also helps to join a choir or other group to become comfortable performing in front of others.

At least half of communication is skilled listening. A good manager mixes with other managers, workers, clients, stockholders, and others outside the firm. He or she listens to recommendations and complaints and acts on them. Active listening requires the asking of questions and feeding back what you've heard to let others know you're truly interested in what they say.

WRITING SKILLS

Managers must also be able to write clearly and precisely. Much of what they want others to do must be communicated through memos, reports, policies, and letters. Much of what was said in the past by phone or letter is now communicated by e-mail or fax. While secretaries often wrote and/or corrected letters in the past, the managers themselves send most e-mail and fax messages. Consequently, organizations everywhere are complaining about many college graduates' inability to write clearly. If students develop good writing skills, they will be miles ahead of the competition. That means taking courses in grammar, composition, and keyboarding. To learn to write, people must practice writing! It helps to write anything: a diary, letters, notes, and so on. With practice, people will develop the ability to write easily—just as they speak. With this skill, they will be more ready for a career in management.

COMPUTER SKILLS

The office of the future will be an office full of computers and related technology. As noted, memos, charts, letters, e-mail and fax messages, and most other communication efforts will involve the computer. The truly efficient manager of the future will be able to effectively use and take advantage of the continuing developments in technology. That includes being able to surf the Internet to find needed facts and figures quickly.

HUMAN RELATIONS SKILLS

A manager works with people, and that means that good managers know how to get along with people, motivate them, and inspire them. People skills are learned by working with people. That means aspiring managers should join student groups, volunteer to help at their church or temple and local charities, and get involved in political organizations. They should try to assume leadership positions where they are responsible for contacting others, assigning them work, and motivating them. Good leaders begin early by assuming leadership positions in sports, community groups, and so on.

TIME MANAGEMENT SKILLS

One of the more important skills for new managers to learn is how to budget their time effectively. There are many demands on managers' time that they need to control: telephone interruptions, visits from colleagues, questions from team members, meetings scheduled by top management, and such. Time management courses or workshops will help you develop such skills as setting priorities, delegating work, choosing activities that produce the most results, doing your work when you're at your best, and dealing with interruptions.

TECHNICAL SKILLS

To rise through the ranks of accounting, marketing, finance, production, or any other functional area, it is important to be proficient in that area. Therefore, students should choose some area of specialization. To rise to top management, it's a good idea to supplement undergraduate studies with an MBA (master of business administration) or some similar degree in government, economics, or hospital administration. More and more students are going on to take advanced degrees, so you too may need such a degree to keep up with your colleagues.

(Critical Thinking Exercise 7-6, Rate Your Management Skills, on page 7.70 gives students an opportunity to evaluate their skill level for these five important skills.

lecture link 7-9

AMERICA'S UPCOMING MANAGEMENT GAP

With unemployment still soaring in double digits, it's difficult to believe that the United States could suffer any sort of labor shortage in the near future. Many companies could face this problem soon enough, though, as upper-management employees begin retiring in droves. By 2015, workers over the age of 55 will make up 20% of the workforce, up from 10% two decades ago. Already the oldest baby boomers are hitting 65 and preparing for retirement. As a result, many companies are worrying about where the next generation of managers will come from once this one has grayed and gone.

The easy solution would be to promote younger managers sooner, but there are signs that the current crop of careerists may not be up to the task just yet. Most 30- to 40-something executives have spent the bulk of their careers languishing in middle-management positions with few perks and little understanding of the company where they work. Job satisfaction for this age group has plummeted in recent years, bottoming out at an all time low of 43%. Matters aren't much better for young grads, either. The turnover rate for workers in their 20s clocked in at a whopping 22% in 2009, more than double that of older employees. In response, companies like Aetna have started mentorship programs to retain and cultivate younger workers.

lecture link 7-10

MANAGED TO DEATH: JAPAN'S ECONOMIC DECLINE

Today, the emerging markets of Brazil, Russia, India, and China command 10.4% of all revenues on *Fortune*'s Global 500 list, up from 0.9% in 1995. Around that same time, Japanese companies boasted 35.2% of all global revenues with a whopping 141 firms placed on *Fortune*'s list. Japan's salad days didn't last forever, of course, as the nation saw its share shrink to 11.2% in 2010, just a shade north of the world's emerging powers.

Japan once typified the ideal image of a burgeoning economic giant with its devotion to quality products, strong corporate leadership, and seemingly unstoppable savvy for global commerce. Somewhere along the way, though, Japan's export-led growth halted, replaced by a stagnation that has contracted the nation's role in the world economy ever since. Incidentally, many of the factors that contributed to Japan's rapid rise also facilitated its fall. For instance, each of Japan's corporations mapped out a clearly defined "Way" deeply entrenched in Japanese cultural values to manage the company. When Japanese businesses expanded overseas they actively sought to keep The Way in place by hiring either fellow Japanese workers or foreigners who would conform exactly to the company's whims. This led to a rash of management catastrophes as executives sought to solve problems on foreign soil in the strict Japanese manner they were taught.

In fact, 98% of corporate officers at Japan's 68 largest global companies are Japanese. The majority of them went to the same four universities and will inevitably spend their whole careers at the same firm. Such homogeneous leadership is unsuitable for a global venture intent on succeeding in markets with contrasting cultures. Ultimately, the unbending devotion of Japanese managers to the social mores and methods of their home country led to their downfall. The same could happen to the world's emerging markets as they branch out of their own backyards and on to the global stage. After all, what works in China won't necessarily succeed in the United States. But Chinese business leaders could learn that fact far too late if their corporate governors are all former classmates and current members of the same country club.[viii]

critical
thinking exercises

Name: _____

Date: _____

critical thinking exercise 7-1
MANAGEMENT FUNCTIONS

Remember the four management functions? They are planning, organizing, leading, and controlling. Think of a job you have now or one you've had in the past. List the managerial activities you have done or observed. If you have never had a paid job, remember that it takes management skills to manage a home, run a baseball team, and lead a church group. Classify each activity of your job according to whether it involved planning, organizing, leading, or controlling.

PLANNING	ORGANIZING	LEADING	CONTROLLING

critical thinking exercise 7-2
CAREER SWOT ANALYSIS

SWOT analysis, the key tool in the strategic planning process, can also be applied to career planning. A SWOT analysis focuses on the internal and external environments, examining strengths and weaknesses in the internal environment and opportunities and threats in the external environment.

Use Figure 7.3, SWOT Matrix, presented on text page 187 and conduct an analysis of your career planning. (SWOT diagrams are also available at numerous websites such as www.quintcareers.com/SWOT_Analysis.html.)ix

1. **STRENGTHS:**
   - What advantages do you have?
   - What do you do well?
   - What relevant resources do you have access to?
   - What do other people see as your strengths?

2. **WEAKNESSES:**
   - What could you improve?
   - What do you do badly?
   - What should you avoid?

3. **OPPORTUNITIES:**
   - Where are the good opportunities facing you?
   - What are the interesting trends you are aware of?
   - What changes in technology and markets are occurring on both a broad and narrow scale?
   - What changes are occurring in social patterns, population profiles, lifestyle changes, and so on?

4. **THREATS:**
   - What obstacles do you face?
   - Are the required specifications for your career changing?
   - Is changing technology threatening your plan?
   - Do you have bad debt or cash-flow problems?
   - Could any of your weaknesses seriously threaten your future?

critical thinking exercise 7-3
CRISIS MANAGEMENT

      This exercise explores management reaction to rapid, unexpected change. Divide the class into groups of five or six. Each group will act as a management team for a large national company faced with a crisis. Have the groups quickly analyze the situation (five or six minutes), decide on an appropriate strategy for coping with the situation, and prepare a brief statement outlining how the company should manage the crisis.

A.   A national consumer foods company has discovered that several batches of its salad dressing have been contaminated with toxic industrial solvent. One person has died and the media are demanding a statement.

B.   At the construction site for a new corporate headquarters, the top floors of the building have collapsed, killing 16 people, including the head of the local union. The cause of the collapse has not been determined, but a local television station has reported that substandard materials have been used in construction.

C.   A hurricane has come ashore near your largest distribution facility days before your marketing department is scheduled to launch the new fall line of clothing. Communications have been cut off to the area and you have not been able to contact anyone at the facility. News media are reporting large-scale damage and loss of life. Your retail managers across the country are worried that the loss of this distribution facility will disrupt deliveries at this critical point.

D.   There has been a massive explosion at a chemical plant, centered in the storage area. The resulting fire is threatening a building where dozens of workers have taken refuge. There are rumors that a terrorist bomb was involved. Casualties and extent of damage are unknown.

E.   A gunman has invaded a large metropolitan bank, killing 4 people and taking 20 employees hostage. He has demanded that bank executives publicly apologize for "crimes against African Americans" or he will blow up the bank. No one knows what weapons he has.

critical thinking exercise 7-4
EVALUATING ALTERNATIVE COURSES

Monmouth Thermics, a subsidiary of General Standard, a large conglomerate, manufactures thermometers. Your primary customers are large companies that purchase the thermometers to use for specialty advertising. Over the last several years, however, low-cost overseas competitors have pulled away many of the company's longtime customers.

General Standard has become concerned about the loss of market share and declining profit. You, as Monmouth general manager, have been asked to put together a recovery plan to present to the General Standard board of directors. Your management team has pulled together the following options:

- **Cut costs by imposing an across-the-board pay cut** for all personnel. This would save enough money to bring the company back to profitability.

- **Expand operations into specialty printing.** Currently the thermometers are sold to other companies for printing. The additional printing cost would add 23¢ to the cost of each unit, but would also add 40¢ to the unit sale price.

- **Expand sales of the current thermometer line** to retail outlets such as Walmart and Target.

- **Manufacture and market a new product** the R&D department has developed, a combination thermometer–barometer housed in an oak case. The product would be marketed through specialty stores. Two new production lines would have to be added for the barometer and for the wood case. The "Thermbarometer" could be manufactured for about $30 per unit and sold for $100.

Use the seven-step decision-making process described in the chapter to decide which option management should present to the General Standard board of directors. Defend your choice.

Name: _____

Date: _____

critical thinking exercise 7-5
THE MOST POWERFUL WOMEN IN BUSINESS

Each year *Fortune* magazine ranks the 50 most powerful women in business. Visit the *Fortune* website (www.fortune.com)[x] and use the listing for the current year to answer the questions below. (Sometimes the Web address for a location changes. You might need to search to find the exact location mentioned.)

1. List the top five most powerful women in business for the latest year. Also give the company for which they work.

    NAME   **COMPANY**

    a. _____   _____

    b. _____   _____

    c. _____   _____

    d. _____   _____

    e. _____   _____

2. Which of the women earns the highest pay? How much?

3. Choose one of the women in the top ten to further research. Give a brief biography.

Name: _____

Date: _____

critical thinking exercise 7-6
RATE YOUR MANAGEMENT SKILLS

Rate yourself on each of these key management skills.

SKILL NEEDED   **PERSONAL EVALUATION**

	Excellent	Good	Fair	Need Work
Verbal skills				
Writing skills				
Computer skills				
Human relations skills				
Time management skills				
Technical skills				

UNDERSTANDING BUSINESS: Instructor's Resource Manual

notes on critical thinking exercise 7-6

Lecture Link 7-8, Learning Management Skills, on page 7.62 discusses these six important management skills.

critical thinking exercise 7-7
ARE LEADERS BORN OR CAN THEY BE TAUGHT?

There is considerable debate on the question, Are individuals born to be leaders or can they be taught? To better understand the leadership equation, answer the questions below and be prepared to discuss the basic concepts that define leadership.

1. What is your initial reaction to the question, Are leaders born or can they be taught?

2. Now, use the Internet and find at least three articles or sites that discuss leadership. Based on your work, how is leadership defined? What are some of the best practices of leaders?

3. Using the Internet, define successful leaders from the past 50 years, the past 25 years, and finally, the leaders of today.

4. Based on your research, what are the general characteristics of leaders? What motivates individuals to become successful leaders?

5. Explain how individuals are taught to become good leaders.

6. Finally, are individuals mostly born or are they taught to become successful leaders? Explain.

critical thinking exercise 7-8

TRAITS OF LEADERS

Leaders possess traits and skills that make them successful. They are effective communicators, skillful planners, and successful motivators. Leaders can be villains or heroes. This exercise examines the skills displayed by famous leaders and gives students the opportunity to use this knowledge to improve their leadership skills.

Groups of five to six people brainstorm a list of famous leaders, and then pick two leaders to compare and contrast. Then the groups profile them in terms of their skills and traits.

QUESTIONS FOR DISCUSSION

1. What criteria did your group use to determine which two leaders you would profile? Describe.

2. In what ways are the leadership styles of these leaders similar? In what ways are they different? Explain.

3. Were you surprised at the similarity or dissimilarity between these leaders? Discuss.

4. Which one of these leaders would you want to work for? Explain your rationale.

bonus cases

bonus case 7-1

DEFENSEWEB EVALUATES A STRATEGIC EXPANSION

DefenseWeb Technologies was on a roll. By 2002 profit margins were strong and clients were happy. But founder Paul Cavanaugh was restless. Annual revenue had flattened at about $2 million, and he worried that his company was hitting a slump. The company's key product is a Web-based software platform used by the U.S. armed forces. One such project is MyArmyLifeToo web portal. MyArmyLifeToo is an online information clearinghouse to support army soldiers and their families.

If the military was so impressed with DefenseWeb's performance, Cavanaugh wondered, could the company target the much larger, and more lucrative, corporate market? The potential new private clients could spur revenue growth and increase the company's value. On the other hand, the Pentagon never bounced a check.

The company had flirted with this expansion strategy for some time. Every time engineers updated the company's flagship software, they were asked to make sure the new version had the potential to work for private-sector clients, keeping the option open. In early 2003, Cavanaugh decided to determine once and for all whether such a move made sense.

To handle the strategic analysis, Cavanaugh hired a new CEO, Doug Burke, a technology industry veteran. Together the two men began exploring DefenseWeb's options. They decided to split the company into two "zones." Cavanaugh would run the government operations, and Burke would investigate a new private-sector strategy. Burke gave himself a six-month timetable. At the end of that time, he would take his findings—good or bad—to the company's board to make the decision.

Burke assigned two full-time technicians to modify DefenseWeb's application for commercial use. He contacted 20 potential clients in the technology sector about adopting the company's software. Six signed on for the pilot program.

While the initial reviews were positive, Burke uncovered roadblocks. The initial six clients were very technology-oriented, but the software would have to be further modified for more mainstream customers. Also, a new marketing and sales force would have to be built to sell to the more cutthroat private sector.[xi]

discussion questions for bonus case 7-1

1. Show how the seven-step decision process could be used in this case.

2. If DefenseWeb expands into the private sector, how would it affect the various stakeholders, such as employees, customers, community, investors, and suppliers?

3. What are the benefits and drawbacks of having a technical person as CEO?

notes on discussion questions for bonus case 7-1

1. *Show how the seven-step decision process could be used in this case.*

    a. Define the situation. The software could be adapted to the civilian market.

    b. Describe and collect information. A six-company pilot program was used.

    c. Develop alternatives. The alternative to going private was to stick to the government.

    d. Develop agreement among those involved. This was a joint decision.

    e. Decide which alternative is best. They decided to try the civilian market.

    f. Do what is indicated. They tried the product at six beta sites.

    g. Determine if the decision was a good one? Yes, but adaptations were needed, they discovered.

2. *If DefenseWeb expands into the private sector, how would it affect the various stakeholders, such as employees, customers, community, investors, and suppliers?*

    Almost all the stakeholders would be affected positively. The stockholders would make more money and so would the employees. The only negative result may be from the government customers who might not get the total, undivided attention they once had.

3. *What are the benefits and drawbacks of having a technical person as CEO?*

    A technical person might not spot the difficulties that customers might have using the product. In fact, that happened. Furthermore, a technical person might not have the people skills needed. But that is easily discovered from past management duties. There is no reason why a technical person couldn't be a wonderful manager.

    Update: The board decided against moving into the private sector. According to Cavanaugh, "It just didn't add up." The private-sector clients that were part of DefenseWeb's pilot program were given the option of continuing to use the software, but most opted to let the trial end. Burke is now courting potential clients like the Army Reserve and scouting out subcontracting opportunities. Neither Burke nor Cavanaugh feel the six-month evaluation was wasted time. The company had been talking about going commercial for a long time. Now that the decision was made, the company was more focused on its original mission.

bonus case 7-2

WHEN EMPLOYEES MAKE THE DECISIONS

W. L. Gore is the maker of the Gore-Tex waterproof fabric found in all sorts of outdoor clothing. Gore-Tex is a unique kind of textile made, basically, out of Teflon. Gore-Tex's pores are hundreds of times too small to let through water droplets. Gore was working for his father's company, which made wires and coatings for wires. He tried making a plumber's tape with a Teflon coating, but the sheet of Teflon material he was using wasn't flexible enough. He got so frustrated that he jerked at it in his hands. When he stretched it that way, it changed its structure and became porous. Gore realized that the material had commercial possibilities and built Gore-Tex around the invention.

W. L. Gore also has a unique organizational structure. There are no directors, line managers, operatives, or secretaries. All the company's employees are referred to as "associates" and share decision-making authority. When a machine operator left W. L. Gore, the human resource department began looking for a replacement. However, before anyone got as far as posting a want ad, the man's former team members met and figured out how they could make do with one less body. They would have to work harder without more pay, but they wanted to do what was best for the enterprise.

The cooperative spirit of this company arises from a unique structure with no fixed hierarchy, few titles, and no formal job descriptions. Any "associate" can speak directly to any other without going through a chain of command. Together the 6,000 associates own the company.

The theory behind employee-ownership programs is that they will transform workers from clock punchers into partners who will be motivated to better serve customers and make things run more efficiently. At the most successful worker-owned firms, the theory is pretty close to reality.

On average, worker-owned companies survive longer, lose fewer workers, enjoy bigger profits, and are more productive than their non-employee-owned competitors. The key to the success of employee-owned companies is openness of information and decision making.

Each worker at Gore enjoys broad discretion to make minor decisions. Bigger ones—hiring and firing, setting compensation—are made by committees whose members constantly shift with the demands of the business. Anyone can start a new project simply by persuading enough people to go along with the idea. Even Bob Gore, chair and son of the founders, has his compensation set by a committee.

The arrangement has its costs. Above all, workers are forced to devote a lot of time to building relationships. Says process technology manager Michael Jones, "At a traditional company, you have one boss to please. Here, you have everyone to please." Few companies go so far; most American firms in which workers own a majority of the stock are organized as conventional hierarchies. But evidence is growing that the most successful firms are those that find some consistent way of empowering workers.[xii]

discussion questions for bonus case 7-2

1. What do you see as the advantages and disadvantages of working for a worker-owned firm?

2. Since there are no hierarchies in worker-owned firms, how would you go about setting the pay scale for people, especially over time? Since there is no hierarchy, there is no way of moving up in the firm. How do you motivate people in such conditions?

3. A worker-owned firm is a radical way of empowering workers. What is the advantage of empowering workers in the first place?

notes on discussion questions for bonus case 7-2

1. *What do you see as the advantages and disadvantages of working for a worker-owned firm?*

   One advantage is that you can learn all the functions of the firm; that prepares you to become an entrepreneur/manager because you have done it all. Another advantage is that you have no boss; on the other hand, you don't have any authority over others either. It is difficult to stand out in a firm where everyone does everything. The tendency is for everyone to want to do the more interesting things, like planning, and for no one to do the menial work, like janitorial work. The disadvantages thus become apparent rather quickly. People will argue over pay, over who does what, and so on. Chaos can quickly develop without hierarchy.

2. *Since there are no hierarchies in worker-owned firms, how would you go about setting the pay scale for people, especially over time? Since there is no hierarchy, there is no way of moving up in the firm. How do you motivate people in such conditions?*

   It is difficult to set pay for people when there is no hierarchy. A new person, potentially, will be doing the same things as a person who has been with the firm for years. So how do you justify paying the senior person more? How do you get a raise? And shouldn't everyone's raise be pretty much the same? How can you distinguish the contribution of one person over another? Worker ownership, therefore, is often more attractive to new people than to older workers who have been around for a while.

3. *A worker-owned firm is a radical way of empowering workers. What is the advantage of empowering workers in the first place?*

   Empowerment is a very powerful way to improve the operations of a firm. All of us know how irritating it can be to deal with a clerk in a store or a front-desk person at a motel who can't make decisions on his or her own. We must wait for a manager to make the decision. Why not train the frontline people to be as knowledgeable as the manager? It would take more time and training, but customers would be happier, workers would be happier, and the firm would need fewer managers. You can imagine how happy you would be if every time you asked someone for something, the person would respond immediately. That may be true, even if the answer is no, as long as you didn't have to wait forever to get that answer.

bonus case 7-3

DECISION MAKING: KLM 4805

At the height of the tourist season, a bomb exploded at the Gran Canaria airport, main airport for the Canary Islands, closing the airport. Air traffic was notified and told to divert air traffic to Los Rodeos airport on Tenerife, including two Boeing 747s—KLM 4805, out of JFK in New York, and Pan Am 1736, out of Amsterdam. Los Rodeos was not prepared for this increased traffic. It was Sunday, and only two air traffic controllers were on duty. The influx of large international aircraft overwhelmed the small airport. The altitude at Los Rodeos was over 2,100 feet, and the airstrips were frequently obscured by clouds and fog. The airport was old and had no ground radar. A new international airport was already under construction on the southern coast of the island to replace the small, outmoded airport.

In the hours after the bombing, the single airstrip at Los Rodeos was overwhelmed with the increased traffic. All traffic had to be directed down the taxiway to the end of the airstrip to take off. The traffic flow was especially complicated as the same airstrip also had to be used for landings.

KLM 4805, a huge 747, taxied to the fueling station to take on 14,500 gallons of jet fuel. The flight crew wanted to take on additional fuel so it would not have to refuel later in the journey. Unfortunately, the jet's wingspread prevented other planes from moving around the stopped plane to begin their take-offs. Pan Am 1736 waited two hours on the tarmac behind KLM waiting for a take-off slot.

KLM crew was headed by Captain Jacob van Zanten, a veteran pilot who routinely trained other KLM pilots. Although he had more than 11,000 hours of flying, his training duties had kept van Zanten out of the cockpit on many occasions. Most of his time was spent in a training simulator. He had flown an average of only 21 hours a month and none in the previous two weeks.

In the hours that Pan Am and KLM spent on the taxiway, weather conditionings had deteriorated. Fog had rolled in, and visibility had fallen to less than 1,000 feet. With no ground radar, pilots were limited to communication by radio with tower control and with each other.

Van Zanten was eager to take off from Tenerife and resume the airline's scheduled flights. Complicating his preparations was the knowledge that his crew was rapidly approaching a time-out. If he was not able to take off quickly, the crew would "time-out," or reach a point at which they would be forced to go off duty. If the time-out occurred, KLM would be forced to pay for the crew and passengers to stay at Los Rodeos until a replacement crew could be sent in.

The taxiway was too small for the 747 jets to use to reach the end of the runway. Instead, both were told to taxi down the active runway, turn, and wait for take-off approval. KLM reached the end first and was told to "hold." Pilot van Zanten pivoted the plane and started winding the engines up for take-off. A crew member in the cockpit noticed the error and asked van Zanten if he heard the hold message. Van Zanten angrily silenced the crew member and temporarily stopped the take-off sequence.

Los Rodeos ATC was unfamiliar with handling large 747s and gave Pan Am instructions to turn on a small turn-off, C3, which would have required the huge plane to make almost a 180-degree turn. Pan Am was using a small sectional map of the airport and listening to instructions from the tower. Just as Pan Am approached the turn-off, pilot Victor Grubbs was distracted by a radio message from KLM stating the plane was "now at take-off." Frantically, both the tower and Pan Am tried to contact KLM to let them know that Pan Am was still on the runway. Tragically, the two messages were silenced by a radio squelch, and KLM did not hear the transmission. Van Zanten released his brakes and accelerated to 180 miles per hour, barreling down the runway toward the Pan Am jumbo jet frantically trying to exit the airstrip. In the KLM cockpit, no crew member was heard questioning van Zanten's decision.

The KLM crew saw the Pan Am jet on the runway and tried to rush the take-off. Pan Am fired its engines and tried to taxi, but both were unsuccessful. KLM clipped the top of the Pan Am jet with its landing gear and slammed into the runway thousands of feet down. Of the 396 passengers on the Pan Am jet, only 61 survived. All 234 passengers and crew on the KLM perished. The role of the 14,700 pounds of jet fuel the KLM took on has been debated since.

The crash remains the world's worst air disaster. Both pilots have been faulted for mistakes made. The KLM crew took off without ATC clearance. The Pan Am pilots failed to follow ATC instructions to exit at turn C3, instead turning at C4 farther down the runway. Both flight crews used nonstandard terminology, such as van Zanten's statement that he was "at take-off." Weather and visibility were also factors. But the bottom line is that 583 people died at a small airport in the Canary Islands, on the ground.[xiii]

discussion questions for bonus case 7-3

1. Identify three points at which the tragedy could have been prevented.

2. What role did communication play in the disaster? Why?

3. Many consumer advocates are pushing for rules that punish airlines for flights delayed more than three hours on the ground. Do you think these rules are a good idea? Why or why not?

notes on discussion questions for bonus case 7-3

1. *Identify three points at which the tragedy could have been prevented.*

    This case illustrates the consequences of flawed decision making. The tragedy could have been prevented if the chain of events was interrupted at any point: if the KLM pilot had decided to load less fuel, if the Pan Am pilot had made the correct turn, if a member of the KLM crew had questioned van Zanten's decision to take off, if all parties had used correct terminology, and so on.

2. What role did communication play in the disaster? Why?

    Poor communication plagued all parties in this case. The difference in languages—Spanish, Dutch, English—was a basic barrier. Also, the KLM pilot used vague terminology ("at take-off") at the end of the runway—did that mean he was waiting at the take-off point or was he actually taking off. Then there is the tragic radio communication squelch, literally interrupting communication.

3. *Many consumer advocates are pushing for rules that punish airlines for flights delayed more than three hours on the ground. Do you think these rules are a good idea? Why or why not?*

    Being stranded on the ground waiting for take-off is frustrating and infuriating. However, it is not fatal. In this case, the KLM crew was rushing to take off partially to prevent "timing-out," in which case the passengers and crew would be required to stay overnight at the small airport. Implementing rules that punish airlines for delays may have unintended, and catastrophic, consequences.

endnotes

[i] *Sources*: Barbara Moses, "Bad Bosses and How to Handle Them," *Globe & Mail,* May 6, 2002; Cori Bolger, "When a Royal Pain Reigns, Morale, Productivity Suffer," *The Clarion-Ledger*, October 14, 2005.

[ii] *Source:* Bill Breen, "The Three Ways of Great Leaders," *Fast Company*, September 2005.

[iii] *Source:* Belinda Luscombe, "The Rise of the Sheconomy," *Time*, November 22, 2010.

[iv] *Source:* Ibid.

[v] *Source:* "CEO Says Victoria's Secret Is Too Sexy," Associated Press/Yahoo News, February 29, 2008.

[vi] *Source:* "Decision Making Tips," Managing a Small Business, www.liraz.com.

[vii] *Sources:* Jon Helyar, "The Recession Is Gone, and the CEO Could Be Next," *Bloomberg Businessweek*, February 3, 2011; William W. Maddux, Adam D. Galinsky, and Carmit T. Tadmor, "Be a Better Manager: Live Abroad," *Harvard Business Review*, September 2010.

[viii] *Source:* J. Stewart Black and Allen J. Morrison, "A Cautionary Tale for Emerging Market Giants," *Harvard Business Review*, September 2010.

[ix] The Internet is a dynamic, changing information source. Web links noted of this manual were checked at the time of publication, but content may change over time. Please review the website before recommending it to your students.

[x] The Internet is a dynamic, changing information source. Web links noted of this manual were checked at the time of publication, but content may change over time. Please review the website before recommending it to your students.

[xi] *Sources*: Rod Kurtz, "The Problem: DefenseWeb's Technology Was a Big Hit with the U.S. Military. Was It Time to Target Corporate America?" *Inc.*, October 2004, pp. 56–58; "DefenseWeb Awarded Follow-On Contract to Enhance MyArmyLifeToo Web Portal, *Business Wire,* December 14, 2005; "DefenseWeb Celebrates 7th Anniversary," *Federal Computer Market Report,* February 14, 2005.

[xii] *Sources*: Laird Harrison, "We're All the Boss," *Time.com*, April 3, 2002; Catroina Ritchie, "A Breath of Fresh Air; Gore-Tex Firm Is Named the UK's Best Employer for Third Year in a Row," *The Daily Mail,* March 6, 2006; "Inventive Bunch Heads to Hall of Fame," *Morning Edition NPR*, May 5, 2005.

[xiii] *Sources:* Steven Cushing, *Fatal Words: Communication Clashes and Aircraft Crashes*, University of Chicago Press, 1997; Macarthur Job, *Air Disaster*, Aerospace Publications, 1995; Valerie Lester, *Fasten Your Seat Belts: History and Heroism in the Pan Am Cabin*, Paladwr Press, 1995; Chris Kilroy, *Special Report: Tenerife*, AirDisaster.com; "The Deadliest Plan Crash," PBS, October 17, 2006; *Joint Report, " K.L.M.-P.A.A., 12.7.1977 (Official Report),"* Project-Tenerife.com.

Structuring Organizations for Today's Challenges

chapter **8**

critical thinking exercises

bonus cases

what's new in this edition

additions to the 10th edition:

- Getting to Know Ursula Burns of Xerox
- Name That Company: K2 Skis
- Social Media in Business: When Twitter and Facebook Are Old School
- Spotlight on Small Business: When Your Workers Work for Someone Else

revisions to the 10th edition:

- Text was revised to eliminate redundancy and tighten discussions.
- Statistical data and examples throughout the chapter were updated to reflect current information.

deletions from the 9th edition:

- Getting to Know Anne Mulcahy, CEO of Xerox
- Name That Company: UPS
- Reaching Beyond Our Borders

brief chapter outline and learning goals

Structuring Organizations for Today's Challenges

Getting To Know URSULA BURNS of XEROX

learning goal 1

Outline the basic principles of organization management.

I. EVERYONE'S REORGANIZING

    A.   Building an Organization from the Bottom Up

learning goal 2

Compare the organizational theories of Fayol and Weber.

II. THE CHANGING ORGANIZATION

    A.   The Development of Organization Design

    B.   Turning Principles into Organization Design

learning goal 3

Evaluate the choices managers make in structuring organizations.

III. DECISIONS TO MAKE IN STRUCTURING ORGANIZATIONS

    A.   Choosing Centralized or Decentralized Authority

    B.   Choosing the Appropriate Span of Control

    C.   Choosing between Tall and Flat Organization Structures

    D.   Weighing the Advantages and Disadvantages of Departmentalization

learning goal 4

Contrast the various organizational models.

IV. ORGANIZATIONAL MODELS

    A.   Line Organizations

    B.   Line-and-Staff Organizations

    C.   Matrix-Style Organizations

lecture outline

Getting to Know URSULA BURNS, CEO of XEROX

Ursula Burns replaced Anne Mulcahy as CEO of Xerox in 2009. She joined Xerox as a summer intern and has risen through the ranks. She had to cut down the size of her ranks to 50,000 shortly after starting as CEO. Then Xerox acquired ACS and created a new challenge for Burns. She hopes to lure more customers to Xerox through this acquisition.

NAME THAT company

This sports equipment company studied the compact-disc industry and learned to use ultra-violet inks to print graphics on skis. It went to the cable television industry to learn how to braid layers of fiberglass and carbon, and adapted that knowledge to make its products. Name that company.

(Students should read the chapter before guessing the company's name: K2 Skis)

learning goal 1

Outline the basic principles of organization management.

I. EVERYONE'S REORGANIZING

A. MANY COMPANIES ARE REORGANIZING.

1. *The text discusses how Procter & Gamble has reorganized to become an innovation leader.*

2. *Other firms are declining—banks, automobile companies, and home-building companies.*

3. **ADJUSTING TO CHANGING MARKETS** is a normal function in a capitalist economy.

4. The key to success is to **REMAIN FLEXIBLE** and to adapt to the changing times.

5. *The text uses the example of Starbucks expanding its menu then reducing it when customers were unhappy with the smell.*

B. BUILDING AN ORGANIZATION FROM THE BOTTOM UP

1. **ORGANIZING THE BUSINESS**

PPT 8-1
Chapter Title

PPT 8-2
Learning Goals

(See complete PowerPoint slide notes on page 8.46.)

PPT 8-3
Ursula Burns

(See complete PowerPoint slide notes on page 8.46.)

PPT 8-4
Name That Company

(See complete PowerPoint slide notes on page 8.47.)

PPT 8-5
Reorganization Is for Everyone

(See complete PowerPoint slide notes on page 8.47.)

lecture link 8-1
SMITH'S FOLLY

A lesson in accountability from Kenneth Olsen, founder of Digital Equipment Corporation (now part of Hewlett-Packard). (See the complete lecture link on page 8.68 of this manual.)

lecture link 8-2
STREAMLINING STARBUCKS

As the recent recession hit and customers weren't keen on spending big bucks for coffee, Starbucks had to respond. (See the complete lecture link on page 8.69 of this manual.)

bonus case 8-1
DARK DAYS AT USPS

With the fall of snail mail, USPS has had to roll with the punches and compete with shipping companies for packages. (See the complete lecture link on page 8.81 of this manual.)

    a. *The text uses the example of starting a lawn-mowing business.*

    b. A first step is **ORGANIZING** (or **STRUCTURING**), deciding what work needs to be done and then dividing up tasks (called **DIVISION OF LABOR).**

    c. Dividing tasks into smaller jobs is called **JOB SPECIALIZATION.**

2. As the business grows, the entrepreneur will hire more workers and will need to organize them into teams or departments.

    a. The process of setting up departments to do specialized tasks is called **DEPARTMEN-TALIZATION**.

    b. Finally, you need to **ASSIGN AUTHORITY AND RESPONSIBILITY** to people so you can control the process.

3. **STRUCTURING AN ORGANIZATION** consists of:

    a. Devising a division of labor

    b. Setting up teams or departments to do specific tasks

    c. Assigning responsibility and authority to people

4. An **ORGANIZATION CHART** shows relation-ships—who is accountable for tasks and who reports to whom.

5. The entrepreneur must monitor the environment to see what competitors are doing and what customers are demanding.

bonus case 8-2
STRUCTURAL COLLAPSE: RESPONSIBILITY AND ACCOUNTABILITY

Because of engineering errors and poor planning, the sky-walks of a newly constructed hotel collapsed, killing over 100 people. (See the complete case, discussion questions, and suggested answers beginning on page 8.83 of this manual.)

PPT 8-6
Structuring an Organization

(See complete PowerPoint slide notes on page 8.47.)

critical thinking exercise 8-1
BUILDING AN ORGANIZATION CHART

This exercise gives a list of employees and asks students to create an organization chart showing a possible chain of command. (See the complete exercise on page 8.76 of this manual.)

MAKING
ethical decisions
(Text page 205)

PPT 8-7
Safety vs. Profit

See complete PowerPoint slide notes on page 8.48.)

Compare the organizational theories of Fayol and Weber.

II. THE CHANGING ORGANIZATION

A. Never before has business changed so quickly, including major changes in the business environment.

1. Managing change has become a critical managerial function.

2. In the past, organizations were designed to make management easier rather than to please the customer.

3. This reliance on rules is called **BUREAUCRACY**.

4. *The text uses the example of the government's response to Hurricane Katrina.*

5. Response to the Gulf oil spill in 2010 was not much better.

B. **THE DEVELOPMENT OF ORGANIZATION DESIGN**

1. Until the 20th century, organizations were small and organized simply.

   a. After the introduction of **MASS PRODUCTION,** business organizations grew complex and difficult to manage.

   b. The bigger the plant, the more efficient production became.

   c. ***ECONOMIES OF SCALE*** describes the situation in which companies can reduce their production costs if they can purchase raw materials in bulk; the average cost of goods goes down as production levels increase.

PPT 8-8
The Changing Organization

(See complete PowerPoint slide notes on page 8.48.)

PPT 8-9
How Much Changes in a Decade?

(See complete PowerPoint slide notes on page 8.48.)

PPT 8-10
Production Changed Organization
Design

(See complete PowerPoint slide notes on page 8.49.)

2. The text discusses two major **ORGANIZATION THEORISTS** and their publications.

    a. **HENRI FAYOL** (*Administration Industrielle et Generale* in France in 1919)

    b. **MAX WEBER** (*The Theory of Social and Economic Organizations* in Germany about the same time)

3. **FAYOL'S PRINCIPLES OF ORGANIZATION**

    a. Fayol introduced principles such as:

        i. **UNITY OF COMMAND**: Each worker is to report to only one boss.

        ii. **HIERARCHY OF AUTHORITY**: One should know to whom to report.

        iii. **DIVISION OF LABOR**: Functions should be divided into areas of specialization.

        iv. **SUBORDINATION OF INDIVIDUAL INTERESTS TO THE GENERAL INTERESTS**: Goals of the organization should be considered more important than personal goals.

        v. **AUTHORITY**: Managers should give orders and expect them to be carried out.

        vi. **DEGREE OF CENTRALIZATION:** The amount of decision-making power vested in top management should vary by circumstances.

        vii. **CLEAR COMMUNICATION CHANNELS**

        viii. **ORDER**: Materials and people should be placed in the proper location.

PPT 8-11
Fayol's Principles

(See complete PowerPoint slide notes on page 8.49.)

      ix. **EQUITY**: A manager should treat employees and peers with respect and justice.

      x. **ESPRIT DE CORPS**: A spirit of pride and loyalty should be created.

  b. For years, these principles have been linked to management.

  c. This led to **RIGID ORGANIZATIONS**.

  d. *The text uses the example of consumer dissatisfaction with government-run DMVs.*

4. **MAX WEBER AND ORGANIZATIONAL THEORY**

  a. Max Weber's book *The Theory of Social and Economic Organizations* appeared in the U.S. in the 1940s.

  b. Weber promoted the **PYRAMID-SHAPED ORGANIZATION STRUCTURE.**

      i. Weber put great trust in managers and felt the less decision making employees had to do, the better.

      ii. This approach makes sense when dealing with uneducated and untrained workers.

  c. **WEBER'S PRINCIPLES** were similar to Fayol's with the addition of:

      i. Job descriptions

      ii. Written rules, decision guidelines, and detailed records

PPT 8-12
Organizations Based on Fayol's
Principles

(See complete PowerPoint slide notes on page 8.49.)

PPT 8-13
Weber's Principles

(See complete PowerPoint slide notes on page 8.50.)

       iii. Consistent procedures, regulations, and policies

       iv. Staffing and promotions based on qualifications

    d. Weber believed large organizations need clearly established rules and guidelines, or **BUREAUCRACY**.

    e. Weber's emphasis on bureaucracy eventually led to **RIGID POLICIES AND PROCEDURES**.

    f. Some organizations today, such as UPS, still thrive on rules and guidelines.

    g. In other organizations, bureaucracy has not been effective.

C. **TURNING PRINCIPLES INTO ORGANIZATION DESIGN**

  1. Managers used the concepts of Fayol and Weber to design organizations so that managers could **CONTROL WORKERS**.

    a. A ***HIERARCHY*** is a system in which one person is at the top of the organization and there is a ranked or sequential ordering from the top down of managers who are responsible to that person.

    b. The ***CHAIN OF COMMAND*** is the line of authority that moves from the top of a hierarchy to the lowest level.

    c. Some organizations have a dozen **LAYERS OF MANAGEMENT** between the chief executive officer and the lowest-level employee.

lecture link 8-3

**IMPLEMENTING THE
TRADITIONAL MANAGERIAL
RULES**

Even if organizations don't always follow the traditional rules, they are aware of the rules and try to adjust accordingly. (See the complete lecture link on page 8.69 of this manual.)

PPT 8-14

Hierarchies and Command

(See complete PowerPoint slide notes on page 8.50.)

PPT 8-15

Typical Organization Chart

TEXT FIGURE 8.1

Typical Organization Chart

(Text page 209)

(See complete PowerPoint slide notes on page 8.50.)

2. **_BUREAUCRACY_** is an organization with many layers of managers who set rules and regulations and oversee all decisions.

3. In a bureaucracy, decision making may take too long to satisfy customers.

4. To make customers happy, firms are reorganizing to give employees more power to make decisions on their own, known as **EMPOWERMENT**.

<u>learning goal 3</u>

Evaluate the choices managers make in structuring organizations

III. DECISIONS TO MAKE IN STRUCTURING ORGANIZATIONS

A. CHOOSING CENTRALIZED OR DECENTRALIZED AUTHORITY

1. **_CENTRALIZED AUTHORITY_** is an organizing structure in which decision-making authority is maintained at the top level of management at the company's headquarters *(text examples: McDonald's and Target)*.

2. However, today's rapidly changing markets tend to favor decentralization and delegation of authority.

3. **_DECENTRALIZED AUTHORITY_** is an organization structure in which decision-making authority is delegated to lower-level managers more familiar with local conditions than headquarters management could be *(text example: JCPenney)*.

B. CHOOSING THE APPROPRIATE SPAN OF CONTROL

1. **_SPAN OF CONTROL_** refers to the optimum number of subordinates a manager supervises or should supervise.

PPT 8-16
Bureaucratic Organizations

(See complete PowerPoint slide notes on page 8.51.)

progress
assessment
(Text page 209)

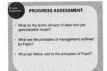

PPT 8-17
Progress Assessment   (See complete PowerPoint slide notes on page 8.51.)

PPT 8-18
Centralization or Decentralization?

(See complete PowerPoint slide notes on page 8.52.)

TEXT FIGURE 8.2
Advantages and Disadvantages of
Centralized versus Decentralized
Management
(Text page 211)

This text figure lists some advantages and disadvantages of centralized versus decentralized authority.

a. At lower levels, a **WIDE SPAN OF CONTROL** is possible.

b. The appropriate span narrows at higher levels of the organization.

2. The span of control **VARIES WIDELY.**

a. The trend now is to expand the span of control as organizations get rid of middle managers.

b. The span of control can be increased through empowerment and the use of technology.

C. **CHOOSING BETWEEN TALL AND FLAT ORGANIZATION STRUCTURES**

1. A _**TALL ORGANIZATION STRUCTURE**_ is one in which the pyramidal organization chart would be quite tall because of the various levels of management.

a. Tall organizations have **MANY LAYERS OF MANAGEMENT.**

b. Communication is distorted as it flows through these layers.

c. The cost of all these managers and support people is high.

2. Because of these problems, organizations have moved toward flatter organizations.

3. A _**FLAT ORGANIZATION STRUCTURE**_ is an organization structure that has few layers of management and a broad span of control.

a. These structures are much **MORE RESPONSIVE TO CUSTOMER DEMANDS** because decision-making power may be given to lower-level employees.

PPT 8-19
Span of Control

(See complete PowerPoint slide notes on page 8.52.)

lecture link 8-4
CHOOSING THE RIGHT SPAN OF CONTROL

Several factors affect the number of people a manager can effectively supervise. (See the complete lecture link on page 8.70 of this manual.)

PPT 8-20
Organizational Structures

(See complete PowerPoint slide notes on page 8.53.)

PPT 8-21
Flat Organizational Structure

TEXT FIGURE 8.3
A Flat Organization Structure
(Text page 211)

(See complete PowerPoint slide notes on page 8.53.)

b. The **FLATTER** organizations became, the larger the **SPAN OF CONTROL** became.

D. **WEIGHING THE ADVANTAGES AND DISADVANTAGES OF DEPARTMENTALIZATION**

1. ___DEPARTMENTALIZATION___ is dividing organizational functions into separate units.

    a. The traditional way to departmentalize is by function.

    b. **FUNCTIONAL STRUCTURE** is the grouping of workers into departments based on similar skills, expertise, or resource use.

2. **ADVANTAGES** of functional departmentalization:

    a. Workers can specialize and work together more effectively.

    b. It may save costs (efficiency).

    c. Skills can be developed in depth.

    d. Resources can be centralized to allow for economies of scale.

    e. There is good coordination within the function.

3. **DISADVANTAGES** of departmentalization:

    a. Departments may not communicate well.

    b. Employees identify with the department rather than the total organization.

    c. Response to external change is slow.

    d. Employees may not be trained in different management responsibilities and become narrow specialists.

TEXT FIGURE 8.4
Advantages and Disadvantages of a Narrow versus a Broad Span of Control
(Text page 212)

This text figure gives some advantages of a narrow versus a wide span of control.

PPT 8-22
Departmentalization

(See complete PowerPoint slide notes on page 8.53.)

PPT 8-23
Advantages of Departmentalization

(See complete PowerPoint slide notes on page 8.54.)

PPT 8-24
Disadvantages of Departmentalization

(See complete PowerPoint slide notes on page 8.54.)

PPT 8-25
Ways to Departmentalize

TEXT FIGURE 8.5
Ways to Departmentalize
(Text page 214)

(See complete PowerPoint slide notes on page 8.54.)

    e. People in the same department tend to think alike (engage in **GROUPTHINK**) and need outside input to become creative.

  4. **LOOKING AT ALTERNATIVE WAYS TO DEPARTMENTALIZE**

    a. By **PRODUCT** *(A book publisher might have departments for trade books, textbooks, and technical books.)*

    b. By **CUSTOMER GROUP** *(A pharmaceutical company might have separate departments that focus on the consumer market, on hospitals, and on doctors.)*

    c. By **GEOGRAPHIC LOCATIONS** *(There may be operations in Asia, Europe, and South America.)*

    d. By **PROCESS** *(A firm that makes leather coats may have one department to cut the leather, another to dye it, and a third to sew the coat.)*

    e. Some firms use a **COMBINATION** of departmental techniques, called **HYBRID FORMS.**

learning goal 4

Contrast the various organizational models.

IV. ORGANIZATIONAL MODELS

  A. There are several ways to structure an organization to accomplish goals.

    1. Traditional organizational models are giving way to new structures, although there may be problems.

PPT 8-26
Ways to Departmentalize

(See complete PowerPoint slide notes on page 8.55.)

lecture link 8-5

OTIS ELEVATORS COME TO THE RESCUE IN JAPAN

By departmentalization by geographic locations, Otis Elevator had teams ready to respond and repair in the wake of the 2011 earthquake and tsunami. (See the complete lecture link on page 8.71 of this manual.)

critical thinking exercise 8-2

HOW DO ORGANIZATIONS GROUP ACTIVITIES?

This exercise asks students to search the websites of several organizations to identify the primary method of departmentalization. (See the complete exercise on page 8.4 of this manual.)

progress assessment
(Text page 215)

PPT 8-27
Progress Assessment

(See complete PowerPoint slide notes on page 8.55.)

PPT 8-28
Four Ways to Structure an Organization

(See complete PowerPoint slide notes on page 8.56.)

2. Some newer models violate traditional management principles.

B. **LINE ORGANIZATIONS**

1. A ***LINE ORGANIZATION*** is an organization that has direct two-way lines of responsibility, authority, and communication running from the top to the bottom of the organization, with all people reporting to only one supervisor *(i.e., the military and small businesses)*.

    a. The line organization has no specialists for management support.

    b. Line managers can issue orders and enforce discipline.

2. **DISADVANTAGES IN LARGE ORGANIZATIONS**:

    a. Too inflexible

    b. Few specialists to advise line employees

    c. Lines of communication too long

    d. Unable to handle complex decisions

3. Such organizations usually become line-and-staff organizations.

C. **LINE-AND-STAFF ORGANIZATIONS**

1. Line-and-staff organizations have both line and staff personnel.

2. ***LINE PERSONNEL*** are employees who are part of the chain of command that is responsible for achieving organizational goals.

PPT 8-29
Line Organizations

(See complete PowerPoint slide notes on page 8.56.)

lecture link 8-6
THE MANHATTAN PROJECT

To build the world's first atomic bomb, the military turned to General Leslie Groves, known for his administrative ability, organizational skill, and decisiveness. (See the complete lecture link on page 8.71 of this manual.)

PPT 8-30
Line Personnel

(See complete PowerPoint slide notes on page 8.56.)

lecture link 8-7
GREATER EFFICIENCY, FEWER JOBS

Line jobs are not always safe. As Campbell's employees saw, with greater efficiency there was less need for large staffs. (See the complete lecture link on page 8.72 of this manual.)

3. ***STAFF PERSONNEL*** are employees who advise and assist line personnel in meeting their goals.

4. Line personnel have **FORMAL AUTHORITY** to make policy decisions; staff have the **AUTHORITY TO ONLY ADVISE** line personnel.

5. **ADVANTAGES OF LINE-AND-STAFF ORGANIZATION:**

   a. Have access to expert advice

   b. Staff positions strengthen the line personnel

D. **MATRIX-STYLE ORGANIZATIONS**

1. Both line and line-and-staff organizations can become **INFLEXIBLE.**

   a. Both structures work well in organizations with relatively unchanging environments and slow product development.

   b. However, high-growth industries now dominate the economy.

   c. In such industries, emphasis is on new product development, creativity, rapid communication, and interdepartmental teamwork.

2. A ***MATRIX ORGANIZATION*** is an organization in which specialists from different parts of the organization are brought together to work on specific projects, but still remain part of a line-and-staff structure.

   a. Matrix organization structures were developed in the aerospace industry.

PPT 8-31
Staff Personnel

(See complete PowerPoint slide notes on page 8.57.)

PPT 8-32
Sample Line-and-Staff
Organization

TEXT FIGURE 8.6
A Sample Line-and-Staff
Organization
(Text page 216)

(See complete PowerPoint slide notes on page 8.57.)

PPT 8-33
Matrix Organizations

(See complete PowerPoint slide notes on page 8.57.)

PPT 8-34
Sample Matrix Organization

TEXT FIGURE 8.7
A Matrix Organization
(Text page 217)

(See complete PowerPoint slide notes on page 8.58.)

   b. The structure is now used in banking, management consulting firms, ad agencies, and school systems.

3. **ADVANTAGES OF MATRIX ORGANIZATIONS**

   a. Flexibility in assigning people to projects

   b. Encourage interorganizational cooperation and teamwork

   c. Can give more creative solutions to problems

   d. More efficient use of organizational resources

4. **DISADVANTAGES OF MATRIX ORGANIZATIONS**

   a. Are costly and complex

   b. Create confusion in employee loyalties

   c. Require good interpersonal skills and cooperative employees and managers

   d. May be only a temporary solution to a long-term problem

5. Although matrix organizations seem to violate some traditional managerial principles, the system functions relatively effectively.

   a. The matrix organization has been adopted in high-tech firms because of its effectiveness.

   b. A potential problem is that the project teams **ARE NOT PERMANENT** and there is little chance for cross-functional learning.

E. **CROSS-FUNCTIONAL SELF-MANAGED TEAMS**

1. One solution to the disadvantage of temporary teams is to establish long-lived teams.

2. *BusinessWeek* magazine survey found that workers prefer working in teams

PPT 8-35
Advantages of Matrix Style

(See complete PowerPoint slide notes on page 8.58.)

PPT 8-36
Disadvantages of the Matrix Style

(See complete PowerPoint slide notes on page 8.58.)

PPT 8-37
Cross-Functional Self-Managed
Teams

(See complete PowerPoint slide notes on page 8.59.)

3. **_CROSS-FUNCTIONAL SELF-MANAGED
TEAMS_** are groups of employees from different
departments who work together on a long-term
basis (as opposed to the temporary teams established in matrix-style organizations).

   a. Usually the teams are **EMPOWERED** to
   make decisions on their own without seeking
   the approval of management.

   b. Self-managed teams reduce the barriers
   between design, engineering, marketing, and
   other functions.

   c. Cross-functional teams work best when leadership is shared.

F. **GOING BEYOND ORGANIZATIONAL BOUNDARIES**

   1. Cross-functional teams work best when customers' input is included.

   2. Some go beyond organizational boundaries to
   include customers, suppliers, and distributors.

   3. Some cross-functional teams share information
   across national boundaries and may be encouraged by the government.

learning goal 5

Identify the benefits of interfirm cooperation and coordination.

V. **MANAGING THE INTERACTIONS AMONG
FIRMS**

   A. **_NETWORKING_** is using communications technology
   and other means to link organizations and allow
   them to work together on common objectives.

<u>bonus case 8-3</u>
**CREATING CROSS-
FUNCTIONAL TEAMS**

The Direct Response Group instigated organizational change to make its people more responsive to the customer. (See the complete case, discussion questions, and suggested answers beginning on page 88.85 of this manual.)

PPT 8-38
Going Beyond Organizational
Boundaries

(See complete PowerPoint slide notes on page 8.59.)

PPT 8-39
Building Successful Teams

(See complete PowerPoint slide notes on page 8.59.)

**progress
assessment**
(Text page 219)

PPT 8-40
Progress Assessment

(See complete PowerPoint slide notes on page 8.60.)

B. **TRANSPARENCY AND VIRTUAL ORGANIZATIONS**

1. The Internet links organizations so closely that each can see what the others are doing in real time.

    a. ***REAL TIME*** is the present moment or the actual time in which something takes place.

    b. **TRANSPARENCY** is a concept that describes a company being so open to other companies working with it that the once-solid barriers between them become see-through, and electronic information is shared as if the companies were one.

    c. Using this integration, two companies can work together as closely as two departments once did.

2. Most organizations are no longer self-sufficient, but are part of a vast network of global businesses.

3. A modern organization chart should show people in different organizations and how they are networked together.

4. Organization structures tend to be flexible and changing.

5. A ***VIRTUAL CORPORATION*** is a temporary networked organization made up of replaceable firms that join and leave as needed.

    a. This concept is very different from traditional organizations.

PPT 8-41
Real-Time Business

(See complete PowerPoint slide notes on page 8.60.)

PPT 8-42
Transparency and Virtual
Corporations

(See complete PowerPoint slide notes on page 8.60.)

PPT 8-43
A Virtual Corporation

TEXT FIGURE 8.8
A Virtual Corporation
(Text page 220)

(See complete PowerPoint slide notes on page 8.61.)

b. Traditional managers often have trouble adapting to rapidly changing structures.

C. **BENCHMARKING AND CORE COMPETENCIES**

1. In the past, each organization had a separate department for each function.

   a. Organizations are now benchmarking each function against the best in the world.

   b. ***BENCHMARKING*** is comparing an organization's practices, processes, and products against the world's best (*example: K2 benchmarked Piezo's technology*).

   c. Companies can also study the best practices of unrelated industries (*example: Wyeth Pharmaceuticals benchmarked the aerospace industry's project management*).

   d. Benchmarking can be used in a direct competitive way, *as when Target compared itself with Wal-Mart.*

2. If the organization can't do as well as the best, it can **OUTSOURCE** the function to an organization that is the best.

   a. **OUTSOURCING** is assigning functions—such as accounting, production, security, and legal work—to outside organizations.

   b. Overseas outsourcing is controversial.

   c. Some functions, such as information management and marketing, may be too important to outsource.

SPOTLIGHT ON

**small
business**

(Text page 221)

PPT 8-44

When Your
Workers Work for
Someone Else

(See complete PowerPoint slide notes on page 8.61.)

PPT 8-45

Benchmarking and Core
Competencies

(See complete PowerPoint slide notes on page 8.62.)

PPT 8-46

Benefits and Concerns of
Healthcare Outsourcing

(See complete PowerPoint slide notes on page 8.62.)

lecture link 8-8

A NEW KIND OF OUTSOURCING

Some communities are finding relief from the very companies that outsourced their old jobs. (See the complete lecture link on page 8.73 of this manual.)

3. **_CORE COMPETENCIES_** are those functions that the organization can do as well or better than any other organization in the world.

   a. *Nike's core competencies are designing and marketing athletic shoes, but it outsources manufacturing.*

   b. *Dell has reversed its outsourcing practices to include call centers in North America.*

VI. ADAPTING TO CHANGE

A. The organization structure must be **ADAPTED TO CHANGES** in the market.

   1. Introducing change into an organization is one of the toughest challenges for managers.

   2. It is difficult for some companies to reinvent themselves in response to changes in the competitive environment.

   3. Painful changes may be necessary—such as U.S. automakers closing plants and reducing staff.

   4. Companies must coordinate the efforts of traditional departments and their Internet staff.

   5. To reach **_DIGITAL NATIVES_** (individuals who grew up with the Internet), companies must retrain older workers in the new technologies *(examples: YouTube, Facebook, Twitter, RSS).*

   6. Target uses a "creative cabinet" to help react effectively to changes in consumer preferences.

B. **RESTRUCTURING FOR EMPOWERMENT**

   1. To implement empowerment, firms often must reorganize dramatically.

PPT 8-47
Which Jobs Will Be Outsourced Next?

(See complete PowerPoint slide notes on page 8.63.)

PPT 8-48
Adapting to Market Changes

(See complete PowerPoint slide notes on page 8.63.)

PPT 8-49
Keep in Touch

(See complete PowerPoint slide notes on page 8.64.)

lecture link 8-9
SETTING UP SHOP ON FACEBOOK

Companies are catering to digital natives by opening up shop on Facebook. (See the complete lecture link on page 8.73 of this manual.)

social
media in business
(Text page 223)

PPT 8-50
When Twitter and Facebook Are Old School

(See complete PowerPoint slide notes on page 8.64.)

2. **_RESTRUCTURING_** is redesigning an organization so that it can more effectively and efficiently serve its customers.

3. A few organizations have turned the traditional organizational structure upside down.

   a. An **_INVERTED ORGANIZATION_** is an organization that has contact people at the top and the chief executive officer at the bottom of the organization chart.

   b. There are few layers of management, and their job is to assist and support frontline people.

   c. Companies using the inverted structure support frontline personnel with internal and external databanks, advances communication systems, and professional assistance.

   d. Frontline people now have to be better educated, better trained, and better paid than in the past.

   e. In more progressive organizations, everyone **SHARES INFORMATION,** giving everyone power.

learning goal 6
Explain how organizational culture can help businesses adapt to change.

VII. CREATING A CHANGE-ORIENTED ORGANIZATIONAL CULTURE

A. Organizational change always causes some **RESISTANCE**.

   1. Firms that adjust best have a change-oriented organizational culture.

PPT 8-51
Restructuring

(See complete PowerPoint slide notes on page 8.64.)

PPT 8-52
Traditional and Inverted
Organizations

TEXT FIGURE 8.9
Comparison of an Inverted
Organizational Structure and a
Traditional Organizational Structure
(Text page 224)

(See complete PowerPoint slide notes on page 8.65.)

2. **_ORGANIZATIONAL (OR CORPORATE) CULTURE_** is the widely shared values within an organization that provide unity and cooperation to achieve common goals.

   a. An organization's culture is reflected in stories, traditions, and myths.

   b. *For example, McDonald's culture emphasizes quality, service, cleanliness, and value.*

   c. An organization's culture can be negative, as with an organization in which no one cares about quality.

3. The very best organizations have cultures that emphasize **SERVICE TO CUSTOMERS.**

   a. The atmosphere is one of friendly, caring people who enjoy working together.

   b. Those companies have **LESS NEED FOR CLOSE SUPERVISION** of employees.

   c. The key to productive culture is **MUTUAL TRUST.**

4. The formal organization structure is just one element of the total organizational system.

B. **MANAGING THE INFORMAL ORGANIZATION**

   1. All organizations have two systems.

      a. The **_FORMAL ORGANIZATION_** is the structure that details lines of responsibility, authority, and position; that is, the structure that appears on the organization chart.

      b. The **_INFORMAL ORGANIZATION_** is the system that develops spontaneously as employees meet and form cliques,

PPT 8-53
Organizational Culture

(See complete PowerPoint slide notes on page 8.65.)

lecture link 8-10
EMPLOYER ICEBREAKING RITUALS

Each organizational culture is different. Foot Levelers has its own practices. (See the complete lecture link on page 8.49 of this manual.)

PPT 8-54
Formal Organization

(See complete PowerPoint slide notes on page 8.65.)

PPT 8-55
Informal Organization

(See complete PowerPoint slide notes on page 8.66.)

relationships, and lines of authority outside the formal organization; that is, the human side of the organization that does not appear on any organization chart.

2. No organization can operate effectively without **BOTH TYPES** of organization.

   a. The **FORMAL ORGANIZATION** can be slow and bureaucratic, while the **INFORMAL ORGANIZATION** can generate creative solutions.

   b. The informal organization is **TOO UN-STRUCTURED AND EMOTIONAL** for decision making, while the formal organization provides guidelines and lines of authority.

3. It is wise to learn quickly who the important people are in the informal organization.

4. The nerve center of the informal organization is the **GRAPEVINE**.

5. Successful managers learn to **WORK WITH THE INFORMAL ORGANIZATION** and use it to the organization's advantage.

6. The informal organization can also be very powerful in resisting management directives.

VIII. SUMMARY

PPT 8-56
Limitations of Informal
Organizations

(See complete PowerPoint slide notes on page 8.66.)

PPT 8-57
Group Norms

(See complete PowerPoint slide notes on page 8.66.)

lecture link 8-11
**MAPPING THE INFORMAL
ORGANIZATION**

The best way to manage informal organizations is to acknowledge their existence and then bring them out into the open. (See the complete lecture link on page 8.74 of this manual.)

bonus case 8-4
OFFICE ALUMNI

Many businesses have set up social networking sites for their "alumni" as the recession takes its toll on American jobs. (See the complete lecture link on page 8.87 of this manual.)

**progress
assessment**
(Text page 226)

PPT 8-58
Progress Assessment

(See complete PowerPoint slide notes on page 8.64.)

PowerPoint slide notes

PPT 8-1
Chapter Title

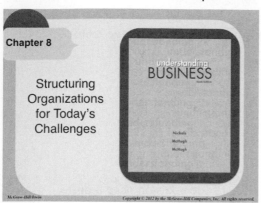

Chapter 8

Structuring
Organizations
for Today's
Challenges

understanding
BUSINESS

Nickels
McHugh
McHugh

PPT 8-2
Learning Goals

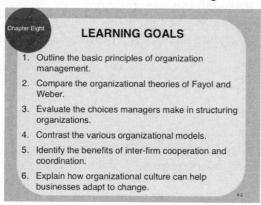

Chapter Eight

LEARNING GOALS

1. Outline the basic principles of organization management.
2. Compare the organizational theories of Fayol and Weber.
3. Evaluate the choices managers make in structuring organizations.
4. Contrast the various organizational models.
5. Identify the benefits of inter-firm cooperation and coordination.
6. Explain how organizational culture can help businesses adapt to change.

PPT 8-3
Ursula Burns

Profile

URSULA BURNS
Xerox

- Started as a summer intern and moved up through Xerox.
- The only female African-American CEO among Fortune's Top 150 Companies.
- Serves on many boards and has been placed on councils by President Obama and Vice-President Biden.

PPT 8-4
Name That Company

Company: K2 Skis

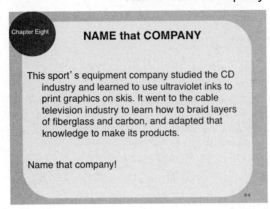

NAME that COMPANY

Chapter Eight

This sport's equipment company studied the CD industry and learned to use ultraviolet inks to print graphics on skis. It went to the cable television industry to learn how to braid layers of fiberglass and carbon, and adapted that knowledge to make its products.

Name that company!

PPT 8-5
Reorganization Is for Everyone

Changing economic times require businesses to alter their approach via reorganization. Using organizational principles is an important aspect to this reorganization.

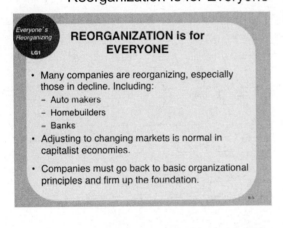

REORGANIZATION is for EVERYONE

Everyone's Reorganizing

LG1

- Many companies are reorganizing, especially those in decline. Including:
  - Auto makers
  - Homebuilders
  - Banks
- Adjusting to changing markets is normal in capitalist economies.

- Companies must go back to basic organizational principles and firm up the foundation.

PPT 8-6
Structuring an Organization

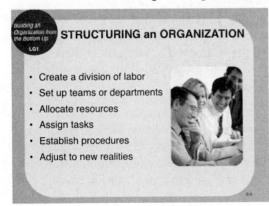

STRUCTURING an ORGANIZATION

Building an Organization from the Bottom Up

LG1

- Create a division of labor
- Set up teams or departments
- Allocate resources
- Assign tasks
- Establish procedures
- Adjust to new realities

PPT 8-7

Safety vs. Profit

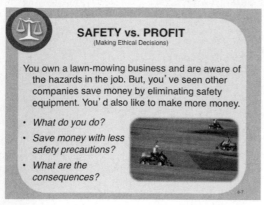

PPT 8-8

The Changing Organization

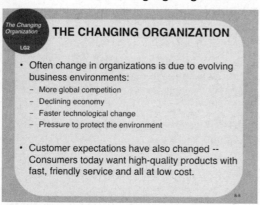

PPT 8-9

How Much Changes in a Decade?

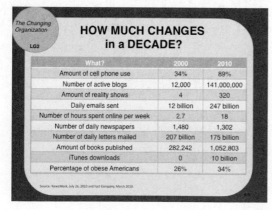

1. This slide shows just how much our country has changed since 2000.

2. Clearly the digital revolution is shown here with the amount of blogs, cell usage, e-mails sent, and so on. Ask the students, Do you expect these numbers to continue to grow? What may this table look like in 2020?

3. The number of daily newspapers and letters sent have dropped. Ask the students, Do you think we will lose more daily newspapers? What about letters? How many still receive letters/cards from grandparents opposed to e-mails or Facebook posts?

PPT 8-10

Production Changed Organization
Design

PRODUCTION CHANGED ORGANZIATION DESIGN

- Mass production of goods led to complexities in organizing businesses.

- **Economies of Scale --** *Companies can reduce their production costs by purchasing raw materials in bulk.*

- The average cost of goods decreases as production levels rise.

PPT 8-11

Fayol's Principles

This slide presents Fayol's principles of organization. Fayol published General and Industrial Management in 1919. Unity of command and hierarchy of authority suggest that each employee reports to one and only one boss. Management courses throughout the world teach these principles, and organizations are designed accordingly. When these principles become rules, policies, and regulations, they create inflexibility which hampers organizations' ability to respond quickly to situations. An example of this inflexibility or a slower response time can be seen in FEMA's response to Hurricane Katrina.

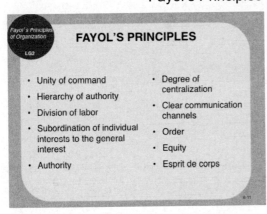

FAYOL'S PRINCIPLES

- Unity of command
- Hierarchy of authority
- Division of labor
- Subordination of individual interests to the general interest
- Authority

- Degree of centralization
- Clear communication channels
- Order
- Equity
- Esprit de corps

PPT 8-12

Organizations Based on Fayol's
Principles

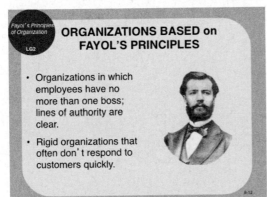

ORGANIZATIONS BASED on FAYOL'S PRINCIPLES

- Organizations in which employees have no more than one boss; lines of authority are clear.

- Rigid organizations that often don't respond to customers quickly.

PPT 8-13
Weber's Principles

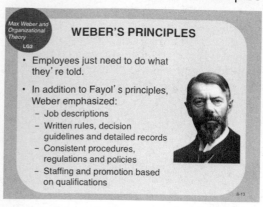

Weber, a German sociologist and economist, wrote The Theory of Social and Economic Organizations. Weber's principles were similar to Fayol's. He emphasized job descriptions, written rules, consistent policies, regulations, and procedures, and staffing and promotions based on qualifications. Weber was in favor of bureaucracy and believed that these principles were necessary for large organizations' effective functioning. However, in today's corporate world, these rules and bureaucracy do not necessarily work. Organizations need to respond to customers and other environmental factors quickly which calls for a creative, flexible, and a quick decision-making process contrary to a bureaucratic process.

PPT 8-14
Hierarchies and Command

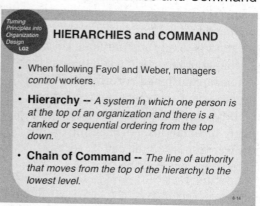

PPT 8-15
Typical Organization Chart

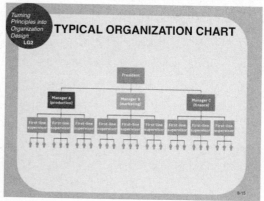

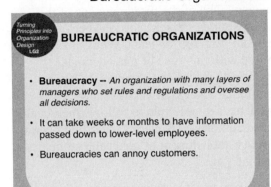

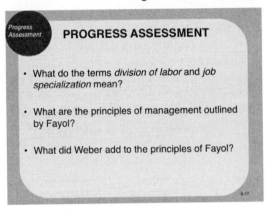

1. *Division of labor* is dividing tasks among workers to complete a job. *Job specialization* is dividing tasks into smaller jobs.

2. Fayol's principles of management are:

   - Unity of command

   - Hierarchy of authority

   - Division of labor

   - Subordination of individual interests to the general interest

   - Authority

   - Degree of centralization

   - Clear communication channels

   - Order

   - Equity

   - Esprit de corps

   - Weber added:

   - Job descriptions

   - Written rules, decision guidelines, and detailed records

   - Consistent procedures, regulations, and policies

   - Staffing and promotion based on qualifications

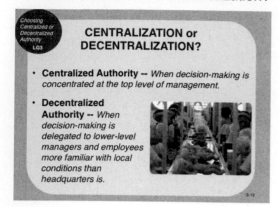

Centralization can be defined as an organizational structure that focuses on retaining control of authority with higher-level managers. One of the disadvantages of this type of management style is slower decisions because of layers of management. Ask the students, What specific problems do you see with this type of management? (Slower decision making means the company is less responsive to both internal and external customer needs.) Share with the students a simple rule to follow when dealing with centralized authority: Decisions regarding overall company policy and establishment of goals and strategies should be made at the top.

Decentralization is an organizational structure that focuses on delegating authority throughout the organization to middle and lower-level managers. The most significant advantage of this form of management style is the empowerment of the employees. Statistics indicate when delegation is practiced in a company, absenteeism, injuries, loyalty, and production improve. Share with the students a simple rule to follow when dealing with decentralized authority: The closer an employee interacts with the customer, the more decentralized the decision making should be. For example, a customer service manager must have the authority to make a decision that will satisfy a customer immediately, not wait until the home office makes a decision.

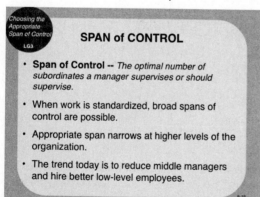

PPT 8-20
Organizational Structures

Many organizations have moved from tall organizations to flat organizations in an effort to increase nimbleness in the marketplace.

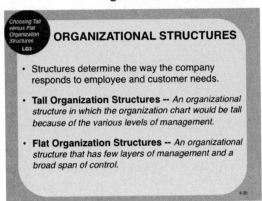

PPT 8-21
Flat Organizational Structure

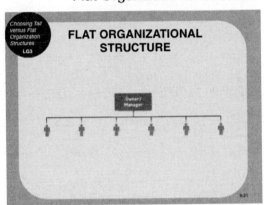

PPT 8-22
Departmentalization

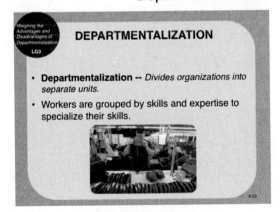

PPT 8-23
Advantages of Departmentalization

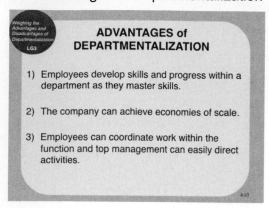

ADVANTAGES of DEPARTMENTALIZATION

1) Employees develop skills and progress within a department as they master skills.

2) The company can achieve economies of scale.

3) Employees can coordinate work within the function and top management can easily direct activities.

PPT 8-24
Disadvantages of Departmentalization

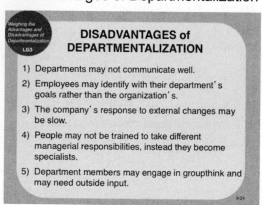

DISADVANTAGES of DEPARTMENTALIZATION

1) Departments may not communicate well.

2) Employees may identify with their department's goals rather than the organization's.

3) The company's response to external changes may be slow.

4) People may not be trained to take different managerial responsibilities, instead they become specialists.

5) Department members may engage in groupthink and may need outside input.

PPT 8-25
Ways to Departmentalize

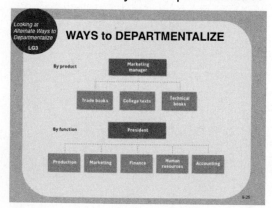

WAYS to DEPARTMENTALIZE

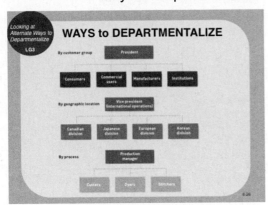

PPT 8-27
Progress Assessment

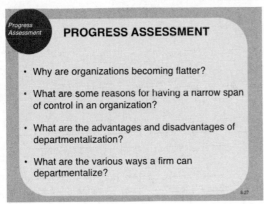

1. Businesses have adopted flatter organizations with fewer layers of management and a broader span of control to quickly respond to customer demands. A flatter organization gives lower-level employees the authority to make decisions directly affecting customers.

2. Span of control refers to the number of subordinates a manager supervises. Generally, the span of control narrows at higher levels because work becomes less standardized and managers need more face-to-face communication.

3. The advantages of departmentalization are that the organization can reduce costs, since employees should be more efficient; employees can develop skills in depth and progress within a department as they master more skills; the company can achieve economies of scale by centralizing all the resources it needs and locating various experts in that particular area; employees can coordinate work within the function; and top management can easily direct and control various departments' activities. The disadvantages of departmentalization are that communication is inhibited; employees may identify with their department's goals rather than the organization's; the company's response may be slowed by departmentalization; employees tend to be narrow specialists; and department members may engage in groupthink and may need input from the outside to become more competitive.

4. An organization can elect to departmentalize in the following ways: customer group, product, functional, geographic, process, and hybrid.

PPT 8-28
Four Ways to Structure an Organization

Traditional business models, such as line organizations and line-and-staff organizations, are giving way to new structures.

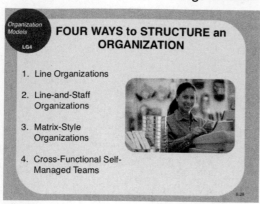

Organization Models
LG4

FOUR WAYS to STRUCTURE an ORGANIZATION

1. Line Organizations

2. Line-and-Staff Organizations

3. Matrix-Style Organizations

4. Cross-Functional Self-Managed Teams

8-28

PPT 8-29
Line Organizations

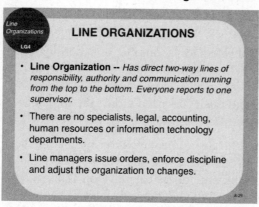

Line Organizations
LG4

LINE ORGANIZATIONS

• **Line Organization** -- *Has direct two-way lines of responsibility, authority and communication running from the top to the bottom. Everyone reports to one supervisor.*

• There are no specialists, legal, accounting, human resources or information technology departments.

• Line managers issue orders, enforce discipline and adjust the organization to changes.

8-29

PPT 8-30
Line Personnel

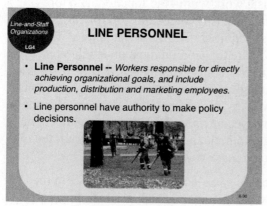

Line-and-Staff Organizations
LG4

LINE PERSONNEL

• **Line Personnel** -- *Workers responsible for directly achieving organizational goals, and include production, distribution and marketing employees.*

• Line personnel have authority to make policy decisions.

8-30

PPT 8-31
Staff Personnel

PPT 8-32
Sample Line-and-Staff Organization

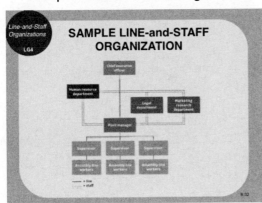

PPT 8-33
Matrix Organizations

The creation of matrix organizations was in response to the inflexibility of other more traditional organizational structures. This structure brings specialists from different parts of the organization to work together temporarily on specific projects.

PPT 8-34

Sample Matrix Organization

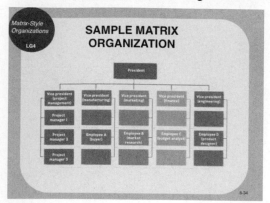

PPT 8-35

Advantages of the Matrix Style

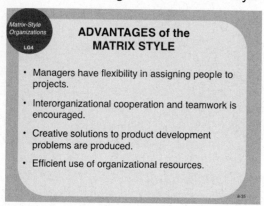

PPT 8-36

Disadvantages of the Matrix Style

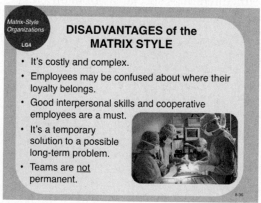

PPT 8-37
Cross-Functional Self-Managed Teams

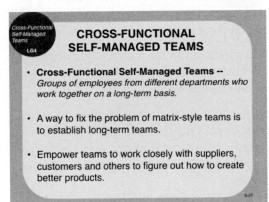

PPT 8-38
Going Beyond Organizational Boundaries

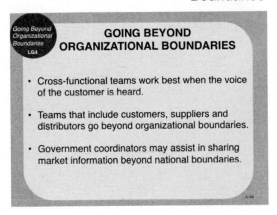

PPT 8-39
Building Successful Teams

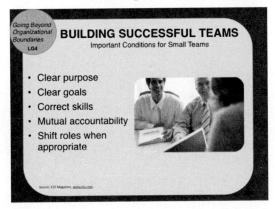

1. This slide presents five important conditions for garnering the maximum benefits of small teams, according to Jon Katzenbach, coauthor of *The Wisdom of Teams*.

2. Ask the students, Which of these five conditions do you believe would be most important in your team experience? Why? *(The most critical factor of these five conditions, according to Katzenbach, is a clear performance purpose for the team.)*

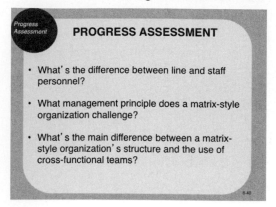

1. Line personnel are responsible for directly achieving organizational goals. Line personnel include production workers, distribution people, and marketing personnel. Staff personnel advise and assist line personnel in meeting their goals.

2. The flexibility inherent in the matrix-style organization directly challenge the rigid line and line-and-staff organization structures.

3. The main difference between matrix-style organization and cross-functional teams is that cross-functional teams tend to be long-lived as compared to the temporary and fluid nature of teams in a matrix-style organization.

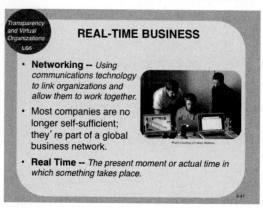

PPT 8-43
A Virtual Corporation

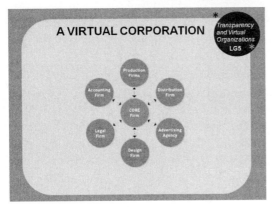

1. This slide illustrates the concept of a virtual corporation as an organizational model that could propel American businesses into the next century.

2. The theory behind the virtual corporation can be understood by picturing a company stripped to its core competencies. All other business functions will be accomplished by:

   - Forming joint ventures

   - Forming temporary alliances with other virtual companies with different areas of expertise

   - Hiring consulting services

   - Outsourcing or subcontracting services

3. Share with the students some other interesting concepts of a virtual corporation:

   - On-demand knowledge workers who operate independently

   - Skill-selling professionals such as engineers, accountants, and human resource experts who manage your projects from their homes through worldwide telecommunications

   Team-building will change as companies hire individuals with expertise in various areas to solve business problems. As a solution is identified, the team will cease to exist.

PPT 8-44
When Your Workers Work for Someone Else

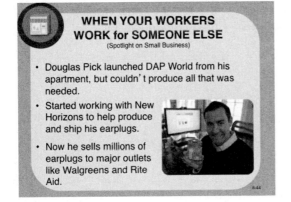

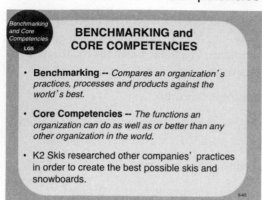

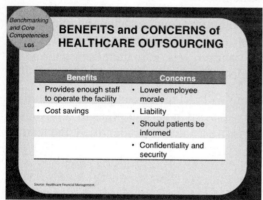

1. This slide identifies the benefits and concerns of healthcare outsourcing.

2. Have the students identify the possible countries to which health care can be outsourced. *(India is used by many hospitals and health care organizations due to availability of knowledge workers.)*

3. Ask the students, Why do you think these countries represent a threat to U.S. jobs? *(Lower wages will result in lower costs.)*

4. Ask the students, What could be outsourced to South Africa? Why? *(South Africa is considered a good choice for customer service centers for French-, English-, and German-speaking customers. The workforce is trained to speak several different languages while wages are low. As a global company dealing with consumer inquiries, the central location of a call center may reduce costs significantly.)*

PPT 8-47

Which Jobs Will Be Outsourced Next?

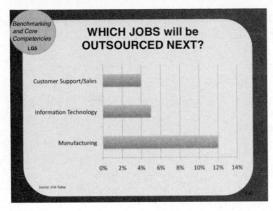

1. This slide supports the previous discussion of out-sourcing by identifying the most common functional areas for which U.S. companies plan on hiring outside organizations. The results are from the TEC International's survey of 1,091 CEOs.

2. As mentioned in previous discussions, the number one reason companies outsource is to reduce costs. This slide shows Manufacturing, Information Technology, and Customer Support/Sales as the largest planned outsourced business categories.

3. Ask the students, Why do you think these categories are outsourced more often? *(Manufacturing can be done a lot cheaper in a country with lower wages. IT and customer support represent functional areas that provide basic or routine types of job performance, unlike sales and marketing, where specific strategies are closely aligned to meet specific customer needs.)*

PPT 8-48

Adapting to Market Changes

PPT 8-49

Keep in Touch

1. Information technology has allowed companies like Amazon to better understand customer needs.

2. Use the three questions on this slide to start a discussion with students in class.

PPT 8-50

When Twitter and Facebook Are Old School

PPT 8-51

Restructuring

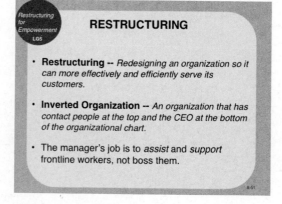

Traditional and Inverted Organizations

1. The inverted organization structure is an alternate to the traditional management layers. The critical idea behind the inverted organization structure is that the managers' job is to support and facilitate the job of the frontline people, not boss them around.

2. Ask the students, What type of organizational structure would they prefer to work under: traditional or inverted? Why?

PPT 8-53
Organizational Culture

When you search for a job, make sure the organizational culture is one you can thrive in.

PPT 8-54
Formal Organization

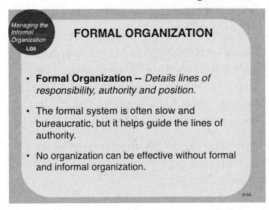

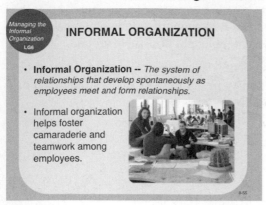

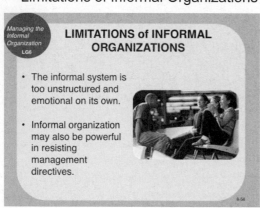

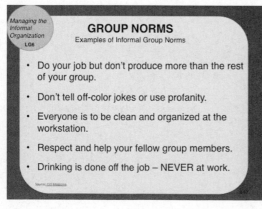

1. Group norms are an interesting topic to discuss in teaching organizational structure. This slide illustrates some informal group norms.

2. Ask the students, Have you ever felt pressure to conform to such informal norms? If you gave in to group pressure not to produce more than the rest of the group, did you feel good about yourself? *(Focus on the self-gratification feeling of a job well done and the corresponding compensation.)*

3. Discuss the importance of informal groups in an organization that become somewhat formal themselves (i.e., labor unions).

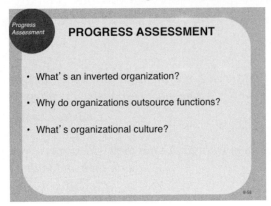

1. Some service-oriented organizations have elected to turn the traditional organizational structure upside down. An inverted organization has employees who come into contact with customers at the top of the organization and the chief executive officer at the bottom. A manager's job is to assist and support frontline people, not tell them what to do.

2. In the past, organizations have often tried to do all functions themselves, maintaining departments for each function including accounting, finance, marketing, and production. If an organization is not able to efficiently perform the function itself it will outsource the function. Outsourcing is the process of assigning various functions, such as accounting, production, security, maintenance, and legal work, to an outside firm. The goal is to retain the functions that the organization considers its core competencies.

3. Organizational or corporate culture is the widely shared values within an organization that create unity and cooperation. Usually the culture of an organization is passed to employees via stories, traditions, and myths.

lecture links

> *"It is not the strongest of the species that survive, nor the most intelligent, but the one most responsive to change."*
>
> *Charles Darwin*

> *"Never tell people how to do things. Tell them what to do and they will surprise you with their ingenuity."*
>
> *General George S. Patton*

> *"When Alexander the Great visited Diogenes and asked whether he could do anything for the famed teacher, Diogenes replied: 'Only stand out of my light.' Perhaps some day we shall know how to heighten creativity. Until then, one of the best things we can do for creative men and women is to stand out of their light."*
>
> *John W. Gardner*

> *"The ability to learn faster than your competitors may be the only sustainable competitive advantage."*
>
> *Arie De Geus, Head of Planning, Royal Dutch Shell*

lecture link 8-1

SMITH'S FOLLY

Kenneth H. Olsen, founder and CEO of Digital Equipment Corporation, was known for his autocratic style. However, at the same time he strongly believed in delegating responsibility, something other computer entrepreneurs have found it difficult to do.

In delegating responsibility, Olsen was always willing to forgive worker mistakes. John F. Smith, Digital's 12th employee and vice president for 20 years, recalls buying a $7,000 soldering machine, a huge investment at the time, that proved unreliable. He says he came in nights and weekends to adjust it so Olsen wouldn't realize his error.

Ultimately, Smith bought a replacement machine, moved the lemon to a vacant storeroom, covered it with a canvas, and thought he had gotten away with it. He served as chief operating officer at Digital Equipment from 1986 through 1994. Much later he came across the machine and idly lifted the covering. He found a hand-lettered sign that read "Smith's folly. [signed] Ken Olsen."

lecture link 8-2

STREAMLINING STARBUCKS

As with thousands of other companies, the recession has been not been kind to Starbucks. Rather than exchange their excess cash for a $4 latte, more and more penny-pinching consumers have begun to place a bigger chunk of their paychecks into their savings accounts. And when people begin to tighten their belts, some of the first things to go are premium goods, such as a cup of expensive coffee. As a result of a 6.6% drop in annual revenue, Starbucks has been forced to close 900 stores as well as renegotiate rents on many others.

Also among Starbucks' list of cost-cutting measures is lean manufacturing, or a streamlining of the company's workforce. To Starbucks' new "vice president of lean thinking" Scott Heydon, such common work occurrences as walking to retrieve a cup of milk or bending over for a scone are unnecessary wastages that end up hurting the store's overall efficiency. By rearranging the locations of necessary items like coffee beans or even an entire pastry case, workers can access those items more readily and thus be able to serve customers faster. Furthermore, as competitors like McDonald's and Dunkin' Donuts find new success in their priced-down premium coffees, Starbucks is hoping to trump its lower prices with quicker service and improved customer relations.

However, the biggest challengers of Starbucks' lean streamlining comes from the baristas themselves, some of whom fear they'll become nothing more than coffee-serving automatons trapped within the machinations of the store's system. But according to Heydon, nothing could be further from the truth. With over 11,000 stores across the country, it would be impossible to convert every single store to the same leaned-down process. Employees are thus encouraged to share ideas for improving store efficiency by drawing from their own work experiences. Regardless of the baristas' qualms, Starbucks has managed to cut $175 million worth of costs last quarter, with a portion of those cuts attributed to "leaning" the company's production method.[i]

lecture link 8-3

IMPLEMENTING THE TRADITIONAL MANAGERIAL RULES

Organizations today don't always follow the traditional rules, but they are aware of the rules and try to adjust accordingly. For example, look at *unity of command*, where each worker is to report to one, and only one, boss. Firms today often have project teams or cross-functional teams where personnel from various functions are brought together under a new boss—the project manager—and thus have two bosses, one back at the department level and the project manager. Firms are aware of potential conflicts, however, and give the project manager full authority to manage the employee, and tell the department manager to release the worker from his or her control until notified otherwise. Similarly, firms have given up much of the idea of *hierarchy*. Workers may well be on the same level as their managers and are not subject to orders as they were in the past. They are often considered as equal parts of the team and no one can give orders to anyone else on the team.

Many companies are doing their best to get rid of the old division of labor among departments. When people work in teams, the old departmental specialization is discouraged. Each employee may be asked to help in design, marketing, and other areas to get a wider perspective. Nonetheless, there is often still a need for *subordination of individual interests to the general interest*. Workers are to think of themselves as a coordinated team. The goals of the team are still more important than the goals of individual workers.

Many managers today are reluctant to give up what they consider to be their right to *give orders* and the power to enforce obedience. Authority and responsibility are related: Whenever authority is exercised, responsibility arises. *Empowerment* means that managers must give workers more authority and responsibility. That means that managers must shift their focus from telling people what to do to guiding, coaching, supporting, motivating, and training employees. Some traditional bosses find it difficult to give up their old roles and have to leave the firm. Furthermore, rather than have *centralized decision making*, more and more firms are delegating authority to lower-level managers.

Some managerial rules have stood the test of time. For example, it is still important to have *clear communication channels*. All workers should be able to reach others in the firm quickly and easily. There should also be *order*. Materials and people should be placed and maintained in the proper location. Finally, there is still a need for equity and espirit de corps. A manager should treat employees and peers with respect and justice, and a spirit of pride and loyalty should be created among people in the firm.[ii]

lecture link 8-4
CHOOSING THE RIGHT SPAN OF CONTROL

No formula exists for determining the ideal span of control. Several factors affect the number of people a manager can effectively supervise. Variables in span of control include the following:

- **Capabilities of the manager.** The more experienced and capable a manager is, the broader the span of control can be. (A large number of workers can report to that manager.)

- **Capabilities of the subordinates.** The more the subordinates need supervision, the narrower the span of control should be. Employee turnover at fast-food restaurants, for example, is often so high that managers must constantly be training new people and thus need a narrow span of control.

- **Geographic closeness.** The more concentrated the work area is, the broader the span of control can be.

- **Functional similarity.** The more similar the functions are, the broader the span of control can be.

- **Need for coordination.** The greater the need for coordination, the narrower the span of control might be.

- **Planning demands.** The more involved the plan, the narrower the span of control might be.

- **Functional complexity.** The more complex the functions are, the narrower the span of control might be.

Other factors to consider include the professionalism of superiors and subordinates and the number of new problems that occur in a day. In business, the span of control varies widely. The number of people reporting to a company president may range from 1 to 80 or more. The trend is to expand the span of control as organizations reduce the number of middle managers and hire more educated and talented lower-level employees. That is all included in the idea of empowerment. It's possible to increase the span of control as employees become more professional, as information technology makes it possible for managers to handle more information, and as employees take on more responsibility for self-management.

lecture link 8-5

OTIS ELEVATORS COME TO THE RESCUE IN JAPAN

Unfortunately the tragedy in Japan continues even after the initial 9.0 earthquake in March 2011. A series of aftershocks and an ongoing nuclear crisis can make any reports of progress toward recovery seem rather hollow. Nevertheless, there's some solace to be found in the fact that this disaster could have been much worse were it not for the ingenuity of the response effort of the government, foreign aid organizations and, perhaps surprisingly, businesses.

For instance, when the president of Otis Elevator Didier Michaud-Daniel heard about the quake, not only did he have 2,400 Japanese employees to worry about, he had 80,000 elevators on his mind as well. Michaud-Daniel wasn't the only one: In the 48 hours following the quake Otis received 13,000 calls from customers about their elevators. Once every employee was accounted for, Michaud-Daniel sent all Otis technicians in southern Japan to the stricken region while everyone else headed to the company's 21 call centers. Their first order of business was to make sure the seismic detectors installed in more than half of Otis's Japanese elevators actually worked. At the first sign of vibration, the specially equipped elevators are designed to return immediately to a building's ground floor.

Thankfully, the detectors worked as planned, leaving approximately 16,700 elevators shut down by the emergency systems. Even more incredibly, Otis received no reports about trapped or injured passengers. Technicians soon restarted all but 300 of the lifts in a seven-day around the clock effort. Though Otis continues to do regular checkups on the effected elevators, they haven't gone within 30 miles of the damaged Fukushima nuclear reactor. Still, the company's careful planning goes to show that the best way to deal with a catastrophe is to anticipate the worst and be prepared.[iii]

lecture link 8-6

THE MANHATTAN PROJECT

As early as 1939 Albert Einstein warned President Franklin Roosevelt that the new field of physics had opened up the possibility of extraordinarily powerful bombs. In the summer of 1942, the government created the Manhattan Engineer District to meet the goal of producing an atomic weapon under the pressure of ongoing global war. The project became known as the Manhattan Project. The story of the bomb's creation involved the extraordinary efforts of scientists, engineers, and military officials. But it is also the story of a massive organizational endeavor.

The project was put under the direction of Brigadier General Leslie Groves of the Army Corps of Engineers. Groves had impressed his superiors with this administrative ability, organizational skill, and decisiveness. Previously Groves had successfully supervised the construction of the Pentagon. (Ironically, construction on the Pentagon began on September 11, 1941.) When he was assigned to head the top secret weapons project, Groves tried to get reassigned, preferring a posting overseas, but was unsuccessful.

Under Groves's direction, secret atomic energy communities were created almost overnight in Oak Ridge, Tennessee, at Los Alamos, New Mexico, and in Hanford, Washington, to house the workers and gigantic new machinery needed to produce the bombs. The weapon itself would be built at the Los Alamos laboratory, under the direction of physicist J. Robert Oppenheimer.

Groves made all the important decisions governing the Manhattan Project himself. He personally recruited Oppenheimer and the other key organization members. Groves drew up the plans for the organization, construction, operation, and security of the project and took all necessary steps to put it into effect. Reporting directly to Secretary of War Henry Stimson and General George Marshall, Groves routinely bypassed traditional lines of authority to ensure the success of the project.

Groves's aggressive management style and determination were key factors to the success of the Manhattan Project. His detractors called him egotistical, brusque, manipulative, and overly authoritative. However, he was decisive and able to cut through the red tape to accomplish his goals.

By the time the bombs were perfected, Germany had surrendered, and some scientists on the project questioned whether to continue bomb development. The project ultimately built four atomic bombs: "Gadget," the test bomb exploded in the New Mexico desert, "Little Boy," dropped on Hiroshima, "Fat Man," dropped on Nagasaki, and bomb no. 4, which was unused.

Based on figures from the Atomic Energy Commission archives, the costs of the project exceeded $1.8 billion. The Oak Ridge gaseous diffusion plant (which obtained the needed uranium isotope) alone cost $512,000,000. The Brookings Institute has translated these figures into current dollars. The four bombs would today cost $20 billion, or $5 billion per bomb. The total value of all bombs, mines, and grenades used in the entirety of World War II, in comparison, was $31.5 billion.[iv]

lecture link 8-7

GREATER EFFICIENCY, FEWER JOBS

After slashing more than 8.2 million jobs during the recession, U.S. companies strived to do more with less by becoming more efficient. Although many businesses' performance still pales in comparison to their pre-recession heydays, expansions abounded in early 2011 with 142 nonfinancial companies on the S&P 500 raising their operating margins. Additionally, annual growth in productivity averaged 3.4% as companies like UPS and Campbell made the most out of every work hour. As a result, employees of these companies seem safe from layoffs for the foreseeable future.

Unfortunately, such efficiency improvements have all but closed the door on future hiring. A tepid economic recovery has forced many companies to operate in recession-mode for the long term, stressing slimming costs instead of investment and expansion. Campbell, for instance, must find $80 million in savings in order to stay profitable and offset inflation. So every day at its factories, floor employees meet with managers to devise ways Campbell can implement its sweeping new efficiency measures. Though these practices will keep jobs safe and the company afloat, they detract focus from innovative measures that could allow Campbell to expand into the new decade. No less than former Fed chair Alan Greenspan fears that this culture of cost cutting will run its course eventually and margins will shrink in its wake.

The story is similar for small businesses. Once the driving force of economic recovery, low demand and tough competition has forced many small businesses to retain a core group of part-timers rather than hiring workers for full salaries. One small Internet retailer said she would need to see a 50% improvement in sales before she could hire anyone full-time. Meanwhile, data gathered from various stock indexes shows small companies that have significantly cut costs or labor are rewarded with greater interest from investors. But like their bigger brethren, small businesses aren't using their capital to innovate. Instead, they're cutting down on health care and payroll taxes by converting workers to contractors or part-time employees rather than bringing in new blood.[v]

lecture link 8-8

A NEW KIND OF OUTSOURCING

With unemployment soaring in the double digits, local governments across the country are scrambling for new ways to create jobs. Ironically, some communities are finding relief from the very companies that were responsible for outsourcing their region's jobs in the first place. For example, like many American cities, Cincinnati lost scores of manufacturing jobs to cheap labor overseas. But Ohio Governor Ted Strickland didn't let bad blood get in the way while he was wooing the Indian tech company Tata Consultancy Services (TCS) to set up offices just outside of Cincinnati. Encouraged by a promise of $19 million in tax credits, TCS agreed. The branch has already hired 300 American employees and plans to employ as many as 1,000 Americans in the future.

While TCS processes data for many American companies, laws prevent it from sending data about the U.S. government or health care projects overseas. As a result, Indian companies like TCS and Wipro Technologies are adding American branches in order to tap into this market. Officials in cities like Dallas, Atlanta, and Minneapolis have been all too happy to court these companies in the hopes of creating jobs for American workers. The cost for setting up shop in the United States is high for Indian companies, with an employee in Ohio making $50,000 a year versus $7,000 for a staffer in Bangalore. Nevertheless, American employees show their value through their knowledge of cultural nuances and their abilities to help their Indian bosses compete against rival American companies.

Still, this brand of domestic outsourcing has its downsides. Though TCS employs 1,300 American workers, it also has 13,000 Indian staffers on work visas employed in the United States. This practice could soon be outlawed, though, as proposed legislation could limit companies with more than 50 U.S.-based employees from using temporary visas for half their American workforce. Furthermore, TCS and Wipro both have admitted that they most likely will not create large amounts of American jobs as the recession has stifled much of their U.S. growth. Even so, as long as jobs are in short supply, expect local governments across the country to continue soliciting Indian companies to set up shop in their regions.[vi]

lecture link 8-9

SETTING UP SHOP ON FACEBOOK

Nearly two decades ago the desktop computer reigned supreme as the must-have technological tool. In time, though, the laptop overtook its stationary sister and thus the mobile age was born. Now consumers have access to an array of smartphones and digital tablets that can send them into cyberspace no matter where they stand. For social networks and retailers alike, the mobile market has already grown to a gargantuan size with no signs that it'll stop anytime soon.

Of its over 500 million users worldwide, Facebook says that more than 200 million people access the site through mobile devices. Mobile stores as well have enjoyed tremendous growth. The online auction house eBay predicts that its mobile sales will double in 2011 to $4 billion. With Facebook's formidable user base and retailers' growing mobile incomes, it was only a matter of time until the two camps joined forces. In January 2011, the London-based retailer ASOS became the first company to set up shop inside Facebook itself. ASOS (which stands for "As Seen on Screen") owns no physical locations, operating solely online. With its new Facebook location, ASOS hopes to capture the interest of mobile Facebookers who may only use the Web on their phone to access the site.

Although many companies use social media to create awareness, this new trend of direct outlets on social platforms could be the future of retail, not just mobile shopping. JCPenney and Delta Airlines have been in talks for months about obtaining a direct presence on Facebook. In three to five years, economists estimate that as much as 15% of total consumer spending may go through social networking sites. Though it's too soon to deem ASOS' Facebook experiment a success, with more than 465,000 "likes" to its name the company seems poised for a fortune if all those friends turn into customers.[vii]

lecture link 8-10

EMPLOYER ICEBREAKING RITUALS

For many fresh hires, a new office environment can seem alien and uninviting. Habits that were commonplace at the employee's previous job may be unacceptable in their new one. Initial interactions with colleagues can be awkward or even hostile, sometimes leading to fissures in working relationships that are difficult to mend. A clear understanding of a company's culture is vital to every employee's success, and sometimes a simple orientation just isn't enough. To help new hires effectively assimilate into the workplace, some companies use initiation rituals to break in their new members. Besides working as an icebreaker, such rituals create an instant bond by establishing the character of the company to the employee through various activities.

For example, at Foot Levelers, a manufacturer of chiropractic products, employees will occasionally notice a sign on the conference room door reading "Rudy in Progress." Inside the room, a group of new hires eat snacks and watch the 1993 football drama *Rudy*, a movie about a tenacious student who strives to play on the Notre Dame gridiron. After the movie ends, Foot Levelers CEO Kent Greenwault collects everyone's impressions on the film and together they compose a list of the traits Rudy utilized to finally gain success. Employees are meant to emulate Rudy's determination and ceaseless work ethic that drove him on even in the bleakest moments. The ritual also clues staffers in on Greenwault's favorite management catchphrase. Whenever an employee comes to a manager with a work problem, the manager will first ask them, "Did you Rudy that?"

Some companies use rituals to test the physical mettle of new staffers. At the Massachusetts-based moving company Gentle Giant, CEO Larry O'Toole requires new hires to join him for a run up and down the steps of Harvard Stadium. First of all, the ritual acts as an effective indicator of the employee's physical capabilities. O'Toole often won't allow new hires onto a moving truck until he has observed them on the steps. Symbolically, though, O'Toole hopes the run shows staffers how he expects them to push themselves even in the most uncomfortable situations.[viii]

lecture link 8-11

MAPPING THE INFORMAL ORGANIZATION

The best way to manage informal organizations is to acknowledge their existence and then bring them out into the open. That is best done through a process known as social network analysis. What you do is chart the flows of information among members of the firm and show those flows using arrows on a chart.

Although it may be tempting to map all the informal networks at one time, that would be difficult to do and the resulting map would be very, very complex. It is more effective for managers to identify those functions or activities in a firm where connectivity is most needed to improve productivity and then map the corresponding networks of people.

How do you collect information from people to make a map of the interrelationships that occur in a firm? One way is to track e-mail correspondence. Another is to simply observe the behavior of people over time. Who visits whose office and how often? The best way may be to administer a simple 10- to 20-minute questionnaire. Questions would vary by firm and the intent of the research, but they would look something like this: "To whom do you talk regularly about work?" "From whom do you get your technical information?" "To whom do you turn for advice before making an important decision?" "With whom are you most likely to discuss a new idea?" Questions can be tailored to the needs of individual managers. The idea is to see who goes to whom for information and support.

There is software available that helps firms create maps that illustrate relationships among employees. Each line on the map indicates a link between two employees and arrows show the direction of the relationship. After a map is drawn, interviews can be conducted to see how such relationships can be used to further the goals of the firm. People are more likely to participate honestly and freely if they know that people who are central to the firm will be compensated accordingly. The goal is not to discover the rumor mill, but to discover who are the real influencers and decision makers in the firm. Which managers are weak and which are strong?

In short, managers can work with employees to discover informal communication networks to optimize those networks and reward those in the firm who others turn to for advice, help, and support. Central connectors link most employees with one another; they provide the expertise that others rely on to get things done. Boundary spanners connect the informal network with other parts of the company or other networks. Peripheral specialists are sought for expertise on selected questions.[ix]

critical thinking exercises

Name: _____

Date: _____

critical thinking exercise 8-1
BUILDING AN ORGANIZATION CHART

Dr. Rea Searge is president of Peabody Researchers, Inc., a pharmaceutical company. Peabody uses a line-and-staff structure to organize its employees. In addition to Dr. Searge, Peabody has the following employees:

> A quality control officer
>
> A vice president of production
>
> 150 research and development employees
>
> A sales force of 100 people
>
> A vice president of finance
>
> Marketing managers for three regions
>
> A vice president of marketing
>
> A director of personnel
>
> A vice president of research and development
>
> Production managers for three product lines
>
> An administrative assistant to the president
>
> A production force of 600 people

On a separate sheet of paper, draw an organization chart for Peabody Researchers, Inc. Use solid lines for line authority–responsibility relationships and dotted lines for staff authority–responsibility relationships. Use the diagram on page 216 of your text as an example.

notes on critical thinking exercise 8-1

The following people are **staff**:

Director of personnel

Vice president of research and development

Administrative assistant to the president

Research and development department

Quality control officer

The rest have **line** positions.

Let the students draw the chart on the board with as little assistance as possible so they can think it through. A possible solution is given on the following page

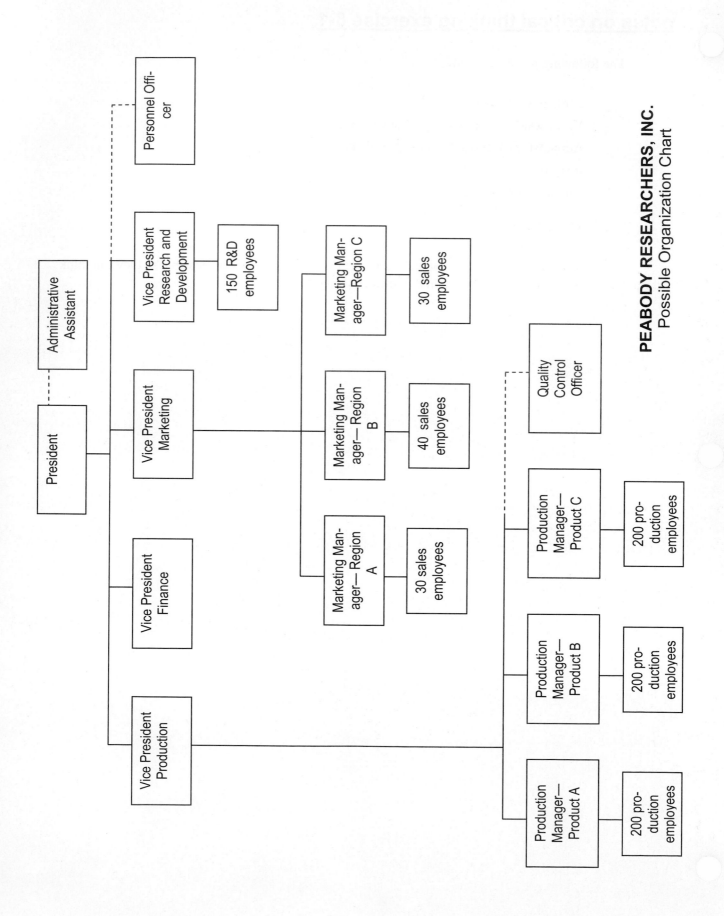

PEABODY RESEARCHERS, INC.
Possible Organization Chart

critical thinking exercise 8-2
HOW DO ORGANIZATIONS GROUP ACTIVITIES?

The Internet has greatly increased access to information about organizations. Corporations use their websites to communicate with investors, customers, and the general public. Just by visiting the company's site you can usually discover the organization's chain of command and approach to departmentalization. Go to the websites for each organization below and identify the primary organizational units. (*Hint:* Look for the "Corporate Information" or "Investor Relations" sections.) Based on that information, speculate on the type of departmentalization used.[x]

1. **COCA-COLA COMPANY**

    Primary Organizational Units:

    Type of Departmentalization Used: _____

2. **THE WALT DISNEY COMPANY**

    Primary Organizational Units:

    Type of Departmentalization Used: _____

3. **THE UNITED METHODIST CHURCH**

    Primary Organizational Units:

    Type of Departmentalization Used: _____

critical thinking exercise 8-2

(continued)

4. **KRAFT FOODS**

Primary Organizational Units:

Type of Departmentalization Used: _____

5. **BOEING**

Primary Organizational Units:

Type of Departmentalization Used: _____

bonus
cases

bonus case 8-1
DARK DAYS AT USPS

Times have been tough for the U.S. Postal Service ever since the average American's e-mail address became just as important as his or her actual address. The government agency reported losses in 14 of the last 16 quarters and is mired in more than $12 billion of debt. In 2009 costs exceeded revenues in USPS's bulk mail service by $2.7 billion, even with the aid of a $3 billion loan from the U.S. Treasury. Were it any other company, USPS would stave off its mounting debt by closing stores, laying off workers, and expanding into new forms of business.

But USPS is far from a normal company. Roadblocks from Congress, labor unions, and regulators often prevent it from making big restructuring decisions. Despite its connection with the government, though, USPS has not received taxpayer dollars for decades. That might not be the case for long. By law USPS cannot incur more than $15 billion in debt. With losses expected to exceed $3 billion next year, the service may need a government bailout by the end of the fiscal year if it is to continue operations.

A bailout may be the only viable option given all the factors standing in the way of real change at USPS. First of all, the agency spends an unsustainable amount on salaries and benefits, usurping 78% of its budget compared to FedEx's 43% and UPS's 61%. Entrenched unions are fighting cutbacks, though, clamoring instead for restoration of jobs that have been outsourced. USPS also desperately needs to shed many of its 32,000 stores. That alarms some local lawmakers who see post offices, especially those named after famous residents, as community institutions. Finally, USPS has forged a paradoxical relationship with its main competitors, FedEx and UPS. While the courier services have sapped much of USPS's business, the agency receives the bulk of its revenue when the courier services use the postal network for last-minute deliveries. Ultimately, USPS needs cash to branch out into new forms of business. Whether that money comes in the form of a bailout or government subsidies remains to be seen.[xi]

discussion questions for bonus case 8-1

1. Should the federal government provide needed funds to USPS?

2. Can USPS become more efficient like UPS and FedEx?

notes on discussion questions for bonus case 8-1

1. *Should the federal government provide needed funds to USPS?*

    We suspect there are many opinions, pro and con, regarding this question. While USPS is certainly an institution that has a place in the U.S. economic system, a significant downsizing may be forthcoming. Given the current state of the U.S. economy it's doubtful taxpayers would favor either a bailout or government subsidy.

2. *Can USPS become more efficient like UPS and FedEx?*

    Changing the culture and operations of USPS will be much harder than you might suspect. As the case notes, many of the excess stores will be difficult to close due to political realities, and layoffs or reduction of services will also cause turmoil politicians may not want to face. USPS needs an infusion of new ideas.

bonus case 8-2

STRUCTURAL COLLAPSE: RESPONSIBILITY AND ACCOUNTABILITY

To publicize its newly opened nightspot, a major hotel instituted weekly "tea dances" in the lobby of the hotel. A local band played 1940s-era music while dancers competed in friendly contests. On a Friday night in July, the band was playing Duke Ellington's "Satin Doll" when two skywalks spanning the lobby of the year-old hotel collapsed. Sixty-five tons of concrete, metal, glass, and dance spectators plunged four floors to the sidewalk below, killing 114 persons and injuring 216 others.

The investigation after the collapse revealed that the collapse resulted from poor judgment and a series of events that, in combination, produced a disastrous result. The study showed a history of oversights, misunderstandings, and safety problems plaguing the 40-story, 780-room luxury hotel during construction and for months after its opening.

Mishaps aren't uncommon on big projects, of course. But this huge project, which was built on an accelerated schedule, encountered a series of accidents and near-accidents during construction. At one point the building's owner dismissed its general contractor and barred an inspection company from bidding on future company projects.

The hotel was erected using the "fast-track" method, a fairly common procedure in which construction proceeds before all drawings are complete. With a $40 million construction loan outstanding and all building costs soaring, the owner wanted the hotel up and open as quickly as practical.

Design changes are common on fast-track projects, making clear communications more critical than usual. The owners of the building had circulated a 27-page procedures manual explaining the proper channels for design changes and approved drawings. But the procedures weren't always followed, and other mistakes slipped in. Because some connections were misplaced on the drawings, for instance, workers installed a sweeping cantilevered stairway without fully attaching it to a wall.

The investigation found that the skywalks fell as a result of a design change made during a telephone call between the structural engineering company and the steel fabricator. Stress calculations would have shown that the redesigned skywalks were barely able to support their own weight, let alone the weight of dozens of dance spectators. However, court depositions of the two engineers who made the telephone redesign indicate that each person assumed it was the other's responsibility to make new calculations, and neither did.

Edward Pfrang, then chief of the structures division of the National Bureau of Standards and a participant in the investigation, says, "One thing that's clear after . . . [this] failure and a few others is that there isn't a clear-cut set of standards and practices defining who is responsible in the construction process."

discussion questions for bonus case 8-2

1.   Who was responsible for the collapse? Explain.

2.   Identify several key time points at which the problem could have been corrected.

notes on discussion questions for bonus case 8-2

1. *Who was responsible for the collapse? Explain.*

   Identifying who is to blame is the function of the legal system. Clearly, many people shared in the blame, but not necessarily legally. Such a case shows the dangers of trying to get a project done quickly instead of safely.

2. *Identify several key time points at which the problem could have been corrected.*

   During construction, during the safety inspection, when the times were set for competition—safety considerations don't take place at any one time. They must be in mind at *all* times.

3. *Is this a failure of planning, organizing, leading, or controlling?*

   This failure occurred at all three stages: (1) At the planning stage because the project was hurried. (2) At the organization stage because responsibility was not made clear. (3) At the control stage because periodic inspections should have found the flaws.

   This case is based on the collapse of the skywalk at the Kansas City Hyatt Regency in 1981. Hundreds of lawsuits were filed against its owner, Hallmark Cards Inc., its operator, Hyatt Hotels Corp, and against the building companies involved. Millions of dollars in damage claims have been paid out.

bonus case 8-3

CREATING CROSS-FUNCTIONAL TEAMS

The Direct Response Group (DRG) at Capital Holding is a direct marketer of life, health, property, and casualty insurance. In the past, it sold a mass-produced product to a mass market. Over time, however, sales slowed, profits eroded, and the company decided it had to refocus its efforts. That meant, for one thing, selling to particular, identifiable customers and giving those customers a customized product/service package that was world class, enabling the company to compete globally.

An analysis of the corporate culture showed that people were more concerned with pleasing their bosses than pleasing the customer. People hoarded information instead of sharing information because the people with information had power. The information system had to be changed to encourage sharing.

Organizational change began with a vision statement that emphasized caring, listening to, and satisfying customers one-on-one. To accomplish that goal, the company formed a cross-functional team to study the sales, service, and marketing processes and completely redesign those functional areas. The idea was to have a world-class customer-driven company. That meant gathering as much information as possible about customers.

Frontline customer-contact people were empowered with user-friendly information systems that made it possible for one contact person, working with a support team, to handle any question that customers had. Management used external databases to get detailed information on some 15 million consumers. The combined internal and external databases were used to develop custom-made products for specific customer groups.

The whole company was focused on satisfying customer wants and needs. That meant changing processes within the firm so that they were geared toward the customer. For example, one case worker is now attached to each customer, and that case worker is responsible for following an application through the entire approval and product design process. Previously, many people handled the application, and no one person was responsible for it.

A pilot program was started whereby a customer-management team was formed to serve 40,000 customers. The team consisted of 10 customer service representatives and their support team (a marketer, an expert in company operations, and an information systems person). Employees are now rewarded for performance, and merit raises are based on team performance to encourage team participation.

discussion questions for bonus case 8-3

1. Are traditional bureaucracies set up to provide custom-made products to individual consumers? Could they be, or is it always better to have customer-oriented teams design such products?

2. Anyone who has worked in team situations has discovered that some members of the team work harder than others; nonetheless, the whole team is often rewarded based on the overall results, not individual effort. How could team evaluations be made so that individual efforts could be recognized and rewarded?

3. What service organizations, private or public, would you like to see become more customer oriented? How could this case be used as a model for that organization?

4. What are some major impediments to implementing customer-oriented teams in service organizations?

notes on discussion questions for bonus case 8-3

1. *Are traditional bureaucracies set up to provide custom-made products to individual consumers? Could they be, or is it always better to have customer-oriented teams design such products?*

    Traditional bureaucracies are organizations that have many layers of management who set rules and regulations and participate in all decisions. Such an organization, by definition, would be unable to swiftly respond to customer needs. Decision making needs to be placed close to the customer, not in successive layers of management.

2. *Anyone who has worked in team situations has discovered that some members of the team work harder than others; nonetheless the whole team is often rewarded based on the overall results, not individual effort. How could team evaluations be made so that individual efforts could be recognized and rewarded?*

    Team contributions are team contributions and difficult to isolate as individual efforts. In fact, the purpose of team organization is to combine the best efforts of many individuals rather than relying on only one. Team members exercise informal pressure to ensure continued quality effort. Such informal pressure is much more effective than organizational efforts.

3. *What service organizations, private or public, would you like to see become more customer oriented? How could this case be used as a model for that organization?*

    The chances are that almost every student's list will contain (1) the U.S. Postal Service and (2) your school. This case shows that the entire organization must be committed to the customer-oriented team approach for it to be effective. Such an approach would be difficult in a public organization such as USPS. The potential for creating a customer-oriented school should be interesting to pursue.

4. *What are some of the major impediments to implementing customer-oriented teams in service organizations?*

    Service organizations are quite different from product-producing organizations in that there is no distance between the production of the service and the customer. The service is created when the customer receives it. Most service organizations already have a customer-oriented focus. This case shows, however, that much improvement can be made in the delivery of that service.

UNDERSTANDING BUSINESS: Instructor's Resource Manual

bonus case 8-4

OFFICE ALUMNI

While few people would describe getting laid off or fired as a "graduating" from their company, many businesses have created social networking sites for their "alumni" as the poor economy continues to take its toll on American jobs. Whether an employee leaves voluntarily or is shown the door with a pink slip, companies like IBM, Lockheed-Martin, and Dow Chemical have created LinkedIn and Facebook sites that allow former workers to keep in touch, even if they move on to competing companies.

Part of the draw of these alumni networks is to provide a centralized spot for "boomerang" employees (those who leave the company only to be hired again later). As the deepening recession forces companies to continue laying off staff, alumni networks keep the connection between company and individual alive. Even if a person does not end up boomeranging, alumni networks have other benefits. Ideas and insights shared between employees new and old on the network can be mutually beneficial. Many sites feature inside industry news and job leads. Some alumni networks even offer exclusive deals on health insurance for former employees.

Many companies are drawn to private social networks because it allows them to track and study the topics being discussed on the site's forums. Using online tools and software, employers can effectively map out the goings on of not only the company, but also the skills and interests of the network's contributors. These tracking methods often help companies find the proper employee to suit their needs. In one such instance, an accounting firm used its tracking software to rehire 31 boomerangs.

As for the disgruntled employees who would rather defame their former employer rather than boomerang back in, trolling and angry dissention appear to be rare occurrences on the alumni networks. Many execs say that a company's most outraged alums choose to air their grievances on sites that are not controlled by the company.[xii]

discussion questions for bonus case 8-4

1. Will the presence of such alumni sites help the image of participating companies?

2. How do the alumni sites serve as a research base for participating companies?

notes on discussion questions for bonus case 8-4

1.   *Will the presence of such alumni sites help the image of participating companies?*

It seems very likely that will be the net effect. The alumni sites are similar to a customer follow-up so highly recommended in marketing.

2.   *How do the alumni sites serve as a research base for participating companies?*

Companies are able to track and study topics discussed on the site's forums. This puts them in touch with the thoughts of employees and ex-employees concerning the company and its operations.

endnotes

[i] *Source:* Julie Jargon, "Latest Starbucks Buzzword: 'Lean' Japanese Techniques," *The Wall Street Journal*, August 4, 2009.

[ii] *Sources:* Allison Overholt, "Health and the Profit Motive," *Fast Company,* February 2003, p. 38; Marty Laubach, "Consent, Informal Organization and Job Rewards: A Mixed Methods Analysis," *Social Forces*, June 1, 2005.

[iii] *Source:* Rachel Layne, "How Otis Elevator Found the Right Floor," *Bloomberg Businessweek*, March 24, 2011.

[iv] *Sources:* "The Costs of the Manhattan Project," The Brookings Institute, www.brook.edu; "The Manhattan Project: A New and Secret World of Human Experimentation," ACHRE Report, Department of Energy, www.eh.doe.gov; Miguel A. Bracchini, "Appendix: Key Figures in the Manhattan Project," University of Texas at Austin, www.me.utexas.edu; Colonel Cole C. Kingseed, "Racing for the Bomb: General Leslie R. Goves, the Manhattan Project's Indispensable Man," *Parameters*, March 22, 2003; Phillip Morrison, "The Manhattan Project's Taskmaster," *American Scientist,* November 1, 2003.

[v] *Sources:* Craig Torres and Anthony Field, "Campbell's Quest for Productivity," *Bloomberg Businessweek*, November 24, 2010; Vivien Lou Chen and Timothy R. Homan, "Small Businesses Keep a Lid on Hiring," *Bloomberg Businessweek*, January 6, 2011.

[vi] *Source:* Mehul Srivastava and Moira Herbst, "The Return of the Outsourced Job," *Bloomberg Businessweek*, January 11, 2010.

[vii] *Source:* Sarah Shannon, "Fashion Retailer ASOS Sets Up Shop on Facebook," *Bloomberg Businessweek*, February 17, 2011.

[viii] *Source:* Leigh Buchanan, "Bizarre Hiring Rituals," *Inc.,* March 1, 2010.

[ix] *Sources:* Rob Cross and Laurence Prusak, "The People Who Make Organizations Go—or Stop," *Harvard Business Review*, June 2002, pp. 105–112; Rob Cross, Nitin Nohria and Andrew Parker, "Six Myths About Informal Networks," *Sloan Management Review*, Spring 2002, pp. 67–75.

[x] The Internet is a dynamic, changing information source. Web links noted of this manual were checked at the time of publication, but content may change over time. Please review the website before recommending it to your students.

[xi] *Source:* Angela Greiling Keane, "A Reckoning Ahead for U.S. Mail," *Bloomberg Businessweek*, December 9, 2010.

[xii] *Source:* Stephen Baker, "You're Fired—But Stay in Touch," *BusinessWeek*, May 4, 2009.

Production
and Operations
Management

chapter **9**

critical thinking exercises

bonus cases

what's new in this edition

additions to the 10th edition:

- Name That Company: Allen-Bradley
- Thinking Green: Key Word: Sustainability
- Reaching Beyond Our Borders: Learning from Germany
- Spotlight on Small Business: Mass Customization of Candy

revisions to the 10th edition:

- Text was revised to eliminate redundancy and tighten discussions.
- Statistical data and examples throughout the chapter were updated to reflect current information.
- Getting to Know Samuel J. Palmisano, CEO and President of IBM

deletions from the 9th edition:

- Name That Company: Ritz-Carlton
- Thinking Green
- Reaching Beyond Our Borders

brief chapter outline
and learning goals

Production and Operations Management

Getting To Know SAMUEL J. PALMISANO of IBM

learning goal 1

Describe the current state of U.S. manufacturing and what manufacturers have done to become more competitive.

I.   MANUFACTURING AND SERVICES IN PERSPECTIVE

A.   Manufacturers and Service Organizations Become More Competitive

learning goal 2

Describe the evolution from production to operations management.

II.   FROM PRODUCTION TO OPERATIONS MANAGEMENT

A.   Operations Management in the Service Sector

learning goal 3

Identify various production processes and describe techniques that improve productivity, including computer-aided design and manufacturing, flexible manufacturing, lean manufacturing, and mass customization.

III.   PRODUCTION PROCESSES

A.   The Need to Improve Production Techniques and Cut Costs
B.   Computer-Aided Design and Manufacturing
C.   Flexible Manufacturing
D.   Lean Manufacturing
E.   Mass Customization

learning goal 4

Describe operations management planning issues including facility location, facility layout, materials requirement planning, purchasing, just-in-time inventory control, and quality control.

IV.   OPERATIONS MANAGEMENT PLANNING

A.   Facility Location

learning goal 5

Explain the use of PERT and Gantt charts to control manufacturing processes.

V. CONTROL PROCEDURES: PERT AND GANTT CHARTS

VI. PREPARING FOR THE FUTURE

VII. SUMMARY

Getting to Know SAMUEL J. PALMISANO, CEO and PRESIDENT of IBM

Sam Palmisano is one of the lifetime IBMers who rose up through the ranks. He became chair in 2002. Palmisano understood that an international company like IBM must always look toward the future, maximize its strengths, and reduce its weaknesses. IBM's strength was its marketing, but it discovered that new-product development and manufacturing were slow and costly. The company has outsourced both functions to concentrate on its marketing strength.

NAME THAT company

This company's robots manufacture, test, and package motor starters—all untouched by human hands. The machines can fill special orders, even for a single item, without slowing down the process. Name that company.

(Students should read the chapter before guessing the company's name: Allen-Bradley.*)*

learning goal 1

Describe the current state of U.S. manufacturing and what manufacturers have done to become more competitive.

I. MANUFACTURING AND SERVICES IN PERSPECTIVE

A. MANUFACTURING AFFECTS THE U.S. ECONOMY

1. The recent recession resulted in increased unemployment and a dramatic fall in the stock market.

   a. The U.S. is still in a leadership position.

   b. Some areas of the country enjoyed economic growth from manufacturing while others experienced declines.

2. **GAINS IN PRODUCTIVITY**

   a. Productivity gains have lowered the number of manufacturing workers that manufacturers need.

lecture notes

PPT 9-1
Chapter Title

PPT 9-2
Learning Goals

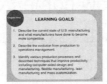

(See complete PowerPoint slide notes on page 9.42.)

PPT 9-3
Learning Goals

(See complete PowerPoint slide notes on page 9.42.)

PPT 9-4
Samuel J. Palmisano

(See complete PowerPoint slide notes on page 9.43.)

PPT 9-5
Name That Company

(See complete PowerPoint slide notes on page 9.43.)

PPT 9-6
Manufacturing in the U.S.

(See complete PowerPoint slide notes on page 9.43.)

PPT 9-7
What's Made in the USA?

(See complete PowerPoint slide notes on page 9.44.)

PPT 9-8
Exporters Extraordinaire

(See complete PowerPoint slide notes on page 9.44.)

    b.   The U.S. economy is no longer manufacturing-based.

    c.   Seventy percent of the U.S. GDP and 85% of its jobs now come from the service sector.

    d.   The service sector has suffered along with manufacturing as a result of the economic downturn.

B. **MANUFACTURERS AND SERVICE ORGANIZATIONS BECOME MORE COMPETITIVE**

    1.   Foreign manufacturers have become competitive by using U.S. technology.

        a.   This helps reduce poverty and open new markets.

        b.   Foreign producers are also moving to the U.S.

    2.   The service sector is gaining in importance.

    3.   To regain a competitive edge, American manufacturers have begun to:

        a.   Focus more on customers

        b.   Maintain closer relationships with suppliers

        c.   Practice continuous improvement

        d.   Focus on quality

        e.   Save on costs through site selection

        f.   Rely on the Internet to unite companies

        g.   Adopt new manufacturing techniques

    4.   Major issues facing American business include service productivity and the use of the Internet.

bonus case 9-1

THE STATE OF AMERICAN MANUFACTURING

American manufacturing has been slowing down for years and economists fear they could eventually lose their edge to foreign competitors. (See the complete case, discussion questions, and suggested answers beginning on page 9.77 of this manual.)

PPT 9-9
Massive Manufacturers

(See complete PowerPoint slide notes on page 9.44.)

lecture link 9-1

THE MILITARY LEARNS FROM NASCAR

Innovative ideas can come from unexpected sources. For example, the military is studying processes used in NASCAR racing. (See the complete lecture link on page 9.63 in this manual.)

thinking green
(Text page 236)

PPT 9-10
Key Word: Sustainability

See complete PowerPoint slide notes on page 9.45.)

lecture link 9-2

MADE IN THE USA, BUT OWNED BY CHINA

Foreign manufacturers are setting up shop in the United States in order to bypass trade barriers and capitalize on government subsidies. (See the complete lecture link on page 9.63 in this manual.)

PPT 9-11
Top-Paying Service Jobs

(See complete PowerPoint slide notes on page 9.45.)

PPT 9-12
Remaining Competitive in Global Markets

(See complete PowerPoint slide notes on page 9.45.)

lecture link 9-3

TOLEDO'S SUNNY FUTURE

To maintain a competitive edge, Toledo, Ohio, is turning away from its glass past and toward solar energy. (See the complete lecture link on page 9.64 in this manual.)

lecture outline

Describe the evolution from production to operations management.

II. FROM PRODUCTION TO OPERATIONS MANAGEMENT

A. **_PRODUCTION_** is the creation of finished goods and services using the factors of production: land, labor, capital, entrepreneurship, and knowledge.

1. Production has usually been associated with **MANUFACTURING**, but this is changing.

   a. **_PRODUCTION MANAGEMENT_** is the term used to describe all the activities managers do to help their firms create goods.

   b. The **SERVICE SECTOR** has grown dramatically.

   c. The U.S. now has a **SERVICE ECONOMY**, one dominated by the service sector.

2. **_OPERATIONS MANAGEMENT_** is a specialized area in management that converts or transforms resources (including human resources) into goods and services.

3. Operations management involves many functions, including inventory management and quality control.

4. Some organizations produce mostly goods *(factories and mines);* others mostly services *(hospitals, schools);* some produce both *(Wendy's).*

B. **OPERATIONS MANAGEMENT IN THE SERVICE SECTOR**

1. *The text uses the example of the Ritz-Carlton and the luxury hotel's operations management.*

REACHING BEYOND
our borders
(Text page 237

PPT 9-13
Learning from
Germany

(See complete PowerPoint slide notes on page 9.46.)

critical thinking
exercise 9-1
**GROUP PROJECT: ORGANIZING
PRODUCTION**

This is a fun exercise to give students firsthand experience in production. (See complete exercise on page 9.69 of this manual.)

PPT 9-14
Production and Production
Management

(See complete PowerPoint slide notes on page 9.46.)

PPT 9-15
Operations Management

(See complete PowerPoint slide notes on page 9.46.)

.

PPT 9-16
Operations Management in the
Service Sector

(See complete PowerPoint slide notes on page 9.47.)

2. The hotel chain created a sophisticated computerized guest recognition program and a Quality Management Program to "certify" employees.

3. In the service industry, operations management is about **CREATING A GOOD EXPERIENCE** for those who use the service.

4. Customers now expect more services (*examples: Internet access and multilingual customer service*).

5. **DELIGHTING CUSTOMERS** has become the quality standard for luxury hotels and other service businesses.

learning goal 3

Identify various production processes and describe techniques that improve productivity, including computer-aided design and manufacturing, flexible manufacturing, lean manufacturing, and mass customization.

III. PRODUCTION PROCESSES

A. PRODUCTION USES BASIC INPUTS TO PRODUCE OUTPUTS

1. Production adds **VALUE**, or **UTILITY**, to materials or processes.

   a. **_FORM UTILITY_** is the value added by the creation of finished goods and services, such as the value added by taking silicon and making computer chips or putting services together to create a vacation package.

   b. Form utility can also be created at the retail level.

2. Andrew S. Grove, former chair of Intel, defines the **THREE BASIC REQUIREMENTS OF PRODUCTION:**

lecture link 9-4
SPEEDING UP THE DRIVE-THROUGH

Fast-food retailers are taking a hard look at the drive-through experience to improve customer satisfaction and increase speed. (See the complete lecture link on page 9.64 of this manual.)

PPT 9-17
There's an App for That

(See complete PowerPoint slide notes on page 9.47.)

progress assessment
(Text page 239)

PPT 9-18
Progress Assessment

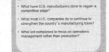

(See complete PowerPoint slide notes on page 9.47.)

PPT 9-19
The Production Process

TEXT FIGURE 9.1
The Production Process
(Text page 239)

(See complete PowerPoint slide notes on page 9.48.)

PPT 9-20
Form Utility

(See complete PowerPoint slide notes on page 9.48.)

    a. To build and deliver products in response to the demands of the customer at a scheduled delivery time

    b. To provide an acceptable quality level

    c. To provide everything at the lowest possible cost

3. **TYPES OF PRODUCTION OPERATIONS**

    a. **_PROCESS MANUFACTURING_** is that part of the production process that physically or chemically changes materials.

    b. The **_ASSEMBLY PROCESS_** is that part of the production process that puts together components.

4. **CONTINUOUS VERSUS INTERMITTENT PROCESSES**

    a. A **_CONTINUOUS PROCESS_** is a production process in which long production runs turn out finished goods over time.

    b. An **_INTERMITTENT PROCESS_** is a production process in which the production run is short and the machines are changed frequently to produce different products.

    c. Today, most new manufacturers use intermittent processes.

B. **THE NEED TO IMPROVE PRODUCTION TECHNIQUES AND CUT COSTS**

1. The goal of manufacturing and process management is to provide high-quality goods and services instantaneously in response to customer demand.

PPT 9-21
Grove's Basic Production
Requirements

(See complete PowerPoint slide notes on page 9.48.)

**critical thinking
exercise 9-2**
PRODUCTION PROCESSES

This exercise asks students to classify several products by the type of manufacturing process used. (See complete exercise on page 9.71 of this manual.)

PPT 9-22
Process and Assembly in
Production

(See complete PowerPoint slide notes on page 9.49.)

PPT 9-23
Key Production Processes

(See complete PowerPoint slide notes on page 9.49.)

PPT 9-24
Minute Made

(See complete PowerPoint slide notes on page 9.49.)

2. **TRADITIONAL ORGANIZATIONS** were not designed to be very responsive to the customer.

3. **MASS PRODUCTION** let producers make a large number of limited varieties of products at a very low cost.

4. Over the years, low cost often came at the **EXPENSE OF QUALITY AND FLEXIBILITY**.

5. Such inefficiencies opened U.S. companies to foreign competition.

6. To meet this competition, companies today must make a wide variety of high-quality custom-designed products at a very low cost.

C. **COMPUTER-AIDED DESIGN AND MANUFACTURING**

1. ***COMPUTER-AIDED DESIGN (CAD)*** is the use of computers in the design of products.

2. ***COMPUTER-AIDED MANUFACTURING (CAM)*** is the use of computers in the manufacturing of products.

3. **CAD/CAM,** the use of both computer-aided design and computer-aided manufacturing, made it possible to custom-design products for small markets.

4. CAD has doubled productivity in many firms.

    a. In the past, computer-aided design machines couldn't talk to computer-aided manufacturing machines.

    b. ***COMPUTER-INTEGRATED MANUFACTURING (CIM)*** is uniting computer-aided design with computer-aided manufacturing.

PPT 9-25
Developments Making U.S.
Companies More Competitive

(See complete PowerPoint slide notes on page 9.50.)

lecture link 9-5

**AMERICA'S ROBOTICS
REBOUND**

Innovative ideas can come from unexpected sources. For example, the military is studying processes used in NASCAR racing. (See complete lecture link on page 9.65 of this manual.)

PPT 9-26
Computer-Aided Design and
Manufacturing

(See complete PowerPoint slide notes on page 9.50.)

PPT 9-27
Computer-Integrated Manufacturing

(See complete PowerPoint slide notes on page 9.50.)

D. **FLEXIBLE MANUFACTURING**

1. ***FLEXIBLE MANUFACTURING*** is designing machines to do multiple tasks so that they can produce a variety of products.

2. *The text uses Allen-Bradley system of robots as an example of flexible manufacturing.*

E. **LEAN MANUFACTURING**

1. ***LEAN MANUFACTURING*** is the production of goods using less of everything compared to mass production.

2. Lean manufacturing uses less human effort, less manufacturing space, less investment in tools, and less engineering time to develop a new product in half the time.

3. A company becomes lean by **CONTINUOUSLY INCREASING THE CAPACITY** to produce more, higher-quality results with fewer resources.

4. Characteristics of lean companies:

   a. They take half the human effort.

   b. They have half the defects in the finished product or service.

   c. They require one-third the engineering effort.

   d. They use half the floor space for the same output.

   e. They carry 90% less inventory.

5. Technology has improved labor productivity, but employees can become frustrated by innovations.

6. More productivity and efficiency will help solve the economic crisis.

PPT 9-28
Flexible Manufacturing

(See complete PowerPoint slide notes on page 9.51.)

PPT 9-29
Lean Manufacturing

(See complete PowerPoint slide notes on page 9.51.)

lecture link 9-6
KODAK LEARNS SPEED

When digital photography gained market share at the expense of film photography, Kodak underwent a difficult restructuring process to clarify strategy and practice lean manufacturing (See the complete lecture link on page 9.65 of this manual.)

PPT 9-30
Mass Customization

(See complete PowerPoint slide notes on page 9.51.)

F. **_MASS CUSTOMIZATION_** means tailoring products to meet the needs of individual customers.

1. **FLEXIBLE MANUFACTURING SYSTEMS** let manufacturers custom-make goods as quickly as mass-produced items.

2. Manufacturers are learning to **CUSTOMIZE THEIR PRODUCTS** for individual customers. *(Custom Foot uses infrared scanners to precisely fit shoes.)*

3. Mass customization of services is actually easier because there is no tangible good that must be adapted. *(Capital Protection Insurance sells customized risk management plans to companies.)*

learning goal 4

Describe operations management planning issues including facility location, facility layout, materials requirement planning, purchasing, just-in-time inventory control, and quality control.

IV. OPERATIONS MANAGEMENT PLANNING

A. Many of the issues covered in operations management planning are the same in both service and manufacturing sectors.

B. **FACILITY LOCATION**

1. **_FACILITY LOCATION_** is the process of selecting a geographic location for a company's operations.

   a. One strategy is to find a site that makes it **EASY FOR CONSUMERS TO USE THE COMPANY'S** service, *such as putting flower shops and banks in supermarkets.*

   b. The ultimate convenience is shopping through the **INTERNET**.

SPOTLIGHT ON small business
(Text page 243)

PPT 9-31
Mass Customization of Candy

(See complete PowerPoint slide notes on page 9.52.)

progress assessment
(Text page 243)

PPT 9-32
Progress Assessment

(See complete PowerPoint slide notes on page 9.52.)

PPT 9-33
Operations Management

(See complete PowerPoint slide notes on page 9.53.)

PPT 9-34
Facility Location

(See complete PowerPoint slide notes on page 9.53.)

bonus case 9-2
A SMALL HOMECOMING BY AMERICAN MANUFACTURERS

Caterpillar is one of several U.S. companies that are bringing factories back to American soil. (See the complete case, discussion questions, and suggested answers beginning on page 9.79 of this manual.)

    c. The most successful service-sector businesses are conveniently located.

C. **FACILITY LOCATION FOR MANUFACTURERS**

  1. Automobile production is shifting from Detroit to southern cities, creating both pockets of unemployment and pockets of rapid growth.

  2. Manufacturers consider:

    a. Labor costs

    b. Availability of resources, including labor

    c. Access to transportation that can reduce time to market

    d. Proximity to suppliers

    e. Proximity to customers

    f. Crime rates

    g. Quality of life for employees

    h. Cost of living

    i. The need to train or retrain the local workforce

  3. Manufacturers often choose sites that are **CLOSE TO INEXPENSIVE LABOR** or to the **RIGHT KIND OF LABOR.**

    a. **LOW-COST LABOR** remains the key reason manufacturers move their plants, even though labor cost is becoming a smaller portion of total production costs.

    b. Firms should maintain the **SAME QUALITY STANDARDS AND FAIR LABOR PRACTICES** wherever they produce.

  4. Another reason for relocating facilities is access to **INEXPENSIVE RESOURCES.**

<u>lecture link 9-7</u>

URBAN AGRICULTURE IN DETROIT

In cities that have lost large manufacturers, civic planners have found new uses for vacant lots. (See the complete lecture link on page 9.66 in this manual.)

<u>bonus case 9-3</u>

ORECK: AFTER THE STORM

Hurricane Katrina affected every organization in its path. This case focuses on Oreck Corporation's decision to close its Mississippi plant at Long Beach. (See the complete case, discussion questions, and suggested answers beginning on page 9.81 of this manual.)

MAKING

ethical

decisions

(Text page 246

PPT 9-35

Stay or Leave

(See complete PowerPoint slide notes on page 9.53.)

5. The most important resource is **PEOPLE**, so companies tend to cluster where they find smart and talented people.

6. **REDUCING TIME TO MARKET,** such as access to modes of transportation, is critical to successful global competition.

7. Locating **CLOSE TO SUPPLIERS** cuts the cost of distribution.

8. Many businesses are **BUILDING FACTORIES OVERSEAS** to get closer to international customers.

9. When U.S. firms select foreign sites, they also study the **QUALITY OF LIFE** for workers and managers.

10. Site selection has become a critical issue in production and operations management.

D. **TAKING OPERATIONS MANAGEMENT TO THE INTERNET**

1. Many rapidly growing companies **OUTSOURCE** engineering, design, manufacturing, and other tasks.

2. Companies are creating an **INTERFIRM** process, creating new relationships with suppliers over the Internet.

3. Coordination between companies can be as close as coordination among departments in a single firm.

E. **FACILITY LOCATION IN THE FUTURE**

1. New developments in information technology are

PPT 9-36

Operations Management on the
Internet

(See complete PowerPoint slide notes on page 9.54.)

**critical thinking
exercise 9-3
SITE SELECTION**

This exercise explores the factors managers consider in choosing the site for manufacturing plants. (See complete exercise on page 9.73 of this manual.)

giving firms and employees more **FLEXIBILITY** in choosing locations.

2. _**TELECOMMUTING**_, working from home via computer, is a major trend.

3. Today, a big incentive to locate in a particular location is the **TAX SITUATION** and **DEGREE OF GOVERNMENT SUPPORT.**

4. Although some states and local governments have higher taxes, they can offer tax reductions and other supports to attract new businesses.

F. **FACILITY LAYOUT**

1. _**FACILITY LAYOUT**_ is the physical arrangement of resources (including people) in the production process.

   a. The facility layout depends on what processes are to be performed.

   b. For **SERVICES**, the layout is usually designed to help the consumer find and buy things.

   c. Increasingly, that means giving customers access via the **INTERNET**.

   d. Many stores are adding **KIOSKS** that help customers find things on the Internet.

2. For **MANUFACTURING PLANTS**, efficient facilities layout can lead to cost savings.

   a. In an **ASSEMBLY LINE LAYOUT** workers do only a few tasks at a time

   b. Many firms are moving toward a **MODULAR LAYOUT**, in which teams of workers combine to produce more complex units of the final product.

PPT 9-37
Future Facility Location

(See complete PowerPoint slide notes on page 9.54.)

lecture link 9-8
WYETH BIOTECH

Wyeth's Biotech unit is using flexible manufacturing and performance bonuses to change the way it produces drugs. (See the complete lecture link on page 9.67 in this manual.)

PPT 9-38
Setting Up the Facility

(See complete PowerPoint slide notes on page 9.54.)

critical thinking exercise 9-4
DESIGNING PLANT LAYOUT

Students are asked to research and design a plant layout for a production firm. (See complete exercise on page 9.75 of this manual.)

PPT 9-39
Facility Layout Options

(See complete PowerPoint slide notes on page 9.55.)

PPT 9-40
Assembly Line Layout

TEXT FIGURE 9.2
Typical Layout Design
(Text page 248)

(See complete PowerPoint slide notes on page 9.55.)

    c. In a **FIXED-POSITION LAYOUT,** workers gather around the product to be completed.

    d. A **PROCESS LAYOUT** is one in which similar equipment and functions are grouped together.

G. **MATERIALS REQUIREMENT PLANNING**

    1. ***MATERIALS REQUIREMENT PLANNING (MRP)*** is a computer-based production management system that uses sales forecasts to make sure the needed parts and materials are available at the right time and place.

    2. **ENTERPRISE RESOURCE PLANNING (ERP)** is a newer version of MRP that combines the computerized functions of all the divisions and subsidiaries of the firm—such as finance, human resources, and order fulfillment—into a single integrated software program that uses a single database.

    3. The result is shorter time between orders and payment plus better customer service.

H. **PURCHASING**

    1. ***PURCHASING*** is the function in a firm that searches for quality material resources, finds the best suppliers, and negotiates the best price for quality goods and services.

    2. In the past, manufacturers dealt with many different suppliers.

    3. Today, they rely more heavily on one or two vendors, and the relationship between suppliers and manufacturers is much closer.

PPT 9-41
Modular Layout

(See complete PowerPoint slide notes on page 9.55.)

PPT 9-42
Process Layout

(See complete PowerPoint slide notes on page 9.56.)

PPT 9-43
Fixed-Position Layout

(See complete PowerPoint slide notes on page 9.56.)

PPT 9-44
MRP and ERP

(See complete PowerPoint slide notes on page 9.56.)

PPT 9-45
Purchasing

(See complete PowerPoint slide notes on page 9.57.)

4. **INTERNET-BASED PURCHASING SERVICES** allow companies to find the best supplies at the best price.

I. **JUST-IN-TIME INVENTORY CONTROL**

1. Holding parts and other items in warehouses is one major cost of production.

2. ***JUST-IN-TIME (JIT) INVENTORY CONTROL*** is a production process in which a minimum of inventory is kept on the premises and parts, supplies, and other needs are delivered just in time to go on the assembly line.

   a. To work effectively, however, JIT requires an accurate production schedule.

   b. Suppliers deliver their products "just in time" to go on the assembly line; a **MINIMUM INVENTORY** is kept.

   c. To work efficiently, JIT requires **CLOSE COORDINATION** among selected suppliers.

3. JIT systems make sure the right **MATERIALS** are at the right **PLACE** at the right time at the cheapest **COST** to meet customer needs.

4. JIT is problematic when there is significant distance between firms. *The text uses the example of Japan's disruption due to the 2010 earthquake and tsunami.*

J. **QUALITY CONTROL**

1. ***QUALITY*** is consistently producing what the customer wants while reducing errors before and after delivery to the customer.

lecture link 9-9
SPYING ON THE GREEN GIANT

In the early years of production, Green Giant managers resorted to spying to learn the secrets of canning. (See the complete lecture link on page 9.67 in this manual.)

PPT 9-46
Inventory Control

(See complete PowerPoint slide notes on page 9.57.)

bonus case 9-4
KAIZEN: REDESIGNING THE MANUFACTURING PROCESS

Manufacturing consultant Anand Sharma advises manufacturers on how to utilize the Japanese concept of kaizen with an American flavor. (See the complete case, discussion questions, and suggested answers beginning on page 9.83 of this manual.)

PPT 9-47
Quality Control

(See complete PowerPoint slide notes on page 9.57.)

a. Historically, quality control was often done at the **END OF THE PRODUCTION LINE** by a quality control department.

b. Quality management occurred after production, when the product has already been produced.

c. Companies realized that quality control should be part of the operations management planning process.

2. Firms now use **MODERN QUALITY CONTROL STANDARDS** such as Six Sigma.

a. *SIX SIGMA QUALITY* is a quality measure that allows only 3.4 defects per million opportunities.

b. *STATISTICAL QUALITY CONTROL (SQC)* is the process some managers use to continually monitor all phases of the production process to ensure that quality is being built into the product from the beginning.

c. *STATISTICAL PROCESS CONTROL (SPC)* is the process of taking statistical samples of product components at each stage of the production process and plotting those results on a graph.

d. Any variances from quality standards are recognized and can be corrected if beyond the set standards.

e. Checking products against standards all along the production process eliminates the need for quality control inspection at the end.

<u>lecture link 9-10</u>
MOTOROLA AND SIX SIGMA

The philosophy of Six Sigma is most closely identified with Jack Welch and GE, but Motorola invented it in the late 1970s. (See the complete lecture link on page 9.45 of this manual.)

PPT 9-48
Statistical Quality Control and
Statistical Process Control

(See complete PowerPoint slide notes on page 9.58)

      f.   This approach to quality control is often called the **DEMING CYCLE** (after the late W. Edwards Deming): **P**lan, **D**o, **C**heck, **A**ct (PDCA).

      g.   Emphasis is placed on **CUSTOMER SATISFACTION**.

K. **THE BALDRIGE AWARDS**

   1. One standard for quality was set with the introduction of the **MALCOLM BALDRIGE NATIONAL QUALITY AWARDS** in 1987.

   2. To qualify, a company has to show quality in **SEVEN KEY AREAS**:

      a.   Leadership

      b.   Strategic planning

      c.   Customer and market focus

      d.   Information and analysis

      e.   Human resources focus

      f.   Process management

      g.   Business results

   3. The focus is shifting to provide **TOP-QUALITY CUSTOMER SERVICE** in all respects.

L. **ISO 9000 AND ISO 14000 STANDARDS**

   1. The **INTERNATIONAL ORGANIZATION FOR STANDARDIZATION (ISO)** is a worldwide federation of national standards bodies that set the global measures for the quality of individual products.

   2. ***ISO 9000*** is the common name given to quality management and assurance standards.

PPT 9-49
The Baldrige Awards

(See complete PowerPoint slide notes on page 9.58.)

PPT 9-50
The Winners Are . . .

(See complete PowerPoint slide notes on page 9.58.)

PPT 9-51
What Is ISO?

(See complete PowerPoint slide notes on page 9.59.)

3. The latest standards are called **ISO 9001:2008.**

4. The **EUROPEAN UNION** is demanding that companies doing business with the EU be certified by ISO standards.

5. **_ISO 14000_** is a collection of the best practices for managing an organization's impact on the environment.

6. Today, ISO 9000 and 14000 standards have been blended so a firm can work on both at once.

learning goal 5

Explain the use of PERT and Gantt charts to control manufacturing processes.

V. CONTROL PROCEDURES: PERT AND GANTT CHARTS

A. The production manager's job is to ensure that products are manufactured and delivered on time.

B. **PROGRAM EVALUATION AND REVIEW TECHNIQUE (PERT)**

1. **_PROGRAM EVALUATION AND REVIEW TECHNIQUE (PERT)_** is a method for analyzing the tasks involved in completing a given project, estimating the time needed to complete each task, and identifying the minimum time needed to complete the total project.

2. **STEPS IN USING PERT**

    a. *Step 1:* Analyzing and sequencing tasks that need to be done

    b. *Step 2:* Estimating the time needed to complete each task

progress
assessment
(Text page 251)

PPT 9-52
Progress Assessment

(See complete PowerPoint slide notes on page 9.59.)

PPT 9-53
PERT

(See complete PowerPoint slide notes on page 9.60.)

PPT 9-54
Steps Involved in PERT

(See complete PowerPoint slide notes on page 9.60.)

    c. *Step 3:* Drawing a PERT network illustrating the information from steps 1 and 2

    d. *Step 4:* Identifying the ***CRITICAL PATH***, the sequence of tasks that takes the longest time to complete. (This is referred to as the **CRITICAL PATH** because a delay in the time needed to complete this path would cause the project or production run to be late.)

3. **DRAWING A PERT CHART**

    a. *The text uses the example of producing a music video.*

    b. **SQUARES** on the chart indicate **COMPLETED TASKS**.

    c. **ARROWS** indicate the **TIME NEEDED** to complete each task.

    d. The path from one completed task to another shows the relationships among tasks.

4. A PERT network can include thousands of events over many months, and is usually done by computer.

5. The ***GANTT CHART*** is a bar graph showing production managers what projects are being worked on and what stage they are in at any given time.

    a. The Gantt chart calculations, once done by hand, are now computerized.

    b. Using a Gantt-like computer program, a manager can trace the production process minute by minute.

critical thinking
exercise 9-5
DRAWING A PERT DIAGRAM

This exercise lets students design a PERT diagram for various production processes. (See complete exercise on page 9.76 of this manual.)

PPT 9-55
PERT Chart for a Music Video

TEXT FIGURE 9.3
PERT Chart for a Music Video
(Text page 252)

(See complete PowerPoint slide notes on page 9.61.)

PPT 9-56
Gantt Charts

(See complete PowerPoint slide notes on page 9.61.)

PPT 9-57
Gantt Chart for a Doll Factory

TEXT FIGURE 9.4
Gantt Chart for a Doll Manufacturer
(Text page 253)

(See complete PowerPoint slide notes on page 9.61.)

VI. PREPARING FOR THE FUTURE

    A. There are tremendous opportunities for careers in operations management.

    B. Relatively few college students major in production and operations management, creating opportunities for those students who do.

VII. SUMMARY

progress
assessment
(Text page 253)

PPT 9-58
Progress Assessment   (See complete PowerPoint slide notes on page 9.62.)

PowerPoint slide notes

Chapter Title

Learning Goals

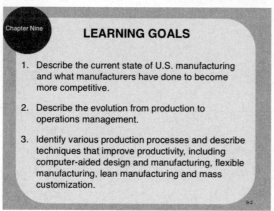

Learning Goals

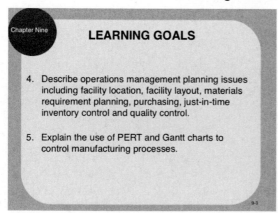

UNDERSTANDING BUSINESS: Instructor's Resource Manual

Company: Allen-Bradley

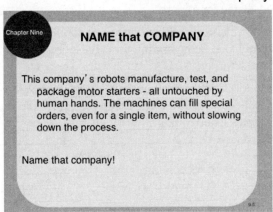

Students are often surprised to read that the United States is the world's leading manufacturer, producing 25% of all goods produced worldwide. To start a discussion ask the students, What items do companies in the United States produce?

PPT 9-7
What's Made in the USA?

1. This slide presents the leading goods manufactured in the United States.

2. Ask the students, Why are the goods on the slide manufactured in the United States? *(Students' answers will vary but should focus on the abundance of certain factors of production and the United States' comparative advantage in the production of capital-intensive products, topics that were covered earlier in the text.)*

3. To determine what goods are manufactured in a particular state use the Bureau of Economic Analysis website (www.bea.gov).

PPT 9-8
Exporters Extraordinaire

1. This slide identifies the 10 leading manufacturing states in terms of amount of products made in the United States for export.

2. Ask the students if they are surprised about any of the states listed being among the largest employers in manufacturing.

3. As mentioned in the previous slide, it might be useful to explore what items are being produced in each of the states listed in this slide by visiting www.bea.gov.

PPT 9-9
Massive Manufacturers

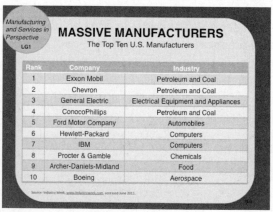

1. This slide presents the top 10 manufacturers (based on revenues) according to *Industry Week*'s list of the 500 largest publicly held U.S. manufacturing companies.

2. One quick observation from this slide—it is dominated by oil and energy companies.

3. Ask the students, How much do you pay per gallon of gas? Does that have any impact on this listing? *(Answer is obvious—the higher the gas price, the more money the oil companies make in both revenues and profits.)*

PPT 9-10
Key Word: Sustainability

KEY WORD:
SUSTAINABILITY
(Thinking Green)

- The market for new green products and services is almost endless.
- Given the rate of population growth, it's important to plan ahead for a world with limited resources.
- Companies like DuPont, Michelin, Chevron and Nokia are working on sustainability projects.
- Procter & Gamble and Kaiser Permanente issue their own mandatory sustainability scorecards to their supply chains.

9-10

PPT 9-11
Top Paying Service Jobs

Manufacturing and Services in Perspective
LG1

TOP PAYING SERVICE JOBS

- The U.S. economy is no longer manufacturing based.
- 85% of jobs are in the service sector.
- The top-paying service jobs in the U.S. are in:
  - Legal services
  - Medical services
  - Entertainment
  - Accounting
  - Finance
  - Management consulting

9-11

PPT 9-12
Remaining Competitive in Global Markets

Manufacturers and Service Organizations Become More Competitive
LG1

REMAINING COMPETITIVE in GLOBAL MARKETS

- U.S. is still the leader in nanotechnology and biotechnology.
- How can U.S. businesses maintain a competitive edge?
  - Focusing on customers
  - Maintaining close relationships with suppliers
  - Practicing continuous improvement
  - Focusing on quality
  - Saving on costs through site selection
  - Relying on the Internet to unite companies
  - Adopting new production techniques.

9-12

The famous economist Joseph Schumpeter believed in continuous improvement and discussed capitalism as a force for creative destruction. If the United States is to remain competitive, the nation as a whole must continually innovate, eschewing old, inefficient industries in favor of capital-intensive knowledge-driven industries.

PPT 9-13
Learning from Germany

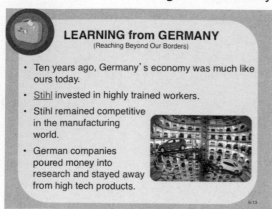

LEARNING from GERMANY
(Reaching Beyond Our Borders)

- Ten years ago, Germany's economy was much like ours today.
- Stihl invested in highly trained workers.
- Stihl remained competitive in the manufacturing world.
- German companies poured money into research and stayed away from high tech products.

PPT 9-14
Production and Production Management

From Production to Operations Management
LG2

PRODUCTION and PRODUCTION MANAGEMENT

- **Production --** *The creation of goods using land, labor, capital, entrepreneurship and knowledge (the factors of production).*
- **Production Management --** *All the activities managers do to help firms create goods.*

PPT 9-15
Operations Management

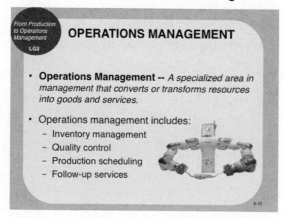

From Production to Operations Management
LG2

OPERATIONS MANAGEMENT

- **Operations Management --** *A specialized area in management that converts or transforms resources into goods and services.*
- Operations management includes:
  - Inventory management
  - Quality control
  - Production scheduling
  - Follow-up services

PPT 9-16
Operations Management in the Service Sector

PPT 9-17
There's an App for That

This slide shows the top iPad apps that help service businesses increase productivity.

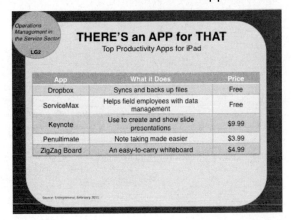

PPT 9-18
Progress Assessment

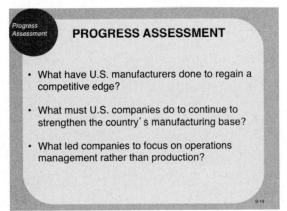

1. Manufacturers have regained a competitive advantage by focusing on the following: satisfying the needs of customers, maintaining a close relationship with suppliers to make sure they are meeting customer needs, practicing continuous improvement, focusing on quality, saving on costs through better site selection, using new technologies, adopting new production techniques.

2. To strengthen the nation's manufacturing base will require an adjustment and recognition of the new realities in manufacturing. This will require focusing on new technologies, such as the green ventures discussed in your textbook.

3. The nature of business has changed dramatically in the past 20 years, forcing companies to focus on operations management. One change is the shift from a manufacturing economy to one dominated by the service industry. Operations management is a more specialized area of management that converts resources into useful outputs.

PPT 9-19
The Production Process

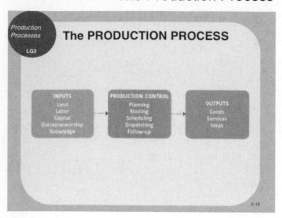

PPT 9-20
Form Utility

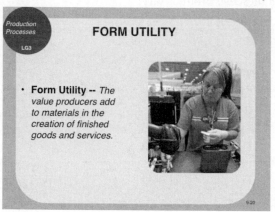

PPT 9-21
Grove's Basic Production Requirements

Andrew Grove is the former chair of computer chip manufacturer Intel.

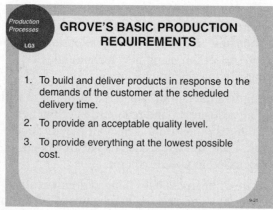

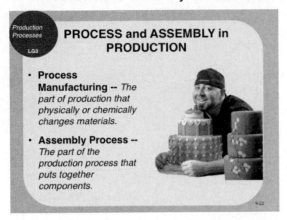

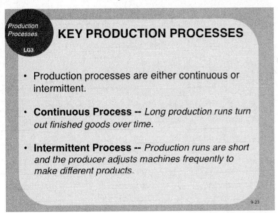

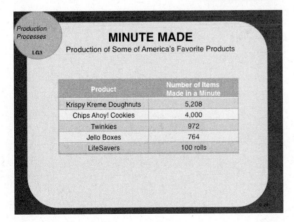

1. This slide presents the production efficiency of various products.

2. Before introducing this slide, it would be interesting to ask the students to take a guess: How many Krispy Kreme Doughnuts or Chips Ahoy! Cookies are made every minute?

3. Again, it is important to reinforce the point that production efficiency directly translates into cost savings and therefore profits.

PPT 9-25
Developments Making U.S.
Companies More Competitive

PPT 9-26
Computer-Aided
Design and Manufacturing

PPT 9-27
Computer-Integrated Manufacturing

PPT 9-28
Flexible Manufacturing

FLEXIBLE MANUFACTURING

- **Flexible Manufacturing** -- *Designing machines to do multiple tasks so they can produce a variety of products.*

- Allen-Bradley uses flexible manufacturing to build motor starters.

- 26 machines and robots build, test and package parts.

9-28

PPT 9-29
Lean Manufacturing

LEAN MANUFACTURING

- **Lean Manufacturing** -- *Using less of everything than in mass production.*

- Compared to others, lean companies:
  - Take half the human effort.
  - Have half the defects in finished products.
  - Require one-third the engineering effort.
  - Use half the floor space.
  - Carry 90% less inventory.

9-29

PPT 9-30
Mass Customization

MASS CUSTOMIZATION

- **Mass Customization** -- *Tailoring products to meet the needs of a large number of individual customers.*

- More manufacturers are learning to customize.

- Mass customization exists in the service sector too.

9-30

PPT 9-31
Mass Customization of Candy

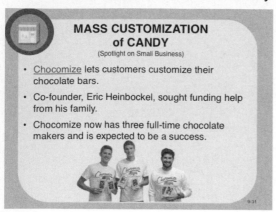

PPT 9-32
Progress Assessment

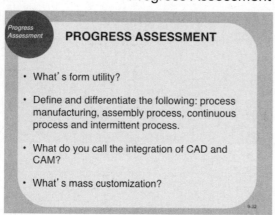

1. Form utility is the value producers add to materials in the creation of finished goods and services. For example, when a company transforms raw steel into the body of an automobile it is creating form utility.

2. Process manufacturing physically or chemically changes materials, such as turning sand into glass or computer chips. The assembly process puts together components to create a product. For example, cars are made through an assembly process that puts together the frame, engine, and other parts. Continuous process involves long production runs turning out finished goods over time. For example, a plant that makes plastic cups is run on a continuous process. Rather than using long runs, an intermittent process involves short runs that respond directly to specific customer orders. An example of this process would include manufacturers of men's custom business suits.

3. The integration of CAD and CAM is referred to as computer-integrated manufacturing or CIM.

4. Mass customization is the process of tailoring products to meet the demands of a large number of individual customers. One example of this process is NIKEiD which allows customers to design athletic shoes by choosing from a variety of colors and designs. For more information on this process go to www.nikeid.nike.com.

OPERATIONS MANAGEMENT

- Operations management planning helps solve problems like:
  - Facility location
  - Facility layout
  - Materials requirement planning
  - Purchasing
  - Inventory control
  - Quality control

9-33

FACILITY LOCATION

- **Facility Location --** *The process of selecting a geographic location for a company's operations.*

- Rising numbers of Internet businesses means brick-and-mortar retailers must find great locations.

9-34

STAY or LEAVE
(Making Ethical Decisions)

- Potential of low-cost labor is very attractive to companies hoping to remain competitive.

- However, shuttering operations and moving can often cause severe economic problems in dependent areas.

- What would you do if you were the CEO of ChildrenWear Industries faced with this problem?

9-35

PPT 9-36

Operations Management on the Internet

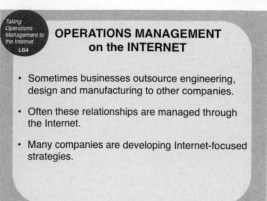

OPERATIONS MANAGEMENT on the INTERNET

Taking Operations Management to the Internet — LG4

- Sometimes businesses outsource engineering, design and manufacturing to other companies.

- Often these relationships are managed through the Internet.

- Many companies are developing Internet-focused strategies.

9-36

PPT 9-37

Future Facility Location

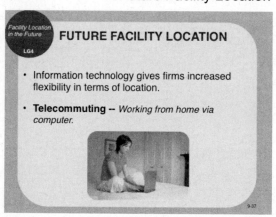

FUTURE FACILITY LOCATION

Facility Location in the Future — LG4

- Information technology gives firms increased flexibility in terms of location.

- **Telecommuting --** *Working from home via computer.*

9-37

PPT 9-38

Setting Up the Facility

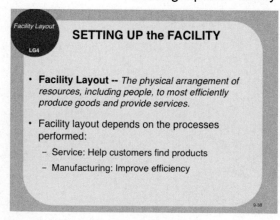

SETTING UP the FACILITY

Facility Layout — LG4

- **Facility Layout --** *The physical arrangement of resources, including people, to most efficiently produce goods and provide services.*

- Facility layout depends on the processes performed:
  - Service: Help customers find products
  - Manufacturing: Improve efficiency

9-38

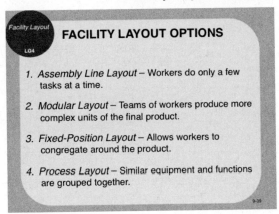

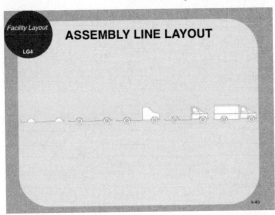

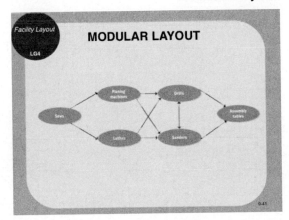

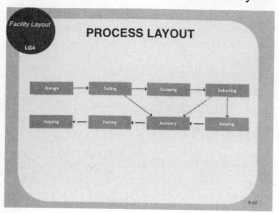

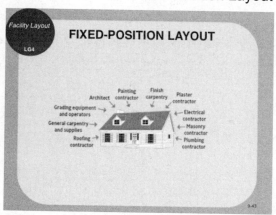

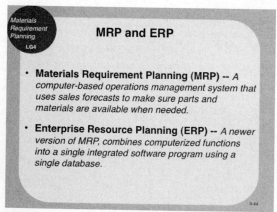

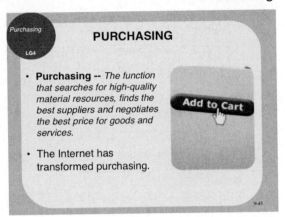

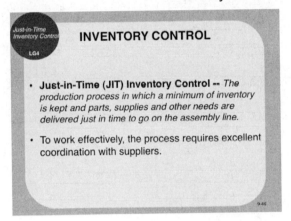

1. A JIT system makes sure the right materials are at the right place at the right time at the cheapest cost to meet both customer and production needs.

2. *To start a discussion with students ask the following question: While the benefits of the JIT system are obvious, what are some of the drawbacks?*

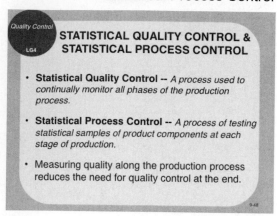

**STATISTICAL QUALITY CONTROL &
STATISTICAL PROCESS CONTROL**

Quality Control
LG4

- **Statistical Quality Control --** *A process used to continually monitor all phases of the production process.*

- **Statistical Process Control --** *A process of testing statistical samples of product components at each stage of production.*

- Measuring quality along the production process reduces the need for quality control at the end.

9-48

The BALDRIGE AWARDS

The Baldrige Awards
LG4

- Companies can apply for awards in these areas:
  - Manufacturing
  - Services
  - Small Businesses
  - Non-Profit/Government
  - Education
  - Healthcare

9-49

THE WINNERS ARE...
2010 Baldrige Award Recipients

The Baldrige Awards
LG4

Company	Category	Where from?
MEDRAD	Manufacturing	Warrendale, PA
Nestlé Purina PetCare	Manufacturing	St. Louis, MO
Freese and Nichols	Small Business	Ft. Worth, TX
K & N Management	Small Business	Austin, TX
Studer Group	Small Business	Gulf Breeze, FL
Advocate Good Samaritan Hospital	Healthcare	Downers Grove, IL
Montgomery County Public Schools	Education	Rockville, MD

Source: National Institute of Standards and Technology, www.quality.nist.gov, accessed June 2011.

1. This slide presents the 2010 Baldrige National Quality Award recipients.

2. Awardees included two manufacturers, three small businesses, one health care system, and one school system.

3. To better understand the process, have students spend time reviewing the www.nist.gov website.

PPT 9-51
What Is ISO?

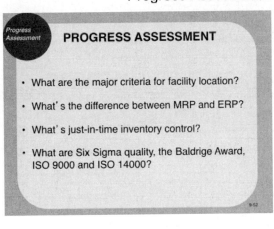

ISO is the world's largest developer and publisher of international standards. The purpose of ISO is to form a bridge between the public and private sectors. ISO is based in Switzerland.

PPT 9-52
Progress Assessment

1. Managers must always consider the customer and the impact on customers' ability to use the company's services and to communicate about their needs. Other criteria that need to be considered include labor costs, availability of resources, access to transportation, proximity to customers, suppliers, crime rates, quality of life for employees, and the cost of living, to mention but a few.

2. Materials requirement planning (MRP) is a computer-based operations management system that uses sales forecasts to make sure needed parts and materials are available at the right time and place. Enterprise resource planning (ERP), a newer version of MRP, combines the computerized functions of all the divisions and subsidiaries of the firm into a single integrated software program that uses a single database.

3. One major expense in the production process is the holding of parts. The goal of just-in-time inventory is to eliminate or reduce that cost. Just-in-time inventory systems keep a minimum of inventory on the premises and deliver parts only as they are needed on the factory floor.

4. Six Sigma is a quality-control standard that sets a benchmark of no more than 3.4 defects per million opportunities. The Baldrige Award was created in 1987 to promote a standard for overall quality in the following areas: manufacturing, services, small business, education, and health care. The award was named after Malcolm Baldrige, the late U.S. secretary of commerce. The International Organization for Standardization, or ISO, is a worldwide

federation of national standards bodies from more than 140 countries. This nongovernmental organization establishes global measures for the quality of individual products. ISO 9000 is the common name given to quality management and assurance standards, while ISO 14000 is a collection of the best practices for managing an organization's environmental impact

PPT 9-53
PERT

The program evaluation and review technique (PERT) was developed in the 1950s with the construction of the Navy's Polaris submarine project.

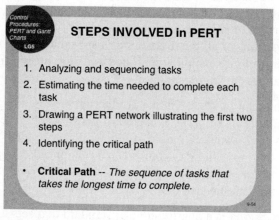

PPT 9-54
Steps Involved in PERT

PPT 9-55

PERT Chart for a Music Video

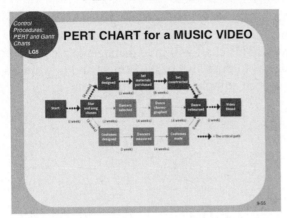

PPT 9-56

Gantt Charts

Henri Gantt created the Gantt chart which allows management to chart workflow and improve worker productivity. The Gantt chart is the forerunner to the modern PERT chart.

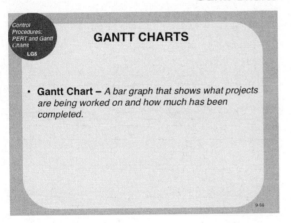

PPT 9-57

Gantt Chart for a Doll Factory

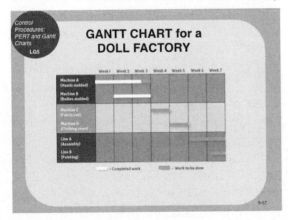

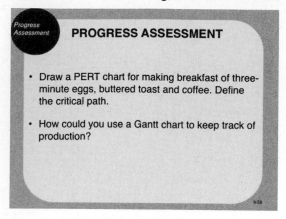

PROGRESS ASSESSMENT

Progress Assessment

- Draw a PERT chart for making breakfast of three-minute eggs, buttered toast and coffee. Define the critical path.

- How could you use a Gantt chart to keep track of production?

9-58

1. To answer this question, refer to Figure 9.3 in the textbook.

2. A Gantt chart is a scheduling mechanism used by manufacturers for measuring production progress. This chart will give management a clear idea as to the status of the project and how much has been completed at any given time.

lecture links

lecture link 9-1

THE MILITARY LEARNS FROM NASCAR

Sometimes production innovations come from unexpected sources. Recently the Pentagon has been consulting with NASCAR professionals on how to improve techniques and equipment. Carlson Technology, which advises NASCAR teams on how to shave seconds off pit stops, has advised the Army National Guard on how to significantly reduce the time it takes to change out a Humvee engine.

The Army is considering using transponders similar to the ones NASCAR installs on cars to monitor its positions in a race. These would allow military commanders to monitor all their vehicles on the battlefield.

One NASCAR innovation has already been put to use on military helicopters. NASCAR racers are equipped with layers of clear plastic sheets on the front of racecar windshields, which crews can quickly tear off when oil or grit blocks the driver's view. These Mylar sheets are now used on Black Hawk helicopters, whose windshields are vulnerable to pitting in desert conditions. A set of layered sheets cost about $1,100, a lot less expensive than the cost of replacing a $15,000 windshield.[i]

lecture link 9-2

MADE IN THE USA, BUT OWNED BY CHINA

Over the past few years, American manufacturing grew in ways that never would have been considered in the nation's industrial heyday. New factories are popping up and expanding all across the country, only they're not being built by American companies. Foreign manufacturers are setting up shop in the United States in order to bypass trade barriers and capitalize on the government's subsidies of alternative energy sources. But most surprisingly, migrating manufacturing to American shores is a dependable way for some companies to save on payroll costs.

For instance, BMW recently hired 1,000 workers for its factory in Greer, South Carolina. Among the applicants were many overqualified candidates, such as a former construction consultant and a manager who oversaw a major distribution center for Target. Despite their previous experience, the $15 an hour floor positions were seen as a boon for the town's many jobless residents. The wages paid to American staffers amounts to about half of what BMW's German employees earn. No one's complaining in Greer, though. Along with the newly added positions, the BMW factory employs 7,000 people and has generated thousands of more jobs in the region at auto part shops and suppliers.

The strangest aspect of this onshoring trend, however, remains the growing presence of Chinese manufacturers on American soil. From the beginning of 2010 through September, Chinese companies invested $2.81 billion in American assets compared to $1.73 billion in all of 2009. Clean energy subsidies and a chance to participate directly in the U.S. market drives many Chinese companies to expand to America. New manufacturing centers constitute the bulk of this new Chinese investment along with interests in retail and resource development. In 2005, such a state of affairs would have been unthinkable as legislators and business leaders alike actively muscled Chinese interests out of the United States. But as many communities furiously attempt to refill their job pools, stamping "Made in the U.S.A." on a Chinese-owned product doesn't seem as offensive anymore.[ii]

lecture link 9-3

TOLEDO'S SUNNY FUTURE

In the 1970s Toledo, Ohio, was a Rust Belt heavyweight. The city reigned as the glass capital of the country and boasted an average per-capita income ranking in the nation's top 10. But like many other cities dependent on manufacturing, deindustrialization hit it hard, causing Toledo's once lofty per-capita income to languish in America's bottom 10 by 2000. Throughout the 1990s civic officials focused on convincing local businesses to stay in town rather than spurring on new industries. But as the recession moved unemployment into double digits, Toledo's governmental and business leaders began to realize that innovation was the only way to bring their city out of its economic doldrums.

In a remarkable partnership among government, academia, and the private sector, Toledo turned away from its glass past and into the sunny future of solar power. Two years ago, a collection of officials from each city sector met and decided that the only way to encourage innovation was to work closely together with few barriers. As a result, the University of Toledo expanded its solar power research staff by hiring top professionals in the field. It also created a solar power business incubator to work with students, professors, and entrepreneurs to build new solar energy companies and manufacturers. Much of the funding granted to these companies and the university came from government subsidies aimed at expanding the solar industry quickly.

Some 6,000 employees now work in Toledo's solar sector. Four solar companies graduated from the University of Toledo's incubator and six more are still working in the program. Owens Community College also played a substantial role in expanding solar manufacturing in Toledo, training 255 solar installers since 2004. Each month members of the city's business, academic, and civic sectors, who aptly dubbed themselves "the partners," meet to discuss Toledo's solar future as well as opportunities in other industries. Although Toledo may not recapture its glory days, through cooperation among its civic leaders it may be able to forge a new identity that will take it through the recession and beyond.[iii]

lecture link 9-4

SPEEDING UP THE DRIVE-THROUGH

The average service time for a fast-food retailer has not changed in recent years. Technical and communication advances have reached a point of diminishing returns. Delivery time is limited by how fast workers can assemble orders, collect payment, and hand out food. Now fast-food retailers are trying to improve the speed of delivery service to customers pulling up at the take-out window.

Drive-through purchases now represent a huge portion of sales. For Burger King, window sales are 70% of total sales. To improve speed, outlets are concentrating on reducing mistakes in orders and making ordering easier.

Pam Farber, daughter of Wendy's founder Dave Thomas, remembers that when she worked at one of her father's fast-food stores in the 1970s, customers were frequently baffled by the drive-through concept. She often had to run outside with a pen and pad to help customers who were confused by the bull-horn speakers.

Customers are now comfortable with the drive-through procedure and expect better and faster service. To improve the ordering process, Wendy's is replacing some text on menus with pictures. It is also placing awnings over menu boards to shield customers from rain and snow. McDonald's and Checkers Drive-In Restaurants have started using confirmation screens, allowing customers to make corrections to their order before pulling up to the window. At McDonald's, that technology has boosted accuracy by more than 11%.

Hyperactive Technologies in Pittsburgh has developed a computer system called "Hyperactive Bob." The system tells managers how much food they need to prepare by counting vehicles in the drive-through line and adjusting for current promotions. McDonald's is also experimenting with outsourcing, using central call centers rather than cashiers to take orders from drive-through customers.[iv]

lecture link 9-5

AMERICA'S ROBOTICS REBOUND

In the early 1960s when America was at the forefront of robotics, a New Jersey company called Unimation unveiled the world's first industrial robot at a GM plant. As the years passed, however, the American robotics industry started to rust. By 1991 the Commerce Department declared, "The U.S. is nearly out of the industrial robot business." Taking up the mantle instead were German, Japanese, and South Korean companies that had blown past their American competition years before.

Today American tech companies are enjoying a revival in the growing business of service robotics. The market is comprised of robots in such varied areas as defense, space, health care, and consumer products. With a market valued at $13 billion worldwide already, the service robot industry is expected to double in size by 2013. And of the approximately 200 top companies currently in operation, 70 hail from the United States. The American robotics renaissance owes a great deal to big defense budgets that financed thousands of aerial drones and unmanned vehicles for Iraq and Afghanistan.

But military might alone isn't responsible for the rise in service robots. Increased computer power coupled with falling prices for laser printers, chips, and other components have made American robots smarter as well as cheaper. Along with a steady flow of $1.2 billion in venture capital from 2000 to 2010, American companies have at last been able to keep pace with their overseas rivals. Still, foreign competitors recognize the threat of the U.S. robotics industry and are spending big on research in order to undercut American firms in the long run. The South Korean government is even spending $607 million on a robotics theme park in order to inspire future engineers. Regardless of the financial might of their rivals, though, American robotics companies could triumph given the tech industry's experience working with third-party developers. Just as Apple has come together with thousands of other operations for its App and iTunes stores, so too could the robotics industry flourish with experts outside their home companies.[v]

lecture link 9-6

KODAK LEARNS SPEED

As digital photography has taken over the consumer photo market, Kodak's profitable film business has gone into a free fall. The company has long invested in digital technologies, going back to a 1976 digital-camera prototype. However, Kodak was slow to accept the shift in consumer preference from film to digital.

In 2004, CEO Daniel Carp announced a huge reorientation for the company, slashing investments in its film business and eliminating nearly a quarter of the company's 64,000-person workforce. Faced with declining profits in its core film business, Kodak embarked on reorganization with dwindling financial resources. It slashed investments in the film business and cut stockholder dividends. Investors bailed out—Kodak's stock prince plunged 18% on the day after the reorganization was announced.

But the painful reorganization has finally borne fruit. Its line of EasyShare digital cameras has grabbed market share from digital competitors. The company now leads in market share, surging ahead of rival Sony. And Carp is slowly changing the old, comfortable culture that the company developed in its hugely profitable era. "We organized the company so it was very clear who was responsible for what," says Kodak COO Antonio Perez.

The company overhauled its manufacturing process as well. Led by Charles Brown, a chemical engineer and long-time Kodak veteran, the company developed a lean production system based on Toyota's continuous-improvement approach. Dubbed the Kodak Operating System (KOS,) it forces managers to look at everything that happens in a plant in terms of waste—waste of time, space, materials. They analyze every step in a process, down to the hand movements of assembly-line workers, to look for a better way. Brown eliminated everything that did not "create value for the customer."

KOS has also led to improvements in product development. In 1997, it took 100 days from the first step of making film to when the yellow box reached the customer. Thanks to Brown's improved system, today's cycle times are half that long.

The restructuring has not been entirely smooth or completely successful. Setbacks have plagued Kodak's medical imaging division. However, CEO Carp believes that the company will emerge stronger. "The strategy is to lead our customers through the transition from traditional products to digital products."[vi]

lecture link 9-7
URBAN AGRICULTURE IN DETROIT

The rundown Detroit of today is a far cry from the industrial behemoth it once was. Less than 900,000 residents remain in a city that once housed 2 million. Civic planners fear that in the coming years the population could drop even lower to 700,000. Approximately 40 square miles of the 139-square-mile metropolis sits almost completely abandoned. Faced with street after street of empty homes, Detroit officials have no choice but to consider radical options in dealing with the city's blighted neighborhoods. As a result, city leaders and local entrepreneurs have proposed that some abandoned neighborhoods be leveled and replaced with, curiously enough, working commercial farms.

Though urban agriculture may run counter to Detroit's long-held reputation as a manufacturing hub, the city may not have any choice if it wants to survive. The city can't just let the vacant land rot, and city-built parks would only add more cost to a broken infrastructure that already can't fund basic services. Farms, on the other hand, would provide the community with jobs, local restaurants with fresh produce, and otherwise forsaken land with a purpose. Perhaps most importantly, though, farms could stimulate development in their adjacent neighborhoods and reduce the volume of excess housing.

So far the urban farming initiative has been met with high anticipation as well substantial opposition. Some community activists accused local businesspeople involved in the proposal, such as money manager John Hantz, of orchestrating a land grab. Others point to Detroit's dubious history of civic revitalization measures that hopelessly backfired. The Renaissance Center office and retail complex, for instance, succeeded only in siphoning tenants out of downtown office buildings. Consequently, 48 of those buildings remain empty. However, if Detroit's urban farming plan works only as a way to generate investor interest in the city, the program would be considered a rousing success in comparison to its many civic disasters. And at this point, any way the city can relieve its staggering 27% jobless rate is met with welcome ears. No one involved with the project believes urban farming will take the city back to its glory days as the "place where cars are made," but it could at least fill something worthwhile into an increasingly empty city.[vii]

lecture link 9-8

WYETH BIOTECH

Big gambles are nothing new to pharmaceutical companies. The next drug in the pipeline may be the cure for AIDS or it may be so flawed it is dropped. Success rates are less than 10% for new drugs in production. Wyeth BioPharma is no exception. But in the 1990s Wyeth hedged its bets acquiring two of the country's most promising biotech companies, Genetics Institute and American Cyanamid, companies working on an unconventional approach. Instead of creating a new drug through the traditional process of R&D, biotech companies cultivate living cells and use them to manufacture complex, large-molecule drugs. Wyeth looked to its two new acquisitions to spread the R&D risk and help change the company's culture. The combination of Wyeth, Genetics Institute, and American Cyanamid was christened Wyeth BioPharma, or Wyeth Biotech.

There are scores of biotech products in the pipeline now, from anti-inflammatory drugs to treatments for cancer. Forty to 45% of Wyeth's revenues now come from biotech. But in addition to the new products, the biotech firms brought something else, a willingness to take risks and rewarding employees not for showing up but for performance. Wyeth took an unprecedented risk in 2003 by creating a new business unit devoted to the company's biotech focus.

The new approach was tested when Mike Kamarck, Wyeth's president for technical operations, spearheaded a program to give performance-based bonuses to workers at a Wyeth Biotech facility in Ireland. Wyeth longtimers wondered what on earth could be gained by giving bonuses to factory workers. But when the Irish workers met all of their stretch performance targets without logging a single hour of overtime, those skeptical senior managers started paying attention. Today, Wyeth's traditional pharma plants in China and Spain are implementing reward-driven compensation programs modeled on the biotech approach.

Another biotech mainstay that Wyeth has adopted is building production equipment that can be repurposed. Wyeth Biotech's scientists have devised ways to manufacture many different drugs using a small number of processes. When one drug's production run is finished, the equipment can switch immediately to the next. This approach lowers the cost of drug development: If a drug doesn't work out, you don't have to shutter that production facility—it can be used to make something else. The typical change-over time from one molecule to another is less than seven days. One senior Wyeth Biotech executive says it can theoretically be done in 24 hours.

The reputation of Wyeth Biotech and the resources of Big Wyeth have also helped secure partnerships with small firms. Drugs are now under development within and outside of the traditional pipeline.[viii]

lecture link 9-9

SPYING ON THE GREEN GIANT

In an official company history, Green Giant Company owned up to the fact that in the early days its own management didn't know how the canning process actually worked. Small canneries of that time hired plant superintendents who kept canning methods a secret from the company as a form of job insurance.

"George F. Winter solved this problem in 1916," says the company history, "by hiding in the rafters of the plant, watching the superintendent at work, and taking notes on his procedures." Winter's feat enabled the company to learn the actual canning process for the first time. Winter went on to become superintendent of production and a member of the board of directors until his retirement in 1954.

lecture link 9-10

MOTOROLA AND SIX SIGMA

The philosophy of Six Sigma is most closely identified with Jack Welch and GE, but Motorola actually invented it. In the late 1970s, Motorola saw its name-making markets—radios, TVs, and semiconductors—challenged or already lost due to the onslaught by Japanese manufacturers. Robert Galvin, son of the Motorola legend Paul Galvin, decided to wage a "quality" war.

Shifting in attitude from "I'd rather whine than fight" to "I'd rather fight than whine," Galvin enlisted all of the company's 50,000 employees in a 10-year crusade to achieve perfect manufacturing processes, eliminating product defects before the products are finished. Dubbed "Six Sigma" (jargon for "perfection"), the theory required an in-depth education on the competition—Asian culture, economics, politics. The staff used a specific "plan-do-check-act" work process. Within one year, Motorola reported a savings of $250 million. In 1988, it won the first Malcolm Baldrige award for quality management from the U.S. Commerce Department.ix

critical thinking exercises

Name: _____

Date: _____

critical thinking exercise 9-1

GROUP PROJECT: ORGANIZING PRODUCTION

You will need about 20 sheets of paper (regular-length scratch paper, old handouts, discarded photocopy paper, etc.) for each student and one large cardboard box for each group of students.

Designate groups of five to six students as "production groups" and one group as "evaluators." Explain that each group is a production team. Each production group's objective is to profitably produce as many *quality* paper airplanes as possible in 15 minutes. The planes' quality is to be judged on the basis of (1) uniformity of design, (2) accuracy, and (3) distance of flight when tossed. Each plane must have a company logo to prevent confusion with the planes of other groups. Completed planes are to be placed in the cardboard box designated for each group.

The evaluation team's task is to determine which production group meets the quality criteria and to verify the production teams' profit. The evaluation team can plan its evaluation process while the production groups are in production. At the end of the 15-minute production period, each production team will calculate the profit for the production run.

Stage 1: **Organizing for production** (10 minutes). Each team will design their product, develop a simple logo, build a prototype, assign duties, and discuss quality criteria: (1) uniformity of design, (2) accuracy, and (3) distance of flight.

Stage 2: **Production** (15 minutes). One member of each team should be designated "Financial Officer"—he or she will keep records of potential revenue and production costs. The rest of the team will be Production Staff, producing as many finished products as possible while meeting quality criteria.

Stage 3: **Profit calculation.** Have each production group use the profit calculation worksheet on the following page to calculate profit. Each production unit (airplane) that meets quality criteria will be purchased for $2.50. Defective products will be valued at $0. Raw materials (paper) cost $1.00 per unit. Production equipment (box) costs $25.00 rental. Each team member will be paid $5.00 in labor cost.

profit calculation worksheet

Each production unit (paper airplane) that meets quality criteria will be purchased for $2.50. Defective products will be valued at $0. Raw materials (paper) cost $1.00 per unit. Production equipment (box) costs $25.00 rental. Each team member will be paid $5.00 in labor cost.

Revenue

_____ acceptable units @ $2.50 _____

Expenses

Raw material costs:

_____ units of raw material @ $1.00 _____
(include defective units)

Equipment cost _____$25.00_____

Labor costs:

_____ team members @ $5.00 each _____

Total Expenses _____

Profit (Loss) _____

(Revenue minus expenses)

critical thinking exercise 9-2
PRODUCTION PROCESSES

The text discusses two types of manufacturing systems: Process manufacturing physically or chemically changes materials. The assembly process puts together components to make a product. Look at each of the products listed below and check whether each was produced using a process manufacturing or assembly system.

PRODUCT	PROCESS MANUFACTURING	ASSEMBLY PROCESS
Orange juice		
Hair brush		
Motor oil		
Computer		
Desk		
Textbook		
Milk		
Dress		
Coal		
Newspaper		
Telephone		

notes on critical thinking exercise 9-2

PRODUCT	PROCESS MANUFACTURING	ASSEMBLY PROCESS
Orange juice	X	
Hair brush		X
Motor oil	X	
Computer		X
Desk		X
Textbook		X
Milk	X	
Dress		X
Coal	X	
Newspaper		X
Telephone		X

critical thinking exercise 9-3
SITE SELECTION

As you drive to school or work, you probably pass a number of manufacturing plants. Choose three of these plants and see if you can figure out why the company chose to locate the plant there. The chart below lists the factors that managers consider in site selection that were discussed in your text. Check the factors that seem to apply to the companies you selected.

FACTOR IN SITE SELECTION	COMPANY A	COMPANY B	COMPANY C
Inexpensive labor			
Plenty of skilled labor			
Abundant and inexpensive resources (water, electricity, wood, coal, etc.)			
Located close to market			
Low cost of land			

<u>critical thinking exercise 9-3</u> (continued)

FACTOR IN SITE SELECTION	COMPANY A	COMPANY B	COMPANY C
Tax and government support			
Access to transportation			

critical thinking exercise 9-4
DESIGNING PLANT LAYOUT

Review the various production layouts presented in text Figure 9.2 on page 248. Choose one of the four products below and design a plant layout for a firm producing that product. To better understand how these products are produced, you can research the subject using the Internet.

Product choices:

Clock radios

Bicycles

Newsprint

Aluminum

Draw your plant design below.

critical thinking exercise 9-5
DRAWING A PERT DIAGRAM

Review the material in the text on developing a PERT diagram (text page 252).

1.   For one of the following production processes, draw a PERT diagram, including estimated completion times. Be sure to include purchasing and transportation elements.

   a.   Painting a house, inside and outside

   b.   Planting and harvesting an acre of corn

   c.   Building a Soapbox Derby racer

   d.   Landscaping a back yard (from bare dirt)

2.   Clearly identify the critical path.

bonus
cases

bonus case 9-1
THE STATE OF AMERICAN MANUFACTURING

Even before the recession, American manufacturing was on the skids. Outsourcing and technological advancements made the American worker obsolete in the eyes of many companies. And just when it seemed like it couldn't get any worse, the recession hit. Since December 2007, the manufacturing sector has lost more than 2 million jobs, roughly one out of seven positions. Nevertheless, the American manufacturing sector generates billions of dollars annually, producing everything from cars to cosmetics to computer chips. In fact, the manufacturing sector's dollar value generally continued to rise throughout 1987 and 2007. Even as jobs disappeared, American manufacturers remained afloat by producing sophisticated goods that can be built by high-skilled workers.

Though American manufacturers are keeping their heads above water at the moment, economists fear they could eventually lose their edge to foreign competitors. That may seem like old news, but the new fear for manufacturers isn't losing jobs, it's losing America's dominance in technological innovation. Foreign companies that produce high-tech items like solar panels and compact fluorescent lights are often doing the design work and product development as well. In recent years the United States began lagging behind in research and development. If this lack of innovation persists, the country could find itself without the necessary infrastructure and suppliers to continue to be a leader in high-tech manufacturing.

Foreign companies also threaten American manufacturers on their own turf. Many of the country's largest manufacturers are actually foreign companies that produce goods within the United States. In fact, approximately 1 of every 12 U.S. manufacturing workers are employed by a foreign company. Still, much of the American manufacturing industry relies on small companies that employ less than 100 workers. These companies usually provide larger companies with small items such as specialized screws. Despite the importance of these manufacturers, economists don't hold much hope that they'll reignite the United States into an industrial powerhouse. Even on a global scale, manufacturing jobs are disappearing from many foreign countries, including China, due to technological improvements.[x]

discussion questions for bonus case 9-1

1. Was the loss of traditional manufacturing inevitable in the U.S. economy?

2. Can the United States hold on to its current manufacturing base?

notes on discussion questions for bonus case 9-1

1. *Was the loss of traditional manufacturing inevitable in the U.S. economy?*

   Economists and business analysts would agree such job losses were inevitable. As discussed in Chapter 1, U.S. businesses evolved from an agricultural economy to today's service and technology-based economy.

2. *Can the United States hold on to its current manufacturing base?*

   As the case notes, this will be difficult. However, so long as American workers remain the most skilled in the world and entrepreneurs continues to innovate with new technologies and products, U.S. manufacturing will survive.

bonus case 9-2

A SMALL HOMECOMING BY AMERICAN MANUFACTURERS

Like many other companies, the recession has not been kind to construction giant Caterpillar Inc. Since late 2008 the company slashed approximately 20,000 U.S. jobs after profits plunged with the stock market. In 2009 Caterpillar cut its worldwide employment further by 17%. Now the company is in recovery mode, trying to level out after such drastic setbacks. One money-saving option for Caterpillar would seem natural for any global industrial conglomerate: move some manufacturing operations overseas to a more cost-effective country. Caterpillar, however, plans to defy the convention by relocating some of its heavy-equipment production facilities from Asia to the United States.

Caterpillar is just one of several U.S. companies that have recently begun "onshoring" some factories back to American soil. Despite outsourcing's cost advantages, the system has long been plagued by quality issues, high shipping costs, and communication difficulties. Plus, with the value of the dollar declining, the cost of importing goods back to the United States has risen, eclipsing the savings of offshoring for some companies. Domestic salaries are getting lower, too, after several trade unions agreed to lower wages in order to encourage more manufacturers to hire.

Still, though onshoring is a growing trend, it is unlikely to increase manufacturing jobs in any significant way. In Caterpillar's plan, for example, the company will consolidate production of construction excavators from two existing factories, one in Japan and the other in Illinois. While the Japanese plant will remain in production to serve the Asian market, the future is foggier for Caterpillar's American plant, which could possibly face job losses. Nevertheless, competition among local governments over where Caterpillar builds its new factory should be fierce as many states try to dig themselves out of debt.[xi]

discussion questions for bonus case 9-2

1. Will "onshoring" become an ongoing trend in the 2010s?

2. Why do states compete so fiercely for new manufacturing operations?

notes on discussion questions for bonus case 9-2

1. *Will "onshoring" become an ongoing trend in the 2010s?*

    Our best guess is that we will see more companies "onshoring" as we slowly pull out of the painful recession of the past few years. However, as the recovery takes hold and competition heats up again, we question whether manufacturers such as Caterpillar will commit to long-term production in the United States.

2. *Why do states compete so fiercely for new manufacturing operations?*

    One simple reason is jobs. The other is that new manufacturing facilities usually mean long-term commitment to a region that generates a constant tax flow. As states painfully discovered, the recession put them in rather deep debt that only increasing tax flows can remedy.

bonus case 9-3

ORECK: AFTER THE STORM

Ten days after Hurricane Katrina tore through Long Beach, Mississippi, the Oreck Corporation reopened the storm-damaged plant where it assembled its widely advertised vacuum cleaners. It hauled in generators, imported trailers to house its workers, and was hailed as a local hero. Oreck's plant, in an industrial park well north of the beach, did not flood, but it suffered damage, losing millions of dollars in inventory, according to Oreck president Thomas A. Oreck.

Then, 16 months later, Oreck announced it would close the plant and move its manufacturing out of the hurricane zone, to a new plant in Cookeville, Tennessee. The move caused an uproar across the region. Local newspapers and state officials, including Mississippi Senator Trent Lott, criticized the relocation.

The company argued it could not get enough insurance to cover the Gulf Coast plant, and could not hire enough skilled workers to replace those who never returned after the storm, mostly because they had nowhere to live. "The decision to move this plant was a very difficult one, a very painful one," said Oreck, the company president. But in late 2006 "we came to realize that conditions on the Gulf Coast had changed in ways that made doing business here very difficult."

Following the storm, finding workers was a challenge all along the coast. Signal International, which makes and repairs offshore drilling rigs, brought 200 welders and other craftsworkers from India to work in its shipyard in Pascagoula, on the eastern end of Mississippi's damaged coast.

Workers who are available are more expensive. High-paying jobs, first in federal recovery programs and then in construction, lured many workers from longtime employers. Fast-food restaurants were forced to pay 50% more than the minimum wage to attract workers.

The job market is good news for displaced workers, who will have no problem finding new jobs. Finding a new owner for the closed Oreck plant will be more difficult in the face of soaring commercial insurance rates. Because the Mississippi legislature passed a bill to limit rate increases for businesses, the remaining businesses face increases of only 100%, rather than the projected 270% rate increase before the act was passed.

The company, which has its headquarters in New Orleans, is owned by private investors and the Oreck family. Oreck said he was grateful to his workers who had helped save the business by getting the plant up and running so quickly. Some government officials are suspicious of the move, perhaps because some tax breaks on the plant were due to expire soon.[xii]

discussion questions for bonus case 9-3

1.   Why was the Oreck move so difficult to accept?

2.   What could the Oreck company have done differently?

3.   What does this decision by Thomas Oreck say about his leadership skills?

4.   Does Oreck have just cause for his decision? Should he have supporters for his decision to move to Tennessee? What decision would you have made considering the situation?

notes on discussion questions for bonus case 9-3

1. *Why was the Oreck move so difficult to accept?*

    In time of crises, those who accept the challenge and work together to make the best of the circumstances are always going to be viewed more favorably. Oreck chose to relocate. The move was a blow to the local economy faced with many uphill battles to turn negative situation into a more positive outcome.

2. *What could the Oreck company have done differently?*

    Most who criticized Oreck see a company owner, who has many resources available to him, not putting these resources to good use. Oreck had an opportunity to not only restructure his business based on the disaster but also to be a conduit to helping other business do the same. His leaving the location now adds to the problems for this area. Instead of contributing to its current needs and future success, he chose to relocate from an economy that supported his business for many years.

3. *What does this decision by Thomas Oreck say about his leadership skills?*

    Unfortunately, Oreck now has disappointed those who expected more from a company president. He chose to neglect his company mission with regard to the needs of the society that has an impact on his business. When companies are interested only in making profits and do not contribute to the betterment of the society they serve in, this sends a bad signal as to the real goals and mission of the company. In the process, Oreck is not seen as a great leader and has left many questions as to his business intentions both in the market he chose to leave and the new market he will soon operate in.

4. *Does Oreck have just cause for his decision? Should he have supporters for his decision to move to Tennessee? What decision would you have made considering the situation?*

    Oreck has his own agenda and it was revealed in his decision to leave Mississippi and relocate to Tennessee. While this is very frustrating to the local patrons and politicians of Mississippi, there will always be those who agree with his strategy to cut losses and get himself into a better situation. Oreck has shown one way to handle this disaster as a decision maker for his company. This is a good time to get students to either to support the decision made by Oreck or to explain how they would have handled the situation given what resources and opportunities he might have had to work with considering his stature and decision-making latitudes as a company president.

bonus case 9-4

KAIZEN: REDESIGNING THE MANUFACTURING PROCESS

Anand Sharma, 55, a personable manufacturing consultant who runs TBM Consulting Group in Durham, North Carolina, has a reputation for finding out what a factory is doing wrong by simply walking through it with the plant manager. Sharma usually asks the manager about the factory's "rhythm." More often than not, the manager expresses puzzlement. But Sharma, like a seasoned orchestra conductor, may already have noted off-tempo components on the plant floor—a machine with a hardly perceptible squeak here, workers laboring at an uneven pace there, too much inventory piled up.

Sharma trusts his senses to point to evidence of bad processes. In addition to looking for obvious signs (Is the plant well lit and clean?), he checks to see if operators at one part of the line are working at a very fast pace while others elsewhere are working slowly or stopping. He observes whether the progress of a part being made can be tracked from beginning to end by line of sight. Says Sharma: "Where other people see complexity, I look at how simple things can be."

The assessment and the walkabout help Sharma and the 72 manufacturing experts who work with him select the best site for their first improvement project in a plant. The TBM experts then come in to eliminate the root causes of problems on the production lines. In the process, they may restructure the whole plant operation. But they don't just tear up things and leave. Unlike consulting firms whose employees depart after a quick fix, TBM often has its experts stay at a plant for years, because it believes that improvement of operations never stops.

Sharma earned an MBA at Boston University. He kept up with manufacturing trends and attended quality-control seminars offered by the founders of the quality movement, W. Edwards Deming and Joseph Juran. By the early 1970s, Sharma was designing better and faster production lines at American Standard. "I was always trying to reach for the next level," he says.

He still had a lot to learn. The revelation of how much better manufacturing can be came in 1979 when Sharma met Toyota manufacturing guru Shigeo Shingo and was invited to see some plants in Japan. What stunned Sharma was the ability of Toyota's workers and others to replace dies on presses in minutes instead of the hours, or even days, that it took in American plants. The Japanese did this, moreover, with a very simple technology that employed compressed air to lift the thousand-pound dies as if they were feathers.

When his division of American Standard was put up for sale, Sharma and three colleagues started TBM Consulting in 1991, operating out of Sharma's home.

Today Sharma applies what he learned from the famous Toyota Production System (TPS) and adds a large dollop of Americanization. TPS is based on a Japanese update of Henry Ford's vision of integrated production. Ford was practicing just-in-time supply of raw materials and parts at the legendary River Rouge plant long before the Japanese popularized the term. TPS evolved during the transition from mass production to mass customization. Unlike the old "push" systems designed to build to inventory, TPS aims to build to customer demand in the shortest possible time and with minimum resources. Its Westernized version is now widely known as lean manufacturing. Sharma goes beyond TPS by combining both lean production and quality elements from Six Sigma into what he calls LeanSigma.

At one level, TPS is built on the concept of kaizen, Japanese for "continuous improvement." TBM experts adjust rigid Japanese methods to freer American ways when they establish kaizen methodology in a plant. In Sharma's approach, for instance, production line workers have a lot more say than Japanese workers about changes on the manufacturing floor. To assure himself of their input, Sharma refuses to work with companies that propose to lay off workers after his system is introduced; that destroys morale, he believes. Any superfluous line workers are assigned other jobs, with some becoming trainers. "We unleash the power of the people," he says.

TPS's initial kaizen study teams are constituted equally of production line workers, managers and supervisors, and office workers. The teams set up model lines and practice the changes before they are introduced on the floor. Sometimes TBM totally reorganizes production, as it did starting in 1998 at the Maytag plant in Cleveland, Tennessee, that makes gas and electric ranges. With no added workers, production of one product line zoomed by 100%. Workers' suggestions are readily accepted and incorporated into Cleveland's new system, which is deemed always open to improvement. That one plant has cut its annual production costs by $7 million and reduced its inventory by $10 million. Says Tom Briatico, vice president and general manager of the Cleveland operation: "Anand Sharma and TBM have skillfully trained us in assembly-line layouts, quick die changes, and, most important, how to manage our operations for daily improvement."[xiii]

discussion questions for bonus case 9-4

1. What concepts from this chapter were implemented by TPS? Do you see the benefits of knowing such concepts now, before you choose a place to work?

2. Notice that introducing change does not necessarily lead to the layoff of workers. They merely become more productive. Who benefits from such changes?

notes on discussion questions for bonus case 9-4

1. *What concepts from this chapter were implemented by TPS? Do you see the benefits of knowing such concepts now, before you choose a place to work?*

   Concepts from the chapter include just-in-time inventory control, lean manufacturing, quality control, facility layout, and organizational change in general. Knowing such concepts can prepare you to find the best-run plants for which to work or to become a consultant to poorly run plants. Studying some chapters that may or may not seem useful or interesting at first has benefits.

2. *Notice that introducing change does not necessarily lead to the layoff of workers. They merely become more productive. Who benefits from such changes?*

   Almost everyone benefits from having plants that are more productive. The workers make more money, the owners make more money, the public gets cheaper goods, and the United States becomes more competitive, keeping more jobs.

endnotes

[i] *Sources:* Douglas Waller, "NASCAR: The Army's Unlikely Adviser," *Time*, July 54, 2005; Stefanie A Gardin, "Army News Service: Army Adopts NASCAR Technology for Helicopters," *Defense AT & L*, May 1, 2005.

[ii] *Sources:* Peter Whoriskey, "A Bargain for BMW Means Jobs for 1,000 in S. Carolina," *The Washington Post*, October 27, 2010; David J. Lynch, "Chinese Plants Grow on U.S. Turf," *Bloomberg Businessweek*, December 28, 2010.

[iii] *Source:* Judy Keen, "Toledo Reinvents Itself as a Solar-Power Innovator," *USA Today*, June 15, 2010.

[iv] *Source:* Associated Press, "Chains Battle Speed Barrier," *The Clarion-Ledger*, January 27, 2006.

[v] *Source:* Brian Bemner, "Rise of the Machines (Again)," *Bloomberg Businessweek*, March 3, 2011.

[vi] *Source:* Unmesh Kher, "Getting Kodak to Focus," *Time Inside Business,* March 2005.

[vii] *Sources:* David Whitford, "Can Farming Save Detroit?" *Fortune*, January 18, 2010; David Runk, "Detroit Is Pondering Radical Renewal Program," Associated Press, March 9, 2010.

[viii] *Source:* Elizabeth Svoboda, "Grand Experiment," *Fast Company*, February 2009.

[ix] *Sources:* Maggie Overfelt, "The Great American Company: Quest for Perfection," *Fortune Small Business*, March 19, 2003; Tam Harbert, "Lean, Mean, Six Sigma Machines: Electronics Companies Have Used Lean Six to Trim Down, But Can It Help Them Pump Up?" *Electronic Business*, June 1, 2006.

[x] *Source:* Allison Linn, "Yes, We Do Still Make Things in America," *MSNBC*, March 15, 2010.

[xi] *Source:* Kris Maher and Bob Tita, "Caterpillar Joins 'Onshoring' Trend," *The Wall Street Journal*, March 12, 2010.

[xii] *Sources:* Leslie Eaton, "Vacuum Maker Hailed as Savior Quits Gulf Town," *The New York Times*, January 15, 2007; J. R. Welsh, "Long Beach Plant Closing Feared," *Sun Herald (Biloxi MS)*, December 2, 2006; Wally Northway, "Oreck Implementing New Call Center Plan, Closing Long Beach Facility," *Mississippi Business Journal*, September 4, 2006.

[xiii] *Sources:* Gene Bylinsky, "A Maestro of the Plant Floor" *Fortune*, March 19, 2001; "Customer Connectivity Gains Are Evidenced in Lean Manufacturing Deployments," *Manufacturing Business Technology*, December 1, 2005; John Welbes, "Reassembling the Assembly Line" *Saint Paul Pioneer Press*, August 9, 2005.

Motivating
Employees

chapter 10

what's new in this edition

additions to the 10th edition:

- Getting to Know Andrew Cherng, Founder and Co-CEO of Panda Express
- Name That Company: UPS
- Social Media in Business: Keeping the Lines Open
- Reaching Beyond Our Borders: Importance of Cultural Competency
- Video Case

revisions to the 10th edition:

- Text was revised to eliminate redundancy and tighten discussions.
- Statistical data and examples throughout the chapter were updated to reflect current information.
- Discussion was expanded on comparisons of generational characteristics in the workplace in section Motivating Employees across Generations.
- Spotlight on Small Business: Small Incentives Can Be Big Motivators

deletions from the 9th edition:

- Getting to Know Sergey Brin and Larry Page, Founders of Google
- Name That Company: Ford
- Legal Briefcase
- Thinking Green

brief chapter outline
and learning goals

Motivating Employees

Getting To Know ANDREW CHERNG of PANDA EXPRESS

I. THE VALUE OF MOTIVATION

learning goal 1

Explain Taylor's theory of scientific management.

    A.   Frederick Taylor: The Father of Scientific Management

learning goal 2

Describe the Hawthorne studies and their significance to management.

    B.   Elton Mayo and the Hawthorne Studies

learning goal 3

Identify the levels of Maslow's hierarchy of needs and apply them to employee motivation.

II. MOTIVATION AND MASLOW'S HIERARCHY OF NEEDS

learning goal 4

Distinguish between the motivators and hygiene factors identified by Herzberg.

III. HERZBERG'S MOTIVATING FACTORS

learning goal 5

Differentiate among Theory X, Theory Y, and Theory Z.

IV. MCGREGOR'S THEORY X AND THEORY Y

    A.   Theory X
    B.   Theory Y

V. OUCHI'S THEORY Z

learning goal 6

Explain the key principles of goal-setting, expectancy, reinforcement, and equity theories.

VI. GOAL-SETTING THEORY AND MANAGEMENT BY OBJECTIVES

VII. MEETING EMPLOYEE EXPECTATIONS: EXPECTANCY THEORY

VIII. REINFORCING EMPLOYEE PERFORMANCE: REINFORCEMENT THEORY

IX. TREATING EMPLOYEES FAIRLY: EQUITY THEORY

learning goal 7

Show how managers put motivation theories into action through such strategies as job enrichment, open communication, and job recognition.

X. PUTTING THEORY INTO ACTION

A.   Motivating through Job Enrichment

B.   Motivating through Open Communication

C.   Applying Open Communication in Self-Managed Teams

D.   Recognizing a Job Well Done

learning goal 8

Show how managers personalize motivation strategies to appeal to employees across the globe and across generations.

XI. PERSONALIZING MOTIVATION

A.   Motivating Employees across the Globe

B.   Motivating Employees across Generations

XII. SUMMARY

Getting to Know **PANDA EXPRESS**

Andrew Cherng is a touchy-feely kind of guy. He frequently hugs his employees at his motivational seminars. Panda Express managers are encouraged to eat a healthy diet, exercise frequently, and attend the seminars. Cherng believes if his employees engage in personal growth, that will lead to Panda Express's financial growth.

NAME THAT company

The employees of this company are told exactly how to do their jobs—and we mean exactly. For instance, they are instructed to carry their keys on their ring finger with the teeth up. If they are considered too slow, a supervisor will shadow them with a stopwatch and clipboard and prod them along. Name that company.

(Students should read the chapter before guessing the company's name: UPS.*)*

I. THE VALUE OF MOTIVATION

A. Satisfaction is an important factor in the workforce.

　1. Happy workers lead to happy customers.

　　a. Unhappy workers may leave.

　　b. Losing an employee can cost the equivalent of 6 to 18 months' salary.

　　c. There are also **"SOFT" COSTS,** such as loss of intellectual capital and decreased morale of remaining workers.

　2. **ENGAGEMENT** describes employees' level of motivation, passion, and commitment.

　　a. **ENGAGED** or **MOTIVATED EMPLOYEES** feel a connection to their company.

　　b. **DISENGAGED WORKERS** have essentially "checked out."

　　c. The lower productivity of disengaged workers costs the U.S. economy about $300 billion a year.

PPT 10-1
Chapter Title

PPT 10-2
Learning Goals

(See complete PowerPoint slide notes on page 10.48.)

PPT 10-3
Learning Goals

(See complete PowerPoint slide notes on page 10.48.)

PPT 10-4
Andrew Cherng

(See complete PowerPoint slide notes on page 10.49.)

PPT 10-5
Name That Company

(See complete PowerPoint slide notes on page 10.49.)

**critical thinking
exercise 10-1**
**MANAGING A FAMILY
BUSINESS**

Management and motivation can be difficult in family firms. This exercise presents such a situation. (See complete exercise on page 10.78 of this manual.)

    d. That number may increase in the near future because of the recent recession and its effect on employee loyalty.

   3. Motivating the right people to **JOIN AND REMAIN WITH THE ORGANIZATION** is a key function of managers.

   4. People are motivated by a variety of things.

    a. An **_INTRINSIC REWARD_** is the personal satisfaction you feel when you perform well and complete goals.

    b. An **_EXTRINSIC REWARD_** is something given to you by someone else as recognition for good work; extrinsic rewards include pay increases, praise, and promotions.

learning goal 1

Explain Taylor's theory of scientific management.

B. **FREDERICK TAYLOR: THE FATHER OF SCIENTIFIC MANAGEMENT**

   1. **FREDERICK TAYLOR'S** book _The Principles of Scientific Management_ was published in 1911.

    a. Taylor's goal was to **INCREASE WORKER PRODUCTIVITY** in order to benefit both the firm and the worker.

    b. The way to improve productivity was through **_SCIENTIFIC MANAGEMENT_**, studying workers to find the most efficient ways of doing things and then teaching people those techniques.

    c. Three elements of his approach were **TIME, METHODS**, and **RULES OF WORK.**

PPT 10-6
Intrinsic Rewards

(See complete PowerPoint slide notes on page 10.49.)

PPT 10-7
Extrinsic Rewards

(See complete PowerPoint slide notes on page 10.50.)

PPT 10-8
Fringe Benefits

(See complete PowerPoint slide notes on page 10.50.)

PPT 10-9
Taylor's Scientific Management

(See complete PowerPoint slide notes on page 10.51.)

PPT 10-10
Taylor's Four Key Principles

(See complete PowerPoint slide notes on page 10.51.)

d. ***TIME-MOTION STUDIES***, begun by Frederick Taylor, study which tasks must be performed to complete the job and the time needed to do each task.

2. Henry L. Gantt, one of Taylor's followers, developed **GANTT CHARTS,** which managers used to plot the work of employees down to the smallest detail.

3. Frank and Lillian Gilbreth used Frederick Taylor's ideas in a study of brick laying.

   a. The ***PRINCIPLE OF MOTION ECONOMY*** is the theory, developed by Frank and Lillian Gilbreth, that every job can be broken down into a series of elementary motions.

   b. They analyzed every motion (**"THERBLIG"**) to make them more efficient.

4. Scientific management viewed **PEOPLE AS MACHINES** that needed to be properly programmed.

   a. There was little concern for the **PSYCHOLOGICAL** or **HUMAN ASPECTS** of work.

   b. In some companies, the emphasis is still on **CONFORMITY TO WORK RULES** rather than on creativity, flexibility, and responsiveness.

   c. *The text uses the example of UPS.*

<u>learning goal 2</u>

Describe the Hawthorne studies and their significance to management.

C. **ELTON MAYO AND THE HAWTHORNE STUDIES**

1. The **HAWTHORNE STUDIES,** begun in 1927, were conducted by Elton Mayo at the Western Electric Company's Hawthorne plant in Cicero, Illinois.

PPT 10-11
Time-Motion Studies

(See complete PowerPoint slide notes on page 10.51.)

PPT 10-12
Are You Stressed?

(See complete PowerPoint slide notes on page 10.52.)

lecture link 10-1
**UPS'S TRUCK DRIVER BOOT
CAMP**

UPS needs to hire 25,000 new drivers to replace retiring employees. Prospective drivers go through intensive training at Integrad. (See the complete lecture link on page 10.71 in this manual.)

PPT 10-13
Taylor and UPS

(See complete PowerPoint slide notes on page 10.52.)

a. The **PURPOSE** of the studies was to determine the best lighting for optimum productivity.

b. The **PRODUCTIVITY** of the experimental group **INCREASED** compared to the control group whether the lighting was bright or dim.

c. The researchers had expected productivity to fall as the lighting was dimmed.

2. A second series of 13 experiments were conducted to see if **OTHER FACTORS**, such as temperature and humidity, contributed to increased production.

a. **PRODUCTIVITY INCREASED** during each of the 13 experimental periods.

b. When conditions were returned to their original status (before the studies were started), **PRODUCTIVITY CONTINUED TO GO UP.** Why?

3. Mayo guessed that some **HUMAN** or **PSYCHOLOGICAL FACTORS** caused the increases.

a. The workers in the test room thought of themselves as a **SOCIAL GROUP**—they felt special and worked hard to stay in the group.

b. The workers were involved in the **PLANNING** of the experiments—they felt that their ideas were respected.

c. The workers enjoyed the **SPECIAL ATMOSPHERE** and **ADDITIONAL PAY** for the increased productivity.

PPT 10-14
Hawthorne Studies: Purpose and Results

(See complete PowerPoint slide notes on page 10.53.)

4. The term ***HAWTHORNE EFFECT*** refers to the tendency for people to behave differently when they know they're being studied.

    a. The results of this study encouraged researchers to **STUDY HUMAN MOTIVATION** and the **MANAGERIAL STYLES** that lead to more productivity.

    b. Mayo's findings led to **NEW ASSUMPTIONS ABOUT EMPLOYEES.**

    c. **MONEY** was found to be a relatively ineffective motivator.

learning goal 3

Identify the levels of Maslow's hierarchy of needs and apply them to employee motivation.

II. MOTIVATION AND MASLOW'S HIERARCHY OF NEEDS

A. MASLOW'S HIERARCHY OF NEEDS

1. Psychologist Abraham Maslow believed that **MOTIVATION ARISES FROM NEED.**

    a. People are motivated to satisfy unmet needs.

    b. Satisfied needs **NO LONGER MOTIVATE.**

    c. Maslow placed needs on a **HIERARCHY** of importance.

2. ***MASLOW'S HIERARCHY OF NEEDS*** is a theory of motivation based on unmet needs, from basic physiological needs to safety, social, and esteem needs to self-actualization needs.

    a. **PHYSIOLOGICAL NEEDS**, basic survival needs including the need for food, water, and shelter

<u>lecture link 10-2</u>
MOTIVATING WITHOUT MONEY

Three ways to motivate employees during lean times. (See the complete lecture link on page 10.72 in this manual.)

<u>critical thinking
exercise 10-2</u>
DOES MONEY MOTIVATE

This exercise involves a debate among small groups as to whether or not money is a motivator. (See complete exercise on page 10.79 of this manual.)

PPT 10-15
Maslow's Theory of Motivation

(See complete PowerPoint slide notes on page 10.53.)

      b. **SAFETY NEEDS,** the need to feel secure at work and at home

      c. **SOCIAL NEEDS**, the need to feel loved, accepted, and part of the group

      d. **ESTEEM NEEDS,** the need for recognition and acknowledgment from others, as well as self-respect and a sense of status or importance

      e. **SELF-ACTUALIZATION NEEDS,** the need to develop to one's fullest potential

B. When one need is satisfied, the person is motivated to do something to satisfy a higher-level need.

    1. A **SATISFIED NEED** is no longer a motivator.

    2. If **LOWER-LEVEL NEEDS** are not met, they may reemerge and take attention away from higher-level needs.

    3. Lower-level needs are met and higher-level needs dominate in **DEVELOPED COUNTRIES**.

C. *The text uses the example of Chip Conley of Joie de Vivre.*

learning goal 4

Distinguish between the motivators and hygiene factors identified by Herzberg.

III. HERZBERG'S MOTIVATING FACTORS

A. **FREDERICK HERZBERG** used interviews to identify the factors that are most effective in generating enthusiastic work effort.

    1. Herzberg surveyed workers to find out how they rank **JOB-RELATED FACTORS**. The results were:

      a. Sense of achievement

PPT 10-16
Maslow's Hierarchy of Needs

TEXT FIGURE 10.1
Maslow's Hierarchy of Needs
(Text page 264)

(See complete PowerPoint slide notes on page 10.53.)

**critical thinking
exercise 10-3**

**TESTING MASLOW'S
HIERARCHY OF NEEDS**

This exercise asks each student to evaluate his or her needs. (See complete exercise on page 10.80 of this manual.)

bonus case 10-1

WHEN FAILURE IS THE NORM

How do you motivate employees when 96% of their projects fail? (See the complete case, discussion questions, and suggested answers beginning on page 10.86 of this manual.)

lecture link 10-3

THE BIG THRILL MOTIVATION

Another facet of motivation involves the individual's tolerance for risk taking. Some individuals have a kind of psychological urge to reach beyond the status quo and seek out novelty, change, and excitement. (See the complete lecture link on page 10.72 in this manual.)

  b. Earned recognition

  c. Interest in the work itself

  d. Opportunity for growth

  e. Opportunity for advancement

  f. Importance of responsibility

  g. Peer and group relationships

  h. Pay

  i. Supervisor's fairness

  j. Company policies and rules

  k. Status

  l. Job security

  m. Supervisor's friendliness

  n. Working conditions

 2. Herzberg noted that the **HIGHEST-RANKING FACTORS DEALT WITH JOB CONTENT.**

 3. Factors relating to job environment were not motivators.

B. **HERZBERG'S CONCLUSIONS**

 1. In Herzberg's theory of motivating factors, ***MOTIVATORS*** are job factors that cause employees to be productive and that give them satisfaction.

 2. ***HYGIENE FACTORS*** are job factors that can cause dissatisfaction if missing but that do not necessarily motivate employees if increased.

 3. The best way to motivate employees is to:

  a. Make the job interesting

  b. Help them achieve their objectives

lecture link 10-4
MCCLELLAND'S ACQUIRED NEEDS THEORY

Psychologist David McClelland proposed that humans acquire different needs over time because of life experiences. He classified these needs that affect motivation in both individuals and organizations. (See the complete lecture link on page 10.73 of this manual.)

PPT 10-17
Herzberg's Motivating Factors

(See complete PowerPoint slide notes on page 10.54.)

PPT 10-18
Job Content

(See complete PowerPoint slide notes on page 10.54.)

PPT 10-19
Job Environment

(See complete PowerPoint slide notes on page 10.55.)

PPT 10-20
Herzberg's Motivators and Hygiene Factors

TEXT FIGURE 10.2
Herzberg's Motivators and Hygiene Factors
(Text page 266)

(See complete PowerPoint slide notes on page 10.55.)

    c. Recognize their achievement through advancement and added responsibility

C. Maslow's hierarchy and Herzberg's two-factor theory are very similar.

learning goal 5

Differentiate among Theory X, Theory Y, and Theory Z.

IV. MCGREGOR'S THEORY X AND THEORY Y

A. **DOUGLAS MCGREGOR** observed that managers' attitudes generally fall into one of two different sets of managerial assumptions: **THEORY X** and **THEORY Y**.

B. TH**EORY X**

    1. The **ASSUMPTIONS** of Theory X management are:

        a. The average person **DISLIKES WORK** and will avoid it if possible.

        b. Because of this dislike, workers must be **FORCED, CONTROLLED, DIRECTED,** or **THREATENED** with punishment to be motivated to put forth the effort to achieve the organization's goals.

        c. The average worker prefers to be directed, wishes to **AVOID RESPONSIBILITY**, has relatively **LITTLE AMBITION**, and wants **SECURITY.**

        d. Primary motivators are **FEAR** and **MONEY.**

    2. The **CONSEQUENCE** of such attitudes is a manager who is very "busy."

        a. Motivation is more **PUNISHMENT** for bad work rather than **REWARD** for good work.

PPT 10-21
Comparison of the Theories of
Maslow and Herzberg

TEXT FIGURE 10.3
Comparison of Maslow's Hierarchy
of Needs and Herzberg's Theory of
Factors
(Text page 266)

(See complete PowerPoint slide notes on page 10.56)

PPT 10-22
Reignite Employees' Drive

(See complete PowerPoint slide notes on page 10.56.)

**progress
assessment**
(Text page 266)

PPT 10-23
Progress Assessment

(See complete PowerPoint slide notes on page 10.56.)

PPT 10-24
Theory X and Theory Y

(See complete PowerPoint slide notes on page 10.57.)

      b.   Theory X managers give workers little responsibility, authority, or flexibility.

      c.   Those were the assumptions behind Taylor's **SCIENTIFIC MANAGEMENT.**

   3.   Theory X management still dominates some organizations.

C. **THEORY Y**

   1.   **THEORY Y** makes entirely different **ASSUMPTIONS** about people:

      a.   Most people **LIKE WORK**; it is as natural as play or rest.

      b.   Most people **NATURALLY WORK TOWARD GOALS** to which they are committed.

      c.   The depth of a person's commitment to goals depends on the perceived **REWARDS** for achieving them.

      d.   Under certain conditions, most people not only accept but **SEEK RESPONSIBILITY.**

      e.   People are capable of using a high degree of **IMAGINATION, CREATIVITY**, and **CLEVERNESS** to solve problems.

      f.   In industry, the average person's **INTELLECTUAL POTENTIAL** is only partially realized.

      g.   People are **MOTIVATED BY A VARIETY OF REWARDS;** each worker is stimulated by a reward unique to that worker.

   2.   Theory Y emphasizes a **RELAXED MANAGERIAL ATMOSPHERE** in which workers are free to set objectives and be flexible.

lecture link 10-5
THE L-FACTOR

According to one author, likability, not intimidation, is the real key to conquering the workplace. (See complete lecture link on page 10.74 of this manual.)

PPT 10-25
Assumptions of Theory X Managers

(See complete PowerPoint slide notes on page 10.57.)

bonus case 10-2
THE SUPERMARKET MANAGER

A new employee takes initiative to identify areas for improvement, but runs into trouble when she approaches her manager with the suggestions. (See the complete case, discussion questions, and suggested answers beginning on page 10.88 of this manual.)

PPT 10-26
Assumptions of Theory Y Managers

(See complete PowerPoint slide notes on page 10.58.)

3. **EMPOWERMENT** is a key technique in meeting these objectives.

4. To be a real motivator, empowerment requires management to:

   a. Find out what people think the problems in the organization are.

   b. Let them design the solutions.

   c. Get out of the way and let them put those solutions into action.

V. OUCHI'S THEORY Z

A. Another reason to adopt a more flexible managerial style is to **MEET COMPETITION** from foreign firms.

B. In the 1980s **WILLIAM OUCHI** researched why Japanese firms seemed to be outperforming American firms.

   1. The Japanese management approach, which he called **TYPE J**, involved:

      a. Lifetime employment

      b. Consensual decision making

      c. Collective responsibility for the outcomes of decisions

      d. Slow evaluation and promotion

      e. Implied control mechanisms

      f. Nonspecialized career paths

      g. Holistic concern for employees

   2. The American management approach, called **TYPE A**, involved:

      a. Short-term employment

      b. Individual decision making

PPT 10-27
Theory Z

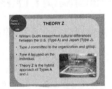

(See complete PowerPoint slide notes on page 10.58.)

      c.   Individual responsibility for the outcomes of decisions

      d.   Rapid evaluation and promotion

      e.   Explicit control mechanism

      f.   Specialized career paths

      g.   Segmented concern for employees

  3. Because American managers would not accept a concept based on another culture, Ouchi recommended a hybrid of the two approaches, **THEORY Z.**

      a.   Long-term employment

      b.   Collective decision making

      c.   Individual responsibility for the outcome of decisions

      d.   Slow evaluation and promotion

      e.   Moderately specialized career path

      f.   Holistic concern for employees

C. Economic changes (including the 2011 earthquake and tsunami) are now forcing Japanese managers to reevaluate the way they conduct business.

  1. Japanese firms need to become more **DYNAMIC** and **MORE EFFICIENT.**

  2. Some Japanese managers are changing the way they do business.

  3. *The text uses the example of how electronics giant Hitachi quit doing company calisthenics.*

  4. Many managers think that conformity has hurt Japanese business.

lecture link 10-6

THE BOSS SETS THE EXAMPLE

The CEO of Japan Airlines rides the city bus to work and eats in the employee dining room. He also cut his own salary when he had to cut employees'. (See the complete lecture link on page 10.74 of this manual.)

PPT 10-28

Theory Z

TEXT FIGURE 10.4

Theory Z: A Blend of American and Japanese Management Approaches
(Text page 269)

(See complete PowerPoint slide notes on page 10.58.)

TEXT FIGURE 10.5

A Comparison of Theories X, Y, and Z
(Text page 270)

This text figure summarizes the key elements in each approach to management.

lecture outline

Explain the key principles of goal-setting, expectancy, reinforcement, and equity theories.

VI. GOAL-SETTING THEORY AND MANAGEMENT BY OBJECTIVES

A. ***GOAL-SETTING THEORY*** is the idea that setting ambitious but attainable goals can motivate workers and improve performance if the goals are accepted, accompanied by feedback, and facilitated by organizational conditions.

1. All organization members should have basic **AGREEMENT ABOUT THE ORGANIZATION'S GOALS** and the specific objectives of each unit.

2. Peter Drucker developed one system in the 1960s called **MANAGEMENT BY OBJECTIVES (MBO)**.

B. ***MANAGEMENT BY OBJECTIVES (MBO)*** is a system of goal setting and implementation that involves a cycle of discussion, review, and evaluation of objectives among top and middle-level managers, supervisors, and employees.

1. Managers:

    a. Formulate goals in cooperation with everyone in the organization

    b. Commit employees to those goals

    c. Monitor results and reward accomplishment

2. *The Department of Defense uses MBO.*

3. Management by objectives is most effective in **RELATIVELY STABLE SITUATIONS.**

lecture link 10-7
WAL-MART GIVES BACK

Walmart shows concern for its communities by giving large charitable contributions. It also works to take care of its employees by helping them further their education through grants. (See the complete lecture link on page 10.75 in this manual.)

lecture link 10-8
SAVING A FORTUNE WITH EMPLOYEE WELLNESS

One way to show concern for employees is to develop wellness programs. Companies such as Johnson & Johnson have also learncd it helps their own pocketbooks as well. (See the complete lecture link on page 10.75 in this manual.)

PPT 10-29
Goal-Setting Theory

(See complete PowerPoint slide notes on page 10.59.)

PPT 10-30
Applying Goal-Setting Theory

(See complete PowerPoint slide notes on page 10.59.)

4. Managers need to understand the difference between helping and coaching subordinates:

    a. **HELPING** tends to make subordinates weak and dependent.

    b. **COACHING** makes them feel capable and part of the team.

5. **HELPING** is working with the subordinate, even doing part of the work if necessary.

6. **COACHING** means acting as a resource— teaching guiding, recommending—but not helping by doing the task.

C. Problems can arise when management uses MBO to **FORCE** managers to commit to goals that are not mutually agreed upon.

VII. MEETING EMPLOYEE EXPECTATIONS: EXPECTANCY THEORY

A. According to **VICTOR VROOM's EXPECTANCY THEORY**, employee expectations can affect an individual's motivation.

1. **_EXPECTANCY THEORY_** is Victor Vroom's theory that the amount of effort employees exert on a specific task depends on their expectations of the outcome.

2. Vroom contends that employees ask **THREE QUESTIONS** before committing maximum effort to a task:

    a. Can I accomplish the task?

    b. If I do accomplish it, what's my reward?

PPT 10-31
Organizations Using MBO

(See complete PowerPoint slide notes on page 10.59.)

PPT 10-32
Expectancy Theory in Motivation

(See complete PowerPoint slide notes on page 10.60.)

    c.   Is the reward worth the effort?

    3.   *The text illustrates this theory by using the example of a student's effort in class.*

    4.   Expectation varies from individual to individual.

B. **FIVE STEPS TO IMPROVE EMPLOYEE PERFORMANCE,** developed by David Nadler and Edward Lawler, state:

    1.   Determine what rewards employees value.

    2.   Determine each employee's desired performance standard.

    3.   Ensure that performance standards are attainable.

    4.   Guarantee rewards tied to performance.

    5.   Be certain that employees consider the rewards adequate.

VIII. REINFORCING EMPLOYEE PERFORMANCE: REINFORCEMENT THEORY

A. ***REINFORCEMENT THEORY*** states that positive and negative reinforcers motivate a person to behave in certain ways.

B. **TYPES OF REINFORCEMENT**

    1.   **POSITIVE REINFORCEMENTS** are rewards such as praise, recognition, or a pay raise.

    2.   **NEGATIVE REINFORCEMENT** includes reprimands, reduced pay, and layoff or firing.

    3.   **EXTINCTION** is trying to stop undesirable behavior by not responding to it.

PPT 10-33
Expectancy Theory

TEXT FIGURE 10.6
Expectancy Theory
(Text page 271)

(See complete PowerPoint slide notes on page 10.60.)

critical thinking
exercise 10-4
**THE MANAGEMENT
CHALLENGE**

Managers at a manufacturing plant are faced with a decision: Motivate employees to significantly increase production or see the plant close. (See complete exercise on page 10.82 of this manual.)

PPT 10-34
Nadler & Lawler's Modification

(See complete PowerPoint slide notes on page 10.60.)

PPT 10-35
Using Reinforcement Theory

(See complete PowerPoint slide notes on page 10.61.)

IX. TREATING EMPLOYEES FAIRLY: EQUITY THEORY

A. ***EQUITY THEORY*** is the idea that employees try to maintain equity between inputs and outputs compared to people in similar positions.

B. When workers do perceive inequity, they will try to **REESTABLISH EQUITABLE EXCHANGES.**

   1. They can **REDUCE** or **INCREASE** their efforts or rationalize the situation.

   2. In the workplace, inequity leads to lower productivity, reduced quality, increased absenteeism, and voluntary resignation.

C. Equity judgments are based on **PERCEPTIONS**, and are therefore subject to errors in perception.

   1. Organizations can try to keep salaries secret, but this often makes things worse.

   2. The best remedy, in general, is clear and frequent communication.

learning goal 7

Show how managers put motivation theories into action through such strategies as job enrichment, open communication, and job recognition.

X. PUTTING THEORY INTO ACTION

A. **MOTIVATING THROUGH JOB ENRICHMENT**

   1. ***JOB ENRICHMENT*** is a motivational strategy that emphasizes motivating the worker through the job itself.

      a. **JOB ENRICHMENT** is based on Herzberg's higher motivators.

      b. **JOB SIMPLIFICATION**, in contrast, produces task efficiency by breaking down the job into

TEXT FIGURE 10.7
Reinforcement Theory
(Text page 272)

This text figure illustrates how a manager can use reinforcement theory to motivate workers.

PPT 10-36
Equity Theory

(See complete PowerPoint slide notes on page 10.61.)

progress
assessment
(Text page 273)

PPT 10-37
Progress Assessment

(See complete PowerPoint slide notes on page 10.61.)

simple steps.

2. The **FIVE CHARACTERISTICS** of work that affect motivation and performance are:

   a. **SKILL VARIETY**, the extent to which a job demands different skills of the person

   b. **TASK IDENTITY**, the degree to which the job requires doing a task with a visible outcome from beginning to end

   c. **TASK SIGNIFICANCE**, the degree to which the job has a substantial impact on the lives of others in the company

   d. **AUTONOMY,** the degree of freedom, independence, and discretion in scheduling work and determining procedures

   e. **FEEDBACK**, the amount of direct, clear information received about job performance

3. **CONTRIBUTIONS:**

   a. **VARIETY, IDENTITY**, and **SIGNIFICANCE** contribute to meaningfulness of the job.

   b. **AUTONOMY** gives people a feeling of responsibility

   c. **FEEDBACK** contributes to a feeling of achievement and recognition.

4. ***JOB ENLARGEMENT*** is a job enrichment strategy that involves combining a series of tasks into one challenging and interesting assignment.

5. ***JOB ROTATION*** is a job-enrichment strategy that involves moving employees from one job to

PPT 10-38
Enriching Jobs

(See complete PowerPoint slide notes on page 10.62.)

PPT 10-39
Motivation on a Budget

(See complete PowerPoint slide notes on page 10.63.)

PPT 10-40
Key Characteristics of Work

(See complete PowerPoint slide notes on page 10.63.)

PPT 10-41
Types of Job Enrichment

(See complete PowerPoint slide notes on page 10.63.)

PPT 10-42
Enrichment by Way of Flexibility

(See complete PowerPoint slide notes on page 10.64.)

another.

B. **MOTIVATING THROUGH OPEN COMMUNICATION**

  1. Create an organizational culture that rewards listening.

  2. Train supervisors and managers to listen.

  3. Use effective questioning techniques.

  4. Remove barriers to open communication

  5. Avoid vague and ambiguous communication.

  6. Make it easy to communicate.

  7. Ask employees what is important to them.

C. **APPLYING OPEN COMMUNICATION IN SELF-MANAGED TEAMS**

  1. Companies with highly motivated workforces usually have **OPEN COMMUNICATION SYSTEMS** and **SELF-MANAGED TEAMS.**

  2. When teams are empowered to make decisions, communication must flow freely.

  3. *The text offers the example of communication among members of self-managed teams at Ford Motor Company.*

  4. To implement such self-managed teams, companies must **REINVENT WORK.**

  5. In doing so, it is essential that managers behave ethically toward all employees.

D. **RECOGNIZING A JOB WELL DONE**

  1. Letting people know you appreciate their work is more powerful than a bonus alone.

  2. Providing advancement opportunity is important in

PPT 10-43
Using Open Communication

(See complete PowerPoint slide notes on page 10.64.)

social
**media in
business**
(Text page 275)

PPT 10-44
Keeping the Lines
Open

(See complete PowerPoint slide notes on page 10.64.)

PPT 10-45
When Too Much Is Too Much

(See complete PowerPoint slide notes on page 10.65.)

bonus case 10-3
MANAGING VOLUNTEERS

How does motivating volunteers differ from managing employees? (See the complete case, discussion questions, and suggested answers beginning on page 10.90 of this manual.)

retaining valuable employees.

3. Recognition can be as simple as noticing positive actions out loud.

4. *The text gives several examples of companies using recognition to motivate employees.*

5. Employees may be motivated by the prospect of future compensation, such as stock options.

6. The same things don't motivate all employees.

learning goal 8

Show how managers personalize motivation strategies to appeal to employees across the globe and across generations.

XI. PERSONALIZING MOTIVATION

A. Managers cannot use one motivational formula for all employees.

1. The motivational effort must be tailored to the individual.

2. Managers' jobs are more complicated now due to working with employees from a variety of cultural backgrounds.

B. **MOTIVATING EMPLOYEES ACROSS THE GLOBE**

1. Different cultures experience motivational approaches differently.

   a. In a high-context culture (Korea, Thailand, and Saudi Arabia), workers build personal relationships and develop group trust before focusing on tasks.

   b. In low-context culture, workers often view

PPT 10-46
Recognizing Good Work

(See complete PowerPoint slide notes on page 10.65.)

lecture link 10-9
RECOGNITION: MAKING HEROES

Companies often make the mistake of equating pay with rewards. The reward for outstanding performance should be a special gain for special achievement. (See the complete lecture link on page 10.76 in this manual.)

PPT 10-47
Work Well with Others

(See complete PowerPoint slide notes on page 10.65.)

PPT 10-48
What's Good for You

(See complete PowerPoint slide notes on page 10.66.)

PPT 10-49
What's Bad for You

(See complete PowerPoint slide notes on page 10.66.)

critical thinking exercise 10-5
WHICH ARE THE BEST COMPANIES TO WORK FOR?

This exercise asks students to use the Internet to research which companies are rated best to work for. (See complete exercise on page 10.83 of this manual.)

lecture link 10-10
POSITIVE FEEDBACK

Employees and managers worry about the same thing: "How can I do a better job?" (See the complete lecture link on page 10.51 of this manual.)

critical thinking exercise 10-6
MOTIVATION SURVEY

This exercise gives the result of a motivation survey for two supervisors and asks students to interpret the results. (See complete exercise on page 10.84 of this manual.)

relationship-building as a waste of time.

2. *Text example: Dow Chemical solved a cross-cultural problem with a Web-based program called Recognition@Dow.*

3. Understanding motivation in global organizations is still a new task for most companies.

C. **MOTIVATING EMPLOYEES ACROSS GENERATIONS**

1. Generations can be classified as follows:

   a. **BABY BOOMERS** (born between 1946 and 1964) experienced economic prosperity and optimism about the future.

   b. **GENERATION X** members (born between 1965 and 1980) were raised with dual-career families and insecurity about a lifelong job.

   c. **GENERATION Y** members (born between 1981 and 2000) are also called "millennials."

   d. The beliefs you accept as a child affect future relationships and management decisions.

2. **GENERATIONAL DIFFERENCES** affect motivation.

   a. Boomer managers need to be flexible with Gen X and Millennial employees.

   b. Employees from this generation will need to use their enthusiasm for change.

   c. Gen Xers tend to focus on career security, not job security, and look for opportunities to

SPOTLIGHT ON
small
business
(Text page 278)

PPT 10-50
Small Incentives
Can Be Big
Motivators

(See complete PowerPoint slide notes on page 10.66.)

PPT 10-51
Motivating Employees across the
Globe

(See complete PowerPoint slide notes on page 10.67.)

REACHING BEYOND
our borders
(Text page 279

PPT 10-52
Importance of
Cultural
Competency

(See complete PowerPoint slide notes on page 10.67.)

PPT 10-53
Motivating across Generations

(See complete PowerPoint slide notes on page 10.67.)

        expand their skills.

3. Generation Xers are now managers themselves.

    a. Gen X managers tend to focus more on results than on hours in the workplace.

    b. They give employees the goals and the parameters of the project and then leave them alone to do their work.

    c. They are better at providing feedback.

4. Each generation questions the **VALUES OF THE NEWER GENERATION.**

5. Millennials tend to share common characteristics:

    a. They are impatient, skeptical, blunt and expressive, image driven, and inexperienced.

    b. Millennials are adaptable, tech savvy, able to grasp new concepts, practiced at multitasking, efficient, and tolerant.

D. In general, motivation will come from the **JOB ITSELF** rather than from external punishments or rewards.

E. Millennials are **"job surfers"** and are not looking for

PPT 10-54

Generation X in the Workplace

(See complete PowerPoint slide notes on page 10.68.)

PPT 10-55

Millennials and the Workplace

(See complete PowerPoint slide notes on page 10.68.)

PPT 10-56

Millennials and the Recession

(See complete PowerPoint slide notes on page 10.68.)

PPT 10-57

Communication across the
Generations

(See complete PowerPoint slide notes on page 10.69.)

PPT 10-58

The Best Companies for Workers

(See complete PowerPoint slide notes on page 10.69.)

lifetime careers.

F. All generations **COMMUNICATE DIFFERENTLY**.

   a. Traditionalists prefer **face-to-face.**

   b. Boomers prefer **meetings or conference calls.**

   c. Gen Xers prefer **e-mail.**

   d. Millennials **prefer social media.**

G. Managers need to give workers what they need to do a good job—the right tools, the right information, and the right amount of cooperation.

XII. SUMMARY

progress
assessment
(Text page 281)

PPT 10-59
Progress Assessment

(See complete PowerPoint slide notes on page 10.69.)

PowerPoint slide notes

PPT 10-1
Chapter Title

PPT 10-2
Learning Goals

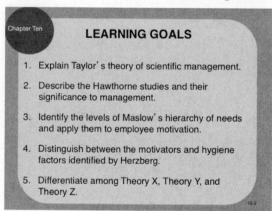

PPT 10-3
Learning Goals

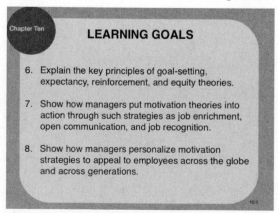

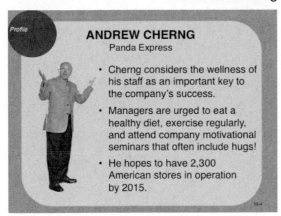

Company: UPS

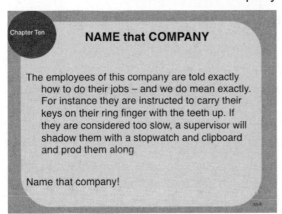

Intrinsic means from within; when you have a drive to succeed and are motivated by purpose, passion, and mission.

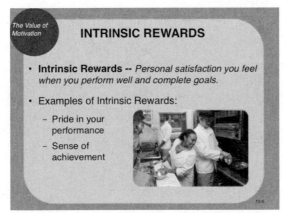

PPT 10-7
Extrinsic Rewards

Extrinsic rewards are often temporary and driven by money, recognition, and results.

PPT 10-8
Fringe Benefits

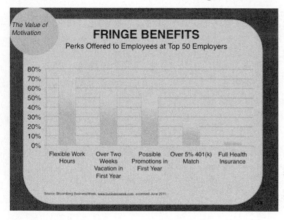

1. This slide displays the most common perks or rewards used by companies to motivate employees.

2. Other examples of extrinsic rewards include the following:

   - Pay

   - Improved working environment or conditions

   - Status

   - Security

3. While these rewards do offer some value, there is much research that indicates many problems with extrinsic motivation. Share with the students some of those ideas:

   - Extrinsic rewards do not produce permanent changes.

   - Extrinsic rewards reduce intrinsic interest.

   - The use of extrinsic rewards can be controlling.

4. Reinforcement of extrinsic rewards can lead to expectations of permanence in the form of job rewards.

Taylor's Scientific Management

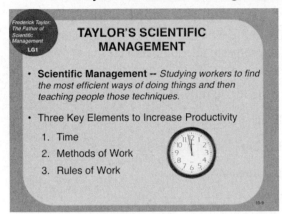

Taylor's Four Key Principles

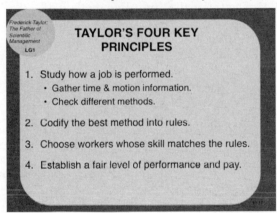

Time-Motion Studies

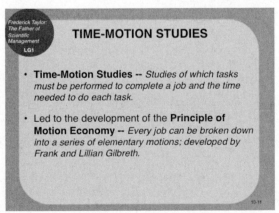

Taylor was looking for the most efficient way or the one right way to do something. Workers were, in a sense, thought of as machines that could be fine-tuned.

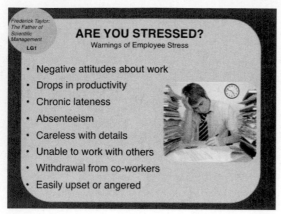

1. Employers can often spot impending stress or on-the-job stress by understanding the signs listed.

2. Ask the students, Have you experienced any of these symptoms when trying to juggle your academic, professional, and personal lives? What did you do to cope with the rigors of stress?

3. Share the following tips for reducing stress:

    *   Learn to plan.

    *   Recognize and accept limits.

    *   Be a positive person.

    *   Learn to tolerate and forgive.

    *   Avoid unnecessary competition.

    *   Get regular exercise.

    *   Learn a systematic, drug-free method of relaxing.

    *   Change your thinking.

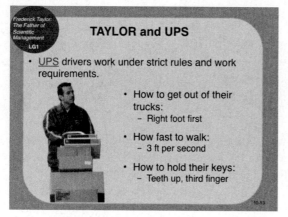

Hawthorne Studies: Purpose and Results

The Hawthorne studies were conducted in Cicero, Illinois, at the Western Electric plant over a six-year period.

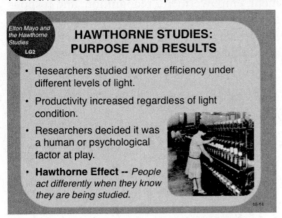

PPT 10-15
Maslow's Theory of Motivation

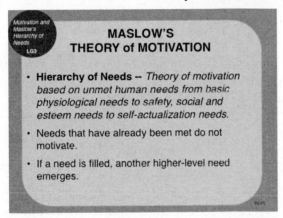

PPT 10-16
Maslow's Hierarchy of Needs

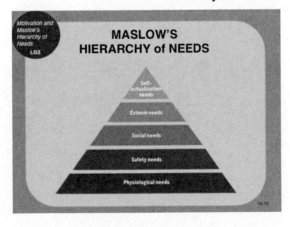

1. This slide reproduces the illustration of Maslow's hierarchy from the chapter.

2. Most people in the class, especially those who have taken basic psychology, may be familiar with Maslow and the premise of human needs hierarchy.

3. Use this opportunity to relate Maslow's needs theory to the work environment:

   • Workers require competitive salaries, benefits, and clean work environments.

   • Employees have the need for security against termination in their jobs and the feeling of being safe against bodily harm while performing their job functions.

   • On the job, workers have the need to feel a part of a successful group, driven by achievement.

- Opportunities within the organization

- Employees seek opportunities for advancement, empowerment, recognition, and responsibility through additional work-related performance. Companies must attempt to satisfy these needs through

PPT 10-17
Herzberg's Motivating Factors

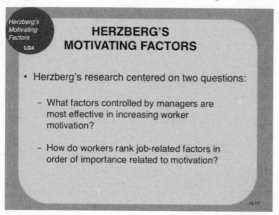

PPT 10-18
Job Content

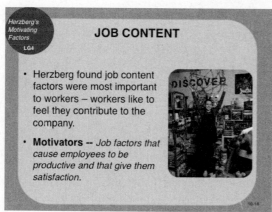

Herzberg's article in the Harvard Business Review, "One More Time: How Do You Motivate Employees?" is a classic and explores his idea of job content in depth.

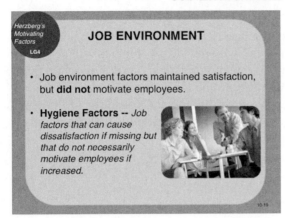

PPT 10-20

Herzberg's Motivators and Hygiene
Factors

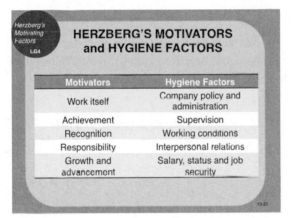

1. This slide illustrates another "needs" theory regarding workers and their job needs.

2. This theory is based on what an organization can do to fulfill the individual needs of workers while motivating them to excel.

3. The key component of Herzberg's work was the opposite of "satisfaction"—"no satisfaction." If the basic hygiene factors were not in place, a worker is not satisfied. To have a satisfied, motivated workforce, a company needs to provide the following:

   - Achievement

   - Recognition

   - Work itself

   - Responsibility

   - Advancement

   - Growth

PPT 10-21

Comparison of the Theories of Maslow
and Herzberg

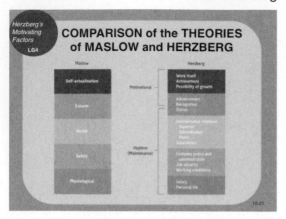

1. This slide gives students a good starting point to see the relationship between Maslow and Herzberg.

2. To start a discussion, ask students if they are motivated by money. Most students will state that money is a real motivating factor. Follow up this discussion with the following question: If you dislike your current job and your boss offers you more money, will it change your feelings about your job in the long run?

PPT 10-22

Reignite Employees' Drive

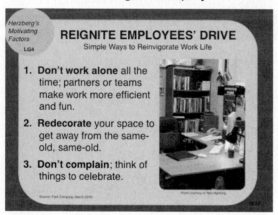

1. Motivators don't have to be big or grand gestures like awards.

2. Employees can motivate themselves.

3. Ask the students, Why do you think redecorating your desk, cube, or office is helpful and reinvigorating?

PPT 10-23

Progress Assessment

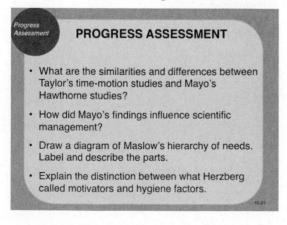

1. Frederick Taylor's time-motion studies measured output. Taylor inspired the Hawthorne studies. Originally Elton Mayo wanted to determine the optimal level of lighting necessary to increase production on the factory floor which is a type of scientific management. He later determined that people who were empowered worked harder. Ultimately Mayo's study brought about behavioral management.

2. The findings at Hawthorne plant in Cicero, Illinois, completely changed how people thought about employees and motivation. One finding was that money was not a primary motivator. These new assumptions led to many theories about the human side of motivation.

3. Students should be able to draw and label Maslow's hierarchy.

4. As Herzberg studied the results of his research, he concluded that motivators made employees productive and gave them satisfaction. These factors related to job content. Hygiene factors related to the job environment could, if left unattended, cause employee dissatisfaction but would not provide long-term motivation. Hygiene factors include such things as pay and working conditions.

PPT 10-24

Theory X and Theory Y

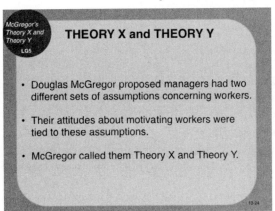

1. Theory X suggests that employees dislike work, avoid responsibility, have little ambition, and are motivated by threat and fear. Theory Y argues that people like work, seek responsibility, and are motivated by empowerment. If a manager believes theory X or Theory Y, he or she would tend to treat the employees accordingly.

2. Ask the students, Would you be a Theory X or Y manager? How do you believe employees should be treated? Would you prefer to work for a Theory X or Y manager? *(The majority if not all would say they would rather work for a Theory Y manager. It should be pointed out that how a manager treats employees is often dictated by the situation. A manager may hold Theory Y values but may have to use Theory X perspective depending on the situation with the employee.)*

PPT 10-25

Assumptions of Theory X Managers

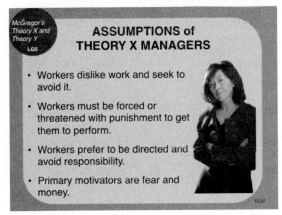

PPT 10-26
Assumptions of Theory Y Managers

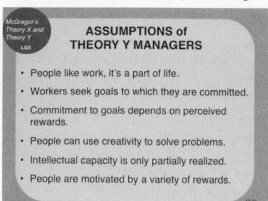

ASSUMPTIONS of THEORY Y MANAGERS

McGregor's Theory X and Theory Y
LG5

- People like work, it's a part of life.
- Workers seek goals to which they are committed.
- Commitment to goals depends on perceived rewards.
- People can use creativity to solve problems.
- Intellectual capacity is only partially realized.
- People are motivated by a variety of rewards.

PPT 10-27
Theory Z

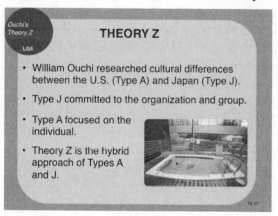

THEORY Z

Ouchi's Theory Z
LG5

- William Ouchi researched cultural differences between the U.S. (Type A) and Japan (Type J).
- Type J committed to the organization and group.
- Type A focused on the individual.
- Theory Z is the hybrid approach of Types A and J.

Demographic changes, the worst recession in their country's history, and fierce global competition have forced Japanese managers to reevaluate the way they conduct business. The effects of the 2011 earthquake on Japanese businesses reinforced the need to change.

PPT 10-28
Theory Z

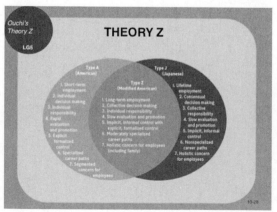

THEORY Z

Ouchi's Theory Z
LG5

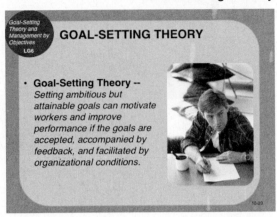

Peter Drucker developed the idea of MBO in his 1954 book *The Practice of Management.*

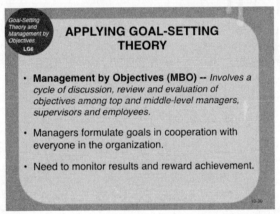

1. Management by objectives (MBO) was popularized by Peter Drucker in the 1950s.

2. Ask the students, What are the benefits of MBO? *(This theory is based on the notion that setting attainable goals with all employees of the organization will create more support for the goals leading to greater motivation.)*

3. *To better understand Peter Drucker visit the following website:* www.druckerinstitute.com/)

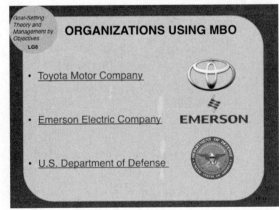

PPT 10-32
Expectancy Theory in Motivation

Victor Vroom developed the expectancy theory.

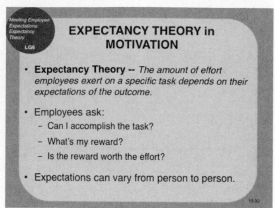

PPT 10-33
Expectancy Theory

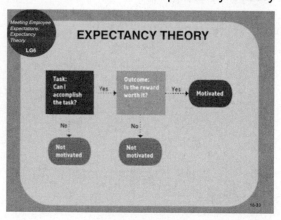

PPT 10-34
Nadler & Lawler's Modification

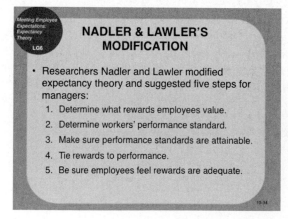

USING REINFORCEMENT THEORY

Reinforcing Employee Performance: Reinforcement Theory
LG6

- **Reinforcement Theory --** *Positive and negative reinforcers motivate a person to behave in certain ways.*

- *Positive* reinforcement includes praise, pay increases and recognition.

- *Negative* reinforcement includes reprimands, reduced pay, and layoff or firing.

- Extinction is a way of trying to stop behavior by not responding to it.

10-35

EQUITY THEORY

Treating Employees Fairly: Equity Theory
LG6

- **Equity Theory --** *Employees try to maintain equity between inputs and outputs compared to others in similar positions.*

- Workers often base perception of their outcomes on a specific person or group.

- Perceived inequities can lead to reduced quality and productivity, absenteeism, even resignation.

10-36

PROGRESS ASSESSMENT

Progress Assessment

- Briefly explain the managerial attitudes behind Theories X, Y and Z.

- Explain goal-setting theory.

- Evaluate expectancy theory. When could expectancy theory apply to your efforts or lack of effort?

- Explain the principles of equity theory.

10-37

1. Theory X assumes the following: People dislike work and will avoid it. Workers must be forced, controlled, directed, or threatened with punishment to make them work toward the organization's goals. Average workers prefer to be directed, wish to avoid responsibility, have little ambition, and want security, and the primary motivators are fear and money. Theory Y managers have completely different views on managing people. Theory Y managers believe that most people like to work; the depth of a person's commitment to goals depends on the perceived rewards for achieving them; under certain circumstances people will seek responsibility; employees tend to be imaginative, creative, and clever; and employees are motivated by a variety of rewards. Theory Z was developed by William Ouchi of UCLA and is a blending of American management style, Theory A, with Japanese management style, Theory J, into Theory Z.

2. The idea behind goal-setting theory is the process of setting attainable goals to motivate employees and improve performance. The key to goal-setting theory is that the goals must be accepted and accompanied by feedback to truly be effective.

3. Victor Vroom created the expectancy theory. His central premise was that the amount of effort employees exert on a specific task depends on their expectations of the outcome. He contends that employees will ask three specific questions before committing maximum effort: Can I accomplish the task? If I do accomplish it, what's my reward? Is the reward worth the effort? Like goal-setting theory the key to expectancy theory is setting attainable goals. If the goal is not attainable employees will simply give up, thus reducing motivation.

4. Equity theory looks at how employees' perceptions of fairness affect their willingness to perform. Employees will try to balance or maintain equity between what they put into the job and what they get out of it, comparing those inputs and outputs to those of others in similar positions.

PPT 10-38
Enriching Jobs

Herzberg argued that factors such as responsibility, achievement, and recognition were more important motivational factors in the long run than pay. He believed that if you wanted to motivate employees you should focus on enriching the job.

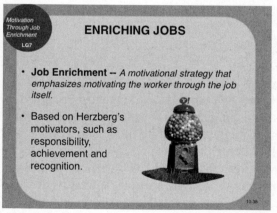

ENRICHING JOBS

- **Job Enrichment** -- *A motivational strategy that emphasizes motivating the worker through the job itself.*

- Based on Herzberg's motivators, such as responsibility, achievement and recognition.

Motivation on a Budget

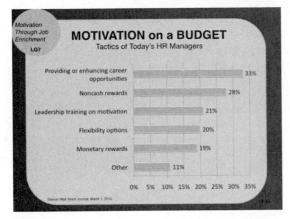

1. In this recent recession, companies have had to ease up on offering monetary rewards for employee performance.

2. Ask the students, Would you be satisfied with these options, excluding monetary rewards?

PPT 10-40
Key Characteristics of Work

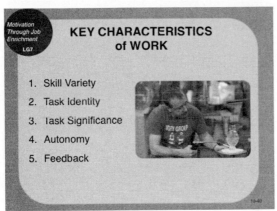

PPT 10-41
Types of Job Enrichment

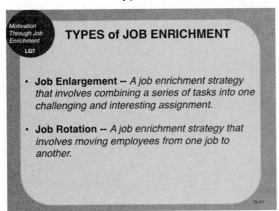

PPT 10-42
Enrichment by Way of Flexibility

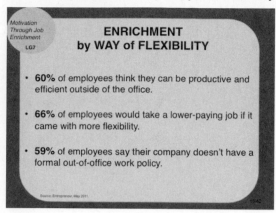

1. Many employees see time outside the office as a perk. This may include work from home, a library, or a remote location.

2. Some companies are following this trend. However, the majority of people surveyed said their company still doesn't offer the option.

3. Ask the students, Would you take a job with lower pay if it meant you could work remotely? Would you prefer to work only in the office?

PPT 10-43
Using Open Communication

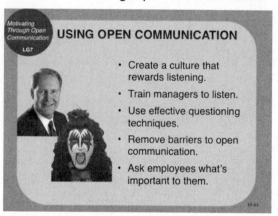

PPT 10-44
Keeping the Lines Open

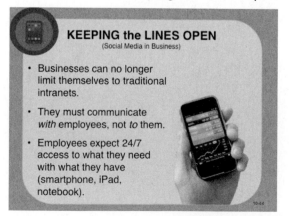

PPT 10-45

When Too Much Is Too Much

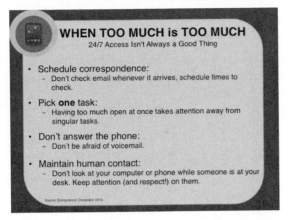

1. We have become accustomed to checking our e-mails, calls, and Facebook wall at all hours of the day.

2. Maintaining constant contact has caused some employees to lose track of the tasks at hand.

3. Ask the students, How often do you check your e-mail? How much time do you spend on Facebook daily? Do you tweet all day? Do you let your phone go to voicemail?

PPT 10-46

Recognizing Good Work

Remember, rewarding performance can come in different formats than money. What are other ways to recognize good performance?

PPT 10-47

Work Well with Others

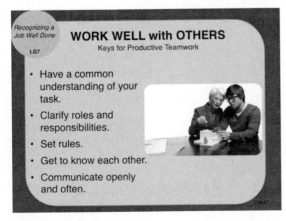

1. This slide presents characteristics of high-performance teams.

2. This list is compiled from the *Wall Street Journal* on high-performance teams.

3. Ask the students in teams to explore these characteristics as they relate to teams they have been on. Which of these characteristics apply to their team and which are lacking? What modifications do they need to make to move toward being a high-performance team?

What's Good for You

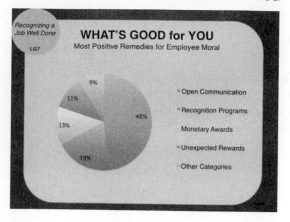

1. This slide offers simple tips for motivating employees in your business.

2. A motto to remember is the Golden Rule: Treat others as you want to be treated.

3. Ask the students where the recommendations in the slide fit in Maslow's or Herzberg's theories.

PPT 10-49
What's Bad for You

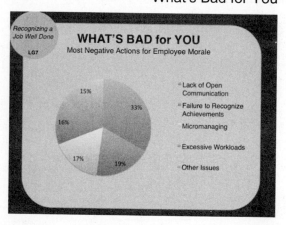

1. This slide ties into the previous slide and offers tips on what to avoid in order to enhance employee morale.

2. Ask students why these factors negatively impact employee morale.

PPT 10-50
Big Motivators for Small Business

Motivating Employees across the Globe

In a globalized world, managers must recognize that what is appropriate in one culture might not work in another.

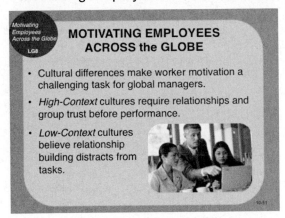

PPT 10-52

Importance of Cultural Competency

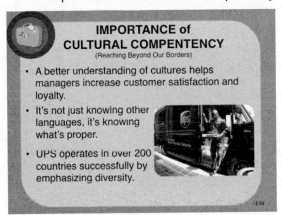

PPT 10-53

Motivating across the Generations

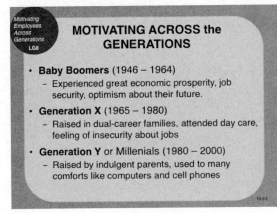

1. Managers must consider cultural differences, and they must also contend with employees in different age groups.

2. To start a discussion ask the students, What issues might you encounter if you manage employees of various generations (baby boomer, Generation X, and Generation Y)?

3. The main constant in the lives of Gen Xers and Millennials is inconstancy. Consider the unprecedented change in the past 10 to 20 years in every area (e.g., economic, technological, scientific, social, and political). Gen Xers and Millennials expect change. It is the absence of change that they find questionable.

PPT 10-54
Generation X in the Workplace

GENERATION X in the WORKPLACE

- Desire economic security but focus more on career security than job security.

- Good motivators as managers due to emphasis on results rather than work hours.

- Tend to be flexible and good at collaboration and consensus building.

- Very effective at giving employee feedback and praise.

PPT 10-55
Millennials and the Workplace

MILLENNIALS and the WORKPLACE

- Tend to be impatient, skeptical, blunt and expressive.

- Are tech-savvy and able to grasp new concepts.

- Able to multi-task and are efficient.

- Highlight a strong sense of commitment.

- Place a high value on work-life balance.

- Fun and stimulation are key job requirements.

PPT 10-56
Millennials and the Recession

MILLENNIALS and the RECESSION

- The recession hurt younger workers more deeply than other workers.

- In July 2010, the unemployment rate was 15.3 percent for those aged 20 to 24, while the overall unemployment rate was 9.5 percent.

Unemployment for 18- to 29-year-olds was the highest it's been in more than three decades. In fact, today Millennials are less likely to be employed than Gen Xers or boomers were at the same age.

PPT 10-57

Communication across the Generations

Ask the students, How might the differences in how the generations prefer to communicate affect the workplace?

PPT 10-58

The Best Companies for Workers

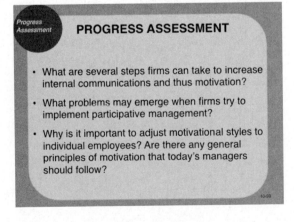

1. This list is generated by *Fortune* magazine.

2. Ask the students, What makes a company "employee friendly"? *(Answers will vary.)*

3. Use the *Fortune* research to profile one or all of the companies, so students can understand what programs these companies have implemented to enhance worker satisfaction.

PPT 10-59

Progress Assessment

1. To increase communication managers can reward listening across the organization, train supervisors and managers to listen using effective questioning techniques, remove barriers to communication, avoid vague and ambiguous communication, make it easy to communicate, and ask employees what is important to them. Focusing on communication is important, but managers can also focus on job enrichment, such as skill variety and task significance.

2. Participative management, if implemented properly, can be successful, but like everything in life there are benefits and weaknesses to this type of management style. One problem with this approach is that it is difficult to implement and workers may spend more time formulating suggestions than actually solving the problem at hand.

3. In today's multicultural workplace managers cannot use one motivational formula for all employees. While they must adjust motivational styles, it is essential that managers give all employees the keys to do a good job: the tools, the right information, and the right amount of cooperation. Motivating employees across cultures and generations can be simple, if managers acknowledge a job well done.

lecture
links

"Motivation is everything. You can do the work of two people, but you can't be two people;
Instead, you have to inspire the next guy down the line and get him to inspire his people."

Lee Iacocca

"Good management is the art of making problems so interesting and their solutions so
constructive that everyone wants to get to work and deal with them."

Paul Hawken

"Motivation is what gets you started. Habit is what keeps you going."

Jim Ryun

"Good judgment comes from bad experience. Experience comes from bad judgment."

Higdon's Law

lecture link 10-1

UPS'S TRUCK DRIVER BOOT CAMP

In the photo caption on page 261, we briefly mentioned the intensive training that prospective UPS drivers must undergo at the company's 11,500-square-foot facility in Landover, Maryland. Called Integrad, the training center has had 1,629 UPS driver candidates go through the program since its 2007 opening. Of that number, only 10% failed. That's great news for UPS, which needs to hire 25,000 new drivers over the next five years to replace retiring baby boomers. The company plans to open another Integrad center in Chicago this summer and eventually expand the training to current drivers instead of just new hires.

At Integrad, candidates are trained in UPS's gargantuan set of driving guidelines, the "340 Methods." Unlike past UPS drivers who were trained in classrooms and by handbooks, Integrad utilizes technology to simulate real-world experiences that the drivers will encounter. For instance, candidates start out driving in a video game where they are taught to spot obstacles. From there they progress to "Clarksville," a UPS-constructed simulation village where drivers, behind the wheel of a real truck, are challenged to complete five deliveries in 19 minutes. Another training module, dubbed the "slip and fall machine," places drivers on a greased tiled runway with a 10-pound box to carry. If that wasn't enough, they're given shoes without tread. Thankfully, candidates wear safety harnesses, as most of them wipe out continuously until they teach themselves to ignore UPS's "2.5 brisk paces per second" rule when on slick surfaces.

Driving candidates spend one week of their 60-day training program at Integrad. In a lot of ways, Integrad is UPS boot camp. Trainees work together in teams and, like the military, get reprimanded as a team when one individual makes a mistake. For example, if a student isn't wearing a clean, ironed UPS uniform or doesn't have his or her keys at the ready, the entire team loses points. For prospective hires, all the hassle is worth it if they can make it to the driver's job. UPS's 99,000 drivers make an average of $74,000 a year, a big step up from the hourly wage of $12.50 that warehouse loaders earn.[i]

lecture link 10-2

MOTIVATING WITHOUT MONEY

How can you motivate employees during lean times? Andrea Nierenberg, founder of the business-consulting firm Nierenberg Group, has some suggestions to motivate workers.

PLUM PROJECTS

Exciting, new assignments can motivate employees more than a few extra dollars. In lean times, most companies are understaffed, so it should be easy to find challenging projects that will allow talented employees to expand their skills and prepare themselves for more responsibility. For example, a junior employee might be asked to join a task force that puts him or her in a key decision-making role.

15 MINUTES OF FAME

Mary Kay Ash, the founder of Mary Kay Cosmetics, used to say, "There are two things people want more than sex and money, and that is praise and recognition." As a result, telling people how their specific contributions make a difference—and making sure others hear about it—is a powerful way to build loyalty. Highlighting employees' accomplishments in a company newsletter should be standard practice. Managers can put an employee in the spotlight by sending newsworthy information about his or her accomplishments to trade publications as well as the person's neighborhood newspaper. Another option is to take out an ad in a trade publication or local newspaper that thanks employees by name for their work on a key project. But keep in mind that some people like public praise and to others, it's embarrassing. Honor employees by learning their preference.

CUSTOMIZED WORK SCHEDULES

In the age of terrorist attacks many people have placed a renewed emphasis on spending time with their loved ones. Employees may be caring for children, elderly parents, friends, or beloved pets. Most will appreciate any efforts made to allow them to adjust their schedules to accommodate these responsibilities. Many bosses find that their employees are more productive when they're not distracted by worries about getting to the daycare center on time or squeezing in a visit to a friend in the hospital during a half-hour lunch break. [ii]

lecture link 10-3

THE BIG THRILL MOTIVATION

Another facet of motivation involves the individual's tolerance for risk taking. Some individuals have a kind of psychological urge to reach beyond the status quo and seek out novelty, change, and excitement. Psychologist Frank Farley, of the University of Wisconsin, has spent 20 years examining what he calls the Type T (thrill-seeking) personality. According to Farley's theory, Big T types are high-profile individuals who seek excitement and stimulation wherever they can find it or create it. For some, the thrills are mostly physical; for others, they're mental.

The degree of risk that individuals are willing to assume spans a broad continuum. Big T personalities, those who continually live on the edge, are at one end of the scale. Little t's, who cling to certainty and predictability, are at the other end. Most people fall somewhere in the middle. But Farley believes it's the Big T segment, a group that makes up an estimated 10 to 30% of the American population, that holds the key to America's future. "Type T's are the people who are likely to have enormous impact on society," he says. "They are the great experimenters in life; they break the rules."

Whether male or female, risk-taking individuals tend to be what Farley calls "transmutative thinkers," adept at shifting from one cognitive process to another, and from the abstract to the concrete and vice versa. Thrill seekers are happiest in jobs that provide change, excitement, and an ample outlet for their creativity. They are often drawn to careers in advertising, journalism, or in the brokerage business, where novelty and uncertainty are a given.

Whether individuals seek risks or avoid them affects not only their own job performance but also boss–employee relationships and coworker production. An organization with too many risk takers can spell trouble. So can an organization top-heavy with cautious, security-minded individuals. A synergistic mix is best. If it's the thrill-seeking visionaries who drive a company with their ideas, it's their more pragmatic peers who help implement those concepts.

Finally, says Farley, "People who are the most successful realize that if they're going to take risks, they're going to fail once in a while."[iii]

lecture link 10-4

MCCLELLAND'S ACQUIRED NEEDS THEORY

Psychologist David McClelland proposed that humans acquire different needs over time as a result of life experiences. He classified these needs that affect motivation in both individuals and organizations:

1. Need for achievement

2. Need for affiliation

3. Need for power

Persons with a high *need for achievement,* according to McClelland's theory, like to work for challenging, but not risky, goals. They like concrete feedback about their work. Rewards, such as salary, are important only as a measure of achievement. They prefer to work alone or with others with a need for achievement. People with a high need for achievement are frequently found in engineering and technical fields; they are generally frustrated in management positions.

People with a *need for affiliation* need harmonious relationships; they desire to form and maintain friendships. They tend to conform to the norms of their group. These individuals prefer work that provides significant personal interactions. They perform well in customer service and client interaction situations.

Persons with a *need for power* are of two types: personal power and institutional power. Those with a need for personal power want to direct others, which can be seen as undesirable. People with a need for institutional power want to organize others to achieve the goals of the organization. Managers with a high need for institutional power are generally more successful that those with a need for personal power.

Just as a manager can use Herzberg's motivating factors to enhance employee performance, recognizing employees' needs can suggest the right types of jobs for individuals. Authors of *Organizational Behavior*, John Schermmerhorn, James Hunt, and Richard Osborn, believe that McClelland's findings are useful when each need is linked with a combination of Herzberg's work preferences such as individual responsibility, challenging but achievable goals, interpersonal relationships, influence over others, and attention and recognition.`

lecture link 10-5
THE L-FACTOR

According to Tim Sanders, a Yahoo executive and author of The Likeability Factor, likability, not intimidation, is the real key to conquering the workplace. Sanders sets forth a how-to plan for an employee trying to get ahead. His philosophy builds on the Dale Carnegie approach, outlined in his 1936 classic How to Win Friends and Influence People. "Men are the worst at this," Sanders reports. "They won't smile."

In business, likability matters. A person who gives others "a sense of joy, happiness, relaxation, or rejuvenation," says Sanders, is more likely to be hired and promoted. He believes that likable bosses, rather than feared bosses, get the best work out of employees. Nastiness translates into less productivity, higher turnover, and a culture of unhappiness.

Sanders calls this element the "L-factor." Raising your L-factor is like improving your physical fitness. The L-factor involves four qualities that aspiring managers need to practice:

1. The first is *friendliness*. "If you are not friendly, you will have to work exponentially harder to be likeable."

2. *Relevance*. A person who has a skill that will help someone else complete a task is relevant.

3. *Empathy*. "Walk a mile in your colleagues' wingtips."

4. *Keep it real*. Colleagues can spot a phony.

Sanders uses the new chair of Sony, Howard Stringer, as a prime example of the success of likability. Stringer, an American, is funny, irreverent, and playful. His positive attitude won over Sony's Japanese executives. That's why they gave him the top leadership at Sony, much to the surprise of the world.

Sanders realizes that many people will have difficulty with implementing the likability principles. For them, Sanders has some basic advice. Strive to be polite, at the very least. No screaming, hanging up phones, slamming doors, and expressing biting sarcasm. The bottom line: "Just be quiet and stop being so unfriendly."[iv]

lecture link 10-6
THE BOSS SETS THE EXAMPLE

The CEO of Japan Airlines represents the differences between the American management approach and the Japanese approach. CEO Haruka Nishimatsu comes to work on the city bus. No corporate jets for him. He believes that management will not work if leaders treat themselves one way and employees another way.

Nishimatsu buys his suits at a discount store because he believes that a boss who wears Armani puts himself at arm's length from his people. While Merrill Lynch boss John Thain spent $1 million decorating his office, Nishimatsu knocked down his office walls so anyone can walk in. Got an idea? Catch him at lunch in the company cafeteria.

All CEOs say that service is important, but Nishimatsu goes a step beyond. He says that if you're having a bad experience, don't get angry with the people you're dealing with—blame it on the people in charge. And Nishimatsu not only talks the talk, he walks the walk. He pops into planes, chats with flight attendants, even sorts the newspapers.

His salary for running the world's 10th largest airline: not millions, but one year as low as $90,000. When he was forced to cut salaries for everyone else, he also cut his own. To him, a leader shares the economic pain.

Nishimatsu says a CEO doesn't motivate by how many millions he makes, but by convincing employees "you're all together in the same boat."v

lecture link 10-7

WAL-MART GIVES BACK

Wal-Mart is often criticized for being too large for smaller retailers to compete with, ultimately causing the underdogs to fold while Wal-Mart picks up their business. The company has also been accused of treating its employees poorly and of bullying its distributors and competitors. While some of these criticisms against Wal-Mart may be justified to some degree, the sheer size of the world's largest retailer also allows it to perform a great deal of good throughout the world.

For example, Wal-Mart recently placed first in a survey measuring the largest charitable cash contributors among American companies. Wal-Mart gave a total of $228.1 million as part of its commitment to donate $2 billion over the next five years to fight world hunger. Wal-Mart's expansive contribution comes at a time when most companies are scaling down their philanthropic efforts as a result of the recession. Donations of cash and products fell 5% in 2010, the first time since 2003 that contributions dropped. Wal-Mart ranks within the 30% who gave more this year while 54% of the 68 surveyed companies gave less.

Wal-Mart is also taking strides toward improving its relationship with its workforce. In June the company announced a joint effort with American Public University (APU) to provide Wal-Mart employees with special grants to defray educational costs with the online college. Wal-Mart will directly provide $50 million to cover tuition and textbooks for its staff. Courses with APU are traditionally low-priced as the college relies on positive word of mouth to increase enrollment in lieu of advertising or a physical campus. Wal-Mart's subsidies almost guarantee that any worker who wants further education can receive it. There's no telling yet how many Wal-Mart workers will take advantage of the program, but with 1.4 million U.S. employees the company could provide a huge boost to APU's current enrollment of 70,600.vi

lecture link 10-8

SAVING A FORTUNE WITH EMPLOYEE WELLNESS

Employee perks are among the first things to go once a company begins tightening its belt. When it comes to employee wellness, however, recent studies show that managers would be better off expanding rather than slashing their current programs. The idea is simple: healthier employees mean fewer sick days and higher efficiency. At one surveyed company, health care costs decreased by $1,421 per participant in its wellness program, amounting to $6 in savings for every dollar invested in the system.

At big companies, returns like that can amount to enormous savings. Johnson & Johnson, for instance, saved $250 million on health care costs over the last 10 years thanks to its wellness program. The amount of cash companies can retain is even greater now thanks to government tax incentives and subsidies available under the new federal health care legislation. Wellness programs also help prevent excessive employee turnover. In 2005, voluntary turnover clocked in at 19% at the Biltmore tourism company. After implementing a wellness program, the rate in the intervening years dropped to 9% in 2009.

Organizing a wellness system consists of much more than plugging in a treadmill and stocking fruit in the break room fridge. First of all, upper management must convey its dedication to the program through its own participation. If employees see their boss exercising, they'll be less self-conscious about taking a break for their own personal fitness. Next, the program must be accessible onsite to maximize its cost-saving potential. Doling out gym memberships is one thing, but for many, convenience reigns supreme when it comes to exercise. Finally, employees should be encouraged, not forced, to participate in the wellness program. Mandates like these only elicit contempt and make employees disinclined to better their bodies.[vii]

lecture link 10-9
RECOGNITION: MAKING HEROES

Rosabeth Moss Kanter, author of the book *The Change Masters*, concluded that companies often make the mistake of equating pay with rewards. Pay is not a reward for outstanding performance; it is compensation for doing the job in the first place. A reward should be a special gain for special achievements. Compensation is a right; recognition is a gift.

Recognition—saying "thank you" in public and perhaps giving a tangible gift along with the words—has multiple functions beyond simple courtesy. To the employee, recognition signifies that someone noticed and someone cares. To the rest of the organization, recognition creates role models—heroes—and communicates the standards: These are the kinds of things that constitute great performance. Kanter's management consulting firm also found a remarkable correlation between recognition and innovation.

Some basic rules should be followed in handing out praise and recognition:

1. **Deliver recognition and reward in an open and publicized way.** If not made public, recognition loses much of its impact and defeats much of the purpose for which it is provided.

2. **Timing is crucial.** Recognize contribution throughout a project. Reward contribution close to the time an achievement is realized. Time delays weaken the impact of most rewards.

3. **Tailor recognition and reward to the unique needs of the people involved.** Have several recognition and reward options to enable managers to acknowledge accomplishment in ways appropriate to the particulars of a given situation.

4. **Deliver recognition in a personal and honest manner.** Avoid providing recognition that is too "slick" or overproduced.

5. **Strive for clear, unambiguous, and well-communicated connection between accomplishments and rewards.** Be sure people understand why they receive awards and the criteria used to determine rewards.

6. **Recognize recognition.** That is, recognize people who recognize others for doing what is best for the company.

Celebrating and publicizing employee achievements need not be expensive. Kanter's research suggests some simple, low-cost ways to make employees "heroes," such as having coffee with an employee or group of employees whom you do not normally see, or letting employees attend important meetings in your place when you're not available.

lecture link 10-10

POSITIVE FEEDBACK

Employees and managers may have different levels of experience, but they worry about the same thing: "How can I do a better job?" Kathryn Lemaire, vice president at the Hay Group, a consulting firm that helps organizations manage people, has some advice. Performance reviews, she says, should not be a single, dreaded day at the end of the year but an ongoing dialogue incorporated into the company's culture. Her advice:

- Employees constantly want to know where they stand in the company, and good managers should clue them in regularly. If someone is doing a good job, give him or her immediate, specific feedback that is genuine, rewarding, and motivating. If there is room to improve what he or she is currently doing, point out how to change and get better. Consistent and honest feedback in small doses throughout the year can alleviate the need for a highly charged annual review.

- Employers usually think they clearly communicate their goals to employees when, in fact, most don't. Sharing your targets and ambitions—and reinforcing those with regular meetings and dialogue—stacks the deck in favor of your employees' living up to expectations. Employees want to do the right thing, but can do so only if they know what the right thing is.

- Empathy is crucial when delivering not-so-pleasant feedback. People who feel forced to defend their self-esteem are less receptive. Focus on specific behavior and remember the goal is to reset direction, not to point out inadequacies.

- Set clear incentives for a job well done. It makes sense that stars should get significantly more than poor performers, but rarely does that actually happen.[viii]

critical thinking exercises

Name: _____

Date: _____

critical thinking exercise 10-1
MANAGING A FAMILY BUSINESS

Nicholas Stavros opened his first restaurant in Cedar City 25 years ago. Stavros's family-style Greek food and atmosphere proved popular, and three additional restaurants were opened in outlying suburbs. One of Papa Nick's children now runs each: Maria's Stavros, Peter's Stavros, and Eric's Stavros. Nick Junior runs the original Nick's Stavros.

The menu is consistent across all four restaurants, but each restaurant features a daily special prepared by the local chef. Customer comment cards consistently rank the quality of food as very high.

Papa Nick now divides his time between the restaurants and the family's real estate holdings. Major decisions are made by Papa Nick. All employees at each restaurant report to the restaurant's Stavros manager, providing some degree of decentralization.

Customer comment cards have begun to show some problem areas at Peter's Stavros Restaurant. Service ratings have fallen to "fair," and many customers have written specific comments about slow service and poor wait service attitude.

Because it is the newest restaurant, Eric's Stavros has received more resources for advertising and promotion. The equipment is also significantly newer than that at the other three restaurants. Over time Maria, Peter, and Nick Junior have come to resent the attention Eric has received. The tension has become so high that the staff at Peter's Stavros does not speak to the staff at Eric's Stavros.

Papa Nick is reviewing two pieces of information. One, the profit margin from restaurant operations has declined over the past year. And, finally, several employees have mentioned their desire to join a union.

Papa Nick has asked your advice for improving the performance of his restaurants. What advice would you give him? Outline a plan of action, with goals and timelines.

critical thinking exercise 10-2
DOES MONEY MOTIVATE?

Divide the class into groups of five or six students. Assign half the groups one of the following hypotheses:

A. Money is an effective motivator.

B. Money does not motivate.

Have each group develop a detailed argument pro or con. After 10 minutes, each group should nominate a debate leader. Give each debate leader 5 minutes to present their arguments to the class. (For large classes, you may have to limit the number of presentations.)

At the end of the presentations, have the entire class vote on which argument they now endorse.

critical thinking exercise 10-3
TESTING MASLOW'S HIERARCHY OF NEEDS

According to Abraham Maslow, we all have certain needs ranging from physical needs to self-actualization. Maslow believed that when needs are unmet, they motivate us to behave a certain way. When the needs are met, they no longer motivate us. He also said that when lower-order needs remain unmet, we give them our attention and don't attend to the higher needs.

Let's test Maslow's theory to see if it holds true. Which needs are you giving your attention to right now (not for the day, not for the future, but for this minute)? Mark the need getting the most attention right now with a "0." Look at each of the other needs; place a check mark next to those that have been met. Each person should do this in private; no need for names on papers.

_____ Self-actualization needs (accomplish goals and develop to potential)

_____ Self-esteem needs (recognition, acknowledgment, and status)

_____ Social needs (feeling loved and part of the group)

_____ Safety needs (security at work and at home)

_____ Physical needs (food, drink, warmth, etc.)

notes on critical thinking exercise 10-3

Tally the results on the board. How many class members are focusing on each need? Have all the lower-level needs for each person been met (checked off)?

What does this information tell you? Are some classmates hungry and concentrating on physical needs? Others may be threatened by this exercise and may be sitting quietly tending to their safety needs. Others may be quite loud and eagerly participating, meeting their social needs. Others are claiming that their ideas are best, searching for recognition. Still others are calmly going about their business knowing that they are doing all they can do and are happy with themselves.

The point is that different things motivate individuals. In order to effectively motivate their employees, managers must listen to their employees, learn what their needs are, and design motivators to meet those needs. For example, if employees are physically uncomfortable or feel unsafe at work, they will pay little attention to meeting company goals unless they perceive that meeting those goals will make them feel comfortable or safe.

critical thinking exercise 10-4
THE MANAGEMENT CHALLENGE

Antonio Lacosta is the plant manager at the North Monticello factory. He has always believed in the abilities of his department heads and let them share in decision making. The four department heads have each been with the company for over 20 years and are very loyal to the organization.

Lacosta called a meeting this morning to inform the department heads of a report just received from the home office. It seems that the North Monticello plant has the highest costs of the 10 plants in the company and has fallen behind in production during the past eight months. This plant is one of the older plants, and the home office will be taking a close look at it. If costs can't be brought under control and production increased by 15% within six months, the North Adams plant will probably be closed. Some senior workers may be transferred to other locations, but most employees will be terminated.

However, if new conditions are met, the company plans to spend over $40 million on new production equipment, and all jobs would be secure. As Lacosta indicated, "If we can do the job over the next six months, this plant will gain a new lease on life. But if we do not, we can expect the company to shut us down permanently. I would like each of you four, as my major department leaders, to call a meeting of your people today to inform them of this situation."

If you were one of the department heads, how would you present the new situation to your workers? Outline the meeting.

critical thinking exercise 10-5

WHICH ARE THE BEST COMPANIES TO WORK FOR?

Despite stories of bad bosses and demotivating bureaucracy, some companies are able to come up with creative ways to keep employees satisfied. Each year the Great Place to Work Institute ranks America's top employers in the annual "Best Companies to Work For." Go to the institute's website (www.greatplacetowork.com/best). [ix] (Sometimes the Web address for a location changes. You might need to search to find the exact location mentioned.)

1.   List the top five companies.

2.   Choose one company from the list and use an Internet search engine (such as www.google.com, www.ask.com, or www.yahoo.com) to research the company. Summarize the company's background and mission.

3.   Follow the links to the institute's listing for the previous year. Are there any companies in common for the two years?

Name: _____

Date: _____

critical thinking exercise 10-6
MOTIVATION SURVEY

Recently Jacobs Construction Company conducted a survey of its supervisors asking them to complete the following form. They were asked to rank each factor from 1 (low) to 10 (high) as to how important each would be in increasing their motivation. The survey results for two of the supervisors are given below.

Factors	Hal Barrington	Frank Ramone	You
Higher wages	2	6	
Better job security	1	8	
Improved benefits	3	9	
Better chance for advancement	8	4	
More challenging work	10	3	
Better supervision	5	1	
More pleasant physical surroundings	6	10	
Better chance to grow and develop job skills	4	5	
More responsibility	9	2	
Better interpersonal relationships	7	7	

1.   Which factors are hygiene factors and which are motivating factors?

2.   Using Maslow's needs hierarchy theory, explain how you would use this information to motivate Hal Barrington.

3.   Using Maslow's needs hierarchy theory, explain how you would use this information to motivate Frank Ramone.

4.   In the final column, rank each factor as to how it would motivate you.

notes on critical thinking exercise 10-6

1. *Which factors are hygiene factors and which are motivating factors?*

    Motivating factors here are better chance for advancement, work that is more challenging, better chance to grow and develop job skills, and more responsibility. These factors cause employees to be productive—they are related to job content. The other factors are hygiene factors—those that have to do with job environment. These factors can cause dissatisfaction if missing, but do not necessarily motivate if increased.

2. *Using Maslow's needs hierarchy theory, explain how you would use this information to motivate Hal Barrington.*

    Barrington is probably trying to satisfy higher-level needs such as esteem and self-actualization. The factor rated highest is more challenging work. "Higher wages" ranks only 2. Money would be an ineffective motivator. Instead, the manager should offer the challenge Barrington desires—maybe give him responsibility for a key new project or for developing a new product.

3. *Using Maslow's needs hierarchy theory, explain how you would use this information to motivate Frank Ramone.*

    Ramone probably still has some lower-level unmet needs. His highest ranking is for more pleasant physical surroundings and improved benefits—a need for security. He also ranks "better personal relationships" high on the survey—a need for belonging. To motivate Ramone, these lower-level needs must be met. Only then can the manager use motivating factors, like more responsibility and challenging work, to improve his productivity.

4. *In the final column, rank each factor as to how it would motivate you.*

    Probably most students will rank higher wages near the top. (There are always student loans to be repaid.) Probably job security and benefits will also be ranked high.

bonus
cases

bonus case 10-1

WHEN FAILURE IS THE NORM

Few companies would accept a 96% failure rate. But in the pharmaceutical industry, a one-digit success rate is the norm. One such company is Pfizer Inc. To find the next big drug, Pfizer spends $152 million a week funding over 400 early-stage drug development projects. Ninety-six percent of those efforts will ultimately bomb. Most compounds prove to be unstable, unsafe, or unsuitable for human use.

Pfizer may have the biggest R&D operation of any company in the world. An army of 13,000 research scientists works out of 16 facilities from California to France to Japan. Pfizer's research budget of $7.9 billion is nearly five times that of the world's largest consumer-products company, Procter & Gamble.

Nancy Hutson is senior vice president of worldwide R&D at Pfizer and the director of Groton Labs, the largest drug-discovery facility on earth. Hutson joined Pfizer as a research scientist in 1981. She spent the next 15 years in drug discovery at Groton Laboratories, spending billions of dollars putting 35 medicines into development. Despite all the time and money, not one of Hutson's drug projects ever made it to market.

How does she manage a workforce that routinely fails? Instead of focusing on the big successes, she encourages the scientists to live for small victories, the small steps that may provide the foundations for an ultimate star drug. When a researcher publishes a paper, or when a lab gets some positive results on a new therapy, it is trumpeted throughout the organization. "Science folks don't live for the big day when a drug makes it to market," she says. "They live for the small moments when you see exciting results in the journals. Small victories help them to deal with the reality that, in all likelihood, there will be no big victory."

In 2000, Pfizer top management launched an effort to reduce the alarming number of failed R&D projects. The company dispatched 600 of its top scientists to find out why so many compounds flunked in clinical trials. The Attrition Task Force visited all Pfizer's worldwide labs, interviewing researchers and compiling a database of doomed projects. The task force eventually helped R&D managers rebalance the company's research projects between high-risk efforts and safer bets. The goal—to cut the research labs' failure rate to 92%. While still a stunning failure rate, this would actually double Pfizer's current R&D success rate, from 4% to 8%.

discussion questions for bonus case 10-1

1. Does the 4% success rate appear to be a good return on the company's investment? What additional information might you need to better answer this question?

2. With such a high failure of idea to market environment, how does this affect the culture of the company? Could you work in such an environment?

3. From your own perspective, how has the drug industry changed in types of products offered? How has this affected advertising?

4. Would Pfizer be a good investment? Why or why not?

UNDERSTANDING BNSINESS: Instructor's Resource Manual

notes on discussion questions for bonus case 10-1

1. *Does the 4% success rate appear to be a good return on the company's investment? What additional information might you need to better answer this question?*

   Four percent success rate is considerably higher than the industry norm and appears to be a very good return for the money spent. However, the amount spent ($7.9 billion) as a percentage to sales would be a better gauge as to how Pfizer compares to other drug companies.

2. *With such a high failure of idea to market environment, how does this affect the culture of the company? Could you work in such an environment?*

   The high failure rate is a byproduct of the industry approval process and is an example of the risk–reward system that is not seen by many companies. Without question, research is very exhausting and many individuals are not compatible with this process. Perseverance and self-confidence are needed to work successfully in this industry.

3. *From your own perspective, how has the drug industry changed in types of products offered? How has this affected advertising?*

   The drug industry has evolved over the years and has created many more options for consumers—for both serious and not so serious illnesses and conditions. Marketing dollars spent by drug companies have steadily risen. The return on this investment appears to be very favorable as more consumers are exposed to drug availability. (This would be a good time for students to name the top two or three drugs that they can easily remember seeing advertised.)

4. *Would Pfizer be a good investment? Why or why not?*

   Pfizer is working to improve its product success rate. While all investments are subject to company performances in the competitive marketplace, it does appear that Pfizer has leadership qualities and market success to be considered a good company to look at for investment purposes.

bonus case 10-2

THE SUPERMARKET MANAGER

Fred Ferrell is the store manager of the Right-Way Supermarket in Beaumont, a small suburban area of some 1,300 families. The store's staff consists of a produce manager, a meat manager and butcher, five checkers, four stockers, and a receiving clerk. The store operates six days per week from 9 a.m. to 9 p.m.

Last week Ferrell hired Amy Caldwell to replace the store's receiving clerk. Since graduating from high school last June, Amy has worked for one other supermarket full-time. She applied for the job at Right-Way to gain new experiences and because the job paid $1 more per hour than she was making at the other store. Amy likes the retail food business and hopes one day to manage a store of her own. She plans to start school again next fall.

After two 10-hour days of training under Mr. Ferrell, Amy felt she knew the operation and procedures well enough to proceed on her own. But Mr. Ferrell thought otherwise. For the rest of Amy's first week, Mr. Ferrell was looking over Amy's shoulder on a regular basis. It seemed that Amy couldn't do anything without Mr. Ferrell's checking it out for himself. Amy's tasks included the receipt, inspection, arrangement, and stacking of inventory received from a central supply warehouse owned and operated by the parent company. She was also responsible for the various inventory control procedures and related paperwork.

Over the weekend between her first and second weeks, Amy studied the inventory procedures and records. She roughed out a system for streamlining the handling and felt she had found a way to reduce the amount of paperwork by combining several forms into one and using the computer system to print forms simultaneously. Amy felt if she could sell these proposals to Mr. Ferrell, not only his store, but all stores in the chain, could benefit. After some hasty calculations, she figured that nearly one hour per day would be saved and several hundred dollars in unnecessary forms could be eliminated.

Amy started work at 6:30 a.m. the following Monday, full of enthusiasm. When Mr. Ferrell arrived at 8:00 a.m., Amy was waiting for him at the door, her notes in hand. Before Amy could speak, however, Ferrell asked her what she was doing up front. Amy replied that she had already handled this morning's deliveries and wanted to talk over a "proposal" with him. Mr. Ferrell pulled a piece of paper out of his pocket and began to go over each item on this checklist with Amy. When he got to item 10 on the list, Amy replied that she would take care of that this afternoon. Ferrell told her to take care of it now. Amy tried again to explain that she had some ideas to speed up the receiving operation. Ferrell replied, "You kids are really something else. You've been here a week and already you're running the place. What makes you think you know a better way? The procedures we use come from downtown. That is good enough for me. Now get to those cases out back."

discussion questions for bonus case 10-2

1.   What motivational approach is Mr. Ferrell using?

2.   Amy has asked your advice. What would you suggest that she do? What are her alternatives?

3.   What advice would you have for the general manager of Right-Way's Supermarket parent corporation?

notes on discussion questions for bonus case 10-2

1. *What motivational approach is Mr. Ferrell using?*

    He is applying the McGregor's Theory X system of motivation. It implies that the average person dislikes work and will avoid it if possible—and will avoid responsibility, with little ambition. Of course, he was wrong on all counts. This theory does work, but only with the kind of people who meet the description of disliking work and so forth.

2. *Amy has asked your advice. What would you suggest that she do? What are her alternatives?*

    Note the timing of her approach to Ferrell—she met him at the door at 8:00 a.m. on Monday morning. Could she have picked a worse time? Amy should wait until the appropriate time—most likely after work—to discuss her ideas with her boss. She should acknowledge the fact that some employees may prosper by merely following the rules, but that she is more ambitious than that and has some ideas. She may submit those ideas in writing so that the boss can implement them without losing face. If there is no response or a negative response to her suggestions, then, and only then, may she take them to a higher-level supervisor. Since this situation is far from unique, it should make for some lively class discussion.

3. *What advice would you have for the general manager of Right-Way's Supermarket parent corporation?*

    Management training is a continuous process and managers who fail to adopt the best motivational strategies need to be eliminated. You could explain the newest concepts, such as employee empowerment, and the motivational techniques that go with them. Theory Y, for example, is much more appropriate for today's more motivated and educated workers.

bonus case 10-3

MANAGING VOLUNTEERS

The executive director of the Oakview Humane Society, Jordan Webster, sometimes wishes he could fire his volunteers. The society has few paid workers and depends on volunteers to handle the day-to-day activities of the shelter.

Lucy is a full-time mother of two toddlers who does volunteer work for the society. She is organized and energetic. Her people skills help maintain positive relationships with local veterinary clinics, which treat the society's resident animals. Lucy spends much of her day running society errands, answering phone calls, and arranging foster homes for animals in need, all while refereeing her two children.

Alice is a 30-something entrepreneur who owns and manages a dinner theater with her husband. She has no children, just three dogs. The theater is open on Thursday, Friday, and Saturday nights. Because of this schedule, she has considerable flexibility and uses her free time to care for animals at the shelter. Alice is also the society adoption coordinator, doing an excellent job of matching pets with prospective adopters. Her manner is a little blunt, and people frequently complain that she is "bossy." Her e-mails to society officers and volunteers are frequently one-line commands to do something.

The two women are jokingly referred to as the "alpha females" because each is strong-willed and outspoken. Unfortunately, they frequently clash over issues, resulting in daily phone calls and e-mails to the director and other society officers. Alice complains that Lucy does not spend enough time at the shelter doing the "dirty work," cleaning pens and changing water. Alice has frequently commented on Lucy's carefree life without a job. Lucy complains that Alice is rude and insensitive and observes that Alice has an easy life with lots of money and free time.

Today Webster ran into Alice at the restaurant. She was furious because Lucy had accepted a stray dog to the society when the pens were already full. "Lucy doesn't help take care of the animals she accepts. She doesn't understand our limitations." Alice has offered to resign for the good of the society.

Webster just got off the phone with Lucy who is threatening to quit because she feels Alice insulted her in an e-mail.

discussion questions for bonus case 10-3

1.   How does managing volunteers differ from managing paid employees?

2.   What incentives can Webster use to motivate volunteers?

3.   What should the director do next, if anything?

notes on discussion questions for bonus case 10-3

1.   How does managing volunteers differ from managing paid employees?

Volunteers cannot be motivated by money because they don't earn any. They can't be bossed around because they can easily quit. In short, volunteers are a real challenge to managers. Conflicts such as those presented in the case are not infrequent. The class may want to introduce some personal experiences or make some up. The idea is to think about management in a nonprofit setting.

2.   *What incentives can Webster use to motivate volunteers?*

The highest-level motivational tool is the job itself. People volunteer at animal shelters and the like because they love being around animals. The second highest motivational tool is recognition for a job well done. This case also brings out "hygiene factors" that cause dissatisfaction if not present, but not motivation if done right. That includes supervision and working conditions and interpersonal relations. For example, a new and nicer boss wouldn't do anything to relieve the problem. Neither would better working conditions.

3.   *What should the director do next, if anything?*

Interpersonal relations are often the most difficult things to manage. The class may enjoy talking about their experiences and what they might do to solve the problem. Would someone have to be "let go"?

endnotes

[i] *Source:* Jennifer Levitz, "UPS Thinks Outside the Box on Driver Training," *The Wall Street Journal*, April 6, 2010.

[ii] *Source*: Andrea Nierenberg, "Motivating Without Money," *Fortune Small Business Online*, October 12, 2004.

[iii] *Sources:* Frank Farley, "The Big T in Personality," *Psychology Today*, May 1, 1986; "The Thrill That Kills," *ABC News,* May 12, 1999; David Sirota et al., "Why Your Employees Are Losing Motivation," *New Straits Times,* April 1, 2006.

[iv] *Source*: Andrea Sachs, "Animals Behave," *Time Inside Business,* May 2005.

[v] *Source:* "Japan Airline Boss Sets Exec Example," *CBS News,* January 29, 2009.

[vi] *Sources:* Noelle Barton DeFazio and Caroline Preston, "Wal-Mart Tops List of Charitable Cash Contributors, AT&T No. 2," *USA Today*, August 9, 2010; Amy Reeves, "Wal-Mart Contract Could Spell Influx of Students for Online School," *Investor's Business Daily*, June 7, 2010.

[vii] *Source:* Leonard L. Berry, Ann M. Mirabito, and William B. Baun, "What's the Hard Return on Employee Wellness Programs?" *Harvard Business Review*, December 2010.

[viii] *Source*: FSB Staff, "Positive Feedback," *Fortune Small Business*, July/August 2002, p. 81

[ix] The Internet is a dynamic, changing information source. Web links noted of this manual were checked at the time of publication, but content may change over time. Please review the website before recommending it to your students.

Human Resource Management: Finding and Keeping the Best Employees

chapter 11

critical thinking exercises   11.93

bonus cases   11.101

what's new in this edition

additions to the 10th edition:

- Getting to Know Mark Parker, CEO of Nike

- Name That Company: Nucor Steel

- Discussion items concerning baby boomers in the workforce and health care added to section The Human Resource Challenge

- Legal Briefcase: The Million Woman Suit against Wal-Mart

- Making Ethical Decisions: Are Unpaid Interns Too Interred?

- Figure Government Legislation Affecting Human Resource Management

- Video Case

revisions to the 10th edition:

- Text was revised to eliminate redundancy and tighten discussions.

- Statistical data and examples throughout the chapter were updated to reflect current information.

- Definition of reverse discrimination revised in section Laws Affecting Human Resource Management and in Glossary.

deletions from the 9th edition:

- Getting to Know Sally Mainquist, President and CEO of Certes Financial Pros

- Name That Company: Wegman's Foods

- Legal Briefcase

- Making Ethical Decisions

- Thinking Green

brief chapter outline and learning goals

Human Resource Management: Finding and Keeping the Best Employees

Getting To Know MARK PARKER, CEO of NIKE

learning goal 1

Explain the importance of human resource management, and describe current issues in managing human resources.

I. WORKING WITH PEOPLE IS JUST THE BEGINNING

    A. Developing the Ultimate Resource

    B. The Human Resource Challenge

learning goal 2

Illustrate the effect of legislation on human resource management.

II. LAWS AFFECTING HUMAN RESOURCE MANAGEMENT

    A. Laws Protecting Employees with Disabilities and Older Employees

    B. Effects of Legislation

learning goal 3

Summarize the five steps in human resource planning.

III. DETERMINING A FIRM'S HUMAN RESOURCE NEEDS

learning goal 4

Describe methods that companies use to recruit new employees, and explain some of the issues that make recruitment challenging.

IV. RECRUITING EMPLOYEES FROM A DIVERSE POPULATION

learning goal 5

Outline the six steps in selecting employees.

V. SELECTING EMPLOYEES WHO WILL BE PRODUCTIVE

    A. Hiring Contingent Workers

learning goal 6

Illustrate employee training and development methods.

VI. TRAINING AND DEVELOPING EMPLOYEES FOR OPTIMUM PERFORMANCE

    A.   **Management Development**

    B.   **Networking**

    C.   **Diversity in Management Development**

learning goal 7

Trace the six steps in appraising employee performance.

VII. APPRAISING EMPLOYEE PERFORMANCE TO GET OPTIMUM RESULTS

learning goal 8

Summarize the objectives of employee compensation programs, and evaluate various pay systems and fringe benefits.

VIII. COMPENSATING EMPLOYEES: ATTRACTING AND KEEPING THE BEST

    A.   **Pay Systems**

    B.   **Compensating Teams**

    C.   **Fringe Benefits**

learning goal 9

Demonstrate how managers use scheduling plans to adapt to workers' needs.

IX. SCHEDULING EMPLOYEES TO MEET ORGANIZATIONAL AND EMPLOYEE NEEDS

    A.   **Flextime Plans**

    B.   **Home-Based Work**

    C.   **Job-Sharing Plans**

learning goal 10

Describe how employees can move through a company: promotion, reassignment, termination, and retirement.

X. MOVING EMPLOYEES UP, OVER, AND OUT

    A.   **Promoting and Reassigning Employees**

    B.   **Terminating Employees**

    C.   **Retiring Employees**

    D.   **Losing Valued Employees**

XI. SUMMARY

lecture outline

Getting to Know MARK PARKER, CEO of NIKE

A champion marathoner, Mark Parker is a shoe designer turned executive. He started at Nike in 1977 and rose through the ranks. After working in many successful design teams, Parker became CEO in 2006. Since then, he has learned he needs to keep his 33,000 employees motivated. Nike's headquarters houses many gym and restaurant facilities plus free on-site child care.

This company is one of the largest U.S. steel producers. It pays its teams bonuses that are calculated on quality—tons of steel that go out the door with no defects. There are no limits on bonuses a team can earn; they usually average about $20,000 per employee each year. Name that company

(Students should read the chapter before guessing the company's name: Nucor Steel)

learning goal 1

Explain the importance of human resource management, and describe current issues in managing human resources.

I. WORKING WITH PEOPLE IS JUST THE BEGINNING.

A. ***HUMAN RESOURCE MANAGEMENT*** is the process of determining human resource needs and then recruiting, selecting, developing, motivating, evaluating, compensating, and scheduling employees to achieve organizational goals.

  1. Historically, human resource management was called "personnel" and managed clerical functions and finding new employees.

  2. The role of HRM has evolved because:

     a. Organizations recognize employees as their ultimate resource.

     b. Changes in the law have rewritten many traditional practices.

PPT 11-1
Chapter Title

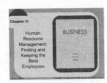

PPT 11-2
Learning Goals

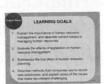

(See complete PowerPoint slide notes on page 11.58.)

PPT 11-3
Learning Goals

(See complete PowerPoint slide notes on page 11.58.)

PPT 11-4
Learning Goals

(See complete PowerPoint slide notes on page 11.59.)

PPT 11-5
Mark Parker

(See complete PowerPoint slide notes on page 11.59.)

PPT 11-6
Name That Company

(See complete PowerPoint slide notes on page 11.59.)

PPT 11-7
Human Resource Management

TEXT FIGURE 11.1
Human Resource Management
(Text page 291)

(See complete PowerPoint slide notes on page 11.60.)

PPT 11-8
Human Resource Management
(HRM)

(See complete PowerPoint slide notes on page 11.60.)

B. **DEVELOPING THE ULTIMATE RESOURCE**

1. The U.S. economy has undergone a major shift from traditional manufacturing industries to service industries that require more **HIGHLY TECHNICAL JOB SKILLS.**

2. Many workers must be retrained for new, more challenging jobs.

3. **EMPLOYEES ARE THE ULTIMATE RESOURCE.**

    a. In the past, the human resource was plentiful, so there was little need to nurture and develop it.

    b. Qualified labor is scarcer today, and that makes recruiting more difficult.

4. For years, most firms assigned the job of recruiting, selecting, training, evaluating, compensating, motivating, and firing people to **FUNCTIONAL DEPARTMENTS.**

5. **HUMAN RESOURCE MANAGEMENT** may be the most critical function in the future because it is responsible for the business's most critical resource—people.

    a. The role of the human resource management is a **FUNCTION OF ALL MANAGERS**, not just one department.

    b. Most human resource functions are **SHARED** between the human resource manager and other managers.

PPT 11-9
Uncovering the Secrets of HRM

(See complete PowerPoint slide notes on page 11.60.)

PPT 11-10
Developing the Firm's Ultimate
Resource

(See complete PowerPoint slide notes on page 11.61.)

C. **THE HUMAN RESOURCE CHALLENGE**

1. The ability of the U.S. business system to compete globally depends on people with good ideas.

2. Some of the **CHALLENGES** and **OPPORTUNITIES** include:

   a. Shortages of people trained to work in high-tech areas

   b. An increasing number of skilled and unskilled workers from declining industries who are unemployed or underemployed

   c. A growing percentage of new workers who are undereducated and unprepared for jobs

   d. A shortage of workers in skilled trades due to retirement of aging baby boomers

   e. An increasing number of baby boomers delaying retirement or moving to lower-level jobs

   f. An increasing number of single-parent and two-income families

   g. A shift in employee attitudes toward work

   h. A declining economy taking a toll on employee morale

   i. More competition from low-wage overseas labor pools

   j. Increased demand for benefits tailored to the individual

   k. Growing concern over health issues, elder care, child care, equal opportunities for people with disabilities, and affirmative action

bonus case 11-1
INCARCERATED CALL
CENTERS

One entrepreneur found a way to transform prisoners into productive members of society both inside and upon release. (See the complete case, discussion questions, and suggested answers beginning on page 11.101 of this manual.)

PPT 11-11
Challenges in Finding High-Level
Workers

(See complete PowerPoint slide notes on page 11.61.)

  l. Changes in healthcare law

  m. A decreased sense of employee loyalty

 3. Significant changes in laws covering HRM have had a major influence.

<u>**learning goal 2**</u>

 Illustrate the effects of legislation on human resource management.

II. LAWS AFFECTING HUMAN RESOURCE MANAGEMENT

 A. Legislation has made hiring, promoting, firing, and managing employee relations complex and subject to legal complications.

  1. Since the 1930s **LEGISLATION AND LEGAL DECISIONS** have greatly affected human resource management.

  2. One of the most important laws ever passed by Congress was the **CIVIL RIGHTS ACT OF 1964**.

   a. **TITLE VII** prohibits discrimination in hiring, firing, compensation, apprenticeships, training, terms, conditions, or privileges of employment based on race, religion, creed, sex, or national origin (age was added later).

   b. Specific language in the law often made its enforcement difficult.

  3. The **EQUAL EMPLOYMENT OPPORTUNITY ACT (EEOA)** was added as an amendment to Title VII in 1972.

   a. It strengthened the **EQUAL EMPLOYMENT OPPORTUNITY COMMISSION (EEOC)**, which issues guidelines for administering

TEXT FIGURE 11.2
Government Legislation Affecting
Human Resource Management
(Text page 293)

PPT 11-12
Civil Rights Act of 1964

(See complete PowerPoint slide notes on page 11.61.)

PPT 11-13
1972 Equal Employment
Opportunity Act (EEOA)

(See complete PowerPoint slide notes on page 11.62.)

equal employment opportunity.

    b. Congress gave the EEOC broad powers to regulate equal employment opportunity.

4. **AFFIRMATIVE ACTION PROGRAMS** are controversial.

    a. ***AFFIRMATIVE ACTION*** refers to employment activities designed to "right past wrongs" by increasing opportunities for minorities and women.

    b. Interpretation of the law was often controversial and enforcement was difficult.

    c. One result has been the perceived ***REVERSE DISCRIMINATION***, or discrimination against dominant or majority group members in hiring or promoting.

    d. Companies have been charged with reverse discrimination when they have been **PERCEIVED** as **UNFAIRLY GIVING PREFERENCE** in hiring or promoting.

5. The **CIVIL RIGHTS ACT OF 1991** expanded the remedies available to victims of discrimination by amending Title VII of the CRA of 1964.

6. The **OFFICE OF FEDERAL CONTRACT COMPLIANCE PROGRAMS (OFCCP)** ensures compliance in firms doing business with the federal government.

PPT 11-14
Controversial Procedures of the
EEOC

(See complete PowerPoint slide notes on page 11.62.)

PPT 11-15
Civil Rights Act of 1991 and
OFCCP

(See complete PowerPoint slide notes on page 11.62.)

B. **LAWS PROTECTING EMPLOYEES WITH DISABILITIES AND OLDER EMPLOYEES**

1. This act, passed in 1973, extended the same protection to people with disabilities.

2. The **AMERICANS WITH DISABILITIES ACT OF 1990 (ADA)** requires that applicants who are disabled be given the same consideration for employment as people without disabilities.

    a. It requires that businesses make **"REASON-ABLE ACCOMMODATIONS"** to people with disabilities.

    b. Most companies can easily and inexpensively make the structural changes needed.

    c. However, companies are having more trouble making **CULTURAL CHANGES** to be accommodating.

    d. A key concept is **ACCOMMODATION**, which means treating people according to their specific needs.

3. In 2008 Congress passed the **AMERICANS WITH DISABILITIES AMENDMENTS ACT.**

    a. This overturned Supreme Court decisions that reduced protections for people with disabilities.

    b. In 2011, the EEOC widened the range of disabilities and shifted the burden of proof of disabilities to owners.

4. The **AGE DISCRIMINATION IN EMPLOYMENT ACT** protects individuals who are 40 years or older from discrimination based on age.

    a. Under the ADEA, it is **UNLAWFUL TO**

PPT 11-16

Laws Protecting Employees with Disabilities

(See complete PowerPoint slide notes on page 11.63.)

PPT 11-17

Age Discrimination in Employment Act (ADEA)

(See complete PowerPoint slide notes on page 11.63.)

DISCRIMINATE AGAINST A PERSON BECAUSE OF AGE with respect to hiring, firing, promotion, layoff, compensation, benefits, job assignments, and training.

    b. The ADEA **OUTLAWED MANDATORY RETIREMENT** in most organizations, but provides exemptions for certain critical jobs.

C. **EFFECTS OF LEGISLATION**

    1. All areas of human resource management are affected by legislation.

    2. **IN SUMMARY**:

        a. Employers must know and act in accordance with the legal rights of their employees.

        b. Legislation affects all areas of human resource management.

        c. It is sometimes legal to go beyond providing equal rights for minorities and women to provide special employment to correct past discrimination.

        d. New court cases and legislation continuously change human resource management; it is important to keep current.

learning goal 3
Summarize the five steps in human resource planning.

III. **DETERMINING A FIRM'S HUMAN RESOURCE NEEDS**

A. **PREPARING A HUMAN RESOURCE INVENTORY** of the organization's employees

B. **PREPARING A JOB**

PPT 11-18
Minding the Law in HRM

(See complete PowerPoint slide notes on page 11.63.)

**legal
briefcase**
(Text page 295)

PPT 11-19
The Million
Woman Suit
against Wal-Mart

(See complete PowerPoint slide notes on page 11.64.)

**progress
assessment**
(Text page 296)

PPT 11-20
Progress Assessment

(See complete PowerPoint slide notes on page 11.64.)

PPT 11-21
Human Resource Planning
Process

(See complete PowerPoint slide notes on page 11.65.)

1. A **_JOB ANALYSIS_** is a study of what is done by employees who hold various jobs.

2. The results of the job analysis are two written statements.

   a. A **_JOB DESCRIPTION_** is a summary of the objectives of a job, the type of work to be done, the responsibilities and duties, the working conditions, and the relationship of the job to other functions.

   b. **_JOB SPECIFICATIONS_** are written summaries of the minimum qualifications required of workers to do a particular job.

C. **ASSESSING FUTURE HUMAN RESOURCE DEMAND**—HR managers must be proactive to anticipate future needs of their organizations.

D. **ASSESSING FUTURE LABOR SUPPLY** in a constantly changing labor market

E. **ESTABLISHING A STRATEGIC PLAN** addressing recruiting, selecting, training and developing, appraising, compensating, and scheduling the labor force

F. Companies are also using advanced technologies to manage the human resource planning process.

learning

Describe methods that companies use to recruit new employees, and explain some of the issues that make recruitment challenging.

IV. **RECRUITING EMPLOYEES FROM A DIVERSE POPULATION**

A. **_RECRUITMENT_** is the set of activities used to obtain a sufficient number of the right people at the right time.

PPT 11-22
What's a Job Analysis?

(See complete PowerPoint slide notes on page 11.65.)

TEXT FIGURE 11.3
Job Analysis
(Text page 297)

This text figure shows a sample job analysis that yields two statements: job descriptions and job specifications.

critical thinking exercise 11-1
EXPANDING THE WORKFORCE

This exercise presents a human resource planning dilemma. Does the increased profit from a business expansion justify increased labor costs? (See complete exercise on page 11.93 of this manual.)

PPT 11-23
Recruiting Employees

(See complete PowerPoint slide notes on page 11.65.)

lecture link 11-1
WHERE HAVE ALL THE WANT ADS GONE?

Traditional newspapers are seeing their classified revenue shrink as classified advertising moved online. (See the complete lecture link on page 11.82 in this manual.)

lecture link 11-2
FINDING GOOGLE PEOPLE

Google is scrambling to find enough people to support its rapid expansion. (See the complete lecture link on page 11.83 in this manual.)

B. **RECRUITING IS CHALLENGING** for several reasons:

   1. Some organizations have policies that demand promotion from within, operate under union regulations, or offer low wages.

   2. It important to hire skilled people who also **FIT IN WITH THE ORGANIZATION'S CULTURE**.

   3. People with the necessary skills may not be available, and must be hired and then trained.

C. Human resource managers turn to many **SOURCES** for assistance.

   1. **INTERNAL SOURCES** involve hiring from within the firm and employee recommendations.

      a. Internal sources are usually less expensive.

      b. Hiring from within helps maintain employee morale.

   2. When it isn't possible to find qualified workers within the company, HR managers must use **EXTERNAL RECRUITMENT** sources.

   3. Recruiting qualified workers may be particularly difficult for small businesses with few staff members.

<u>**learning goal** 5</u>

Outline the six steps in selecting employees.

V. **SELECTING EMPLOYEES WHO WILL BE PRODUCTIVE**

A. **_SELECTION_** is the process of gathering information and deciding who should be hired, under legal guidelines, for the best interest of the individual and the organization.

SPOTLIGHT ON
small
business
(Text page 300)

PPT 11-24
It's Not Easy
Being Small

(See complete PowerPoint slide notes on page 11.66.)

critical thinking
exercise 11-2
MANAGEMENT SELECTION

This exercise asks the students to consider several applicants for two job openings and decide whom to hire. (See complete exercise on page 11.96 of this manual.)

critical thinking
exercise 11-3
JOB SEARCH VIA THE INTERNET

This Internet exercise explores online job search engines such as Monster.com. (See complete exercise on page 11.98 of this manual.)

PPT 11-25
Employee Sources

TEXT FIGURE 11.4
Employee Sources
(Text page 299)

(See complete PowerPoint slide notes on page 11.66.)

PPT 11-26
Selection

(See complete PowerPoint slide notes on page 11.66.)

1. The selection process is a key element in human resource management.

2. Selection expenses can cost one and one-half of an employee's annual salary.

B. **STEPS OF THE SELECTION PROCESS**

1. **OBTAINING A COMPLETE APPLICATION FORM**

   a. Legal guidelines limit the kinds of questions that may appear on an application form.

   b. Allowed information includes the applicant's educational background, past work experience, career objectives, and other qualifications.

   c. Many large organizations use an automated program, Workforce Acquisition, to screen applicants.

2. **CONDUCTING INITIAL AND FOLLOW-UP INTERVIEWS**

   a. A human resource department staff member often screens applicants in a first interview.

   b. Potential employees are then interviewed by the manager who will supervise the new employee.

   c. Both HRM and functional managers must be careful to avoid missteps in interview questioning.

3. **GIVING EMPLOYMENT TESTS**

   a. Some organizations continue to use tests to measure basic competencies in **SPECIFIC JOB SKILLS**, although testing has been severely criticized.

lecture link 11-3
MAKING AN IMPRESSION WITH VIDEO RESUMES

In the age of intense competition, job seekers are doing what they can to stand out from the crowd and be selected. (See the complete lecture link on page 11.84 in this manual.)

PPT 11-27
Steps in the Selection Process

(See complete PowerPoint slide notes on page 11.67.)

lecture link 11-4
INTERVIEW BLUNDERS

There are a few questions that interviewers should never ask prospective employees. Here's an explanation of what to do should the interviewer ask such questions. (See the complete lecture link on page 11.84 of this manual.)

lecture link 11-5
MEMORABLE JOB INTERVIEWS

In a survey, executives revealed some of the more unusual interviews they had conducted. (See complete lecture link on page 11.86 of this manual.)

PPT 11-28
Oops!

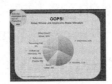

(See complete PowerPoint slide notes on page 11.67.)

lecture link 11-6
PERSONALITY TESTING FOR JOB APPLICANTS

About 30% of employers use a version of personality tests in hiring. (See the complete lecture link on page 11.87 of this manual.)

lecture link 11-7
BACKGROUND CHECKS: SECURITY AND PRIVACY ISSUES

Today's heightened concerns for security coupled with improved technology means background checking has become more widely used. Do these checks violate applicants' rights? (See the complete lecture link on page 11.87 in this manual.)

lecture link 11-8
THE INVASIVE DANGERS OF FACEBOOK

The personalization of Facebook is great for personal use. However, it can be detrimental to job seekers. (See the complete lecture link on page 11.88 in this manual.)

    b. It is important that the test be **DIRECTLY RELATED** to the job.

    c. Employment tests have been criticized because of the potential for illegal discrimination.

    d. Many companies test potential employees in **ASSESSMENT CENTERS** where applicants perform tasks of the actual job.

4. **CONDUCTING BACKGROUND INVESTIGATIONS** helps determine which candidates are most likely to succeed in a given position.

    a. Most organizations investigate an applicant's work record, school records, credit history, and references.

    b. Services such as LexisNexis let prospective employers conduct background checks and verify work experience of applicants.

5. **OBTAINING RESULTS FROM PHYSICAL EXAMS**

    a. Medical tests cannot be given to screen out individuals.

    b. In some states, physical exams can be given only **AFTER AN OFFER OF EMPLOYMENT HAS BEEN ACCEPTED**.

    c. Preemployment testing to detect drug or alcohol abuse or for AIDS screening is controversial.

6. **ESTABLISHING TRIAL (PROBATIONARY) PERIODS** allows organizations to hire an employee conditionally.

7. The selection process is difficult but helps ensure that new employees meet requirements in all relevant areas.

C. **HIRING CONTINGENT WORKERS**

1. Sometimes it is more cost-effective to hire contingent workers when a company has a varying need for employees.

   a. **_CONTINGENT WORKERS_** include part-time workers, temporary workers, seasonal workers, independent contractors, interns, and co-op students.

2. **REASONS TO USE CONTINGENT WORKERS:**

   a. The firm has a varying need for employees.

   b. The full-time employees are on leave.

   c. There is a peak demand for labor.

   d. Quick service to customers is a priority.

3. Companies also tend to hire more contingent workers in an uncertain economy.

4. Contingent workers receive **FEW BENEFITS** and **EARN LESS** than permanent workers do.

   a. Many temporary workers are offered full-time positions.

   b. Managers view using temporary workers as a way of finding good hires.

5. Although exact data are unavailable, the use of contingency workers appears to be increasing.

6. Many people, such as college students, find that temporary work offers them more **FLEXIBILITY** than a permanent position.

<u>bonus case 11-2</u>
SHOULD YOU HIRE BACK A FORMER EMPLOYEE?

Former employees sometimes ask employers to hire them back. Is this a good idea? (See the complete case, discussion questions, and suggested answers beginning on page 11.103 of this manual.)

PPT 11-29
Hiring Contingent Workers

(See complete PowerPoint slide notes on page 11.67.)

PPT 11-30
Why Hire Contingent Workers?

(See complete PowerPoint slide notes on page 11.68.)

PPT 11-31
Students and the Contingent Workforce

(See complete PowerPoint slide notes on page 11.68.)

MAKING
ethical
decisions
(Text page 304)

PPT 11-32
Are Unpaid Interns Too Interred?

(See complete PowerPoint slide notes on page 11.68.)

7. "Temping" may be a more secure situation in an era of downsizing.

Illustrate employee training and development methods.

VI. TRAINING AND DEVELOPING EMPLOYEES FOR OPTIMUM PERFORMANCE

A. DESIGNING TRAINING AND DEVELOPMENT PROGRAMS

1. ***TRAINING AND DEVELOPMENT*** involves all attempts to improve performance by increasing an employee's ability to perform.

2. Spending for employee training is a good investment because it:

   a. Leads to higher retention rates

   b. Increases productivity

   c. Improves job satisfaction among employees

3. **TRAINING** focuses on short-term skills.

4. **DEVELOPMENT** focuses on long-term abilities.

5. The process of **CREATING TRAINING AND DEVELOPMENT PROGRAMS** includes:

   a. **ASSESSING THE NEEDS** of the organization and the skills of the employees to determine training needs

   b. **DESIGNING TRAINING ACTIVITIES** to meet the identified needs

   c. **EVALUATING THE EFFECTIVENESS** of the training

progress
assessment
(Text page 303)

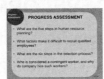

PPT 11-33
Progress Assessment.   (See complete PowerPoint slide notes on page 11.69.)

PPT 11-34
Training and Developing
Employees

(See complete PowerPoint slide notes on page 11.69.)

PPT 11-35
Three Steps of Training and
Development

(See complete PowerPoint slide notes on page 11.70.)

B. **TRAINING AND DEVELOPMENT ACTIVITIES**

1. _**ORIENTATION**_ is the activity that introduces new employees to the organization; to fellow employees; to their immediate supervisors; and to the policies, practices, and objectives of the firm.

2. **ON-THE-JOB TRAINING**

   a. _**ON-THE-JOB TRAINING**_ is training at the workplace that lets the employee learn by doing, or by watching others for a while, and then imitating them.

   b. Salespeople are often trained by watching experienced salespeople perform (**SHADOWING**).

   c. This type of training is **EASY AND EFFECTIVE** for learning low-skill, repetitive jobs but can **BE DISASTROUS** if used in areas demanding more knowledge and expertise.

   d. Cost-effective on-the-job training programs can be created using **INTRANETS.**

   e. Computer systems can monitor workers' input and provide feedback.

3. **APPRENTICE PROGRAMS**

   a. _**APPRENTICESHIP PROGRAMS**_ are training programs during which a learner works alongside an experienced employee to master the skills and procedures of a craft.

   b. In many skilled crafts, a new worker is required to serve several years as an **APPRENTICE.**

PPT 11-36
Most Commonly Used Training and
Development Activities

(See complete PowerPoint slide notes on page 11.70.)

    c. Workers who successfully complete an apprenticeship earn the classification of **JOURNEYMAN.**

    d. There may be more, but shorter, apprenticeship programs in the future, as jobs require more intense training.

4. ***OFF-THE-JOB TRAINING*** are internal or external training programs away from the workplace that develop any of a variety of skills or to foster personal development.

5. ***ONLINE TRAINING*** consists of training programs in which employees "complete" classes via the Internet.

    a. Educational institutes offer **DISTANCE LEARNING** programs.

    b. Employers can offer consistent content tailored to specific training needs.

6. ***VESTIBULE TRAINING*** (near-the-job training) is done in schools where employees are trained on equipment similar to that used on the job.

7. ***JOB SIMULATION*** is the use of equipment that duplicates the job conditions and tasks so that trainees can learn skills before attempting them on the job.

C. **MANAGEMENT DEVELOPMENT**

1. **MANAGERS NEED SPECIAL TRAINING**: They must learn communication, planning, and human relations skills.

PPT 11-37
Developing Effective Managers

(See complete PowerPoint slide notes on page 11.70.)

PPT 11-38
Why Good Employees Quit

(See complete PowerPoint slide notes on page 11.71.)

2. ***MANAGEMENT DEVELOPMENT*** is the process of training and educating employees to become good managers and then monitoring the progress of their managerial skills over time.

3. **MANAGEMENT DEVELOPMENT PROGRAMS** include the following:

    a. **ON-THE-JOB COACHING** by a senior manager

    b. **UNDERSTUDY POSITIONS** as assistants to higher-level managers who participate in planning and other managerial functions

    c. **JOB ROTATION** exposing managers to different functions of the organization

    d. **OFF-THE-JOB COURSES AND TRAINING** exposing managers to the latest concepts and creating a sense of camaraderie

D. **NETWORKING**

1. ***NETWORKING*** is the process of establishing and maintaining contacts with key managers in one's own organization and in other organizations and using those contacts to weave strong relationships that serve as informal development systems.

2. A ***MENTOR*** is an experienced employee who supervises, coaches, and guides lower-level employees by introducing them to the right people and generally being their organizational sponsors.

3. Most mentoring is **INFORMAL**, but many organizations use a formal system of assigning mentors.

PPT 11-39
Using Networks and Mentoring

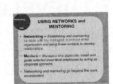

(See complete PowerPoint slide notes on page 11.71.)

    4. Networking goes beyond the business environment and can start with making educational contacts.

  E. **DIVERSITY IN MANAGEMENT DEVELOPMENT**

    1. Since most older managers are male, women often have more difficulty finding mentors and entering the network.

    2. "Men only" clubs were declared illegal by the U.S. Supreme Court, allowing women **ACCESS TO AREAS WHERE CONTACTS ARE MADE.**

    3. African American and Hispanic managers are also learning the benefits of networking.

    4. Other ethnic groups can also use networking.

    5. **PRINCIPLES TO DEVELOP FEMALE AND MINORITY MANAGERS:**

      a. Grooming women and minorities for management positions is more than a legal or moral issue—it is about bringing in more talent.

      b. The best women and minorities will become harder to attract and retain.

      c. Having more women and minorities means that businesses can serve female and minority customers better.

learning goal 7

Trace the six steps in appraising employee performance.

VII. APPRAISING EMPLOYEE PERFORMANCE TO GET OPTIMUM RESULTS

  A. A **_PERFORMANCE APPRAISAL_** is an evaluation that measures employee performance against established standards to make decisions about promotions, compensation, additional training, or firing.

<u>critical thinking
exercise 11-4</u>

DIVERSITY IN MANAGEMENT

This exercise directs students to the federal government's Bureau of Labor Statistics website to identify the current statistics on the percentage of minority managers in the workforce. (See complete exercise on page 11.99 of this manual.)

<u>critical thinking
exercise 11-5</u>

**BEST COMPANIES FOR
WORKING MOMS**

Working Mother magazine ranks the best companies for working mothers. This exercise directs students to research the Internet for the year's current winners. (See complete exercise on page 11.100 of this manual.)

PPT 11-40
Appraising Performance on the Job

(See complete PowerPoint slide notes on page 11.71.)

B. **SIX STEPS OF PERFORMANCE APPRAISALS**:

1. **ESTABLISHING PERFORMANCE STANDARDS** that are understandable, measurable, and reasonable

2. **COMMUNICATING THOSE STANDARDS** to employees

3. **EVALUATING PERFORMANCE**

4. **DISCUSSING RESULTS WITH EMPLOYEES**

5. **TAKING CORRECTIVE ACTION** or providing feedback

6. **USING THE RESULTS TO MAKE DECISIONS**

C. The latest form of performance appraisal is the **360-DEGREE REVIEW** because it uses feedback from all directions in the organization: up, down, and all around.

learning goal 8

Summarize the objectives of employee compensation programs, and evaluate various pay systems and fringe benefits.

VIII. COMPENSATING EMPLOYEES: ATTRACTING AND KEEPING THE BEST

A. Companies compete for employees.

1. **COMPENSATION** is one of the main marketing tools used to attract qualified employees.

   a. The long-term success of a firm may depend on how well it can **CONTROL EMPLOYEE COSTS** and **OPTIMIZE EMPLOYEE EFFICIENCY**.

   b. For service operations, the cost of labor is the largest cost item.

PPT 11-41
Six Steps of Performance
Appraisals

(See complete PowerPoint slide notes on page 11.72.)

PPT 11-42
Major Uses of Performance
Appraisals

(See complete PowerPoint slide notes on page 11.72.)

lecture link 11-9
**MICROSOFT REVISES
PERFORMANCE APPRAISALS**

Microsoft's dreaded forced curve review is being modified to make the appraisal system fairer. (See the complete lecture link on page 11.89 in this manual.)

PPT 11-43
Performance Appraisal Mistakes

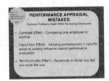

(See complete PowerPoint slide notes on page 11.72.)

TEXT FIGURE 11.5
Conducting Effective Appraisals
and Reviews
(Text page 309)

This text figure illustrates how managers can make performance appraisals more meaningful.

**progress
assessment**
(Text page 308)

PPT 11-44
Progress Assessment

(See complete PowerPoint slide notes on page 11.73.)

PPT 11-45
Compensation Programs

(See complete PowerPoint slide notes on page 11.73.)

    c. Manufacturing firms in some industries have asked employees to take reductions in wages to make the firm more competitive.

    d. **COMPENSATION** and **BENEFIT PACKAGES** are being given special attention.

    e. Corporate downsizing has made tailoring compensation packages more important than ever.

2. The **OBJECTIVES** of compensation and benefit programs include:

    a. **ATTRACTING THE KINDS OF PEOPLE NEEDED** in sufficient numbers

    b. Providing employees with the **INCENTIVE TO WORK EFFICIENTLY AND PRODUCTIVELY**

    c. **KEEPING VALUED EMPLOYEES** from leaving the company

    d. **MAINTAINING A COMPETITIVE POSITION** by keeping costs low by increasing productivity

    e. Providing employees with some sense of **FINANCIAL SECURITY**

B. **PAY SYSTEMS**

1. An organization's pay system can have a dramatic effect on efficiency and productivity.

2. Many companies use the **HAY SYSTEM.**

    a. Compensation is based on job tiers, each of which has a strict pay range.

PPT 11-46
Types of Pay Systems

(See complete PowerPoint slide notes on page 11.74.)

    b. The system is set up on a **POINT BASIS**
with three key factors:

        i. Know-how

        ii. Problem solving

        iii. Accountability

  3. Another system lets workers pick their own pay system.

C. **COMPENSATING TEAMS**

  1. Compensating teams is a complex issue.

  2. Measuring and rewarding individual performance on teams is tricky.

    a. Pay based strictly on **INDIVIDUAL PERFORMANCE** erodes team cohesiveness.

    b. Experts recommend basing pay on **TEAM PERFORMANCE.**

  3. **SKILL-BASED PAY** is related to the growth of both the individual and the team.

    a. Base pay is raised when team members learn and apply **NEW SKILLS.**

    b. The skill-based pay system is complex, and it is difficult to correlate skill acquisition to bottom-line gains.

  4. In **GAIN-SHARING SYSTEMS**, bonuses are based on improvements over a performance baseline.

  5. It is important to **REWARD INDIVIDUAL TEAM PLAYERS**, as well.

D. **FRINGE BENEFITS**

  1. ***FRINGE BENEFITS*** are benefits such as sick-leave pay, vacation pay, pension plans, and

TEXT FIGURE 11.6
Pay Systems
(Text page 311)

This text figure outlines some of the most common pay systems.

PPT 11-47
Compensating Teams

(See complete PowerPoint slide notes on page 11.74.)

health plans that represent additional compensation to employees beyond base wages.

    a. In recent years fringe benefit programs have grown faster than wages.

    b. Benefits account for about **30% OF PAYROLLS** today.

    c. To avoid higher taxes, many employees want more fringe benefits instead of more salary.

2. **FRINGE BENEFIT PACKAGES**

    a. Fringe benefit packages can include recreation facilities, company cars, paid sabbaticals, and day care.

    b. Employees want packages to include dental care, mental health care, elder care, legal counseling, eye care, and short workweek.

3. **SOFT BENEFITS** help workers maintain the balance between work and family life by freeing them from spending time on errands.

4. Some companies offer ***CAFETERIA-STYLE FRINGE BENEFITS***, a fringe benefit plan that allows employees to choose the benefits they want up to a certain dollar amount.

5. Because of the cost of administering benefit programs, many companies are contracting with outside companies (**OUTSOURCING**) to run their benefit plans.

lecture link 11-10

KEEPING TALENTED EMPLOYEES: IT'S THE FRINGE THAT COUNTS

Celeste Volz Ford has created a novel array of fringe benefits to retain talented aerospace engineers. (See the complete lecture link on page 11.61 of this manual.)

PPT 11-48

Fringe Benefits on the Job

(See complete PowerPoint slide notes on page 11.74.)

PPT 11-49

Healthcare, a Perk Not to Be Taken Lightly

(See complete PowerPoint slide notes on page 11.75.)

PPT 11-50

Who Pays for Employee Benefits?

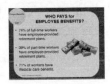

(See complete PowerPoint slide notes on page 11.75.)

PPT 11-51

The Range of Fringe Benefits

(See complete PowerPoint slide notes on page 11.75.)

PPT 11-52

Special Perks at Dreamworks

(See complete PowerPoint slide notes on page 11.76.)

PPT 11-53

Cafeteria-Style and Soft Benefits

(See complete PowerPoint slide notes on page 11.76.)

6. Managing benefits can be especially complicated when employees are located **IN OTHER COUNTRIES**.

learning goal 9

Demonstrate how managers use scheduling plans to adapt to workers' needs.

IX. SCHEDULING EMPLOYEES TO MEET ORGANIZATIONAL AND EMPLOYEE NEEDS

A. Managers and workers are demanding more flexibility and responsiveness from their jobs.

B. **FLEXTIME PLANS**

1. A ***FLEXTIME PLAN*** is a work schedule that gives employees some freedom to choose when to work, as long as they work the number of required hours or complete assigned tasks.

2. Most flextime plans include some ***CORE TIME***, a period when all employees are expected to be at their job stations.

    a. Flextime plans are designed to allow employees to **ADJUST TO WORK–LIFE DEMANDS,** such as two-income families.

    b. Companies find that **FLEXTIME** boosts employee productivity and morale.

3. There are **DISADVANTAGES**, as well.

    a. It does not work in assembly-line processes or for shift work.

    b. Managers often have to work longer days in order to supervise employees.

    c. Flextime makes communication more difficult.

PPT 11-54
Let's Go to the Beach!

(See complete PowerPoint slide notes on page 11.76.)

REACHING BEYOND
our borders
(Text page 313)

PPT 11-55
Working
Worldwide

(See complete PowerPoint slide notes on page 11.77.)

lecture link 11-11
ENCOURAGING HEALTHY
WORK–LIFE BALANCE

Ernst & Young is trying to get employees to work smarter and balance work and family. (See the complete lecture link on page 11.91 of this manual.)

PPT 11-56
Flexible Scheduling Plans

(See complete PowerPoint slide notes on page 11.77.)

PPT 11-57
Using Flextime Plans

(See complete PowerPoint slide notes on page 11.77.)

PPT 11-58
A Flextime Chart

TEXT FIGURE 11.7
A Flextime Chart
(Text page 314)

(See complete PowerPoint slide notes on page 11.78.)

lecture link 11-12
THE DANGERS OF FLEXTIME

Workers with flextime schedules are growing increasingly worried about the states of their jobs. (See he complete lecture link on page 11.91 of this manual.)

    d. Some employees could abuse the system.

  4. A ***COMPRESSED WORKWEEK*** is a work schedule that allows an employee to work a full number of hours per week but in fewer days.

    a. Employees enjoy working only four days.

    b. But some employees get tired working such long hours, and productivity could decline.

C. HOME-BASED WORK

  1. Nearly 10 million U.S. workers work from home at least once a month.

    a. About 12% of businesses use some home-based work.

    b. Home-based workers can choose their own hours, interrupt work for family tasks, and take time out for personal reasons.

  2. To be successful, a home-based worker must have the discipline to stay focused on the work.

  3. Telecommuting can **SAVE COSTS** for employers.

  4. Many businesses are doing away with the concept of one seat per employee.

    a. When companies reduce the number of offices, employees use "**HOT-DESKING**" to share office space.

    b. Some firms use home-based call agents rather than in-house operators or less-qualified offshore call centers.

PPT 11-59
Compressed Workweeks

(See complete PowerPoint slide notes on page 11.78.)

PPT 11-60
Home-Based Work

(See complete PowerPoint slide notes on page 11.78.)

PPT 11-61
Virtually There

(See complete PowerPoint slide notes on page 11.79.)

PPT 11-62
Going Nowhere Fast

(See complete PowerPoint slide notes on page 11.79.)

bonus case 11-3
**HUMAN RESOURCE PLANNING
AND WOMEN WORKERS**

This case explores how employers are incorporating benefits to attract and retain more women and minorities. (See the complete case, discussion questions, and suggested answers beginning on page 11.105 of this manual.)

TEXT FIGURE 11.8
Benefits and Challenges of Home-Based Work
(Text page 315)

This text figure outlines the benefits and challenges of home-based work to organizations, individuals, and society.

D. **JOB-SHARING PLANS**

1. _**JOB SHARING**_ is an arrangement whereby two part-time employees share one full-time job.

2. Job sharing lets parents work part-time while their children are in school.

3. **BENEFITS INCLUDE:**

   a. Employment opportunities for those who cannot or prefer not to work full-time

   b. An enthusiastic and productive workforce

   c. Reduced absenteeism and tardiness

   d. Ability to schedule people into peak demand periods

   e. Retention of experienced employees

4. **DISADVANTAGES** include having to hire, train, motivate, and supervise twice as many people.

5. Most firms have found that the benefits of job sharing outweigh the disadvantages.

learning goal 10

Describe how employees can move through a company: promotion, reassignment, termination, and retirement.

X. MOVING EMPLOYEES UP, OVER, AND OUT

A. Employees don't always stay in the position they were initially hired to fill.

B. **PROMOTING AND REASSIGNING EMPLOYEES**

1. Promotions are **COST-EFFECTIVE** ways to improve **EMPLOYEE MORALE**.

2. With flatter corporate structures today, more workers transfer **OVER** to a new position than move **UP** to one.

PPT 11-63
Job-Sharing Benefits

(See complete PowerPoint slide notes on page 11.79.)

PPT 11-64
Moving Employees

(See complete PowerPoint slide notes on page 11.80.)

C. **TERMINATING EMPLOYEES**

1. Human resource managers are struggling to manage layoffs and firings due to downsizing and global trends.

2. The **COST OF TERMINATING** employees is so high that managers choose to use **TEMPORARY EMPLOYEES** or **OUTSOURCE** certain functions.

3. **EMPLOYMENT AT WILL**

   a. The doctrine of **"EMPLOYMENT AT WILL"** meant that managers had as much freedom to fire workers as workers had to leave voluntarily.

   b. Most states now have employment laws that **LIMIT THE "AT WILL" DOCTRINE** to protect employees from wrongful firing.

   c. This legislation has restricted management's ability to terminate employees.

D. **RETIRING EMPLOYEES**

1. Another tool used to downsize companies is to offer early retirement benefits, called **GOLDEN HANDSHAKES**, to entice older workers to resign.

2. Offering early retirement benefits rather than laying off employees **INCREASES THE MORALE OF THE SURVIVING EMPLOYEES**.

3. Retiring senior workers increases **PROMOTION OPPORTUNITIES** for younger employees.

PPT 11-65
Terminating Employees

(See complete PowerPoint slide notes on page 11.80.)

TEXT FIGURE 11.9
How to Avoid Wrongful Discharge
Lawsuits
(Text page 317)

This text figure gives advice about how to minimize the chance of wrongful discharge lawsuits.

bonus case 11-4
**THE DEPARTMENT STORE
DILEMMA**

What should a manager do when a bureaucratic snafu threatens to cause the termination of a valuable worker? (See the complete case, discussion questions, and suggested answers beginning on page 11.107 of this manual.)

  E. **LOSING VALUED EMPLOYEES**

    1. Some employees will inevitably choose to leave the organization.

    2. One way to learn why employees leave is to have a third party conduct an **EXIT INTERVIEW**.

    3. There are now Web-based exit interview systems.

XI. SUMMARY

lecture link 11-13
USING THE EXIT INTERVIEW FOR FEEDBACK

One often overlooked way of getting employment feedback is through the exit interview. (See the complete lecture link on page 11.92 of this manual.)

**progress
assessment**
(Text page 318)

PPT 11-66
Progress Assessment

(See complete PowerPoint slide notes on page 11.80.)

PowerPoint slide notes

PPT 11-1
Chapter Title

PPT 11-2
Learning Goals

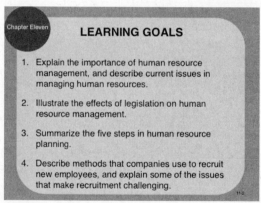

LEARNING GOALS

1. Explain the importance of human resource management, and describe current issues in managing human resources.

2. Illustrate the effects of legislation on human resource management.

3. Summarize the five steps in human resource planning.

4. Describe methods that companies use to recruit new employees, and explain some of the issues that make recruitment challenging.

PPT 11-3
Learning Goals

LEARNING GOALS

5. Outline the six steps in selecting employees.

6. Illustrate employee training and development methods.

7. Trace the six steps in appraising employee performance.

8. Summarize the objectives of employee compensation programs, and evaluate pay systems and fringe benefits.

PPT 11-4
Learning Goals

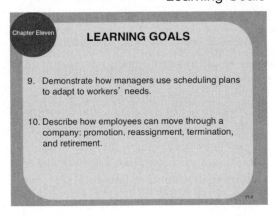

LEARNING GOALS

Chapter Eleven

9. Demonstrate how managers use scheduling plans to adapt to workers' needs.

10. Describe how employees can move through a company: promotion, reassignment, termination, and retirement.

11-4

PPT 11-5
Mark Parker

Profile

MARK PARKER
Nike

- Started as shoe designer, rose to CEO in 2006.

- The 7,000 workers at Nike's headquarters have access to two gyms, an Olympic-size pool, five restaurants, and have free on-site childcare.

- Named one of the 100 Best Places to Work in 2006, 2007 and 2008.

11-5

PPT 11-6
Name That Company

Company: Nucor Steel

NAME that COMPANY

Chapter Eleven

This company is one of the largest U.S. steel producers. It pays its teams bonuses that are calculated on quality—tons of steel that go out the door with no defects. There are no limits on bonuses a team can earn; they usually average around $20,000 per employee each year.

Name that company!

11-6

Human Resource Management

Human resource management is more than hiring employees. It involves a multitude of tasks and responsibilities. This slide gives some insight into the various roles the HRM department has now assumed. Business leaders in many companies understand the effect management of human capital can have in creating a competitive advantage in the marketplace.

PPT 11-8

Human Resource Management (HRM)

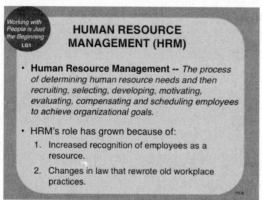

PPT 11-9

Uncovering the Secrets of HRM

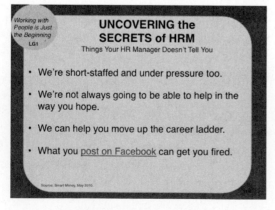

1. This slide shows that the HR department can help or hurt your career.

2. Some folks will approach HR with every little problem they encounter. However, with the decline in employment, HR departments are often under pressure to get more pressing things taken care of.

3. If you want to succeed in a company, make sure the HR staff knows you and **likes** you. They can help you move up.

4. Click the link on the slide and surf through various Facebook posts that have gotten people fired. This will help promote class discussion.

5. Ask the students, Do you think the terminations described in the stories link on the slide were justified?

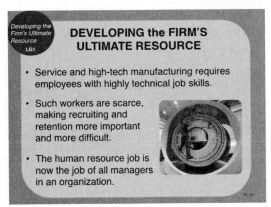

**DEVELOPING the FIRM'S
ULTIMATE RESOURCE**

*Developing the
Firm's Ultimate
Resource*
LG1

- Service and high-tech manufacturing requires
  employees with highly technical job skills.

- Such workers are scarce,
  making recruiting and
  retention more important
  and more difficult.

- The human resource job is
  now the job of all managers
  in an organization.

PPT 11-11

Challenges in Finding High-Level
Workers

Demographic changes are creating a challenging environment for HR managers, requiring companies to come up with creative ways to attract, develop, and retain employees.

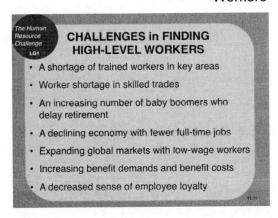

**CHALLENGES in FINDING
HIGH-LEVEL WORKERS**

*The Human
Resource
Challenge*
LG1

- A shortage of trained workers in key areas

- Worker shortage in skilled trades

- An increasing number of baby boomers who
  delay retirement

- A declining economy with fewer full-time jobs

- Expanding global markets with low-wage workers

- Increasing benefit demands and benefit costs

- A decreased sense of employee loyalty

PPT 11-12

Civil Rights Act of 1964

The Civil Rights Act of 1964 was a significant piece of legislation and directly brought the federal government into human resource management.

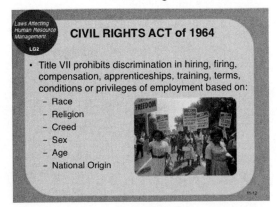

CIVIL RIGHTS ACT of 1964

*Laws Affecting
Human Resource
Management*
LG2

- Title VII prohibits discrimination in hiring, firing,
  compensation, apprenticeships, training, terms,
  conditions or privileges of employment based on:
  - Race
  - Religion
  - Creed
  - Sex
  - Age
  - National Origin

PPT 11-13
1972 Equal Employment Opportunity Act (EEOA)

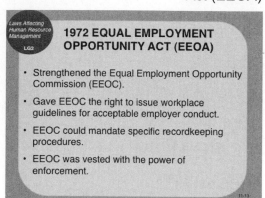

1972 EQUAL EMPLOYMENT OPPORTUNITY ACT (EEOA)

- Strengthened the Equal Employment Opportunity Commission (EEOC).
- Gave EEOC the right to issue workplace guidelines for acceptable employer conduct.
- EEOC could mandate specific recordkeeping procedures.
- EEOC was vested with the power of enforcement.

PPT 11-14
Controversial Procedures of the EEOC

Ask the students, Did affirmative action create reverse discrimination against whites and males by unfairly giving preference to females and minorities?

CONTROVERSIAL PROCEDURES of the EEOC

- **Affirmative Action** -- *Policy designed to "right past wrongs" by increasing opportunities for minorities and women.*
- **Reverse Discrimination** -- *Discriminating against members of a dominant or majority group (e.g. whites or males) usually as a result of policies designed to correct previous discrimination against minority or disadvantaged groups.*
- This policy has been at the center of many debates and lawsuits.

PPT 11-15
Civil Rights Act of 1991 and OFCCP

CIVIL RIGHTS ACT of 1991 and OFCCP

- Civil Rights Act of 1991
  - Amended Title VII and gave victims of discrimination the right to a jury trial and possible damages.
- Office of Federal Contract Compliance Programs (OFCCP)
  - Ensures that employers doing business with the federal government comply with the nondiscrimination and affirmative action laws.

PPT 11-16
Laws Protecting Employees with Disabilities

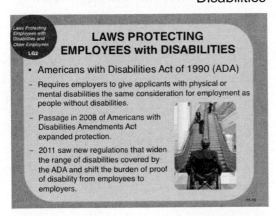

LAWS PROTECTING EMPLOYEES with DISABILITIES

Laws Protecting Employees with Disabilities and Older Employees LG2

- Americans with Disabilities Act of 1990 (ADA)
  - Requires employers to give applicants with physical or mental disabilities the same consideration for employment as people without disabilities.
  - Passage in 2008 of Americans with Disabilities Amendments Act expanded protection.
  - 2011 saw new regulations that widen the range of disabilities covered by the ADA and shift the burden of proof of disability from employees to employers.

PPT 11-17
Age Discrimination in Employment Act (ADEA)

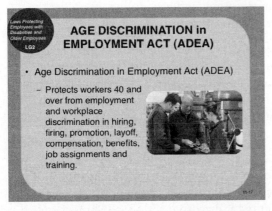

AGE DISCRIMINATION in EMPLOYMENT ACT (ADEA)

Laws Protecting Employees with Disabilities and Older Employees LG2

- Age Discrimination in Employment Act (ADEA)
  - Protects workers 40 and over from employment and workplace discrimination in hiring, firing, promotion, layoff, compensation, benefits, job assignments and training.

PPT 11-18
Minding the Law in HRM

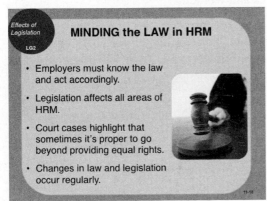

MINDING the LAW in HRM

Effects of Legislation LG2

- Employers must know the law and act accordingly.
- Legislation affects all areas of HRM.
- Court cases highlight that sometimes it's proper to go beyond providing equal rights.
- Changes in law and legislation occur regularly.

PPT 11-19
The Million Woman Suit against
Wal-Mart

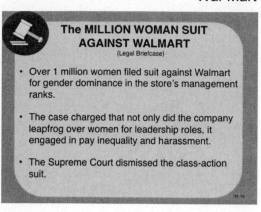

Although the Supreme Court ruled in favor of Wal-Mart, the Court did not decide whether Wal-Mart had, in fact, discriminated against the women; only that they could not proceed as a class.

PPT 11-20
Progress Assessment

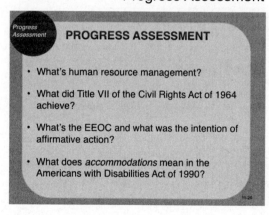

1. Human resource management is the process of determining the needs of the organization and then recruiting, selecting, developing, motivating, evaluating, compensating, and scheduling employees to achieve organizational goals.

2. Title VII prohibits discrimination in hiring, firing, compensation, apprenticeships, training, terms, conditions, or privileges of employment based on race, religion, creed, sex, or national origin. At a later date age discrimination was added to the act.

3. The Equal Employment Opportunity Commission was created by the Civil Rights Act. The EEOC was permitted to issue guidelines for acceptable employer conduct in administering equal employment opportunity. Affirmative action is the most controversial policy of the EEOC and was designed to "right past wrongs" by increasing opportunities for minorities and women.

4. Employers are required to make "reasonable accommodations" for employees with disabilities, such as modifying equipment or widening doorways.

PPT 11-21
Human Resource Planning Process

HUMAN RESOURCE PLANNING PROCESS

Determining a Firm's Human Resource Needs LG3

1) Preparing a human resource inventory of employees.
2) Preparing a job analysis.
3) Assessing future human resource demand.
4) Assessing future labor supply.
5) Establishing a strategic plan.

11-21

PPT 11-22
What's a Job Analysis?

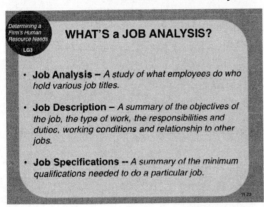

WHAT'S a JOB ANALYSIS?

Determining a Firm's Human Resource Needs LG3

- **Job Analysis** – *A study of what employees do who hold various job titles.*

- **Job Description** – *A summary of the objectives of the job, the type of work, the responsibilities and duties, working conditions and relationship to other jobs.*

- **Job Specifications** -- *A summary of the minimum qualifications needed to do a particular job.*

11-22

PPT 11-23
Recruiting Employees

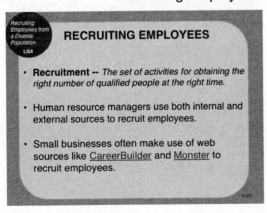

RECRUITING EMPLOYEES

Recruiting Employees from a Diverse Population LG4

- **Recruitment** -- *The set of activities for obtaining the right number of qualified people at the right time.*

- Human resource managers use both internal and external sources to recruit employees.

- Small businesses often make use of web sources like CareerBuilder and Monster to recruit employees.

11-23

PPT 11-24
It's Not Easy Being Small

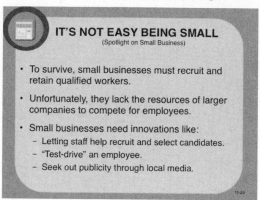

PPT 11-25
Employee Sources

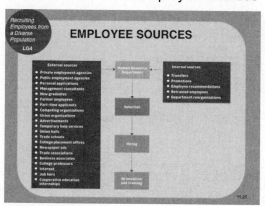

Job candidates can come from internal and external sources. In order to attract qualified employees from external sources, many employers offer referral bonuses to employees who refer a new employee to the company.

PPT 11-26
Selection

PPT 11-27

Steps in the Selection Process

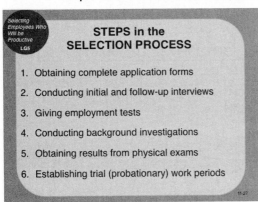

STEPS in the SELECTION PROCESS

Selecting Employees Who Will be Productive — LG5

1. Obtaining complete application forms
2. Conducting initial and follow-up interviews
3. Giving employment tests
4. Conducting background investigations
5. Obtaining results from physical exams
6. Establishing trial (probationary) work periods

PPT 11-28

Oops!

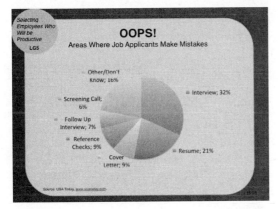

OOPS!
Areas Where Job Applicants Make Mistakes

Selecting Employees Who Will be Productive — LG5

Other/Don't Know; 16%
Screening Call; 6%
Follow Up Interview; 7%
Reference Checks; 9%
Cover Letter; 9%
Interview; 32%
Resume; 21%

Source: USA Today, www.usatoday.com

1. This slide presents the job application areas where the applicants make the most mistakes.

2. The results are based on the survey of over 1,400 CFOs of U.S. companies with 20 or more employees.

3. The top two areas where applicants make the most mistakes are interviews and resumes.

4. Ask the students, What are your experiences with interviews or resume errors? How many of you follow up after an interview?

PPT 11-29

Hiring Contingent Workers

HIRING CONTINGENT WORKERS

Hiring Contingent Workers — LG5

- **Contingent Workers** -- *Include part-time and temporary workers, seasonal workers, independent contractors, interns and co-op students.*

- There are about 5.7 million contingent workers in the U.S.

- Majority of contingent workers are under 25.

SPIRIT

PPT 11-30
Why Hire Contingent Workers?

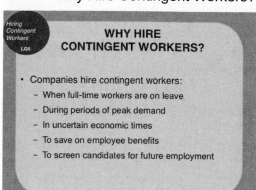

WHY HIRE CONTINGENT WORKERS?

Hiring Contingent Workers LG5

- Companies hire contingent workers:
  - When full-time workers are on leave
  - During periods of peak demand
  - In uncertain economic times
  - To save on employee benefits
  - To screen candidates for future employment

11-30

PPT 11-31
Students and the Contingent Workforce

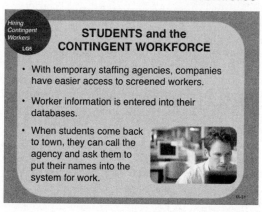

STUDENTS and the CONTINGENT WORKFORCE

Hiring Contingent Workers LG5

- With temporary staffing agencies, companies have easier access to screened workers.

- Worker information is entered into their databases.

- When students come back to town, they can call the agency and ask them to put their names into the system for work.

11-31

PPT 11-32
Are Unpaid Interns Too Interred?

ARE UNPAID INTERNS TOO INTERRED?
(Making Ethical Decisions)

- With few entry-level positions available, interns can end up in an unpaid position for as long as six months with no chance of advancement.

- Some businesses give interns lots of responsibility; a Toronto paper fired all paid staff and replaced them with unpaid interns.

- Is it ethical for companies to use unpaid interns if they know they don't have jobs to offer or if the unpaid internships replace paid jobs?

11-32

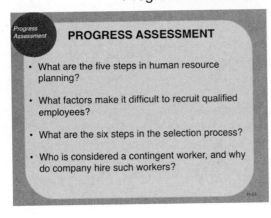

1. The five steps in human resource planning are (1) preparing a human resource inventory of the organization's employees, (2) preparing a job analysis, (3) assessing future human resource demand, (4) assessing future labor supply, and (5) establishing a strategic plan.

2. Some factors that make it difficult to recruit qualified employees include organizational policies that demand promotions from within, union regulations, and low wages.

3. The six steps in the selection process are (1) obtaining complete application forms, (2) conducting initial and follow-up interviews, (3) giving employment tests, (4) conducting background investigations, (5) obtaining results from physical exams, and (6) establishing a trial period.

4. Contingent workers include part-time workers, temporary workers, seasonal workers, independent contractors, interns, and co-op students. Contingent workers are sometimes hired in an uncertain economic climate, when full-time workers are on leave, when there is peak demand for labor or products, and when quick service is necessary.

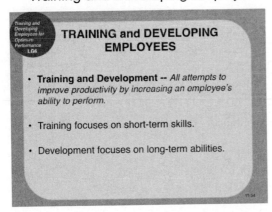

PPT 11-35
Three Steps of Training and Development

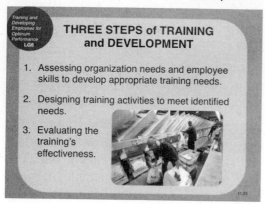

THREE STEPS of TRAINING and DEVELOPMENT

Training and Developing Employees for Optimum Performance LG6

1. Assessing organization needs and employee skills to develop appropriate training needs.

2. Designing training activities to meet identified needs.

3. Evaluating the training's effectiveness.

PPT 11-36
Most Commonly Used Training and Development Activities

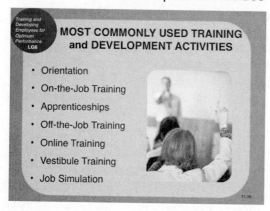

MOST COMMONLY USED TRAINING and DEVELOPMENT ACTIVITIES

Training and Developing Employees for Optimum Performance LG6

- Orientation
- On-the-Job Training
- Apprenticeships
- Off-the-Job Training
- Online Training
- Vestibule Training
- Job Simulation

PPT 11-37
Developing Effective Managers

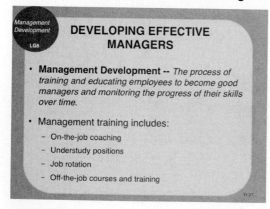

DEVELOPING EFFECTIVE MANAGERS

Management Development LG6

- **Management Development --** *The process of training and educating employees to become good managers and monitoring the progress of their skills over time.*

- Management training includes:
  - On-the-job coaching
  - Understudy positions
  - Job rotation
  - Off-the-job courses and training

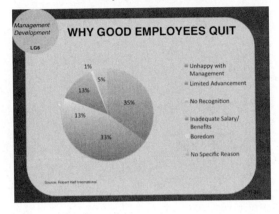

1. This slide presents some of the reasons why good employees quit.

2. Ask the students, Why is it important for managers to understand why employees leave a company? *(It translates directly into the bottom line of the organization. The higher the turnover, the higher the costs for recruiting, selecting, training, and development, etc.)*

3. Ask the students, What are other reasons why employee retention is important? *(Some other reasons may be morale of the workers, ability to recruit, reputation and image of the company, etc.)*

4. Ask the students, Would you like to work at a place that feels like it has a revolving door?

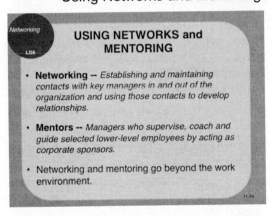

Many students are familiar with social networking but are unfamiliar with career networking. Ask the students, How can you use sites like Facebook, YouTube, and Twitter to establish and maintain contacts with key managers in and out of the organization?

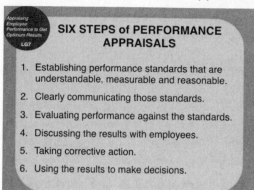

SIX STEPS of PERFORMANCE APPRAISALS

1. Establishing performance standards that are understandable, measurable and reasonable.

2. Clearly communicating those standards.

3. Evaluating performance against the standards.

4. Discussing the results with employees.

5. Taking corrective action.

6. Using the results to make decisions.

11-41

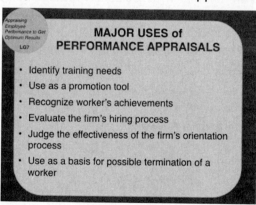

MAJOR USES of PERFORMANCE APPRAISALS

- Identify training needs
- Use as a promotion tool
- Recognize worker's achievements
- Evaluate the firm's hiring process
- Judge the effectiveness of the firm's orientation process
- Use as a basis for possible termination of a worker

1. This slide gives students insight as to the importance of regular performance appraisals.

2. To start a discussion on performance appraisals, ask students to discuss the 360-degree review.

3. After the discussion use the next slide to walk students through some of the problems associated with performance appraisals.

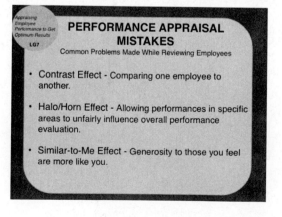

PERFORMANCE APPRAISAL MISTAKES
Common Problems Made While Reviewing Employees

- Contrast Effect - Comparing one employee to another.

- Halo/Horn Effect - Allowing performances in specific areas to unfairly influence overall performance evaluation.

- Similar-to-Me Effect - Generosity to those you feel are more like you.

1. This slide highlights some of the problems made while reviewing employees.

2. Ask the students, How can managers avoid some of the issues discussed in this slide?

3. To start a discussion about performance appraisals and teams ask the students, Do you think it is fair to have your own performance appraised based on the work of others on your team?

PPT 11-44
Progress Assessment

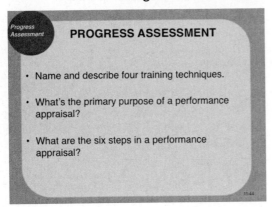

1. Off-the-job training occurs away from the workplace and consists of internal or external programs to develop any of a variety of skills or to foster personal development. An apprenticeship program involves a student or apprentice working alongside an experienced employee to master the skills and procedures of a craft. Vestibule training or near-the-job training is done in a classroom with equipment similar to that used on the job so employees learn proper methods and safety procedures before assuming a specific job assignment. Job simulation is the use of equipment that duplicates job conditions and tasks so trainees can learn skills before attempting them on the job.

2. The primary purpose of a performance appraisal is to determine whether workers are doing an effective and efficient job, with a minimum of errors and disruptions.

3. The six steps in a performance appraisal are (1) establishing performance standards, (2) communicating those standards, (3) evaluating performance, (4) discussing results with employees, (5) taking corrective action, and (6) using the results to make decisions.

PPT 11-45
Compensation Programs

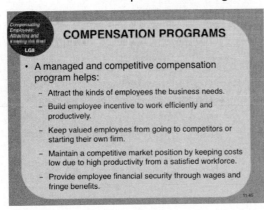

When accepting a job offer, students should consider not just the salary but the entire compensation package.

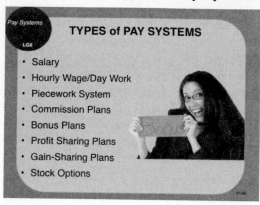

1. Skill-based pay is increased when teams learn and apply new skills. Gain sharing bases team bonuses on improvements over previous performance.

2. Nucor Steel calculates bonuses on quality—tons of steel that go out the door with no defects. There are no limits on bonuses a team can earn; they usually average around $20,000 per employee each year.

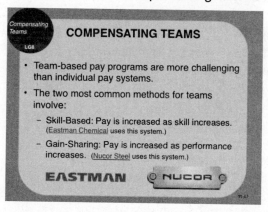

The rising cost of health care and the cost of employer-provided health insurance is unsustainable in the long term. This requires both management and employees to create systems that keep costs down, but still provide meaningful coverage. This could include employee wellness programs and/or higher deductibles.

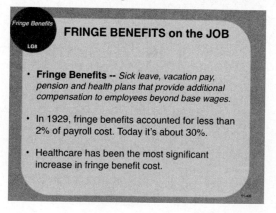

PPT 11-49

Healthcare, a Perk Not to Be Taken Lightly

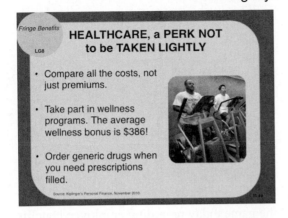

1. Many companies now ask their employees to pitch in for health care costs.

2. This slide shows students how to cope with those costs and find what's best for them.

PPT 11-50

Who Pays for Employee Benefits?

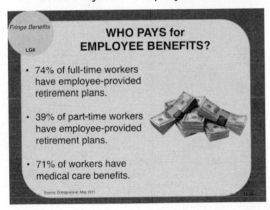

1. *Entrepreneur* used statistics from the Bureau of Labor Statistics to create this list.

2. Ask the students, Did you think more Americans had retirement plans sponsored by their employer? What about health care?

PPT 11-51

The Range of Fringe Benefits

PPT 11-52
Special Perks at Dreamworks

Employee perks can take different shapes. Companies like Dreamworks try to offer benefits to keep the work environment loose and creative.

PPT 11-53
Cafeteria-Style and Soft Benefits

The name of the game today regarding employee benefits is creativity!

PPT 11-54
Let's Go to the Beach!

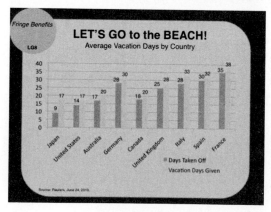

1. This slide presents a comparison of number of vacation days given and used per year in different countries.

2. France leads with an average of 38 vacation days given per year, whereas the United States ties for last with just 17 days.

3. Even though the United States comes in last with only 17 days, an interesting fact to share with the students is that most Americans don't even use these 17 days.

4. Ask the students, What impact does this benefit of number of vacation days have on recruiting at an international level? *(Most should be able to identify that domestically, it may not have much of an impact. Internationally, however, potential candidates would compare the different countries—especially if they are from one of the countries that offers a much higher number of vacation days, such as Italy, France, or Germany. This may have an impact on the organization's ability to recruit.)*

PPT 11-55
Working Worldwide

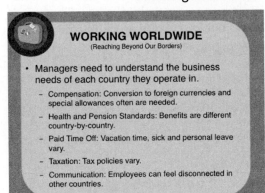

WORKING WORLDWIDE
(Reaching Beyond Our Borders)

- Managers need to understand the business needs of each country they operate in.
  - Compensation: Conversion to foreign currencies and special allowances often are needed.
  - Health and Pension Standards: Benefits are different country-by-country.
  - Paid Time Off: Vacation time, sick and personal leave vary.
  - Taxation: Tax policies vary.
  - Communication: Employees can feel disconnected in other countries.

11-55

PPT 11-56
Flexible Scheduling Plans

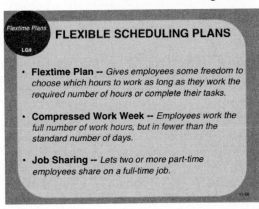

Flextime Plans

FLEXIBLE SCHEDULING PLANS

LG9

- **Flextime Plan --** *Gives employees some freedom to choose which hours to work as long as they work the required number of hours or complete their tasks.*

- **Compressed Work Week --** *Employees work the full number of work hours, but in fewer than the standard number of days.*

- **Job Sharing --** *Lets two or more part-time employees share on a full-time job.*

11-56

PPT 11-57
Using Flextime Plans

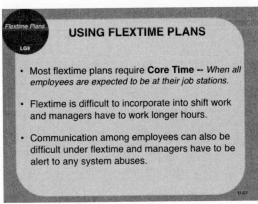

Flextime Plans

USING FLEXTIME PLANS

LG9

- Most flextime plans require **Core Time --** *When all employees are expected to be at their job stations.*

- Flextime is difficult to incorporate into shift work and managers have to work longer hours.

- Communication among employees can also be difficult under flextime and managers have to be alert to any system abuses.

11-57

PPT 11-58
A Flextime Chart

Flextime gives employees some freedom and empowers them to work when it best meets their schedule. The benefits are obvious and often lead to a more motivated workforce.

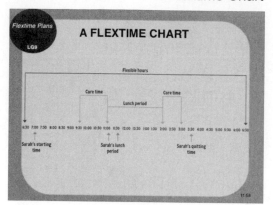

PPT 11-59
Compressed Work Weeks

PPT 11-60
Home-Based Work

Bank of America's program adds up to a $100 million a year savings and employees in the program work remotely about 60% of the time.

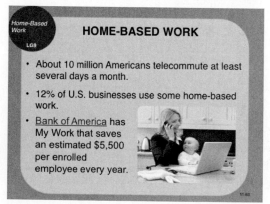

PPT 11-61

Virtually There

Click on these links to visit pages containing useful tools for working outside the office.

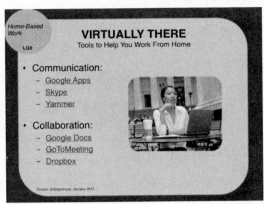

PPT 11-62

Going Nowhere Fast

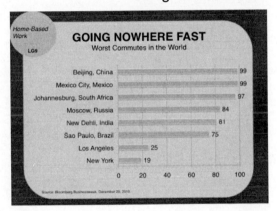

1. IBM ranked cities from 1 to 100 (100 being the worst). Factors included traffic, road rage, and grid-lock.

2. Sixty-nine percent of commuters in Beijing have said traffic has been so bad some days, they turned around and went home.

3. New York and Los Angeles ranked rather low on the list considering they're notorious for having U.S. traffic problems.

4. Those in Moscow normally spend 2.5 to 3 hours in their cars. Ask the students, Would you travel 2.5 hours just to get to and from work? Would flex-time be more beneficial for these workers?

PPT 11-63

Job-Sharing Benefits

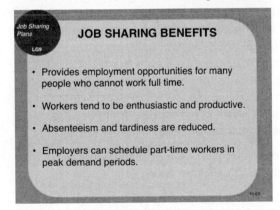

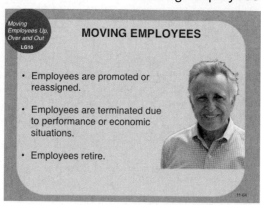

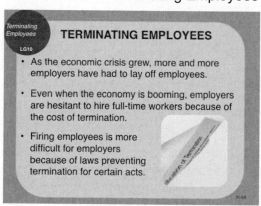

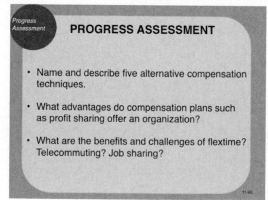

1. Alternative compensation techniques include:
   (1) commission Plans - rewarding employees with a percentage of sales, (2) bonus plans - rewarding employees with payment based on achievement of a predetermined goal, (3) profit sharing plans - giving employees the ability to share in a percentage of the company's profit, (4) gain-sharing plans - bonus is based on improvements over previous performance, and (5) stock options - granting employees shares of stocks based on performance.

2. The hope is that profit sharing plans will motivate employees to think like owners.

3. Flextime benefits include allowing employees to adjust to work/life demands. Challenges of flextime include not being applicable for all businesses, making communication more difficult, and creating the possibility of resentment if employees abuse the system. Telecommuting benefits include cost saving for employers and allows employees to manage work/life demands. Challenges of telecommuting

include that it requires disciplined employees to stay focused and communication with employees may suffer. Job sharing benefits include employment opportunities for those who cannot (or prefer not to) work full-time, reduced absenteeism and tardiness, retention of experienced workers and ability to schedule workers during peak times. Challenges of job sharing include the need to hire, train, motivate, and supervise at least twice as many employees.

lecture
links

"Never fear the want of business. A man who qualifies himself well for his calling, never fails of employment."

Thomas Jefferson

"The first quality that is needed is audacity."

Winston Churchill

"If each of us hires people who are smaller than we are, we shall become a company of dwarfs. But if each of us hires people who are bigger than we are, we shall become a company of giants."

David Ogilvy

"Every organization has an allotted number of positions to be filled by misfits."

Owens' Theory of Organizational Deviance (Murphy's Law)

"Once a misfit leaves, another one will be recruited."

Owens' Corollary

lecture link 11-1

WHERE HAVE ALL THE WANT ADS GONE?

In 2000, the Sunday *Boston Globe* had about 100 pages of help-wanted classified ads. In 2011, it had three. What happened?

The want ads have moved online. The *Fortune* 1000, companies with at least 2,500 employees, have by and large stopped doing business with the newspapers. These ads accounted for about one-third of the newspapers' classified revenue. In the past, IBM ran full-page ads for key positions. Now it spends its money online. Newspapers are scrambling to hold onto their small- and medium-sized business classifieds.

But the online job sites now have their sights set on this market, also. Andrew McKelvey, CEO of Monster.com, the biggest online job search company, thinks that it's only a matter of time before even those companies switch to online recruiting. "When the 50-year-old manager of the Brown Shoe Co. loses an employee, what does he do? He reaches for the phone to put an ad in the paper because that's what he's always done. What's his son going to do? Flip open his laptop." Monster.com is trying to speed up this evolutionary process, targeting HR professionals in smaller companies.

Monster.com is also looking overseas for its future. The company has developed a site in India and bought online job sites in China and Korea. McKelvey admits he was late in realizing the potential in Asia and passed up an opportunity to enter the Chinese market in the early 1990s. The company can no longer ignore the largest country in the world. He believes that China will generate more online recruiting revenue than the United States in the next decade.

Monster.com is seeing more listings at the high end, with some salaries up to $325,000. The site lists CFO positions and some small-company CEO openings that pay $100,000. Skilled and hourly listings are also growing. "Of the 50,000 resumes we get a day, more than half come from blue-collar workers," says McKelvey.

Even more inventive job posting solutions may be coming. Monster.com's research and development labs are working on applications for cell phones. McKelvey envisions job seekers looking for jobs and being notified of new openings on mobile phones. With the high cell phone usage in China, this looks like a promising strategy.[i]

lecture link 11-2
FINDING GOOGLE PEOPLE

Have you ever made a profit from a catering business or a dog walking enterprise? Do you prefer to work alone or in groups? Have you ever set a world record in anything? The right answers could help get you a job at Google.

Google has tried to hire people with straight-A report cards and double 800s on their SATs. Now it is starting to look for more well-rounded candidates, like those who have published books or started their own clubs.

Desperate to hire more engineers and sales representatives to staff its rapidly growing search and advertising business, Google—in typical eccentric fashion—has created an automated way to search for talent among the more than 100,000 job applications it receives each month. It is starting to ask job applicants to fill out an elaborate online survey that explores their attitudes, behavior, personality, and biographical details going back to high school. The questions range from the age when applicants first got excited about computers to whether they have ever tutored or ever established a nonprofit organization. The answers are fed into a series of formulas created by Google's mathematicians that calculate a score—from zero to 100—meant to predict how well a person will fit into its chaotic and competitive culture.

"As we get bigger, we find it harder and harder to find enough people," said Laszlo Bock, Google's vice president for people operations. "With traditional hiring methods, we were worried we will overlook some of the best candidates."

As a result, Bock has been trying to make the company's rigorous screening process more efficient. Until now, head hunters said, Google largely turned up its nose at engineers who had less than a 3.7 grade-point average. (Those who wanted to sell ads could get by with a 3.0 average, head hunters said.) And it often would take two months to consider candidates, submitting them to more than half a dozen interviews.

Unfortunately, most of the academic research suggests that the factors Google has put the most weight on   grades and interviews—are not an especially reliable way of hiring good people. "Interviews are a terrible predictor of performance," Bock said. So Google set out to find out if there were any bits of life experience or personality it could use to spot future stars.

In 2006, Google asked every employee who had been working at the company for at least five months to fill out a 300-question survey. Some questions were factual: What programming languages are you familiar with? What Internet mailing lists do you subscribe to? Some looked for behavior: Is your work space messy or neat? And some looked at personality: Are you an extrovert or an introvert? And some fell into no traditional category in the human resources world: What magazines do you subscribe to? What pets do you have?

The data from this initial survey were then compared with 25 separate measures of each employee's performance. Again there were traditional yardsticks—the employees' reviews, both by supervisors and peers, and their compensation—and some oddball ones.

One score was what the company called "organizational citizenship," that is, things you do that aren't technically part of your job but make Google a better place to work. When all this was completed, Dr. Todd Carlisle, who designed the survey, analyzed the two million data points the survey collected. Among the first results was confirmation that Google's obsession with academic performance was not always correlated with success at the company. "Sometimes too much schooling will be a detriment to you in your job," according to Carlisle.

Indeed, there was no single factor that seemed to identify the top workers for every single job title. But Dr. Carlisle was able to create several surveys that he believed would help find candidates in specific areas—engineering, sales, finance, and human resources. He plans to use the survey for every applicant soon.

Even as Google tries to hire more people faster, it wants to make sure that its employees will fit into its freewheeling culture. The company boasts that only 4% of its workforce leaves each year, less than other Silicon Valley companies. And it works hard to retain people, with free food, time to work on personal projects, and other goodies. Stock options and grants certainly encourage employees to stay long enough to take advantage of the company's surging share price.[ii]

lecture link 11-3

MAKING AN IMPRESSION WITH VIDEO RESUMES

In this age of intense employment competition, many job seekers do whatever they can to set themselves apart from the pack. One of the newer ways to do that is to create a video resume (CV). A one-page CV can tell an employer about an applicant's basics qualifications, but offers little room for his or her personality. Companies that need an employee who can interact well with people often require an indication of a person's social skills on the resume. If an applicant's vibrant character doesn't exactly shine through in his or her job history, a multimedia resume can help flesh out those blank spots.

Nevertheless, video resumes are not a traditional way to list one's qualifications. In a 2008 survey of senior executives from the nation's top 1,000 companies, only 24% said they accepted video resumes. Some bosses even claim they've tossed out applications with video resumes if their inbox is too full. But as the years have passed and personal video technology has grown dramatically, more and more employers are starting to take multimedia resumes just as seriously as written ones. In this day and age, though, producing a film of one's every thought is as easy as ranting in front of a webcam and publishing the footage to YouTube with the click of a button. Video resumes should be polished and professional, which can be a feat for a budding careerist armed only with iMovie.

Luckily, a number of websites are available to help job seekers create a professional-quality video resume. BriteTab.com, for instance, allows users to embed pictures and videos into their standard resume. InterviewStudio.com leads the user in a mock interview where the person's answers make up the bulk of the video. The site even gives vital production tips, such as telling the user where to position their head in front of the camera. Each of these websites charges a monthly access fee. And just because a job seeker makes a video resume using one of these sites doesn't mean he or she is guaranteed the job. Poor lighting or shoddy sound is still a possibility even with the help of these sites. Recruiters warn that distracting production deficiencies often do the potential job seeker more harm than if they just would have sent a standard resume.[iii]

lecture link 11-4

INTERVIEW BLUNDERS

The following are a few questions interviewers should never ask prospective employees:

- Are you married/single/engaged/divorced/dating anyone?
- Do you have/plan to have children?
- How old are you?
- When was the last time you were thrown in jail?
- Do you rent or own your home?

- Have you ever declared bankruptcy?
- How does someone like you get in and out of airports (to an applicant with a mobility disability)?
- Would you move if your spouse's employment required a move?
- What do your parents or what does your spouse do for a living?
- What church do you attend?
- How tall are you?
- What color are your eyes?
- Did you get any workers' comp from your last job?
- How would someone your age fit in with young people?
- How did you pay for your education?
- Were you admitted to college under an affirmative action program?
- What is your cultural background?
- How has the AIDS epidemic affected you?
- Do you usually wear jewelry/makeup?

Why can't you ask these questions? Because

1. They are not job-related.
2. They are often directed to members of groups that have suffered past discrimination.

Interviewees typically do not think they are in a position to refuse to answer the question. What should an interviewee do if the interviewer asks such questions?

Stay calm. Be objective and dispassionate. The interviewer probably does not intend to offend you, and will respond well to your graceful handling of the question.

Respond professionally. Gently lead the questioner in the way that he or she should go.

Never respond directly to the question asked. For example, if the interviewer asks, "Do you plan to have children?" you might assume that he or she is really interested in your commitment to your career. You can respond, "It is natural for employers to be concerned about any new employee's commitment to the job. I have demonstrated my commitment by interning during the summer, working part-time while in school, taking on the additional responsibilities of working in. . . ."

Ask the interviewer a question. If you aren't able to redirect the interviewer's question (i.e., the question is asked again after you've given a response like above), ask "How is that question job-related?" or "Why do you ask?" Respond to that answer.

Do not feel guilty about not answering. The interviewer's questions were out of line, not your response. Many interviewees feel ashamed when interviewers ask offensive, personal, or discriminatory questions; interviewers rarely do. If the interviewer has asked you questions that made you uncomfortable, he or she has probably offended other applicants as well.

Of course, there are many more issues involving job recruitment cover by federal law. To learn more, visit the EEOC website at www.eeoc.gov.

lecture link 11-5

MEMORABLE JOB INTERVIEWS

Everybody wants to put their best foot forward at a job interview, but the pressure of the interview can sometimes make interviewees lose their common sense. Here are a few mishaps that are good enough for a gag reel:

- One candidate arrived at an early morning interview and asked to use the interviewer's phone. She then faked a coughing fit as she called in sick to her boss.

- A hiring manager called a job seeker and asked him to bring several copies of his resume and three references to an interview. An hour before the interview, the applicant called back and asked to reschedule because his references couldn't come with him.

- One candidate apologized for being late, said he accidentally locked his clothes in his closet.

- A balding candidate abruptly asked to be excused. He returned to the office in a few minutes later wearing a hairpiece.

- An applicant wore an iPod to the job interview and explained she could listen to the interviewer and the music at the same time.

- When an interviewer offered to answer any questions the job seeker had, the applicant asked, "What happens if I wake up in the morning and don't feel like going to work?"

- An interviewer asked a job candidate, "What do you know about us?" He leaned back in his chair and replied, "Not much. Why don't you fill me in?"

- After answering the first few questions, an interviewee picked up his cell phone and called his parents to let them know how the interview was going.

- Shortly after sitting down, another interviewee brought out a line of cosmetics and started a strong sales pitch.

- At the end of one interview, the candidate said she was interested in the position but would have to check with her boyfriend. Then she said, "He's waiting outside. Can he come in and say hello?"

- When one applicant was asked why she wanted to work for the company, she replied, "I really want to work close to Bloomingdales."

- A man brought in his five children and cat.

- The company was actually pursuing one candidate. He was impressive on the phone, and an interview was set up at a five-star restaurant. He showed up dressed inappropriately and smacked chewing gum as he talked. When the gum fell out of his mouth onto the table, it became stuck to the tablecloth and then to a linen napkin. He wasn't hired.

- When asked why she was leaving her current job, an interviewee said, "My manager was a jerk. All managers are jerks."

- One applicant said "if I hired him, I'd soon learn to regret it."

- An executive search recruiter asked a candidate, a previous accounting manager, what their ideal job would be. The candidate responded with, "A *Playboy* photographer."

- One candidate disparaged his former boss during an interview, not noticing that the interviewer and the former boss had the same last name and were related.

- When asked about loyalty, an applicant showed the interviewer a tattoo of his girlfriend's name.

- During an interview, a call came in from the applicant's wife. The interviewer heard: "Which company? How much? When do I start?" The interviewer said, "I assume you're not interested in continuing our interview?" He promptly replied, "That depends on whether you'll pay me more." He wasn't hired, and it turned out there was no other job offer. His conversation was a scam to get a higher offer.[iv]

lecture link 11-6

PERSONALITY TESTING FOR JOB APPLICANTS

A job applicant today is likely to be asked to take a personality test. At least 30% of employers—from Wal-Mart to DuPont—use a version of personality tests in hiring. Even CEOs get tested. Carly Fiorina reported took a 900-question test before landing the top job at Hewlett-Packard. In that case the benefit, however, is debatable since Fiorina was fired in 2004.

Personality testing is becoming an attractive method of retaining employees. Turnover averages about 15% of the workforce and costs at least a quarter of a departing worker's salary. Many of these tests claim to predict a worker's "fit" with the job and company culture, hopefully increasing chances of keeping the new employee. Computerization has made these tests easier and cheaper to administer. The 2,500 companies in the industry earn about $400 million a year.

Personality tests screen for five basic personality traits: extroversion, agreeableness, emotional stability, conscientiousness, and openness to experience. There are two types of personality tests—"screen-out" and "screen-in." Screen-out tests like the Minnesota Multiphasic Personality Inventory (MMPI) are used to uncover tendencies toward problems such as substance abuse. Screen-in tests, such as the California Psychological Inventory, can help find the right person for the job by attempting to predict how someone will behave. The Myers-Briggs test is used by employers on existing employees to measure leadership and teamwork skills.

No test is an infallible predictor of behavior, however. Applicants can try to answer questions to make themselves look attractive. But improved testing techniques have made this more difficult, often by analyzing questions to uncover a pattern.v

lecture link 11-7

BACKGROUND CHECKS: SECURITY AND PRIVACY ISSUES

Traditionally, employers have used background checks to screen applicants so they can find the best new employees. Today's heightened concerns for security coupled with improved technology means background checking has become more widely used.

Current events illustrate some of the reasons for this increase. Child abuse and abductions prompted the enactment of new laws that require background checks for anyone seeking to work or to volunteer to work with children. After the corporate scandals of the early 2000s, executives, directors, and officers face a higher degree of scrutiny. The threat of terrorist attacks has led to tightened security and screening of candidates to work at airports, train stations, and car rental agencies.

Another reason for increased scrutiny in the hiring process—negligent hiring suits are on the rise. If an employee's actions hurt someone, the employer may be liable. A company in Pennsylvania lost a lawsuit when it failed to perform a check that would have uncovered an applicant's history of inappropriate behavior to women. The increase in the crime of identity theft has employers checking to be sure applicants are who they say they are. (This is a double-edged sword, as some applicants have been the victims of identity theft and unknowingly lost potential jobs because of false information on their records.) Federal and state laws require background checks for certain jobs; for instance, in the health care industry, and of anyone seeking to work with children and individuals who are elderly or disabled.

With companies increasingly relying on preemployment background checks, it's important to get the information right. But the background checking industry lacks consistent standards, which can cause errors that can disqualify reputable job applicants. One applicant for an Office Depot cashier position was rejected when a criminal background check revealed a lengthy history of drug convictions in Washington, although she had never been to the state. She fought for six weeks to clear her name and eventually got the job.

Even more disturbing are the cases in which preemployment screening misses something important. In 2005, FedEx Corp. was accused of hiring a sex offender who was later charged with molesting an eight-year-old boy while at work. FedEx did a background check on the employee, but it did not reveal his criminal history.

Background screeners say it can be difficult to uncover criminal histories. The FBI's criminal database is generally not public, except for law enforcement and similar organizations. In the FedEx case, the employee worked in Connecticut but had a criminal record in Maine. Searching across state and county jurisdictions is virtually impossible. Records are scattered across the 3,142 counties in the United States.

Despite the necessity of these background checks, applicants are not without rights. For example, employers need to obtain written consent from applicants before performing background checks. The Fair Credit Reporting Act requires a specific notification of rights and notice that a consumer report (background check) is being performed by an outside company. If there is "adverse action" (the candidate is not hired, for instance) because of information obtained on the consumer report, the person must be notified that he or she is entitled to request a copy of the report.

There are time limits on disclosure of some information. Bankruptcies may not be considered after 10 years. Civil suits, civil judgments, records of arrest, paid tax liens, accounts placed for collection, and any other negative information (except criminal convictions) may not be reported after 7 years.

Some information requires the authorization of the subject. Education records and military service records are confidential except for "directory information" such as name, dates, degrees, and military rank. Medical records are confidential, and the subject's specific permission is required for release. The Americans with Disabilities Act allows potential employers to inquire only about an applicant's ability to perform specific job functions.

While the Internet has made it possible for employers to perform basic checks with their computer and a credit card, labor lawyers caution against depending on websites since information obtained may not be complete or up-to-date. For instance, an arrest may show up but the acquittal or dropped charges may not.

A national task force funded by the Justice Department has been established to recommend national standards for screening companies. The standards cannot come too soon.vi

lecture link 11-8

THE INVASIVE DANGERS OF FACEBOOK

There is a double-edged sword when it comes to social networking websites. To their credit, sites like Facebook and LinkedIn allow users to easily keep in touch with friends and business contacts. But what seems at first like a private interaction between a closed network of friends is actually very public. After all, once something is posted online, it often gets copied to a cache that can still be accessed even after the object has been deleted. Furthermore, social networking sites frequently receive criticism for their lax or even invasive privacy practices. The most notable culprit is Facebook, which has been under fire as of late for its shaky privacy standards.

In April 2010, Facebook announced it was adding a new feature to its site called "instant personalization." The idea was to link the interests listed in a user's profile to outside websites and other Facebook pages. For example, if a person listed "bowling" as one of his or her favorite activities, then the next time that person visited Yelp.com, one of Facebook's partner sites, he or she would find content about bowling on the home site. The instant personalization feature also turns each one of the user's interests into a separate Facebook page that can be accessed by anyone. So if a college student lists "Jagermeister" as one of his key interests, then he would automatically become a fan of Jagermeister on Facebook. The problem is that person's information could then be viewed by people outside his network, such as family members or job recruiters.

Many Facebook users consider this use of their profiles as an invasion of their privacy. They also feared that the website tie-ins could be exploited to hack into users' accounts like e-mail phishers do. As such, Facebook immediately implemented an opt-out policy, but that didn't solve the entire problem. A user must also opt out of instant personalization on each of Facebook's partner sites, such as Pandora.com or Microsoft Docs. If you'd like to find out how private your Facebook information is, you can use this website to measure just how private your page is:www.reclaimprivacy.org/.[vii]

lecture link 11-9

MICROSOFT REVISES PERFORMANCE APPRAISALS

In April 2005, Steven A. Ballmer knew he had an epic morale problem on his hands at Microsoft. The company's new operating system, Vista, had been repeatedly delayed and shares of Microsoft stock had drifted sideways after years of spectacular growth. The outlook of the workforce was darkening.

Ballmer decided he needed a new human resource chief, someone who would help improve the mood. Instead of promoting another HR professional, Ballmer looked outside the HR department and hired Lisa Brummel, a veteran product manager.

According to Brummel, her first weeks felt as though she were flying at night without instruments. At first she was receiving about two e-mails a day from employees. "There was no communication with employees—none," she says. "It was a gulf." Internal surveys—which at most companies help inform HR policy—presented a picture of a happy, contented workforce. Brummel didn't buy the rosy findings. "People weren't connected to the company or our mission anymore," she says.

Brummel started an internal blog to get people talking and created a portal on the intranet where people could suggest solutions to HR shortcomings. She held focus groups and mined her network of on-the-ground intelligence agents: the people, from managers to coders, she had come to know since joining the company in 1989.

Time and again, Brummel heard the same refrain: HR was a black box; it had to open up and get employee input. People loathed the performance review system. They wanted clarity on compensation, more direction on how to get promoted, and better managers.

Brummel's most radical change was the overhaul of the performance review. Employees dreaded Microsoft's ranking system for all the usual reasons: It pitted coworkers against one another at a time when the company needed to be more collaborative; it was unfair; it made frank evaluations less likely.

Here Brummel faced high-level opposition. Ballmer believed that the "forced curve" review—giving a few people the top grade, most a pass, and laggards failing marks—was the key to Microsoft's we-take-the-hills culture. When Brummel approached Ballmer about an overhaul, she met with steely resistance.

Microsoft has always had two rankings: one measuring annual performance and one that captures long-term potential. A forced curve applied to both. To get Ballmer on board, Brummel created a new system that preserved the positive aspects—grades and the chance for stars to win bigger paychecks—while canceling out the negatives. No longer would the first ranking—employee's yearly performance—be subject to the curve. Raises and bonuses would be tied to that ranking. Bosses would have freedom to pass out whatever grades they wanted.

The second, long-term potential ranking determines stock awards. A terrific manager who goes to a struggling division might get a lower grade on the first ranking but would get stock for his or her potential to turn things around.

In the first year, Brummel's policies reduced turnover from 10 to 8.3%. Despite Ballmer's early fears, the new performance rating system has not led to grade inflation. The company successfully released the Vista operating system (although initial market acceptance was disappointing) and its stock price rebounded.viii

lecture link 11-10

KEEPING TALENTED EMPLOYEES: IT'S THE FRINGE THAT COUNTS

When Celeste Volz Ford started Stellar Solutions, an aerospace engineering services firm, she used her talent in problem solving and analytical approach to create the "ideal" working environment for her employees. Studying what had and had not worked over her career in aerospace technology, she selected an array of employee perks designed to balance the long hours and deadline pressures inherent in the highly technical field.

Stellar's 55 full-time employees and 20 part-timers are spread out from Colorado to Washington, DC, so Ford tries hard to encourage a sense of camaraderie. On someone's first day at work, Ford sends a cookie bouquet and arranges for all area employees to take the new person to lunch. On birthdays and work anniversaries, she sends cards.

The company's benefit package reinforces Ford's vision of pampering talented employees. In addition to medical, disability, and life insurance, Stellar offers maternity and paternity leave, tuition reimbursement, and generous retirement contributions. Ford donates $1,000 a year to each employee's charity of choice.

Every worker also receives an individual benefit account. A lump sum equal to 25% of each employee's salary goes into a modified flexible spending account that can be drawn on for extra medical expenses, child care, counseling, even vacation. Rather than assigning a specific number of days off for holidays, sick days, and personal days, employees get six weeks of vacation to take as they please. In addition, Ford requires that employees spend a week on training or conferences or they won't receive their full bonus.

At the peak of the high-tech bubble, many of Stellar's employees were being recruited by dot.com start-ups. To retain her highly trained employees, Ford gave workers a stake in Stellar Ventures, a capital fund she created to invest in start-ups and spin-offs.

Ford sums up her vision in one sentence: "We satisfy our customers' critical needs while realizing our dream jobs." As proof of her approach, her first two bosses now work for her.ix

lecture link 11-11

ENCOURAGING HEALTHY WORK–LIFE BALANCE

When it comes to work, Americans have a little problem: We don't know when to say when. Nearly half of American workers put in more than 50 hours a week on the job. A quarter work all year without taking a vacation.

The American work ethic has been hijacked by a culture that encourages overwork, says Joe Robinson, author of Work to Live: The Guide to Getting a Life. We say we like to work hard and play hard, but we don't actually leave much time for play. We survive layoffs only to be saddled with multiple jobs. Then, hoping to protect those jobs, we put in late nights and long weekends and defer comp time or time off. In the process, we become, if not workaholics, then lousy employees: tired, depressed, mistake prone, resentful, and eventually burned out.

Ernst & Young, the professional services firm, is trying to get employees to work smarter, not longer. "People used to wear overtime on their sleeve like a badge of honor," says audit partner John Beatrice. "But we realized that was no way to live." Employees, women in particular, were leaving the firm.

Now E&Y encourages employees to create flexible schedules that accommodate both their personal and their professional lives. Some work full-time from January to March, then a reduced schedule the rest of the year. Others leave work early to pick up kids from school, then work from home later. More importantly, employees in the flexible work program aren't considered second-class citizens, says Maryella Gockel, the firm's flexibility strategy leader. Since the mid-1990s, 54 have been promoted to partner, director, or principle.

Such strategies are still in the minority. They work only when people see their bosses doing the same. This is one reason E&Y partner John Beatrice is assistant coach for the hockey team at Randolph High School, in Randolph, New Jersey. There are days he leaves the office at 2:30 to make an afternoon game, and he expects his audit teams to pursue similar outside interests. "We think you'll do a better job, and you'll be more focused, if you have other things going on in your life." That is, we need to put our work in context. At best, Robinson says, we should consider our relationship with work in the same terms as any other relationship. "If you don't have a perimeter, you'll get walked on," he says.x

lecture link 11-12

THE DANGERS OF FLEXTIME

During a time when many employed Americans fear the loss of their jobs, the millions of people who either telecommute or work on flextime schedules may have the most to worry about. Reduced time workers and telecommuters fear that they may be the first heads on the chopping block. In some cases their paranoia is warranted. Certain hard-nosed executives sometimes translate a lack of face time with bosses and unorthodox work hours as a lack of commitment. Other execs have simply cut out all flexible work arrangements altogether, preferring to have all employees in-house and under the supervision of the higher-ups during this time of crisis.

But other less stringent managers see an innate benefit in flexible schedules and telecommuters. Such arrangements offer savings on real estate and office costs, and workers are often more productive when their schedules better fit their lifestyles. One part-timer at a Burlingame, California, consulting firm was so productive as a reduced time worker that her boss kept her onboard while more senior full-timers were shown the door. Some businesses are seeing such advantages in flextime scheduling that they're structuring all new working plans to cut costs. In a 2009 survey of 700 companies, 21 to 32% surveyed are implementing part-time shifts or instituting four-day compressed workweeks as a means of reducing overhead.

Normally, in a recession the number of employees working flexibly falls only to recover as the economy rebounds. Indeed, the number of flextime workers shrank from 9.2 million in 2006 to 8.7 million in 2009. Whether or not more companies will restructure their work plans to accommodate more flexible scheduling remains to be seen, but in the meantime those managers who fire flextime workers first on the stereotype that they are less committed won't have such an easy road ahead. Discrimination complaints to the Equal Employment Opportunity Commission about firing part-timers are rising. For example, EEOC recently held hearing on bias against people with caregiving duties. [xi]

lecture link 11-13

USING THE EXIT INTERVIEW FOR FEEDBACK

Getting feedback on problems is the only way to prevent them from recurring. One often-overlooked way of getting this feedback is through the exit interview. Interviews with employees who voluntarily leave the organization serve a dual purpose. For employees, exit interviews are a chance to say many things they haven't been able to say before. For employers, the interviews can be an excellent source of information. Many companies, however, do not conduct exit interviews, or conduct them ineffectively.

A good exit interview should consist of structured and unstructured questions. If the employee is counting on a reference, he or she may be unwilling to be too truthful. To put the employee at ease and get honest information, some human resource professionals recommend writing the reference in advance and letting the employee know at the beginning of the interview. Then questions such as the following can be used to get honest information about the company as a whole.

"What did you like most about working here?" This helps gain insight into how the employee perceives the corporate culture. At AT&T, one of the answers most frequently heard is that employees appreciated the benefits package. When exiting employees mention this, it reaffirms to the company that the investment in benefits is paying off.

"What do you feel good about having accomplished?" This helps determine what responsibilities gave the employee a sense of accomplishment.

"If you were in charge here, what would you change?" This question is used to give the employee a chance to figuratively change the work environment. Prepare for a candid answer.

"What best helped you achieve your goals?" This is where managers find out which employee-support systems are working and which are not. If, for example, the vice president's open door policy was useful in getting some project underway, the policy could be encouraged among other senior managers.

"What did you dislike about the work environment here?" An exit interview survey at a Boston hospital showed that 20% said they had problems with the work schedule and 15% said they disliked their direct supervisor. This information encouraged hospital administrators to implement schedule alternatives and management training for supervisors.

Finally, the exit interview information should be *used*. Managers at AT&T produce a twice-yearly, in-depth analysis of exit interview findings, which are presented to the senior vice president of human resources. The information is used to reexamine policies, make suggestions for change, and generally help retain skilled employees. Some of the best ideas have come from people who are leaving.

critical
thinking exercises

Name: _____

Date: _____

critical thinking exercise 11-1
EXPANDING THE WORKFORCE

You are the human resource manager for Kaiser Electronics, Inc. Kaiser is considering expanding its operations in order to double its current $1.5 million in sales in five years. This means production must double. It will require expanding the workforce and payroll. You have been asked to project the staffing levels and payroll costs necessary to expand. You report that in addition to the current workforce, the following personnel will be required:

Two additional sales representatives

Two additional secretaries (both Level 6)

Ten additional assembly-line operators (Level 4) for the production department

Three additional materials handlers (Level 4) for the production department

One additional assembly-line supervisor (Level 14)

Now you must estimate the costs of adding these personnel to the payroll. Use the chart "Future Payroll Estimates" to compute your projection figures (assume the current pay scales remain unchanged). Then use the chart to answer the following questions:

1. What will be the projected annual payroll cost?

2. If Kaiser does double its sales in five years, what percentage of sales will payroll be in five years? What percentage is it today?

3. Would you recommend the expansion? Why or why not?

<u>critical thinking exercise 11-1</u> (continued)

FUTURE PAYROLL ESTIMATES

POSITION	PAY SCALE	PRESENT STAFF	PRESENT PAYROLL	PROJECTED STAFF	PROJECTED PAYROLL
Management					
Level 24	$65,000	1	$65,000	_____	_____
Level 18	$45,000	1	$45,000	_____	_____
Clerical					
Level 10	$21,000	2	$42,000	_____	_____
Level 6	$16,000	3	$48,000	_____	_____
Production					
Level 14	$26,000	3	$78,000	_____	_____
Level 10	$19,000	1	$19,000	_____	_____
Level 8	$16,000	2	$32,000	_____	_____
Level 5	$13,000	2	$26,000	_____	_____
Level 4	$11,000	13	$143,000	_____	_____
Sales					
Level 10	$26,000	5	$130,000	_____	_____
Totals		36	$628,000	_____	_____

notes on critical thinking exercise 11-1

POSITION	PAY SCALE	PRESENT STAFF	PRESENT PAYROLL	PROJECTED STAFF	PROJECTED PAYROLL
Management					
Level 24	$65,000	1	$65,000	1	$65,000
Level 18	$45,000	1	$45,000	1	$45,000
Clerical					
Level 10	$21,000	2	$42,000	2	$42,000
Level 6	$16,000	3	$48,000	5	$80,000
Production					
Level 14	$26,000	3	$78,000	4	$104,000
Level 10	$19,000	1	$19,000	1	$19,000
Level 8	$16,000	2	$32,000	2	$32,000
Level 5	$13,000	2	$26,000	2	$26,000
Level 4	$11,000	13	$143,000	26	$286,000
Sales					
Level 10	$26,000	5	$130,000	7	$182,000
Totals		36	$628,000	50	$881,000

1. *What will be the projected annual payroll cost?*

    Projected annual payroll cost is $881,000.

2. *If Kaiser does double its sales in five years, what percentage of sales will payroll be in five years? What percentage is it today?*

    Projected percentage of sales: $881,000 ÷ 3,000,000 = 29%

    Current percentage of sales: $628,000 ÷ 1,500,000 = 41.9%.

3. *Would you recommend the expansion? Why or why not?*

    Yes, the cost figures are good and the potential is good. The percentage of sales devoted to payroll expenses will decrease significantly with the expansion. Looked at another way, by spending an additional $253,000 in payroll costs, the company can earn an additional $1,500,000 in revenue—not a bad return on investment.

critical thinking exercise 11-2
MANAGEMENT SELECTION

You are vice president of a medium-sized corporation that believes strongly in promoting from within. You have two jobs to fill:

- General manager, Midwestern Division.

- Project manager, Internet marketing

On your desk are four resumes:

Peter Evans, 49. Evans, a white male, has been with the company for 18 years. He has been in charge of the information technology department for the past 10 years. His employees praise him for his easygoing management style and computer skills. He is married with three children.

Anylla Padova, 35. Padova, a white female, has been with the company for 10 years. She started working in the shipping department, spent 4 years in sales, and for the past 3 years has been the manager of the company's Mexico City office. She is fluent in Spanish and French.

Jacques Davidson, 29. Davidson, an African American male, has worked for the company for 3 years as supervisor in the production department. Production efficiency in his work crew is the highest in the company. Prior to joining the company, Davidson worked at a petrochemical refinery as supervisor.

Jocinta Fernandez, 23. Fernandez, a Hispanic American female, recently received an MBA from the state university. Her undergraduate degree is in marketing. She has worked for the company as an intern while attending school.

1.   Analyze each job. What types of skills do you think each position would require?

2.   What do you think of the company's policy of promoting from within? Should you consider outside applicants for either of these positions? Why or why not?

3.   Which of the four applicants would you hire for each position? Why?

4.   Which employee characteristics should *not* be considered?

notes on critical thinking exercise 11-2

1. *Analyze each job. What types of skills do you think each position would require?*

    The position for general manager requires all the management skills described in Chapter 7. Strong conceptual and organizational skills are important.

    The position of Internet project manager requires more technical skills and training.

2. *What do you think of the company's policy of promoting from within? Should you consider outside applicants for either of these positions? Why or why not?*

    Hiring from within is good for the motivation of current employees. The company also knows the individual's track record, strengths, and weaknesses. However, hiring from outside sources brings new ideas into the organization. It may also be necessary when key skills are not available within the organization.

3. *Which of the four applicants would you hire for each position? Why?*

    This will be an individual decision. Keep in mind that some facts included in the resume descriptions should not be considered in the selection decision—for instance, race, sex, and marital status.

4. *Which employee characteristics should* not *be considered?*

    Characteristics that do not affect job performance—race, sex, marital status, number of children—should not be considered.

critical thinking exercise 11-3
JOB SEARCH VIA THE INTERNET

Go to the website for Monster.com (www.monster.com).[xii] (Sometimes the Web address for a location changes. You might need to search to find the exact location mentioned.)

1.   Use the search by geographic location (or by zip code) to pull up job openings in your home city. List the three jobs that most interest you and/or match your skills and education.

2.   Follow links to career resources (or job search resources). Which tools would be helpful to you in a job search?

3.   Go to other online employment agencies such as www.jobsearch.org, www.careerbuilder.com, or www.hotjobs.com. Which site provides the information you need to search for a job?

4.   Why would a company place an employment listing using an online employment service rather than place an ad in a newspaper or trade journal?

<u>critical thinking exercise 11-4</u>
DIVERSITY IN MANAGEMENT

The text discusses the increasing diversity in the management field. Go to the federal government's Bureau of Labor Statistics website and find the current statistics (www.bls.gov/cps).[xiii] (Sometimes the Web address for a location changes. You might need to search to find the exact location mentioned.)

Under the category "Characteristics of the employed," choose "Employed persons by occupation, race, and sex."

1. What percentage of white females are in executive, administrative, and managerial positions?

2. What percentage of black males are in executive, administrative, and managerial positions?

3. What percentage of the entire workforce is in executive, administrative, and managerial positions?

4. Is the percentage of women managers increasing from the previous year or decreasing?

5. Is the percentage of black managers increasing from the previous year or decreasing?

critical thinking exercise 11-5
BEST COMPANIES FOR WORKING MOMS

An important segment of the worker pool is the working mother. Companies that want to attract and/or retain these employees have found creative ways to adjust to the flexibility that raising children can require. Each year *Working Mother* magazine publishes a list of the best companies to work for. Top considerations for inclusion are flexible scheduling, child-care options, and time off for new parents. Companies were scored on 500 different items in their application for inclusion on the list. The companies also had to provide supporting documentation.

Go to the website for *Working Mother* magazine (www.workingmother.com).[xiv] (Sometimes the Web address for a location changes. You might need to search to find the exact location mentioned.)

1. List the top 10 companies for working women for the current year.

2. Choose one of the winners and research the company.

    a. Are any members of the top management female? If so, who?

    b. Find the company's mission statement. (*Hint:* Look for the "investor relations" section.) Does the mission reflect the company's concern for working mothers? If it does, how?

3. Go back to the *Working Mother* site and locate winners for previous years. Are there any companies that have won more than once? If so, list them.

bonus
cases

bonus case 11-1

INCARCERATED CALL CENTERS

Overcrowding, skyrocketing costs, and high recidivism rates cripple the American penal system. But even with the nation's penitentiaries in such a state, at least one entrepreneur found a way to transform prisoners into productive members of society, both behind bars and on the outside. James Hooker is the founder and CEO of Televerde, a company that seeks businesses willing to buy complex, multimillion-dollar software from tech giants like Cisco, NetApp, and Hitachi. At the heart of Televerde's operation are 250 incarcerated women who work at four different call centers within the Arizona State Penitentiary in Perryville.

Purchased by Hooker in 1995, Televerde grew from a six-person call center running out of a trailer into a profitable operation taking in $12.1 million annually. Detractors claim that Hooker's unconventional staff is robbing law-abiding citizens of work in this already rough job market. But Hooker is quick to point out that the facts read differently. Televerde employees make the federal minimum wage of $7.25, with one-third of each prisoner's salary going back into the system for room and board. Also, the recidivism rate of Televerde alumni is amazingly low. Over the last 14 years only 11% of released Televerde employees have gone back to jail. This is remarkably better than the national average of 40% of female felons returning to custody within just three years. Alumni from the Perryville prison also come out with a heap of savings, averaging $15,000 per prisoner.

Hooker hires back approximately 25% of his former inmate staff after their release. Many obtain their high school diploma, a requirement for employment at Televerde, while incarcerated, with one former prisoner even going on to obtain her MBA at Arizona State University. Besides its contributions to the lives of its employees and the Perryville prison in general, Televerde simply runs a better operation than its competitors. In a study conducted comparing Televerde with a rival company, Televerde delivered five times as many high-quality leads than its competitor. Hooker attributes this to his staff, whom he claims are "50 times more motivated than someone on the outside." [xv]

discussion questions for bonus case 11-1

1. Could the Televerde system work in other states?

2. What is a key strength of the Televerde system?

notes on discussion questions for bonus case 11-1

1.   *Could the Televerde system work in other states?*

There doesn't seem to be any reason that the Televerde system could not work in other states given the fact that penal systems across the nation are expensive and in horrid shape. Whether employers would be willing to spend the money to set up the system could be a sticking point.

2.   *What is a key strength of the Televerde system?*

Televerde provides inmates an opportunity to save money and develop a marketable skill they can transfer to the outside world. Its greatest benefits to society are the reduction of costs to house prisoners and the reduction in the recidivism rate.

bonus case 11-2

SHOULD YOU HIRE A FORMER EMPLOYEE?

When one of Santera Systems' top engineers left the telecom upstart for another hot tech company, CEO David Heard tried to convince the employee he was making the wrong move. That engineer should have listened. Heard's former star showed up at Santera only four months later looking for his old job back. Turned out his new employer wasn't so hot after all. "He came back, hat in hand, and said 'I made a mistake,'" says Heard.

You could call them prodigal employees—workers who leave in search of greener pastures, only to return to the fold when things don't work out as planned. The tech meltdown and the unstable economy have forced a growing group of newly displaced workers to knock on their former employers' doors.

Good people, however, are hard to find, and prodigal employees should be welcomed back—if there is a position to fill. But it's not such a clear-cut decision for small businesses. Since employee relationships tend to be tighter-knit at smaller firms, a company's productivity can easily unravel when the boss shows signs of favoritism. In Santera's case, CEO Heard felt rehiring the engineer would harm his efforts to build a culture long on longevity and short on greed. "Part of me thought, 'Bring him back—he's a smart guy,'" Heard says, "but you don't want to reward his behavior. It doesn't send the right message to the employees who stuck with you."

Small-company CEOs and managers must be extra sensitive to their employees' morale if they do decide to bring back a wayward worker. Recruiting experts suggest lining up allies to be advocates for the returning employee before—and after—his or her first day back. That helps the rest of the team understand why the "ex" is back home and helps the old newcomer feel more comfortable. They also recommend giving the whole team a project to pursue together.

In many cases, bringing back a former employee can be an unexpected boon for a small company. Sterling Communications executive Chris Corcoran was happy to rehire a qualified account supervisor who had left months earlier for a dot-com that went bust. He was pleasantly surprised to discover she came back with a better understanding of business as a result of wearing many hats at the tech company. "She had matured and become a much better counselor to our clients."[xvi]

discussion questions for bonus case 11-2

1.   What would be the advantages and disadvantages of hiring a former employee in larger organizations? In small firms?

2.   How valid were David Heard's concerns about the effect of returning employees on the company's culture?

3.   At which level of the organization should the rehire decision be made—supervisory, middle management, or upper management?

notes on discussion questions for bonus case 11-2

1.   *What would be the advantages and disadvantages of hiring a former employee in larger organizations? In small firms?*

It may be easier to hire back an employee in large organizations, but only after discussion with the other employees. They may welcome a great worker back. It depends greatly on the circumstances. Students should be able to think through such issues. That's what these cases demand. In a small firm, hiring people back can have more severe consequences for promotions and such. Discuss.

2.   *How valid were David Heard's concerns about the effect of returning employees on the company's culture?*

His comments were valid. Bringing people back can harm the whole atmosphere in a company. On the other hand, it may be a good opportunity to show the returning worker and those who stay that the company is loyal to its workers and will bring you back. Of course, the whole subject needs to be discussed with other employees first.

3.   *At which level of the organization should the rehire decision be made—supervisory, middle management, or upper management?*

All levels should be involved because all levels are affected—not just managers, but employees too. Eventually, there should be a policy on such issues so that everyone is not forced to agonize over each decision.

bonus case 11-3

HUMAN RESOURCE PLANNING AND WOMEN WORKERS

The steadily increasing flow of women into the workforce has caused human resource planners and chief executive officers to consider women's needs more carefully when doing human resource planning.

Affirmative action laws are partially responsible for increasing the number of women in the workplace. Another cause of the influx of women is demographics: The workforce is no longer expanding in the traditional way, since population growth has slowed. As companies expand and the population doesn't, HR managers will have to hire more women and minorities to fill their needs for employees. This is causing some employers to incorporate benefits in their overall benefit package that are especially addressed to women.

Among the more important issues for both males and females is how to balance work and family. The 1993 Family and Medical Leave Act gives employees the right to 12 weeks of unpaid leave for parental leave or family medical leave. Upon return, an employee must be returned to the same or equivalent position.

Maternity leave is a controversial area of human resources. Some say women should be guaranteed paid maternity leave. These groups claim that when women leave their jobs to have children it has a negative effect on their careers that doesn't affect men. Women thus lose seniority since career ladders are not designed for people who take leave.

Some companies now offer women benefits in a "cafeteria plan." Basically, that means that women are able to choose from a variety of benefits to suit their individual needs. A parent may choose parental leave, for example, while a single woman may choose an extra week of vacation.

Child care is another area where companies are beginning to provide assistance to parents. IBM, for example, has set up a referral service to help employees find day care in the community. Other countries, such as France, Belgium, Italy, Israel, and Canada, have day care systems that are subsidized by the government to help ease the financial burden on parents. In many cases, the salary of a working mother in the United States may barely cover the cost of keeping a child in day care.

Other benefits that can help parents manage work while raising a family—flextime, part-time work with partial benefits, and job sharing—can also benefit employers. These benefits reduce the need for parents to spend time at work dealing with family issues.

Flextime allows workers to come in during a two-hour period and leave within a two-hour period, as long as they are at work between certain hours (known as core time). A new arrangement for part-time workers allows them to reduce their work time and keep some proportion of their benefits. With job sharing, two workers share a job and a salary, along with benefits.

A company called Chicken Soup in Minneapolis provides day care for ill children so that parents won't have to stay home from work when a child is ill. Many large corporations, such as 3M, Dayton Hudson, and First Bank Systems, have provided funding for the project.

discussion questions for bonus case 11-3

1.   Have companies done enough to adjust to women in the workplace?

2.   Which of the issues mentioned so far do you feel is most important? Why?

3.   What else could companies do, if anything, to assist women workers? Would you recommend that they do that?

notes on discussion questions for bonus case 11-3

1. *Have companies done enough to adjust to women in the workplace?*

   Some companies have, but many have done little or nothing. In the future, all companies will have to do something because women will make up a huge part of the labor force, especially in the service sector. Focus should be on families, not just women.

2. *Which of the issues mentioned so far do you feel is most important? Why?*

   The most important issue is freedom to choose options in benefits. Not all families have children and need day care, flextime, and so on. Also, too much emphasis on families is unfair to those without families. Flexible systems can be fair to all.

3. *What else could companies do, if anything, to assist women workers? Would you recommend that they do that?*

   It is not wise to focus on women in isolation. It is best to study families, work, and home situations. More work may be done at home and sent over computer lines to work. More part-time and flextime schedules could be made. The women and men in the class may have several good suggestions.

bonus case 11-4

THE DEPARTMENT STORE DILEMMA

"This is a rough decision," said Stan Wheatley, store manager and vice president of Bassfield Department Store. Bassfield, a large urban retailer with 350 employees, is a family-owned business that has operated in Levittston for over 30 years. Wheatley believes strongly in delegating authority to lower levels of management. However, Adele Stafford, manager of the women's sportswear department, has recently referred a problem to him.

Six weeks ago, Mary Alice Brooks, aged 23, was hired as a temporary employee. She has an outstanding personality and immediately made friends with the senior workers in the department, as well as with other salespersons and clerks in the store. Moreover, she is an exceptional salesperson who relates well to customers. In fact, many had gone out of their way to tell Adele Stafford how much they enjoyed dealing with Mary Alice. After Mary Alice's two-week temporary period, her manager requested that she be hired on a full-time basis; Mary Alice's husband has recently undergone major surgery, so Mary Alice was glad to have full-time work.

Four days ago, Bill Chavez, personnel manager of the store, realized that Mary Alice had not taken the medical exam required of all full-time employees. When Mary Alice took the exam that afternoon, she didn't pass it due to an existing heart condition. Because of restrictions in the company's medical insurance program, she could not be hired. Chavez told Stafford that Mary Alice would have to be terminated. Stafford, women's sportswear manager, argues strongly that an exception be made in Mary Alice's case. Several employees have also told the personnel manager that it is unfair to Mary Alice to release her now, since it was his own oversight. Also, they argue that the company should be willing to help people in situations such Mary Alice's, since they have an EEOC program and have even hired some employees with disabilities in the past.

But Chavez, the personnel manager, says that Mary Alice must go. The rule is that all permanent employees must pass the physical, and Mary Alice did not.

Stafford appealed the decision to Wheatley, the store manager, who said he would let her know something the next day. As he ponders a way out of the dilemma, Wheatley is aware of the results of a survey on his desk: 42% of the employees say that they would consider joining a union if one attempted to organize the store.

discussion questions for bonus case 11-4

1. What are the key issues in the case?

2. Develop several realistic alternatives for Wheatley to consider.

3. What decision do you recommend that Wheatley make?

notes on discussion questions for bonus case 11-4

1. *What are the key issues in the case?*

   It is a good idea to let students develop this case. They should consider that the company policy is to have everyone pass a physical. Policies are there for just such cases—so that managers don't have to make decisions over and over again with hard cases. But the human side also needs to be considered, as does the effect on existing employees and customers.

2. *Develop several realistic alternatives for Wheatley to consider.*

   A store manager is very concerned with sales and profit; therefore, it would be hard to let go a stellar sales performer. Among the alternatives:

   a. Seek a second opinion from another physician to determine the exact extent of Mary Alice's condition.

   b. Look into purchasing a supplemental health insurance policy for Mary Alice.

   c. Waive the insurance restriction and hire Mary Alice anyway.

   d. Reduce Mary Alice's hours below full-time status so the restriction would not apply.

   e. Find another insurance company.

   f. Fire Mary Alice.

3. *What decision do you recommend that Wheatley make?*

   I have used this case in my Intro classes several times over two decades. With very few exceptions, students have decided to keep Mary Alice on despite the manager's recommendation. A few want to fire Chavez. Some think the employees should unionize to protect themselves from unfair practices. Most want to find a middle ground that lets Mary Alice keep her job with some modifications to the policy.

   One practical idea suggested is to involve the employees in the decision-making process, perhaps creating an ad hoc committee made up of managers, employees, and knowledgeable consultants. If employees are given all the facts, they can make an educated decision. A decision reached with employee input would be more likely to be accepted by workers than one dictated by management. Explain that insurance premiums are based on the combined experience of the group covered. In a large organization, one expensive medical problem will be spread out over a large number of covered workers. In a small business, however, one person's health costs can drive up premiums very quickly. Would employees be willing to accept higher insurance premiums to keep this valuable worker?

   A very important point to consider: Is this policy even legal? Can you reject a potential employee because of a medical problem? Does this violate the Americans with Disabilities Act? If you fire Mary Alice, are you opening your company to a wrongful termination lawsuit?

endnotes

[i] *Sources*: Jeremy Caplan, "Resume Mogul," *Time Inside Business,* February 2006, and *Boston Globe*, August 14, 2011.

[ii] *Sources*: Saul Hansell, "Google's Answer to Filling Jobs: New Algorithm," *The New York Times*, January 3, 2007; Julie Masis, "Google Clicks with Job-Seekers," *Boston Globe*; August 12, 2007; Amanda Fung, "Google, Rivals Hunt for Sales Staff in NY," *Crain's New York Business*, July 31, 2006; "Silicon Valley Upstart Google Grows into the Not-So-Little Engine That Could," *The Philadelphia Inquirer,* January 4, 2004.

[iii] *Source:* Alina Dizik, "Wooing Job Recruiters with Video Resumes," *The Wall Street Journal*, May 20, 2010.

[iv] *Sources*: Rachel Farrell, "Interviewees Say the Darndest Things," *CareerBuilder,* September 15, 2010; Alicia Dennis, "'Cow Car' Isn't Just an Interviewer's Tall Tale," *Austin Business Journal*, January 31, 2003; Press release, "Note to Job Candidates: Avoid Bringing Doughnuts, Dogs, and Dates to the Interview," *Officeteam.com*, September 25, 2002.

[v] *Sources*: Steve Bates, " Personality Counts: Psychological Tests Can Help Peg the Job Applicants Best Suited for Certain Jobs," *HR Magazine;* February 1, 2002; Ariana Eunjung Cha, "Employers Relying on Personality Tests to Screen Applicants," *The Washington Post*, March 27, 2005; Lisa Takeuchi Cullen, "SATS for J-O-B-S," *Time*, April 3, 2006.

[vi] *Sources*: Gwen Shaffer, "Background Checks on the Rise at Companies," *Philadelphia Business Journal*, March 28, 2003; David Hench, "Requests Surge for Criminal Histories," *Maine Sunday Telegram*, December 1, 2002; *Employment Background Checks: A Jobseeker's Guide*, Privacy Rights Clearinghouse, Revised April 2003; "Background Checks by Companies Spark Worries," *The Clarion-Ledger,* Associated Press, December 30, 2005.

[vii] *Source:* Helen A. S. Popkin, "Facebook: The Evil Interface," *MSNBC.com,* May 3, 2010.

[viii] *Sources:* Benjamin J. Romano, "Microsoft Exec Puts Her Stamp on Human Resources,*" Seattle Times*, October 9, 2006; Dina Bass, "Microsoft Spends More to Keep Staff," *International Herald Tribune,* May 20, 2006; Sean P. Means, "Pixar Genius, Lasseter, Is a Fresh Infusion for Disney," *Salt Lake Tribune,* June 11, 2006; Michelle Conlin and Jay Greene, "How to Make a Microserf Smile," *BusinessWeek,* September 10, 2007.

[ix] *Sources:* Julie Sloane, "The Best Bosses: The Iconoclast," *Fortune Small Business*, October 2003; "U.S. Lags World in Fringe Benefits," United Press International, June 18, 2004; Joe D. Jones, "On the Fringe: Benefit Costs Continue Steep Climb," *Mississippi Business Journal*, February 27, 2006.

[x] *Source*: Chuck Salter, "Solving the Real Productivity Crisis," *Fast Company,* January 2004, p. 37.

[xi] *Source:* Sue Shellenbarger, "Does Avoiding a 9-to-5 Grind Make You a Target for Layoffs?" *The Wall Street Journal*, April 22, 2009.

[xii] The Internet is a dynamic, changing information source. Web links noted of this manual were checked at the time of publication, but content may change over time. Please review the website before recommending it to your students.

[xiii] The Internet is a dynamic, changing information source. Web links noted of this manual were checked at the time of publication, but content may change over time. Please review the website before recommending it to your students.

[xiv] The Internet is a dynamic, changing information source. Web links noted of this manual were checked at the time of publication, but content may change over time. Please review the website before recommending it to your students.

[xv] *Source:* Victoria Barret, "Salvation at the Call Center," *Forbes*, June 28, 2010.

[xvi] *Source:* Stephanie N. Mehta, "Prodigal Son," *Fortune Small Business*, July/August 2002, p. 77.

Dealing with Union and Employee–Management Issues

chapter 12

critical thinking exercises

critical thinking exercises   12.73

bonus cases   12.78

what's new in this edition

additions to the 10th edition:

- Getting to Know David Stern, Commissioner of the National Basketball Association

- Name That Company: Bright Horizons

- Subsection Public Sector Union Membership in section Labor Unions from Different Perspectives

- Subsection Union Organizing Campaigns with reorganized discussions of NRLB and EFCA added in section Labor Legislation and Collective Bargaining

- Spotlight on Small Business: The Triangle Fire

- Legal Briefcase: Executive Pay Remains on the Rise

- Video case

revisions to the 10th edition:

- Text was revised to eliminate redundancy and tighten discussions.

- Statistical data and examples throughout the chapter were updated to reflect current information.

- Discussion of unions' recent status revised in section Employee–Management Issues.

deletions from the 9th edition:

- Getting to Know Roger Goodell, commissioner of the National Football League

- Name That Company: James P. Hoffa

- Reaching Beyond Our Borders

- Legal Briefcase

- Spotlight on Small Business

brief chapter outline
and learning goals

Dealing with Union and Employee–Management Issues

Getting To Know DAVID STERN of THE NATIONAL BASKETBALL ASSOCIATION (NBA)

I. EMPLOYEE–MANAGEMENT ISSUES

learning goal 1

Trace the history of organized labor in the United States.

II. LABOR UNIONS FROM DIFFERENT PERSPECTIVES

   A. The History of Organized Labor

   B. Public Sector Union Membership

learning goal 2

Discuss the major legislation affecting labor unions.

III. LABOR LEGISLATION AND COLLECTIVE BARGAINING

   A. Union Organizing Campaigns

learning goal 3

Outline the objectives of labor unions.

   B. Objectives of Organized Labor over Time

   C. Resolving Labor–Management Disagreements

   D. Mediation and Arbitration

learning goal 4

Describe the tactics used by labor and management during conflicts, and discuss the role of unions in the future.

IV. TACTICS USED IN LABOR–MANAGEMENT CONFLICTS

   A. Union Tactics

   B. Management Tactics

   C. The Future of Unions and Labor–Management Relations

learning goal 5

Assess some of today's controversial employee–management issues, such as executive compensation, pay equity, child care and elder care, drug testing, and violence in the workplace.

V. CONTROVERSIAL EMPLOYEE–MANAGEMENT ISSUES

    A.   **Executive Compensation**

    B.   **Pay Equity**

    C.   **Sexual Harassment**

    D.   **Child Care**

    E.   **Elder Care**

    F.   **Drug Testing**

    G.   **Violence in the Workplace**

VI. SUMMARY

Getting to Know DAVID STERN of THE NATIONAL BASKETBALL ASSOCIATION (NBA)

Over his three decades with the NBA, Stern has led the league to huge growth from local ticket sales to globalization. Labor issues, however, have been a sore spot. Stern has presided over five employee lockouts. As of this writing, he is teetering on his sixth.

NAME THAT company

As the number of women in the workplace began growing rapidly about 25 years ago, this company recognized that providing child care benefits would be a real advantage for companies. Today, it is the largest provider of child care at worksites, operating about 700 child care centers for 400 companies including 90 companies in the Fortune 500. Name that company.

(Students should read the chapter before guessing the company's name: Bright Horizon)

I.   EMPLOYEE–MANAGEMENT ISSUES

A.   The relationship of employees and their managers has always been complex.

B.   A **UNION** is an employee organization whose main goal is representing its members in employee–management negotiation of job-related issues.

   1.   Public sector unions have been in the news recently.

   2.   **PUBLIC SECTOR UNIONS** represent government employees like teachers, firefighters, and police.

   3.   Workers originally formed unions to protect themselves from intolerable working conditions and unfair treatment.

   4.   Labor unions are largely responsible for minimum wage laws, child-labor laws, and other significant worker benefits.

PPT 12-1
Chapter Title

PPT 12-2
Learning Goals

(See complete PowerPoint slide notes on page 12.46.)

PPT 12-3
Learning Goals

(See complete PowerPoint slide notes on page 12.46.)

PPT 12-4
David Stern

(See complete PowerPoint slide notes on page 12.47.)

PPT 12-5
Name That Company

(See complete PowerPoint slide notes on page 12.47.)

PPT 12-6
Organized Labor

(See complete PowerPoint slide notes on page 12.47.)

PPT 12-7
Public Sector Labor Unions

(See complete PowerPoint slide notes on page 12.48.)

5. However, unions have failed to regain their previous power, and membership declined.

6. **REASONS FOR UNION DECLINE:**

   a. Some suggest that global competition, the shift to a service economy, and changes in management philosophy have caused the decline.

   b. The decline may also be because objectives have been achieved.

learning goal 1

Trace the history of organized labor in the United States.

II. LABOR UNIONS FROM DIFFERENT PERSPECTIVES

A. Your opinion about unions usually depends upon which side of the management fence you are on.

B. Most historians generally do agree on the reason unions were started in the first place.

   1. The **INDUSTRIAL REVOLUTION** moved workers out of the field and into the factories.

   2. Workers learned that **STRENGTH THROUGH UNITY** (unions) could lead to improved job conditions, better wages, and job security.

   3. But some argue that for organized labor the real issue of protecting workers has become secondary.

   4. Critics also argue that the current legal system and management philosophy reduce the risk of unsafe or oppressive conditions.

PPT 12-8
Public Sector Jobs

(See complete PowerPoint slide notes on page 12.48.)

lecture link 12-1
THE COMPLICATED LEGACY OF HENRY FORD

Henry Ford founded the Ford Motor Company in 1903, producing an inexpensive, all-purpose car, the model T. Throughout its history the company's dealings with the union were complex and contradictory. (See the complete lecture link on page 12.65 in this manual.)

PPT 12-9
Goals of Organized Labor

(See complete PowerPoint slide notes on page 12.48.)

critical thinking exercise 12-1
ARE UNIONS GOOD OR BAD FOR BUSINESS?

This exercise asks the student to consider unions from both the manager's and the union member's perspective. (See complete exercise on page 12.73 of this manual.)

C. THE HISTORY OF ORGANIZED LABOR

1. As early as 1792, **CORDWAINERS** (shoemakers) met to discuss labor issues in Philadelphia.

    a. The cordwainers were a **_CRAFT UNION_**, that is, an organization of skilled workers in a particular craft or trade.

    b. A craft union usually met to achieve a specific goal and then disbanded.

2. The Industrial Revolution changed the economic structure of the U.S.

    a. With the Industrial Revolution intensified, labor problems were **NO LONGER SHORT TERM.**

    b. Workers who failed to produce lost their jobs.

    c. The average workweek in 1900 was 60 hours.

    d. Wages were low, child labor existed, and unemployment benefits were nonexistent.

    e. There was a need for an organization that would attack **LONG-TERM PROBLEMS** such as child labor and subsistence wages.

3. The first national labor organization was the **_KNIGHTS OF LABOR_** formed by **URIAH SMITH STEPHENS** in 1869.

    a. It included employers as well as workers, and promoted social, labor, and economic causes.

    b. After they were blamed for the Haymarket Square bombing in 1886, the Knights of Labor fell from prominence.

PPT 12-10
History of Organized Labor

(See complete PowerPoint slide notes on page 12.49.)

SPOTLIGHT ON
small
business
(Text page 327)

PPT 12-11
The Triangle Fire

(See complete PowerPoint slide notes on page 12.49.)

PPT 12-12
Emergence of Labor Organizations

(See complete PowerPoint slide notes on page 12.49.)

4. The **AMERICAN FEDERATION OF LABOR
   (AFL)** was formed in 1886 under the leadership of
   SAMUEL GOMPERS.

   a. The ***AMERICAN FEDERATION OF LABOR
      (AFL)***, an organization of **MANY INDIVIDUAL
      CRAFT UNIONS,** championed fundamental
      labor issues.

   b. An unauthorized committee in the AFL began
      to organize workers in ***INDUSTRIAL UNIONS,***
      labor organizations of unskilled and semi-
      skilled workers in mass-production industries
      such as automobiles and mining.

5. When the AFL rejected these unions, **JOHN
   LEWIS,** president of the **UNITED MINE WORK-
   ERS UNION**, formed a new, rival organization.

   a. The ***CONGRESS OF INDUSTRIAL ORGANI-
      ZATIONS (CIO),*** a union organization of un-
      skilled workers, broke off from the AFL in 1935
      and rejoined it in 1955.

   b. Membership in the CIO soon rivaled that of
      the AFL.

   c. The AFL and CIO struggled for power in the
      labor movement until the **TWO ORGANIZA-
      TIONS MERGED** in 1955 under the leader-
      ship of **GEORGE MEANY**.

   d. Recently, the AFL-CIO's influence has weak-
      ened but it's trying to regain strength.

   e. In 2005 seven unions left the AFL-CIO and
      formed a coalition called Change to Win.

PPT 12-13
Industrial Unions

(See complete PowerPoint slide notes on page 12.50.)

6. The AFL-CIO maintains affiliations with 56 national and international labor unions and has about 12.2 million members.

D. **PUBLIC SECTOR UNION MEMBERSHIP**

1. For the first time, **7.6 million of the 14.7 million union members** work in the government.

2. Unfortunately, huge state and local revenue losses have put pressure on governments to cut wages and benefits.

3. Today, at least **17 states** are trying to restrict union rights.

learning goal 2

Discuss the major legislation affecting labor unions.

III. **LABOR LEGISLATION AND COLLECTIVE BARGAINING**

A. The growth and influence of organized labor in the U.S. has depended on two major factors: the **LAW** and **PUBLIC OPINION.**

1. The **NORRIS-LAGUARDIA ACT** paved the way for union growth.

   a. It prohibited employees from using contracts that forbid union activities.

   b. A _**YELLOW-DOG CONTRACT**_ is a type of contract that requires employees to agree as a condition of employment not to join a union; prohibited by the Norris-LaGuardia Act.

2. The **NATIONAL LABOR RELATIONS ACT** (or **WAGNER ACT)** provided legal justification for union activities.

PPT 12-14
Public Unions

(See complete PowerPoint slide notes on page 12.50.)

lecture link 12-2
UNION UPROAR IN WISCONSIN

Cash-strapped states are struggling with budget cuts and public unions. (See the complete lecture link on page 12.66 in this manual.)

PPT 12-15
Effects of Laws on Labor Unions

(See complete PowerPoint slide notes on page 12.50.)

TEXT FIGURE 12.1
Major Legislation Affecting Labor–
Management Relations
(Text page 329)

This text figure shows the five major federal laws that have had a significant impact on labor unions' activities.

    a. ***COLLECTIVE BARGAINING*** is the process whereby union and management representatives form a labor–management agreement, or contract, for workers.

    b. The Wagner Act expanded labor's right to collectively bargain.

B. **UNION ORGANIZING CAMPAIGNS**

    1. The Wagner Act also established the **NATIONAL LABOR RELATIONS BOARD (NLRB)**, to oversee labor–management relations.

        a. ***CERTIFICATION*** is the formal process whereby a union is recognized by the NLRB as the bargaining agent for a group of employees.

        b. ***DECERTIFICATION*** is the process by which workers take away a union's right to represent them.

        c. The Wagner Act provided clear procedures for both.

learning goal 3

Outline the objectives of labor unions.

C. **OBJECTIVES OF ORGANIZED LABOR OVER TIME**

    1. Union objectives change over time due to shifts in social and economic trends.

        a. Throughout the 1980s, objectives shifted to **JOB SECURITY** and **UNION RECOGNITION.**

        b. The 1990s and early 2000s also focused on job security, but the biggest issue is **GLOBAL COMPETITION.**

PPT 12-16
Collective Bargaining and the
Public Sector

(See complete PowerPoint slide notes on page 12.51.)

PPT 12-17
Forming a Union in the Workplace

(See complete PowerPoint slide notes on page 12.51.)

TEXT FIGURE 12.2
Steps in Union-Organizing and
Decertification Campaigns
(Text page 330)

This text figure describes the steps involved in a union-organizing campaign leading to certification.

**critical thinking
exercise 12-2**
UNION NEGOTIATIONS

This exercise simulates the negotiations that occur between labor and management in reaching a contract agreement. (See complete exercise on page 12.75 of this manual.)

PPT 12-18
Why Join a Union?

(See complete PowerPoint slide notes on page 12.51.)

    c.   The AFL-CIO opposed the North Atlantic Free Trade Association **(NAFTA)** in 1994 and the Central American Free Trade Agreement **(CAFTA)** fearing union workers would lose jobs to nations with **LOWER LABOR COSTS**.

    d.   Organized labor has strongly opposed the increase in offshore outsourcing.

2.   The ***NEGOTIATED LABOR–MANAGEMENT AGREEMENT*** (the ***LABOR CONTRACT***) is the agreement that sets the tone and clarifies the terms under which management and labor agree to function over a period of time.

3.   **COMMON ISSUES IN LABOR–MANAGEMENT AGREEMENTS**

    a.   A ***UNION SECURITY CLAUSE*** is a provision in a negotiated labor–management agreement that stipulates that employees who benefit from a union must either join or pay dues to the union.

    b.   A ***CLOSED SHOP AGREEMENT*** was a clause in a labor–management agreement that specified workers had to be members of a union before being hired (was outlawed by the Taft-Hartley Act in 1947).

    c.   The ***UNION SHOP AGREEMENT*** is a clause in a labor–management agreement that says workers do not have to be members of a union to be hired, but must agree to join the union within a prescribed period.

PPT 12-19
Labor–Management Agreements

(See complete PowerPoint slide notes on page 12.52.)

TEXT FIGURE 12.3
Issues in a Negotiated Labor–
Management Agreement
(Text page 331)

This text figure gives a list of topics commonly negotiated by labor and management during contract talks.

PPT 12-20
Union Security Agreements

(See complete PowerPoint slide notes on page 12.52.)

TEXT FIGURE 12.4
Different Forms of Union
Agreements
(Text page 332)

This text figure explains four common types of union agreements.

      d. The **_AGENCY SHOP AGREEMENT_** is a clause in a labor–management agreement that says employers may hire nonunion workers; employees are not required to join the union but must pay a union fee.

    4. The **TAFT-HARTLEY ACT** gave states the right to pass right-to-work laws.

      a. Twenty-two states have passed **_RIGHT-TO-WORK LAWS_** that give workers the right, under an open shop, to join or not join a union if it is present.

      b. An **_OPEN SHOP AGREEMENT_** is an agreement in right-to-work states that gives workers the option to join or not join a union, if one exists in their workplace.

    5. Future labor negotiations will include issues such as job security, child and elder care, offshore outsourcing, immigration policies, etc.

D. RESOLVING LABOR–MANAGEMENT DISAGREE-MENTS

    1. The negotiated agreement becomes the basis for union–management relations.

    2. Labor and management do not always agree on the interpretation of the labor–management agreement.

    3. If such a disagreement cannot be resolved, a grievance may be filed.

    4. A **_GRIEVANCE_** is a charge by employees that management is not abiding by the terms of the negotiated labor agreement.

PPT 12-21
Right-to-Work Laws

(See complete PowerPoint slide notes on page 12.52.)

<u>bonus case 12-1</u>
DO RIGHT-TO-WORK LAWS HELP STATES?

A major debate has been, Does passage of right-to-work laws make a difference in a state's economy? (See the complete case, discussion questions, and suggested answers beginning on page 12.78 of this manual.)

PPT 12-22
States with Right-to-Work Laws

TEXT FIGURE 12.5
States with Right-to-Work Laws
(Text page 332)

(See complete PowerPoint slide notes on page 12.53.)

PPT 12-23
Resolving Disagreements

(See complete PowerPoint slide notes on page 12.53.)

5. The vast majority of grievances are resolved by shop stewards.

6. **_SHOP STEWARDS_** are union officials who work permanently in an organization and represent employee interests on a daily basis.

E. **MEDIATION AND ARBITRATION**

1. The **_BARGAINING ZONE_** is the range of options between the initial and final offers that each party will consider before negotiations dissolve or reach an impasse.

2. If negotiations don't result in an alternative within this bargaining zone, mediation may be necessary.

3. **_MEDIATION_** is the use of a third party, called a mediator, who encourages both sides to continue negotiating and often makes suggestions for re-solving the dispute.

4. The mediator makes **SUGGESTIONS**, not **DECI-SIONS**, for settling the dispute.

5. The National Mediation Board provides federal mediators when requested by both sides.

6. **_ARBITRATION_** is the agreement to bring in an impartial third party (single arbitrator or a panel) to render a binding decision in a labor dispute.

7. Many negotiated labor–management agreements call for the use of arbitration in disputes.

learning goal 4

Describe the tactics used by labor and management during conflicts, and discuss the role of unions in the future.

PPT 12-24
Using Mediation and Arbitration

(See complete PowerPoint slide notes on page 12.53.)

PPT 12-25
The Grievance Resolution Process

TEXT FIGURE 12.6
The Grievance Resolution Process
(Text page 333)

(See complete PowerPoint slide notes on page 12.54.)

IV. TACTICS USED IN LABOR–MANAGEMENT CONFLICTS

A. Both sides use specific tactics if labor and management reach an impasse in collective bargaining.

B. **UNION TACTICS**

1. The strike has always been the most powerful tactic unions use to achieve their objectives.

   a. A ***STRIKE*** is a union strategy in which workers refuse to go to work; the purpose is to further workers' objectives after an impasse in collective bargaining.

   b. Strikes can slow down or stop operations in a company.

   c. Strikers may also **PICKET**, or walk around outside the firm carrying signs and talking with the public about the issues in the labor dispute.

   d. Strikes have led to resolution of labor disputes, but have also generated violence and **RESIDUAL BITTERNESS**.

   e. The public often realizes how important a worker is when he or she goes on strike.

   f. Many states **PROHIBIT JOB ACTIONS** by state workers even though they can unionize.

   g. Often police, teachers, or others engage in **SICKOUTS** (or the **BLUE FLU**) when union members don't strike but refuse to come to work on the pretext of illness.

2. Under the provisions of the Taft-Hartley Act, the president can request a **COOLING-OFF PERIOD**

PPT 12-26
Tactics Used in Conflicts

(See complete PowerPoint slide notes on page 12.54.)

PPT 12-27
Strike and Boycotts

(See complete PowerPoint slide notes on page 12.54.)

to prevent a strike in a critical industry.

    a. In a ***COOLING-OFF PERIOD***, workers in a critical industry return to their jobs while the union and management continue negotiations.

    b. Cooling-off periods can last up to 80 days.

    c. The 2007–2008 strike by the Screenwriters Guild lasted 100 days and shut down many TV shows.

3. Very **FEW LABOR DISPUTES LEAD TO A STRIKE**, but it still remains a powerful weapon.

4. **PRIMARY AND SECONDARY BOYCOTTS**

    a. A ***PRIMARY BOYCOTT*** is when a union encourages both its membership and the general public not to buy the products of a firm involved in a labor dispute.

    b. A ***SECONDARY BOYCOTT*** is an attempt by labor to convince others to stop doing business with a firm that is the subject of the primary boycott.

    c. Labor unions can legally authorize **PRIMARY** boycotts, but the Taft-Hartley Act prohibits the use of **SECONDARY** boycotts.

C. **MANAGEMENT TACTICS**

1. A ***LOCKOUT*** (rarely used today) is an attempt by management to pressure on unions by temporarily closing the business.

<u>lecture link 12-3</u>
ADDITIONAL LABOR–MANAGEMENT TACTICS

In addition to those discussed in the text, there are other tools that labor and management use in certification campaigns. (See the complete lecture link on page 12.67 in this manual.)

PPT 12-28
Tactics Used in Conflicts

(See complete PowerPoint slide notes on page 12.55.)

PPT 12-29
Lockouts, Injunctions, and Strikebreakers

(See complete PowerPoint slide notes on page 12.55.)

2. An **_INJUNCTION_** is a court order directing some-one to do something or refrain from doing some-thing.

   a. Management can seek injunctions to order striking workers back to work or limit the number of pickets.

   b. To get an injunction, management must show "just cause."

3. The use of **_STRIKEBREAKERS_**, workers hired to do the jobs of striking workers until the labor dis-pute is resolved, has been a source of hostility in labor relations.

D. **THE FUTURE OF UNIONS AND LABOR–MANAGEMENT RELATIONS**

1. Organized labor is at a crossroads—only 7.4% of workers in the private sector are unionized.

2. Many unions have even granted **_GIVEBACKS_**, concessions made by union members to management.

3. The largest labor union in the U.S. is the **SER-VICE EMPLOYEES INTERNATIONAL UNION (SEIU)** with 2.2 million members.

4. To grow, unions will have to **BROADEN THE TYPE OF WORKERS** they represent.

5. Unions have taken on **NEW ROLES** helping man-agement in training workers and redesigning jobs.

MAKING

ethical
decisions
(Text page 336)

PPT 12-30
Walking a Fine
Line

(See complete PowerPoint slide notes on page 12.55.)

lecture link 12-4
RESHAPING THE UNION TO SAVE THE UNION

One union leader, Andy Stern, thinks the old labor union model is broken. His union, the Employees International Union, broke away from the AFL-CIO in 2005 to build a better organization. (See the complete lecture link on page 12.68 of this manual.)

PPT 12-31
Challenges Facing Labor Unions

(See complete PowerPoint slide notes on page 12.56.)

PPT 12-32
Labor Unions in the Future

(See complete PowerPoint slide notes on page 12.56.)

lecture link 12-5
UNIONS TURN TO THE SERVICE INDUSTRY FOR GROWTH

This reading focuses on how labor unions can reverse their membership slide—organize service workers. (See complete lecture link on page 12.69 of this manual.)

PPT 12-33
Union Membership by State

TEXT FIGURE 12.7
Union Membership by State
(Text page 337)

(See complete PowerPoint slide notes on page 12.56.)

progress assessment
(Text page 337)

PPT 12-34
Progress Assessment

(See complete PowerPoint slide notes on page 12.57.)

lecture outline

Assess some of today's controversial employee–management issues, such as executive compensation, pay equity, child care and elder care, drug testing, and violence in the workplace.

V. CONTROVERSIAL EMPLOYEE–MANAGEMENT ISSUES

A. EXECUTIVE COMPENSATION

1. The U.S. free-market system was built using incentives such as large salaries for performance.

2. However, today's government, boards of directors, stockholders, unions, and employees have argued that executive compensation is **GETTING OUT OF LINE.**

   a. The average total compensation for a CEO is $9.2 million.

   b. Even after adjustments for inflation, this is an enormous increase over time.

3. In the past, an executive's compensation and bonuses were determined by the **FIRM'S PROFITABILITY** or **INCREASE IN STOCK PRICE.**

   a. The assumption is that the CEO will improve the performance of the company and raise the price of the firm's stock.

   b. Today, many executives receive **STOCK OPTIONS** (the ability to buy the company stock at a set price at a later date) or **RESTRICTED STOCK** (issued directly to the CEO).

      i. Stock options account for 50% of CEO compensation.

      ii. Restricted stock adds 25%.

PPT 12-35
Compensating Executives

(See complete PowerPoint slide notes on page 12.58.)

legal briefcase
(Text page 339)

PPT 12-36
Executive Pay Remains on the Rise

(See complete PowerPoint slide notes on page 12.58.)

PPT 12-37
Play Ball!

(See complete PowerPoint slide notes on page 12.59.)

bonus case 12-2
PENSION PLANS UNDER ATTACK

Faced with losses in the billions of dollars, a few U.S. airlines have declared bankruptcy. Some, such as United, have walked away from pension obligations in an attempt to regain profitability. (See the complete case, discussion questions, and suggested answers beginning on page 12.80 of this manual.)

      iii. The financial crisis allowed executives to obtain stock options at very low prices. As the market recovered, the options became very lucrative.

    c. The problems arise when executives are handsomely compensated, even when the company doesn't do well.

    d. Poor executives can often leave the company yet still receive huge monetary benefits. *Mark Hurd of HP walked away with $40 million after resigning because of a sexual harassment violation.)*

4. The late management consultant Peter Drucker suggested that CEOs should not earn much more than **20 TIMES** as much as the company's lowest-paid employee.

    a. Not many companies followed his advice.

    b. Today, the average chief executive of a major corporation makes **400 TIMES THE PAY OF AN AVERAGE HOURLY WORKER**.

5. Global comparisons:

    a. European CEOs typically earn 50% less than U.S. executives.

    b. In Europe, workers are entitled to seats on the board of directors according to a process called **CO-DETERMINATION.**

    c. The U.S. public is now pressing for full disclosure concerning executive compensation.

critical thinking
exercise 12-3
EXECUTIVE PAY WATCH

This exercise further explores the issue of executive compensation by having students visit the AFL-CIO site and gather current pay data. (See complete exercise on page 12.77 of this manual.)

lecture link 12-6
REVAMPING EXECUTIVE PAY

Throughout this recent recession, few things have stirred as much emotion as disproportionate bonuses given to executives. (See the complete lecture link on page 12.69 of this manual.)

PPT 12-38
Compensating Executives in the Future

(See complete PowerPoint slide notes on page 12.59.)

6. The recent financial crisis increased pressure on boards of directors to rein in executive compensation.

7. However, most U.S. executives are responsible for multibillion-dollar corporations and work 70+ hours a week.

    a. Many executives guide their companies to prosperity.

    b. Good CEOs are a scarce commodity.

B. **PAY EQUITY**

1. The **EQUAL PAY ACT OF 1963** requires companies to pay equal pay to women and men who do the same job.

2. **PAY EQUITY** is the concept that people in jobs that require similar levels of education, training, or skills should receive equal pay.

    a. This goes beyond equal pay for equal work.

    b. The issue of pay equity centers on comparing the **VALUE OF JOBS**, which shows that "women's" jobs tend to pay less.

3. A 1980s concept called **COMPARABLE WORTH** has recently been reintroduced.

    a. **COMPARABLE WORTH** required that people in jobs that require similar levels of education, training, or skills should receive equal pay.

    b. It is difficult to determine whether comparable worth creates greater equality or simply chaos.

<u>lecture link 12-7</u>

THE MALE EMPLOYMENT DROUGHT

Though women seem to still be earning less than their male counterparts, not all is rosy in the world of male employment. (See the complete lecture link on page 12.70 in this manual.)

PPT 12-39
The Question of Pay Equity

(See complete PowerPoint slide notes on page 12.59.)

PPT 12-40
Equal Pay for Equal Work

(See complete PowerPoint slide notes on page 12.60.)

PPT 12-41
The Salary Gender Gap

(See complete PowerPoint slide notes on page 12.60.)

4. Women earn approximately **81%** of what men earn.

    a. Once this difference could be explained because women only worked 50 to 60% of their available years.

    b. Today, such extended leaves by women are rarer.

    c. One reason for the disparity is that many women devote more time to their families and accept lower paying jobs with flexible hours.

5. There is evidence that **EDUCATION** and knowledge-based skills are reducing women's inequality.

    a. In many fields women now earn as much as men.

    b. Young women in urban areas earn **8% more** than male counterparts due to high college graduation rates.

    c. Today women earn almost **60% of all bachelors and masters awarded**.

    d. However, inequities still exist for women with children.

C. **SEXUAL HARASSMENT**

1. ***SEXUAL HARASSMENT*** refers to unwelcome sexual advances, requests for sexual favors, and other conduct of a sexual nature (verbal or physical) that create a hostile work environment.

2. **SEXUAL HARASSMENT** becomes **ILLEGAL** when:

    a. An employee's submission to such conduct is made either explicitly or implicitly a term or

PPT 12-42
What's Sexual Harassment?

(See complete PowerPoint slide notes on page 12.60.)

PPT 12-43
Kinds of Sexual Harassment

(See complete PowerPoint slide notes on page 12.61.)

CONDITION OF EMPLOYMENT or an employee's submission to or rejection of such conduct is used as the basis for employment decisions affecting the worker's status.

b. The conduct unreasonably interferes with a worker's job performance or creates an **INTIMIDATING, HOSTILE, OR OFFENSIVE WORKING ENVIRONMENT.**

3. Both men and women are covered under the **CIVIL RIGHTS ACT** of 1991 that governs sexual harassment.

   a. In 1997 the Supreme Court ruled that **SAME-SEX HARASSMENT** should be treated the same.

   b. The number of complaints filed with the EEOC has fallen off.

4. In 1996, the U.S. Supreme Court broadened the scope of what can be considered a hostile work environment.

5. Recent cases have introduced the concept of a **HOSTILE WORKPLACE**, which is any workplace where a particular behavior that is unwelcome, or that would offend a reasonable person, occurs.

6. Managers and workers are now much more sensitive to comments and behavior of a sexual nature.

   a. One of the major problems is that workers and managers often know a policy concerning sexual harassment exists, but they **HAVE NO IDEA WHAT IT SAYS.**

PPT 12-44

You Make the Call . . .

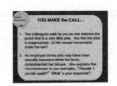

(See complete PowerPoint slide notes on page 12.61.)

b. One expert suggests that companies **REQUIRE SEXUAL HARASSMENT WORK-SHOPS** for all employees.

c. Foreign companies doing business in the U.S. are not immune from sexual harassment charges.

d. Many companies have set up rapid effective grievance procedures and promptly react to an employee's allegations of harassment.

D. **CHILD CARE**

1. Child care is an increasingly important workplace issue.

2. The percentage of women in the workforce with children under 18 has reached 75%. There are now more women than men in the workforce.

3. These trends cause concerns:

   a. Absences related to child care already cost businesses billions of dollars annually.

   b. There is also the question of who will pay for these services.

4. Federal child care assistance has not risen significantly since the passage of the **WELFARE REFORM ACT OF 1996.**

5. Many companies are now **PROVIDING CHILD CARE** for their employees.

6. **COMPANIES ARE OFTEN PROVIDING:**

   a. Discount arrangements with national child care chains

   b. Vouchers for payments of child care expenses

PPT 12-45
Facing Child Care Issues

(See complete PowerPoint slide notes on page 12.62.)

PPT 12-46
Businesses' Response to Child Care

(See complete PowerPoint slide notes on page 12.62.)

      c.   Referral services

      d.   On-site child care centers

      e.   Sick-child centers

E. **ELDER CARE**

   1. Currently there are about **40 million Americans over 65**.

      a.   Over the next 20 years, it's expected that number will grow to **70 million**.

      b.   These workers will not be concerned with child care.

      c.   Instead, they face the responsibility of caring for older parents and other relatives.

   2. About 65 million U.S. workers provide care for an older family member.

   3. Employees with elder care responsibilities need medical, legal, and insurance information, as well as the full support of their companies.

      a.   Some firms offer elder care programs *(examples: DuPont and JPMorgan Chase)*.

      b.   Unfortunately, few U.S. companies now provide any elder care benefits.

   4. **ELDER CARE PROVIDERS** are generally older and more experienced employees who are often more critical to the company than the younger workers effected by childcare problems.

   5. With an aging workforce, this issue will continue to be important.

F. **DRUG TESTING**

   1. Fortunately, the spread of AIDS has declined in the U.S., although it remains a challenge.

PPT 12-47

Increasing Elder Care Challenges

(See complete PowerPoint slide notes on page 12.62.)

PPT 12-48

Elder Care in the Modern Household

(See complete PowerPoint slide notes on page 12.63.)

2. Some companies feel that alcohol and drug abuse are even more serious workplace issues because **SUBSTANCE ABUSE** involves more workers.

   a. Alcohol is the most widely used drug in the workplace, with 6.5% of full-time employees believed to be heavy drinkers.

   b. Approximately 40% of industrial injuries and fatalities can be linked to use of alcohol.

   c. About 8% of employed adults use illicit drugs.

3. Individuals who use drugs are **THREE AND A HALF TIMES** more likely to be involved in **WORKPLACE ACCIDENTS.**

4. The National Institute of Health estimates that each drug abuser can cost an employer $10,000 annually.

5. Over 80% of major companies now test workers and job applicants for substance abuse.

G. **VIOLENCE IN THE WORKPLACE**

   1. Employers are also struggling with a growing trend of violence in the workplace.

   2. Homicides account for 16% of all workplace deaths.

   3. Although some believe the problem is overblown by the media, workplace violence is all too real.

   4. Other organizations recognize the threat and hire managers with **STRONG INTERPERSONAL SKILLS** to deal with growing employee violence.

PPT 12-49
Drug Use in the Workplace

(See complete PowerPoint slide notes on page 12.63.)

lecture link 12-8
**RECESSION INCREASES
WORKPLACE SUICIDES**

An employee stock ownership plan turns workers into owners. When the plan works, the employee/owners benefit. But there are many potential problems. (See the complete lecture link on page 12.71 in this manual.)

PPT 12-50
Violence in the Workplace

(See complete PowerPoint slide notes on page 12.63.)

PPT 12-51
Warning Signs of Possible Workplace Violence

(See complete PowerPoint slide notes on page 12.64.)

lecture link 12-9
**EMPLOYEE STOCK OWNERSHIP
PLANS**

An employee stock ownership plan turns workers into owners. When the plan works, the employee/owners benefit. But there are many potential problems. (See the complete lecture link on page 12.71 in this manual.)

**progress
assessment**
(Text page 345)

PPT 12-52
Progress Assessment

(See complete PowerPoint slide notes on page 12.64.)

PowerPoint slide notes

PPT 12-1
Chapter Title

PPT 12-2
Learning Goals

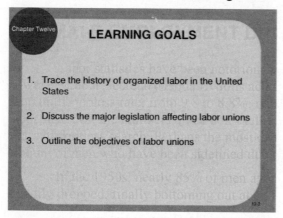

PPT 12-3
Learning Goals

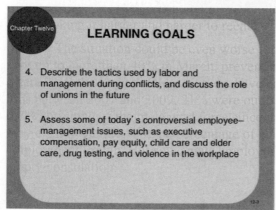

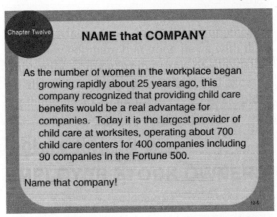

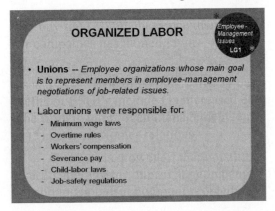

Many of the benefits that workers enjoy today are due to the battles unions have fought over the past 100 years. Students are often surprised that a little over 100 years ago the average workweek was between 60 to 80 hours. The 40 hour workweek is a direct result of unions.

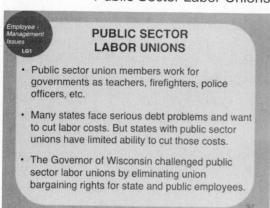

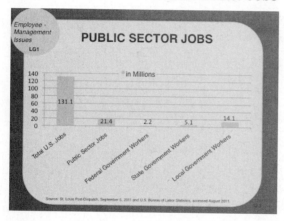

1. This slide shows the amount of public sector jobs in today's U.S. workforce.

2. Of the 131.1 million total U.S. jobs (nonfarm), the public sector holds 21.4 million jobs.

3. Federal government workers statistic excludes postal workers.

4. Local government workers statistic excludes teachers.

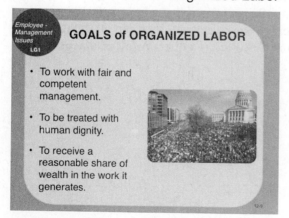

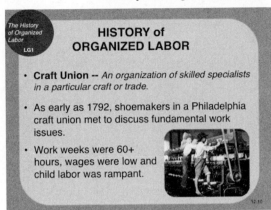

HISTORY of ORGANIZED LABOR

- **Craft Union** -- *An organization of skilled specialists in a particular craft or trade.*

- As early as 1792, shoemakers in a Philadelphia craft union met to discuss fundamental work issues.

- Work weeks were 60+ hours, wages were low and child labor was rampant.

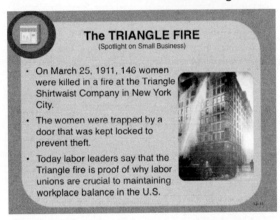

The TRIANGLE FIRE
(Spotlight on Small Business)

- On March 25, 1911, 146 women were killed in a fire at the Triangle Shirtwaist Company in New York City.

- The women were trapped by a door that was kept locked to prevent theft.

- Today labor leaders say that the Triangle fire is proof of why labor unions are crucial to maintaining workplace balance in the U.S.

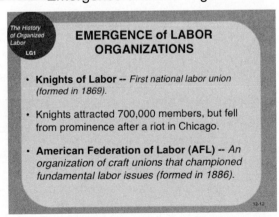

EMERGENCE of LABOR ORGANIZATIONS

- **Knights of Labor** -- *First national labor union (formed in 1869).*

- Knights attracted 700,000 members, but fell from prominence after a riot in Chicago.

- **American Federation of Labor (AFL)** -- *An organization of craft unions that championed fundamental labor issues (formed in 1886).*

INDUSTRIAL UNIONS

The History of Organized Labor
LG1

- **Industrial Unions --** *Labor unions of unskilled or semiskilled workers in mass production industries.*

- **Congress of Industrial Organizations (CIO) --** *Union organization of unskilled workers; broke away from the AFL in 1935 and rejoined in 1955.*

- The <u>AFL-CIO</u> today has affiliations with 56 unions and has about 12.2 million members.

12-13

PUBLIC UNIONS

Public Sector Union Membership
LG1

- For the first time in U.S. history, 7.6 million of the 14.7 union members work in government.

- Taxpayers, not stockholders, are paying the cost of union workers wages and benefits.

- The huge state and local government revenue losses caused by the economic crisis put pressure to reduce wage and benefit costs.

12-14

EFFECTS of LAWS on LABOR UNIONS

Labor Legislation and Collective Bargaining
LG2

- Labor unions' growth and influence has been very dependent on public opinion and law.

- The Norris-LaGuardia Act helped unions by prohibiting the use of **Yellow-Dog Contracts --** *A type of contract that required employees to agree to NOT join a union.*

- **Collective Bargaining --** *The process whereby union and management representatives form an agreement, or contract, for employees.*

12-15

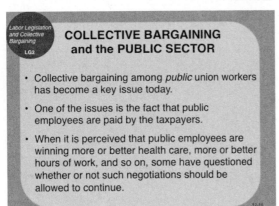

The National Labor Relations Act (often referred to as the Wagner Act) created the NLRB.

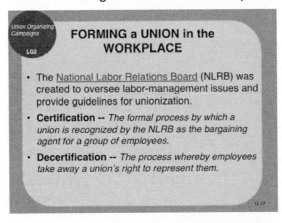

1. This slide lists some of the key reasons why a person might consider joining a union.

2. The power of unions has waned as the economy has shifted from an industrial economy into a service-based economy.

3. Ask the students, Are unions necessary in today's modern working environment?

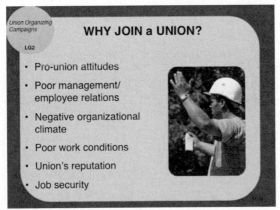

LABOR/MANAGEMENT AGREEMENTS

Objectives of Organized Labor Over Time
LG3

- **Negotiated Labor-Management Agreement (Labor Contract)** -- *Sets the terms under which labor and management will function over a period of time.*

- **Union Security Clause** -- *Stipulates workers who reap union benefits must either join the union or pay dues to the union.*

UNION SECURITY AGREEMENTS

Objectives of Organized Labor Over Time
LG3

- **Closed Shop Agreement** -- *Specified workers had to be members of a union before being hired for a job.*

- **Union Shop Agreement** -- *Declares workers don't have to be members of a union to be hired, but must agree to join the union within a specific time period.*

- **Agency Shop Agreement** -- *Allows employers to hire nonunion workers who don't have to join the union, but must pay fees.*

RIGHT-to-WORK LAWS

Objectives of Organized Labor Over Time
LG3

- **Right-to-Work Laws** -- *Legislation that gives workers the right, under an open shop, to join or not to join a union.*

- The Taft-Hartley Act of 1947 granted states the power to outlaw union shop agreements.

- **Open Shop Agreement** -- *Agreement in right-to-work states that gives workers the right to join or not join a union, if one exists in their workplace.*

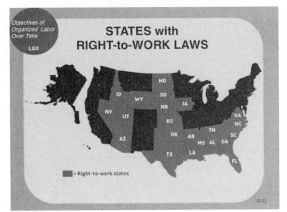

This map can be used as the basis for an interesting classroom exercise. The United States' auto industry has been in the news with the financial difficulties of General Motors and Chrysler well chronicled. Have students use the Internet to research the location of any new auto plants in the United States. Research will uncover that many new auto-related jobs are in right-to-work states. For example, a recent article in the Boston Globe profiled Alabama's auto-related job growth. In 2001, Alabama had 21,000 auto-related jobs; that number now stands at over 48,000. Many would argue that this trend of relocating in the southeast is due to the states' right-to-work laws.

PPT 12-23
Resolving Disagreements

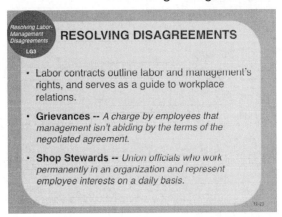

PPT 12-24
Using Mediation and Arbitration

In 2011, the National Football League and National Football League Players Association asked for the assistance of a federal mediator in their attempt to forge a new contract between the players and the league.

PPT 12-25

The Grievance Resolution Process

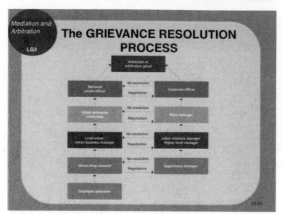

PPT 12-26

Tactics Used in Conflicts

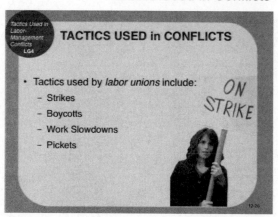

PPT 12-27

Strikes and Boycotts

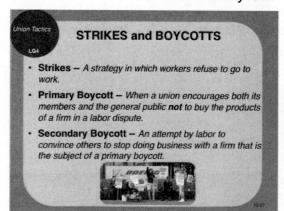

PPT 12-28
Tactics Used in Conflicts

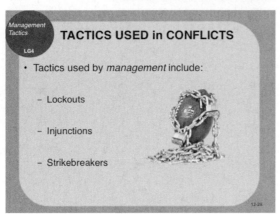

PPT 12-29
Lockouts, Injunctions, and Strikebreakers

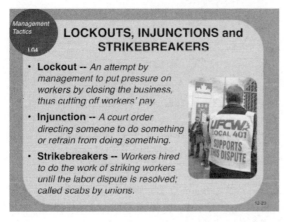

Employers have had the right to replace striking workers since a 1938 Supreme Court ruling, but this tactic was used infrequently until the 1980s.

PPT 12-30
Walking a Fine Line

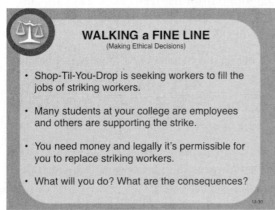

Challenges Facing Labor Unions

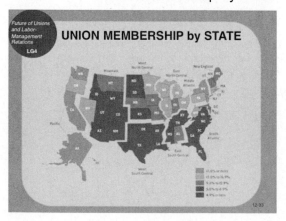

The percentage of union membership has fallen over the past 50 years. In 1945, 35.5% of all workers were unionized; today that number stands at only 12.4%.

Labor Unions in the Future

Both public and private sector union members now face challenges as they try to maintain any remaining wage and fringe benefit gains achieved in past negotiations.

Union Membership by State

1. The slide presents union membership by state in the United States.

2. Washington, California, New York, Hawaii, and Alaska lead the states, with unionization rates greater than 17%.

3. Most of the southern states (Arkansas, Louisiana, Tennessee, Mississippi, North Carolina, South Carolina, Virginia, and Georgia) have the lowest percentage of union workers, with unionization rates less than 4.9%.

4. Today the largest union in the United States is the Service Employees International Union (SEIU), with 2.2 million members.

PPT 12-34
Progress Assessment

PROGRESS ASSESSMENT

Progress Assessment

- What are the major laws that affected union growth, and what does each one cover?
- How do changes in the economy affect the objectives of unions?
- What are the major tactics used by unions and by management to assert their power in contract negotiations?
- What types of workers do unions need to organize in the future?

12-34

1. The major laws that affected union growth are as follows:

- The Norris-LaGuardia Act prohibited employers from using contracts that forbid union activities and paved the way for union growth in the United States.

- The National Labor Relations Act or Wagner Act allowed collective bargaining and created the National Labor Relations Board.

- The Fair Labor Standards Act set a minimum wage and maximum basic hours for work.

- The Labor–Management Relations Act or Taft-Hartley Act amended the Wagner Act and permitted states to pass laws prohibiting compulsory union membership, set up methods to deal with strikes that impact national health and safety, and prohibited closed shop agreements and wage payments for work not performed (featherbedding). This law weakened union power in the United States.

- The Labor–Management Report and Disclosure Act or Landrum-Griffin Act amended the Taft-Hartley Act and Wagner Act, guaranteed individual rights of union members in dealing with their union such as the right to nominate candidates for union office, vote in union elections, attend and participate in union meetings, vote on union business, and examine union records and accounts. The goal of this legislation was to eliminate union corruption.

2. Unions and their objectives have frequently shifted with social and economic trends. In the 1970s the primary objective was additional pay and benefits, while in the 1980s unions focused on job security. During the 1990s and 2000s job security remained a key issue as unions tried to cope with global competition and outsourcing.

3. The major tactics used by unions include strikes, boycotts, work slowdowns, and pickets. Management tactics include lockouts, injunctions, and the bringing in of strikebreakers.

(continued)

PPT 12-34
Progress Assessment
(continued)

What types of workers do unions hope to organize in the future? To remain relevant, unions must attract new members. This includes more professional, female, and foreign-born workers. Both the Teamsters Union and Service Employees International Union have started to target workers in health care, technology, and finance.

PPT 12-35
Compensating Executives

Peter Drucker suggested CEO pay should be no more than 20 times the lowest-paid employee. The average is now 400 times.

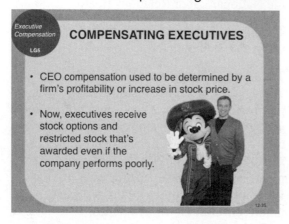

PPT 12-36
Executive Pay Remains on the Rise

With unemployment still high, would companies be better off hiring new workers instead of using their newly found profits for executive pay?

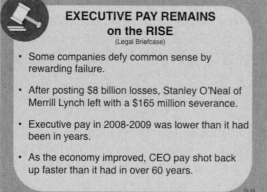

PPT 12-37
Play Ball!

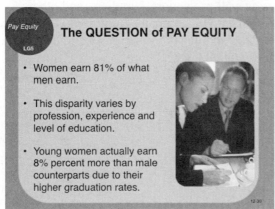

1. Ask the students, What do you expect to make when you graduate? What do these minimum salaries say about what society values? *(Student answers will vary.)*

2. Ask the students, Why are the minimum and highest salaries paid to female basketball players so much lower than the male players?

PPT 12-38
Compensating Executives in the Future

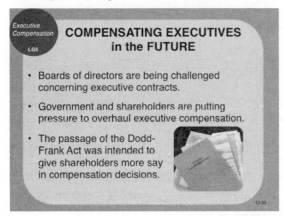

PPT 12-39
The Question of Pay Equity

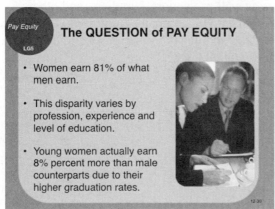

PPT 12-40
Equal Pay for Equal Work

1. This slide presents the Equal Pay Act factors that justify pay differences: skill, effort, responsibility, and working conditions. The Equal Pay Act prohibits unequal pay to men and women who perform jobs that require substantially the same skills, efforts, responsibilities, and so on.

2. Ask the students, Is it fair that different genders receive different pay? *(Most students will say "NO.")*

3. Yet, in the United States women earn only about 80% of what men earn. There are, however, significant disparities by profession, education level, and other factors.

PPT 12-41
The Salary Gender Gap

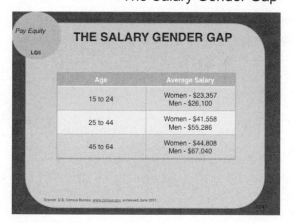

1. This slide presents the inequity in earnings: what women of certain ages earn compared with the average salary earned by a male in the same age range.

2. Ask the students, What are some of the reasons behind this salary gender gap? *(Student answers will vary, but could include issues like women working part time to raise children or women leaving the workforce due to family issues.)*

3. If time permits, have students read Chapter 3 of Thomas Sowell's awarding-winning book *Economic Facts and Fallacies*, which explores this issue in depth and will provide for a rich classroom discussion.

PPT 12-42
What's Sexual Harassment?

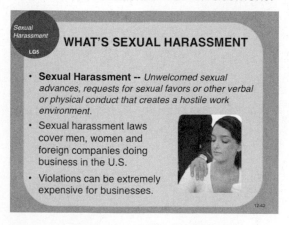

Students should realize that sexual harassment covers all employees as well as vendors, suppliers, and others who come in contact with company employees. Businesses need to take all allegations seriously and develop a protocol for investigating each claim.

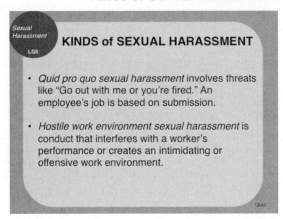

PPT 12-44
You Make the Call . . .

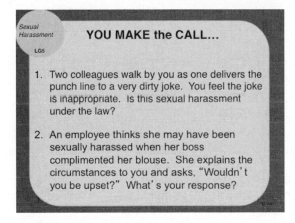

1. Ask the students, Have you felt uncomfortable in situations that can be described as sexual harassment? How about the male students in class?

2. Discuss the situations on the slide with students and then specifically discuss what constitutes sexual harassment.

3. For the conduct to be considered illegal under specific conditions:

   - The employee's submission to such conduct must be explicitly or implicitly made a term or condition of employment, or an employee's submission to or rejection of such conduct must be used as the basis for employment decisions affecting the worker's status.

   - The conduct must unreasonably interfere with a worker's job performance or create an intimidating, hostile, or offensive work environment.

PPT 12-45
Facing Childcare Issues

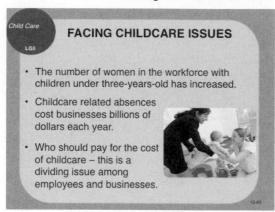

FACING CHILDCARE ISSUES

Child Care
LG5

- The number of women in the workforce with children under three-years-old has increased.
- Childcare related absences cost businesses billions of dollars each year.
- Who should pay for the cost of childcare – this is a dividing issue among employees and businesses.

PPT 12-46
Businesses Response to Child Care

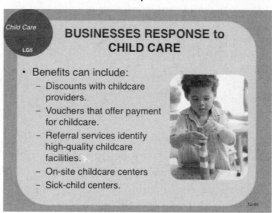

BUSINESSES RESPONSE to CHILD CARE

Child Care
LG5

- Benefits can include:
  - Discounts with childcare providers.
  - Vouchers that offer payment for childcare.
  - Referral services identify high-quality childcare facilities.
  - On-site childcare centers
  - Sick-child centers.

PPT 12-47
Increasing Elder Care Challenges

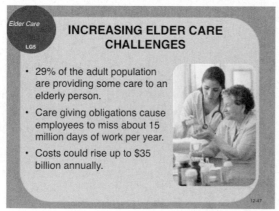

INCREASING ELDER CARE CHALLENGES

Elder Care
LG5

- 29% of the adult population are providing some care to an elderly person.
- Care giving obligations cause employees to miss about 15 million days of work per year.
- Costs could rise up to $35 billion annually.

As the population ages, caring for one's parents and other relatives will be a bigger employment-related issue. Proactive companies will develop benefits to meet this challenge.

PPT 12-48

Elder Care in the Modern Household

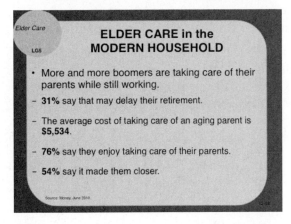

1. As boomers' parents age, more and more have started bringing them into their homes.

2. 25% of boomers expect to live with their parents again.

3. Ask the students, Do you think this will delay more retirements? What does this mean for the young workforce?

PPT 12-49

Drug Use in the Workplace

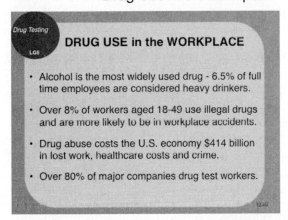

PPT 12-50

Violence in the Workplace

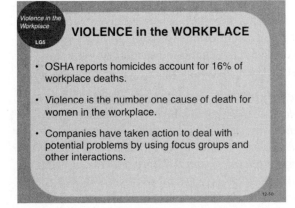

Warning Signs of Possible Workplace
Violence

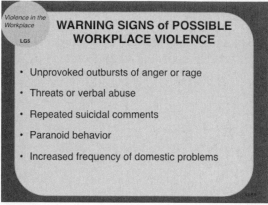

1. Managers and workers must be on the lookout for possible signs of workplace violence.

2. Most companies do not have formal training or a formal policy to deal with workplace violence.

3. Ask the students to discuss the following question: What actions can management take to prevent workplace violence? *(Firms that maintain positive employee relations tend to experience fewer problems. The key to prevention of workplace violence is being proactive.)*

Progress Assessment

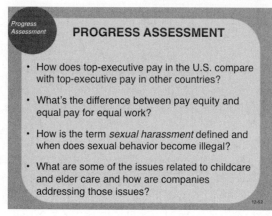

1. Executive pay in the United States is significantly higher than in other countries. For example, the typical European CEOs earn only about 40% of what their U.S. counterparts make.

2. Equal pay for equal work refers to giving equal pay to men and women who do the same job. This concept was codified in the 1963 Equal Pay Act. Pay equity goes beyond this concept and says people in jobs that require similar levels of education, training, or skills should receive equal pay. For example, the pay of an occupation traditionally considered a women's job, such as a bank teller, should pay the same as a truck driver typically considered a man's job.

3. *Sexual harassment* refers to any unwelcome sexual advance, requests for sexual favors, and other verbal or physical conduct of a sexual nature that creates a hostile work environment. This behavior is considered illegal if the conduct unreasonably interferes with a worker's job performance or creates an intimidating, hostile, or offensive work environment. It is also considered illegal if the sexual harassment constitutes a quid pro quo.

4. *Issues of child care or elder care are of concern to employers, since these issues account for reduced productivity, absenteeism, and high turnover. Another issue to consider is who pays for the care of a child or an aging parent. Companies are addressing these issues by arranging discounts at national child care chains, subsidizing payment for child care, developing referral services to identify high-quality providers of care, creating on-site child care centers or sick child centers, offering health-spending accounts that allow workers to set aside pretax dollars for elder care expenses, and offering flexible work schedules.*

lecture
links

lecture link 12-1

THE COMPLICATED LEGACY OF HENRY FORD

Henry Ford founded the Ford Motor Company in 1903, producing an inexpensive, all-purpose car, the Model T. His company grew rapidly after the Model T became an instant success. The close relationship he enjoyed with his skilled workers deteriorated as he installed the assembly line and hired unskilled workers. In 1913, dissatisfaction among workers resulted in labor turnover of over 380% in one year alone. A small number of workers joined the International Workers of the World, which served as an outlet for the workers' hostility.

On January 14, 1914, Henry Ford shocked the industry by raising the average wage for his workers from $2.34 to $5.00 per day. Although this, overnight, made Ford known as the defender of the worker, Ford's motives were more complex. He believed that the more money he paid to workers, the more of his cars would be bought. Although he paid his workers attractive salaries when they worked, he felt little responsibility for their continued employment and laid them off when necessary.

During this early period, Ford instituted other worker benefits that were revolutionary. He created a Safety and Health Department in 1914 and opened the Henry Ford Trade School in 1916 so that boys could learn a trade while attending school. Another farsighted policy was the hiring workers with partial disabilities, ex-criminals, people who were epileptic, and individuals who were former mental patients. In 1934, approximately 34% of Ford workers were physically disabled.

Also instituted was the Ford Sociology Department that counseled workers and management alike. It gave workers advice on how to budget money and served as a protection for them when unscrupulous salesmen descended on them after they had received their paychecks. The Sociology Department also conducted a Language School to teach foreign-born workers the English language. Labor appreciated his reforms, and supported Ford in his unsuccessful campaign for the U.S. Senate in 1918. Many experts feel that Ford's reforms were the only labor reforms in the early part of the century.

But Ford was inconsistent in his dealings with his workers. During the 1920s, Ford instituted a cost-saving campaign. The assembly line was increased in speed so that workers performed their jobs in less time. Discipline was strict, and workers were driven to work as hard as possible. Even the Sociology Department was disbanded. The Ford Service Police, a 3,000-person group, was created to enforce the speed-up and other discipline measures. Workers who were involved in union activities were often physically assaulted.

Ford, who was once hailed as the workers' hero, was now viewed as a reactionary. During the Great Depression, layoffs in all industries resulted in massive unemployment. In March 1932, the Ford Hunger March took place. Several hundred workers marched on Ford, demanding a six-hour workday, two daily rest periods, and an unemployment bonus of $50 per worker. The marchers were greeted by gunfire that resulted in four deaths. Henry Ford steadfastly maintained a hostile attitude toward any union activities.

The Wagner Act was passed in 1935, establishing a national policy of protecting the rights of workers to organize and collectively bargain. Under the protection of the Wagner Act, the United Automobile Workers began a systematic campaign to organize the automobile industry. By 1937, they had succeeded, except for Ford.

In May 1937, the UAW began its campaign to unionize Ford. Walter Reuther headed the campaign and planned to distribute circulars to Ford workers on their way home. The union members stationed themselves on a bridge over a road leading to the Ford Rouge River plant. Ford Service Police ordered them to leave, and when the union supporters started to comply, the police attacked them. The Battle of the Bridge ended with Reuther and several others, including women, requiring hospitalization.

Even though Ford prevented unionization one more time, time was running out. When the UAW began another organizing effort in 1941, it succeeded. After the head of the Ford Service Police fired eight Rouge River workers for union activities, the workers spontaneously walked off their jobs. They surrounded the plant and refused to let food and water be sent in to the Ford Service Police in the plant. On April 11, 1941, Henry Ford agreed to recognize the union.

lecture link 12-2

UNION UPROAR IN WISCONSIN

As America's manufacturing might has waned, so too has the power of its unions. But you couldn't tell that from looking at the Wisconsin capital building in Madison lately. In early 2011, Governor Scott Walker was embroiled in a battle with the state's public workers over new legislation that would significantly reduce take-home pay and collective bargaining rights.

The governor claimed that a $137 million deficit and potential $3.6 billion hole in the next two-year budget has given him little choice but to make drastic cuts. While public workers and the state's unions agreed that some of the financial cuts must be made, they fiercely fought to retain their collective bargaining rights. After enduring months of budget trims and layoffs, Governor Walker's mid-February proposal proved to be the last straw. Democratic representatives of the state senate walked out on the session debating the bill. Soon protestors filled the capital as teachers, civil servants, and union allies railed against the bill that would raise the amount workers pay for health insurance and rob them of their voice in future labor debates.

In fact, many see the events]in Madison as a portent for things to come in other cash-strapped states. With a new crop of Republican governors in office, union boosters fear this latest assault on workers' rights could spread across the nation and cripple unions irrevocably. As a result, leaders of the nation's biggest unions have set aside their differences and effectively unionized together to fund the protest in Wisconsin as well as any other that may pop up in the future. The aim of the campaign is to raise $30 million for paid media and lobbying against the efforts of lawmakers who try to eliminate public employees' collective bargaining rights.[i]

lecture link 12-3

ADDITIONAL LABOR–MANAGEMENT TACTICS

ADDITIONAL TOOLS USED BY LABOR TO FIGHT MANAGEMENT

In addition to those discussed in the text, other tools that labor uses in its efforts to achieve concessions and "fair treatment" from management include:

1. **Slowdowns.** Slowdowns occur when workers decrease their work output voluntarily to let management know of their dissatisfaction.

2. **Blue flu.** A form of slowdown occurs when a large number of workers suddenly "become ill" and call in sick. The end result is a slowdown in productivity—at least, until the workers are back on their jobs. Public sector employees often use the blue flu as a tool against management.

3. **Sabotage.** Putting glass soda bottles inside car doors, slipping faulty bearings into machines, slashing tires, and even planting live grenades under the beds of managers—as has been done in past wars—are ways of showing workers' dissatisfaction with a company and causing it to lose money, as well as public support and confidence in its products.

4. **Political power.** Endorsements from labor unions are often very important to elected officials. The threat of withholding support or promise of actively providing advocacy can be an effective weapon, especially in the areas where elected officials have large union constituencies or sympathizers to the union movement.

5. **Financial influence.** Unions can contribute funds to the campaigns of elected officials that support labor issues and withhold support from those who are known for their anti-union voting patterns. Unions also have large pension funds and operating accounts that they can deposit in supportive financial institutions and invest in organizations that treat their workers and unions fairly. Unions can also withdraw their pension funds and operating accounts from institutions that show an anti-union bias.

6. **Publicity battles.** With growing media attention to business events, union leaders have become adept in presenting their causes to the public, seeking sympathy, understanding, and support. A classic case where a union used publicity to try to persuade the public to go against a company was the Amalgamated Clothing and Textile Workers Union going against J.P. Stevens, the huge textile firm. The Steelworkers Union tried to wage a publicity campaign against U.S. Steel (now USX). PATCO sought public support in the air controllers strike but did not get much of it.

ADDITIONAL TOOLS USED BY MANAGEMENT TO FIGHT LABOR

In addition to those discussed in the text, management has the following tools to combat labor:

1. **Harassment of union members and their families.** The goal is to get the members to drop out of the unions or become less active in supporting union causes. Harassment may be direct or subtle, using many subliminal techniques.

2. **Modern "yellow dogs."** Companies can often gauge the feelings of employees regarding unions and try to discourage them from joining as a condition of employment. While this practice is illegal, it still exists.

3. **Political power.** Companies, like unions, have vast resources that can be used to contribute workers and money to elected officials who advocate their causes or to try to defeat pro-union officials.

4. **Financial power.** Companies can direct their financial resources to institutions that are pro-business and withhold investments from organizations that have a pro-union bias.

5. **Pacts and mutual support organizations**. Sometimes firms within a given industry share information about union strategies before collective bargaining begins. They decide to unite to hold down wage-cost increases and thwart union demands. They often agree to help each other financially in case one of them is confronted with a strike; because increases in wages at one firm can spread to another.

6. **Publicity.** Large firms have established public relations departments and teams that can procure favorable news stories at no cost. Management can use publicity and promotion adeptly to persuade the public that its cause is the correct one in disputes with labor.

7. **Two-tier wage systems.** Two-tier wage systems maintain present workers at existing pay levels and even give them a raise, while new workers are brought in at substantially lower wages. Unions in the aerospace industry are beginning to rebel against two-tier systems at Boeing, Lockheed, and other companies.

8. **Plant closings.** The ultimate weapon an employer has is to close the business if workers do not accept the terms offered. Employers may then move to other locations—simply cease operations entirely—or sell to new owners who demand wage cuts that the workers, who have suffered economic losses from the strike, accept in order to get back to work.

lecture link 12-4

RESHAPING THE UNION TO SAVE THE UNION

Andrew Stern, president of the powerful Service Employees International Union (SEIU), has been a labor activist and innovator for more than 30 years. His commitment to the labor cause underwent a renewal after the unexpected death of his 13-year-old daughter Cassie in 2002. After Cassie passed away of complications from spinal surgery, Stern realized that something in him had awakened.

"Cassie gave me the courage to have the voice," he explains. He started speaking more forcefully, and openly. "I lost a lot of my concern about what people thought of me," he says.

"My greatest fear," Stern says, "is not having the courage to take on a fight, whether it's the labor movement, the Democratic Party, or anybody else who stands in the way of workers doing well." After Cassie's death, the question taunted him: "What am I so scared about?"

Stern took his revolution into the leadership of the giant AFL-CIO. He wanted the federation to merge some of its small unions with larger ones. Stern also wanted to recruit more aggressively and across entire sectors, not just at individual workplaces. His wanted to work with businesses in labor negotiations by reducing their fears of being undercut by competing workplaces. He believed that the AFL-CIO could do it because his own union had done it. Membership in the SEIU has tripled since the 1980s to 1.8 million.

Then in 2005, he stunned the American labor movement when he led the SEIU and six other unions to defect from the AFL-CIO. Stern effectively split the union in two, peeling off about 40% of its membership.

Unlike the typical union boss, Stern understands the economics of globalization. He believes that it is necessary to take the labor movement far beyond the workplace. Stern believes that the labor union model built in the 1930s is failing. "Do we try to revive that model?" he asks, "or do we say, 'The economy is different now, and workers need different kinds of organizations'?"

According to Stern, labor has slipped into a form of economic Darwinism. He feels that the global economy has made things worse, with multinationals competing to find the cheapest labor, minus unions—what he refers to as the "Wal-Mart effect." For workers to thrive, big labor has to act as big business does: go global, recruit without borders, and unionize workers across entire economic sectors.

He even had a model for the new workers' organization: AARP. He envisions a new national membership and advocacy organization for millions of working people having the clout in Washington that AARP does now. A labor group like that could be very appealing to the 92% of private sector workers who have no interest in traditional bargaining, but still worry about losing their jobs.

Surveys show that Americans want unions but are afraid their employers will retaliate, including illegally firing organizers for their activities. Workers, Stern says, are devalued, and he is trying to change the way Americans view labor and the economy as a whole.[ii]

lecture link 12-5

UNIONS TURN TO THE SERVICE INDUSTRY FOR GROWTH

Unions now represent only 13.2% of the labor force. If the figure goes much lower, unions may become irrelevant as a force in business. The answer, many union organizers believe, is to organize service workers. Most of the nation's job growth between now and the end of the century will be in service businesses. The question is whether or not unions will be able to win over service workers. There is some evidence that they will.

Ralph Whitehead from the University of Massachusetts calls service workers "new-collar workers." Their ranks include clerical workers, insurance agents, keypunchers, nurses, teachers, mental health aides, computer technicians, loan officers, auditors, and salespeople. There are some 20 million such workers, more than the AFL-CIO's current 13 million members.

To reach these workers, labor has to broaden its traditional bread and butter (money) appeals to include quality-of-work concerns such as career development, professional autonomy, and technological change. Thus, unions may push issues such as pay equity, career ladders, child care, job training, and stress management. Workers will also have to be won over by successful union marketing. Most service workers are unfamiliar with unions, and there is some resistance to union organizing. Nonetheless, unions have made some progress.

A Harris Survey found a growing discontent among nonunion workers over pay and job-advancement opportunities. More than 75% feel that unions generally improve pay and working conditions. The survey indicated that 53% of nonunion service workers would react favorably to union representation. Some unions have had success recruiting service workers, including the Service Employees Union, the Hotel Employees and Restaurant Employees Union, and the National Union of Hospital and Health Care Employees.

One union that is doing a particularly good job of listening to employee needs and adjusting to them is the American Federation of State, County, and Municipal Employees (AFSCME). The union's campaign emphasizes issues such as workplace dignity and safety, pay equity, and career development. One worker who joined voiced a complaint that many new computer workers have. She keys information from tax forms into computers, and her work is monitored to see if she meets daily goals. If not, she receives warnings. This is a return to the management styles of Frederick Taylor and Scientific Management, and is greatly resented by some workers.

lecture link 12-6

REVAMPING EXECUTIVE PAY

In an unsettling era, few things have managed to stir up as much ire as the disproportionate bonuses given to many of the nation's most inept executives. For example, Countrywide Financial's Angelo Mozilo, who received $103 million in bonuses and unloaded $169 million worth of stock as his business crumbled, achieved infamy on CNBC's "Worst American CEOs of All Time" list. The executive bonuses handed out to TARP-aided AIG caused such an uproar that the company had to position extra security guards at the doors of several offices in response to numerous death threats and angry letters. As the horror stories of enormous executive greed become commonplace, experts ask: How can high-level executives be compensated in a manner proportionate to their job performance?

Miami's World Fuel Services provides a good example for calculating executive salaries the right way. Under the company's executive pay plan, CEO Paul Stebbins's equity grants are tied up in restricted stock that won't vest for years. Additionally, two-thirds of Stebbins's net-worth, $23 million, is wrapped up in World Fuel stock, thus intimately connecting his own compensation with the performance of the company. According to Stanford corporate governance professor David Larcker, companies can judge job performance by accounting measures like profit gains as well as by nonfinancial indicators like customer satisfaction and employee turnover.

For decades, companies judged their own executive salaries on that of their peers. Rather than awarding good work, 86% of S&P corporations said they based their executive pay on what other groups of similar companies compensated their bosses. Over the years, an ever-increasing game of corporate one-upmanship occurred, bloating executive salaries from 40 times average worker pay in 1980 to 433 times in 2007. While this method is obviously flawed in itself, Nordstrom president Blake Nordstrom uses a variation to effectively regulate his own compensation. A portion of his pay is granted in performance shares that vest every three years, but only when the company's total shareholder return is positive and above the average among its retail peers. Along with his $59 million in company shares, Nordstrom's financial well-being is tied with his company both by itself and in relation to its peers, which could prove to be a welcomed solution for eliminating corruption at the highest level of business management.[iii]

lecture link 12-7
THE MALE EMPLOYMENT DROUGHT

Labor statistics have been notoriously dire since the economic collapse of 2008. In April 2011, however, Labor Secretary Hilda L. Solis actually had some good news to report. She said the four-month drop in the jobless rate, from 9.8 to 8.8%, represented its largest decline since 1984. But, as with most labor statistics, the numbers alone don't tell the whole story. Many people gave up hunting for a job after years of fruitless search. Perhaps the most disturbing facet of today's labor crisis, however, is the vast amount of men who have been sidelined due to a lack of employment opportunities.

In the 1950s, nearly 85% of men aged 16 to 64 were employed. Over the years that number has steadily dropped, finally bottoming out at an all-time low of less than 65%. Traditionally during recessions the employment-to-population ratio for men drops and does not return to its previous high during recoveries. Given the severity of the latest recession, the recent slump has been even worse than usual. Oftentimes unemployed men are workers who would have bounced back in a normal job market. But with total recovery almost entirely out of the picture, many men are on a path of joblessness that could go well into the future. As they remain on the bench indefinitely they begin to lose skills, confidence, and contacts, making it harder and harder to reenter the workforce.

The situation could be even worse for young black men. The jobless rate for black male teens shot up to more than 40% in March, preventing many from so much as getting a foot in the door let alone a career off the ground. Older workers have had it rough as well. Of those aged 55 to 64 who lost their jobs between 2007 and 2009, 21% were out of the workforce entirely by January 2010. All this led to a 0.7% shrinking of the male workforce since unemployment hit its peak in October 2009. One silver lining may exist in the fact that the percentage of employed males has rebounded more than women since the employment trough. But since male employment fell off so much to begin with, it's little more than an empty consolation.[iv]

lecture link 12-8

RECESSION INCREASES WORKPLACE SUICIDES

In May 2010 many Americans were shocked to learn about a wave of suicides at a Chinese factory that produces iPhones and iPods. However, workplace-related tragedies are being reported in ever-increasing numbers on the homefront as well. Workplace suicides jumped by 28%, from 196 cases in 2007 to 251 cases, in 2008—their highest level since the government first started tracking the numbers. Even worse, experts project that workplace suicides and attempted suicides are up 75% from their 2008 levels.

The majority of these cases appear to be directly related to the current economic downturn. According to the clinical director of Harris, Rothman International, suicide and suicide attempts surged after the 2008 stock crash. And in a recessive economy, anxiety runs high and causes some people to fall into a depressive state. People desperate to keep their jobs work longer hours for less pay just to appear more driven to management. Colleagues can be perceived as a threat to an employee's livelihood, turning the workplace into a toxic environment. For some, even the smallest change in the office system can drive them to the brink. One suicidal worker, for example, took his own life after being assigned to a new boss after the layoffs of the company's other managers.

Furthermore, reports of the economy's recovery have only made matters worse for desperate workers. Media spots about the resurgence of America's financial sector make workers more dejected when they compare that good news with the unchanged reality of their own daily lives. According to Pace University, some warning signs of suicidal individuals include long periods of depression or sadness, verbal altercations at work or home, and excessive substance abuse. If you or someone you know is harboring thoughts about harming themselves, please call the National Suicide Hotline at 1-800-273-8255.[v]

lecture link 12-9

EMPLOYEE STOCK OWNERSHIP PLANS

No matter how hard workers fight for better pay, they will never become as wealthy as the people who actually own the company. At least that is the theory behind employee stock ownership plans (ESOPs). An ESOP enables employees to buy part or total ownership of the firm. Louis O. Kelso, a San Francisco lawyer and economist, conceived the idea of ESOPs about 50 years ago. His plan was to turn workers into owners by selling them stock. Using this concept, he helped the employees of a newspaper buy their company. Since then, the idea of employees taking over all or some of the ownership of their companies has gained favor—there are approximately 11,500 ESOPs today.

Employee participation in ownership has emerged as an important issue in many different industries and every type of company. Many people consider ESOPs examples of capitalism at its best. Some benefits of ESOPs include (1) increased employee motivation, (2) shared profitability through ownership of the firm, (3) improved management–employee relations, (4) higher employee pride in the organization, and (5) better customer relations.

The fact is, however, that not all ESOPs work as planned. When used correctly, ESOPs can be a powerful strategy for improving company profitability and increasing employee satisfaction, participation, and income. But potential problems with ESOPs include (1) lack of employee stock voting rights within the firm, (2) lack of communication between management and employees, (3) little or no employee representation on the company board of directors, and (4) lack of job security assurances.

The saga of Weirton Steel illustrates what can happen when an ESOP goes wrong. In 1983, the employees of Weirton Steel voted to take a 20% pay cut to save their jobs. Through an ESOP they purchased the ailing company. Full of hope and confidence, the workers believed their sacrifices would eventually secure their future. Weirton became the largest ESOP in the United States.

Things looked good initially. Weirton earned about $500 million profit between 1984 and 1990, of which workers shared $170 million. The mill also provided 8,000 jobs. Several observers described the mill's participative practices in glowing terms.

However, profits then steadily turned to into large losses, $230 million in 1993, $320 million in 2001, and almost $700 million in 2003. Management cut the workforce by two-thirds, and Weirton's worker-owners lost their investments. In May 2003, the company filed bankruptcy.

Today Weirton's stock is practically worthless, thousands of jobs have been eliminated, and the company's officers and directors have been subject to multiple lawsuits. Members of top management were criticized for bad accounting and personal enrichment, while the employee-owners watched their net worth erode year after year. Long before Arthur Andersen's poor auditing became legendary, the firm's auditors helped Weirton Steel's management waste millions of the employee-owners' value.[vi]

critical
thinking exercises

Name: _____

Date: _____

critical thinking exercise 12-1

ARE UNIONS GOOD OR BAD FOR BUSINESS?

What do managers and workers think about unions? Find out by interviewing one manager of a business that is organized by a labor union and one union member (this exercise is more interesting if the manager and union member work for the same company.) Use the following questions as a guideline. Compare your results with your classmates' findings.

MANAGER	UNION MEMBER
1. What do you think is good about management's relationship with the union?	1. What do you think is good about the union's relationship with management?
2. What do you think is bad about the relationship?	2. What do you think is bad about the relationship?
3. How are things different in the company now than before the union was organized?	3. How are things different in the company now than before the union was organized?

notes on critical thinking exercise 12-1

This exercise is especially interesting in a town dominated by union workers or one that is having union difficulties. In any case, it gets students involved with talking with real people about real perceptions and takes learning out into the real world. Classroom discussions can only supplement, not replace, learning on your own.

critical thinking exercise 12-2
UNION NEGOTIATIONS

Let's get a feel for how employee–management negotiations work. Divide the class into three groups: managers, union representatives, and observers. The task of the managers and the union representatives is to agree on salary rates for the next contract. The task of the observers is to "critique" the negotiation process used (Did one group make an error? Could a particular confrontation been handled a better way?).

Here's the situation:

You work for Frigid Refrigerator Enterprise Systems. Employees of FRES earn 15% above the average of other workers in the industry. Management feels FRES is losing its ability to compete because its labor costs are too high. The obvious solution: ask labor to reduce labor costs either by reducing salaries, reducing the number of workers, or a combination of both. Now it's time to reach an employee–management agreement. Keep in mind that "frozen" negotiations will mean an arbitrator (your professor) will make a binding decision that both groups must accept—things will go better for you if you settle these yourselves!

MANAGEMENT DEMANDS ⟶	COMPROMISED SETTLEMENT	⟵ UNION DEMANDS

notes on critical thinking exercise 12-2

     The instructor should stay out of this as much as possible to let the students decide the issues and resolve them. The instructor can assume the arbitrator position only at the end, not along the way. See how many options the groups can come up with to be sure that everyone feels they are being treated fairly. Be sure that the students act out the role assigned and aren't too wishy-washy in their demands.

Name: _____

Date: _____

critical thinking exercise 12-3
EXECUTIVE PAY WATCH

Visit the AFL–CIO website at www.aflcio.org.[vii] Navigate through the site and find information regarding salaries of CEOs of major corporations in the United States. (Sometimes the Web address for a location changes. You might need to search to find the exact location mentioned.)

1.   What is the average CEO compensation for the latest year?

2.   Which CEO received the largest total compensation package? How much?

3.   Who is the highest-paid CEO in the information technology industry? In the financial industry? In the industrial industry?

4.   List the top three executive retirement packages.

5.   The text states that the average CEO of a major corporation makes 180 times as much as the average hourly worker. What is the current ratio of average hourly workers to CEO pay rates?

bonus
cases

bonus case 12-1

DO RIGHT-TO-WORK LAWS HELP STATES?

The year is 1947 and the U.S. Senate and House of Representatives are considering legislation to deal with an unsettled labor–management situation affecting the U.S. economy. Since the end of World War II, organized labor and employers have experienced a host of problems. Strikes in the oil, automobile, steel, and coal industries have occurred, causing President Harry Truman to call a national labor–management conference to find a formula for industrial peace. Still, this unsettled labor–management situation greatly strengthened opposition to the Wagner Act Congress passed in 1935.

Since the passage of the Wagner Act, labor unions had insisted on the legality of the closed shop (which demanded that workers be members of a labor union before obtaining a job). Senator Robert Taft of Ohio and Congressman Fred Hartley of New Jersey argued that the equity between organized labor and management intended by the Wagner Act was out of balance. Together they proposed the Labor Management Relations Act to counter what was perceived as the growing power of labor unions. Organized labor vigorously opposed the legislation and President Truman promised to veto the bill. However, on June 23, 1947, after overriding a presidential veto, the Taft-Hartley Act became law.

The concept of reaching a balance between labor and management led to provisions in the bill that dealt with "unfair labor practices" that applied to unions and management. Practices such as refusing to bargain in good faith, engaging in secondary boycotts, stopping work over jurisdictional or interunion disputes, and charging excessive initiation fees to keep members out of a union were considered unfair labor practices. Special rules that allowed the president to call for a "cooling-off" period or waiting period were also written into the law for handling controversies or strikes that could threaten national health or safety. The Taft-Hartley Act also made the closed shop illegal.

Organized labor denounced the entire Taft-Hartley Act as a "slave labor" law. However, unions were particularly troubled with Section 14(b) of the legislation. Section 14(b) enabled states to pass right-to-work laws that would permit limitations on union shop and union security agreements. Labor "affectionately" called the provision "right-to-wreck" laws and promised to fight such legislation in states where it was proposed. To date, 22 states have passed legislation authorizing the open shop agreement in the workplace. Oklahoma was the last state to pass right-to-work legislation in 2001.

A major question that's been debated since passage of the Taft-Hartley Act is, Does passage of right-to-work laws make a difference in a state's economy? Former Governor Frank Keating of Oklahoma, who supported the right-to-work legislation in his state, says Oklahoma experienced "a blizzard of interest after passage of the right-to-work law." A study by the Mackinac Center for Public Policy in Michigan states, "right-to-work laws increase labor productivity by requiring labor unions to earn the support of each worker since workers are able to decide for themselves whether or not to pay dues." Dennis Donovan, a corporate-location consultant in Edison, New Jersey, says that among manufacturers choosing facilities among numerous states, having a right-to-work law is a precondition for about one-third of the companies. Labor unions take an opposite view and claim that workers in right-to-work states earn on average less than union employees and work under less worker-friendly conditions. Unions claim the real purpose of right-to-work laws is to roll back the achievements earned by organized labor. This issue promises to be strongly debated in the 21st century.[viii]

discussion questions for bonus case 12-1

1.   If given a choice, would you elect to join a labor union or not join? What are the reasons for your decision?

2.   With today's protections under the law available to workers, do you believe that unions have outlived their usefulness?

3.   Is your home state or the state in which you now live a right-to-work state? How do you feel about economic development and growth in your state? If your state is not a right-to-work state, would you support a right-to-work law if it were put to a popular vote?

notes on discussion questions for bonus case 12-1

1.   *If given a choice, would you elect to join a labor union or not join? What are the reasons for your decision?*

This may or may not be a critical case in your class, depending on the unionization of the workforce in your area and whether or not yours is a right-to-work state. If it is a major issue, let students debate these questions as long as they like. Getting involved in a course is critical, and this is one way to get participation.

2.   *With today's protections under the law available to workers, do you believe that unions have outlived their usefulness?*

Unions are still popular among those who feel they are being poorly paid and mistreated. That's why the number one union is that of teachers. Nurses and doctors are also being courted. What other groups do students believe could benefit from unionization in their area?

3.   *Is your home state or the state in which you now live a right-to-work state? How do you feel about economic development and growth in your state? If your state is not a right-to-work state, would you support a right-to-work law if it were put to a popular vote?*

This is a major issue in some states and a nonissue in others. Depending on the circumstances, let students debate this issue, again, as long as they are interested. If there is no interest, go on to another case.

bonus case 12-2

PENSION PLANS UNDER ATTACK

The U.S. airline industry has never recovered from 9/11. Since the terrorist attacks, the industry has been in a free fall. Record fuel costs, the lowest fares since the early 1990s, and stiff competition have caused the air carriers to lose billions of dollars. The industry as a whole has lost $30 billion. To keep the carriers from economic collapse, labor unions have agreed to millions of dollars in concessions and wage cutbacks.

Hardest hit is United Airlines, which has lost $10 billion by itself. But even the labor concessions were not enough to keep United out of bankruptcy court. Looming large in the equation are the pension obligations to retiring flight attendants, mechanics, and pilots. When it faced the bankruptcy judge in 2002, United had pension obligations of $9.8 billion. This staggering sum was owed to present and future retirees under the terms of their contracts.

United argued that it was financially unable to pay these benefits, and the bankruptcy court agreed. The airline walked away from the pension obligation, the equivalent of taking $267,000 from each pilot, flight attendant, and mechanic.

The Pension Benefit Guaranty Corporation (PBGC), the government agency created in 1975 to bail out domestic companies that default on pension obligations, will pick up the tab for United's pension plans. The PBGC is funded through an employer premium that is essentially a tax on employers to fund pension plans. PBGC believes that U.S. pension plans are underfunded by more than $450 billion, with companies in financial trouble liable for nearly $100 billion of this amount. The PBGC collects roughly $560 million a year from the private sector, far short of the amount needed to pay the pensions of companies that have fallen on hard times. The agency's resources will be exhausted within a few years.

Because of the United pension fiasco, some members of Congress warned that taxpayers may someday have to bail out the deficit-riddled government pension agency. "Taxpayers had better buckle up, because we will be in for a bumpy ride of bailout after bailout, as more and more corporations dump their pension plan obligations on the PBGC," said U.S. Representative Jan Schakowsky. The PBGC is already operating at a deficit of more than $23 billion.

While preserving some of United's pension benefits, the bankruptcy settlement hit workers and retirees hard. Federal regulations limit the amount of pension payments the PBGC can make to a maximum of about $45,000 a year. The highest-paid United workers, such as pilots, face pension cuts of up to 50%. The pilots also face a catch-22: Under one federal law, they are not allowed to work after age 60; under another, the proportion of their pension guaranteed by the PBGC is sharply reduced if they retire before age 65.

The former United pension plan covers 120,000 current and retired United workers. Bankruptcy Judge Eugene Wedoff approved the pension plan over the objections of several unions. He called it "the least bad" of the available choices, since it gives unprofitable United the best chance to keep functioning. United's CFO, Jake Brace, said the verdict was important but that it "was not a joyous day" for the airline.

Employees and retirees are bitter about what they perceive as an inequity of sacrifice. While workers take huge cuts in pension benefits, United CEO Glen Tilton has a $4.5 million annual pension guaranteed by his employment contract with the company.[ix]

discussion questions for bonus case 12-2

1. What ethical and economic issues are raised by this case?

2. Since Social Security will not be fully funded in the future and company pensions may be in doubt, what should a student do to prepare for retirement? Is this a union–management issue that is easily resolved?

3. Does the government backing of pension programs create a "moral hazard"? What is a moral hazard anyhow?

notes on discussion questions for bonus case 12-2

1. *What ethical and economic issues are raised by this case?*

   It may not seem ethical for a company to not pay its pension obligations, but United was bankrupt. It had no choice. The government has assumed the role of backup in such cases, but is it ethical for you and me to cover the losses caused by decision making at United? If one airline fails to pay its obligations, won't all the other airlines do the same to stay competitive? And won't other companies be tempted to do the same? Should the government get out of the pension-backing business? Students should enjoy debating this one.

2. *Since Social Security will not be fully funded in the future and company pensions may be in doubt, what should a student do to prepare for retirement? Is this a union–management issue that is easily resolved?*

   Students should not rely on Social Security or pensions for their secure retirement. Instead, they should begin a dramatic savings plan now to cover their retirement needs. You may refer them to the personal finance bonus chapter for more information on this topic. Is there any way that employees can force companies to keep their pension promises? Good discussion point!

3. *Does the government backing of pension programs create a "moral hazard" What is a moral hazard anyhow?*

   Students should learn what a moral hazard is, so this is as good a time as any to discuss it. A moral hazard occurs when an attempt to do good encourages bad behavior from others. For example, forgiving the debts of one poor country could encourage other poor countries not to pay their debts and to incur additional debts that they would also not pay. Such potentially bad motivation is called a moral hazard. In this case, the moral hazard is that all major companies may be tempted to bail out of their pension plans to increase profits.

endnotes

[i] *Sources:* Monica Davey and Steve Greenhouse, "Angry Demonstrations in Wisconsin as Cuts Loom," *The New York Times*, February 16, 2011; Kris Maher and Melanie Trottman, "Sparring Unions Now Working as One," *The Wall Street Journal*, February 24, 2011.

[ii] *Sources*: Matt Miller, "Blowing Up the Union to Save the Union," *Fortune*, August 22, 3005; Clayton Nall, "Gompers's Ghost and Labor's New Look," *The Washington Post*, September 4, 2005; Lynne Duke, "Love, Labor, Loss: A Child's Death Stirred Andrew Stern to Challenge Himself—and Unionism," *The Washington Post*, January 3, 2006.

[iii] *Source:* Emily Lambert, "The Right Way to Pay," *Forbes*, May 11, 2009.

[iv] *Source:* Peter Coy, "The Hidden Job Crisis for American Men," *Bloomberg Businessweek*, April 7, 2011.

[v] *Source:* Eve Tahmincioglu, "Workplace Suicides on the Rise," *MSNBC*, June 1, 2010.

[vi] *Sources*: Amey Stone, "The Joys of an ESOP," *BusinessWeek,* November 1, 2004; Lois Alete Fundis, "A Short History of the Weirton Area," Mary H. Weir Public Library, Weirton, W.Va.; The ESOP Association, www.esopassociation.org.

[vii] The Internet is a dynamic, changing information source. Web links noted of this manual were checked at the time of publication, but content may change over time. Please review the website before recommending it to your students.

[viii] *Sources:* Kathy Chen, "Wooing Companies: Do 'Right-to-Work' Laws Make a Difference?" *The Wall Street Journal*, July 10, 2002, p. B3; Ashley Friedman, "University of Michigan Study Shows 'Right-to-Work' Laws Help States," *University Wire*, June 10, 2002.